P9-CFV-987

The
Random
House
Basic Dictionary

French-English
English-French

**The
Random
House
Basic Dictionary**

French-English
English-French

**Edited by
Francesca L.V. Langbaum**

University of Virginia

**Under the General Editorship of
Professor Robert A. Hall, Jr.**

Cornell University

The Ballantine Reference Library

Ballantine Books · New York

Copyright © 1981, 1954 by Random House, Inc.

All rights reserved under International and Pan-American Copyright Conventions. Published in the United States by Ballantine Books, a division of Random House, Inc., New York, and simultaneously in Canada by Random House of Canada Limited, Toronto.

Library of Congress Catalog Card Number: 54-5962

ISBN 0-345-33712-3

This edition published by arrangement with Random House, Inc.

Previously published as *The French Vest Pocket Dictionary* and *The Random House French Dictionary*.

Manufactured in the United States of America

First Ballantine Books Edition: August 1981
Sixteenth Printing: August 1993

Concise Pronunciation Guide

The following concise guide describes the approximate pronunciation of the letters and frequent combinations of letters occurring in the French language. A study of it will enable the reader to pronounce French adequately most of the time. While the guide cannot list all the exceptions to the established pronunciations, or cover the manner in which adjacent words affect each other in speech, such exceptions and variations will readily be learned as one develops facility in the language.

French Letter	Description of Pronunciation
a, à	Between *a* in *calm* and *a* in *hat*.
â	Like *a* in *calm*.
ai	Like *e* in *bed*.
au	Like *oa* in *coat*.
b	As in English. At end of words, usually silent.
c	Before *e*, *i*, *y*, like *s*. Elsewhere, like *k*. When *c* occurs at the end of a word and is preceded by a consonant, it is usually silent.
ç	Like *s*.
cc	Before *e*, *i*, like *x*. Elsewhere, like *k*.
ch	Usually like *sh* in *short*. *ch* is pronounced like *k* in words of Greek origin; before *a*, *o*, and *u;* and before consonants.
d	At beginning and in middle of words, as in English. At end of words, usually silent.
e	At end of words, normally silent; indicates that preceding consonant letter is pronounced. Between two single consonant sounds, usually silent. Elsewhere, like English *a* in *sofa*.
é	Approximately like *a* in *hate*.

French Letter	Description of Pronunciation
è, ê, ei	Like *e* in *bed*.
eau	Like *au*.
ent	Silent when it is the third person plural ending.
er (end of words)	At end of words of more than one syllable, usually like *a* in *hate*, the *r* being silent; otherwise like *air* in *chair*.
es	Silent at end of words.
eu	A vowel sound not found in English; like French *e*, but pronounced with the lips rounded as for *o*.
ez	At end of words, almost always like English *a* in *hate*, the *z* being silent.
f	As in English; silent at the end of a few words.
g	Before *e*, *i*, *y*, like *z* in *azure*. Elsewhere, like *g* in *get*. At end of words, usually silent.
gn	Like *ni* in *onion*.
gu	Before *e*, *i*, *y*, like *g* in *get*. Elsewhere, like *g* in *get* plus French *u* (see below).
h	In some words, represents a slight tightening of the throat muscles (in French, called "aspiration"). In most words, silent.
i, î	Like *i* in *machine*.
ill	(-il at end of words) like *y*

French Letter	Description of Pronunciation	French Letter	Description of Pronunciation
	in *yes,* in many but not all words.		See above under *er.*
j	Like *z* in *azure.*	s	Generally, like *s* in *sea.* Single *s* between vowels, like *z* in *zone.* At end of words, normally silent.
k	As in English.		
l	As in English, but always pronounced "bright," with tongue in front of mouth.		
		sc	Before *e* or *i,* like *s.* Elsewhere, like *sk.*
m, n	When double, and when single between two vowel letters or at beginning of word, like English *m* and *n* respectively. When single at end of syllable (at end of word or before another consonant), indicates nasalization of preceding vowel.	t	Approximately like English *t,* but pronounced with tongue tip against teeth. At end of words, normally silent. When followed by *ie, ion, ium, ius,* and other diphthongs beginning with a vowel, *t* generally is like English *s* in *sea* (unless the *t* itself is preceded by an *s* or an *x*).
o	Usually like *u* in English *mud,* but rounder. When final sound in word, and often before *s* and *z,* like *ô.*		
ô	Approximately like *oa* in *coat.*	th	Like *t.*
		u, û	A vowel sound not found in English; like the *i* in *machine* but with lips rounded as for *ou.*
oe, oeu	Like *eu.*		
oi	Approximately like a combination of the consonant *w* and the *a* of *calm.*	ue	After *c* or *g* and before *il,* like *eu.*
		v	As in English.
ou, oû, où	Like *ou* in *tour.*	w	Usually like *v;* in some people's pronunciation, like English *w.*
p	At end of words, usually silent. Between *m* and *t, m* and *s, r* and *s,* usually silent. Elsewhere, as in English.	x	Generally sounds like *ks;* but when the syllable *ex* begins a word and is followed by a vowel, *x* sounds like *gz.* At end of words, usually silent.
pn, ps	Unlike English, when *pn* and *ps* occur at the beginning of words the *p* is usually sounded.		
ph	Like *f.*	y	Generally like *i* in *machine;* but when between two vowels, like *y* in *yes.*
qu	Usually like *k.*		
r	A vibration either of the uvula, or of the tip of the tongue, against the upper front teeth.	z	Like *z* in *zone.* At end of words, often silent (see above under *ez*).

Note on Pronunciation

A few minutes' study of the *Concise Pronunciation Guide* will enable you to pronounce most French words without having to look each word up in the dictionary. For the relatively few cases in which the pronunciation does not follow the usual pattern, this dictionary provides a transcription in simple and familiar symbols.

ă   bat

ā   cape

â   dare

ä   calm

å   [a vowel intermediate in quality between the *a* of *cat* and the *a* of *calm*, but closer to the former]

ĕ   set

ē   bee

ĭ   big

.ī   bite

N   [a symbol used to indicate nasalized vowels. There are four such vowels in French, found in *un bon vin blanc* (œN bōN văN bläN)]

ŏ   hot

ŏ   no

ô   order

œ   [a vowel made with the lips rounded in position for *o* as in *over*, while trying to say *a* as in *able*]

oi   oil

ŏŏ   book

ōō   ooze

ou   loud

ŭ   up

ū   cute

û   burn

Y   [a vowel made with the lips rounded in position for *ōō* as in *ooze*, while trying to say *e* as in *easy*]

ə   [indicates the sound of *a* in *alone*, *e* in *system*, *i* in *easily*, *o* in *gallop*, *u* in *circus*]

Irregular Verbs

Infinitive	Pres. Part.	Past Part.	Pres. Indic.	Future
aller	allant	allé	vais	irai
asseoir	asseyant	assis	assieds	assiérai
atteindre	atteignant	atteint	atteins	atteindrai
avoir	ayant	eu	ai	aurai
battre	battant	battu	bats	battrai
boire	buvant	bu	bois	boirai
conduire	conduisant	conduit	conduis	conduirai
connaître	connaissant	connu	connais	connaîtrai
courir	courant	couru	cours	courrai
craindre	craignant	craint	crains	craindrai
croire	croyant	cru	crois	croirai
devoir	devant	dû	dois	devrai
dire	disant	dit	dis	dirai
dormir	dormant	dormi	dors	dormirai
écrire	écrivant	écrit	écris	écrirai
envoyer	envoyant	envoyé	envoie	enverrai
être	étant	été	suis	serai
faire	faisant	fait	fais	ferai
falloir	———	fallu	(il) faut	(il) faudra
joindre	joignant	joint	joins	joindrai
lire	lisant	lu	lis	lirai
mettre	mettant	mis	mets	mettrai
mourir	mourant	mort	meurs	mourrai
naître	naissant	né	nais	naîtrai
ouvrir	ouvrant	ouvert	ouvre	ouvrirai
plaire	plaisant	plu	plais	plairai
pleuvoir	pleuvant	plu	(il) pleut	(il) pleuvra
pouvoir	pouvant	pu	peux	pourrai
prendre	prenant	pris	prends	prendrai
recevoir	recevant	reçu	reçois	recevrai
rire	riant	ri	ris	rirai
savoir	sachant	su	sais	saurai
suffire	suffisant	suffi	suffis	suffirai
suivre	suivant	suivi	suis	suivrai
tenir	tenant	tenu	tiens	tiendrai
valoir	valant	valu	vaux	vaudrai
venir	venant	venu	viens	veindrai
vivre	vivant	vécu	vis	vivrai
voir	voyant	vu	vois	verrai
vouloir	voulant	voulu	veux	voudrai

Abbreviations

abbr.	abbreviation	*med.*	medical
adj.	adjective	*mil.*	military
adv.	adverb	*n.*	noun
art.	article	*naut.*	nautical
comm.	commercial	*pl.*	plural
conj.	conjunction	*pred.*	predicate
eccles.	ecclesiastical	*prep.*	preposition
f.	feminine	*pron.*	pronoun
fig.	figurative	*sg.*	singular
geom.	geometry	*tr.*	transitive (used only with
gramm.	grammar, grammatical		verbs which also have
interj.	interjection		reflexive use to indicate
intr.	intransitive		intransitive meaning)
lit.	literal, literally	*vb.*	verb
m.	masculine		

Useful Phrases

Good day. Bonjour.
Good evening. Bonsoir.
Good night. Bonne nuit.
Good bye. Au revoir.
How are you? Comment allez-vous?
Fine, thank you. Très bien, merci.
Glad to meet you. Enchanté de faire votre connaissance.
Thank you very much. Merci beaucoup.
You're welcome. Pas de quoi.
Please. S'il vous plaît.
Good luck. Bonne chance.
To your health. A votre santé.

Please help me. Aidez-moi, s'il vous plaît.
Do you understand? Comprenez-vous?
I don't understand. Je ne comprends pas.
Speak slowly, please. Parlez lentement, s'il vous plaît.
Please repeat. Répétez, s'il vous plaît.
I don't speak French. Je ne parle pas français.
Do you speak English? Parlez-vous anglais?
Does anyone here speak English? Y a-t-il quelqu'un qui parle anglais?
How do you say...in French? Comment dit-on...en français?

What is your name? Comment vous appelez-vous?
My name is... Je m'appelle...
I am an American. Je suis américain.

How is the weather?   Quel temps fait-il?
What time is it?   Quelle heure est-il?
What is it?   Qu'est-ce que c'est?

How much does this cost?   Combien est ceci?
It is too expensive.   C'est trop cher.
I want to buy...   Je voudrais acheter...

I want to eat.   Je voudrais manger.
Can you recommend a restaurant?   Pouvez-vous recommander un restaurant?
I am hungry.   J'ai faim.
Check, please.   L'addition, s'il vous plaît.
Is there a hotel here?   Y a-t-il un hôtel ici?

Where is...?   Oú est...?
What is the way to...?   Quelle est la route de...?
Take me to...   Conduisez-moi à...
I need...   J'ai besoin de...
I am ill.   Je suis malade.
Please call a doctor.   Appelez un docteur, s'il vous plaît.
I want to send a telegram.   Je voudrais envoyer un télégramme.
Where can I change money?   Où puis-je changer de l'argent?
Will you accept checks?   Acceptez-vous des chèques?
What is the postage?   Quel est l'affranchissement?

Right away.   Tout de suite.
Help!   Au secours!
Come in.   Entrez.
Stop.   Arrêtez.
Hurry.   Dépêchez-vous.
Go on.   Continuez.
Right.   A droite.
Left.   A gauche.
Straight ahead.   Tout droit.

Signs

Attention Caution		**Ralentir** Go Slow	
Danger Danger		**Défense de fumer** No smoking	
Sortie Exit		**Défense d'entrer** No admittance	
Entrée Entrance		**Dames** Women	
Halte, Arrêtez Stop		**Hommes** Men	
Fermé Closed		**Lavabos, toilettes** Lavatory	
Ouvert Open			

Weights and Measures

The French use the *Metric System* of weights and measures, a decimal system in which multiples are shown by the prefixes **déci-** (one-tenth); **centi-** (one hundredth); **milli-** (one thousandth); **hecto-** (hundred); and **kilo-** (thousand).

1 centimètre	=	.3937 inch
1 mètre	=	39.37 inches
1 kilomètre	=	.621 mile
1 centigramme	=	.1543 grain
1 gramme	=	15.432 grains
100 grammes	=	3.527 ounces
1 kilogramme	=	2.2046 pounds
1 tonne	=	2,204 pounds
1 centilitre	=	.338 ounce
1 litre	=	1.0567 quart (liquid);
	=	.908 quart (dry)
1 kilolitre	=	264.18 gallons

Numerals

Cardinal

1 un, une	22 vingt-deux	77 soixante-dix-sept
2 deux	23 vingt-trois	78 soixante-dix-huit
3 trois	24 vingt-quatre	79 soixante-dix-neuf
4 quatre	25 vingt-cinq	80 quatre-vingts
5 cinq	26 vingt-six	81 quatre-vingt-un
6 six	27 vingt-sept	82 quatre-vingt-deux
7 sept	28 vingt-huit	90 quatre-vingt-dix
8 huit	29 vingt-neuf	91 quatre-vingt-onze
9 neuf	30 trente	92 quatre-vingt-douze
10 dix	31 trente et un	
11 onze	32 trente-deux	100 cent
12 douze	40 quarante	101 cent un
13 treize	50 cinquante	102 cent deux
14 quatorze	60 soixante	200 deux cents
15 quinze	70 soixante-dix	300 trois cents
16 seize	71 soixante et onze	301 trois cent un
17 dix-sept	72 soixante-douze	1,000 mille
18 dix-huit	73 soixante-treize	5,000 cinq mille
19 dix-neuf	74 soixante-quartorze	1,000,000 un million
20 vingt	75 soixante-quinze	
21 vingt et un	76 soixante-seize	

Ordinal

1st	premier, première	19th	dix-neuvième
2nd	deuxième, second	20th	vingtième
3rd	troisième	21th	vingt-et-unième
4th	quatrième	22nd	vingt-deuxième
5th	cinquième	30th	trentième
6th	sixième	40th	quarantième
7th	septième	50th	cinquantième
8th	huitième	60th	soixantième
9th	neuvième	70th	soixante-dixième
10th	dixième	80th	quatre-vingtième
11th	onzième	90th	quatre-vingt-dixième
12th	douzième		
13th	treizième	100th	centième
14th	quatorzième	101st	cent-unième
15th	quinzième	102nd	cent-deuxième
16th	seizième	300th	trois-centième
17th	dix-septième	1,000th	millième
18th	dix-huitième	1,000,000th	millionième

Days of the Week

Sunday	dimanche
Monday	lundi
Tuesday	mardi
Wednesday	mercredi
Thursday	jeudi
Friday	vendredi
Saturday	samedi

Months

January	janvier	July	juillet
February	février	August	août
March	mars	September	septembre
April	avril	October	octobre
May	mai	November	novembre
June	juin	December	décembre

French-English

A

à, *prep.* at, in, to.
abaisser, *vb.* depress, lower.
abandon, *n.m.* desertion, abandonment.
abandonné, *adj.* forlorn.
abandonner, *vb.* forsake, leave (desert). s'a., give up, resign oneself.
abasourdir, *vb.* astound.
abattage, *n.m.* slaughter.
abattement, *n.m.* depression, dejection.
abattre, *vb.* depress, reduce; slaughter. s'a., alight.
abbaye, *n.f.* abbey.
abbé, *n.m.* abbot.
abbesse, *n.f.* abbess.
abcès, *n.m.* abscess.
abdiquer, *vb.* abdicate.
abdomen, *n.m.* abdomen.
abeille, *n.f.* bee.
aberration, *n.f.* aberration.
abîme, *n.m.* abyss.
abîmer, *vb.* injure, spoil.
abject, *adj.* abject, low.
aboiement, *n.m.* barking.
abolir, *vb.* abolish.
abolition, *n.f.* abolition.
abominable, *adj.* vile, objectionable.
abondamment, *adv.* fully.
abondance, *n.f.* plenty.
abondant, *adj.* plentiful. peu a., scanty.
abonder de, *vb.* abound in.
abonnement, *n.m.* subscription.
abonner, *vb.* s'a., subscribe.
abord, 1. *n.m.* approach. 2. *adv.* d'a., at first.
aborder, *vb.* accost.
aboutir, *vb.* end (in).
aboyer, *vb.* bark.
abréger, *vb.* abridge, shorten, abbreviate.
abréviation, *n.f.* abbreviation.
abri, *n.m.* shelter. à l'a. de, safe from.
abricot, *n.m.* apricot.
abriter, *vb.* shelter.
abrupt (-pt), *adj.* steep.
absence, *n.f.* absence.
absent, *adj.* absent. rester a., stay away.
absenter, *vb.* s'a., go away.
abside, *n.f.* apse.
absinthe, *n.f.* absinthe.
absolu, *adj.* utter, absolute.
absolution, *n.f.* absolution.
absorbant, *adj. and n.m.* absorbent.
absorbé dans, *adj.* intent on.
absorber, *vb.* engross, absorb. s'a. dans, pore over.
absorption, *n.f.* absorption.
absoudre, *vb.* absolve.
abstenir, *vb.* forbear. s'a. de, abstain from.

abstinence, *n.f.* abstinence.
abstraction, *n.f.* abstraction.
abstrait, *adj.* abstract.
absurde, *adj.* absurd, preposterous.
absurdité, *n.f.* nonsense, absurdity.
abus, *n.m.* abuse.
abuser de, *vb.* abuse.
académie, *n.f.* academy.
académique, *adj.* academic.
acajou, *n.m.* mahogany.
accablant, *adj.* oppressive.
accabler, *vb.* overwhelm, burden.
accaparer, *vb.* get a corner on.
accélération, *n.f.* acceleration.
accélérer, *vb.* quicken, hurry.
accent, *n.m.* stress, emphasis, accent.
accentuer, *vb.* accentuate, accent, emphasize.
acceptable, *adj.* acceptable.
acceptation, *n.f.* acceptance.
accepter, *vb.* accept, admit.
accepteur, *n.m.* accepter.
accès, *n.m.* access, approach; fit (of anger); bout (of fever).
accessible, *adj.* accessible.
accessoire, *n.m. and adj.* accessory, adjunct.
accident, *n.m.* crash, accident.
accidentel, *adj.* accidental.
acclamation, *n.f.* acclamation.
acclamer, *vb.* acclaim, cheer.
accommoder, *vb.* accommodate.
accompagnement, *n.m.* accompaniment.
accompagner, *vb.* accompany, go with.
accompli, *adj.* accomplished, complete, perfect.
accomplir, *vb.* accomplish, achieve, fulfill, carry out, perform.
accomplissement, *n.m.* performance, fulfillment, achievement, accomplishment.
accord, *n.m.* agreement, harmony; settlement; chord, tune. être d'a., agree, concur.
accorder, *vb.* grant, bestow; allow; tune. s'a., agree.
accouchement, *n.m.* delivery.
accoucher, *vb.* deliver.
accoucheur, *n.m.* médecin-a., obstetrician.
accouder, *vb.* s'a., lean.
accourir, *vb.* flock, run up.
accoutumer, *vb.* accustom.
accréditer, *vb.* accredit.
accrocher, *vb.* hook, hitch.
accroissement, *n.m.* growth, addition.
accroître, *vb.* increase.
accroupir, *vb.* s'a., squat, crouch.
accueil, *n.m.* reception, greeting.
accueillir, *vb.* receive, greet.
accumuler, *vb.* heap up.

accusateur, *n.m.* accuser.
accusatif, *n.m.* accusative.
accusation, *n.f.* accusation.
accusatrice, *n.f.* accuser.
accusé, *n.m.* defendant.
accuser, *vb.* arraign, accuse.
acharné, *adj.* eager, fanatical.
achat, *n.m.* purchase.
acheminer, *vb.* start (toward).
acheter, *vb.* buy.
acheteur, *n.m.* buyer.
achèvement, *n.m.* completion.
achever, *vb.* complete, finish, achieve.
acide, *adj. and n.m.* acid.
acidité, *n.f.* acidity.
acier, *n.m.* steel.
acoustique, *n.f.* acoustics.
acquérir, *vb.* acquire, get, obtain.
acquiescement, *n.m.* acquiescence, compliance.
acquiescer à, *vb.* acquiesce, consent.
acquisition, *n.f.* acquisition, purchase.
acquittement, *n.m.* acquittal.
acquitter, *vb.* acquit.
âcre, *adj.* sharp.
acrobate, *n.m.f.* acrobat.
acte, *n.m.* act. a. notarié, deed. a. de naissance, birth certificate.
acteur, *n.m.* actor.
actif, 1. *n.m.* assets (comm.). 2. *adj.* active.
action, *n.f.* action, deed, act; (comm.) share.
action de contrôle en retour, *n.f.* feedback.
actionnaire, *n.m.* shareholder.
actionner, *vb.* operate.
activement, *adv.* busily.
activer, *vb.* activate, fan, hurry.
activité, *n.f.* activity.
actrice, *n.f.* actress.
actualités, *n.f.pl.* newsreel.
actuel, *adj.* present.
actuellement, *adv.* now, at present.
acuponcture, *n.f.* acupuncture.
adaptation, *n.f.* adaptation.
adapter, *vb.* adapt, fit, adjust, suit.
addition, *n.f.* addition, bill.
additionnel, *adj.* additional.
additionner, *vb.* add.
adhérent, *n.m.* follower.
adhérer, *vb.* cleave, adhere.
adhésif, *adj.* adhesive.
adieu, *n.m. and interj.* goodbye, farewell. faire ses adieux, take one's leave.
adjacent, *adj.* adjacent.
adjectif, *n.m.* adjective.
adjoint, *n.m.* fellow-worker, associate.
adjuger, *vb.* grant.
admettre, *vb.* allow, admit, grant.
administrateur, *n.m.* administrator, director, manager.

administratif, *adj.* administrative.

administration, *n.f.* administration, direction.

administrer, *vb.* administer, manage.

admirable, *adj.* admirable.

admirateur, *n.m.* admirer.

admiration, *n.f.* admiration.

admirer, *vb.* admire.

admission, *n.f.* confession, admission.

adolescence, *n.f.* adolescence.

adolescent, *adj. and n.m.f.* adolescent.

adonner, *vb.* s'a. à, indulge in, become addicted to.

adopter, *vb.* adopt.

adoption, *n.f.* adoption.

adoration, *n.f.* adoration.

adorer, *vb.* worship, adore.

adosser, *vb.* s'a. à, lean on.

adoucir, *vb.* soothe.

adresse, *n.f.* address; skill, ability.

adresser, *vb.* address (a letter); direct. s'a. à, apply to.

adroit, *adj.* skillful, clever, handy.

adulte, *adj. and n.m.f.* adult.

adultère, *n.m.* adultery.

adultérer, *vb.* adulterate.

adverbe, *n.m.* adverb.

adversaire, *n.m.f.* opponent.

adverse, *adj.* adverse.

adversité, *n.f.* adversity.

aéré, *adj.* airy.

aérer, *vb.* air (a room).

aérien, *adj.* aerial.

aérogare, *n.f.* airline (city) station.

aeroglisseur, *n.m.* hovercraft.

aéroport, *n.m.* airport.

affable, *adj.* affable.

affaiblir, *vb.* weaken.

affaire, *n.f.* affair, matter; deal; *(pl.)* business. se tirer d'a., manage (somehow). homme d'a.s, businessman.

affairé, *adj.* busy.

affaissement, *n.m.* collapse.

affaisser, *vb.* s'a., collapse.

affamé, *adj.* hungry, famished.

affamer, *vb.* starve.

affectation, *n.f.* affectation.

affecter, *vb.* affect.

affection, *n.f.* affection.

affectueux, *adj.* affectionate.

affermir, *vb.* strengthen.

affété, *adj.* finicky.

affiche, *n.f.* poster.

afficher, *vb.* post.

affilier, *vb.* affiliate.

affinité, *n.f.* affinity.

affirmatif, *adj.* affirmative.

affirmation, *n.f.* statement.

affirmer, *vb.* assert, state, maintain, testify, affirm.

affliction, *n.f.* affliction.

affligé, *adj.* sorrowful.

affliger, *vb.* distress, afflict, grieve.

affluent, *n.m.* tributary.

affluer, *vb.* flow into.

affoler, *vb.* drive mad.

affranchir, *vb.* free.

affranchissement, *n.m.* postage.

affréter, *vb.* charter (boat).

affreusement, *adv.* terribly.

affreux, *adj.* dreadful, terrible, horrid, dire.

affront, *n.m.* affront, insult.

affronter, *vb.* confront, face.

afin, *1.* a. de, *prep.* in order to. *2. conj.* a. que, so that.

Africain, *n.m.* African.

africain, *adj.* African.

Afrique, *n.f.* Africa.

agacer, *vb.* vex, irritate.

âge, *n.m.* age. d'un certain â., elderly. le moyen â., the Middle Ages.

âgé, *adj.* aged.

agence, *n.f. (comm.)* agency.

agenouiller, *vb.* s'a., kneel.

agent, *n.m.* agent. a. de police, policeman. a. de change, stockbroker.

aggraver, *vb.* aggravate.

agile, *adj.* nimble.

agir, *vb.* act. s'a. de, be a question of.

agitateur, *n.m.* agitator.

agitation, *n.f.* excitement, disturbance, commotion, flutter.

agité, *adj.* upset, excited.

agiter, *vb.* agitate, wave, wag, shake, stir. s'a., toss, flutter.

agneau, *n.m.* lamb.

agonie, *n.f.* agony.

agrafe, *n.f.* clasp.

agrafer, *vb.* clasp.

agrandir, *vb.* enlarge.

agréable, *adj.* likable, pleasant, enjoyable, agreeable.

agréer, *vb.* accept, consent.

agrégation, *n.f.* aggregation, fellowship.

agrément, *n.m.* pleasure.

agresseur, *n.m.* aggressor.

agressif, *adj.* aggressive.

agression, *n.f.* aggression.

agricole, *adj.* agricultural.

agriculture, *n.f.* agriculture.

ahurir, *vb.* bewilder, fluster.

aide, *n.f.* help, aid.

aider, *vb.* help, aid.

aïeul (à yœl), *n.m.* grandfather.

aïeule (à yœl), *n.f.* grandmother.

aïeux, *n.m.pl.* ancestors.

aigle, *n.m.f.* eagle.

aiglefin, *n.m.* haddock.

aigre, *adj.* sour.

aigu, *adj.* shrill, keen, pointed.

aiguille, *n.f.* needle.

aiguisé, *adj.* keen.

aiguiser, *vb.* sharpen.

ail (à ē) *n.m.* garlic.

aile, *n.f.* wing.

ailleurs, *adv.* elsewhere. d'a., in addition, anyhow.

aimable, *adj.* kind, pleasant, amiable.

aimant, *n.m.* magnet.

aimer, *vb.* love, like.

aine, *n.f.* groin.

aîné (ē nā), *1. adj. and n.m.* elder. *2. adj.* eldest, senior.

ainsi, *adv.* thus, so.

air, *n.m.* air, looks. en plein air, in the open air.

aire, *n.f.* area.

aise, *n.f.* ease, comfort. à l'a., comfortable.

aisé, *adj.* substantial, well-to-do; easy.

aisselle, *n.f.* armpit.

ajourner, *vb.* put off. s'a., adjourn.

ajouter, *vb.* add.

ajustage, *n.m.* fitting.

ajuster, *vb.* fit, fix, adjust.

alarme, *n.f.* alarm.

alarmer, *vb.* alarm.

album, *n.m.* album.

alcool (-kôl), *n.m.* alcohol.

alcoolique (-kôl-), *adj.* alcoholic.

alcôve, *n.f.* alcove.

alentours, *n.m.pl.* neighborhood, surroundings.

alerte, *adj.* spry, active, alert.

algèbre, *n.f.* algebra.

aliéné, *n.m.* lunatic.

aliéner, *vb.* alienate.

aligner, *vb.* line up.

aliment, *n.m.* food.

alimentation, *n.f.* feeding.

alimenter, *vb.* feed.

alinéa, *n.m.* paragraph.

aliter, *vb.* confine to bed.

allée, *n.f.* path, avenue, aisle.

allégation, *n.f.* allegation.

alléger, *vb.* lighten, soothe.

allégresse, *n.f.* glee, delight, mirth.

alléguer, *vb.* plead, allege.

Allemagne, *n.f.* Germany.

Allemand, *n.m.* German (person).

allemand, *1. n.m.* German (language). *2. adj.* German.

aller, *vb.* go. s'en a., go away. a. à, fit. se laisser a., drift. a. bien, fare well. a. mal, fare ill. a. et retour, round trip.

alliage, *n.m.* alloy.

alliance, *n.f.* alliance, union.

allié, *1. n.m.* ally, relation. *2. adj.* allied.

allier, *vb.* ally. s'a. à, join with.

allô, *interj.* hello.

allocation, *n.f.* allowance.

allonger, *vb.* lengthen, prolong.

allons, *interj.* well, come now.

allouer, *vb.* grant.

allumer, *vb.* light.

allumette, *n.f.* match.

allure, *n.f.* pace, gait.

allusion, *n.f.* hint, allusion. faire a. à, allude to.

almanach (-nä), *n.m.* almanac.

alors, *1. adv.* then. *2. conj.* a. que, when.

alouette, *n.f.* lark.

alphabet, *n.m.* alphabet.

altérer, *vb.* change.

alternatif, *adj.* alternate.

alternative, *n.f.* alternative.

alterner, *vb.* alternate.

Altesse, *n.f.* Highness (title).

altitude, *n.f.* altitude.

aluminium, *n.m.* aluminum.

amabilité, n.f. kindness.

amalgamer, vb. amalgamate.

amande, n.f. kernel; almond.

amant, n.m. lover.

amas, n.m. hoard, mass.

amasser, vb. hoard, gather, amass.

amateur, n.m. amateur.

ambassade, n.f. embassy.

ambassadeur, n.m. ambassador.

ambassadrice, n.f. ambassadress.

ambigu m., ambiguë f. adj. ambiguous.

ambiguïté, n.f. ambiguity.

ambitieux, adj. ambitious.

ambition, n.f. ambition.

ambre, n.m. amber.

ambulance, n.f. ambulance.

âme, n.f. soul.

amélioration, n.f. improvement.

améliorer, vb. improve.

aménager, vb. fit up.

amende, n.f. fine. mettre à l'a., fine.

amendement, n.m. amendment.

amender, vb. amend.

amener, vb. bring, lead.

amer (-r), adj. bitter.

Américain, n.m. American.

américain, adj. American.

Amérique, n.f. America.

A. du Nord, North America.

A. du Sud, South America.

amertume, n.f. bitterness.

ameublement, n.m. furniture.

ami m., amie f. n. friend.

amical, adj. friendly, amicable.

amidon, n.m. starch.

amiral, n.m. admiral.

amitié, n.f. friendship.

ammoniaque, n.f. ammonia.

amniocentèse, n.f. amniocentesis.

amoindrir, vb. lessen, reduce.

amollir, vb. soften.

amortir, vb. deaden, soften.

amour, n.m. love.

amoureux, 1. n.m. lover. 2. adj. in love, amorous.

amour-propre, n.m. vanity, pride, conceit.

ample, adj. ample, spacious.

ampleur, n.f. plenty, compass.

amplifier, vb. increase, enlarge, develop.

ampoule, n.f. blister; (electric) bulb.

amputer, vb. amputate.

amusement, n.m. fun, pastime, entertainment.

amuser, vb. entertain. s'a., have a good time.

amygdale, n.f. tonsil.

an, n.m. year.

analogie, n.f. analogy.

analogue, adj. similar, analogous.

analyse, n.f. analysis.

analyser, vb. analyze.

anarchie, n.f. anarchy.

anatomie, n.f. anatomy.

ancêtre, n.m. forefather, ancestor.

anche, n.f. reed.

anchois, n.m. anchovy.

ancien m., ancienne f. adj. ancient, old, former.

ancre, n.f. anchor.

ancrer, vb. anchor.

âne m., ânesse f. n. ass, donkey.

anéantir, vb. annihilate, destroy.

anecdote, n.f. anecdote.

anesthésique, adj. and n.m. anesthetic.

ange, n.m. angel.

Anglais, n.m. Englishman.

anglais, adj. and n.m. English.

Anglaise, n.f. Englishwoman.

angle, n.m. angle, corner.

Angleterre, n.f. England.

angoissant, adj. in anguish.

angoisse, n.f. agony, pang, anguish.

anguille, n.f. eel.

anguleux, adj. angular.

anicroche, n.f. hitch.

animal, n.m. and adj. animal.

animation, n.f. animation.

animer, vb. enliven, animate.

animosité, n.f. animosity.

anneau, n.m. ring, circle.

année, n.f. year; vintage.

annexe, n.f. annex.

annexer, vb. annex.

annexion, n.f. annexation.

anniversaire, n.m. anniversary, birthday.

annonce, n.f. advertisement, announcement.

annoncer, vb. advertise, announce.

annotation, n.f. annotation.

annoter, vb. annotate.

annuaire, n.m. directory.

annuel, adj. yearly, annual.

annulation, n.f. cancellation.

annuler, vb. cancel, void, annul.

ânonner, vb. stammer.

anonyme, adj. anonymous.

anormal, adj. irregular, abnormal.

anse, n.f. handle; bay.

antagonisme, n.m. antagonism.

antarctique, adj. antarctic.

antécédent, adj. and n.m. antecedent.

antécédents, n.m.pl. record.

antenne, n.f. antenna.

antérieur, adj. previous; fore, front.

anthracite, n.m. anthracite.

antichambre, n.f. entrance hall.

anticipation, n.f. anticipation.

anticiper, vb. anticipate.

antidote, n.m. antidote.

antilope, n.f. antelope.

antinucléaire, adj. antinuclear.

antipathie, n.f. antipathy.

antiquaire, n.m. antique dealer.

antique, adj. ancient, antiquated, antique.

antiquité, n.f. antiquity.

antiseptique, adj. and n.m. antiseptic.

antre, n.m. den.

anxiété, n.f. anxiety, worry.

anxieux, adj. anxious.

août (oo), n.m. August.

apaiser, vb. allay, quiet, appease.

apathie, n.f. apathy.

apercevoir, vb. perceive. s'a. de, realize.

aperçu, n.m. outline.

apéritif, n.m. appetizer.

apitoyer, vb. move (emotionally).

aplanir, vb. even off.

aplatir, vb. flatten.

aplomb, n.m. poise, boldness.

apoplexie, n.f. apoplexy.

apostolique, adj. apostolic.

apôtre, n.m. apostle.

apparaître, vb. appear.

appareil, n.m. gear, appliance, device. a. photographique, camera.

apparence, n.f. appearance, looks.

apparent, adj. noticeable, apparent.

apparition, n.f. appearance, ghost.

appartement, n.m. apartment.

appartenir, vb. belong, pertain.

appât, n.m. bait.

appel, n.m. call, appeal.

appeler, vb. call, summon, appeal. s'a., be named.

appendice, n.m. appendix.

appétit, n.m. appetite.

applaudir, vb. applaud.

applaudissements, n.m.pl. applause.

applicable, adj. applicable.

application, n.f. application, industry.

appliqué, adj. industrious.

appliquer, vb. apply (put on), stick. s'a., work hard.

appointements, n.m.pl. salary.

apporter, vb. bring, fetch.

apposer, vb. affix.

appréciable, adj. appreciable.

appréciation, n.f. appreciation.

apprécier, vb. appreciate, value.

appréhension, n.f. apprehension.

apprendre, vb. learn. a. à, teach (to). a. par cœur, memorize.

apprenti, n.m. apprentice.

apprentissage, n.m. apprenticeship.

apprêt, n.m. preparation.

apprêter, vb. s'a., prepare, get ready.

apprivoiser, vb. tame.

approbation, n.f. endorsement, approval, approbation.

approche, n.f. approach.

approcher, vb. s'a. de, approach, go toward.

approfondir, vb. deepen.

appropriation, n.f. appropriation.

approprier, vb. s'a., take over, appropriate.

approuver, vb. approve.

approvisionnement, n.m. supply.

approximatif, adj. approximate.

appui, n.m. support.

appuyer (-pwè-), vb. support, endorse, advocate. **a. sur,** emphasize.

après, 1. adv., prep. after. **2.** conj. **a. que,** after. **d'a.,** according to.

après-demain, n.m. day after tomorrow.

après-midi, n.m.f. afternoon.

âpreté, n.f. harshness, bitterness.

à-propos, n.m. fitness.

apte à, adj. apt, suitable for.

aptitude, n.f. fitness, ability, aptitude.

aqualit, n.m. waterbed.

aquarelle (-kwà-), n.f. water color.

aquarium (-kwà-), n.m. aquarium.

aquatique (-kwà-), adj. aquatic.

aqueux, adj. watery.

Arabe, n.m.f. Arab, Arabian.

arabe, 1. n.m. Arabic. **2.** adj. Arab, Arabian, Arabic.

arachide, n.f. peanut.

araignée, n.f. spider. **toile d'a.,** cobweb.

arbitrage, n.m. arbitration.

arbitraire, adj. arbitrary.

arbitre, n.m.f. umpire, arbitrator.

arbitrer, vb. arbitrate.

arbre, n.m. tree.

arbrisseau, n.m. shrub.

arc (-k), n.m. arc, arch, bow.

arcade, n.f. arcade.

arc-boutant, n.m. flying buttress.

arc-en-ciel, n.m. rainbow.

archaïque (àrk-), adj. archaic.

arche, n.f. arch (of bridge); ark.

archet, n.m. bow.

archevêque, n.m. archbishop.

archipel, n.m. archipelago.

architecte, n.m. architect.

architectural, adj. architectural.

architecture, n.f. architecture.

archives, n.f.pl. files, archives.

arctique, adj. arctic.

ardemment, adv. eagerly.

ardent, adj. eager, fiery, ardent.

ardeur, n.f. ardor.

ardoise, n.f. slate.

arène, n.f. arena, ring.

argent, n.m. silver, money.

argenterie, n.f. silverware.

Argentin, n.m. Argentine.

argentin, adj. Argentine.

argile, n.f. clay.

argot, n.m. slang.

argument, n.m. argument (reasoning).

argumenter, vb. argue (reason).

aride, adj. arid.

aristocrate, n.m.f. aristocrat.

aristocratie, n.f. aristocracy.

aristocratique, adj. aristocratic.

arithmétique, n.f. arithmetic.

arme, n.f. weapon; arm.

armée, n.f. army.

armement, n.m. armament.

arme nucléaire, n.f. nuclear weapon.

armer, vb. arm.

armistice, n.m. armistice.

armoire, n.f. cupboard, closet, wardrobe.

armure, n.f. armor.

aromatique, adj. aromatic.

arome, n.m. flavor, aroma.

arpenter, vb. pace.

arracher, vb. snatch.

arrangement, n.m. arrangement, settlement.

arranger, vb. settle, trim, fix, arrange.

arrestation, n.f. arrest, apprehension. **en état d'a.,** under arrest.

arrêt, n.m. stop.

arrêté, n.m. decree.

arrêter, vb. stop, check, halt, arrest.

arrière, adv. behind, back. **en a.,** backward. **marche a.,** reverse (gear).

arriéré, 1. n.m. arrear. **2.** adj. backward.

arrière-garde, n.f. rear guard.

arrivée, n.f. arrival.

arriver, vb. happen, reach, arrive.

arrogance, n.f. arrogance.

arrogant, adj. arrogant.

arroger, vb. arrogate, assume.

arrondir, vb. round off.

arrondissement, n.m. district.

arroser, vb. water, sprinkle, baste (meat).

arsenal, n.m. arsenal.

arsenic, n.m. arsenic.

art, n.m. art. **beaux-arts,** fine arts.

artère, n.f. artery.

artichaut, n.m. artichoke.

article, n.m. article, item, entry. **a. de fond,** editorial.

articulation, n.f. joint, articulation.

articuler, vb. articulate.

artifice, n.m. artifice.

artificiel, adj. artificial.

artificieux, adj. artful.

artillerie, n.f. artillery.

artisan, n.m. craftsman, artisan.

artiste, n.m. artist.

artistique, adj. artistic.

as (às), n.m. ace.

ascenseur, n.m. elevator.

ascension, n.f. ascent (of a mountain).

Asiatique, n.m.f. Asian.

asiatique, adj. Asian.

Asie, n.f. Asia.

asile, n.m. haven, refuge, asylum.

aspect (-pè), n.m. looks, appearance, aspect.

asperger, vb. sprinkle.

asperges, n.f.pl. asparagus.

asphalte, n.m., asphalt.

aspirateur, n.m. vacuum cleaner.

aspiration, n.f. aspiration, longing.

aspirer, vb. aspire, breathe.

assaillant, n.m. assailant.

assaillir, vb. assail, attack.

assaisonner, vb. season.

assassin, n.m. assassin, murderer.

assassinat, n.m. assassination, murder.

assassiner, vb. assassinate, murder.

assaut, n.m. assault, attack.

assemblage, n.m. collection.

assemblée, n.f. congregation, assembly.

assembler, vb. convene, gather. **s'a.,** assemble.

assentiment, n.m. assent.

asseoir, vb. seat. **s'a.,** sit down.

assertion, n.f. assertion.

asservir, vb. enslave.

assez (de), n. and adv. enough (of); pretty much.

assidu, adj. assiduous, industrious.

assiduité, n.f. industry.

assiéger, vb. besiege.

assiette, n.f. plate.

assigner, vb. assign.

assimiler, vb. assimilate.

assis, adj. seated.

assistance, n.f. those present.

assister à, vb. attend, be present at.

association, n.f. soccer; association, company; connection.

associé, 1. n.m. partner, associate. **2.** adj. associated.

associer, vb. associate.

assombrir, vb. s'a., grow dark.

assommer, vb. murder, slaughter.

Assomption, n.f. Assumption (eccles.).

assortiment, n.m. assortment.

assortir, vb. match; tune.

assoupir, vb. s'a., get drowsy.

assourdir, vb. deafen.

assujetti, adj. subject.

assujettir, vb. subject.

assumer, vb. assume.

assurance, n.f. assurance, insurance.

assuré, adj. sure.

assurer, vb. insure; assure. **s'a. de,** make certain.

assureur, n.m. insurer.

astérisque, n.m. asterisk.

astre, n.m. star.

astronaute, n.m. astronaut.

astronome, n.m. astronomer.

astronomie, n.f. astronomy.

astucieux, adj. tricky.

atelier, n.m. studio, (work)shop.

athée, n.m.f. atheist.
athlète, n.m.f. athlete.
athlétique, adj. athletic.
atlantique, adj. Atlantic.
atlas (-s), n.m. atlas.
atmosphère, n.f. atmosphere.
atmosphérique, adj. atmospheric.
atome, n.m. atom.
atomique, adj. atomic.
atroce, adj. atrocious, outrageous.
atrocité, n.f. atrocity.
attachement, n.m. attachment, affection.
attacher, vb. tie, fasten, join, attach.
attaque, n.f. attack.
attaquer, vb. attack.
attardé, adj. belated.
attarder, vb. s'a., linger, delay.
atteindre, vb. reach, attain; strike.
atteint, adj. stricken.
atteinte, n.f. reach. hors d'a., out of reach.
attelage, n.m. team.
atteler, vb. hitch up, harness.
attendre, vb. wait (for), await. s'a. à, expect.
attendrir, vb. soften, move. se laisser a., relent.
attendrissement, n.m. feeling, emotion.
attentat, n.m. criminal attack, outrage.
attente, n.f. expectation, wait.
attentif, adj. thoughtful, attentive.
attention, n.f. notice, heed, attention. faire a., heed, pay attention.
atténuer, vb. extenuate.
atterrir, vb. land.
attester, vb. attest.
attirer, vb. attract, entice, lure.
attitude, n.f. attitude.
attouchement, n.m. touch.
attraction, n.f. attraction.
attrait, n.m. charm.
attraper, vb. catch.
attrayant, adj. attractive.
attribuer, vb. ascribe, attribute.
attribut, n.m. attribute, characteristic.
attrister, vb. grieve.
au m., à la f., aux pl. prep. to the, in the.
aube, n.f. dawn.
auberge, n.f. inn.
aubergine, n.f. eggplant.
aubergiste, n.m. innkeeper.
aucun, pron. none.
aucunement, adv. not at all.
audace, n.f. audacity.
audacieux, adj. daring, bold.
au-dessous, 1. adv. below. 2. prep. au-d. de, beneath, under.
au-dessus, 1. adv. above. 2. prep. au-d. de, over, above.
audience, n.f. audience.
audiovisuel, adj. audiovisual.
auditoire, n.m. audience, assembly.

auge, n.f. trough.
augmentation, n.f. increase, raise, rise.
augmenter, vb. increase.
augure, n.m. omen, augury. de bon a., auspicious. de mauvais a., ominous.
augurer, vb. augur.
aujourd'hui, adv. today.
aumône, n.f. alms.
aumônier, n.m. chaplain.
auparavant, adv. before (time).
auprès de, prep. next, near, beside.
auréole, n.f. halo.
aurore, n.f. dawn.
auspice, n.m. auspice.
aussi, adv. too, also; so, as; therefore.
austère, adj. austere, severe.
austérité, n.f. austerity.
Australie, n.f. Australia.
Australien, n.m. Australian.
australien, adj. Australian.
autant, adv. so much as much. a. que, as (so) much as. d'a. que, since. a. plus, so much the more.
autel, n.m. altar.
auteur, n.m. author, originator.
authentique, adj. true, genuine, authentic.
auto, n.f. auto.
autobus (-s), n.m. bus.
automatique, adj. automatic.
automne (-tôn), n.m. fall.
automobile, n.f. automobile.
autonomie, n.f. autonomy.
autorisation, n.f. license, authorization.
autoriser, vb. authorize.
autoritaire, adj. authoritative.
autorité, n.f. authority.
autour, 1. adv. around. 2. prep. a. de, around.
autre, 1. adj. other. 2. pron. other, else. l'un l'a., one another. quelqu'un d'a., someone else.
autrefois, adv. formerly.
autrement, adv. otherwise.
Autriche, n.f. Austria.
Autrichien, n.m. Austrian.
autrichien, adj. Austrian.
autruche, n.f. ostrich.
autrui, pron. someone else, others.
auxiliaire, adj. auxiliary.
avalanche, n.f. avalanche.
avaler, vb. swallow.
avance, n.f. advance. d'a., beforehand. en a., fast (clock).
avancé, adj. forward, advanced.
avancement, n.m. advance; advancement; promotion.
avancer, vb. proceed; come or go forward or onward.
avances, n.f.pl. advance. faire des a. à, make approaches to.
avant, 1. n.m. fore, bow. 2. adv., prep. before. 3. conj. a. que, before. en a., forward, onward. en a. de, ahead of.
avantage, n.m. advantage.

avantageux, adj. advantageous; favorable; profitable.
avant-bras, n.m. forearm.
avant-garde, n.f. vanguard.
avant-hier (-yâr), n.m. day before yesterday.
avant-toit, n.m. eaves.
avare, 1. n.m.f. miser. 2. adj. miserly, stingy.
avarice, n.f. avarice.
avec, prep. with.
avenant, adj. comely. à l'a., accordingly.
avenir, n.m. future.
Avent, n.m. (eccles.) Advent.
aventure, n.f. adventure.
aventurer, vb. s'a., take a chance.
aventureux, adj. adventurous.
aventurier, n.m. adventurer.
avenue, n.f. avenue.
averse, n.f. shower.
aversion, n.f. aversion, dislike.
avertir, vb. notify, warn.
avertissement, n.m. warning.
avertisseur d'incendie, n.m. fire alarm.
aveu, n.m. admission, confession.
aveugle, adj. blind.
aveuglement, n.m. blindness.
aveuglément, adv. blindly.
aveugler, vb. blind.
aviateur, n.m. flier, aviator.
aviation, n.f. air force, aviation.
avide, adj. eager, greedy, avid.
avidité, n.f. greediness.
avilir, vb. debase, disgrace.
avion, n.m. airplane. a. de bombardement, bomber. par a., via air mail.
avis, n.m. notice, opinion, advice (comm.).
aviser, vb. inform, notify. s'a. (de), decide.
avocat, n.m. lawyer; advocate.
avoine, n.f. oat.
avoir, vb. have. il y a, ago.
avortement, n.m. abortion.
avoué, n.m. attorney, lawyer.
avouer, vb. confess, admit, avow.
avril (-l), n.m. April.
axe, n.m. axis.
ayatollah, n.m. ayatollah.
azur, n.m. azure, blue.
azuré, adj. azure.

B

babeurre, n.m. buttermilk.
babil, n.m. babble.
babiller, vb. babble.
bâbord, n.m. (naut.) port.
babouin, n.m. baboon.
bac, n.m. ferryboat. passage en b., ferry.
bachelier, n.m. graduate.
bacille (-l), n.m. bacillus.
bactérie, n.f. bacterium.
bactériologie, n.f. bacteriology.
badaud, adj. silly.

bagages, *n.m.pl.* luggage.

bagatelle, *n.f.* trifle.

bague, *n.f.* ring.

baguette, *n.f.* wand, stick; long, thin loaf of bread.

baie, *n.f.* bay, creek; berry.

baigner, *vb.* bathe.

baigneur, *n.m.* bather.

baignoire, *n.f.* bathtub.

bail, *n.m.* lease.

bâillement, *n.m.* yawn.

bâiller, *vb.* yawn.

bâillon, *n.m.* gag.

bain, *n.m.* bath.

baïonnette, *n.f.* bayonet.

baiser, *n.m. and vb.* kiss.

baissé, *adj.* downcast.

baisser, *vb.* lower, sink.

bal, *n.m.* ball.

balai, *n.m.* broom. **b. à laver,** mop.

balance, *n.f.* scales, balance.

balancement, *n.m.* rocking, swinging.

balancer, *vb.* rock, swing, sway. **se b.,** roll, hover.

balayer, *vb.* sweep.

balbutier, *vb.* stammer.

balcon, *n.m.* balcony.

baldaquin, *n.m.* canopy.

baleine, *n.f.* whale.

ballade, *n.f.* ballad.

balle, *n.f.* bullet, ball; bale.

ballet, *n.m.* ballet.

ballon, *n.m.* balloon.

ballot, *n.m.* bundle.

ballotter, *vb.* shake.

balsamique, *adj.* balmy.

bambou, *n.m.* bamboo.

ban, *n.m.* ban. **mettre au b.,** ban.

banal, *adj.* trite.

banane, *n.f.* banana.

banc, *n.m.* bench.

bandage, *n.m.* bandage.

bande, *n.f.* strip, stripe; pack, gang, band.

bande vidéo, *n.f.* videotape.

bandit, *n.m.* bandit, robber, knave.

banlieue, *n.f.* suburbs.

bannière, *n.f.* banner.

bannir, *vb.* banish.

bannissement, *n.m.* banishment.

banque, *n.f.* bank. **billet de b.,** banknote.

banqueroute, *n.f.* bankruptcy.

banqueroutier, *n.* bankrupt.

banquet, *n.m.* banquet, feast.

banquier, *n.m.* banker.

baptême (bä těm), *n.m.* christening, baptism.

baptiser (bä tě-), *vb.* christen, baptize.

Baptiste (bä těst), *n.m.* Baptist.

baptistère (bä tès-), *n.m.* baptistery.

bar, *n.m.* bar; bass (fish).

baraque, *n.f.* booth, stall.

baratter, *vb.* churn.

barbare, **1.** *n.m.f.* barbarian. **2.** *adj.* barbarian, barbarous, wild.

barbarie, *n.f.* cruelty.

barbe, *n.f.* beard.

barbouiller, *vb.* daub, blur.

baromètre, *n.m.* barometer.

baron, *n.m.* baron.

barque, *n.f.* boat.

barrage, *n.m.* dam.

barre, *n.f.* bar, rail(ing). **b. du gouvernail,** helm.

barreau, *n.m.* bar.

barrer, *vb.* shut out.

barricade, *n.f.* barricade.

barrière, *n.f.* gate; bar, barrier; fence.

barrique, *n.f.* barrel, cask.

bas, *n.m.* stocking.

bas *m.,* **basse** *f. adj.* base, low, soft. *n.m.* **b.,** down(ward), downstairs. **b. côté,** aisle.

bascule, *n.f.* seesaw. **chaise à b.,** rocking-chair.

base, *n.f.* base, basis.

basse, *n.f.* bass (voice).

basse-cour, *n.f.* barnyard.

bassesse, *n.f.* baseness.

bassin, *n.m.* basin, dock.

bataille, *n.f.* battle.

bataillon, *n.m.* battalion.

bâtard, *adj. and n.m.* bastard.

bateau, *n.m.* boat.

bâtiment, *n.m.* building.

bâtir, *vb.* build.

bâton, *n.m.* stick, staff.

battant, *n.m.* flap, door.

batte, *n.f.* bat.

battement, *n.m.* beat.

batterie, *n.f.* battery.

battre, *vb.* beat, strike; flap, pulsate. **se b.,** fight.

baume, *n.m.* balm.

bavard, *adj.* talkative, gossipy.

bavardage, *n.m.* gossip, chatter.

bavarder, *vb.* gossip, chat(ter).

bavette, *n.f.* bib.

bazar, *n.m.* bazaar.

béatitude, *n.f.* bliss.

beau, bel *m.,* **belle** *f. adj.* beautiful, handsome, fair, lovely, fine. **avoir beau,** (to do something) in vain. **faire beau, be fine** (weather).

beaucoup (de), *adj.* a lot, a great deal; much, many. **de b.,** by far.

beau-frère, *n.m.* brother-in-law.

beau-père, *n.m.* father-in-law.

beauté, *n.f.* beauty. **grain de b.,** mole.

bébé, *n.m.* baby.

bec, *n.m.* beak, bill; spot; burner.

bêche, *n.f.* spade.

bêcher, *vb.* dig.

becqueter, *vb.* peck.

bée, *adj.* **rester bouche b.,** stand gaping.

bégayer, *vb.* stammer.

bêler, *vb.* bleat.

Belge, *n.m.f.* Belgian.

belge, *adj.* Belgian.

Belgique, *n.f.* Belgium.

bélier, *n.m.* ram.

belle-fille, *n.f.* daughter-in-law.

belle-mère, *n.f.* mother-in-law; stepmother.

belligérant, *adj. and n.m.* belligerent.

bénédiction, *n.f.* blsessing, benediction.

bénéfice, *n.m.* benefit, advantage, profit.

bénéficier, *vb.* benefit, profit.

bénin *m.,* **bénigne** *f. adj.* benign.

bénir, *vb.* bless.

béquille, *n.f.* crutch.

berceau, *n.m.* cradle, bower.

bercer, *vb.* rock.

berge, *n.f.* bank.

berger, *n.m.* shepherd.

besogne, *n.f.* (piece of) work.

besoin, *n.m.* need, want. **avoir b.,** need.

bestiaux, *n.m.pl.* cattle.

bétail, *n.m.* cattle, animals.

bête, 1. *n.f.* beast, animal. **2.** *adj.* stupid, dumb.

bêtise, *n.f.* nonsense.

béton, *n.m.* concrete.

betterave, *n.f.* beet.

beurre, *n.m.* butter.

bévue, *n.f.* blunder, boner.

biais, *n.m.* slant; bias. **en b.,** at an angle.

bibelot, *n.m.* trinket.

biberon, *n.m.* baby's bottle.

Bible, *n.f.* Bible.

bibliothèque, *n.f.* library; bookcase.

biblique, *adj.* biblical.

bicyclette, *n.f.* bicycle. **faire de la b.,** cycle.

bidon, *n.m.* can.

bien, *n.m.* good; *(pl.)* goods, property, estate. **faire du b. à,** benefit.

bien, *adv.* well. **b. entendu,** of course. **aller b.,** be well. **vouloir b.,** be willing. **b. que,** although.

bien-aimé, *n.m.f. and adj.* darling.

bien-être, *n.m.* welfare.

bienfaisant, *adj.* beneficent, kind, humane.

bienfait, *n.m.* benefit.

bienfaiteur, *n.m.* benefactor.

bienheureux, *adj.* blessed.

bientôt, *adv.* soon.

bienveillance, *n.f.* benevolence, kindness.

bienveillant, *adj.* benevolent, kindly.

bienvenu, *adj.* welcome.

bière, *n.f.* beer, ale.

biffer, *vb.* cancel, erase.

bifteck, *n.m.* beefsteak.

bigamie, *n.f.* bigamy.

bigot, *n.m.* bigot.

bigoterie, *n.f.* bigotry.

bijou, *n.m.* jewel.

bijouterie, *n.f.* jewelry.

bile, *n.f.* bile. **se faire de la b.,** worry.

billard, *n.m.* billiards.

bille, *n.f.* marble (toy).

billet, *n.m.* ticket, note. **b. de banque,** banknote.

billion (-l-), *n.m.* billion.

biographie, *n.f.* biography.

biologie, *n.f.* biology.

biscuit, *n.m.* biscuit.

bizarre, *adj.* queer, odd, strange, quaint.

blâme, *n.m.* blame.

blâmer, *vb.* blame.

blanc *m.,* **blanche** *f. adj.* white, blank. **en b.,** blank.

blancheur, *n.f.* whiteness.

blanchir, *vb.* whiten.

blanchisserie, *n.f.* laundry.

blasé, *adj.* sophisticated.

blasphème, *n.m.* blasphemy.

blasphémer, *vb.* curse, blaspheme.

blatte, *n.f.* cockroach.

blé, *n.m.* wheat.

blême, *adj.* pale.

blesser, *vb.* wound, hurt, injure.

blessure, *n.f.* wound, hurt, injury.

bleu, *adj.* blue.

bloc, *n.m.* pad, block.

blocus (-s), *n.m.* blockade.

blond, *adj.* fair, blond(e).

bloquer, *vb.* block.

blottir, *vb.* se b., cower.

blouse, *n.f.* blouse.

blue jeans, *n.m.pl.* blue jeans.

bluff, *n.m.* bluff.

bluffeur, *n.m.* bluffer.

bobine, *n.f.* spool, reel.

bœuf (bœf), *n.m.* ox, beef. **jeune b.,** steer.

Bohême, *n.f.* Bohemia.

bohème, **1.** *n.m.f.* bohemian, happy-go-lucky person. **2.** *n.f.* artistic underworld. **3.** *adj.* bohemian.

Bohémien, *n.m.* Bohemian; gypsy.

bohémien, *adj.* Bohemian.

boire, *vb.* drink. **b. à petits coups,** sip.

bois, *n.m.* wood, forest, lumber.

boiserie, *n.f.* woodwork.

boisseau, *n.m.* bushel.

boisson, *n.f.* beverage, drink.

boîte, *n.f.* box; can (food). **b. aux lettres,** mail-box.

boiter, *vb.* limp.

boiteux, *adj.* lame.

bol, *n.m.* bowl.

bombardement, *n.m.* bombardment.

bombarder, *vb.* bomb, bombard.

bombe, *n.f.* bomb, shell.

bombe à neutrons, *n.f.* neutron bomb.

bon *m.,* **bonne** *f. adj.* good, kind. **de b. heure,** early. **b. marché,** cheap.

bon, *n.m.* bond.

bonbon, *n.m.* candy, bonbon.

bond, *n.m.* bound, leap.

bonder, *vb.* overcrowd, jam.

bondir, *vb.* bound, leap, spring.

bonheur, *n.m.* happiness.

bonhomme, *n.m.* fellow.

bonjour, *interj. and n.m.* good morning.

bonne, *n.f.* maid.

bonnement, *adv.* simply.

bonnet, *n.m.* cap, hood.

bonsoir, *interj. and n.m.* good evening.

bonté, *n.f.* kindness, goodness.

bord, *n.m.* edge, rim, brim **b. du toit,** eaves.

border, *vb.* bound, edge, border, hem.

borne, *n.f.* bound, limit.

borner, *vb.* bound, limit.

bosquet, *n.m.* clump (trees).

bosse, *n.f.* bump.

bosselure, *n.f.* dent.

bossu, *adj.* hunchbacked.

botanique, *n.f.* botany.

botte, *n.f.* boot; bunch.

bottine, *n.f.* boot.

bouche, *n.f.* mouth.

boucher, *vb.* stop up.

boucher, *n.m.* butcher.

boucherie, *n.f.* butcher shop.

bouchon, *n.m.* cork.

boucle, *n.f.* curl, loop, buckle. **b. d'oreille,** earring.

boucler, *vb.* curl.

bouclier, *n.m.* shield.

bouder, *vb.* sulk.

boue, *n.f.* mud.

bouée, *n.f.* buoy.

boueur, *n.m.* scavenger.

boueux, *adj.* muddy.

bouffée, *n.f.* puff.

bouffon, *n.m.* clown, fool.

bouffonnerie, *n.f.* antic(s).

bouger, *vb.* stir, move, budge.

bougie, *n.f.* candle.

bouillir, *vb.* boil.

bouilloire, *n.f.* kettle.

bouillon, *n.m.* broth.

bouillonner, *vb.* bubble.

bouillotte, *n.f.* kettle.

boulanger, *n.m.* baker.

boulangerie, *n.f.* bakery.

boule, *n.f.* ball.

bouleau, *n.m.* birch.

bouledogue, *n.m.* bulldog.

boulevard, *n.m.* boulevard.

bouleversement, *n.m.* upset.

bouleverser, *vb.* upset, overturn.

bouquet, *n.m.* cluster, bunch, bouquet.

bouquiniste, *n.m.* (secondhand) bookseller.

bourbeux, *adj.* sloppy.

bourdon, *n.m.* bumblebee.

bourdonnement, *n.m.* buzz.

bourdonner, *vb.* hum, buzz.

bourg, *n.m.* borough, village.

bourgeois, *adj.* middle-class, bourgeois.

bourgeoisie, *n.f.* middle class.

bourgeon, *n.m.* bud.

bourgeonner, *vb.* bud.

bourre, *n.f.* stuffing.

bourreau, *n.m.* executioner, hangman; brute.

bourrelet, *n.m.* pad.

bourrer, *vb.* stuff, pad.

bourru, *adj.* gruff.

bourse, *n.f.* purse, bag; stock exchange; scholarship, fellowship.

boursoufler, *vb.* bloat.

bousculer, *vb.* jostle.

bousiller, *vb.* bungle.

boussole, *n.f.* compass.

bout, *n.m.* end, tip, butt, stub.

bouteille, *n.f.* bottle.

boutique, *n.f.* shop.

bouton, *n.m.* button, bud; pimple.

boutonnière, *n.f.* buttonhole.

boxe, *n.f.* boxing.

boxeur, *n.m.* boxer.

boycotter, *vb.* boycott.

bracelet, *n.m.* bracelet.

braconnier, *n.m.* poacher.

brailler, *vb.* bawl.

braise, *n.f.* coals, embers.

brancard, *n.m.* stretcher.

branche, *n.f.* branch, bough, limb.

brandir, *vb.* brandish.

branler, *vb.* waver.

braquer, *vb.* aim, point.

bras, *n.m.* arm.

brasse, *n.f.* fathom.

brasser, *vb.* brew.

brasserie, *n.f.* brewery, beerjoint.

bravade, *n.f.* bravado.

brave, *adj.* fine, good, brave.

braver, *vb.* brave, face, defy.

bravoure, *n.f.* courage.

brebis, *n.f.* lamb.

brèche, *n.f.* breach, gap.

bref, **1.** *adj.m.,* **brève** *f.* brief, short. **2.** *adv.* in short.

Brésil, *n.m.* Brazil.

brevet, *n.m.* commission. **b. d'invention,** patent.

bribe, *n.f.* scrap, bit.

bride, *n.f.* bridle.

brider, *vb.* curb.

bridge, *n.m.* bridge (game).

brièveté, *n.f.* brevity.

brigade, *n.f.* brigade.

brigadier, *n.m.* corporal.

brigand, *n.m.* robber, knave.

brillant, *adj.* brilliant, bright, glowing.

briller, *vb.* shine, glisten, glare.

brin, *n.m.* blade (grass).

brindille, *n.f.* twig.

brioche, *n.f.* bun.

brique, *n.f.* brick.

briquet, *n.m.* pierre à b., flint.

brise, *n.f.* breeze.

briser, *vb.* break, shatter, smash.

britannique, *adj.* British.

brocart, *n.m.* brocade.

broche, *n.f.* spit, spindle; brooch.

brochure, *n.f.* pamphlet.

broder, *vb.* embroider.

broderie, *n.f.* embroidery.

bronchite, *n.f.* bronchitis.

bronze, *n.m.* bronze.

broquette, *n.f.* tack.

brosse, *n.f.* brush.

brosser, *vb.* brush.

brouhaha, *n.m.* uproar.

brouillard, *n.m.* fog, mist.

brouiller, *vb.* jumble, embroil;

scramble (eggs). se b., quarrel.

brouillon, n.m. (rough) draft.

broussailles, n.f.pl. brushwood.

brouter, vb. browse.

broyer, vb. crush.

bruine, n.f. drizzle.

bruiner, vb. drizzle.

bruissement, n.m. rustle.

bruit, n.m. noise, clatter; report, rumor.

brûler, vb. burn.

brume, n.f. mist. b. légère, haze.

brumeux, adj. foggy, misty.

brun, adj. brown.

brune, adj. and n.f. brunette.

brusque, adj. abrupt, curt, blunt, gruff, brusque.

brut, adj. crude, gross.

brutal, adj. brutal, savage.

brutalité, n.f. brutality.

brute, n.f. brute.

bruyant, adj. noisy, loud.

bruyère, n.f. heath, heather.

bûche, n.f. log.

bûcheron, n.m. wood-cutter.

budget, n.m. budget.

buffet, n.m. buffet.

buffle, n.m. buffalo.

buis, n.m. box (tree).

buisson, n.m. bush, shrub, thicket.

buissonneux, adj. bushy.

bulbe, n.m. bulb.

bulle, n.f. bubble; (papal) bull.

bulletin, n.m. bulletin, ticket.

bureau, n.m. office, bureau; desk. b. de location, box-office.

burin, n.m. chisel.

burlesque, adj. ludicrous.

buste, n.m. bust.

but, n.m. aim, goal, purpose.

butin, n.m. spoils, booty.

butte, n.f. hill, knoll.

buvard, n.m. blotter.

C

ça, pron. that.

cabane, n.f. cabin, hut.

cabaret, n.m. cabaret, tavern.

cabine, n.f. cabin, booth.

cabinet, n.m. closet; office. c. de toilette, lavatory. c. de travail, study.

câble, n.m. cable, rope.

câbler, vb. cable.

câblogramme, n.m. cablegram.

cacao, n.m. cocoa.

cacher, vb. hide, conceal. se c., lurk.

cachet, n.m. seal.

cadavre, n.m. corpse.

cadeau, n.m. gift, present.

cadence, n.f. cadence.

cadet, 1. n.m. cadet. 2. adj. junior.

cadran, n.m. dial.

cadre, n.m. frame.

café, n.m. coffee; café.

cage, n.f. cage.

cahier, n.m. notebook.

caille, n.f. quail.

caillot, n.m. clot.

caillou, n.m. pebble.

caisse, n.f. crate, case, box.

caissier, n.m. cashier, teller.

cajoler, vb. coax.

calamité, n.f. calamity.

calcium, n.m. calcium.

calcul, n.m. calculation.

calculer, vb. figure, reckon, calculate.

cale, n.f. hold.

calembour, n.m. pun.

calendrier, n.m. calendar.

calibre, n.m. caliber.

calicot, n.m. calico.

callosité, n.f. callus.

calme, n.m. and adj. quiet, calm.

calmer, vb. soothe, quiet, calm.

calomnie, n.f. slander.

calomnier, vb. slander.

calorie, n.f. calorie.

calotte, n.f. crown (of hat).

Calvaire, n.m. Calvary.

camarade, n.m.f. comrade, companion, mate.

camaraderie, n.f. companionship, fellowship.

cambrioleur, n.m. burglar.

camion, n.m. truck.

camoufler, vb. camouflage.

camp, n.m. camp.

campagnard, 1. n. countryman, peasant. 2. adj. peasant.

campagne, n.f. country; campaign.

camper, vb. camp.

camphre, n.m. camphor.

Canada, n.m. Canada.

Canadien, n.m. Canadian.

canadien, adj. Canadian.

canaille, n.f. rabble; scoundrel.

canal, n.m. channel, canal.

canapé, n.m. sofa, couch; canapé.

canard, n.m. duck.

canari, n.m. canary.

cancer (-r), n.m. cancer.

cancérogène, adj. carcinogenic.

candeur, n.f. purity; candor.

candidat, n.m. candidate, applicant.

candidature, n.f. candidacy.

candide, adj. frank, open, candid.

canevas, n.m. canvas. gros c., burlap.

canin, adj. canine.

canne, n.f. cane, stick.

canneberge, n.f. cranberry.

cannelle, n.f. cinnamon.

cannibale, adj. and n.m.f. cannibal.

canoë (-ō ă), n.m. canoe.

canon, n.m. cannon.

canot, n.m. boat, canoe. c. automobile, motorboat.

cantaloup, n.m. cantaloupe.

cantique, n.m. hymn.

canton, n.m. district, canton.

caoutchouc (-choo), n.m. rubber.

cap (-p), n.m. cape (headland).

capable, adj. efficient, fit, capable, competent.

capacité, n.f. capability, capacity.

cape, n.f. cape (clothing).

capitaine, n.m. captain.

capital, n.m. and adj. capital.

capitale, n.f. capital (city).

capitaliser, vb. capitalize.

capitalisme, n.m. capitalism.

capitaliste, n.m.f. capitalist.

caporal, n.m. corporal.

capote, n.f. hood.

câpre, n.f. caper.

caprice, n.m. whim, fancy.

capricieux, adj. fickle, capricious.

capsule, n.f. capsule.

captif, adj. and n.m. captive.

captiver, vb. captivate, charm.

captivité, n.f. captivity.

capture, n.f. capture.

capturer, vb. capture.

capuchon, n.m. hood.

car, conj. for.

caractère, n.m. character, nature, disposition; type.

caractériser, vb. characterize; distinguish; mark.

caractéristique, adj. characteristic.

carafe, n.f. decanter, water-bottle.

caramel, n.m. caramel.

carat, n.m. carat.

caravane, n.f. caravan.

carbone, n.m. carbon.

carboniser, vb. char.

carburateur, n.m. carburetor.

carcasse, n.f. shell; carcass.

cardinal, n.m. cardinal.

carême, n.m. Lent.

caresse, n.f. caress.

caresser, vb. fondle, stroke, caress.

cargaison, n.f. cargo.

caricature, n.f. caricature.

carie, n.f. decay.

carillon, n.m. chime.

carillonner, vb. chime.

carnaval, n.m. carnival.

carnet, n.m. notebook.

carnivore, adj. carnivorous.

carotte, n.f. carrot.

carré, n.m. and adj. square.

carreau, n.m. diamond (cards); pane; tile.

carrefour, n.m. crossroads.

carrière, n.f. career; scope; quarry.

carriole, n.f. (light) cart.

carrosse, n.m. coach.

carte, n.f. chart, map, card. c. de crédit, n.f. credit card. c. du jour, bill of fare.

carton, n.m. cardboard; box, carton.

cartouche, n.f. cartridge.

cas, n.m. case; event.

case, n.f. pigeonhole; hut, shed.

caserne, n.f. barracks.

casque, n.m. helmet.

casquette, n.f. cap.

cassable, *adj.* breakable.

casse-croûte, *n.m.* snack.

casser, *vb.* break, crack.

casserole, *n.f.* pan.

cassette, *n.f.* 1. casket. 2. cassette.

cassis, *n.m.* black currant.

caste, *n.f.* caste.

castor, *n.m.* beaver.

casuel, *adj.* casual.

catalogue, *n.m.* catalogue.

cataracte, *n.f.* cataract.

catarrhe, *n.m.* catarrh.

catastrophe, *n.f.* disaster, catastrophe.

catéchisme, *n.m.* catechism.

catégorie, *n.f.* category.

cathédrale, *n.f.* cathedral.

catholicisme, *n.m.* Catholicism.

catholique, *adj.* Catholic.

cauchemar, *n.m.* nightmare.

cause, *n.f.* case; cause.

causer, *vb.* chat; cause.

causerie, *n.f.* chat, talk.

causette, *n.f.* chat.

caution, *n.f.* bail, security.

cavalerie, *n.f.* cavalry.

cavalier, *n.m.* rider, horseman; escort.

cave, *n.f.* cellar, cavern.

cavité, *n.f.* cavity.

ce (sə), cet (sèt) *m.*, cette (sèt) *f.*, ces (sā) *pl. adj.* that, this.

ceci, *pron.* this.

cécité, *n.f.* blindness.

céder, *vb.* yield, give in, cede.

cèdre, *n.m.* cedar.

ceindre, *vb.* gird.

ceinture, *n.f.* belt, sash.

cela, *pron.* that.

célébration, *n.f.* celebration.

célèbre, *adj.* famous, noted.

célébrer, *vb.* celebrate.

célébrité, *n.f.* celebrity.

céleri, *n.m.* celery.

céleste, *adj.* heavenly, celestial.

célibataire, 1. *n.m.* bachelor. 2. *adj.* single.

celle, *pron. f.* See celui.

cellule, *n.f.* cell.

celluloïd (-lô ēd), *n.m.* celluloid.

celtique, *adj.* Celtic.

celui *m.*, celle *f.*, ceux *m.pl.*, celles *f.pl. pron.* the one. celui-ci, this one; the latter. celui-là, that one; the former.

cendre, *n.f.* ashes, cinders.

cendrier, *n.m.* ash-tray.

censeur, *n.m.* censor.

censure, *n.f.* censure.

censurer, *vb.* censor.

cent, *adj.* and *n.m.* hundred. pour c., percent.

centaine, *n.f.* hundred.

centenaire, *adj.* and *n.m.* centenary, centennial.

centième, *adj.* hundredth.

centigrade, *adj.* centigrade.

centimètre, *n.m.* centimeter.

central, *adj.* central.

centraliser, *vb.* centralize.

centre, *n.m.* center.

cependant, *adv.* however, still, yet.

cercle, *n.m.* circle, ring, hoop; club.

cercueil, *n.m.* coffin.

céréale, *adj.* and *n.f.* cereal.

cérémonial, *adj.* and *n.m.* ceremonial.

cérémonie, *n.f.* ceremony. sans c., informal.

cérémonieux, *adj.* formal, ceremonious.

cerf (sèr), *n.m.* deer.

cerf-volant, *n.m.* kite.

cerise, *n.f.* cherry.

certain, *adj.* certain, sure; *(pl.)* some.

certes, *adv.* indeed.

certificat, *n.m.* credentials; certificate.

certifier, *vb.* certify.

certitude, *n.f.* certainty, assurance.

cerveau, *n.m.* brain.

cervelle, *n.f.* brains.

cessation, *n.f.* stopping, cessation.

cesser, *vb.* stop, desist, cease.

cession, *n.f.* assignment (law).

cet, cette, *pron.* See ce.

chacun, *pron.* everybody, everyone; each; apiece.

chagrin, 1. *n.m.* grief, vexation. 2. *adj.* fretful.

chagriner, *vb.* grieve.

chaîne, *n.f.* chain; range.

chaînon, *n.m.* link.

chair, *n.f.* flesh.

chaire, *n.f.* pulpit; chair (university).

chaise, *n.f.* chair.

chaland, *n.m.* barge.

châle, *n.m.* shawl.

chaleur, *n.f.* warmth, heat, glow.

chaloupe, *n.f.* launch.

chambre, *n.f.* room, chamber; House (parliament). c. à coucher, bedroom.

chameau, *n.m.* camel.

chamois, *n.m.* chamois.

champ, *n.m.* field.

champignon, *n.m.* mushroom.

champion, *n.m.* champion.

championnat, *n.m.* championship.

chance, *n.f.* luck, risk, chance.

chanceler, *vb.* stagger, reel.

chancelier, *n.m.* chancellor.

chandail, *n.m.* sweater.

chandelier, *n.m.* candlestick.

chandelle, *n.f.* candle.

change, *n.m.* exchange.

changeant, *adj.* changeable.

changement, *n.m.* change, shift.

changer, *vb.* alter, shift, change.

chanson, *n.f.* song.

chant, *n.m.* song, chant. c. du coq, cock-crow.

chantage, *n.m.* blackmail.

chanter, *vb.* sing, chant.

chanteur, *n.m.* singer.

chantier, *n.m.* (work)yard.

chaos (k-), *n.m.* chaos.

chaotique (k-), *adj.* chaotic.

chapeau, *n.m.* hat, bonnet.

chapelle, *n.f.* chapel.

chaperon, *n.m.* chaperon.

chapiteau, *n.m.* capital.

chapitre, *n.m.* chapter.

chapon, *n.m.* capon.

chaque, *adj.* every, each.

char, *n.m.* chariot. c. d'assaut, (military) tank.

charbon, *n.m.* coal. c. de bois, charcoal.

charge, *n.f.* load, charge.

charger, *vb.* load, burden, charge.

chariot, *n.m.* wagon; baggage cart.

charisme, *n.m.* charisma.

charitable, *adj.* charitable.

charité, *n.f.* charity.

charlatan, *n.m.* charlatan.

charmant, *adj.* delightful, lovely, charming.

charme, *n.m.* spell, charm.

charmer, *vb.* charm.

charnel, *adj.* carnal.

charnu, *adj.* fleshy.

charpente, *n.f.* framework.

charpentier, *n.m.* carpenter.

charretier, *n.m.* carter.

charrette, *n.f.* cart.

charrue, *n.f.* plow.

charte, *n.f.* charter.

chasse, *n.f.* hunt(ing), chase.

châsse, *n.f.* shrine.

chasser, *vb.* hunt, chase; drive away.

chasseur, *n.m.* hunter; bellboy.

châssis, *n.m.* (window) sash.

chaste, *adj.* chaste.

chasteté, *n.f.* chastity.

chat, *m.*, chatte *f. n.* cat.

châtaigne, *n.f.* chestnut.

château, *n.m.* mansion, castle.

châtier, *vb.* punish, chastise.

chatouiller, *vb.* tickle.

chatouilleux, *adj.* ticklish.

chaud, *adj.* hot, warm.

chaudière, *n.f.* boiler.

chauffage, *n.m.* heating.

chauffer, *vb.* heat, warm.

chauffeur, *n.m.* driver, chauffeur.

chaumière, *n.f.* cottage.

chaussée, *n.f.* road.

chausser, *vb.* wear shoes. se c., put on shoes.

chaussette, *n.f.* sock.

chaussure, *n.f.* footgear.

chauve, *adj.* bald.

chauve-souris, *n.f.* bat.

chaux, *n.f.* lime.

chavirer, *vb.* capsize.

chef, *n.m.* leader, chief.

chef-d'œuvre (shē-), *n.m.* masterpiece.

chemin, *n.m.* road. c. de fer, railway. à mi-c., halfway. c. de table, table-runner.

chemineau, *n.m.* tramp.

cheminée, *n.f.* fireplace, chimney; funnel.

chemise, *n.f.* shirt. c. de nuit, nightgown.

chêne, *n.m.* oak.

chenille, *n.f.* caterpillar.

chèque, *n.m.* check.

chèque de voyage, *n.m.* traveller's check.

cher (-r), *adj.* dear, expensive.

chercher, *vb.* seek, look for, search. **aller c.**, fetch.

chère, *n.f.* fare.

chéri, *adj. and n.m.* beloved, darling.

chérir, *vb.* cherish.

cheval, *n.m.* horse. **à c.**, on horseback. **monter à c.**, ride (horseback). **fer à c.**, horseshoe.

chevaleresque, *adj.* chivalrous.

chevalerie, *n.f.* chivalry.

chevalet, *n.m.* easel; knight.

chevalier, *n.m.* knight.

cheveu, *n.m.*, *pl.* **cheveux**, hair.

cheville, *n.f.* ankle; peg.

chèvre, *n.f.* goat.

chevreau, *n.m.* kid.

chevreuil, *n.m.* roe.

chevron, *n.m.* rafter.

chevroter, *vb.* quaver.

chevrotine, *n.f.* buckshot.

chez, *prep.* at . . .'s (house, office, shop, etc.).

chic, *adj.* stylish.

chien, *n.m.* dog.

chienne, *n.f.* bitch.

chiffon, *n.m.* rag.

chiffonner, *vb.* crumple.

chiffre, *n.m.* figure.

chiffrer, *vb.* figure.

Chili, *n.m.* Chile.

Chilien, *n.m.* Chilean.

chilien, *adj.* Chilean.

chimie, *n.f.* chemistry.

chimiothérapie, *n.f.* chemotherapy.

chimique, *adj.* chemical.

chimiste, *n.m.f.* chemist.

Chine, *n.f.* China.

Chinois, *n.m.* Chinese (person).

chinois, **1.** *n.m.* Chinese (language). **2.** *adj.* Chinese.

chiquenaude, *n.f.* flip.

chirurgie, *n.f.* surgery.

chirurgien, *n.m.* surgeon.

chloroforme (k-), *n.m.* chloroform.

choc, *n.m.* shock, clash, brunt.

chocolat, *n.m.* chocolate.

chœur (k-), *n.m.* choir, chorus.

choisir, *vb.* choose, select, pick.

choix, *n.m.* choice.

chômage, *n.m.* stoppage (of work).

choquer, *vb.* shock, clash.

choral (k-), *adj.* choral.

chose, *n.f.* thing, matter. **quelque c.**, anything.

chou, *n.m.* cabbage.

chou-fleur, *n.m.* cauliflower.

choyer, *vb.* pamper.

chrétien (k-), *adj. and n.m.* Christian.

chrétienté (k-), *n.f.* Christendom.

christianisme (k-), *n.m.* Christianity.

chronique (k-), **1.** *n.f.* chronicle. **2.** *adj.* chronic.

chronologique (k-), *adj.* chronological.

chrysanthème (k-), *n.m.* chrysanthemum.

chuchoter, *vb.* whisper.

chute, *n.f.* fall, drop, downfall.

cible, *n.f.* target.

cicatrice, *n.f.* scar.

cidre, *n.m.* cider.

ciel, *n.m.*, *pl.* **cieux**, heaven, sky.

cierge, *n.m.* (church) candle.

cigale, *n.f.* locust.

cigare, *n.m.* cigar.

cigarette, *n.f.* cigarette.

cigogne, *n.f.* stork.

ci-joint, *adj.* enclosed.

cil (-l), *n.m.* eyelash.

cime, *n.f.* top, summit.

ciment, *n.m.* cement.

cimenter, *vb.* cement.

cimetière, *n.m.* churchyard, cemetery.

cinéma, *n.m.* cinema.

cinglant, *adj.* scathing.

cinq (-k), *adj. and n.m.* five.

cinquante, *adj. and n.m.* fifty.

cinquième, *adj. and n.m.* fifth.

cintre, *n.m.* semicircle; arch.

circonférence, *n.f.* circumference.

circonscription, *n.f.* c. **électorale**, borough.

circonscrire, *vb.* circumscribe.

circonstance, *n.f.* event, circumstance. **c. critique**, emergency.

circuit, *n.m.* circuit. **hors c.**, disconnected.

circulaire, *adj.* circular.

circulation, *n.f.* traffic, circulation.

circuler, *vb.* circulate, turn, revolve.

cire, *n.f.* wax.

cirer, *vb.* polish, shine.

cireur, *n.m.* bootblack.

cirque, *n.m.* circus.

cisailles, *n.f.pl.* shears.

ciseau, *n.m.* chisel; (*pl.*) scissors.

ciseler, *vb.* chisel.

citadelle, *n.f.* citadel.

citation, *n.f.* quotation, citation.

cité, *n.f.* city. **droit de c.**, citizenship.

citer, *vb.* quote, cite.

citoyen, *n.m.* citizen.

citron, *n.m.* lemon. **c. pressé**, lemonade.

citrouille, *n.f.* pumpkin.

civil (-l), **1.** *n.m.* civilian. **2.** *adj.* civil.

civilisation, *n.f.* civilization.

civilisé, *adj.* civilized.

civiliser, *vb.* civilize.

civique, *adj.* civic.

clair, *adj.* clear, bright. **c. de lune**, moonlight.

clairière, *n.f.* glade, clearing.

clairon, *n.m.* bugle.

clameur, *n.f.* clamor, outcry.

clandestin, *adj.* clandestine.

clapoteux, *adj.* choppy (sea).

claque, *n.f.* slap.

claquement, *n.m.* smack.

claquer, *vb.* slap, smack, chatter (teeth), bang.

clarifier, *vb.* clarify.

clarinette, *n.f.* clarinet.

clarté, *n.f.* clarity; light.

classe, *n.f.* class.

classement, *n.m.* classification.

classer, *vb.* classify, order, file, grade.

classeur, *n.m.* file.

classification, *n.f.* classification.

classifier, *vb.* classify.

classique, *adj.* classic, classical.

clause, *n.f.* clause.

clavicule, *n.f.* collarbone.

clef (klä), **clé**, *n.f.* key.

clémence, *n.f.* clemency.

clément, *adj.* merciful.

clerc, *n.m.* clerk.

clergé, *n.m.* clergy.

clérical, *adj.* clerical.

cliché, *n.m.* cliché; snapshot.

client, *n.m.* customer, patron, client.

clientèle, *n.f.* customers, practice.

cligner (de l'œil), *vb.* wink.

clignoter, *vb.* blink, wink.

climat, *n.m.* climate.

climatisation, *n.f.* air-conditioning.

climatiser, *vb.* air-condition.

clin, *n.m.* c. **d'œil**, wink.

clinique, **1.** *n.f.* clinic. **2.** *adj.* clinical.

cloche, *n.f.* bell.

clocher, *n.m.* belfry. **de c.**, parochial.

cloison, *n.f.* partition.

cloître, *n.m.* cloister, convent.

clôture, *n.f.* fence.

clou, *n.m.* nail.

clouer, *vb.* nail, tack.

club (-b), *n.m.* club.

coaguler, *vb.* coagulate.

coalition, *n.f.* coalition.

coasser, *vb.* croak (frogs).

cocaïne, *n.f.* cocaine.

cochon, *n.m.* pig.

coco, *n.m.* **noix de c.**, coconut.

cocon, *n.m.* cocoon.

code, *n.m.* code; laws.

code postal, *n.m.* zip code.

cœur, *n.m.* heart.

coffre, *n.m.* bin; coffer.

cogner, *vb.* bump, strike, run into, knock (down).

cohérent, *adj.* coherent.

cohésion, *n.f.* cohesion.

coiffer, *vb.* dress (hair).

coiffeur, *n.m.* hairdresser, barber.

coiffure, *n.f.* hair-do.

coin, *n.m.* corner, wedge.

coïncidence (kŏ ăn-), *n.f.* coincidence.

coïncider (kŏ ăn-), *vb.* coincide.

col, *n.m.* collar; pass.

colère, n.f. anger, temper. en c., angry.

colimaçon, n.m. snail.

colis, n.m. parcel.

collaborateur, n.m. fellow-worker.

collaboration, n.f. assistance, collaboration.

collaborer, vb. work together, collaborate.

collant, n.m. panty hose.

collatéral, adj. and n.m. collateral.

colle, n.f. glue, paste.

collecte, n.f. collection.

collectif, adj. collective.

collection, n.f. collection.

collectionneur, n.m. collector.

collège, n.m. college.

collègue, n.m.f. colleague.

coller, vb. glue, paste, stick.

collier, n.m. necklace; collar (dog).

colline, n.f. hill.

collision, n.f. collision.

colombe, n.f. dove.

colon, n.m. settler, colonist.

colonel, n.m. colonel.

colonial, adj. colonial.

colonie, n.f. settlement, colony.

coloniser, vb. colonize.

colonne, n.f. column.

coloré, adj. colorful.

colorer, vb. color.

colossal, adj. huge, colossal.

colosse, n.m. giant, colossus.

colporter, n.m. peddle.

colporteur, n.m. peddler.

combat, n.m. fight, battle. hors de c., disabled.

combattant, adj. and n.m. combatant.

combattre, vb. fight.

combien (de), adv. how much, how many.

combinaison, n.f. combination, slip, B.V.D.'s.

combiner, vb. devise, combine.

comble, n.m. climax, top.

combler, vb. heap up, fill.

combustible, 1. n.m. fuel. 2. adj. combustible.

combustion, n.f. combustion.

comédie, n.f. comedy.

comédien, n.m. actor, comedian.

comestible, adj. edible.

comète, n.f. comet.

comique, adj. funny, comic(al).

comité, n.m. committee.

commandant, n.m. major, commander.

commande, n.f. order; commission.

commandement, n.m. command, commandment.

commander, vb. order, command.

commanditer, vb. finance.

comme, 1. adv. as, how. 2. prep. as, like. c. il faut, proper, decent.

commémoratif, adj. memorial.

commémorer, vb. commemorate.

commençant, n.m. beginner.

commencement, n.m. beginning, start.

commencer, vb. begin, start.

comment, adv. how.

commentaire, n.m. comment, commentary.

commentateur, n.m. commentator.

commenter, vb. comment on.

commerçant, n.m. trader.

commerce, n.m. trade, commerce.

commercer, vb. trade.

commercial, adj. commercial.

commettre, vb. commit.

commis, n.m. clerk.

commissaire, n.m. commissary, commissioner.

commission, n.f. errand, commission.

commode, 1. n.f. dresser, bureau. 2. adj. handy, convenient, comfortable.

commodité, n.f. convenience.

commun, adj. joint, common.

communauté, n.f. community.

commune, n.f. commune, town(ship).

communicatif, adj. communicative.

communication, n.f. communication.

communion, n.f. communion.

communiquer, vb. communicate.

communisme, n.m. communism.

communiste, adj. and n.m.f. communist.

compacité, n.f. compactness.

compact (-kt), adj. compact.

compagne, n.f. mate, companion.

compagnie, n.f. company.

compagnon, n.m. mate, fellow, companion.

comparable, adj. comparable.

comparaison, n.f. comparison.

comparaître, vb. appear.

comparatif, adj. and n.m. comparative.

comparer, vb. compare.

compartiment, n.m. compartment.

compas, n.m. compass.

compassion, n.f. sympathy, compassion.

compatible, adj. compatible.

compatissant, adj. sympathetic, compassionate.

compatriote, n.m.f. compatriot.

compensation, n.f. amends; compensation.

compenser, vb. compensate.

compétence, n.f. qualification, efficiency, competence.

compiler, vb. compile.

complaire, vb. please.

complaisance, n.f. kindness, compliance.

complaisant, adj. obliging, kind.

complément, n.m. object; complement.

complet, 1. n.m. suit. 2. adj. full, thorough, complete.

compléter, vb. complete.

complexe, adj. and n.m. complex.

complexité, n.f. complexity.

complication, n.f. complication.

complice, n.m.f. party to, accomplice.

compliqué, adj. intricate, involved, complicated.

compliquer, vb. complicate.

complot, n.m. plot.

comporter, vb. se c., act, behave.

composant, adj. and n.m. component.

composé, adj. and n.m. compound.

composer, vb. compound, compose.

compositeur, n.m. composer.

composition, n.f. essay, theme, composition.

compote, n.f. stewed fruit.

compréhensif, adj. comprehensive.

compréhension, n.f. comprehension.

comprendre, vb. understand, realize, comprise, include. c. mal, misunderstand.

compresse, n.f. compress.

compression, n.f. compression.

comprimer, vb. compress.

compromettre, vb. compromise.

compromis, n.m. compromise.

comptabilité, n.f. accounting, bookkeeping.

comptable, n.m. accountant.

compte, n.m. account, count. rendre c. de, account for. tenir c. de, allow for.

compter, vb. count, reckon. c. sur, rely on.

compteur, n.m. meter.

comptoir, n.m. counter.

comte, n.m. count.

comtesse, n.f. countess.

concave, adj. concave.

concéder, vb. grant, concede.

concentration, n.f. concentration.

concentrer, vb. condense, concentrate.

concept (-pt), n.m. concept.

conception, n.f. conception.

concernant, prep. concerning.

concerner, vb. concern.

concert, n.m. concert.

concession, n.f. grant, license, admission, concession.

concevable, adj. conceivable.

concevoir, vb. conceive, imagine.

concierge, n.m.f. janitor, doorkeeper, porter.

concile, n.m. council.

conciliation, n.f. conciliation.

concilier, *vb.* reconcile, conciliate.

concis, *adj.* concise.

conclsion, *n.f.* conciseness.

concluant, *adj.* conclusive.

conclure, *vb.* complete, conclude, infer.

conclusion, *n.f.* conclusion.

concombre, *n.m.* cucumber.

concourir, *vb.* concur, contribute, contend.

concours, *n.m.* contest.

concret, *adj.* concrete.

concurrence, *n.f.* competition.

concurrent, *n.m.* rival, competitor.

condamnation (-dâ nä-), *n.f.* conviction, condemnation, sentence.

condamner (-dâ nä), *vb.* convict, doom, condemn, sentence.

condensation, *n.f.* condensation.

condenser, *vb.* condense.

condescendance, *n.f.* condescension.

condescendre, *vb.* condescend.

condition, *n.f.* condition.

conditionnel, *adj. and n.m.* conditional.

conditionner, *vb.* condition.

condoléance, *n.f.* condolence. **faire ses c.s à**, condole with.

condominium, *n.m.* condominium.

conducteur, *n.m.* conductor.

conduire, *vb.* lead, take, drive, conduct. **se c.**, behave, act.

conduite, *n.f.* behavior, conduct.

cône, *n.m.* cone.

cône de charge *n.m.* warhead.

confection, *n.f.* making (e.g. clothes); ready-made garment.

confédération, *n.f.* confederacy, confederation.

confédéré, *adj. and n.m.* confederate.

conférence, *n.f.* lecture, talk, conference.

conférer, *vb.* confer, grant.

confesser, *vb.* confess, admit.

confesseur, *n.m.* confessor.

confession, *n.f.* denomination, confession.

confiance, *n.f.* trust, belief, confidence. **digne de c.**, dependable.

confiant, *adj.* confident.

confidence, *n.f.* confidence.

confident, *n.m.* confidant.

confidentiel, *adj.* confidential.

confier, *vb.* confide, entrust. **se c. à**, trust.

confiner, *vb.* confine, limit.

confirmation, *n.f.* confirmation.

confirmer, *vb.* confirm.

confiserie, *n.f.* confectionery.

confisquer, *vb.* confiscate.

confiture, *n.f.* jam, jelly.

conflit, *n.m.* conflict.

confondre, *vb.* confuse, confound.

conforme, *adj.* similar.

conformer, *vb.* conform. **se c. à**, comply with.

conformité, *n.f.* accordance.

confort, *n.m.* comfort.

confortable, *adj.* cozy, snug, comfortable.

confronter, *vb.* confront.

confus, *adj.* confused.

confusion, *n.f.* confusion.

congé, *n.m.* discharge; leave of absence.

congédier, *vb.* discharge, dismiss.

congélateur, *n.m.* freezer.

congeler, *vb.* congeal.

congestion, *n.f.* congestion.

conglomération, *n.f.* conglomeration.

congrès, *n.m.* congress, assembly, conference.

conjecture, *n.f.* guess, conjecture.

conjonction, *n.f.* conjunction.

conjugaison, *n.f.* conjugation.

conjuguer, *vb.* conjugate.

conjuration, *n.f.* conspiracy.

conjurer, *vb.* conspire, plot.

connaissance, *n.f.* knowledge, acquaintance. **sans c.**, unconscious. **faire la c. de**, meet.

connaisseur, *n.m.* connoisseur.

connaître, *vb.* be acquainted with, know.

connexion, *n.f.* connection.

conquérir, *vb.* conquer.

conquête, *n.f.* conquest.

consacrer, *vb.* consecrate, devote, dedicate, hallow.

conscience, *n.f.* conscience, consciousness.

consciencieux, *adj.* conscientious.

conscient, *adj.* conscious.

conscription, *n.f.* draft.

conscrit, *adj. and n.m.* conscript.

consécration, *n.f.* consecration.

consécutif, *adj.* consecutive.

conseil, *n.m.* advice, counsel; council, board; staff.

conseiller, **1.** *vb.* advise, counsel. **2.** *n.m.* advisor.

consentement, *n.m.* consent.

consentir, *vb.* consent, assent, accede.

conséquence, *n.f.* outgrowth, result, consequence.

conséquent, *adj.* consequent, consistent. **par c.**, consequently.

conservateur, *adj. and n.m.* conservative.

conservation, *n.f.* conservation.

conserve, *n.f.* conserve, pickle.

conserver, *vb.* conserve, keep; preserve, can.

considérable, *adj.* considerable.

considération, *n.f.* consideration.

considérer, *vb.* consider.

consigne, *n.m.* check-room; (*mil.*) orders.

consigne automatique, *n.f.* (luggage) locker.

consigner, *vb.* consign.

consistance, *n.f.* consistency.

consistant, *adj.* consistent.

consister, *vb.* consist.

consolateur, *n.m.* comforter.

consolation, *n.f.* comfort, solace.

console, *n.f.* bracket.

consoler, *vb.* comfort, console.

consolider, *vb.* consolidate, strengthen.

consommateur, *n.m.* consumer.

consommation, *n.f.* consumption; end, consummation.

consommé, *adj.* consummate.

consommer, *vb.* consummate, complete, consume.

consomption, *n.f.* consumption.

consonne, *n.f.* consonant.

conspirateur, *n.m.* conspirator.

conspiration, *n.f.* conspiration.

conspirer, *vb.* conspire.

constamment, *adv.* continually, constantly.

constance, *n.f.* constancy, firmness.

constant, *adj.* constant, firm.

constater, *vb.* observe, state as a fact.

constellation, *n.f.* constellation.

consternation, *n.f.* dismay.

consterné, *adj.* aghast.

consterner, *vb.* dismay.

constipation, *n.f.* constipation.

constituant, *adj.* constituent.

constituer, *vb.* constitute.

constitution, *n.f.* constitution.

constitutionnel, *adj.* constitutional.

constructeur, *n.m.* builder.

constructif, *adj.* constructive.

construction, *n.f.* construction.

construire, *vb.* construct, build.

consul, *n.m.* consul.

consulat, *n.m.* consulate.

consultation, *n.f.* consultation.

consulter, *vb.* consult.

consumer, *vb.* consume.

contact (-kt), *n.m.* touch, contact.

contagieux, *adj.* contagious.

contagion, *n.f.* contagion.

contaminer, *vb.* contaminate.

conte, *n.m.* tale, story.

contemplation, *n.f.* contemplation.

contempler, *vb.* survey, observe, contemplate.

contemporain, *adj.* contemporary.

contenance, *n.f.* compass, capacity.

contenir, *vb.* hold, restrain, contain.

content de, *adj.* glad of, contented with. **c. de soi-même**, complacent.

contentement, *n.m.* content-

(ment), satisfaction. **c. de soi-même**, complacency.

contenter, vb. please, satisfy.

contenu, n.m. contents.

conter, vb. tell.

contester, vb. challenge (dispute), object to, contest.

contexte, n.m. context.

contigu, adj. adjoining.

continent, n.m. continent.

continental, adj. continental.

contingent, n.m. quota.

continu, adj. continuous.

continuation, n.f. continuation, continuance.

continuel, adj. continual.

continuer, vb. carry on, keep on, go on, continue.

continuité, n.f. continuity.

contour, n.m. outline.

contourner, vb. go round.

contracter, vb. contract.

contraction, n.f. contraction.

contradiction, n.f. discrepancy, contradiction.

contradictoire, adj. contradictory.

contraindre, vb. coerce, force.

contrainte, n.f. compulsion.

contraire, 1. n.f. reverse. 2. adj. contrary. **au c.**, on the contrary.

contrarier, vb. thwart, vex, annoy, oppose, keep (from).

contrariété, n.f. annoyance.

contraste, n.m. contrast.

contraster, vb. contrast.

contrat, n.m. contract.

contre, prep. against.

contre-balancer, vb. counterbalance.

contrebande, n.f. smuggling; contraband.

contre-cœur, adv. **à c.**, unwillingly.

contredire, vb. contradict.

contrée, n.f. district, province.

contrefaire, vb. forge, counterfeit.

contrefort, n.m. buttress.

contremaître, n.m. foreman.

contre-partie, n.f. counterpart.

contrepoids (-pwä), n.m. counterbalance.

contribuer, vb. contribute.

contribution, n.f. share, contribution; tax.

contrôle, n.m. check.

contrôle des naissances, n.m. birth control, contraception.

contrôler, vb. control, check.

contrôleur, n.m. checker, collector.

controverse, n.f. controversy.

convaincre, vb. convince.

convaincu, adj. positive.

convalescence, n.f. convalescence.

convenable, adj. becoming, appropriate, suitable, congenial.

convenance, n.f. convenience.

convenir à, vb. suit, fit, befit, agree.

convention, n.f. convention; contract.

conventionnel, adj. conventional.

converger, vb. converge.

conversation, n.f. talk, conversation.

converser, vb. talk, converse.

conversion, n.f. conversion, change.

convertir, vb. convert, transform.

convexe, adj. convex.

conviction, n.f. conviction.

convive, n.m. guest, companion.

convoi, n.m. convoy, funeral procession.

convoiter, vb. covet.

convoitise, n.f. covetousness.

convoquer, vb. summon, call.

convulsion, n.f. convulsion.

coopératif (kŏ ŏ-), adj. coöperative.

coopération (kŏ ŏ-), n.f. coöperation.

coopérative (kŏ ŏ-), n.f. coöperative.

coopérer (kŏ ŏ-), vb. coöperate.

coordonner (kŏ ôr-), vb. coördinate.

copie, n.f. copy.

copier, vb. copy.

copieux, adj. copious.

coq (-k), n.m. rooster.

coque, n.f. **œuf à la c.**, boiled egg.

coquille, n.f. shell.

coquin, adj. and n.m. rogue, rascal.

cor, n.m. horn; corn.

corail, n.m., pl. **coraux**, coral.

corbeau, n.m. raven, crow.

corbeille, n.f. basket.

corde, n.f. rope, string, cord.

cordial, adj. hearty, cordial.

cordon, n.m. rope.

cordonnier, n.m. shoemaker.

Corée, n.f. Korea.

corne, n.f. horn.

corneille, n.f. crow.

cornemuse, n.f. bagpipe.

cornichon, n.m. gherkin.

corporation, n.f. corporation.

corporel, adj. bodily.

corps, n.m. body.

corpulent, adj. burly.

corpuscule (-sk-), n.m. corpuscle.

correct (-kt), adj. right, correct.

correction, n.f. correction, correctness.

corrélation, n.f. correlation.

correspondance, n.f. (train) connection; similarity; correspondence.

correspondant, 1. n.m. correspondent. 2. adj. similar, corresponding.

correspondre, vb. correspond.

corriger, vb. mend, reclaim, correct.

corroborer, vb. corroborate.

corroder, vb. corrode.

corrompre, vb. bribe, corrupt.

corrompu, adj. corrupt.

corruption, n.f. bribery, graft, corruption.

corsage, n.m. bodice.

corset, n.m. corset.

cortège, n.m. procession.

cosmétique, adj. and n.m. cosmetic.

cosmopolite, adj. and n.m.f. cosmopolitan.

costume, n.m. attire, dress.

cote, n.f. quotation.

côte, n.f. rib; coast.

côté, n.f. side, way. **mettre de c.**, put to one side (save; discard). **à c. de**, beside.

côtelette, n.f. chop, cutlet.

coton, n.m. cotton.

cou, n.m. neck.

couche, n.f. layer, bed; stratum; diaper.

coucher, vb. put to bed. **se c.**, lie down; set.

couchette, n.f. bunk, berth.

coucou, n.m. cuckoo.

coude, n.m. elbow.

coudoyer, vb. jostle.

coudre, vb. sew, stitch.

couler, vb. flow, sink, run; cast (metal).

couleur, n.f. hue, color; suit (cards).

couloir, n.m. corridor.

coup, n.m. blow, stroke, hit, bump, knock, cast. **c. de feu**, discharge (gun). **c. d'œil**, glance, look. **c. de pied**, kick. **c. de poing**, punch.

coupable, adj. guilty, to blame.

coupe, n.f. cut; goblet. **c. de cheveux**, haircut.

couper, vb. cut.

couple, n.f. couple, pair.

coupler, vb. couple.

coupon, n.m. remnant; coupon.

coupure, n.f. cut, clipping.

cour, n.f. court(yard).

courage, n.m. bravery, pluck, courage.

courageux, adj. brave.

couramment, adv. fluently.

courant, 1. adj. current. **peu c.**, unusual. **au c.**, well informed. 2. n.m. stream, current. **c. d'air**, draft.

courbe, n.f. curve, sweep.

courber, vb. bend, curve.

courbure, n.f. curvature.

coureur, n.m. runner.

courir, vb. run.

couronne, n.f. crown, wreath.

couronnement, n.m. coronation.

couronner, vb. crown.

courrier, n.m. mail.

courroie, n.f. strap.

courroux, n.m. wrath.

cours, n.m. course.

course, n.f. race, errand.

court, adj. short.

courtepointe, n.f. quilt.

courtier, n.m. broker.

courtisan, *n.m.* courtier.
courtois, *adj.* courteous.
courtoisie, *n.f.* courtesy.
cousin, *n.m.* cousin.
coussin, *n.m.* cushion.
coussinet, *n.m.* bearing.
coût, *n.m.* cost.
couteau, *n.m.* knife.
coutellerie, *n.f.* cutlery.
coûter, *vb.* cost.
coûteux, *adj.* expensive, costly.
coutume, *n.f.* custom.
couture, *n.f.* seam. **haute couture,** high fashion.
couturière, *n.f.* dressmaker.
couvée, *n.f.* brood.
couvent, *n.m.* convent.
couver, *vb.* brood, hatch; smolder.
couvercle, *n.m.* lid, cover.
couvert, 1, *n.m.* cover. **2.** *adj.* covered, cloudy.
couverture, *n.f.* blanket, cover; *(pl.)* bedclothes.
couvrir, *vb.* cover.
crabe, *n.m.* crab.
crachat, *n.m.* spit.
cracher, *vb.* spit.
craie, *n.f.* chalk.
craindre, *vb.* fear.
crainte, *n.f.* fear, dread, awe.
craintif, *adj.* fearful, apprehensive.
cramoisi, *adj. and n.m.* crimson.
crampe, *n.f.* cramp.
crampon, *n.m.* cramp, crampiron.
cramponner, *vb.* se c., cling.
crâne, *n.m.* skull.
crapaud, *n.m.* toad.
craquement, *n.m.* crack.
craquer, *vb.* crack.
cratère, *n.m.* crater.
cravate, *n.f.* necktie.
crayon, *n.m.* pencil.
créance, *n.f.* belief. **lettres de c.,** credentials.
créancier, *n.m.* creditor.
créateur *m.,* **créatrice** *f.* **1.** *adj.* creative. **2.** *n.* creator.
création, *n.f.* creation.
créature, *n.f.* creature.
crédit, *n.m.* credit.
credo, *n.m.* creed.
crédule, *adj.* credulous.
créer, *vb.* create.
crème, *n.f.* cream, custard.
crêpe, *n.f.* pancake; crepe.
crépuscule (-sk-)**,** *n.m.* dusk.
crête, *n.f.* ridge, crest.
crétin, *n.m.* dunce.
cretonne, *n.f.* cretonne.
creuser, *vb.* dig.
creuset, *n.m.* crucible.
creux, *adj. and n.m.* hollow.
crevasse, *n.f.* crevice.
crever, *vb.* burst; die.
crevette, *n.f.* shrimp.
cri, *n.m.* cry, call.
crible, *n.m.* sieve.
crier, *vb.* yell, shout.
crime, *n.m.* crime.
criminel, *adj.* criminal.
crinière, *n.f.* mane.

crise, *n.f.* crisis.
cristal, *n.m.* crystal.
cristallin, *adj.* crystalline.
cristalliser, *vb.* crystallize.
critérium, *n.m.* criterion.
critique, 1, *n.m.* critic. **2.** *n.f.* criticism. **3.** *adj.* critical.
critiquer, *vb.* criticize.
croasser, *vb.* croak.
croc (-ô)**,** *n.m.* hook.
croche, *n.f.* quaver (music).
crochet, *n.m.* bracket, hook.
crochu, *adj.* hooked.
crocodile, *n.m.* crocodile.
croire, *vb.* believe.
croisade, *n.f.* crusade.
croisé, *n.m.* crusader.
croiser, *vb.* cross.
croiseur, *n.m.* cruiser.
croisière, *n.f.* cruise.
croissance, *n.f.* growth.
croissant, *n.m.* crescent.
croître, *vb.* grow.
croix, *n.f.* cross.
croquant, *adj.* crisp.
croquet, *n.m.* croquet.
croquis, *n.m.* sketch.
crosse, *n.f.* (golf) club.
crotale, *n.m.* rattlesnake.
crouler, *vb.* fall apart.
croup, *n.m.* croup.
croupir, *vb.* wallow.
croûte, *n.f.* crust.
croûton, *n.m.* crouton.
croyable, *adj.* believable.
croyance, *n.f.* belief.
croyant, *n.m.* believer.
cru, *adj.* raw.
cruauté, *n.f.* cruelty.
cruche, *n.f.* pitcher.
crucifier, *vb.* crucify.
crucifix, *n.m.* crucifix.
cruel, *adj.* cruel.
cryochirurgie, *n.f.* cryosurgery.
Cuba, *n.m.* Cuba.
Cubain, *n.m.* Cuban.
cubain, *adj.* Cuban.
cube, *n.m.* cube.
cubique, *adj.* cubic.
cueillir, *vb.* pick.
cuiller, *n.f.* spoon. **c. à thé,** teaspoon. **c. à bouche,** tablespoon.
cuillerée, *n.f.* spoonful.
cuir, *n.m.* leather.
cuirassé, *n.m.* battleship.
cuire, *vb.* cook; sting, smart.
cuisine, *n.f.* kitchen, cooking.
cuisinier, *n.m.* cook.
cuisse, *n.f.* thigh.
cuivre, *n.m.* copper **c. jaune,** brass.
cul-de-sac, *n.m.* blind alley.
culotte, *n.f.* breeches.
culpabilité, *n.f.* guilt.
culte, *n.m.* worship; cult.
cultiver, *vb.* cultivate; grow, raise.
culture, *n.f.* culture, cultivation; farming.
cure, *n.f.* cure.
curé, *n.m.* (parish) priest.
curieux, *adj.* curious.
curiosité, *n.f.* curiosity, curio.
cursif, *adj.* cursive.

cuticule, *n.f.* cuticle.
cuve, *n.f.* vat.
cuver, *vb.* ferment.
cuvette, *n.f.* (wash) basin.
cuvier, *n.m.* washtub.
cycle, *n.m.* cycle.
cycliste, *n.m.f.* cyclist.
cyclomoteur, *n.m.* moped.
cyclone, *n.m.* cyclone.
cygne, *n.m.* swan.
cylindre, *n.m.* cylinder.
cylindrique, *adj.* cylindrical.
cymbale, *n.f.* cymbal.
cynique, 1. *n.m.* cynic. **2.** *adj.* cynical.
cynisme, *n.m.* cynicism.
cyprès, *n.m.* cypress.
czar, *n.m.* czar.

D

dactylographe, *n.m.f.* typist.
daigner, *vb.* deign.
daim, *n.m.* buck.
daine, *n.f.* doe.
dais, *n.m.* canopy.
dalle, *n.f.* slab, flag(stone).
dame, *n.f.* lady.
damner (dä nä)**,** *vb.* damn.
Danemark, *n.m.* Denmark.
danger, *n.m.* danger.
dangereux, *adj.* dangerous.
Danois, *n.m.* Dane.
danois, *adj. and n.m.* Danish.
dans, *prep.* in, into.
danse, *n.f.* dance.
danser, *vb.* dance.
danseur, *n.m.* dancer.
dard, *n.m.* dart.
date, *n.f.* date.
dater, *vb.* date.
datte, *n.f.* date.
davantage, *adv.* more, further.
de, *prep.* of, from, by, about; some.
dé, *n.m.* die; thimble.
débarquer, *vb.* land.
débarrasser, *vb.* rid.
débat, *n.m.* debate.
débattre, *vb.* canvass; debate.
débit, *n.m.* delivery (speech); sale; debit.
débiter, *vb.* sell (retail).
débiteur, *n.m.* debtor.
déblayer, *vb.* clear.
déborder, *vb.* overflow.
déboucher, *vb.* flow (into).
débourser, *vb.* disburse.
debout, *adv.* up. **être d.,** stand.
débris, *n.m.pl.* wreck, debris.
début, *n.m.* beginning, first appearance, debut.
débuter, *vb.* make one's first appearance; begin.
décadence, *n.f.* decay, decadence.
décaféiné, *adj.* decaffeinated.
décapiter, *vb.* behead.
décéder, *vb.* die.
décembre, *n.m.* December.
décence, *n.f.* decency.
décent, *adj.* decent.

déception, *n.f.* disappointment.

décerner, *vb.* award.

décès, *n.m.* death.

décevoir, *vb.* disappoint.

décharge, *n.f.* discharge.

décharger, *vb.* unload, discharge.

décharné, *adj.* gaunt.

déchausser, *vb.* take off shoes.

déchets (-à), *n.m.pl.* waste.

déchets nucléaires, *n.m.pl.* nuclear waste.

déchiffrer, *vb.* decipher.

déchirer, *vb.* tear, rend.

déchirure, *n.f.* tear, rent.

décibel, *n.m.* decibel.

décider, *vb.* prevail upon, decide.

décimal, *adj.* decimal.

décisif, *adj.* decisive.

décision, *n.f.* decision.

déclamer, *vb.* recite.

déclaration, *n.f.* statement, declaration.

déclarer, *vb.* state, declare.

déclin, *n.m.* ebb.

décliner, *vb.* decline.

décolorer, *vb.* bleach, fade.

décomposer, *vb.* spoil, decompose.

déconcerter, *vb.* baffle, disconcert, embarrass.

décongestionnant, *adj.* decongestant.

décontracté, *adj.* relaxed.

décoratif, *adj.* decorative.

décoration, *n.f.* decoration, trimming.

décorer, *vb.* decorate.

décors, *n.m.pl.* scenery.

découper, *vb.* carve (meat).

découragé, *adj.* despondent.

découragement, *n.m.* discouragement.

décourager, *vb.* dishearten, discourage.

découverte, *n.f.* discovery.

découvreur, *n.m.* discoverer.

découvrir, *vb.* uncover detect, discover.

décrépit, *adj.* decrepit.

décret, *n.m.* decree.

décréter, *vb.* enact.

décrire, *vb.* describe.

dédaigneux, *adj.* scornful.

dédain, *n.m.* scorn, disdain.

dedans, *n.m.* inside, within.

dédicace, *n.f.* dedication.

dédier, *vb.* dedicate.

déduction, *n.f.* deduction.

déduire, *vb.* infer, deduce, deduct.

défaire, *vb.* undo.

défaite, *n.f.* defeat.

défaut, *n.m.* flaw, fault, failure, lack. à d. de, for want of.

défectueux, *adj.* faulty, defective.

défendeur, *n.m.* defendant.

défendre, *vb.* forbid, defend.

défense, *n.f.* prohibition, plea, defense.

défenseur, *n.m.* advocate, defender.

défensif, *adj.* defensive.

déférer, *vb.* defer.

défi, *n.m.* challenge, defiance.

défiance, *n.f.* mistrust.

déficit (-t), *n.m.* deficit.

défier, *vb.* challenge, defy. se d. de, mistrust.

défigurer, *vb.* deface.

défiler, *vb.* march off.

défini, *adj.* definite.

définir, *vb.* define.

définitif, *adj.* final, definitive.

définition, *n.f.* definition.

déformer, *vb.* distort, deform.

défraîchi, *adj.* dingy.

défricher, *vb.* reclaim.

défunt, *n.m.* and *adj.* deceased.

dégagé, *adj.* breezy.

dégât, *n.m.* damage.

dégénérer, *vb.* degenerate.

dégoût, *n.m.* distaste, disgust.

dégoûtant, *adj.* foul, disgusting.

dégoûter, *vb.* disgust.

dégoutter, *vb.* drip.

dégradation, *n.f.* degradation.

dégrader, *vb.* degrade.

degré, *n.m.* degree, step.

déguisement, *n.m.* disguise.

déguiser, *vb.* disguise.

dehors, *adv.* (out)doors, outside. en d. de, apart from.

déifier, *vb.* deify.

déité, *n.f.* deity.

déjà, *adv.* already.

déjeter, *vb.* make unsymmetrical.

déjeuner, *n.m.* and *vb.* lunch, breakfast. petit d., breakfast.

déjouer, *vb.* foil, thwart.

delà, *adv.* beyond. au d. de, over, past, beyond.

délabrement, *n.m.* decay.

délabrer, *vb.* ruin, wreck.

délacer, *vb.* unlace.

délai, *n.m.* delay.

délaissement, *n.m.* desertion.

délaisser, *vb.* desert.

délassement, *n.m.* relaxation.

délasser, *vb.* refresh.

délateur, *n.m.* informer.

délavé, *adj.* faded, pallid.

délayer, *vb.* dilute with water.

délectable, *adj.* delicious.

délectation, *n.f.* enjoyment.

délecter, *vb.* delight.

délégation, *n.f.* delegation.

délégué, *n.m.* delegate.

déléguer, *vb.* delegate.

délester, *vb.* relieve of ballast.

délétère, *adj.* harmful; offensive.

délibératif, *adj.* deliberative.

délibération, *n.f.* deliberation.

délibéré, *adj.* deliberate.

délibérer, *vb.* deliberate.

délicat, *adj.* dainty, delicate.

délicatesse, *n.f.* delicacy.

délices, *n.f.pl.* delight.

délicieux, *adj.* delicious.

délié, *adj.* slender; keen.

délier, *vb.* untie.

délimiter, *vb.* mark the limits of.

délinéer, *vb.* delineate.

délinquant, 1. *n.m.* delinquent, offender. 2. *adj.* delinquent.

délirant, *adj.* delirious.

délire, *n.m.* frenzy.

délirer, *vb.* rave.

délit, *n.m.* offense, crime.

délivrance, *n.f.* rescue, deliverance.

délivrer, *vb.* rescue, set free, deliver.

déloger, *vb.* dislodge.

déloyal, *adj.* disloyal.

déloyauté, *n.f.* disloyalty.

déluge, *n.m.* deluge.

déluré, *adj.* clever, cute.

démagogue, *n.m.* demagogue.

demain, *adv.* tomorrow.

demande, *n.f.* application, request, inquiry, claim. d. en mariage, proposal.

demander, *vb.* ask, request. se d., wonder.

demandeur, *n.m.* plaintiff.

démangeaison, *n.f.* itch.

démanger, *vb.* itch.

démanteler, *vb.* dismantle.

démarcation, *n.f.* demarcation.

démarche, *n.f.* walk, bearing; step.

démarrage, *n.m.* start.

démarrer, *vb.* unmoor; start off.

démarreur, *n.m.* (self-)starter.

démasquer, *vb.* unmask; expose, reveal.

démêler, *vb.* disentangle.

démembrement, *n.m.* dismemberment.

démembrer, *vb.* dismember.

déménagement, *n.m.* moving.

déménager, *vb.* move.

déménageur, *n.m.* furniture mover.

démence, *n.f.* insanity.

démener, *vb.* struggle.

dément, *adj.* insane.

démenti, *n.m.* denial.

démentir, *vb.* give the lie to.

démesuré, *adj.* measureless, immense.

démettre, *vb.* se d. (de), resign.

demeure, *n.f.* abode.

demeurer, *vb.* dwell.

demi, *n.m.* and *adj.* half.

demi-cercle, *n.m.* semicircle.

demi-dieu, *n.m.* demigod.

demi-frère, *n.m.* stepbrother.

demi-heure, *n.f.* half an hour.

démilitariser, *vb.* demilitarize.

demi-place, *n.f.* half price; half fare.

demi-saison, *adj.* between-season.

demi-sœur, *n.f.* stepsister.

demi-solde, *n.f.* half-pay.

démission, *n.f.* resignation.

démobilisation, *n.f.* demobilization.

démobiliser, *vb.* demobilize.

démocrate, *n.m.f.* democrat.

démocratie, *n.f.* democracy.

démocratique, *adj.* democratic.

démodé, *adj.* old-fashioned.

demoiselle, *n.f.* young lady. d. d'honneur, bridesmaid.

démolir, vb. demolish.

démolition, n.f. demolition.

démon, n.m. demon.

démonétiser, vb. demonetize.

démoniaque, adj. demonic.

démonstratif, adj. effusive, demonstrative.

démonstration, n.f. demonstration.

démonter, vb. unhorse; dismantle.

démontrable, adj. demonstrable.

démontrer, vb. demonstrate.

démoralisation, n.f. demoralization.

démoraliser, vb. demoralize.

démouler, vb. remove from a mold.

démuni, adj. short of, lacking.

dénationaliser, vb. denationalize.

dénaturer, vb. denature.

dénégation, n.f. denial.

dénigrer, vb. disparage.

dénivelé, adj. not level.

dénombrement, n.m. enumeration; census.

dénombrer, vb. count.

dénomination, n.f. denomination.

dénommer, vb. name.

dénoncer, vb. report, denounce.

dénonciation, n.f. denunciation.

dénoter, vb. denote.

dénouement, n.m. result, outcome.

dénouer, vb. untie.

denrée, n.f. ware, produce.

dense, adj. dense.

densité, n.f. density.

dent, n.f. tooth. **mal de d.s,** toothache. **brosse à d.s,** toothbrush.

dental, adj. dental.

denté, adj. cogged.

dentelle, n.f. lace.

dentifrice, n.m. tooth paste or powder.

dentiste, n.m. dentist.

dentition, n.f. dentition.

denture, n.f. set of natural teeth.

dénuder, vb. denude.

dénué, adj. destitute, bare.

dénuement, n.m. destitution.

dénuer, vb. divest.

dépannage, n.m. emergency repairs.

dépareillé, adj. odd (unmatched).

départ, n.m. departure.

département, n.m. department.

départir, vb. divide in shares.

dépasser, vb. outrun, pass.

dépayser, vb. bewilder, confuse.

dépêche, n.f. dispatch.

dépêcher, vb. se d., hurry.

dépeindre, vb. portray.

dépendance, n.f. annex (to a building).

dépendant, adj. dependent.

dépendre, vb. depend.

dépens, n.m.pl. expenses.

dépense, n.f. expenditure, expense.

dépenser, vb. spend, expend.

dépérir, vb. waste away; decline.

dépecer, vb. dismember.

dépit, n.m. spite. **en d. de,** despite.

déplacement, n.m. displacement.

déplacer, vb. displace, move, shift.

déplaire à, vb. displease.

déplaisant, adj. displeasing.

déplanter, vb. transplant.

déplantoir, n.m. trowel.

déplier, vb. unfold.

déploiement, n.m. deployment.

déplorable, adj. wretched, deplorable.

déplorer, vb. deplore.

déployer, vb. deploy.

déplumer, vb. pluck.

déportation, n.f. deportation.

déportements, n.m.pl. misconduct.

déporter, vb. deport.

déposant, n.m. depositor.

déposer, vb. deposit, set down, depose.

dépositaire, n.m.f. trustee.

déposséder, vb. oust; dispossess.

dépôt, n.m. deposit, depot. **d. de vivres,** commissary.

dépouille, n.f. hide, skin, pelt.

dépouiller, vb. strip. se d. de, shed.

dépourvu, adj. devoid; needy.

dépoussiéreur, n.m. vacuum cleaner.

dépravation, n.f. depravity.

dépraver, vb. deprave.

dépréciation, n.f. depreciation.

déprécier, vb. depreciate, cheapen.

déprédation, n.f. depredation.

dépression, n.f. depression.

déprimer, vb. depress.

depuis, adv. and prep. since. **d. que,** conj. since.

députation, n.f. delegation.

député, n.m. representative, deputy.

déraciner, vb. uproot, eradicate.

déraison, n.f. unreason.

déraisonnable, adj. unreasonable.

dérangement, n.m. disturbance.

déranger, vb. disturb, trouble.

derechef, adv. once again.

dérégler, vb. upset, disorder.

dérider, vb. smooth; cheer up.

dérision, n.f. derision. **tourner en d.,** deride.

dérivation, n.f. derivation, etymology.

dérive, n.f. drift. **à la d.,** adrift.

dériver, vb. derive; drift.

dernier, adj. last, latter.

dernièrement, adv. lately.

dérober, vb. rob. se d., steal away.

dérouiller, vb. remove the rust from.

dérouler, vb. unroll, unfold.

déroute, n.f. rout.

dérouter, vb. mislead; confuse.

derrière, n.m., adv. and prep. behind.

derviche, n.m. dervish.

dès, prep. since. **d. que,** conj. as soon as.

désabuser, vb. disillusion.

désaccord, n.m. disagreement.

désaccoutumer, vb. break of a habit.

désaffecter, vb. put (church) to secular use.

désagréable, adj. nasty, distasteful.

désagrégation, n.f. disintegration.

désaligné, adj. out of alignment.

désaltérer, vb. quench (one's) thirst.

désappointement, n.m. disappointment.

désappointer, vb. disappoint.

désapprobation, n.f. disapproval.

désapprouver, vb. disapprove.

désarmement, n.m. disarmament.

désarmer, vb. disarm.

désarroi, n.m. disorder.

désastre, n.m. disaster.

désastreux, adj. disastrous.

désavantage, n.m. disadvantage.

désaveu, n.m. denial.

désavouer, vb. disown.

descendance, n.f. descent.

descendant, 1. n.m. offspring, descendant. 2. adj. downward, descending.

descendre, vb. go down, come down, alight, descend.

descente, n.f. raid; descent.

descriptif, adj. descriptive.

description, n.f. description.

désembarquer, vb. disembark, unload.

désenchanter, vb. disenchant.

désenivrer, vb. sober up.

désert, n.m. wilderness, desert.

déserter, vb. desert.

déserteur, n.m. deserter.

désertion, n.f. desertion.

désespéré, adj. hopeless, forlorn, desperate.

désespérer, vb. despair.

désespoir, n.m. desperation, despair.

déshabiller, vb. undress.

déshériter, vb. disinherit.

déshonnête, adj. improper, indecent.

déshonneur, n.m. disgrace, dishonor.

déshonorant, adj. dishonorable.

déshonorer, vb. disgrace, dishonor.

déshydrater, vb. dehydrate.

désignation, n.f. nomination.

désigner, vb. appoint, nominate; point out; designate.

désillusion, n.f. disillusion.

désinfectant, n.m. disinfectant.

désinfecter, vb. disinfect, fumigate.

désinfection, n.f. disinfection.

désintégration, n.f. disintegration.

désintegrer, vb. disintegrate.

désintéressé, adj. unselfish.

désintéressement, n.m. unselfishness.

désir, n.m. desire, wish.

désirable, adj. desirable.

désirer, vb. desire, wish.

désireux, adj. desirous.

désistement, n.m. withdrawal.

désobéir à, vb. disobey.

désobéissance, n.f. disobedience.

désobéissant, adj. disobedient.

désœuvré, adj. idle.

désolation, n.f. desolation.

désolé, adj. disconsolate; desolate.

désoler, vb. desolate.

désordonné, adj. disorderly.

désordonner, vb. upset, confuse.

désordre, n.m. disorder.

désorganisation, n.f. disorganization.

désorganiser, vb. disorganize.

désormais, adv. henceforth.

despote, n.m. despot.

despotique, adj. despotic.

despotisme, n.m. despotism.

dessécher, vb. dry out, parch; drain.

dessein, n.m. plan, intent.

desserrer, vb. loosen.

dessert, n.m. dessert.

dessin, n.m. drawing, design, sketch.

dessinateur, n.m. designer.

dessiner, vb. draw, design. se d., loom.

dessous, n.m. underside. en d., au-d. de, beneath, underneath.

dessus, n.m. top. en d., au-d. de, above. d. de lit, bedspread.

destin, n.m. fate, destiny.

destinataire, n.m.f. addressee.

destination, n.f. destination. à d. de, bound for.

destinée, n.f. destiny.

destiner, vb. destine, intend.

destituer, vb. dismiss.

destructif, adj. destructive.

destruction, n.f. destruction.

désuet, adj. obsolete.

désuétude, n.f. disuse.

désunion, n.f. disunion.

désunir, vb. disconnect.

détaché, adj. loose.

détachement, n.m. detachment.

détacher, vb. detach. se d., stand out.

détail, n.m. item, particular, detail. au d., at retail.

détective, n.m. detective.

déteindre, vb. run (of colors).

détenir, vb. detain.

détente, n.f. 1. trigger. 2. (politics) détente.

détention, n.f. custody, detention.

détérioration, n.f. deterioration.

détériorer, vb. deteriorate.

détermination, n.f. determination.

déterminer, vb. determine, fix.

détestable, adj. detestable, hateful.

détester, vb. abhor, loathe, detest.

détonation, n.f. detonation.

détoner, vb. detonate.

détour, n.m. turn; detour.

détourné, adj. devious.

détourner, vb. turn away; divert; avert; embezzle.

détresse, n.f. trouble, distress.

détriment, n.m. detriment.

détroit, n.m. strait.

détruire, vb. destroy.

dette, n.f. debt.

deuil, n.m. mourning.

deux, adj. and n.m. two. tous les d., both.

deuxième, adj. second.

deux-points, n.m. colon.

dévaliser, vb. rob.

dévaliseur, n.m. robber.

devancer, vb. be ahead of.

devant, 1. n.m. front. 2. prep. before, in front of.

devanture, n.f. window, (shop) front.

dévastation, n. devastation.

dévaster, vb. devastate.

déveine, n.f. bad luck.

développement, n.m. development.

développer, vb. develop.

devenir, vb. become.

déverser, vb. divert.

dévêtir, vb. undress, disrobe.

déviation, n.f. deviation.

dévider, vb. unwind.

dévier, vb. turn away.

deviner, vb. guess.

devinette, n.f. puzzle, riddle.

devis, n.m. estimate.

devise, n.f. motto.

dévisser, vb. unscrew.

dévoiler, vb. unveil, disclose, reveal.

devoir, n.m. duty.

devoir, vb. owe; be supposed to; have to; (conditional) ought.

dévorer, vb. devour.

dévot, adj. devout.

dévotion, n.f. devotion.

dévoué, adj. devoted.

dévouement, n.m. devotion.

dévouer, vb. dedicate, devote.

dextérité, n.f. dexterity.

diabétique, adj. and n. diabetic.

diable, n.m. devil.

diablerie, n.f. mischief.

diabolique, adj. diabolic.

diacre, n.m. deacon.

diacritique, adj. diacritic.

diadème, n.m. diadem.

diagnostic, n.m. diagnosis.

diagnostiquer, vb. diagnose.

diagonal, adj. diagonal.

diagramme, n.m. diagram.

dialectal, adj. dialect.

dialecte, n.m. dialect.

dialogue, n.m. dialogue.

dialoguer, vb. converse, talk together.

diamant, n.m. diamond.

diamétral, adj. diametric.

diamètre, n.m. diameter.

diaphane, adj. diaphanous.

diaphragme, n.m. diaphragm.

diarrhée, n.f. diarrhea.

diathermie, n.f. diathermy.

diatribe, n.f. diatribe.

dictateur, n.m. dictator.

dictature, n.f. dictatorship.

dictée, n.f. dictation.

dicter, vb. dictate.

diction, n.f. diction.

dictionnaire, n.m. dictionary.

dicton, n.m. maxim, proverb.

didactique, adj. didactic.

dièse, n.f. and n.m. sharp.

diète, n.f. diet.

diététique, adj. dietetic.

Dieu, n.m. God.

diffamant, adj. libelous.

diffamateur, n.m. libeler.

diffamation, n.f. libel.

diffamer, vb. defame.

différence, n.f. difference.

différenciation, n.f. differentiation.

différencier, vb. differentiate.

différend, n.m. difference, dispute.

différent, adj. different.

différer, vb. defer; differ.

difficile, adj. arduous, hard; difficult; fastidious.

difficilement, adv. with difficulty.

difficulté, n.f. trouble; difficulty.

difficulté psychologique, n.f. hangup.

difforme, adj. deformed.

difformité, n.f. deformity.

diffus, adj. diffuse.

diffusion, n.f. spread, diffusion.

digérer, vb. digest.

digestible, adj. digestible.

digestif, adj. and n.m. digestive.

digestion, n.f. digestion.

digital, adj. digital.

digitaline, n.f. digitalis.

digne, adj. worthy.

dignitaire, n.m. dignitary.

dignité, n.f. dignity.

digression, n.f. digression.

digue, n.f. dike, dam.

dilapidation, n.f. waste.

dilater, vb. expand, dilate.

dilemme, n.m. dilemma.

dilettante, n.m. amateur.

diligence, n.f. diligence.

diligent, adj. diligent.

diluer, vb. dilute.

dilution, *n.f.* dilution.

dimanche, *n.m.* Sunday.

dimension, *n.f.* dimension.

diminuer, *vb.* lessen, decrease, diminish.

diminutif, *adj. and n.m.* diminutive.

diminution, *n.f.* decrease.

dindon, *n.m.* turkey.

dîner, 1. *n.m.* dinner. **2.** *vb.* dine.

dîneur, *n.m.* diner.

diphtérie, *n.f.* diphtheria.

diphtongue, *n.f.* diphthong.

diplomate, *n.m.* diplomat.

diplomatie, *n.f.* diplomacy.

diplomatique, *adj.* diplomatic.

diplôme, *n.m.* diploma.

dipsomane, *n.m.* dipsomaniac.

dipsomanie, *n.f.* dipsomania.

dire, *vb.* say, tell. **vouloir d.,** mean. **c'est-à-d.,** namely; that is.

direct, *adj.* direct.

directement, *adv.* directly.

directeur, *n.m.* manager, director.

directif, *adj.* guiding.

direction, *n.f.* management, leadership, direction.

directorate, *n.f.* directorate.

dirigeable, *adj. and n.m.* dirigible.

dirigeant, *adj.* ruling.

diriger, *vb.* manage, boss, steer, direct.

discernable, *adj.* barely visible.

discernement, *n.m.* discernment, judgment.

discerner, *vb.* discern.

disciple, *n.m.* follower, disciple.

disciplinaire, *adj.* disciplinary.

discipline, *n.f.* discipline.

discipliner, *vb.* discipline.

disco, *adj.* disco.

discontinuer, *vb.* discontinue.

disconvenance, *n.f.* unsuitability.

discordance, *n.f.* discord.

discorde, *n.f.* discord.

discothèque, *n.f.* discotheque.

discourir, *vb.* speak one's views.

discours, *n.m.* speech, oration, talk, discourse.

discourtois, *adj.* discourteous.

discrédit, *n.m.* disrepute.

discréditer, *vb.* disparage.

discret, *adj.* discreet.

discrétion, *n.f.* discretion.

disculper, *vb.* exonerate.

discursif, *adj.* discursive.

discussion, *n.f.* argument, discussion.

discutable, *adj.* debatable.

discuter, *vb.* argue, debate, discuss.

disette, *n.f.* famine.

diseur, *n.m.* talker.

disgrâce, *n.f.* disgrace.

disgracier, *vb.* put out of favor.

disjoindre, *vb.* sever, disjoint.

dislocation, *n.f.* dislocation.

disloquer, *vb.* dislocate.

disparaître, *vb.* disappear.

disparate, *adj.* unlike; badly matched.

disparition, *n.f.* disappearance.

dispendieux, *adj.* expensive.

dispensaire, *n.m.* dispensary.

dispensation, *n.f.* dispensation.

dispense, *n.f.* military exemption.

dispenser, *vb.* dispense.

disperser, *vb.* scatter, disperse.

dispersion, *n.f.* dispersal.

disponible, *adj.* available.

disposé, *adj.* disposed. **d. d'avance,** predisposed. **peu d.,** reluctant.

disposer, *vb.* dispose, settle.

dispositif, *n.m.* device.

disposition, *n.f.* arrangement, disposal, disposition.

disproportionné, *adj.* disproportionate.

dispute, *n.f.* row, fight, quarrel, dispute.

disputer, *vb.* dispute. **se d.,** quarrel.

disqualifier, *vb.* disqualify.

disque, *n.m.* disk, record.

dissemblable, *adj.* unlike.

dissemblance, *n.f.* dissimilarity.

dissension, *n.f.* dissension.

dissentiment, *n.m.* dissent.

disséquer, *vb.* dissect.

dissertation, *n.f.* essay.

dissimulation, *n.f.* pretense.

dissimuler, *vb.* dissemble, pretend.

dissipation, *n.f.* dissipation.

dissiper, *vb.* dispel, waste, dissipate.

dissolu, *adj.* dissolute.

dissolution, *n.f.* dissolution.

dissoudre, *vb.* dissolve.

dissuader, *vb.* dissuade.

distance, *n.f.* distance.

distancer, *vb.* outdistance.

distant, *adj.* distant.

distillation (-l-), *n.f.* distillation.

distiller (-l-), *vb.* distill.

distillerie (-l-), *n.f.* distillery.

distinct (-kt), *adj.* distinct.

distinctif, *adj.* distinctive.

distinction, *n.f.* distinction.

distingué, *adj.* distinguished.

distinguer, *vb.* discriminate; make out; distinguish.

distraction, *n.f.* distraction, pastime.

distraire, *vb.* distract, amuse. **se d.,** have fun.

distrait, *adj.* absent-minded.

distribuer, *vb.* give out, deal out, distribute.

distributeur, *n.m.* distributor.

distribution, *n.f.* distribution; delivery; cast.

district (-trèk), *n.m.* district.

dit, *adj.* called.

divaguer, *vb.* ramble.

divan, *n.m.* davenport, couch.

divergence, *n.f.* divergence.

diverger, *vb.* diverge.

divers, *adj.* various.

diversion, *n.f.* diversion.

diversité, *n.f.* diversity.

divertir, *vb.* divert, entertain. **se d.,** enjoy oneself.

divertissement, *n.m.* diversion.

dividende, *n.m.* dividend.

divin, *adj.* divine.

divinateur, *n.m.* soothsayer.

divinité, *n.f.* divinity.

diviser, *vb.* part, divide.

divisible, *adj.* divisible.

division, *n.f.* division.

divorce, *n.m.* divorce.

divorcer, *vb.* divorce.

divulguer, *vb.* divulge.

dix (-s), *adj. and n.m.* ten.

dix-huit (-z-), *adj. and n.m.* eighteen.

dix-huitième (-z-), *adj. and n.m.f.* eighteenth.

dixième (-z-), *adj. and n.m.* tenth.

dix-neuf (-z-), *adj. and n.m.* nineteen.

dix-sept (-s-), *adj. and n.m.* seventeen.

dizaine, *n.f.* (group of) ten.

docile, *adj.* docile.

docilité, *n.f.* docility.

docte, *adj.* learned, wise.

docteur, *n.m.* doctor.

doctorat, *n.m.* doctorate.

doctrine, *n.f.* doctrine.

document, *n.m.* document.

documenter, *vb.* document.

dodu, *adj.* plump.

dogmatique, *adj.* dogmatic.

dogme, *n.m.* dogma.

dogue, *n.m.* watchdog.

doigt (dwä), *n.m.* finger. **d. de pied,** toe.

doit, *n.m.* debit.

dollar, *n.m.* dollar.

domaine, *n.m.* domain, property.

dôme, *n.m.* dome.

domestique, 1. *n.m.f.* servant. **2.** *adj.* domestic.

domicile, *n.m.* residence.

dominant, *adj.* dominant.

domination, *n.f.* sway, domination, dominion.

dominer, *vb.* rule, dominate.

domino, *n.m.* domino.

dommage, *n.m.* injury, damage. **c'est d.,** that's too bad. **quel d.!,** what a pity!

dompter, *vb.* tame, subdue.

don, *n.m.* gift.

donateur, *n.m.* donor.

donation, *n.f.* donation.

donc (-k), *adv.* therefore.

donjon, *n.m.* dungeon.

donne, *n.f.* deal (cards).

donner, *vb.* give.

donneur, *n.m.* giver.

dont, *pron.* whose.

dorénavant, *adv.* hereafter.

dorer, *vb.* gild.

dorloter, *vb.* coddle.

dormant, *adj.* dormant; asleep.

dormir, *vb.* sleep.

dos, *n.m.* back.

dose, *n.f.* dose.

doser, *vb.* decide the amount.

dossier, *n.m.* record.

dot (-t), *n.f.* dowry.

doter, *vb.* endow.

douaire, *n.m.* dowry.

douane, *n.f.* customs, custom house.

douanier, *n.m.* customs officer.

double, *adj. and n.m.* double. **faire le d. de,** duplicate.

doubler, *vb.* double.

doublure, *n.f.* lining.

doucement, *adv.* gently.

doucereux, *adj.* sugary; oversweet.

douceur, *n.f.* sweetness, gentleness, meekness.

douche, *n.f.* shower bath; douche.

douer, *vb.* endow.

douille, *n.f.* socket.

douleur, *n.f.* pain, ache, sorrow, grief.

douloureux, *adj.* painful.

doute, *n.m.* doubt.

douter, *vb.* doubt. **se d. de,** suspect.

douteux, *adj.* dubious, doubtful, questionable.

douve, *m.,* *n.f.* ditch.

doux, *m.,* **douce** *f.* *adj.* soft, sweet, gentle, mild, meek.

douzaine, *n.f.* dozen.

douze, *adj. and n.m.* twelve.

douzième, *adj. and n.m.* twelfth.

doyen, *n.m.* dean.

dragon, *n.m.* dragon; dragoon.

draguer, *vb.* dredge.

drainage, *n.m.* drainage.

drainer, *vb.* drain.

dramatique, *adj.* dramatic.

dramatiser, *vb.* dramatize.

dramaturge, *n.m.* playwright.

drame, *n.m.* drama.

drap, *n.m.* sheet.

drapeau, *n.m.* flag.

draper, *vb.* drape.

draperie, *n.f.* drapery.

drapier, *n.m.* clothier.

dresser, *vb.* draw up.

dressoir, *n.m.* dresser.

drogue, *n.f.* drug.

droguer, *vb.* drug.

droit, 1. *n.m.* right; law; claim. 2. *adj. and adv.* (up)right, straight, fair. **d. d'auteur,** copyright.

droite, *n.f.* right. **à d.,** (to the) right.

drôle, *adj.* funny.

du, *m.,* **de la,** *f.,* **des,** *pl. prep.* some, any.

dû *m.,* **due** *f.* *adj.* due.

duc, *n.m.* duke.

duché, *n.m.* dukedom.

duchesse, *n.f.* duchess.

ductile, *adj.* ductile.

duel, *n.m.* duel.

duelliste, *n.m.* duellist.

dûment, *adv.* duly.

dune, *n.f.* dune.

duo, *n.m.* duet.

dupe, *n.f.* dupe.

duper, *vb.* trick.

duperie, *n.f.* trickery.

duplicité, *n.f.* duplicity.

dur, *adj.* hard, tough.

durabilité, *n.f.* durability.

durable, *adj.* lasting, durable.

durant, *prep.* during.

durcir, *vb.* harden.

durcissement, *n.m.* hardening.

durée, *n.f.* duration.

durement, *adv.* hard, harshly, strongly.

durer, *vb.* last.

dureté, *n.f.* hardness.

duvet, *n.m.* down.

duveté, *adj.* downy.

dynamique, *adj.* dynamic.

dynamite, *n.f.* dynamite.

dynamo, *n.f.* dynamo.

dynastie, *n.f.* dynasty.

dynastique, *adj.* dynastic.

dysenterie, *n.f.* dysentery.

dyslexie, *n.f.* dyslexia.

dyspepsie, *n.f.* dyspepsia.

E

eau, *n.f.* water. **faire e.,** leak.

eau-de-vie, *n.f.* brandy.

eau-forte, *n.f.* nitric acid.

ébahir, *vb.* amaze.

ébahissement, *n.m.* amazement.

ébarber, *vb.* trim, clip.

ébauche, *n.f.* outline.

ébaucher, *vb.* outline.

ébène, *n.m.* ebony.

ébénisterie, *n.f.* cabinet work.

éblouir, *vb.* dazzle.

éboulement, *n.m.* cave-in.

ébouriffer, *vb.* ruffle.

ébranler, *vb.* shake.

ébriété, *n.f.* drunkenness.

écaille, *n.f.* scale.

écarlate, *adj. and n.f.* scarlet.

écart, *n.m.* separation. **à l'é.,** aloof.

écarté, *adj.* isolated; lonely.

écartement, *n.m.* gap, separation.

écarter, *vb.* set aside.

ecclésiastique, *adj. and n.m.* ecclesiastic.

écervelé, *adj.* scatterbrained.

échafaud, *n.m.* scaffold.

échafaudage, *n.m.* scaffolding.

échancrure, *n.f.* scallop, notch.

échange, *n.m.* exchange.

échangeable, *adj.* exchangeable.

échanger, *vb.* exchange.

échantillon, *n.m.* sample.

échappatoire, *n.f.* loophole.

échappement, *n.m.* exhaust.

échapper, *vb.* escape.

écharde, *n.f.* splinter.

écharpe, *n.f.* scarf, sling.

échasse, *n.f.* stilt.

échauder, *vb.* scald.

échauffer, *vb.* heat up.

échéance, *n.f.* maturity.

échecs (-shē), *n.m.pl.* chess.

échelle, *n.f.* ladder, scale.

échelon, *n.m.* step; echelon.

échevelé, *adj.* dishevelled.

échine, *n.f.* spine.

échiner, *vb.* work like a slave.

écho (-kō), *n.m.* echo.

échoir, *vb.* fall due.

échoppe, *n.f.* booth, stall.

échouer, *vb.* fail. **faire é.,** frustrate.

éclabousser, *vb.* splash.

éclair, *n.m.* flash.

éclairage, *n.m.* lighting.

éclaircie, *n.f.* clearing.

éclaircir, *vb.* clear up.

éclairer, *vb.* (en)lighten, light, clear up, clarify.

éclaireur, *n.m.* scout.

éclat, *n.m.* chip, splinter; burst; brilliance, radiance, glamour.

éclatant, *adj.* bursting; loud; brilliant.

éclatement (de pneu), *n.m.* blowout.

éclater, *vb.* burst out.

éclectique, *adj.* eclectic.

éclipse, *n.f.* eclipse.

éclipser, *vb.* eclipse.

éclore, *vb.* hatch, open, blossom.

écluse, *n.f.* lock.

écœurer, *vb.* disgust.

école, *n.f.* school.

écolier, *n.m.* schoolboy.

écologie, *n.f.* ecology.

écologique, *adj.* ecological.

écologiste, *n.m.* ecologist; environmentalist.

économe, *adj.* economical.

économie, *n.f.* economy. **é. politique,** economics.

économique, *adj.* economic(al).

économiser, *vb.* economize.

économiste, *n.m.* economist.

écope, *n.f.* ladle.

écoper, *vb.* ladle or bail out.

écorce, *n.f.* bark.

écorcher, *vb.* skin.

écorchure, *n.f.* gall.

Écossais, *n.m.* Scotchman, Scotsman.

écossais, *adj.* Scotch, Scottish.

Écosse, *n.f.* Scotland.

écot, *n.m.* share.

écouler, *vb.* drain. **s'é.,** flow, elapse.

écouter, *vb.* listen (to).

écouteur, *n.m.* listener.

écran, *n.m.* screen.

écraser, *vb.* crush.

écrémer, *vb.* skim.

écrevisse, *n.f.* crayfish.

écrier, *vb.* **s'é.,** exclaim.

écrin, *n.m.* case, box.

écrire, *vb.* write. **machine à é.,** typewriter.

écrit, *n.m.* written.

écriteau, *n.m.* notice.

écritoire, *n.f.* inkstand.

écriture, *n.f.* writing, scripture.

écrivain, *n.m.* writer.

écrou, *n.m.* nut.

écrouler, *vb.* **s'é.,** fall to pieces.

écru, *adj.* natural.

écu, *n.m.* shield.

écuelle, n.f. bowl, dish.
écume, n.f. lather, foam.
œcuménique, adj. ecumenical.
écureuil, n.m. squirrel.
écurie, n.f. stable.
écusson, n.m. escutcheon.
écuyer (-kwē-), n.m. squire.
édenté, adj. toothless.
édifice, n.m. building.
édifier, vb. build; edify.
édit, n.m. edict.
éditeur, n.m. publisher.
édition, n.f. edition.
éditorial, adj. editorial.
éducateur, n.m. educator.
éducation, n.f. breeding, education.
éduquer, vb. educate.
effacer, vb. erase, efface.
effectif, adj. effective, actual.
effectivement, adv. effectively.
effectuer, vb. effect.
efféminé, adj. effeminate.
effet, n.m. effect; (pl.) belongings. en e., as a matter of fact, indeed.
efficace, adj. effective.
efficacité, n.f. efficacy.
effigie, n.f. effigy.
effleurer, vb. skim, graze.
effondrement, n.m. collapse.
effondrer, vb. s'e., collapse, sink.
efforcer, vb. s'e., endeavor, try hard.
effort, n.m. endeavor, strain, exertion, effort.
effrayant, adj. fearful.
effrayer, vb. frighten, scare, startle.
effréné, adj. unrestrained; frantic.
effroi, n.m. fright.
effronté, adj. brazen.
effronterie, n.f. effrontery.
effusion, n.f. shedding.
égal, adj. even, equal, same.
également, adv. equally.
égaler, vb. equal.
égaliser, vb. equalize.
égalité, n.f. equality, evenness.
égard, n.m. regard, consideration, esteem. à l'é. de, as for. plein d'é.s, considerate.
égaré, adj. astray.
égarement, n.m. aberration.
égarer, vb. mislay, bewilder. s'é., go astray, get lost.
égayer, vb. cheer up.
église, n.f. church.
égoïsme, n.m. selfishness, egoism.
égoïste, adj. selfish.
égorger, vb. kill.
égotisme, n.m. egotism.
égout, n.m. sewer.
égoutter, vb. drain; drip.
égratignure, n.f. scratch.
Egypte, n.f. Egypt.
Égyptien, n.m. Egyptian.
égyptien, adj. Egyptian.
éhonté, adj. brazen, shameless.
élaboration, n.f. working out, elaboration; data processing.
élaborer, vb. draft, elaborate.

élan, n.m. elk; zest.
élancer, vb. s'é., dash.
élargir, vb. widen, increase, enlarge.
élasticité, n.f. elasticity.
élastique, adj. and n.m. elastic.
électeur, n.m. voter.
électif, adj. elective.
élection, n.f. election.
électoral, adj. electoral.
électricien, n.m. electrician.
électricité, n.f. electricity.
électrique, adj. electric, electrical.
électrocardiogramme, n.m. electrocardiogram.
électrocuter, vb. electrocute.
élégance, n.f. elegance.
élégant, adj. elegant, smart, stylish.
élégie, n.f. elegy.
élément, n.m. element.
élémentaire, adj. elementary.
éléphant, n.m. elephant.
élevage, n.m. breeding.
élévation, n.f. elevation.
élève, n.m.f. pupil.
élevé, adj. lofty.
élever, vb. raise. s'é., arise, soar.
éleveur, n.m. breeder.
élider, vb. elide.
éligibilité, n.f. eligibility.
éligible, adj. eligible.
élimination, n.f. elimination.
éliminer, vb. eliminate.
élire, vb. elect.
élite, n.f. elite.
elle, pron.f. she, her; (pl.) they, them (f.).
elle-même, pron. herself.
éloge, n.m. praise.
éloigné, adj. remote.
éloignement, n.m. distance.
éloigner, vb. take away. s'é., go away, recede.
éloquence, n.f. eloquence.
éloquent, adj. eloquent.
élu, adj. chosen.
éluder, vb. evade, elude.
émacié, adj. emaciated.
émail, n.m., pl. émaux, enamel.
émancipation, n.f. emancipation.
émanciper, vb. emancipate.
émaner, vb. emanate.
emballer, vb. pack.
embarcation, n.f. craft.
embargo, n.m. embargo.
embarquer, vb. embark.
embarras, n.m. embarrassment, trouble, fix.
embarrassant, adj. embarassing, awkward.
embarrasser, vb. embarrass.
embaumé, adj. balmy.
embaumer, vb. perfume, embalm.
embellir, vb. beautify.
embêter, vb. bore, irritate.
emblème, n.m. emblem.
embolie, n.f. embolism.
embouchure, n.f. mouth.
embourber, vb. bog.

embranchement, n.m. junction.
embrasser, vb. embrace, kiss.
embrayage, n.m. clutch.
embrouillement, n.m. tangle, mix-up.
embrouiller, vb. perplex, entangle.
embrun, n.m. spray.
embuscade, n.f. ambush.
émeraude, n.f. emerald.
émerger, vb. emerge.
émerveiller, vb. astonish.
émettre, vb. emit, send forth, issue.
émeute, n.f. riot.
émietter, vb. crumble.
émigrant, n.m. emigrant.
émigration, n.f. emigration.
émigré, n.m. political exile.
émigrer, vb. (e)migrate.
éminemment, adv. eminently.
éminence, n.f. eminence.
éminent, adj. eminent.
émission, n.f. issue.
emmagasinage, n.m. storage.
emmagasiner, vb. store.
emmener, vb. take away.
émotif, adj. emotional.
émotion, n.f. emotion, feeling.
émotionnable, adj. emotional.
émotionner, vb. thrill.
émoussé, adj. blunt.
émouvant, adj. moving.
émouvoir, vb. move.
empaler, vb. impale.
empan, n.m. span.
emparer, vb. s'e. de, take possession of.
empêchement, n.m. prevention.
empêcher, vb. prevent, stop, hinder, inhibit.
empereur, n.m. emperor.
empêtrer, vb. entangle.
emphase, n.f. emphasis.
emphatique, adj. emphatic.
empléter, vb. encroach, trespass.
empire, n.m. empire.
empirique, adj. empirical.
emplette, n.f. purchase. faire des e.s, shop.
emploi, n.m. employment, use; job.
employé, n.m. employee, clerk, (public) servant.
employer, vb. employ, use.
employeur, n.m. employer.
empois, n.m. starch.
empoisonné, adj. poisonous.
empoisonner, vb. poison.
emporter, vb. take away. s'e., get angry.
empreinte, n.f. print, impression.
empressé, adj. solicitous.
empressement, n.m. eagerness.
empresser, vb. s'e., be eager.
emprise, n.f. expropriation.
emprisonnement, n.m. imprisonment.
emprisonner, vb. imprison.
emprunt, n.m. loan.
emprunter à, vb. borrow from.
emprunteur, n.m. borrower.

ému, adj. touched, stirred.

émule, n. rival, competitor.

en, 1. prep. in, into. 2. adv. thence; of it; some, any.

encadrer, vb. frame.

en-cas, n.m. reserve.

enceinte, adj.f. pregnant.

encens, n.m. incense.

enchaîner, vb. chain.

enchantement, n.m. enchantment.

enchanter, vb. delight, charm, enchant.

enchère, n.f. bid. vente aux e.s, auction.

enclore, vb. fence in, enclose.

enclos, 1. n.m. enclosure, 2. adj. shut in.

enclume, n.f. anvil.

encoche, n.f. notch.

encoller, vb. paste.

encombrant, adj. cumbersome.

encombré, adj. crowded.

encombrement, n.m. congestion.

encombrer, vb. crowd, clutter, block up.

encontre, adv. à l'e., toward, counter (to).

encore, adv. still, yet, again.

encourageant, adj. encouraging.

encouragement, n.m. encouragement.

encourager, vb. encourage, urge, promote.

encourir, vb. incur.

encre, n.f. ink.

encrier, n.m. inkwell.

encyclopédie, n.f. encyclopedia.

endetté, adj. indebted.

endiguer, vb. dam up.

endive, n.f. chicory.

endolori, adj. painful.

endommager, vb. damage.

endormi, adj. asleep.

endormir, vb. put to sleep. s'e., go to sleep.

endossement, n.m. endorsement.

endosser, vb. endorse.

endroit, n.m. place.

enduire, vb. smear, daub.

endurance, n.f. endurance.

endurant, adj. patient.

endurcir, vb. harden.

endurcissement, n.m. hardening.

énergie, n.f. energy.

énergique, adj. energetic.

énervant, adj. enervating.

énervé, adj. nervous.

enfance, n.f. childhood. première e., infancy.

enfant, n.m.f. child.

enfantement, n.m. childbirth.

enfanter, vb. bear (children).

enfantillage, n.m. childishness.

enfantin, adj. childish.

enfariner, vb. coat with flour.

enfer (-r), n.m. hell.

enfermer, vb. shut in.

enfiévrer, vb. excite, inspire.

enfin, adv. finally, at last.

enflammer, vb. inflame.

enfler, vb. swell.

enflure, n.f. swelling.

enfoncer, vb. sink.

enfouir, vb. bury.

enfourchure, n.f. bifurcation; crotch of a tree.

enfreindre, vb. violate.

enfuir, vb. s'e., run away, flee, elope.

enfumer, vb. fill or cover with smoke.

engageant, adj. personable, charming.

engagement, n.m. pledge, agreement, engagement.

engager, vb. hire, engage. s'e., volunteer.

engelure, n.f. chilblain.

engendrer, vb. beget.

engin, n.m. machine; engine, motor.

englober, vb. include.

engloutir, vb. devour.

engorgement, n.m. choking.

engouement, n.m. infatuation.

engouffrer, vb. engulf.

engourdir, vb. dull.

engrais, n.m. fertilizer.

engraisser, vb. fatten.

engraver, vb. strand or ground (a ship).

engrenage, n.m. gear.

engrener, vb. engage (gears).

enhardir, vb. make bolder.

énigmatique, adj. enigmatic.

énigme, n.f. riddle, puzzle, enigma.

enivrant, adj. intoxicating.

enivrement, n.m. intoxication.

enivrer, vb. intoxicate. s'e., get drunk.

enjambée, n.f. stride.

enjamber, vb. stride.

enjeu, n.m. stake.

enjoindre, vb. enjoin; call upon.

enjôlement, n.m. cajolery.

enjôler, vb. cajole.

enjoliver, vb. beautify.

enjoué, adj. playful.

enjouement, n.m. playfulness.

enlacer, vb. entwine; interlace; embrace.

enlaidir, vb. make or become ugly.

enlevable, adj. detachable.

enlèvement, n.m. removal, abduction.

enlever, vb. take away, remove, abduct.

enneigé, adj. snow-covered.

ennemi, adj. and n.m. enemy.

ennoblir, vb. exalt; ennoble.

ennui (-nwè), n.m. nuisance, bore, bother; boredom.

ennuyer, vb. bore, annoy, vex, bother, irk.

ennuyeux, adj. boring, tedious, dull.

énoncer, vb. enunciate.

énonciation, n.f. enunciation.

énorme, adj. enormous.

énormité, n.f. enormity.

enquérir, vb. inquire.

enquête, n.f. inquiry.

enraciner, vb. root. s'e., take root.

enragé, adj. rabid.

enrageant, adj. infuriating.

enrager, vb. be, go mad. s'e., get angry.

enregistrement, n.m. registration, recording; checking.

enregistrer, vb. record, register, list; check (luggage).

enrichir, vb. enrich.

enrober, vb. coat, envelop.

enrôlement, n.m. enlistment, enrollment.

enrôler, vb. enlist, enroll.

enroué, adj. hoarse.

enrouement, n.m. hoarseness.

enrouler, vb. s'e., roll up, twist, wind.

enseigne, n.f. sign, ensign.

enseignement, n.m. teaching, instruction.

enseigner, vb. teach.

ensemble, 1. n.m. set. 2. adv. together.

ensevelir, vb. bury.

ensoleillé, adj. sunny.

ensommeillé, adj. sleepy.

ensuite, adv. then, next, afterwards.

ensuivre, vb. s'e., ensue.

entablement, n.m. entablature.

entacher, vb. taint, besmirch.

entailler, vb. hack (notch).

entamer, vb. begin.

entassement, n.m. accumulation.

entasser, vb. heap up.

ente, n.f. scion (horticulture).

entendement, n.m. understanding, sense.

entendre, vb. hear, understand. s'e., get on together.

entendu, adj. understood, agreed. bien e., of course.

enténébré, adj. gloomy.

entente, n.f. understanding, agreement.

enterrement, n.m. burial.

enterrer, vb. bury.

entêté, adj. perverse.

entêtement, n.m. stubbornness.

entêter, vb. s'e., be stubborn, insist.

enthousiasme, n.m. enthusiasm.

enthousiaste, 1. n.m.f. enthusiast. 2. adj. enthusiastic. e. de, keen on.

entichement, n.m. infatuation.

entier, adj. whole, complete, entire.

entité, n.f. entity.

entonnoir, n.m. funnel.

entorse, n.f. sprain.

entourage, n.m. circle of friends; surroundings.

entourer, vb. surround, encircle.

entournure, n.f. armhole.

entr'acte, n.m. intermission.

entr'aide, n.f. mutual assistance.

entrailles, *n.f.pl.* bowels.

entrain, *n.m.* zest.

entraîner, *vb.* draw along; involve, entail; coach, train.

entraîneur, *n.m.* coach.

entrant, *adj.* incoming.

entraver, *vb.* clog.

entre, *prep.* among, between.

entre-clos, *adj.* ajar.

entre-deux, *n.m.* interval.

entrée, *n.f.* admission, entry; main course.

entreface, *n.f.* interface.

entregent, *n.m.* tact; spirit.

entrelacer, *vb.* interlace.

entremets (-mè), *n.m.* (side) dish.

entremetteur, *n.m.* intermediary.

entreposer, *vb.* store.

entreposeur, *n.m.* warehouseman.

entrepôt, *n.m.* warehouse.

entreprenant, *adj.* enterprising.

entreprendre, *vb.* undertake.

entrepreneur, *n.m.* contractor. e. de pompes funèbres, undertaker.

entreprise, *n.f.* concern, undertaking.

entrer (dans), *vb.* enter, come in, go in. laisser e., admit.

entretenir, *vb.* entertain. s'e., converse.

entretien, *n.m.* maintenance; conference; talk, conversation.

entrevoir, *vb.* glimpse.

entrevue, *n.f.* interview.

entr'ouvert, *adj.* ajar.

entr'ouvrir, *vb.* open halfway.

énumération, *n.f.* enumeration.

énumérer, *vb.* enumerate.

envahir, *vb.* invade.

envahissement, *n.m.* invasion.

enveloppe, *n.f.* envelope, wrapping.

envelopper, *vb.* envelop, wrap, enfold.

envers, 1. *n.m.* wrong side. 2. *prep.* toward.

enviable, *adj.* enviable.

envie, *n.f.* envy, desire. avoir e. de, want to, feel like.

envier, *vb.* envy.

envieux, *adj.* envious.

environ, *prep. and adv.* around, about; approximately.

environnement, *n.m.* surroundings.

environnementaliste, *n.m.* environmentalist.

environner, *vb.* surround.

envisager, *vb.* consider.

envoi, *n.m.* shipment, sending.

envoler, *vb.* s'e., fly away.

envoyé, *n.m.* envoy.

envoyer, *vb.* send.

enzyme, *n.f.* enzyme.

éon, *n.m.* eon.

épais, *adj.* thick.

épaisseur, *n.f.* thickness.

épaissir, *vb.* thicken.

épancher, *vb.* shed (blood).

épanouir, *vb.* s'é., bloom.

épargne, *n.f.* savings.

épargner, *vb.* save, spare.

éparpiller, *vb.* scatter.

épars, *adj.* scattered, sparse.

éparvin, *n.m.* spavin.

épatant, *adj.* (*colloq.*) grand.

épate, *n.f.* swagger.

épatement, *n.m.* amazement.

épater, *vb.* amaze.

épaule, *n.f.* shoulder.

épaulette, *n.f.* epaulette.

épée, *n.f.* sword.

épeler, *vb.* spell.

épellation, *n.f.* spelling.

éperdu, *adj.* distracted.

éperlan, *n.m.* smelt.

éperon, *n.m.* spur.

éperonner, *vb.* spur.

épervier, *n.m.* hawk.

épeuré, *adj.* frightened.

éphémère, *adj.* ephemeral, fleeting.

épice, *n.f.* spice.

épicé, *adj.* spicy.

épicerie, *n.f.* grocery.

épicier, *n.m.* grocer.

épidémie, *n.f.* epidemic.

épiderme, *n.m.* epidermis.

épidermique, *adj.* epidermal.

épier, *vb.* spy.

épigramme, *n.f.* epigram.

épilatoire, *n.m. and adj.* depilatory.

épilepsie, *n.f.* epilepsy.

épileptique, *adj. and n.* epileptic.

épilogue, *n.m.* epilogue.

épinards (-nar), *n.m.pl.* spinach.

épine, *n.f.* spine, thorn. é. dorsale, spinal column.

épinet, *n.f.* spinet.

épineux, *adj.* thorny.

épingle, *n.f.* pin. é. à cheveux, hairpin. é. anglaise, safety pin.

épingler, *vb.* pin.

épique, *adj.* epic.

épiscopal, *adj.* Episcopal.

épisode, *n.m.* episode.

épisodique, *adj.* episodic.

épistolaire, *adj.* epistolary.

épitaphe, *n.f.* epitaph.

épithète, *n.f.* epithet.

épitomé, *n.m.* epitome.

épître, *n.f.* epistle.

éploré, *adj.* tearful.

épointé, *adj.* dull, blunted.

éponge, *n.f.* sponge.

éponger, *vb.* sponge up.

épopée, *n.f.* epic.

époque, *n.f.* epoch.

époufflé, *adj.* breathless, panting.

épouiller, *vb.* delouse.

épouse, *n.f.* wife.

épouser, *vb.* marry.

épouseur, *n.m.* suitor.

épousseter, *vb.* dust.

époussette, *n.f.* duster.

épouvantable, *adj.* terrible.

épouvante, *n.f.* fright.

épouvanter, *vb.* frighten.

époux, *n.m.* husband.

épreindre, *vb.* squeeze.

éprendre, *vb.* s'é., fall in love.

épreuve, *n.f.* trial, test, ordeal, proof.

éprouver, *vb.* experience.

éprouvette, *n.f.* test tube.

épuisant, *adj.* exhausting.

épuisement, *n.m.* exhaustion.

épuiser, *vb.* exhaust.

épuration, *n.f.* purification.

épurer, *vb.* purify.

équanimité (-kwa-), *n.f.* equanimity.

équateur (-kwa-), *n.m.* equator.

équation (-kwa-), *n.f.* equation.

équatorial (-kwa-), *adj.* equatorial.

équestre, *adj.* equestrian.

équidistant, *adj.* equidistant.

équilibre, *n.m.* poise.

équilibrer, *vb.* balance.

équilibriste, *n.* tight-rope walker.

équinoxe, *n.m.* equinox.

équinoxial, *adj.* equinoctial.

équipage, *n.m.* crew.

équipe, *n.f.* team, crew, gang, shift.

équipement, *n.m.* equipment.

équiper, *vb.* equip.

équitable, *adj.* fair.

équité, *n.f.* equity.

équivalent, *adj. and n.m.* equivalent.

équivaloir, *vb.* equal in value.

équivoque, *adj.* equivocal.

érable, *n.m.* maple.

éradication, *n.f.* eradication.

érafure, *n.m.* scratch; graze.

érailler, *vb.* unravel.

ère, *n.f.* era.

érection, *n.f.* erection; construction.

éreintant, *adj.* exhausting.

éreinter, *vb.* exhaust.

erg, *n.m.* erg.

ériger, *vb.* erect.

ermitage, *n.m.* hermitage.

ermite, *n.m.* hermit.

éroder, *vb.* erode.

érosif, *adj.* erosive.

érosion, *n.f.* erosion.

érotique, *adj.* erotic.

errant, *adj.* wandering.

erratique, *adj.* erratic.

errer, *vb.* wander; err.

erreur, *n.f.* mistake, error.

erroné, *adj.* erroneous.

éructation, *n.f.* belch.

éructer, *vb.* belch.

érudit, *adj.* learned, scholarly.

érudition, *n.f.* learning.

éruption, *n.f.* rash, eruption.

érysipèle, *n.m.* erysipelas.

escabeau, *n.m.* stool.

escadrille, *n.f.* (ships) flotilla; (airplanes) squadron.

escadron, *n.m.* squadron.

escalader, *vb.* scale; escalate.

escalier, *n.m.* stairs.

escalope, *n.f.* cutlet.

escamotage, *n.m.* legerdemain.

escamoteur, *n.m.* conjurer, magician.

escapade, *n.f.* escapade.

escarcelle, *n.f.* wallet.

escargot, n.m. snail.
escarole, n.f. endive.
escarpé, adj. abrupt.
escarpement, n.m. steepness.
eschare, n.f. scab; bedsore.
esclandre, n.m. slander.
esclavage, n.m. slavery.
esclave, n.m.f. slave.
escompte, n.m. discount.
escorte, n.f. escort.
escorter, vb. escort.
escouade, n.f. squad.
escrime, n.f. fencing.
escrimer, vb. fight.
escrimeur, n.m. swordsman.
escroc (-ô), n.m. swindler.
escroquer, vb. swindle.
escroquerie, n.f. swindle.
esculent, adj. esculent.
espace, n.m. space.
espacé, adj. at great intervals.
espacer, vb. space out.
espadon, n.m. swordfish.
Espagne, n.f. Spain.
Espagnol, n.m. Spaniard.
espagnol, adj. and n.m. Spanish.
espalier, n.m. espalier.
espèce, n.f. species, kind; (pl.) cash.
espérance, n.f. hope.
espéranto, n.m. Esperanto.
espérer, vb. hope.
espiègle, adj. mischievous.
espièglerie, n.f. mischief.
espion, n.m. spy.
espionnage, n.m. espionage.
espionner, vb. spy on.
esplanade, n.f. esplanade.
espoir, n.m. hope.
esprit, n.m. spirit, mind, wit.
Saint-E., Holy Ghost.
esquif, n.m. skiff.
Esquimau n.m., Esquimaude f.n. Eskimo.
esquimau, adj. Eskimo.
esquinancie, n.m. quinsy.
esquinter, vb. exhaust, tire out.
esquisse, n.f. sketch.
esquisser, vb. sketch.
esquiver, vb. shirk.
essai, n.m. essay, attempt; experiment; assay.
essaim, n.m. swarm.
essaimer, vb. swarm.
essayer, vb. try; assay.
essence, n.f. gasoline; essence.
essentiel, adj. essential.
esseulement, n.m. solitude.
essieu, n.m. axle.
essor, n.m. flight.
essorer, vb. dry.
essoufflé, adj. breathless.
essoufflement, n.m. breathlessness.
essuie-glace, n.m. windshield wiper.
essuyer, vb. wipe.
est (-t), n.m. east.
estacade, n.f. stockade.
estafette, n.m. courier.
estafier, n.m. bodyguard.
estagnon, n.m. oil drum.
estaminet, n.m. bar, taproom.
estampe, n.f. engraving.

estampille, n.f. trademark.
esthète, n.m. esthete.
esthétique, adj. aesthetic.
estimable, adj. estimable.
estimateur, n.m. estimator; appraiser.
estimatif, adj. estimated.
estimation, n.f. estimate.
estime, n.f. esteem; estimation.
estimer, vb. esteem; estimate, value, rate.
estival, adj. of summer.
estivant, n.m. summer tourist.
estiver, vb. spend the summer.
estoc, n.m. tree trunk.
estomac (mä), n.m. stomach.
estourbir, vb. kill.
estrade, n.f. platform; stage.
estropié, 1. n.m. cripple. 2. adj. crippled.
estropier, vb. cripple.
estuaire, n.m. estuary.
esturgeon, n.m. sturgeon.
et, conj. and.
étable, n.f. barn.
établi, n.m. worktable.
établir, vb. settle, establish.
établissement, n.m. establishment.
étage, n.m. floor, story.
étagère, n.f. whatnot shelf.
étain, n.m. tin.
étal, n.m. butcher shop.
étalage, n.m. display.
étalager, vb. display.
étaler, vb. display, spread.
étalon, n.m. standard.
étameur, n.m. tinsmith.
étamine, n.f. coarse muslin; stamen.
étampe, n.f. stamp.
étamper, vb. stamp.
étanche, adj. impervious.
étancher, vb. quench, stanch.
étang, n.m. pond.
étape, n.m. stage.
état, n.m. state.
état-major, n.m. staff.
États-Unis, n.m.pl. United States.
été, n.m. summer.
éteindre, vb. extinguish, put out.
éteint, adj. extinct.
étendage, n.m. clotheslines.
étendard, n.m. standard.
étendre, vb. extend, spread, reach.
étendu, adj. extensive.
étendue, n.f. extent.
éternel, adj. everlasting.
éterniser, vb. perpetuate.
éternité, n.f. eternity.
éternuement, n.m. sneeze.
éternuer, vb. sneeze.
éther (-r), n.m. ether.
éthéré, adj. ethereal.
Éthiopie, n.f. Ethiopia.
éthique, n.f. ethics.
ethnique, adj. ethnic.
étinceler, vb. sparkle.
étincelle, n.f. spark, sparkle.
étincellement, n.m. sparkle, glitter.
étiolement, n.m. atrophy.

étioler, vb. blanch.
étiqueter, vb. label.
étiquette, n.f. label, tag; etiquette.
étirer, vb. stretch out.
étoffe, n.f. stuff, material, cloth.
étoffer, vb. stuff.
étoile, n.f. star.
étoiler, vb. bespangle.
étonnement, n.m. astonishment.
étonner, vb. astonish.
étouffé, adj. braised.
étouffer, vb. smother.
étourdi, adj. thoughtless.
étourdir, vb. daze.
étourdissant, adj. dazing.
étourdissement, n.m. dizziness.
étrange, adj. strange.
étranger, n. and adj. alien.
étranglement, n.m. strangulation.
étrangler, vb. strangle.
étrave, n.f. stem, bow.
être, 1. n.m. being. 2. vb. be.
étrécir, vb. shrink.
étreindre, vb. clasp.
étreinte, n.f. clasp, hug, embrace.
étrier, n.m. stirrup.
étrille, n.f. currycomb.
étroit, adj. narrow.
Étrusque, n.m.f. Etruscan.
étrusque, adj. Etruscan.
étude, n.f. study.
étudiant, n.m. student.
étudier, vb. study.
étui, n.m. 1. case. 2. needle case.
étuve, n.f. steam room.
étymologie, n.f. etymology.
étymologique, adj. etymological.
eucalyptus, n.m. eucalyptus.
eucharistie, n.f. eucharist.
eunuque, n.m. eunuch.
euphémique, adj. euphemistic.
euphémisme, n.m. euphemism.
euphonie, n.f. euphony.
euphonique, adj. euphonic.
euphorie, n.f. euphoria.
Europe, n.f. Europe.
Européen, n.m. European.
européen, adj. European.
euthanasie, n.f. euthanasia.
eux, pron. them.
évacuable, adj. able to be evacuated.
évacuation, n.f. evacuation.
évacuer, vb. evacuate.
évader, vb. s'é., escape.
évaluateur, n.m. appraiser.
évaluation, n.f. appraisal.
évaluer, vb. evaluate, rate, assess.
évangélique, adj. evangelic.
évangéliste, n.m. evangelist.
évangile, n.m. gospel.
évanouir, vb. s'é., fade away; faint.
évaporation, n.f. evaporation.
évaporer, vb. evaporate.
évasif, adj. evasive.
évasion, n.f. escape.

évêché, n.m. bishopric.

éveil, n.m. alertness.

éveillé, adj. sprightly.

éveiller, vb. wake.

événement, n.m. event.

éventail, n.m. fan.

éventrer, vb. disembowel.

éventualité, n.f. eventuality.

éventuel, adj. possible.

éventuellement, adv. eventually.

évêque, n.m. bishop.

éviction, n.f. eviction.

évidemment, adv. evidently.

évidence, n.f. evidence. en é., conspicuous.

évident, adj. obvious, evident.

évider, vb. scoop out.

évier, n.m. sink.

évincer, vb. oust.

éviscérer, vb. eviscerate, disembowel.

évitable, adj. avoidable.

éviter, vb. avoid.

évocation, n.f. evocation.

évolution, n.f. evolution.

évoquer, vb. evoke.

exact (-kt), adj. exact, precise.

exactement, adv. exactly.

exactitude, n.f. precision.

exagération, n.f. exaggeration.

exagérer, vb. exaggerate.

exaltant, adj. exciting.

exaltation, n.f. exaltation.

exalté, adj. impassioned.

exalter, vb. exalt, elate.

examen, n.m. examination.

examiner, vb. examine.

exaspération, n.f. exasperation.

exaspérer, vb. exasperate, aggravate.

excavateur, n.m. steam shovel.

excavation, n.f. excavation.

excaver, vb. excavate.

excédent, n.m. excess; overweight.

excéder, vb. exceed.

excellence, n.f. excellence, excellency, highness.

excellent, adj. excellent.

exceller, vb. excel.

excentrique, adj. eccentric.

excepté, prep. except.

excepter, vb. except.

exception, n.f. exception.

exceptionnel, adj. exceptional.

excès, n.m. excess.

excessif, adj. excessive, extreme.

exciser, vb. excise; cut out.

excitabilité, n.f. excitability.

excitable, adj. excitable.

excitant, adj. exciting.

exciter, vb. excite.

exclamatif, adj. exclamatory.

exclamation, n.f. exclamation.

exclamer, vb. exclaim.

exclure, vb. exclude.

exclusif, adj. exclusive.

exclusion, n.f. exclusion.

excommunication, n.f. excommunication.

excommunier, vb. excommunicate.

excorier, vb. excoriate.

excrément, n.m. excrement.

excréter, vb. excrete.

excrétion, n.f. excretion.

excursion, n.f. excursion.

excursionniste, n. excursionist.

excusable, adj. excusable.

excuse, n.f. plea, excuse.

excuser, vb. excuse. s'e. de, apologize for.

exécuter, vb. perform, enforce.

exécuteur, n.m. executor.

exécutif, adj. and n.m. executive.

exécution, n.f. performance, enforcement, execution.

exemplaire, 1. n.m. copy. 2. adj. exemplary.

exemple, n.m. instance, example.

exempt, adj. exempt.

exempt de droits, adj. duty-free.

exempter, vb. exempt.

exemption, n.f. exemption.

exerçant, adj. practicing.

exercer, vb. exercise, drill, train. s'e., practice.

exercice, n.m. exercise, drill, practice.

exhalation, n.f. exhalation.

exhaler, vb. exhale.

exhaustion, n.f. exhaust.

exhiber, vb. show, present; exhibit.

exhibition, n.f. exhibition.

exhortation, n.f. exhortation.

exhorter, vb. exhort.

exhumer, vb. exhume.

exigence, n.f. requirement.

exiger, vb. require, exact, demand.

exil (-l), n.m. exile.

exilé, n.m. exile.

exiler, vb. banish.

existant, adj. existent.

existence, n.f. existence.

exister, vb. exist.

exode, n.m. exodus.

exonération, n.f. exoneration.

exonérer, vb. exonerate.

exorbitant, adj. exorbitant.

exorciser, vb. exorcise.

exotique, adj. exotic.

expansible, adj. expansible.

expansif, adj. expansive.

expansion, n.f. expansion.

expatriation, n.f. expatriation.

expatrié, n. exile, expatriate.

expectorant, n.m. and adj. expectorant.

expectorer, vb. expectorate.

expédient, n.m. makeshift.

expédier, vb. dispatch.

expéditif, adj. expeditious.

expédition, n.f. dispatch; expedition, shipment.

expérience, n.f. experience, experiment.

expérimental, adj. experimental.

expérimentation, n.f. experimentation.

expérimenté, adj. practiced, experienced.

expert, adj. and n.m. expert.

expiable, adj. expiable.

expiation, n.f. atonement.

expier, vb. atone for.

expiration, n.f. expiration.

expirer, vb. expire.

explétif, n. and adj. expletive.

explicatif, adj. explanatory.

explication, n.f. explanation.

explicite, adj. explicit, clear.

expliquer, vb. explain.

exploit, n.m. feat, exploit.

exploitation, n.f. exploitation, working.

exploiter, vb. exploit.

explorateur, n.m. explorer.

exploratif, adj. exploratory.

exploration, n.f. exploration.

explorer, vb. explore.

explosible, adj. explosive.

explosif, adj. and n.m. explosive.

explosion, n.f. blast, explosion.

exportation, n.f. export, exportation.

exporter, vb. export.

exposé, n.m. account, statement.

exposer, vb. expound, expose, exhibit.

exposition, n.f. exposition, exposure, show, display.

exprès, 1. n.m. special delivery. 2. adj. express. 3. adv. on purpose.

expressif, adj. expressive.

expression, n.f. expression.

exprimable, adj. expressible.

exprimer, vb. express.

exproprier, vb. expropriate.

expulser, vb. expel.

expulsion, n.f. expulsion.

expurgation, n.f. expurgation.

expurger, vb. expurgate.

exquis, adj. exquisite.

exsuder, vb. exude.

extase, n.f. ecstasy.

extasier, vb. s'e. sur, rave about.

extatique, adj. ecstatic.

extensif, adj. extensive.

extension, n.f. extension.

exténuation, n.f. extenuation.

exténuer, vb. extenuate, exhaust.

extérieur, 1. n.m. exterior. 2. adj. exterior, outer.

extérieurement, adv. externally.

extermination, n.f. extermination.

exterminer, vb. exterminate.

externat, n.m. day school.

externe, adj. external.

exterritorialité, n.f. extraterritoriality.

extincteur, n.m. fire extinguisher.

extinction, n.f. extinction.

extirper, vb. extirpate, root out.

extorquer, vb. extort.

extorsion, n.f. extortion.

extra-, prefix extra.

extraction, *n.m.* extraction; descent.

extrader, *vb.* extradite.

extradition, *n.f.* extradition.

extra-fin, *adj.* extremely fine.

extraire, *vb.* extract.

extrait, *n.m.* extract, abstract.

extraordinaire, *adj.* extraordinary, unusual.

extraordinairement, *adv.* extraordinarily.

extravagance, *n.f.* extravagance.

extravagant, *adj.* extravagant.

extrême, *adj. and n.m.* extreme.

extrémiste, *n.* extremist.

extrémité, *n.f.* extremity.

extrinsèque, *adj.* extrinsic.

extroverti, *n.* extrovert.

extrusion, *n.f.* extrusion.

exubérance, *n.f.* exuberance.

exubérant, *adj.* exuberant.

exultation, *n.f.* exultation.

exulter, *vb.* exult.

F

fable, *n.f.* fable.

fabliau, *n.m.* fabliau.

fabricant, *n.m.* maker, manufacturer.

fabricateur, *n.m.* forger.

fabrication, *n.f.* make.

fabrique, *n.f.* factory.

fabriquer, *vb.* manufacture.

fabuleux, *adj.* fabulous.

fabuliste, *n.f.* fabulist.

façade, *n.f.* front.

face, *n.f.* face. en f. de, opposite. faire f. à, confront.

facétie, *n.f.* joke, prank.

facétieux, *adj.* facetious.

facette, *n.f.* facet.

fâché, *j.* angry; sorry.

fâcher, *vb.* anger, offend, grieve. se f., get angry.

fâcherie, *n.f.* quarrel, argument.

fâcheux, *adj.* upleasant.

facial, *adj.* facial.

facile, *adj.* easy.

facilité, *n.f.* fluency, ease.

faciliter, *vb.* facilitate, make easy.

façon, *n.f.* way, manner, fashion. de f. à, so as to.

faconde, *n.f.* glibness; fluency.

façonner, *vb.* shape, fashion.

facsimilé, *n.m.* facsimile.

facteur, *n.m.* factor, element; mailman.

factice, *adj.* artificial.

factieux, *adj.* factious; quarrelsome.

faction, *n.f.* faction, party.

factionnaire, *n.m.* sentry.

facture, *n.f.* invoice, bill.

facturer, *vb.* bill; send an invoice to.

facultatif, *adj.* optional.

faculté, *n.f.* faculty.

fadaise, *n.f.* nonsense.

fade, *adj.* insipid.

fadeur, *n.f.* insipidity.

fagot, *n.m.* bundle.

faible, *adj.* weak, faint, dim, feeble.

faiblement, *adv.* feebly, weakly.

faiblesse, *n.f.* weakness, frailty, dimness.

faiblir, *vb.* weaken.

failli, *adj. and n.m.* bankrupt.

faillibilité, *n.f.* fallibility.

faillible, *adj.* fallible.

faillir, *vb.* fail.

faillite, *n.f.* bankrupcy.

faim, *n.f.* hunger.

fainéant, *n.m.* loafer.

faire, *vb.* make, do. f. part, inform. f. mal à, hurt. f. voir, show.

faisable, *adj.* feasible.

faisan, *n.m.* pheasant.

fait, *n.m.* fact. tout à f., wholly.

falaise, *n.f.* cliff.

fallacieux, *adj.* fallacious.

falloir, *vb.* be necessary. comme il faut, decent.

falot, *n.m.* lamp.

falsificateur, *n.* forger; falsifier.

falsification, *n.f.* falsification.

falsifier, *vb.* falsify.

fameux, *adj.* famous.

familiariser, *vb.* familiarize.

familiarité, *n.f.* familiarity.

familier, *adj.* familiar.

familièrement, *adv.* familiarly.

famille, *n.f.* family, household.

famine, *n.f.* famine.

fanatique, *adj. and n.m.* fanatic.

fanatisme, *n.m.* fanaticism.

faner, *vb.* fade.

fanfare, *n.f.* fanfare.

fanfaronnade, *n.f.* boast.

fange, *n.f.* filth; vice.

fantaisie, *n.f.* fancy, fantasy.

fantastique, *adj.* fantastic.

fantoche, *n.m.* puppet.

fantôme, *n.m.* phantom, ghost.

faon, *n.m.* fawn.

farce, *n.f.* stuffing; farce.

farceur, *n.m.* jokester.

farcir, *vb.* stuff.

fard, *n.m.* facial makeup.

fardeau, *n.m.* burden.

farinacé, *adj.* farinaceous.

farine, *n.f.* meal, flour.

farniente, *n.m.* idleness.

farouche, *adj.* fierce, sullen, shy.

fascinant, *adj.* fascinating.

fascination, *n.f.* fascination.

fascine, *n.f.* faggot (of wood).

fasciner, *vb.* fascinate.

fascisme, *n.m.* fascism.

fasciste, *n.m.* fascist.

faste, *n.m.* ostentation.

fastidieux, *adj.* dull.

fat, *adj.* foppish.

fatal, *adj.* mortal; fatal.

fatalisme, *n.m.* fatalism.

fataliste, *n.m.f.* fatalist.

fatalité, *n.f.* fatality; misfortune.

fatigant, *adj.* tiring.

fatigue, *n.f.* weariness.

fatiguer, *vb.* tire.

fatuité, *n.f.* smugness.

faubourg, *n.m.* suburb.

faubourien, *adj.* suburban.

faucher, *vb.* mow.

faucheur, *n.m.* reaper, mower.

faucille, *n.f.* sickle.

faucon, *n.m.* hawk.

fauconneau, *n.m.* young falcon.

fauconnerie, *n.f.* falconry.

faufil, *n.m.* basting thread.

faufiler, *vb.* baste.

faune, *n.f.* fauna; wildlife.

faussaire, *n.* forger; liar.

faussement, *adv.* falsely.

fausser, *vb.* pervert, warp, distort.

fausset, *n.m.* falsetto; spigot, faucet.

fausseté, *n.f.* falseness.

faute, *n.f.* fault, mistake. f. de, for want of.

fauteuil, *n.m.* armchair.

fautif, *adj.* faulty, wrong.

fauve, *adj.* wild.

faux, 1. *n.m.* forgery. 2. *f.* scythe.

faux *m.*, fausse *f. adj.* false, wrong, spurious, counterfeit.

faux-filet, *n.m.* sirloin.

faveur, *n.f.* favor. en f. de, on behalf of.

favorable, *adj.* conducive, favorable.

favorablement, *adv.* favorably.

favori, *n.m.* whisker.

favori *m.*, favorite *f. adj. and n.* favorite.

favoriser, *vb.* favor.

favoritisme, *n.m.* favoritism.

fayot, *n.m.* kidney bean.

féal, *adj.* faithful.

fébrile, *adj.* feverish.

fécal, *adj.* fecal.

fécond, *adj.* fertile.

féconder, *vb.* fertilize.

fécondité, *n.f.* fertility.

féculent, *adj.* starchy.

fédéral, *adj.* federal.

fédéraliser, *vb.* federalize.

fédéraliste, *n. and adj.* federalist.

fédération, *n.f.* confederacy, federation.

fédérer, *vb.* federate.

fée, *n.f.* fairy.

féerie, *n.f.* fairyland.

féerique, *adj.* fairylike.

feindre, *vb.* feign, pretend.

fêler, *vb.* crack.

félicitation, *n.f.* congratulation.

félicité, *n.f.* bliss.

féliciter (de), *vb.* congratulate (on).

félin, *adj.* feline.

félon, *adj.* disloyal.

femelle, *adj. and n.f.* female.

féminin, *adj.* female, feminine.

femme, *n.f.* woman, wife. f. de chambre, chambermaid.

fémoral, *adj.* femoral.

fendille, *n.f.* crack.

fendiller, *vb.* se f., crack.

fendoir, *n.m.* cleaver.

fendre, *vb.* split, rip.

fenêtre, *n.f.* window.

fenil, *n.m.* hayloft.

fente, *n.f.* crack, rip, split.

féodal, *adj.* feudal.

féodalité, *n.f.* feudalism.

fer (-r), *n.m.* iron. **chemin de f.,** railway. **fil de f.,** wire. **f. à cheval,** horseshoe.

fermail, *n.m.* brooch, clasp.

ferme, *n.f.* farm. **maison de f.,** farmhouse.

ferme, *adj.* firm, steady, fast.

fermement, *adv.* firmly.

fermentation, *n.f.* fermentation.

fermenter, *vb.* ferment.

fermer, *vb.* close. **f. à clef,** lock.

fermeté, *n.f.* firmness.

fermier, *n.m.* farmer.

féroce, *adj.* fierce.

férocité, *n.f.* ferocity.

ferraille, *n.f.* old iron.

ferreux, *adj.* ferrous.

ferrique, *adj.* ferric.

fertile, *adj.* fertile.

fertilisant, *n.m.* fertilizer.

fertilisation, *n.f.* fertilization.

fertiliser, *vb.* fertilize.

fertilité, *n.f.* fertility.

férule, *n.f.* cane, rod.

fervemment, *adv.* fervently.

fervent, *adj.* fervent.

ferveur, *n.f.* fervor.

fesse, *n.f.* buttock.

fessée, *n.f.* spanking.

fesser, *vb.* spank.

festin, *n.m.* feast.

festiner, *vb.* feast.

feston, *n.m.* festoon.

fête, *n.f.* feast, party. **jour de f.,** holiday.

fêter, *vb.* fete.

fétiche, *n.m.* fetish.

fétide, *adj.* fetid.

feu, *n.m.* fire. **f. de joie,** bonfire. **f. d'artifice,** fireworks. **prendre f.,** catch fire. **coup de f.,** shot.

feu, *adj.* late (deceased).

feuillage, *n.m.* foliage.

feuille, *n.f.* leaf, sheet, foil.

feuilleter, *vb.* skim (book).

feutre, *n.m.* felt.

fève, *n.f.* bean.

février, *n.m.* February.

fez, *n.m.* fez.

fi, *interj.* fie!

fiacre, *n.m.* cab.

fiançailles, *n.f.pl.* engagement, betrothal.

fiancé, *n.m.* fiancé.

fiancer, *vb.* betroth.

fiasco, *n.m.* fiasco.

fibre, *n.f.* fiber.

fibreux, *adj.* fibrous.

ficelle, *n.f.* string, twine.

fiche, *n.f.* slip (of paper).

ficher, *vb.* se f. de, care nothing about.

fichier, *n.m.* card index.

fichu, *adv.* ruined.

fictif, *adj.* fictitious.

fiction, *n.f.* fiction.

fidèle, *adj.* faithful.

fidélité, *n.f.* fidelity, loyalty, allegiance.

fief, *n.m.* feud.

fiel, *n.m.* gall.

fiente, *n.f.* dung.

fier (-r), *adj.* proud.

fier, *vb.* se f., trust.

fierté, *n.f.* trust.

fièvre, *n.f.* fever.

fiévreux, *adj.* feverish.

fifre, *n.m.* fife(r).

figer, *vb.* coagulate.

figue, *n.f.* fig.

figuratif, *adj.* figurative.

figure, *n.f.* face, figure.

figurer, *vb.* figure, imagine. se f., fancy.

fil (-l), *n.m.* thread, string. **f. de fer,** wire.

filament, *n.m.* filament.

filature, *n.f.* spinning-mill.

file, *n.f.* file.

filer, *vb.* spin.

filet, *n.m.* net.

filial, *adj.* filial.

filin, *n.m.* rope.

fille, *n.f.* daughter. **jeune f.,** girl. **vieille f.,** old maid.

film, *n.m.* film.

filmer, *vb.* film.

filou, *n.m.* thief.

fils (fês), *n.m.* son.

filtrant, *adj.* filterable.

filtration, *n.f.* filtration.

filtre, *n.m.* filter.

filtrer, *vb.* filter.

fin, 1. *n.f.* end. **2.** *adj.* fine; sharp; clever.

final, *adj.* final.

finaliste, *n.* finalist.

finalité, *n.f.* finality.

finance, *n.f.* finance.

financer, *vb.* finance.

financier, 1. *n.m.* financier. **2.** *adj.* financial.

finasser, *vb.* finesse.

finir, *vb.* finish.

Finlande, *n.f.* Finland.

Finnois, *n.m.* Finn.

finnois, *adj.* and *n.m.* Finnish.

firmament, *n.m.* firmament.

firme, *n.f.* company.

fiscal, *adj.* fiscal.

fissure, *n.f.* fissure.

fixation, *n.f.* fixation.

fixe, *adj.* set, fixed.

fixer, *vb.* fix, secure, settle.

fixité, *n.f.* fixity.

flaccidité, *n.f.* flabbiness.

flacon, *n.m.* bottle.

flagellation, *n.f.* flagellation.

flageller, *vb.* flog.

flagrant, *adj.* flagrant.

flair, *n.m.* flair.

flairer, *vb.* smell.

flamand, *adj.* Flemish.

flambant, *adj.* flaming.

flambeau, *n.m.* torch.

flambée, *n.f.* blaze.

flamber, *vb.* blaze.

flamboyant, *adj.* flaming; flamboyant.

flamboyer, *vb.* flame, flare.

flamme, *n.f.* flame.

flanc, *n.m.* side, flank.

flanchet, *n.m.* flank (of beef).

flanelle, *n.f.* flannel.

flâner, *vb.* saunter, stroll, loiter, loaf.

flâneur, *n.m.* idler.

flanquer, *vb.* flank.

flasque, *n.f.* puddle.

flasque, *adj.* flabby.

flatter, *vb.* flatter.

flatterie, *n.f.* flattery.

flatteur, *n.m.* flatterer.

fléau, *n.m.* scourge, plague.

flèche, *n.f.* arrow.

fléchir, *vb.* bend.

flegmatique, *adj.* phlegmatic.

flegme, *n.m.* phlegm.

flet, *n.m.* flounder.

flétan, *n.m.* halibut.

flétrir, *vb.* wilt, wither.

fleur, *n.f.* flower, blossom, bloom.

fleuret, *n.m.* foil.

fleuri, *adj.* flowery.

fleurir, *vb.* flower, bloom, blossom.

fleuriste, *n.m.f.* florist.

fleuve, *n.m.* river.

flexibilité, *n.f.* flexibility.

flexible, *adj.* flexible.

flirt (-t), *n.m.* flirtation.

flirter, *vb.* flirt.

flocon, *n.m.* flake.

florissant, *adj.* prosperous, flourishing.

flot, *n.m.* wave. **à flot,** afloat.

flottant, *adj.* floating; irresolute.

flotte, *n.f.* fleet.

flottement, *n.m.* fluctuation; wavering.

flotter, *vb.* float.

flou, *adj.* hazy, indistinct.

fluctuation, *n.f.* fluctuation.

fluctuer, *vb.* fluctuate.

fluet *m.,* **fluette** *f.* *adj.* thin, delicate.

fluide, *adj.* and *n.m.* fluid, liquid.

fluidité, *n.f.* fluidity.

flûte, *n.f.* flute.

flûté, *adj.* soft; flute-like.

flux, *n.m.* flow, flux.

fluxion, *n.f.* inflammation.

foi, *n.f.* faith; trust.

foie, *n.m.* liver.

foin, *n.m.* hay.

foire, *n.f.* fair.

fois, *n.f.* time. **à la f.,** at once.

foison, *n.f.* abundance.

foisonner, *vb.* abound.

folâtre, *adj.* frisky.

folâtrer, *vb.* frolic.

folichon, *adj.* playful.

folie, *n.f.* mania, madness, folly.

folklore, *n.m.* folklore.

follement, *adv.* foolishly.

follet, *adj.* merry, playful.

fomenter, *vb.* foment.

foncé, *adj.* dark.

foncer, *vb.* deepen.

fonction, *n.f.* function.

fonctionnaire, n.m. official, civil servant.

fonctionnement, n.m. operation, working.

fonctionner, vb. function, work.

fonctions, n.f.pl. office.

fond, n.m. bottom, (back)ground. à f., thorough(ly). au f., fundamentally.

fondamental, adj. basic, fundamental.

fondateur, n.m. founder.

fondation, n.f. foundation, establishment.

fondé, adj. authentic; (comm.) funded.

fondement, n.m. foundation.

fonder, vb. found.

fonderie, n.f. foundry.

fondre, vb. melt, fuse.

fondrière, n.f. bog.

fonds, n.m. fund.

fongus (-s), n.m. fungus.

fontaine, n.f. fountain.

fonte, n.f. melting.

fonts, n.m.pl. font.

football, n.m. football.

footing, n.m. walking.

forain, n.m. peddler.

forçat, n.m. convict.

force, n.f. strength, force; emphasis.

forcé, adj. forced, far-fetched.

forcément, adv. of necessity.

forcené, adj. frantic.

forcer, vb. force, compel.

forcir, vb. thrive.

forer, vb. bore, drill.

forestier, n.m. forest ranger.

foret, n.m. drill.

forêt, n.f. forest.

foreuse, n.f. drill.

forfait, n.m. crime; forfeit; contract.

forfaiture, n.f. mishandling.

forfanterie, n.f. bragging.

forge, n.f. forge.

forger, vb. forge.

forgeron, n.m. blacksmith.

forgeur, n.m. forger; inventor.

formaliser, vb. offend.

formaliste, adj. formal; precise.

formalité, n.f. formality, ceremony.

formation, n.f. formation.

forme, n.f. shape, form.

formel, adj. formal.

former, vb. form, shape.

formidable, adj. terrible, formidable.

formule, n.f. formula, form.

formuler, vb. formulate, draw up.

fort, 1. n.m. fort. **2.** adj. strong, loud. **3.** adv. hard.

forteresse, n.f. fort(ress).

fortifiant, n.m. strengthening.

fortification, n.f. fortification.

fortifier, vb. strengthen.

fortuit, adj. accidental.

fortuité, n.f. fortuitousness.

fortune, n.f. fortune.

fortuné, adj. lucky, fortunate.

fosse, n.f. pit.

fossé, n.m. ditch; dike.

fossette, n.f. dimple.

fossile, n.m. fossil.

fossoyer, vb. dig a trench.

fou m., **folle** f. adj. mad, crazy, demented.

foudre, n.m. thunderbolt.

foudroyant, adj. terrifying, crushing.

foudroyer, vb. crush, blast.

fouet, n.m. whip, lash.

fouetter, vb. flog, whip.

fougère, n.f. fern.

fougue, n.f. dash.

fougueux, adj. fiery, impetuous.

fouille, n.f. excavation.

fouiller, vb. ransack.

fouillis, n.m. litter, mess.

fouir, vb. dig, burrow.

foulard, n.m. scarf.

foule, n.f. crowd, mob.

fouler, vb. trample.

foulure, n.f. sprain, wrench.

four, n.m. oven.

fourbe, 1. n.m. knave. **2.** adj. scheming.

fourberie, n.f. knavery.

fourbir, vb. polish.

fourche, n.f. fork.

fourgon, n.m. wagon.

fourmi, n.f. ant.

fourmillement, n.m. swarming; tingling.

fourmiller, vb. mill; swarm.

fourneau, n.m. stove, furnace.

fournée, n.f. batch.

fourniment, n.m. equipment.

fournir de, vb. supply, furnish.

fournisseur, n.m. tradesman.

fournitures, n.f.pl. supplies.

fourrage, n.m. fodder, forage.

fourrager, vb. forage.

fourré, adj. lined (of clothing); thick; wooded.

fourreau, n.m. sheath.

fourrer, vb. thrust in. se f., interfere, meddle.

fourreur, n.m. furrier.

fourrure, n.f. fur.

fourvoyer, vb. mislead.

foyer, n.m. focus, hearth. f. domestique, home.

frac, n.m. dress coat.

fracas, n.m. crash; rattle; noise; ado.

fracasser, vb. se f., shatter.

fraction, n.f. fraction.

fracture, n.f. fracture.

fracturer, vb. break, fracture.

fragile, adj. brittle, delicate, frail, fragile.

fragilité, n.f. fragility.

fragment, n.m. fragment.

fragmenter, vb. divide up.

fraîcheur, n.f. freshness, coolness.

fraîchir, vb. freshen.

frais, n.m.pl. expense(s), cost, fee.

frais m. **fraîche** f. adj. fresh, cool.

fraise, n.f. strawberry; ruffle.

framboise, n.f. raspberry.

franc, 1. n.m. franc. **2.** adj.m., **franche** f. frank, open.

Français, n.m. Frenchman.

français, adj. and n.m. French.

Française, n.f. Frenchwoman.

France, n.f. France.

franchement, adv. frankly.

franchir, vb. clear, cross.

franchise, n.f. frankness.

franciser, vb. make French.

franc-maçon, n.m. Freemason.

franc-parler, n.m. frankness.

franc-tireur, n.m. sniper; freelancer.

frange, n.f. fringe.

frangible, adj. breakable.

frapper, vb. strike, hit, rap, knock. f. du pied, stamp.

frasque, n.f. prank.

fraternel, adj. brotherly.

fraterniser, vb. fraternize.

fraternité, n.f. brotherhood.

fraude, n.f. fraud.

frauder, vb. defraud.

fraudeur, n.m. smuggler.

frauduleux, adj. fraudulent.

frayer, vb. open up; rub.

frayeur, n.f. fright.

fredaine, n.f. prank.

fredonner, vb. hum.

frégate, n.f. frigate.

frein, n.m. brake, check.

freiner, vb. brake; restrain.

frelater, vb. adulterate.

frêle, adj. frail.

frelon, n.m. hornet.

frémir, vb. tremble. **faire f.**, thrill.

frémissement, n.m. shiver, thrill.

frêne, n.m. ash (tree).

frénésie, n.f. frenzy.

frénétique, adj. frantic.

fréquemment, adv. often.

fréquence, n.f. frequency.

fréquent, adj. frequent.

fréquenter, vb. frequent, associate with.

frère, n.m. brother.

fresque, n.f. fresco.

fret, n.m. freight.

fréter, vb. charter (ship); freight.

frétillant, adj. lively.

frétiller, vb. wag; quiver.

fretin, n.m. young fish.

frette, n.f. hoop.

friand, adj. dainty; fond (of).

friandise, n.f. love of delicacies.

fricoter, vb. cook, stew.

friction, n.f. friction.

frictionner, vb. chafe.

frigo, n.m. frozen meat.

frigorifier, vb. freeze, refrigerate.

frileux, adj. chilly; susceptible to cold.

frime, n.f. pretense, sham.

fringant, adj. lively, frisky.

friper, vb. crush, rumple.

fripier, n.m. second-hand clothing dealer.

fripon, 1. *adj.* knavish. 2. *n.m.* rascal.

friponnerie, *n.f.* roguery.

kripouille, *n.f.* rascal.

frire, *vb.* fry.

frisé, *adj.* curly.

friser, *vb.* curl.

frisoir, *n.m.* (hair) curler.

frisson, *n.m.* shudder, shiver.

frissonnement, *n.m.* shudder; shivering.

frissonner, *vb.* shudder, shiver.

frites, *n.f.pl.* (potato) chips.

friture, *n.f.* frying.

frivole, *adj.* frivolous.

frivolité, *n.f.* frivolity.

froc, *n.m.* (monk's) frock.

froid, *n.m. and adj.* cold. **un peu f.,** chilly. **avoir f.,** be cold.

froideur, *n.f.* coldness.

froissé, *adj.* bruised. **être f. de,** resent.

froissement, *n.m.* crumpling, rustling, jostling.

froisser, *vb.* crease, wrinkle; bruise, hurt.

frôler, *vb.* graze.

fromage, *n.m.* cheese.

froment, *n.m.* wheat.

froncement, *n.m.* puckering, contraction.

froncer, *vb.* pucker. **f. les sourcils,** frown.

frondaison, *n.f.* foliage.

fronde, *n.f.* sling.

fronder, *vb.* sling; censure.

front, *n.m.* forehead.

frontière, *n.f.* boundary, border, frontier.

frottement, *n.m.* rubbing.

frotter, *vb.* rub.

frou-frou, *n.m.* rustle.

fructueux, *adj.* fruitful.

frugal, *adj.* frugal.

frugalité, *n.f.* frugality.

fruit, *n.m.* fruit.

fruiterie, *n.f.* fruit store.

fruitier, *n.m.* fruit seller.

fugace, *adj.* fleeting.

fugitif, *adj.* fugitive.

fuir, *vb.* flee; shun; leak.

fuite, *n.f.* escape, flight; leak.

fumée, *n.f.* smoke.

fumer, *vb.* smoke.

fumeur, *n.m.* one who smokes.

fumeux, *adj.* smoky.

fumier, *n.m.* dung.

funèbre, *adj.* funereal.

funérailles, *n.f.pl.* funeral.

funeste, *adj.* disastrous.

fureter, *vb.* pry.

fureur, *n.f.* fury.

furie, *n.f.* fury.

furieux, *adj.* furious.

furtif, *adj.* sly.

fuseau, *n.m.* spindle.

fusée, *n.f.* rocket.

fuser, *vb.* melt, spread.

fusil, *n.m.* rifle.

fusilier (-zèl yä), *vb.* shoot.

fusion, *n.f.* merger; meltdown.

fusionner, *vb.* merge.

futé, *adj.* cunning, crafty.

futile, *adj.* futile.

futur, *n.m. and adj.* future.

futurologie, *n.f.* futurology.

fuyant, *adj.* passing, transitory, fugitive.

fuyard, *n.* fugitive.

G

gâcher, *vb.* mess.

gâchette, *n.f.* trigger.

gage, *n.m.* pledge, wage.

gageure, *n.f.* bet.

gagnant, *n.m.* winner.

gagner, *vb.* earn, gain, win, beat (in a game).

gai, *adj.* cheerful, cheery, merry, gay.

gaieté, *n.f.* mirth, cheer, merriment, gaiety.

gaillard, *adj.* hearty, sound.

gain, *n.m.* gain, profit.

gaine, *n.f.* girdle.

galant, 1. *n.m.* beau. 2. *adj.* gallant, civil, courteous. **g. homme,** gentleman.

galanterie, *n.f.* courtesy, compliment.

galbe, *n.m.* outline, contour.

galère, *n.f.* galley, ship.

galerie, *n.f.* gallery, balcony (theater).

galet, *n.m.* boulder.

gallon, *n.m.* gallon.

galon, *n.m.* stripe, braid.

galop, *n.m.* gallop.

galoper, *vb.* gallop.

gambader, *vb.* frolic.

gamin, *n.m.* boy, urchin.

gamme, *n.f.* scale.

gangster (-r), *n.m.* gangster.

gant, *n.m.* glove.

ganterie, *n.f.* glove shop.

garage, *n.m.* garage.

garagiste, *n.m.* garage keeper.

garant, *n.m.* sponsor.

garantie, *n.f.* guarantee, pledge.

garantir, *vb.* guarantee, pledge, warrant.

garçon, *n.m.* boy; waiter; bachelor; flight attendant.

garçonnière, *n.f.* bachelor's apartment.

garde, *n.f.* watch, guard, custody. **prendre g. à,** beware of. **avant-g.,** vanguard. **g. du corps,** bodyguard.

garde-boue, *n.m.* fender.

garde-feu, *n.m.* fender (fireplace).

garde-manger, *n.m.* pantry.

garder, *vb.* guard, keep, mind.

gardeur, *n.m.* keeper.

gardien, *n.m.* keeper, guard, watchman, guardian.

gare, 1. *n.f.* station. 2. *interj.* look out!

garer, *vb.* garage, park.

gargariser, *vb.* se **g.,** gargle.

gargarisme, *n.m.* gargle.

garni, *adj.* furnished, garnished.

garnir, *vb.* trim, garnish.

garnison, *n.f.* garrison.

garniture, *n.f.* fittings.

gars, *n.m.* chap.

gaspillage, *n.m.* waste.

gaspiller, *vb.* waste, squander.

gâteau, *n.m.* cake. **g. de miel,** honeycomb. **g. sec,** cookie.

gâter, *vb.* spoil.

gâterie, *n.f.* excessive indulgence.

gâteux, *adj.* senile.

gauche, *adj. and n.f.* left. **à g.,** on or to the left. *adj.* awkward, clumsy.

gaucherie, *n.f.* clumsiness.

gaufre, *n.f.* waffle.

gaule, *n.f.* pole.

gausser, *vb.* se **g. de,** mock, banter.

gaz (-z), *n.m.* gas.

gaze, *n.f.* gauze.

gazeux, *adj.* gassy, gaseous.

gazon, *n.m.* turf, lawn.

gazouillement, *n.m.* warble, twitter.

géant, *n.m.* giant.

geindre, *vb.* moan, whine.

gelé, *adj.* frozen.

gelée, *n.f.* jelly, frost.

geler, *vb.* freeze.

gémir, *vb.* groan, wail, moan.

gémissement, *n.m.* groan, moan.

gênant, *adj.* troublesome, bothersome.

gencive, *n.f.* gum.

gendarme, *n.m.* policeman.

gendarmerie, *n.f.* police force.

gendre, *n.m.* son-in-law.

gêne, *n.f.* trouble, uneasiness. **être à la g.,** be uneasy.

gêné, *adj.* uneasy.

généalogie, *n.f.* pedigree.

gêner, *vb.* hinder, be in the way, embarrass, bother.

général, *n.m. and adj.* general, overhead (*comm.*). **quartier g.,** headquarters.

généraliser, *vb.* generalize.

généralissime, *n.m.* commander-in-chief.

généralité, *n.f.* generality.

génération, *n.f.* generation.

généreusement, *adv.* generously.

généreux, *adj.* generous, liberal.

générosité, *n.f.* generosity.

génial, *adj.* of genius, highly original.

génie, *n.m.* genius; engineer corps. **soldat du g.,** engineer.

genièvre, *n.m.* gin.

génisse, *n.f.* heifer.

genou, *n.m.* knee; (*pl.*) lap.

genre, *n.m.* kind, gender.

gens, *n.m.f.pl.* people, persons, folk.

gentiane, *n.f.* gentian.

gentil *m.,* **gentille** *f.* *adj.* pleasant, nice.

gentilhomme, *n.m.* nobleman, peer.

gentillesse, *n.f.* prettiness, gracefulness.

géographie, *n.f.* geography.

géographique, *adj.* geographical.

géologie, *n.f.* geology.

géométrie, *n.f.* geometry.

géométrique, *adj.* geometric.

gérance, *n.f.* managership.

géranium, *n.m.* geranium.

gérant, *n.m.* manager, director, superintendent.

gerbe, *n.f.* sheaf.

gerçure, *n.f.* chap.

gérer, *vb.* manage.

germain, *adj.* first (of cousins).

germe, *n.f.* germ.

germer, *vb.* sprout.

gésir, *vb.* lie.

geste, *n.m.* gesture.

gesticuler, *vb.* gesticulate.

gestion, *n.f.* management.

gibier, *n.m.* game.

giboulée, *n.f.* sudden storm, hailstorm.

gicler, *vb.* spurt.

gifler, *vb.* slap.

gigantesque, *adj.* great, huge.

gigue, *n.f.* leg; jig.

gilet, *n.m.* vest. g. de dessous, undershirt.

gingembre, *n.m.* ginger.

girofle, *n.m.* clou de g., clove.

giron, *n.m.* lap.

gitane, *n.m.f.* gypsy.

gîte, *n.m.* lodging, bed.

givre, *n.m.* frost.

glabre, *adj.* smooth-shaven.

glaçage, *n.m.* frosting.

glace, *n.f.* ice, ice cream; mirror.

glacer, *vb.* freeze.

glacial, *adj.* icy.

glacier, *n.m.* glacier.

glacière, *n.f.* icebox.

glacis, *n.m.* slope.

glaçon, *n.m.* block of ice.

glaise, *n.f.* clay.

gland, *n.m.* acorn.

glande, *n.f.* gland.

glaner, *vb.* glean.

glapir, *vb.* yelp; screech.

glas, *n.m.* knell.

glissade, *n.f.* slide, slip.

glissant, *adj.* slippery.

glisser, *vb.* slide, slip. se g., creep, sneak.

global, *adj.* entire.

globe, *n.m.* globe. g. de l'œil, eyeball.

gloire, *n.f.* glory.

glorieux, *adj.* glorious.

glorifier, *vb.* glorify.

glose, *n.f.* criticism; gloss.

glossaire, *n.m.* glossary.

glousser, *vb.* cluck.

gluant, *adj.* sticky.

gobelet, *n.m.* goblet.

gober, *vb.* swallow.

goéland, *n.m.* seagull.

golfe, *n.m.* gulf.

gomme, *n.f.* gum; eraser.

gommeux, *adj.* gummy.

gond, *n.m.* hinge.

gonfler, *vb.* inflate; swell.

gonfleur, *n.m.* tire pump.

gorge, *n.f.* throat; gorge.

gorger, *vb.* cram.

gosier, *n.m.* throat.

gosse, *n.m.f.* kid (child).

gothique, *adj.* Gothic.

goudron, *n.m.* tar.

gouffre, *n.m.* gulf, abyss.

goulu, *adj.* gluttonous.

gourde, *n.f.* flask.

gourmand, 1. *n.m.* glutton. 2. *adj.* greedy.

gourmander, *vb.* scold.

gourmandise, *n.f.* greediness.

gourmer, *vb.* curb.

gourmet, *n.m.* epicure.

gourmette, *n.f.* curb (horse).

gourou, *n.m.* guru.

gousse, *n.f.* shell, pod.

goût, *n.m.* taste, relish.

goûter, 1. *n.m.* snack. 2. *vb.* taste, relish.

goutte, *n.f.* drop; gout.

goutteux, *adj.* gouty.

gouttière, *n.f.* gutter.

gouvernail, *n.m.* rudder, helm.

gouvernante, *n.f.* governess, housekeeper.

gouvernement, *n.m.* government.

gouverner, *vb.* govern, rule, steer.

gouverneur, *n.m.* governor.

grabuge, *n.m.* squabble.

grâce, *n.f.* grace. faire g. de, spare.

gracier, *vb.* pardon.

gracieux, *adj.* graceful, gracious.

grade, *n.m.* grade, rank.

gradin, *n.m.* step, tier.

graduel, *adj.* gradual.

graduer, *vb.* graduate.

grain, *n.m.* grain, seed, berry, kernel. g. de beauté, mole.

graine, *n.f.* seed, berry.

graissage, *n.m.* greasing.

graisse, *n.f.* grease, fat.

graisser, *vb.* grease.

grammaire, *n.f.* grammar.

gramme, *n.m.* gram.

grand, *adj.* big, great, tall. grand'chose, much.

grandement, *adv.* grandly, greatly.

grandeur, *n.f.* size, height, greatness.

grandiose, *adj.* grand.

grandir, *vb.* grow.

grand'mère, *n.f.* grandmother.

grand-père, *n.m.* grandfather.

grange, *n.f.* barn.

granit (-t), *n.m.* granite.

graphique, *adj.* chart.

grappe, *n.f.* bunch, cluster.

gras m., grasse f. *adj.* fat, stout.

grassement, *adj.* plentifully.

grasset, *adj.* plump.

grassouillet, *adj.* plump.

gratification, *n.f.* bonus.

gratifier, *vb.* bestow.

gratin, *n.m.* burnt part.

gratitude, *n.f.* gratitude.

gratte-ciel, *n.m.* skyscraper.

gratter, *vb.* scrape, scratch.

gratuit, *adj.* free.

grave, *adj.* grave.

graveleux, *adj.* gritty.

graver, *vb.* engrave.

graveur, *n.m.* engraver.

gravier, *n.m.* gravel.

gravir, *vb.* climb.

gravité, *n.f.* gravity.

graviter, *vb.* gravitate.

gravure, *n.f.* engraving. g. à l'eau-forte, etching.

gré, *n.m.* pleasure.

Grec m., Grecque f. *n.* Greek (person).

grec, *n.m.* Greek (language).

grec m., grecque f. *adj.* Greek.

Grèce, *n.f.* Greece.

gréement, *n.m.* rig.

gréer, *vb.* rig.

greffier, *n.m.* clerk.

grêle, 1. *n.f.* hail. 2. *adj.* thin, slight.

grêler, *vb.* hail.

grêlon, *n.m.* hailstone.

grelotter, *vb.* shiver.

grenier, *n.m.* attic.

grenouille, *n.f.* frog.

grève, *n.f.* strike. se mettre en g., strike, *vb.*

gréviste, *n.m.f.* striker.

gribouiller, *vb.* scribble.

grief, *n.m.* grievance.

grièvement, *adv.* seriously.

griffe, *n.f.* claw, clutch.

griffer, *vb.* seize; scratch.

griffonner, *vb.* scribble.

grignoter, *vb.* nibble.

gril, *n.m.* grill.

grillade, *n.f.* broiling.

grille, *n.f.* grate, gate.

griller, *vb.* broil, roast, toast.

grillon, *n.m.* cricket.

grimace, *n.f.* grimace.

grimacer, *vb.* make faces.

grimer, *vb.* make up.

grimper, *vb.* climb.

grincer, *vb.* creak, grate, grind.

gris, *adj.* gray; drab; drunk.

griser, *vb.* get drunk.

grive, *n.f.* thrush.

grogner, *vb.* growl, snarl, grumble.

grommeler, *vb.* mutter.

gronder, *vb.* scold, nag; roar, rumble.

gros m., grosse f. *adj.* overly large; gross, stout, rough. en g., wholesale.

groseille, *n.f.* currant.

grosseur, *n.f.* size, thickness.

grossier, *adj.* coarse, crude, gross.

grossièreté, *n.f.* coarseness.

grossir, *vb.* magnify, grow.

grotesque, *adj.* grotesque.

grouiller, *vb.* stir, swarm.

groupe, *n.m.* group, party; cluster.

groupement, *n.m.* grouping.

grouper, *vb.* group.

grue, *n.f.* crane.

gué, *n.m.* ford. traverser à g., wade.

guêpe, *n.f.* wasp.

guère, *adv.* hardly.

guérir, *vb.* cure, heal.

guérison, *n.f.* cure.

guerre, *n.f.* war.

guerrier, *adj.* warlike.

guetter, *vb.* watch (for).

gueule, *n.f.* mouth.

gueux, *n.m.* beggar, tramp.

guichet, *n.m.* ticket-window.

guide, *n.m.* guide(book).

guider, *vb.* guide.

guillotine, *n.f.* guillotine.

guingan, *n.m.* gingham.

guirlande, *n.f.* garland.

guise, *n.f.* way, manner.

guitare, *n.f.* guitar.

gymnase, *n.m.* gymnasium.

H

habile, *adj.* clever, skillful, smart, able.

habileté, *n.f.* craft, ability.

habillement, *n.m.* apparel.

habillements masculins, *n.m.pl.* menswear.

habiller, *vb.* dress.

habilleur *m.*, **habilleuse** *f.* *n.* dresser.

habit, *n.m.* coat; attire; (*pl.*) clothes.

habitant, *n.m.* inhabitant, resident.

habitation, *n.f.* dwelling.

habiter, *vb.* inhabit, live.

habitude, *n.f.* habit, practice. **d'h.**, customarily. **avoir l'h. de**, be accustomed to.

habituel, *adj.* customary, usual.

habituer, *vb.* get used to.

hâbleur, *n.m.* boaster.

hache, *n.f.* ax.

hacher, *vb.* mince, chop, hack up.

hachette, *n.f.* hatchet.

hachis, *n.m.* hash.

hagard, *adj.* haggard.

haie, *n.f.* hedge.

haillon, *n.m.* rag.

haine, *n.f.* hatred.

haineux, *adj.* hating.

haïr, *vb.* hate.

haïssable, *adj.* hateful.

halage, *n.m.* towage.

hâle, *n.m.* tan, sunburn.

haleine, *n.f.* breath.

haler, *vb.* haul, tow.

hâler, *vb.* tan. **se h.**, become sunburned.

haleter, *vb.* pant, gasp.

halle, *n.f.* market.

halte, *n.f.* halt.

hamac, *n.m.* hammock.

hameau, *n.m.* hamlet.

hameçon, *n.m.* hook.

hampe, *n.f.* handle.

hanche, *n.f.* hip.

hangar, *n.m.* shed.

hanter, *vb.* haunt.

hantise, *n.f.* obsession.

happer, *vb.* snap.

harcèlement, *n.m.* hassle, harassment.

harceler, *vb.* worry, bother; hassle; harass.

hardes, *n.f.pl.* togs.

hardi, *adj.* bold.

hardiesse, *n.f.* boldness.

hareng, *n.m.* herring.

hargneux, *adj.* cross, snarling.

haricot, *n.m.* bean.

harmonie, *n.f.* harmony.

harmonieux, *adj.* harmonious.

harmoniser, *vb.* put in tune, harmonize.

harnacher, *vb.* harness.

harnais, *n.m.* harness.

harpe, *n.f.* harp.

harpin, *n.m.* boat hook.

hasard, *n.m.* chance. **au h.** or **par h.**, at random.

hasarder, *vb.* venture.

hasardeux, *adj.* hazardous, unsafe.

hâte, *n.f.* haste, hurry. **à la h.**, hastily.

hâter, *vb.* hasten, hurry.

hâtif, *adj.* early, hasty.

haussement, *n.m.* raising; shrug.

hausser, *vb.* raise; shrug.

haussier, *n.m.* bull (stock exchange).

haut, **1.** *n.m.* top. **2.** *adj.* high, loud. **à haute voix**, aloud. **en haut**, up, above.

hautain, *adj.* haughty, lofty, proud.

hautbois, *n.m.* oboe.

haute fidélité, *n.f.* high fidelity.

hauteur, *n.f.* height; haughtiness. **être à la h. de**, be up to.

hauturier, *adj.* sea-going.

hâve, *adj.* wan, gaunt.

havre, *n.m.* haven.

havresac, *n.m.* knapsack.

hebdomadaire, *adj.* weekly.

héberger, *vb.* shelter.

bébété, *adj.* dull.

hébreu, **1.** *n.m.* Hebrew (language). **2.** *adj.* Hebrew.

hein, *interj.* huh?

hélas (-s), *interj.* alas!

héler, *vb.* call, hail.

hélice, *n.f.* propeller.

hélicoptère, *n.m.* helicopter.

helvétique, *adj.* Swiss.

hémisphère, *n.m.* hemisphere.

hémorragie, *n.f.* hemorrhage.

hennir, *vb.* neigh.

héraut, *n.m.* herald.

herbage, *n.m.* grass, pasture.

herbe, *n.f.* grass, herb; marijuana. **mauvaise h.**, weed.

herbeux, *adj.* grassy.

héréditaire, *adj.* hereditary.

hérésie, *n.f.* heresy.

hérétique, **1.** *n.m.f.* heretic. **2.** *adj.* heretic, heretical.

hérisser, *vb.* bristle.

hérisson, *n.m.* hedgehog.

héritage, *n.m.* inheritance.

hériter, *vb.* inherit.

héritier, *n.m.* heir.

hermétique, *adj.* (sealed) tight.

hermine, *n.f.* ermine.

hernie, *n.f.* hernia.

héroïne, *n.f.* heroine.

héroïque, *adj.* heroic.

héroïsme, *n.m.* heroism.

héros, *n.m.* hero.

hertz, *n.m.* hertz.

hésitation, *n.f.* hesitation.

hésiter, *vb.* hesitate, waver, falter.

hétérosexuel, *adj.* heterosexual.

hêtre, *n.m.* beech.

heure, *n.f.* hour; time. **de bonne h.**, early.

heureusement, *adv.* happily, luckily.

heureux, *adj.* glad, happy; lucky, fortunate; successful.

heurt, *n.m.* blow, shock.

heurter, *vb.* collide (with).

heurtoir, *n.m.* (door) knocker.

hibou, *n.m.* owl.

hideux, *adj.* hideous.

hier (-r), *adv.* yesterday.

hilare, *adj.* hilarious.

hilarité, *n.f.* hilarity.

Hindou, *n.m.* Hindu.

hindou, *adj.* Hindu.

hippodrome, *n.m.* race course.

hippopotame, *n.m.* hippopotamus.

hirondelle, *n.f.* swallow.

hispanique, *adj.* Hispanic.

hisser, *vb.* hoist.

histoire, *n.f.* history, story; to-do, fuss.

historien, *n.m.* historian.

historique, *adj.* historic.

hiver (-r), *n.m.* winter.

hiverner, *vb.* s'h., hibernate.

hocher, *vb.* shake, nod.

hochet, *n.m.* rattle.

hoirie, *n.f.* inheritance.

Hollandais, *n.m.* Hollander, Dutchman.

hollandais, *adj. and n.m.* Dutch.

Hollande, *n.f.* Holland; the Netherlands.

hologramme, *n.m.* hologram.

holographie, *n.f.* holography.

homard, *n.m.* lobster.

hommage, *n.m.* homage.

hommasse, *adj.* mannish.

homme, *n.m.* man. **h. d'affaires**, businessman.

homogène, *adj.* of the same kind, homogeneous.

homosexuel, *adj.* homosexual.

Hongrie, *n.f.* Hungary.

Hongrois, *n.m.* Hungarian (person).

hongrois, **1.** *n.m.* Hungarian (language). **2.** *adj.* Hungarian.

honnête, *adj.* honest.

honnêteté, *n.f.* honesty, fairness.

honneur, *n.m.* honor, credit.

honorable, *adj.* honorable.

honoraires, *n.m.pl.* fee.

honorer, *vb.* honor.

honte, *n.f.* shame. **avoir h. de**, be ashamed of. **faire h. à.**, shame.

honteux, *adj.* ashamed; shameful.

hôpital, *n.m.* hospital.

hoquet, *n.m.* hiccup.

horaire, *n.m.* timetable.

horde, *n.f.* horde.

horizon, *n.m.* horizon.

horizontal, *adj.* horizontal.

horloge, *n.f.* clock.

horloger, *n.m.* watchmaker.

hormis, *prep.* except.

horreur, *n.f.* horror.

horrible, *adj.* horrible, ghastly.

horrifier, *vb.* horrify.

horrifique, *adj.* hair-raising.

horripiler, *vb.* annoy.

hors-bord, *n.m.* outboard boat.

hors de, *prep.* out of, outside.

horticole, *adj.* horticultural.

hospice, *n.m.* refuge.

hospitalier, *adj.* hospitable.

hospitaliser, *vb.* hospitalize; shelter.

hospitalité, *n.f.* hospitality.

hostie, *n.f.* (eccles.) host.

hostile, *adj.* hostile.

hostilité, *n.f.* hostility.

hôte, *n.m.* host; guest.

hôtel, *n.m.* hotel; mansion. h. de ville, city hall.

hôtelier, *n.m.* innkeeper.

hôtesse, *n.f.* hostess.

hôtesse de l'air, *n.f.* stewardess, flight attendant.

hotte, *n.f.* basket carried on back.

houblon, *n.m.* hop.

houe, *n.f.* hoe.

houer, *vb.* hoe.

houille, *n.f.* coal.

houillère, *n.f.* coal mine.

houle, *n.f.* surge.

houleux, *adj.* stormy, rough.

houppe, *n.f.* tuft; powder puff.

hourra, *n.m.* cheer.

housse, *n.f.* covering.

houx, *n.m.* holly.

hublot, *n.m.* porthole.

huer, *vb.* shout, hoot.

huile, *n.f.* oil.

huiler, *vb.* oil.

huileux, *adj.* oily.

huissier, *n.m.* usher.

huit, *adj. and n.m.* eight.

huitième, *adj. and n.m.f.* eighth.

huître, *n.f.* oyster.

humain, *adj.* human, humane.

humanitaire, *adj.* humanitarian.

humanité, *n.f.* humanity.

humble, *adj.* lowly, humble.

humecter, *vb.* moisten.

humer, *vb.* suck up, sniff up.

humeur, *n.f.* humor; mood, temper.

humide, *adj.* damp, humid.

humidité, *n.f.* moisture.

humiliation, *n.f.* humiliation.

humilier, *vb.* humiliate, humble.

humilité, *n.f.* humility.

humoristique, *adj.* humorous.

humour, *n.m.* humor.

hune, *n.f.* (naut.) top.

huppe, *n.f.* tuft, crest.

hurlement, *n.m.* noise, howling.

hurler, *vb.* howl, roar, yell.

hutte, *n.f.* hut, shed.

hybride, *adj. and n.m.* hybrid.

hydrogène, *n.m.* hydrogen.

hyène, *n.f.* hyena.

hygiène, *n.f.* sanitation, hygiene.

hygiénique, *adj.* hygienic.

hymne, *n.m.* hymn; *n.f.* church hymn.

hypnotiser, *vb.* hypnotize.

hypocondriaque, *adj. and n.* hypochondriac.

hypocrisie, *n.f.* hypocrisy.

hypocrite, 1. *n.m.f.* hypocrite. 2. *adj.* hypocritical.

hypothèque, *n.f.* mortgage.

hypothéquer, *vb.* mortgage.

hypothèse, *n.f.* hypothesis.

hystérectomie, *n.f.* hysterectomy.

hystérie, *n.f.* hysteria.

hystérique, *adj.* hysterical.

I

ici, *adv.* here. d'i., hence.

ictère, *n.m.* jaundice.

idéal, *adj. and n.m.* ideal.

idéaliser, *vb.* idealize.

idéalisme, *n.m.* idealism.

idéaliste, *n.m.f.* idealist.

idée, *n.f.* idea, notion.

identification, *n.f.* identification.

identifier, *vb.* identify.

identique (à), *adj.* identical (with).

identité, *n.f.* identity.

idéologie, *n.f.* ideology.

idiome, *n.m.* idiom.

idiot, *adj. and n.m.* idiot(ic).

idiotie, *n.f.* idiocy.

idiotisme, *n.m.* idiom.

idolâtrer, *vb.* idolize.

idole, *n.f.* idol.

idyllique, *adj.* idyllic.

if, *n.m.* yew.

ignare, *adj.* ignorant.

ignoble, *adj.* ignoble.

ignorance, *n.f.* ignorance.

ignorant, *adj.* ignorant.

ignorer, *vb.* not know.

il (el), *pron.* he, it; (pl.) they.

île, *n.f.* island.

illégal (-l-), *adj.* illegal.

illégitime (-l-), *adj.* illegitimate.

illettré (-l-), *adj.* illiterate.

illicite (-l-), *adj.* illicit.

illimité (-l-), *adj.* boundless.

illogique (-l-), *adj.* illogical.

illuminer (-l-), *vb.* light, illuminate.

illusion (-l-), *n.f.* illusion, delusion.

illustration (-l-), *n.f.* illustration.

illustre (-l-), *adj.* illustrious, famous.

illustrer (-l-), *vb.* illustrate.

image, *n.f.* picture.

imaginaire, *adj.* fancied, imaginary.

imaginatif, *adj.* imaginative.

imagination, *n.f.* imagination.

imaginer, *vb.* imagine.

imam, *n.m.* imam.

imbattable, *adj.* unbeatable.

imbécillité, *n.f.* imbecility; stupidity.

imberbe, *adj.* beardless.

imbiber, *vb.* soak, steep.

imbu, *adj.* imbued; steeped.

imitation, *n.f.* imitation, copy.

imiter, *vb.* imitate, copy; mimic.

immaculé, *adj.* immaculate.

immangeable, *adj.* uneatable.

immatériel, *adj.* incorporeal.

immatriculer, *vb.* matriculate.

immédiat, *adj.* immediate.

immense, *adj.* immense, great, huge.

immensité, *n.f.* immensity.

immeuble, *n.m.* real estate.

imminent, *adj.* imminent.

immiscer, *vb.* s'i., meddle, interfere.

immixtion, *n.f.* mixing; interference.

immobile, *adj.* motionless.

immoler, *vb.* sacrifice. s'i., sacrifice oneself.

immonde, *adj.* filthy.

immoral, *adj.* immoral.

immortaliser, *vb.* immortalize.

immortalité, *n.f.* immortality.

immortel, *adj. and n.m.* immortal.

immuable, *adj.* unchangeable.

immunité, *n.f.* immunity.

impair, *adj.* odd.

impalpable, *adj.* intangible.

imparfait, *adj. and n.m.* imperfect.

impartial, *adj.* impartial.

impasse, *n.f.* dead end.

impassible, *adj.* impassive.

impatience, *n.f.* impatience.

impatient, *adj.* impatient.

impatienter, *vb.* provoke.

impayable, *adj.* invaluable; very funny.

impeccable, *adj.* faultless.

impécunieux, *adj.* impecunious.

impénétrable, *adj.* impenetrable.

impératif, *adj. and n.m.* imperative.

impératrice, *n.f.* empress.

imperceptible, *adj.* imperceptible.

impérial, *adj.* imperial.

impérialisme, *n.m.* imperialism.

impérieux, *adj.* domineering.

impérissable, *adj.* imperishable.

imperméabiliser, *vb.* waterproof.

imperméable, 1. *n.m.* raincoat. 2. *adj.* waterproof.

impertinence, *n.f.* impertinence.

impertinent, *adj.* saucy.

impétueux, *adj.* headlong, impetuous.

impie, *adj.* impious.

impitoyable, *adj.* merciless, pitiless, ruthless.

impliquer, *vb.* involve, imply.

implorer, *vb.* implore, beg.

impoli, *adj.* rude, impolite, discourteous.

impolitesse, *n.f.* discourtesy.

impopulaire, *adj.* unpopular.

importance, *n.f.* significance, importance.

important, *adj.* momentous, important.

importateur, *n.m.* importer.

importation, *n.f.* import.

importer, *vb.* matter; import.

importun, *adj.* tiresome, bothersome, importunate.

importuner, *vb.* pester, keep bothering.

importunité, *n.f.* importunity.

imposable, *adj.* taxable.

imposer (à), *vb.* impose (on); tax; enforce.

imposition, *n.f.* imposition.

impossibilité, *n.f.* impossibility. **dans l'i. de**, unable to.

impossible, *adj.* impossible.

imposteur, *n.m.* fraud (person), faker, impostor.

imposture, *n.f.* imposture, deception.

impôt, *n.m.* tax, tariff.

impotent, *adj.* weak, infirm.

impôt sur les ventes, *n.m.* sales tax.

imprécis, *adj.* imprecise.

imprégner, *vb.* impregnate, imbue.

imprenable, *adj.* impregnable.

impression, *n.f.* print, impression.

impressionnable, *adj.* sensitive, impressionable.

impressionnant, *adj.* impressive.

impressionner, *vb.* affect.

imprévoyance, *n.f.* improvidence.

imprévoyant, *adj.* not foresighted.

imprévu, *adj.* unexpected, unforeseen.

imprimé, *n.m.* printed matter.

imprimer, *vb.* impress; print.

imprimerie, *n.f.* printery, printing.

imprimeur, *n.m.* printer.

improbable, *adj.* improbable.

improbité, *n.f.* dishonesty.

improductif, *adj.* unproductive.

impromptu, *adv., adj and n.m.* impromptu.

impropre, *adv.* improper, unfit.

improviste, *adv.* **à l'i.,** all of a sudden.

imprudence, *n.f.* indiscretion.

impudence, *n.f.* impudence.

impudicité, *n.f.* lewdness.

impuissance, *n.f.* impotence.

impuissant, *adj.* impotent, powerless, helpless.

impulsif, *adj.* impulsive.

impulsion, *n.f.* impulse, spur.

impunément, *adv.* with impunity.

impunité, *n.f.* impunity.

impur, *adj.* impure.

impureté, *n.f.* impurity.

imputer, *vb.* impute.

inabordable, *adj.* inaccessible.

inaccoutumé, *adj.* unusual.

inachevé, *adj.* unfinished.

inactif, *adj.* inactive, indolent.

inadvertance, *n.f.* oversight.

inanimé, *adj.* lifeless.

inanité, *n.f.* uselessness.

inaperçu, *adj.* unperceived.

inattaquable, *adj.* unassailable.

inattendu, *adj.* unexpected.

inavouable, *adj.* unavowable, shameful.

incalculable, *adj.* countless, incalculable.

incapable, *adj.* unable.

incarcérer, *vb.* imprison.

incarnat, *adj.* flesh-colored, rosy.

incarner, *vb.* embody.

incartade, *n.f.* insult, prank.

incendie, *n.m.* fire.

incendier, *vb.* set fire to.

incertain, *adj.* uncertain.

incertitude, *n.f.* suspense.

incessamment, *adv.* incessantly; immediately.

inceste, *n.m.* incest.

incident, *n.m.* incident.

incinérer, *vb.* cremate; incinerate.

incision, *n.f.* incision.

inciter, *vb.* incite.

inclinaison, *n.f.* slope.

inclination, *n.f.* bow, nod; propensity.

incliner, *vb.* slant, nod, bow. **s'i.,** lean.

inclure, *vb.* include, enclose.

inclus, *adj.* included. **ci-inclus,** enclosed, herewith.

inclusif, *adj.* inclusive.

incolore, *adj.* colorless.

incomber, *vb.* devolve upon.

incommode, *adj.* uncomfortable, inconvenient.

incommoder, *vb.* inconvenience.

incomparable, *adj.* incomparable.

incompatible, *adj.* incompatible.

incompétence, *n.f.* incompetence.

incomplet, *adj.* imperfect, unfinished.

incompris, *adj.* unappreciated, not understood.

inconduite, *n.f.* misconduct.

inconnu, *adj.* unknown.

inconscient, *adj. and n.m.* unconscious.

inconséquent, *adj.* inconsistent.

inconsidéré, *adj.* thoughtless.

inconsistant, *adj.* weak, inconsistent.

inconstant, *adj.* inconstant.

incontestable, *adj.* unquestionable.

incontesté, *adj.* unquestioned.

incontinent, 1. *adj.* incontinent. **2.** *adv.* immediately.

incontrôlable, *adj.* not verifiable.

inconvenance, *n.f.* impropriety.

inconvénient, *n.m.* inconvenience.

incorporer, *vb.* embody.

incorrect, *adj.* incorrect.

incriminer, *vb.* accuse.

incroyable, *adj.* incredible.

incroyant, *n.m.* unbeliever.

inculper, *vb.* charge, accuse.

inculte, *adj.* uncultivated, unkempt.

incurable, *adj.* incurable.

incurie, *n.f.* carelessness, neglect.

Inde, *n.f.* India.

indécis, *adj.* doubtful, vague, dim.

indéfini, *adj.* indefinite.

indéfinissable, *adj.* nondescript.

indéfrisable, *n.f.* permanent wave.

indélicat, *adj.* indelicate.

indélicatesse, *n.f.* indelicacy; blunder.

indépendance, *n.f.* independence.

indépendant, *adj.* independent.

index (-ks), *n.m.* index; forefinger.

indicateur, *n.m.* timetable.

indicatif, *adj. and n.m.* indicative.

indicatif interurbain, *n.m.* area code.

indication, *n.f.* indication.

indice, *n.m.* sign, proof.

indicible, *adj.* unspeakable, inexpressible.

Indien, *n.m.* Indian.

indien, *adj.* Indian.

indifférence, *n.f.* indifference.

indifférent, *adj.* indifferent.

indigène, *n.m.f.* native.

indigent, *adj.* destitute.

indigeste, *adj.* indigestible.

indignation, *n.f.* indignation, anger.

indigne, *adj.* worthless, unworthy.

indigné, *adj.* indignant.

indigner, *vb.* anger.

indiquer, *vb.* indicate, point out.

indirect, *adj.* indirect.

indiscret, *adj.* indiscreet.

indiscutable, *adj.* indisputable.

indispensable, *adj.* indispensable, essential.

indisposer, *vb.* indispose; set against.

indisposition, *n.f.* ailment.

indistinct, *adj.* indistinct.

individu, *n.m.* individual, person.

individuel, *adj.* individual.

indomptable, *adj.* adamant, unconquerable.

indu, *adj.* undue; not ordinary.

induire, *vb.* induce; infer.

indulgence, *n.f.* indulgence.
indulgent, *adj.* lenient, indulgent.
indûment, *adv.* unduly.
industrie, *n.f.* industry.
industriel, *adj.* industrial.
inébranlable, *adj.* immovable, firm.
inédit, *adj.* unpublished.
inefficace, *adj.* ineffectual.
inégal, *adj.* uneven, unequal.
inégalité, *n.f.* inequality, irregularity.
inepte, *adj.* inept, stupid.
ineptie, *n.f.* inept action.
inépuisable, *n.f.* inexhaustible.
inertie, *n.f.* inertia.
inestimable, *adj.* priceless.
inévitable, *adj.* inevitable.
inexact, *adj.* inexact.
inexécutable, *adj.* impracticable.
inexplicable, *adj.* inexplicable.
inexprimable, *adj.* inexpressible.
infaillible, *adj.* infallible.
infâme, *adj.* infamous.
infamie, *n.f.* infamy.
infanterie, *n.f.* infantry.
infatigable, *adj.* untiring.
infécond, *adj.* barren, sterile.
infect, *adj.* infected, rotten.
infecter, *vb.* infect.
infection, *n.f.* infection.
inférieur, *adj. and n.m.* inferior, low(er).
infernal, *adj.* infernal.
infester, *vb.* infest.
infidèle, *adj.* disloyal, unfaithful, false.
infidélité, *n.f.* infidelity.
infime, *adj.* lowest; mean.
infini, *adj. and n.m.* infinite.
infinité, *n.f.* infinity.
infirme, *adj. and n.m.f.* invalid.
infirmer, *vb.* invalidate, weaken.
infirmière, *n.f.* nurse.
infirmité, *n.f.* infirmity.
inflammation, *n.f.* inflammation.
inflation, *n.f.* inflation.
infliger, *vb.* inflict.
influence, *n.f.* influence.
influent, *adj.* influential.
information, *n.f.* inquiry; (*pl.*) news.
informatique, *n.f.* computer science.
informatiser, *vb.* computerize.
informe, *adj.* shapeless.
informer, *vb.* inform. **i. de.** acquaint with.
infraction, *n.f.* breach.
infructueux, *adj.* fruitless.
infuser, *vb.* infuse. **faire i.,** brew.
ingambe, *adj.* nimble.
ingénieur, *n.m.* engineer.
ingénieux, *adj.* ingenious.
ingéniosité, *n.f.* ingenuity.
ingénu, *adj.* naïve, ingenuous.
ingrat, *adj.* ungrateful.
ingrédient, *n.m.* ingredient.
inguérissable, *adj.* incurable.

inhabile, *adj.* awkward, incapable.
inhiber, *vb.* inhibit.
inhospitalier, *adj.* inhospitable.
inhumain, *adj.* cruel, inhuman.
inimitié, *n.f.* enmity.
inique, *adj.* unfair.
initial, *adj.* initial.
initiale, *n.f.* initial.
initiative, *n.f.* initiative.
initier, *vb.* initiate.
injecté, *adj.* **i. de sang,** bloodshot.
injecter, *vb.* inject.
injection, *n.f.* injection.
injonction, *n.f.* injunction.
injures, *n.f.pl.* abuse.
injurier, *vb.* abuse, insult.
injurieux, *adj.* abusive, insulting, offensive.
injuste, *adj.* unfair.
injustice, *n.f.* injustice.
inlassable, *adj.* untiring.
inné, *adj.* innate.
innocence, *n.f.* innocence.
innocent, *adj.* innocent.
innocenter, *vb.* declare innocent.
innombrable, *adj.* countless.
innovation, *n.f.* innovation.
inoccupé, *adj.* idle; unoccupied.
inoculer, *vb.* inoculate.
inodore, *adj.* odorless.
inoffensif, *adj.* innocuous, harmless.
inondation, *n.f.* flood.
inonder, *vb.* flood.
inopiné, *adj.* unexpected.
inoubliable, *adj.* unforgettable.
inouï, *adj.* unheard-of.
inquiet, *adj.* restless, anxious, uneasy.
inquiéter, *vb.* trouble. **s'i.,** worry.
inquiétude, *n.f.* misgiving, worry.
insaisissable, *adj.* imperceptible.
insalubre, *adj.* unhealthy.
inscription, *n.f.* incription, entry.
inscrire, *vb.* inscribe; enter.
insecte, *n.m.* bug, insect.
insensé, *adj.* mad.
insensible, *adj.* insensible; unfeeling.
inséparable, *adj.* inseparable.
insérer, *vb.* insert.
insigne, *n.m.* badge, sign.
insignifiant, *adj.* petty, insignificant.
insinuer, *vb.* hint.
insipide, *adj.* tasteless, dull.
insistance, *n.f.* insistence.
insister, *vb.* insist.
insolation, *n.f.* susntroke.
insolence, *n.f.* insolence.
insolite, *adj.* unusual.
insomnie, *n.f.* insomnia.
insondable, *adj.* bottomless.
insouciant, *adj.* casual, careless.
insoumis, *adj.* unsubdued.

inspecter, *vb.* examine, survey.
inspecteur, *n.m.* inspector.
inspection, *n.f.* inspection.
inspiration, *n.f.* inspiration.
inspirer, *vb.* inspire.
instable, *adj.* temperamental, unsteady, unstable.
installer, *vb.* install.
instamment, *adv.* urgently.
instance, *n.f.* entreaty; instance.
instant, *n.m.* instant. **à l'i., at once.**
instantané, *adj.* instantaneous.
instinct, *n.m.* instinct.
instinctif, *adj.* instinctive.
instituer, *vb.* institute.
instituteur, *n.m.* teacher.
institution, *n.f.* institution, institute.
institutrice, *n.f.* teacher.
instructeur, *n.m.* teacher.
instructif, *adj.* instructive.
instruction, *n.f.* education, instruction; (*pl.*) directions.
instruire, *vb.* educate, teach, instruct.
instrument, *n.m.* instrument.
instrumentation, *n.f.* orchestration.
insu, *n.m.* **à l'i. de,** unknown to.
insuccès, *n.m.* failure.
insuffisance, *n.f.* deficiency.
insuffisant, *adj.* deficient.
insulaire, 1. *n.m.* islander. 2. *adj.* insular.
insulte, *n.f.* affront, insult.
insulter, *vb.* affront, insult.
insurgé, *adj. and n.m.* insurgent.
insurger, *vb.* **s'i.,** revolt.
insurmontable, *adj.* insuperable.
intact (-kt), *adj.* intact.
intarissable, *adj.* inexhaustible.
intègre, *adj.* upright.
intégrité, *n.f.* integrity.
intellect, *n.m.* intellect.
intellectuel, *adj. and n.m.* intellectual.
intelligence, *n.f.* intelligence.
intelligent, *adj.* intelligent.
intelligible, *adj.* intelligible; audible.
intempérie, *n.f.* inclemency (of weather).
intempestif, *adj.* untimely.
intendance, *n.f.* administration.
intendant, *n.m.* director.
intendante, *n.f.* matron.
intense, *adj.* intense.
intensif, *adj.* intensive.
intensité, *n.f.* intensity.
intention, *n.f.* intention.
intentionné, *adj.* intentioned.
intentionnel, *adj.* intentional.
intercéder, *vb.* intercede.
intercepter, *vb.* intercept.
interdire, *vb.* forbid.
intéressant, *adj.* interesting.
intéresser, *vb.* interest, concern, affect.
intérêt, *n.m.* interest.

intérieur, adj. and n.m. interior.

interjection, n.f. interjection.

interloquer, vb. embarrass.

intermède, n.m. interlude.

intermédiaire, adj. and n.m.f. intermediate.

interminable, adj. interminable.

internat, n.m. boarding school.

international, adj. international.

interne, 1. adj. internal. 2. n.m. resident student.

interner, vb. intern.

interpellation, n.f. questioning.

interpeller, vb. ask.

interposer, vb. interpose.

interprétation, n.f. interpretation.

interprète, n.m.f. interpreter.

interpréter, vb. interpret.

interrogateur, 1. n.m. examiner. 2. adj. questioning.

interrogation, n.f. interrogation.

interrogatoire, n.m. cross-examination.

interroger, vb. question.

interrompre, vb. interrupt.

interrupteur, n.m. switch.

interruption, n.f. break, intermission, interruption.

intervalle, n.m. interval.

intervenir, vb. interfere.

intervention, n.f. interference.

intervertir, vb. transpose.

interview, n.m. or f. interview.

interviewer, vb. interview.

intestin, n.m. bowels.

intimation, n.f. notification.

intime, adj. intimate.

intimer, vb. notify.

intimider, vb. daunt, intimidate.

intimité, n.f. intimacy.

intituler, vb. entitle.

intolérance, n.f. intolerance.

intonation, n.f. intonation.

intoxication, n.f. poisoning.

intoxiquer, vb. poison.

intraitable, adj. intractable, difficult to deal with.

intrépide, adj. fearless.

intrigant, 1. adj. intriguing. 2. n.m. schemer.

intrigue, n.f. plot, intrigue.

intriguer, vb. intrigue; puzzle.

introduction, n.f. introduction.

introduire, vb. introduce, insert.

introuvable, adj. unfindable.

intrus, n.m. intruder.

intrusion, n.f. intrusion; trespass.

intuitif, adj. intuitive.

intuition, n.f. intuition.

inusité, adj. unusual.

inutile, adj. useless, needless.

invalide, 1. n.m.f. invalid. 2. adj. disabled, invalid.

invalider, vb. invalidate.

invasion, n.f. invasion.

invectiver, vb. abuse, revile.

inventaire, n.m. inventory.

inventer, vb. invent.

inventeur, n.m. inventor.

invention, n.f. invention.

inventorier, vb. inventory, catalogue.

inverse, adj. inverted, inverse.

investigateur, 1. adj. searching. 2. n.m. investigator.

investigation, n.f. investigation, inquiry.

investir, vb. invest.

invétéré, adj. inveterate.

invincible, adj. invincible.

invisible, adj. invisible.

invitation, n.f. invitation.

invité, n.m. guest.

inviter, vb. invite, ask.

involontaire, adj. involuntary.

invoquer, vb. call upon.

invraisemblable, adj. improbable.

iode, n.m. iodine.

Irak, n.m. Iraq.

Iran, n.m. Iran.

iris (-s), n.m. iris.

irisé, adj. iridescent.

Irlandais, n.m. Irishman.

irlandais, adj. Irish.

Irlande, n.f. Ireland.

ironie, n.f. irony.

ironique, adj. ironical.

irradier, vb. radiate.

irraisonnable, adj. irrational.

irréfléchi, adj. thoughtless, rash.

irrégulier, adj. irregular.

irréligieux, adj. irreligious.

irrésistible, adj. irresistible.

irrésolu, adj. irresolute.

irrespectueux, adj. disrespectful.

irrévérence, n.f. direspect.

irrigation, n.f. irrigation.

irriguer, vb. irrigate.

irritation, n.f. irritation.

irriter, vb. irritate, anger, provoke.

Islam, n.m. Islam.

islamique, adj. Islamic.

isolateur, adj. insulating.

isolement, n.m. isolation.

isoler, vb. isolate.

Israël, n.m. Israel.

Israéli, n.m. Israeli.

issue, n.f. issue, outlet, outcome.

isthme, n.m. isthmus.

Italie, n.f. Italy.

Italien, n.m. Italian (person).

italien, 1. n.m. Italian (language). 2. adj. Italian.

italique, 1. n.m. italics. 2. adj. italic.

itinéraire, n.m. route, itinerary.

ivoire, n.m. ivory.

ivre, adj. drunk, intoxicated.

ivresse, n.f. drunkenness, intoxication.

ivrogne, n.m. drunkard.

ivrognerie, n.f. drunkenness.

J

jaboter, vb. prattle.

jacasser, vb. chatter.

jachère, n.f. fallow.

jacinthe, n.f. hyacinth.

jadis (-s), adv. formerly.

jaillir, vb. gush, spurt.

jaillissement, n.m. gush, spurt.

jais, n.m. jet (mineral).

jalon, n.m. staff; landmark.

jalonner, vb. mark out.

jalouser, vb. envy.

jalousie, n.f. jealousy.

jaloux, adj. jealous.

jamais, adv. ever, never.

jambe, n.f. leg.

jambière, n.f. legging.

jambon, n.m. ham.

jante, n.f. rim.

janvier, n.m. January.

Japon, n.m. Japan.

Japonais, n.m. Japanese (person).

japonais, 1. n.m. Japanese (language). 2. adj. Japanese.

japper, vb. yelp.

jaquette, n.f. jacket.

jardin, n.m. garden.

jardinage, n.m. gardening.

jardinier, n.m. gardener.

jarre, n.f. jar.

jarretière, n.f. garter.

jaser, vb. jabber.

jatte, n.f. bowl.

jaunâtre, adj. yellowish.

jaune, 1. adj. yellow. 2. n.m. yolk (of egg).

jaunir, vb. turn yellow.

jaunisse, n.f. jaundice.

jazz, n.m. jazz.

je (j.), pron. I.

jeans, n.m.pl. jeans.

jésuite, n.m. Jesuit.

jet, n.m. jet (water, gas).

jetée, n.f. pier.

jeter, vb. throw.

jeton, n.m. token.

jeu, n.m. play, game. mettre en j., stake.

jeudi, n.m. Thursday.

jeune, adj. young, youthful.

jeûne, n.m. fast.

jeûner, vb. fast.

jeunesse, n.f. youth.

joaillerie, n.f. jewelry.

joaillier, n.m. jeweler.

jobard, n.m. fool.

joie, n.f. joy.

joindre, vb. join.

joint, n.m. joint.

jointure, n.f. joint (esp. of the body).

joli, adj. pretty.

joliment, adv. prettily; awfully.

jonc, n.m. rush.

joncher, vb. scatter.

jonction, n.f. junction.

jongler, vb. juggle.

jongleur, n.m. juggler.

jonquille, n.f. jonquil.

joue, n.f. cheek.

jouer, vb. play.

jouet, n.m. toy.

joueur, n.m. player.

joufflu, adj. chubby.

joug (-g), n.m. yoke.

jouir de, vb. enjoy.

jouissance, n.f. enjoyment.

jouisseur, *n.m.* pleasure-seeker.

jour, *n.m.* day, daylight. **j. de fête,** holiday. **point du j.,** dawn.

journal, *n.m.* newspaper, journal, diary.

journalier, *adj.* daily.

journalisme, *n.m.* journalism.

journaliste, *n.m.* journalist.

journée, *n.f.* day.

journellement, *adv.* daily.

joute, *n.f.* joust.

jovialité, *n.f.* jollity.

joyau, *n.m.* jewel.

joyeux, *adj.* joyful.

jubilé, *n.m.* jubilee.

jubiler, *vb.* exult.

judaïsme, *n.m.* Judaism.

judiciaire, *adj.* judicial, legal.

judicieux, *adj.* wise, judicious.

juge, *n.m.* judge.

jugement, *n.m.* judgment, reason. **mettre en j.,** try.

juger, *vb.* judge.

jugulaire, *adj.* jugular.

Juif *m.,* Juive *f. n.* Jew.

juif *m.,* juive *f. adj.* Jewish.

juillet, *n.m.* July.

juin, *n.m.* June.

jumeau *m.,* jumelle *f. adj. and n.* twin.

jumeler, *vb.* couple, join.

jumelles, *n.f.pl.* opera glasses.

jument, *n.f.* mare.

jupe, *n.f.* skirt.

jupon, *n.m.* petticoat.

jurer, *vb.* swear.

juridiction, *n.f.* jurisdiction.

juridique, *adj.* judicial.

jurisconsulte, *n.m.* jurist, lawyer.

jurisprudence, *n.f.* jurisprudence.

juriste, *n.m.* jurist.

juron, *n.m.* oath.

jury, *n.m.* jury.

jus, *n.m.* juice, gravy.

jusque, *prep.* up to. **jusqu'à,** as far as, until. **jusqu'ici,** hitherto.

juste, **1.** *adj.* just, fair, right. **2.** *adv.* just.

justement, *adv.* precisely, exactly.

justesse, *n.f.* accuracy, precision.

justice, *n.f.* justice, fairness.

justifiant, *adj.* justifying.

justification, *n.f.* justification.

justifier, *vb.* justify.

juteux, *adj.* juicy.

juvénile, *adj.* juvenile.

K

kangourou, *n.m.* kangaroo.

karaté, *n.m.* karate.

képi, *n.m.* cap.

kermesse, *n.f.* fair.

kif, *n.m.* marijuana.

kilogramme, *n.m.* kilogram.

kilohertz, *n.m.* kilohertz.

kilométrage, *n.m.* mileage.

kilomètre, *n.m.* kilometer.

kilométrique, *adj.* kilometric.

kiosque, *n.m.* kiosk; newsstand; bandstand.

klaxon, *n.m.* car horn.

kyrielle, *n.f.* litany.

L

la, *pron.* her.

là, *adv.* there.

là-bas, *adv.* yonder, out there.

labeur, *n.m.* labor.

laboratoire, *n.m.* laboratory.

laborieux, *adj.* industrious, laborious.

labour, *n.m.* plowing.

labourer, *vb.* plow.

labyrinthe, *n.m.* maze.

lac, *n.m.* lake.

lacérer, *vb.* lacerate; tear up.

lacet, *n.m.* shoelace; winding.

lâche, **1.** *n.m.f.* coward. **2.** *adj.* cowardly, loose.

lâchement, *adv.* loosely, shamefully.

lâcher, *vb.* loosen, let go. **l. pied,** give ground, flee.

lâcheté, *n.f.* cowardice.

lacis, *n.m.* network.

laconique, *adj.* laconic.

lacrymogène, *adj.* gaz l., tear gas.

lacté, *adj.* milky.

lacune, *n.f.* gap, blank.

ladre, *adj.* stingy, mean.

lagune, *n.f.* lagoon.

laid, *adj.* ugly.

laideron, *n.m.* ugly person.

laideur, *n.f.* ugliness.

lainage, *n.m.* woolen goods.

laine, *n.f.* wool.

laineux, *adj.* wooly; downy.

laïque (à ĕk), *n.m.* layman.

laisse, *n.f.* leash.

laisser, *vb.* let, leave.

laisser-aller, *n.m.* freedom, negligence.

laissez-passer, *n.m.* pass.

lait, *n.m.* milk.

laitage, *n.m.* dairy foods.

laiterie, *n.f.* dairy.

laiteux, *adj.* milky.

laitier, *n.m.* milkman.

laiton, *n.m.* brass.

laitue, *n.f.* lettuce.

lambeau, *n.m.* rag.

lambin, *adj.* slow, dawdling.

lame, *n.f.* blade.

lamé, *adj.* gold- or silver-trimmed.

lamelle, *n.f.* (microscope) slide.

lamentable, *adj.* sad, grievous.

lamentation, *n.f.* lamentation.

lamenter, *vb.* mourn, lament.

laminer, *vb.* laminate.

lampe, *n.f.* lamp. **l. de poche,** flashlight.

lamper, *vb.* drink, gulp.

lampion, *n.m.* Chinese lantern.

lampiste, *n.m.* lamplighter.

lance, *n.f.* lance.

lancer, *vb.* hurl; launch.

lanceur, *n.m.* pitcher.

lancinant, *adj.* throbbing (of pain).

lande, *n.f.* wasteland, moor.

langage, *n.m.* language.

langoureux, *adj.* languishing.

langue, *n.f.* tongue, language.

languette, *n.f.* tonguelike strip.

langueur, *n.f.* languor.

languir, *vb.* pine, languish.

languissant, *adj.* languid.

lanière, *n.f.* strap, thong.

lanterne, *n.f.* lantern.

lapider, *vb.* stone; abuse.

lapin, *n.m.* rabbit.

laps, *n.m.* lapse of time.

lapsus (-sys), *n.m.* slip.

laquais, *n.m.* footman, lackey.

laque, *n.f.* shellac; hairspray.

larcin, *n.m.* larceny, theft.

lard, *n.m.* bacon, fat.

larder, *vb.* lard; pierce.

large, *adj.* wide.

largeur, *n.f.* width.

larguer, *vb.* loosen, let go.

larme, *n.f.* tear.

larmoyer, *vb.* weep, whimper.

larron, *n.m.* thief.

las, *adj.* weary.

lascif, *adj.* lewd, wanton.

laser, *n.m.* laser.

lasser, *vb.* weary.

latéral, *adj.* lateral.

Latin, *n.m.* Latin (person).

latin, **1.** *n.m.* Latin (language). **2.** *adj.* Latin.

latte, *n.f.* lath.

laurier, *n.m.* bay, laurel.

lavabo, *n.m.* lavatory.

lavande, *n.f.* lavender.

lavandière, *n.f.* laundress.

lavement, *n.m.* enema.

laver, *vb.* wash.

lavette, *n.f.* dishrag.

laxatif, *n.m.* laxative.

le (lə), *m.,* la *f.,* les *pl.* **1.** *art.* the. **2.** *pron.* him, her, it.

lécher, *vb.* lick.

leçon, *n.f.* lesson.

lecteur, *n.m.* reader.

lecture, *n.f.* reading.

légal, *adj.* lawful, legal.

légaliser, *vb.* legalize.

légalité, *n.f.* legality.

légataire, *n.m.* legatee.

légation, *n.f.* legation.

légendaire, *adj.* legendary.

légende, *n.f.* legend; inscription.

léger, *adj.* light.

légèreté, *n.f.* lightness.

légion, *n.f.* legion.

législateur, *n.m.* legislator.

législatif, *adj.* legislative.

législation, *n.f.* legislation.

législature, *n.f.* legislature.

légitime, *adj.* legitimate, lawful.

legs, *n.m.* bequest.

léguer, *vb.* bequeath.

légume, *n.m.* vegetable.

lendemain, *n.m.* the next day.

lent, *adj.* slow.

lenteur, *n.f.* slowness.

lentille, *n.f.* lentil; lens.
lèpre, *n.f.* leprosy.
lépreux, 1. *adj.* leprous. 2. *n.* leper.
lequel, *pron.* which, who.
les, *pron.* them.
lesbien, *adj.* Lesbian.
lesbienne, *n.f.* Lesbian.
léser, *vb.* wrong, hurt.
lésine, *n.f.* stinginess.
lésion, *n.f.* wrong; lesion.
lessive, *n.f.* laundry.
lessiveuse, *n.f.* washing machine.
lest (-t), *n.m.* ballast.
leste, *adj.* nimble, clever.
lettre, *n.f.* letter.
lettré, *adj.* lettered, literate.
leur, 1. *pron.* to them; le leur, la leur, theirs. 2. leur *m.f.*, leurs *pl. adj.* their.
leurre, *n.m.* lure, trap.
leurrer, *vb.* lure.
levain, *n.m.* yeast, leaven.
levée, *n.m.* embankment, levy.
lever, *vb.* raise. se l., get up.
levier, *n.m.* lever.
lèvre, *n.f.* lip.
lévrier, *n.m.* greyhound.
lexique, *n.m.* lexicon.
lézard, *n.m.* lizard.
lézarde, *n.f.* crevice.
liaison, *n.f.* connection, linkage.
liant, *adj.* supple; affable.
liasse, *n.f.* file.
libelle, *n.m.* libel.
libeller, *vb.* draw up, word.
libéral, *adj.* liberal.
libérateur, *n.m.* rescuer.
libérer, *vb.* free.
liberté, *n.f.* freedom, liberty.
libertin, 1. *adj.* wanton. 2. *n.* libertine.
libraire, *n.m.* bookseller.
librairie, *n.f.* bookstore.
libre, *adj.* free.
libre-échange, *n.m.* free trade.
licence, *n.f.* license.
licencié, *n.m.* licensee; holder of university degree.
licencieux, *adj.* licentious.
licite, *adj.* lawful.
licorne, *n.f.* unicorn.
licou, *n.m.* halter.
lie, *n.f.* dreg.
liège, *n.m.* cork.
lien, *n.m.* bond, link, tie.
lier, *vb.* bind, tie, link.
lierre, *n.m.* ivy.
lieu, *n.m.* place. au l. de, instead of.
lieu-commun, *n.m.* commonplace.
lieue, *n.f.* league.
lieutenant, *n.m.* lieutenant.
lièvre, *n.m.* hare.
ligne, *n.f.* line.
lignée, *n.f.* offspring.
ligoter, *vb.* bind up.
ligue, *n.f.* league.
liguer, *vb.* league.
lilas, *n.m.* lilac.
limaçon, *n.m.* snail.
lime, *n.f.* file; lime (fruit).

limer, *vb.* file.
limier, *n.m.* bloodhound.
limitation, *n.f.* limitation.
limitation des naissances, *n.f.* birth control, contraception.
limite, *n.f.* limit, border.
limiter, *vb.* limit, confine.
limon, *n.m.* mud, slime.
limonade, *n.f.* lemon soda.
limoneux, *adj.* muddy.
limpide, *adj.* clear, limpid.
lin, *n.m.* flax.
linceul, *n.m.* shroud.
linéaire, *adj.* lineal.
linge, *n.m.* linen, wash.
lingerie, *n.f.* linen goods, underwear.
linguistique, *adj.* linguistic.
linon, *n.m.* lawn (sheer linen).
linteau, *n.m.* lintel.
lion, *n.m.* lion.
lippu, *adj.* thick-lipped.
liqueur, *n.m.* liquid, liqueur.
liquidation, *n.f.* liquidation, settling.
liquide, *adj. and n.m.* liquid, fluid.
liquider, *vb.* liquidate.
liquoreux, *adj.* sweet.
lire, *vb.* read.
lis (-s), *n.m.* lily.
liséré, *n.m.* piping, border.
liseur, *n.m.* reader.
liseuse, *n.f.* bookmark.
lisible, *adj.* legible.
lisière, *n.f.* edge.
lisse, *adj.* smooth.
lisser, *vb.* smooth.
liste, *n.f.* list, roll.
lit, *n.m.* bed.
litanie, *n.f.* litany.
lit-cage, *n.f.* (folding) cot.
lit de la mer, *n.m.* seabed.
literie, *n.f.* bedding.
litière, *n.f.* litter.
litige, *n.m.* litigation.
litigieux, *adj.* litigious.
litre, *n.m.* liter.
littéraire, *adj.* literary.
littéral, *adj.* literal.
littérature, *n.f.* literature.
liturgie, *n.f.* liturgy.
livide, *adj.* livid.
livraison, *n.f.* delivery. l. contre remboursement, C.O.D.
livre, *n.f.* pound.
livre, *n.m.* book.
livre broché, *n.m.* paperback.
livrée, *n.f.* livery.
livrer, *vb.* deliver.
livresque, *adj.* bookish, from books.
livreur, *n.m.* delivery man.
local, *adj.* local.
localiser, *vb.* locate.
localité, *n.f.* locality.
locataire, *n.m.f.* tenant.
location, *n.f.* action or price of renting.
loch (-k), *n.m.* log.
locomotive, *n.f.* locomotive.
locuste, *n.f.* locust.
locution, *n.f.* locution, phrase.
loge, *n.f.* box.
logement, *n.m.* lodging.

loger, *vb.* lodge.
logique, 1. *n.f.* logic. 2. *adj.* logical.
logis, *n.m.* dwelling.
loi, *n.f.* law.
loin, *adv.* far, away.
lointain, *adj.* distant.
loir, *n.m.* dormouse.
loisible, *adj.* optional, allowable.
loisir, *n.m.* leisure.
Londres, *n.m.* London.
long m., longue f. *adj.* long.
longe, *n.f.* leash; loin (of veal).
longer, *vb.* go along.
longeron, *n.m.* beam, girder.
longitude, *n.f.* longitude.
longtemps, *adv.* long.
longueur, *n.f.* length.
lopin, *n.m.* small piece, plot.
loquace, *adj.* talkative.
loque, *n.f.* morsel, rag.
loquet, *n.m.* latch.
loqueteux, *adj.* tattered.
lorgner, *vb.* glance at; ogle.
lorgnon, *n.m.* glasses.
loriot, *n.m.* oriole.
lors, *adv.* then. l. de, at the time of.
lorsque, *conj.* when.
losange, *n.m.* diamond, lozenge.
lot, *n.m.* lot, prize.
loterie, *n.f.* raffle, lottery.
lotion, *n.f.* lotion.
lotir, *vb.* divide, apportion.
louable, *adj.* praiseworthy.
louage, *n.m.* hire.
louange, *n.f.* praise.
louche, *adj.* shady.
loucher, *vb.* squint.
louer, *vb.* praise; hire, rent.
loueur, *n.m.* one who rents.
loup, *n.m.* wolf.
loupe, *n.f.* magnifying glass.
louper, *vb.* spoil, botch.
loup-garou, *n.m.* werewolf.
lourd, *adj.* heavy.
lourdaud, *n.m.* clod.
lourdeur, *n.f.* heaviness, dullness.
loyal, *adj.* loyal.
loyauté, *n.f.* loyalty.
loyer, *n.m.* rent.
lubricité, *n.f.* lewdness.
lubrifier, *vb.* lubricate.
lucarne, *n.f.* attic window.
lucide, *adj.* lucid.
lucidité, *n.f.* clearness.
luciole, *n.f.* firefly.
lueur, *n.f.* gleam.
lugubre, *adj.* doleful, dismal, lugubrious.
lui, *pron.* he; to him, to her.
lui-même, *pron.* himself, itself.
luire, *vb.* gleam.
luisant, *adj.* shiny.
lumière, *n.f.* light.
lumineux, *adj.* luminous.
lunaire, *adj.* lunar.
lunatique, *adj.* whimsical.
lundi, *n.m.* Monday.
lune, *n.f.* moon. l. de miel, honeymoon. clair de l., moonlight.

lunetier, *n.m.* optician.

lunettes, *n.f.pl.* glasses.

lustre, *n.m.* chandelier; luster; five-year period.

lustrer, *vb.* polish, gloss.

luth, *n.m.* lute.

lutiner, *vb.* tease.

lutte, *n.f.* strife, struggle, contest.

lutter, *vb.* struggle, contend.

luxe, *n.m.* luxury.

luxer, *vb.* dislocate.

luxueux, *adj.* luxurious.

luxure, *n.f.* lust.

luzerne, *n.f.* alfalfa.

lycée, *n.m.* high school.

lycéen, *n.m.* high-school student.

lymphatique, *adj.* lymphatic.

lynchage, *n.m.* lynching.

lyncher, *vb.* lynch.

lyre, *n.f.* lyre.

lyrique, *adj.* lyric.

M

M. (abbr. for **Monsieur**), *n.m.* Mr.

macabre, *adj.* macabre, ghastly.

macédoine, *n.f.* salad; mixture.

macérer, *vb.* macerate, soak.

mâcher, *vb.* chew.

machin, *n.m.* thing, gadget.

machinal, *adj.* mechanical.

machination, *n.f.* plot, scheme.

machine, *n.f.* machine. **m. à copier,** copier. **m. à écrire,** typewriter.

machiner, *vb.* plot.

machiniste, *n.m.* machinist.

mâchoire, *n.f.* jaw.

mâchonner, *vb.* mumble, munch.

maçon, *n.m.* mason.

macules, *n.f.* spot, blot.

madame, *n.f.* madam, Mrs.

madeleine, *n.f.* light cake.

mademoiselle, *n.f.* Miss.

madone, *n.f.* Madonna.

mafia, *n.f.* mafia.

magasin, *n.m.* store.

mages, *n.m.pl.* wise men.

magicien, *n.m.* magician.

magie, *n.f.* magic.

magique, *adj.* magic.

magistrat, *n.m.* magistrate.

magnanime, *adj.* magnanimous.

magnat, *n.m.* magnate.

magnétique, *adj.* magnetic.

magnétophone, *n.m.* tape recorder.

magnificence, *n.f.* magnificence.

magnifique, *adj.* magnificent.

mahométan, *adj.* Mohammedan.

mai, *n.m.* May.

maigre, *adj.* lean, thin, meager.

maigrir, *vb.* lose weight.

maille, *n.f.* stitch; mesh.

maillot, *n.m.* shorts; T-shirt.

main, *n.f.* hand. **sous la m.,** handy.

main-d'œuvre, *n.f.* manpower.

maintenant, *adv.* now. **dès m.,** henceforth.

maintenir, *vb.* maintain.

maintien, *n.m.* upkeep; behavior.

maire, *n.m.* mayor.

mairie, *n.m.* city hall.

mais, *conj.* but.

maïs (mä ēs), *n.m.* corn.

maison, *n.f.* house.

maisonnée, *n.f.* household.

maître, *n.m.* master, teacher.

maîtresse, *n.f.* mistress, teacher.

maîtrise, *n.f.* mastery.

maîtriser, *vb.* master, overcome.

majesté, *n.f.* majesty.

majestueux, *adj.* majestic.

majeur, *adj.* major.

majordome, *n.m.* majordomo.

majorer, *vb.* increase price, over-price.

majorité, *n.f.* majority.

majuscule, *n.f.* capital.

mal, 1. *n.m.* harm, ill, evil. **2.** *adv.* badly. **faire m. à,** hurt. **avoir m. à,** have a pain in.

malade, 1. *n.m.f.* sick person, patient. **2.** *adj.* sick.

maladie, *n.f.* disease, illness, sickness.

maladif, *adj.* sickly.

maladresse, *n.f.* awkwardness.

maladroit, *adj.* awkward.

malaise, *n.m.* discomfort.

malappris, *adj.* ill-bred.

malaria, *n.f.* malaria.

malavisé, *adj.* indiscreet, ill-advised.

malchance, *n.f.* bad luck, mishap.

maldonne, *n.f.* misdeal.

mâle, *adj. and n.m.* male.

malédiction, *n.f.* curse.

maléfice, *n.m.* witchery, evil spell.

malencontre, *n.f.* unlucky incident.

malencontreux, *adj.* unlucky.

malentendu, *n.m.* misunderstanding.

malfaiteur, *n.m.* malefactor.

malfamé, *adj.* ill-famed.

malgré, *prep.* despite.

malhabile, *adj.* awkward, dull.

malheur, *n.m.* misfortune, accident.

malheureux, *adj.* unfortunate, unhappy, miserable.

malhonnête, *adj.* dishonest.

malhonnêteté, *n.f.* dishonesty.

malice, *n.f.* mischief, malice.

malicieux, *adj.* malicious, roguish.

malin *m.,* **maligne** *f. adj.* malignant; sharp, sly.

malingre, *adj.* sickly, puny.

malintentionné, *adj.* ill-disposed.

malle, *n.f.* trunk.

mallette, *n.f.* small suitcase.

malotru, *n.m.* boor, lout.

malpropre, *adj.* messy.

malpropreté, *n.f.* messiness.

malsain, *adj.* unhealthy.

malséant, *adj.* improper.

maltraiter, *vb.* misuse.

malveillant, *adj.* malevolent.

malvenu, *adj.* without any right.

malversation, *n.f.* embezzlement.

maman, *n.f.* mamma.

mamelle, *n.f.* udder.

mammifère, *n.m.* mammal.

manche, *n.m.* handle. *f.* sleeve. **La M.,** the English Channel.

manchette, *n.f.* cuff.

manchon, *n.m.* muff.

mandarine, *n.f.* tangerine.

mandat, *n.m.* warrant, writ, mandate. **m.-poste,** money order.

mandataire, *n.m.* agent, proxy.

mander, *vb.* send for, inform.

manège, *n.m.* horsemanship.

manette, *n.f.* handle, lever.

mangeable, *adj.* eatable.

mangeoire, *n.f.* manger.

manger, *vb.* eat.

maniable, *adj.* manageable; easygoing.

maniaque, 1. *n.m.* maniac. **2.** *adj.* maniac, maniacal.

manie, *n.f.* mania.

manier, *vb.* handle, wield.

manière, *n.f.* manner.

maniéré, *adj.* affected.

manière de vivre, *n.f.* life style.

manifestation, *n.f.* demonstration.

manifeste, *adj.* manifest, evident, overt.

manifester, *vb.* manifest, show.

manigance, *n.f.* trick, intrigue.

manipuler, *vb.* manipulate.

manivelle, *n.f.* crank; winch.

mannequin, *n.m.* dummy.

manœuvre, *n.f.* maneuver.

manoir, *n.m.* country house, estate.

manquant, 1. *adj.* missing. **2.** *n.m.* absentee.

manque, *n.m.* lack.

manquer, *vb.* miss, lack, fail.

mansarde, *n.f.* attic.

mansuétude, *n.f.* mildness, kindness.

manteau, *n.m.* cloak, coat.

manucure, *n.m.f.* manicurist.

manuel, *adj. and n.m.* manual.

manufacture, *n.f.* manufacture.

manuscrit, *adj. and n.m.* manuscript.

manutention, *n.f.* management.

maquereau, *n.m.* mackerel.

maquette, *n.f.* preliminary sketch or model.

maquillage, *n.m.* make-up.

maquis, *n.m.* scrub land; guerrilla fighters.

maquisard, *n.m.* guerrilla fighter.

marais, *n.m.* marsh.

marâtre, *n.f.* stepmother.

maraude, *n.f.* marauding.
marbre, *n.m.* marble.
marchand, *n.m.* merchant.
marchander, *vb.* bargain, haggle.
marchandises, *n.f.pl.* goods.
marche, *n.f.* march, step.
marché, *n.m.* market, bargain. **bon m.,** cheap.
marchepied, *n.m.* running-board.
marcher, *vb.* walk, step, march, run (machine).
marcheur, *n.m.* pedestrian.
mardi, *n.m.* Tuesday.
mare, *n.f.* pool.
marécage, *n.m.* bog.
marécageux, *adj.* marshy.
maréchal, *n.m.* marshal.
marée, *n.f.* tide.
mareyeur, *n.m.* fish seller.
margarine, *n.f.* margarine.
marge, *n.f.* margin.
margelle, *n.f.* edge, brink.
marguerite, *n.f.* daisy.
mari, *n.m.* husband.
mariage, *n.m.* marriage.
marié, 1. *n.m.* bridegroom. **2.** *adj.* married.
mariée, *n.f.* bride.
marie-jeanne, *n.f.* marijuana.
marier, *vb.* marry.
marijuana, *n.f.* marijuana.
marin, 1. *n.m.* sailor. **2.** *adj.* marine. **fusilier m.,** marine.
marinade, *n.f.* mixture for pickling.
marine, *n.f.* navy.
mariner, *vb.* pickle.
marionnette, *n.f.* puppet.
maritime, *adj.* marine.
marmite, *n.f.* pot.
marmiter, *vb.* blast (with gunfire).
marmot, *n.m.* urchin, brat.
marmotter, *vb.* mumble.
marotte, *n.f.* fad.
marque, *n.f.* brand, mark.
marquer, *vb.* mark.
marqueur, *n.m.* marker, scorekeeper.
marquis, *n.m.* marquis.
marraine, *n.f.* godmother; sponsor.
marron, *n.m.* chestnut; brown.
marronier, *n.m.* chestnut tree.
mars (-s), *n.m.* March.
marteau, *n.m.* hammer.
marteler, *vb.* hammer.
martial, *adj.* warlike.
martre, *n.m.* marten.
martyr, *n.m.* martyr.
martyre, *n.m.* martyrdom.
marxisme, *n.m.* marxism.
mascarade, *n.f.* masquerade.
mascotte, *n.f.* mascot.
masculin, *adj.* masculine.
masque, *n.m.* mask.
masquer, *vb.* mask.
massacre, *n.m.* slaughter.
massage, *n.m.* massage.
masse, *n.f.* mass.
masser, *vb.* mass; massage.
massif, *adj.* massive, solid.
massue, *n.f.* club.

mastiquer, *vb.* chew.
mat (-t), *adj.* dull.
mât (mä), *n.m.* mast.
matelas, *n.m.* mattress.
matelot, *n.m.* sailor.
matérialiser, *vb.* materialize.
matérialisme, *n.m.* materialism.
matérialiste, *adj.* and *n.m.f.* materialist, materialistic.
matériaux, *n.m.pl.* stuff, materials.
matériel, *adj.* material, real.
maternel, *adj.* native; maternal.
maternité, *n.f.* maternity.
mathématique, *adj.* mathematical.
mathématiques, *n.f.pl.* mathematics.
matière, *n.f.* matter. **table des m.s,** index.
matin, *n.m.* morning.
mâtin, *n.m.* big dog.
matinal, *adj.* early.
matinée, *n.f.* morning.
matineux, *adj.* rising early.
matois, *adj.* cunning, sly.
matou, *n.m.* tomcat.
matraque, *n.f.* heavy club.
matrice, *n.f.* womb.
matricule, *n.f.* roster, registration.
matriculer, *vb.* enroll, register.
matrimonial, *adj.* marital.
mâture, *n.f.* masts (of boats).
maturité, *n.f.* maturity.
maudire, *vb.* curse.
maudit, *adj.* cursed, miserable.
maugréer, *vb.* curse, grumble.
maussade, *adj.* glum, sullen, cross.
mauvais, *adj.* bad.
maxime, *n.f.* maxim.
maximum, *n.m.* maximum.
me (mə), *pron.* me, myself.
méandre, *n.m.* winding.
mécanicien, *n.m.* mechanic, engineer.
mécanique, *adj.* mechanical.
mécaniser, *vb.* mechanize.
mécanisme, *n.m.* mechanism, machinery.
mécano, *n.m.* mechanic.
méchamment, *adv.* maliciously.
méchanceté, *n.f.* wickedness, malice.
méchant, *adj.* wicked, malicious.
mèche, *n.f.* lock; wick, fuse.
mécompte, *n.m.* error, disappointment.
méconnaissable, *adj.* unrecognizable.
méconnaître, *vb.* fail to recognize.
mécontent, *adj.* discontented.
mécontentement, *n.m.* discontent.
mécontenter, *vb.* dissatisfy.
mécréant, *n.m.* unbeliever.
médaille, *n.f.* medal.
médaillon, *n.m.* locket.
médecin, *n.m.* physician.

médecine, *n.f.* medicine.
médiateur, *n.m.* mediator; ombudsman (in France).
médiation, *n.f.* mediation.
médical, *adj.* medical.
médicament, *n.m.* medicament.
médicinal, *adj.* medicinal.
médiéval, *adj.* medieval.
médiocre, *adj.* mediocre.
médiocrité, *n.f.* mediocrity.
médire, *vb.* slander, defame.
médisance, *n.f.* slander.
méditation, *n.f.* meditation.
méditer, *vb.* meditate, muse, brood.
méditerrané, *adj.* Mediterranean.
médium, *n.m.* medium.
méduse, *n.f.* jellyfish.
méduser, *vb.* stupefy.
méfait, *n.m.* crime, misdeed.
méfiance, *n.f.* distrust.
méfiant, *adj.* distrustful.
méfier, *vb.* **se m. de,** distrust.
mégarde, *n.f.* heedlessness.
mégère, *n.f.* vixen, shrew.
mégot, *n.m.* cigarette butt.
meilleur, *adj.* better, best.
mélancolie, *n.f.* melancholy.
mélancolique, *adj.* melancholy.
mélange, *n.m.* mixture.
mélasse, *n.f.* molasses.
mêlée, *n.f.* struggle.
mêler, *vb.* mix. **se m. de,** meddle in.
mélèze, *n.m.* larch.
mellifu, *adj.* sweet, honeyed.
mélodie, *n.f.* melody.
mélodieux, *adj.* melodious.
mélodique, *adj.* melodic.
mélodrame, *n.m.* melodrama.
mélomane, *n.m.* lover of music.
melon, *n.m.* melon.
membrane, *n.f.* membrane.
membre, *n.m.* member, limb.
membrure, *n.f.* frame, limbs.
même, 1. *adj.* same, very, self. **moi-m.,** myself; **lui-m.,** himself, etc. **2.** *adv.* even. **de m.,** likewise. **tout de m.,** notwithstanding. **mettre à m. de,** enable to.
mémento, *n.m.* memento, notebook.
mémoire, *n.f.* memory, memoir.
mémorable, *adj.* memorable.
mémorandum, *n.m.* memorandum.
mémorial, *n.m.* memorial; memoirs.
menaçant, *adj.* threatening.
menace, *n.f.* threat.
menacer, *vb.* threaten.
ménage, *n.m.* household.
ménagement, *n.m.* discretion.
ménager, 1. *n.m.* manager. **2.** *vb.* manage.
ménagère, *n.f.* housewife, housekeeper.
ménagerie, *n.f.* menagerie.
mendiant, *n.m.* beggar.
mendicité, *n.f.* begging.

mendier, vb. beg.

menées, n.f.pl. schemes.

mener, vb. lead.

ménestrel, n.m. minstrel.

ménétrier, n.m. country fiddler.

meneur, n.m. leader, ringleader.

méningite, n.f. meningitis.

menottes, n.f.pl. handcuffs.

mensonge, n.m. falsehood, lie.

mensonger, adj. false, deceptive.

mensualité, n.f. remittance paid monthly.

mensuel, adj. monthly.

mensurable, adj. measurable.

mental, adj. mental.

mentalité, n.f. mentality.

menterie, n.f. lie.

menteur, n.m. liar.

menthe, n.f. mint.

mention, n.f. mention.

mentionner, vb. mention.

mentir, vb. lie.

menton, n.m. chin.

menu, 1. n.m. menu. 2. adj. little, minute.

menuet, n.m. minuet.

menuiserie, n.f. woodwork.

menuisier, n.m. carpenter.

méprendre, vb. se m., be mistaken.

mépris, n.m. contempt, scorn.

méprisable, adj. mean, contemptible.

méprisant, adj. contemptuous.

méprise, n.f. mistake, misunderstanding.

mépriser, vb. scorn, despise.

mer (-r), n.f. sea. mal de m., seasickness.

mercanti, n.m. profiteer.

mercantile, adj. mercantile.

mercenaire, adj. and n.m. mercenary.

mercerie, n.f. haberdashery.

merci, n.m. thanks, mercy.

mercredi, n.m. Wednesday.

mercure, n.m. mercury.

mère, n.f. mother.

méridien, n.m. meridian.

méridional, adj. southern.

meringue, n.f. meringue.

méritant, adj. meritorious.

mérite, n.m. merit, desert.

mériter, vb. merit, deserve.

méritoire, adj. meritorious.

merle, n.m. blackbird.

merveille, n.f. marvel.

merveilleux, adj. wonderful, marvelous.

mésalliance, n.f. misalliance.

mésallier, vb. marry badly.

mésaventure, n.f. accident, mishap.

mesdames, pl. of madame.

mesdemoiselles, pl. of mademoiselle.

mésestime, n.f. low opinion or repute.

mésintelligence, n.f. difficulty, discord.

mesquin, adj. shabby, mean, stingy.

mesquinerie, n.f. meanness.

message, n.m. message.

messager, n.m. messenger.

messe, n.f. Mass.

Messie, n.m. Messiah.

messieurs, pl. of monsieur.

mesurage, n.m. measurement.

mesure, n.f. measure. à m. que, as.

mesuré, adj. measured, cautious.

mesurer, vb. measure.

métairie, n.f. small farm.

métal, n.m. metal.

métallique, adj. metallic.

métallurgie, n.f. metallurgy.

métamorphose, n.f. transformation.

métaphore, n.f. metaphor.

métaphysique, 1. n.f. metaphysics. 2. adj. metaphysical.

métayer, n.m. small farmer.

météore, n.m. meteor.

météorologie, n.f. meteorology.

métèque, n.m. alien.

méthode, n.f. method.

méthodique, adj. methodical, systematic.

méticuleux, adj. meticulous.

métier, n.m. loom; craft, trade.

métis, adj. hybrid, crossbred.

métrage, n.m. measurement.

mètre, n.m. meter.

métrique, adj. metric.

métro, n.m. subway.

métropole, n.f. metropolis; native land.

métropolitain, adj. metropolitan.

mets, n.m. food, dish.

mettable, adj. wearable.

metteur, n.m. m. en scène, play director.

mettre, vb. put, place, set. se m. à, begin.

meuble, n.m. piece of furniture; (pl.) furniture.

meubler, vb. furnish, outfit.

meule, n.f. stack.

meunier, n.m. miller.

meurtre, n.m. murder.

meurtrier, n.m. murderer.

meurtrière, n.f. murderess.

meurtrir, vb. bruise.

meurtrissure, n.f. bruise.

meute, n.f. dog pack; mob.

Mexicain, n.m. Mexican.

mexicain, adj. Mexican.

Mexique, n.m. Mexico.

mezzanine, n.f. mezzanine.

mi, adj. mid, half.

miaou, n.m. mew.

miauler, vb. mew.

mica, n.m. mica.

miche, n.f. loaf of bread.

micro, n.m. microphone.

microbe, n.m. microbe.

microfiche, n.f. microfiche.

microforme, n.f. microform.

microphone, n.m. microphone.

microscope, n.m. microscope.

microscopique, adj. microscopic.

midi, n.m. noon; south.

midinette, n.f. young saleswoman, business woman.

mie, n.f. crumb.

miel, n.m. honey.

mielleux, adj. honeyed, sweet.

mien, pron. le mien, la mienne, mine.

miette, n.f. crumb.

mieux, adv. better, best.

mièvre, adj. affected.

mignard, adj. dainty, mincing.

mignon, 1. adj. delicate, dainty. 2. n.m.f. darling.

migraine, n.f. headache.

migration, n.f. migration.

mijoter, vb. cook slowly, simmer.

mil (mêl), num. thousand.

milice, n.f. militia.

milieu, n.m. middle, center, environment.

militaire, adj. military.

militant, adj. militant.

militarisme, n.m. militarism.

militer, vb. militate.

mille (-l), 1. n.m. mile. 2. adj. and n.m. thousand.

millet, n.m. millet.

millier (-l-), n.m. thousand.

milligramme (-l-), n.m. milligram.

million (-l-), n.m. million.

millionnaire (-l-), adj. and n.m.f. millionaire.

mime, n.m. mime, mimic.

mimique, adj. mimic.

minable, adj. shabby, poor.

minauder, vb. simper.

mince, adj. slender, slight, thin.

minceur, n.f. slimness.

mine, n.f. mine; mien; lead.

miner, vb. mine; wear away; weaken.

minéral, n.m. ore.

minéral, adj. and n.m. mineral.

mineur, 1. n.m. miner. 2. adj. and n.m. minor.

miniature, n.f. miniature.

miniaturiser, vb. miniaturize.

minier, adj. of mines.

minime, adj. very small.

minimum, n.m. minimum.

ministère, n.m. ministry, department, board.

ministériel, adj. ministerial.

ministre, n.m. minister. premier m., premier.

minorité, n.f. minority.

minotier, n.m. miller.

minuit, n.m. midnight.

minuscule, adj. minute.

minute, n.f. minute.

minutie, n.f. trifle; care with details.

minutieux, adj. minute.

mioche, n.m.f. urchin.

miracle, n.m. miracle.

miraculeux, adj. miraculous.

mirage, n.m. mirage.

mirer, vb. aim at, look at.

mirifique, adj. wonderful.

miroir, n.m. mirror.

miroiter, vb. glisten.

misanthrope, 1. n.m. misanthrope. 2. *adj.* misanthropic.

mise, *n.f.* putting; mode. **mise en scène,** setting.

miser, *vb.* bid.

misérable, *adj.* miserable, wretched, squalid.

misère, *n.f.* misery.

miséreux, *adj.* poor, miserable.

miséricorde, *n.f.* mercy.

miséricordieux, *adj.* merciful.

misogyne, 1. *n. m.* misogynist. **2. woman-hating;** misogynist.

missel, *n.m.* missal.

mission, *n.f.* mission.

missionnaire, *adj. and n.m.f.* missionary.

missive, *adj.* missive.

mitaine, *n.f.* mitten.

mite, *n.f.* moth.

miteux, *adj.* shabby.

mitiger, *vb.* moderate.

mitoyen, *adj.* midway; jointly owned.

mitrailleuse, *n.f.* machine gun.

mixte, *adj.* mixed, joint.

Mlle. (abbr. for **Mademoiselle**), *n.f.* Miss.

Mme. (abbr. for **Madame**), *n.f.* Mrs.

mobile, *adj.* movable.

mobilier, *adj.* movable.

mobilisation, *n.f.* mobilization.

mobiliser, *vb.* mobilize.

mobilité, *n.f.* mobility; instability.

mode, *n.f.* fashion, mode, mood; *(pl.)* millinery. **à la m.,** fashionable.

modèle, *n.m.* model, pattern.

modeler, *vb.* model, shape.

modelliste, *n.m.f.* dress designer.

modérateur, *n.m.* moderator.

modération, *n.f.* moderation.

modéré, *adj.* moderate.

modérer, *vb.* check, moderate.

moderne, *adj.* modern.

moderniser, *vb.* modernize.

modernité, *n.f.* modernity.

modeste, *adj.* modest.

modestie, *n.f.* modesty.

modicité, *n.f.* small quantity.

modification, *n.f.* alteration.

modifier, *vb.* modify, qualify.

modique, *adj.* moderate, unimportant.

modiste, *n.f.* milliner.

modulation, *n.f.* modulation.

moduler, *vb.* modulate.

moelle, *n.f.* marrow.

moelleux (mwä ly), *adj.* mellow, soft.

mœurs (-s), *n.f.pl.* manner(s), custom.

moi, 1. *n.m.* ego. **2.** *pron.* me.

moignon, *n.m.* stump.

moindre, *adj.* less, lesser, least.

moine, *n.m.* monk.

moineau, *n.m.* sparrow.

moins, *adv.* less, least. **au m.,** at least. **à m. que,** unless.

moire, *n.f.* watered silk.

mois, *n.m.* month.

moisi, *adj.* moldy.

moisir, *vb.* mold.

moisissure, *n.f.* mold.

moisson, *n.f.* harvest, crop.

moissonner, *vb.* reap, harvest.

moissonneur, *n.m.* harvester.

moissonneuse, *n.f.* reaping machine.

moite, *adj.* moist.

moiteur, *n.f.* dampness.

moitié, *n.f.* half. **à m.,** half, *adv.*

molaire, *adj. and n.f.* molar.

môle, *n.m.* pier.

molécule, *n.f.* molecule.

molester, *vb.* molest.

mollah, *n.m.* mullah.

molasse, *adj.* flabby, soft.

mollesse, *n.f.* softness, weakness.

mollet, 1. *adj.* soft. **œufs mollets,** soft-boiled eggs. **2.** *n.m.* calf of leg.

molletière, *n.f.* legging.

molleton, *n.m.* heavy flannel.

mollir, *vb.* soften, slacken.

mollusque, *n.m.* mollusc.

moment, *n.m.* moment.

momentané, *adj.* momentary.

mon m., ma f., mes *pl. adj.* my.

monacal, *adj.* pertaining to monks.

monarchie, *n.f.* monarchy.

monarchiste, *n.m.* monarchist.

monarque, *n.m.* monarch.

monastère, *n.m.* monastery.

monastique, *adj.* monastic.

monceau, *n.m.* pile.

mondain, *adj.* worldly.

monde, *n.m.* world, people. **tout le m.,** everybody, everyone. **mettre au m.,** bear.

mondial, *adj.* world-wide.

monétaire, *adj.* monetary.

moniteur, *n.m.* monitor.

monnaie, *n.f.* money, change, currency. **Hôtel de la M.,** mint.

monnayer, *vb.* mint.

monocle, *n.m.* monocle.

monogramme, *n.m.* monogram.

monologue, *n.m.* monologue.

monologuer, *vb.* soliloquize.

monoplan, *n.m.* monoplane.

monopole, *n.m.* monopoly.

monopoliser, *vb.* monopolize.

monosyllabe, *n.m.* monosyllable.

monosyllabique, *adj.* monosyllabic.

monotone, *adj.* monotonous.

monotonie, *n.f.* monotony, dullness.

monseigneur, *n.m.* title of honor; My Lord.

monsieur, *n.m.,* **messieurs,** *pl.* gentleman, sir; Mr.

monstre, *n.m.* monster.

monstrueux, *adj.* monstrous.

monstruosité, *n.f.* monstrosity.

mont, *n.m.* mount, hill.

montage, *n.m.* carrying up.

montagnard, *n.m.* mountaineer.

montagne, *n.f.* mountain.

montagneux, *adj.* mountainous.

montant, *n.m.* amount.

mont-de-piété, *n.m.* pawnshop.

monté, *adj.* mounted, supplied.

montée, *n.f.* ascent, rise, climb.

monter, *vb.* go up, mount, climb, rise.

montre, *n.f.* watch; display. **m.-bracelet,** wrist watch.

montrer, *vb.* show.

montreur, *n.m.* showman.

montueux, *adj.* hilly.

monture, *n.f.* mount.

monument, *n.m.* monument.

monumental, *adj.* monumental.

moquer, *vb.* **se m. de,** make fun of, mock, laugh at.

moquerie, *n.f.* mockery, ridicule.

moqueur, *adj.* mocking.

moral, *adj.* ethical, moral.

morale, *n.f.* morals, morality, morale.

moraliser, *vb.* moralize.

moraliste, *n.m.f.* moralist.

moralité, *n.f.* morals, morality.

morbide, *adj.* morbid.

morceau, *n.m.* piece, bit, morsel. **gros m.,** lump, chunk.

morceler, *vb.* cut up.

mordant, *adj.* pointed.

mordiller, *vb.* nibble.

mordre, *vb.* bite.

morfondre, *vb.* chill.

morgue, *n.f.* morgue.

moribond, *adj.* dying.

morne, *adj.* bleak, dismal, dreary.

morose, *adj.* morose.

morosité, *n.f.* moroseness.

morphine, *n.f.* morphine.

morphinomane, *n.* drug addict.

morphologie, *n.f.* morphology.

mors, *n.m.* horse's bit.

morse, *n.m.* walrus.

morsure, *n.f.* bite.

mort, 1. *n.m.* dummy, dead man. **2.** *n.f.* death. **3.** *adj.* dead.

mortaise, *n.f.* mortise.

mortalité, *n.f.* mortality.

mortel, 1. *adj.* deadly, mortal.

morte-saison, *n.f.* off season.

mortier, *n.m.* mortar.

mortifier, *vb.* mortify.

mort-né, *adj.* still-born.

mortuaire, *adj.* mortuary.

morue, *n.f.* cod.

mosaïque (-à čk), *n.f.* mosaic.

Moscou, *n.m.* Moscow.

mosquée, *n.f.* mosque.

mot, *n.m.* word; cue.

moteur, *n.m.* motor.

motif, *n.m.* motive.

motion, *n.f.* motion.

motiver, *vb.* motivate, justify.

motocyclette, *n.f.* motorcycle.

motocycliste, *n.m.* motorcyclist.

motte, *n.f.* clod.

mou, m., molle *f. adj.* soft.

mouchard, *n.m.* spy.

moucharder, vb. spy.

mouche, n.f. fly.

moucher, vb. blow the nose.

moucheron, n.m. gnat.

moucheté, adj. spotted.

moucheture, n.f. spot.

mouchoir, n.m. handkerchief.

moudre, vb. grind.

moue, n.f. pout, wry face.

mouette, n.f. gull.

moufette, n.f. skunk.

moufle, n.f. mitten.

mouillage, n.m. wetting.

mouillé, adj. wet.

mouiller, vb. soak.

moulage, n.m. cast (from mold).

moule, n.m. mold.

mouler, vb. mold.

mouleur, n.m. molder.

moulin, n.m. mill.

mouhure, n.f. molding.

mourant, adj. dying.

mourir, vb. die.

mouron, n.m. pimpernel.

mousquetaire, n.m. musketeer.

mousse, n.f. moss; foam, lather.

mousseline, n.f. muslin.

mousser, vb. foam, froth.

mousseux, adj. foaming.

mousson, n.m. monsoon.

moustache, n.f. mustache, whisker.

moustiquaire, n.f. mosquito net.

moustique, n.m. mosquito.

moutarde, n.f. mustard.

mouton, n.m. sheep; mutton.

moutonner, vb. curl; make wooly.

mouture, n.f. grinding.

mouvant, adj. moving, shifting.

mouvement, n.m. movement, stir.

mouvoir, vb. move.

moyen, 1. n.m. means, medium. 2. adj. middle, average.

moyennant, prep. by means of.

moyenne, n.f. average.

Moyen Orient, n.m. Middle East.

muabilité, n.f. changeability.

mue, n.f. molting; changing (esp. of voice).

muer, vb. molt (animals); break, change (voice).

muet m., muette f. adj. dumb, mute.

mufle, n.m. cad.

mugir, vb. roar, bellow.

mugissement, n.m. roaring, bellowing.

muguet, n.m. lily of the valley.

mulâtre, n.m. and adj. mulatto.

mulet, n.m. mule.

muletier, n.m. muleteer.

mulot, n.m. field mouse.

multinational, adj. multinational.

multiple, adj. multiple, manifold.

multiplicande, n.m. multiplicand.

multiplication, n.f. multiplication.

multiplicité, n.f. multiplicity.

multiplier, vb. multiply.

multitude, n.f. multitude.

municipal, adj. municipal.

municipalité, n.f. municipality.

munificence, n.f. munificence, liberality.

munificent, adj. very generous.

munir, vb. provide, supply.

munitionner, vb. provision, supply.

munitions (de guerre), n.f.pl. ammunition.

muqueux, adj. mucous.

mur, n.m. wall.

mûr, adj. ripe, mature.

muraille, n.f. wall.

mural, adj. mural.

mûre (de ronce), n.f. blackberry.

mûrier, n.m. mulberry tree.

mûrir, vb. ripen, mature.

murmure, n.m. murmur.

murmurer, vb. murmur.

musarder, vb. waste time, dawdle.

muscade, n.f. nutmeg.

muscle, n.m. muscle.

musculaire, adj. muscular.

musculeux, adj. muscular.

muse, n.f. muse.

museau, n.m. muzzle.

musée, n.m. museum.

museler, vb. muzzle; gag.

muselière, n.f. muzzle.

muser, vb. trifle, dawdle.

musical, adj. musical.

musicien, adj. and n.m. musical, musician.

musique, n.f. music.

musulman, adj. and n.m. Mohammedan.

mutabilité, n.f. mutability.

mutation, n.f. change, replacement.

mutilation, n.f. mutilation.

mutiler, vb. mutilate, mangle, mar.

mutin, adj. refractory, mutinous.

mutiner, vb. se m., mutiny, revolt.

mutinerie, n.f. mutiny.

mutisme, n.m. muteness, lack of speech.

mutuel, adj. mutual.

myope, adj. near-sighted.

myopie, n.f. near-sightedness.

myosotis, n.m. forget-me-not.

myriade, n.f. myriad.

myrrhe, n.f. myrrh.

myrte, n.m. myrtle.

mystère, n.m. mystery.

mystérieux, adj. mysterious, weird.

mysticisme, n.m. mysticism.

mystification, n.f. hoax.

mystifier, vb. mystify.

mystique, adj. mystic.

mythe, n.m. myth.

mythique, adj. mythical.

mythologie, n.f. mythology.

N

nabot, n.m. dwarf.

nacre, n.f. mother-of-pearl.

nacré, adj. pearly.

nage, n.f. act of swimming.

nageoire, n.f. fin.

nager, vb. swim.

nageur, n.m. swimmer.

naguère, adv. a short time ago.

naïf (nä ĕf) m., naïve f. adj. naïve.

nain, adj. and n.m. dwarf.

naissance, n.f. birth.

naissant, adj. beginning, newborn.

naître, vb. be born.

naïveté (nä ĕv-), n.f. simplicity.

nantir, vb. give as security; furnish.

nantissement, n.m. pledge, guarantee.

naphte, n.m. naphtha.

nappe, n.f. tablecloth.

narcisse, n.m. daffodil.

narcotique, n.m. narcotic.

narguer, vb. defy, flout.

narine, n.f. nostril.

narrateur, n.m. narrator, storyteller.

narration, n.f. narrative, recital.

narrer, vb. narrate, relate.

nasal, adj. nasal.

naseau, n.m. nostril.

nasiller, vb. talk with a nasal voice.

nasse, n.f. fish trap.

natal, adj. native.

natalité, n.f. rate of birth.

natation, n.f. swimming.

natif, n.m. and adj. native.

nation, n.f. nation.

national, adj. national.

nationalisation, n.f. nationalization.

nationaliser, vb. nationalize.

nationalisme, n.m. nationalism.

nationalité, n.f. nationality.

nativité, n.f. nativity.

naturaliser, vb. naturalize; (of animals) stuff.

naturalisme, n.m. naturalism, naturalness.

naturaliste, n.m. naturalist.

nature, n.f. nature.

naturel, 1. n.m. nature. 2. adj. natural.

naufrage, n.m. shipwreck.

naufragé, adj. shipwrecked.

nauséabond, adj. nauseous, offensive.

nausée, n.f. nausea.

nautique, adj. nautical.

naval, adj. naval.

navet, n.m. turnip.

navette spatiale, n.f. space shuttle.

navigable, adj. navigable.

navigateur, n.m. navigator, seaman.

navigation, n.f. seafaring, navigation.

naviguer, *vb.* sail, navigate.

navire, *n.m.* ship.

navrant, *adj.* distressing, causing grief.

navrer, *vb.* wound, grieve.

né, *adj.* born.

néanmoins, *adv.* yet, nevertheless, however.

néant, *n.m.* nothing(ness).

nébuleux, *adj.* cloudy; worried.

nécessaire, *adj.* requisite, necessary.

nécessité, *n.f.* necessity. **n. préalable,** prerequisite.

nécessiter, *vb.* make necessary or imperative.

nécessiteux, *adj.* needy.

nécrologe, *n.m.* obituary.

nef, *n.f.* nave.

néfaste, *adj.* ill-omened, unlucky.

négatif, *adj.* negative.

négation, *n.f.* negation; negative word.

négative, *n.f.* negative argument or opinion.

négligé, **1.** *adj.* neglected, sloppy. **2.** *n.m.* state of undress.

négligeable, *adj.* negligible.

négligence, *n.f.* neglect.

négligent, *adj.* negligent.

négliger, *vb.* overlook, neglect.

négoce, *n.m.* commerce, trade.

négociable, *adj.* negotiable.

négociant, *n.m.* merchant.

négociation, *n.f.* negotiation.

négocier, *vb.* negotiate.

nègre, *adj. and n.m.* Black.

négresse, *n.f.* Black.

neige, *n.f.* snow.

neiger, *vb.* snow.

neigeux, *adj.* snowy.

néon, *n.m.* neon.

néophyte, *n.m.* neophyte, convert.

néphrite, *n.f.* nephritis.

nerf (nèr), *n.m.* nerve.

nerveux, *adj.* nervous.

nervosité, *n.f.* nervousness.

net (-t) *m.,* **nette** *f. adj.* net, clear, clean, neat.

netteté, *n.f.* clearness, neatness.

nettoyer, *vb.* clean, cleanse, scour.

nettoyeur, *n.m.* one who or that which cleans.

neuf, *adj. and n.m.* nine.

neuf *m.,* **neuve** *f. adj.* brand-new.

neutraliser, *vb.* counteract.

neutralité, *n.f.* neutrality.

neutre, *adj. and n.m.* neutral.

neutron, *n.m.* neutron.

neuvième, *adj. and n.m.* ninth.

neveu, *n.m.* nephew.

névralgie, *n.f.* neuralgia.

névrite, *n.f.* neuritis.

névrose, *n.f.* neurosis.

névrosé, *adj. and n.m.* neurotic.

nez, *n.m.* nose.

ni, *conj.* nor. **ni . . . ni . . .,** neither . . . nor . . . .

niais, *adj.* foolish.

niaiserie, *n.f.* silliness, trifle.

niche, *n.f.* alcove.

nichée, *n.f.* brood.

nicher, *vb.* se n., nestle.

nickel, *n.m.* nickel.

nid, *n.m.* nest.

nièce, *n.f.* niece.

nielle, *n.f.* wheat blight.

nier, *vb.* deny.

nigaud, *n.m.* fool, simpleton.

nihilisme, *n.m.* nihilism.

nimbe, *n.m.* halo.

n'importe, *interj.* never mind.

nippes, *n.f.pl.* old clothes.

nitrate, *n.m.* nitrate.

niveau, *n.m.* level. **au n. de,** level with.

niveler, *vb.* make level; survey.

nivellement, *n.m.* leveling, surveying.

noble, **1.** *n.m.* nobleman, peer. **2.** *adj.* noble.

noblesse, *n.f.* nobility.

noce, *n.f.* wedding. **faire la n.,** revel.

noceur, *n.m.* gay blade.

nocif, *adj.* harmful.

noctambule, *n.m.* sleep-walker, prowler.

nocturne, *adj.* nocturnal.

Noël (nō ěl), *n.m.* Christmas; carol.

nœud (nœ), *n.m.* knot.

noir, *adj. and n.m.* black.

noircir, *vb.* blacken.

noisetier, *n.m.* hazel (tree).

noisette, **1.** *n.f.* hazelnut. **2.** *adj.* light reddish brown.

noix, *n.f.* nut, walnut.

nolis, *n.m.* freight.

nom, *n.m.* name; noun.

nomade, *adj.* wandering, roaming.

nombre, *n.m.* number.

nombrer, *vb.* number.

nombreux, *adj.* numerous, manifold.

nombril, *n.m.* navel.

nominal, *adj.* nominal.

nominatif, *adj. and n.m.* nominative.

nomination, *n.f.* nomination, appointment.

nommément, *adv.* particularly, namely.

nommer, *vb.* name, nominate, appoint.

non, *adv.* no. **non plus,** neither.

non-aligné, *adj.,* non-aligned.

nonchalamment, *adv.* carelessly, nonchalantly.

nonchalant, *adj.* nonchalant.

non-combattant, *adj. and n.m.* non-combatant.

nonne, *n.f.* nun.

nonobstant, *prep.* in spite of, notwithstanding.

nonpareil, *adj.* unequaled.

non-sens, *n.m.* nonsense.

nord, *n.m.* north.

normal, *adj.* normal.

normand, *adj.* Norman; equivocal.

norme, *n.f.* norm.

Norvège, *n.f.* Norway.

Norvégien, *n.m.* Norwegian (person).

norvégien, **1.** *n.m.* Norwegian (language). **2.** *adj.* Norwegian.

nostalgie, *n.f.* nostalgia.

notabilité, *n.f.* notability.

notable, **1.** *n.m.* notable. **2.** remarkable, notable.

notaire, *n.m.* lawyer, notary.

notamment, *adv.* particularly.

notation, *n.f.* notation.

note, *n.f.* note, bill.

noter, *vb.* note.

notice, *n.f.* notice, review.

notification, *n.f.* notification.

notifier, *vb.* notify.

notion, *n.f.* notion.

notoire, *adj.* notorious.

notoriété, *n.f.* notoriety.

notre *sg.,* **nos** *pl. adj.* our.

nôtre, *pron.* le n., ours.

nouer, *vb.* tie.

noueux, *adj.* knotty.

nouilles, *n.f.pl.* noodles.

nourrice, *n.f.* (wet-)nurse.

nourricier, *adj.* nourishing; of nursing.

nourrir, *vb.* feed, nourish, foster.

nourriture, *n.f.* food, nourishment.

nous, *pron.* we, us, ourselves.

nouveau *m.,* **nouvelle** *f. adj.* new, fresh. **de n.,** anew.

nouveauté, *n.f.* novelty.

nouvel an, *n.m.* new year.

nouvelle, *n.f.* news.

nouvellement, *adv.* recently, newly.

novembre, *n.m.* November.

novice, *n.m.f.* novice.

noviciat, *n.m.* novitiate.

noyade, *n.f.* drowning.

noyau, *n.m.* kernel, nucleus.

noyer, *vb.* drown.

noyer, *n.m.* walnut (tree).

nu, *adj.* naked, bare.

nuage, *n.m.* cloud; gloom.

nuageux, *adj.* cloudy.

nuance, *n.m.* shade, degree.

nucléaire, *adj.* nuclear.

nudité, *n.f.* bareness.

nuire à, *vb.* injure, harm.

nuisible, *adj.* injurious, hurtful.

nuit, *n.f.* night.

nul, *adj.* no, none; void. **nulle part,** nowhere.

nullement, *adv.* not at all.

nullité, *n.f.* nonentity.

numéral, *adj. and n.m.* numeral.

numérique, *adj.* numerical.

numéro, *n.m.* number.

nu-pieds, *adv.* barefoot.

nuptial, *adj.* bridal.

nuque, *n.f.* nape.

nutritif, *adj.* nutritious.

nutrition, *n.f.* nutrition.

nylon, *n.m.* nylon.

nymphe, *n.f.* nymph.

O

oasis (-s), n.f. oasis.
obéir à, vb. obey.
obéissance, n.f. obedience.
obéissant, adj. obedient.
obélisque, n.m. obelisk.
obérer, vb. burden with debt.
obèse, adj. obese.
obésité, n.f. obesity.
objecter, vb. object.
objectif, adj. and n.m. objective.
objection, n.f. objection.
objet, n.m. object.
obligation, n.f. obligation.
obligatoire, adj. compulsory, mandatory, binding.
obligeance, n.f. obligingness.
obliger, vb. oblige, accommodate.
oblique, adj. slanting; devious.
oblitération, n.f. obliteration.
oblitérer, vb. obliterate.
oblong, adj. oblong.
obscène, adj. filthy, obscene.
obscénité, n.f. obscenity.
obscur, adj. obscure, dark, dim.
obscurcir, vb. darken, obscure.
obscurcissement, n.m. darkening, state of being obscure.
obscurément, adv. obscurely.
obscurité, n.f. darkness, dimness, obscurity.
obséder, vb. harass, haunt.
obsèques, n.f.s.pl. funeral.
obséquieusement, adv. obsequiously.
obséquieux, adj. obsequious.
observance, n.f. observance.
observateur, n.m. observer.
observation, n.f. observation, remark.
observer, vb. observe, watch.
obsession, n.f. obsession.
obstacle, n.m. obstacle, bar.
obstétrical, adj. obstetrical.
obstination, n.f. stubbornness.
obstiné, adj. obstinate, stubborn.
obstiner, vb. s'o., persist.
obstruction, n.f. obstruction.
obstruer, vb. obstruct, stop up.
obtempérer, vb. obey.
obtenir, vb. obtain, get.
obtention, n.f. obtaining.
obtus, adj. obtuse, dull, stupid.
obus (-s), n.m. shell.
obusier, n.m. howitzer.
occasion, n.f. opportunity, chance; bargain.
occasionnel, adj. occasional.
occasionner, vb. cause, bring about.
occident, n.m. west.
occidental, adj. western.
occulte, adj. occult.
occupant, n.m. occupant, tenant.
occupation, n.f. pursuit, occupation.
occupé, adj. busy.

occuper, vb. occupy, busy. s'o. de, attend to.
occurrence, n.f. occurrence.
océan, n.m. ocean.
océanique, adj. oceanic.
ocre, n.f. ochre.
octave, n.f. octave.
octobre, n.m. October.
octroyer, vb. grant.
oculaire, adj. ocular.
oculiste, n.m. oculist.
ode, n.f. ode.
odeur, n.f. odor, scent, perfume.
odieux, adj. hateful, obnoxious, odious.
odorant, adj. having a fragrant odor.
odorat, n.m. (sense of) smell.
œil, n.m., pl. yeux, eye. coup d'o., glance.
œillade, n.f. wink, quick look.
œillère, n.f. eyetooth.
œillet, n.m. carnation.
œuf, n.m. egg.
œuvre, n.f. work.
offensant, adj. offensive.
offense, n.f. offense.
offenser, vb. offend.
offenseur, n.m. offender.
offensif, adj. offensive.
offensive, n.f. offensive.
offensivement, adv. offensively.
office, n.m. office, pantry; (church) service.
officiant, n.m. one who officiates.
officiel, adj. official.
officier, 1. n.m. officer; mate. 2. vb. officiate.
officieux, adj. officious.
offrande, n.f. offering.
offre, n.f. offer.
offrir, vb. offer, present.
offusquer, vb. obscure, shadow, irritate.
ogre, n.m. ogre.
oie, n.f. goose.
oignon (ô nyôN), n.m. onion, bulb.
oindre, vb. anoint.
oiseau, n.m. bird.
oiselet, n.m. small bird.
oiseux, adj. idle, empty, useless.
oisif, adj. idle.
oisillon, n.m. young bird.
oisiveté, n.f. idleness.
oléagineux, adj. oily.
olivâtre, adj. olive-colored.
olive, n.f. olive.
olivier, n.m. olive tree.
olympique, adj. Olympic.
ombilical, adj. umbilical.
ombrage, n.m. shade.
ombragé, adj. shady.
ombrager, vb. shade.
ombrageux, adj. suspicious, doubtful.
ombre, n.f. shade, shadow.
ombreux, adj. shady.
omelette, n.f. omelet.
omettre, vb. omit.
omission, n.f. omission.

omnibus (-s), n.m. bus.
omnipotent, adj. omnipotent.
omoplate, n.f. shoulder blade.
on, pron. one (indef. subj.).
once, n.f. ounce.
oncle, n.m. uncle.
onction, n.f. unction.
onctueux, adj. unctuous.
onde, n.f. wave.
ondé, adj. wavy.
ondoyer, vb. wave.
ondulation, n.f. wave. o. permanente, permanent wave.
onduler, vb. wave.
onéreux, adj. burdensome.
ongle, n.m. (finger)nail.
onglée, n.f. numb feeling.
onguent, n.m. salve, ointment.
onomatopée, n.f. onomatopœia.
onze, adj. and n.m. eleven.
onzième, adj. and n.m.f. eleventh.
opacité, n.f. opacity.
opale, n.f. opal.
opaque, adj. opaque.
opéra, n.m. opera.
opérateur, n.m. operator.
opération, n.f. operation, transaction.
opératoire, adj. operative.
opéré, n. patient undergoing surgery.
opérer, vb. operate.
opérette, n.f. operetta.
opiner, vb. hold or express an opinion.
opiniâtre, adj. stubborn.
opiniâtreté, n.f. stubbornness.
opinion, n.f. opinion.
opium, n.m. opium.
opportun, adj. timely.
opportunité, n.f. timeliness.
opposé, adj. opposite, averse.
opposer, vb. oppose. s'o. à, oppose, resist.
opposition, n.f. opposition.
oppresser, vb. weigh heavily on.
oppresseur, n.m. oppressor.
oppressif, adj. oppressive.
oppression, n.f. oppression.
opprimer, vb. oppress.
opprobre, n.m. disgrace, infamy.
opter, vb. select, decide.
opticien, n.m. optician.
optimisme, n.m. optimism.
optimiste, 1. adj. optimistic. 2. n.m.f. optimist.
option, n.f. option.
optique, adj. optic.
opulence, n.f. opulence, riches.
opuscule, n.m. small work.
or, 1. n.m. gold. 2. conj. now.
oracle, n.m. oracle.
orage, n.m. storm.
orageusement, adv. turbulently, stormily.
orageux, adj. stormy.
oraison, n.f. prayer, oration.
oral, adj. oral.
orange, n.f. orange.
oranger, n.m. orange tree.

orateur, n.m. speaker, orator.

oratoire, adj. oratorical. art o., oratory.

orbe, n.m. orb, sphere.

orbite, n.m. orbit, socket (as of eye).

orchestre (-k-), n.m. orchestra, band.

orchestrer (-k-), vb. orchestrate.

orchidée, n.f. orchid.

ordinaire, adj. and n.m. ordinary.

ordinal, adj. and n.m. ordinal.

ordinateur, n.m. computer.

ordonnance, n.f. prescription, ordinance, decree.

ordonné, adj. orderly, tidy.

ordonner, vb. order, ordain, bid, command.

ordre, n.m. order. de premier o., first-rate.

ordure, n.f. filth, garbage, refuse.

ordurier, adj. foul.

oreille, n.f. ear.

oreiller, n.m. pillow.

oreillons, n.m.pl. mumps.

orfèvrerie, n.f. gold or silver jewelry.

organdi, n.m. organdy.

organe, n.m. organ.

organique, adj. organic.

organisateur, 1. n.m. organizer. 2. adj. organizing.

organisation, n.f. organization, arrangement.

organiser, vb. organize.

organisme, n.m. organism.

organiste, n.m.f. organist.

orge, n.f. barley.

orgelet, n.m. sty (of eye).

orgie, n.f. orgy.

orgue, n.f. organ.

orgueil, n.m. pride.

orgueilleux, adj. proud, haughty.

Orient, n.m. Orient, East.

Oriental, n.m. Oriental.

oriental, adj. Oriental, eastern.

orienter, vb. orient.

orifice, n.m. orifice, hole.

originaire, adj. original, native.

originairement, adv. originally.

original, 1. n.m. queer person. 2. adj. original.

originalement, adv. originally; unusually.

originalité, n.f. originality.

origine, n.f. origin, source.

originel, adj. original.

oripeau, n.m. tinsel, showy clothes.

orme, n.m. elm.

orné, adj. ornate.

ornement, n.m. ornament, adornment, trimming.

ornemental, adj. ornamental.

ornementation, n.f. ornamentation.

orner, vb. adorn, trim.

ornière, n.f. rut, track.

ornithologie, n.f. ornithology.

orphelin, n.m. orphan.

orphelinat, n.m. orphanage.

orphéon, n.m. choral group.

orteil, n.m. toe.

orthodoxe, adj. orthodox.

orthodoxie, n.f. orthodoxy.

orthographe, n.f. spelling, orthography.

orthographier, vb. spell.

ortie, n.f. nettle.

os, n.m. bone.

oscillant, adj. oscillating.

oscillation, n.f. sway.

osciller, vb. fluctuate, oscillate.

osé, adj. attempted, bold.

oser, vb. dare.

osier, n.m. willow.

ossature, n.f. bony structure, skeleton.

ossements, n.m.pl. human remains.

osseux, adj. bony.

ossifier, vb. ossify.

ostensible, adj. ostensible.

ostentation, n.f. ostentation.

ostraciser, vb. ostracize.

otage, n.m. hostage.

ôter, vb. take off, take away.

ou, conj. or. ou . . . ou . . ., either . . . or . . . .

où, adv. where.

ouailles, n.f.pl. religious congregation.

ouater (wä-), vb. pad.

oubli, n.m. forgetfulness, oblivion.

oublier, vb. forget.

oublieux, adj. forgetful.

ouest (wèst), n.m. west.

oui (wè), adv. yes.

oui-dire, n.m. gossip, hearsay.

ouïe, n.f. gill.

ouïr, vb. hear.

ouragan, n.m. hurricane.

ourler, vb. hem.

ourlet, n.m. hem.

ours (-s), n.m. bear. o. blanc, polar bear.

ourson, n.m. bear cub.

outil, n.m. tool, implement.

outillage, n.m. quantity of tools, plant.

outiller, vb. supply with tools.

outrage, n.m. outrage.

outrageant, adj. outrageous.

outrager, vb. outrage, affront.

outrance, n.f. extreme degree. à o. to the very end.

outre, adv. and prep. beyond. en o., besides, furthermore.

outré, adj. excessive, extreme.

outrecuidant, adj. excessively bold and forward.

outre-mer, adv. across the seas.

outrer, vb. overdo, irritate.

ouvert, adj. open.

ouverture, n.f. opening, gap; overture.

ouvrable, adj. work, workable.

ouvrage, n.m. work.

ouvrer, vb. work.

ouvreuse, n.f. usher or usherette.

ouvrier, n.m. workman; (pl.) labor.

ouvrir, vb. open.

ouvroir, n.m. work room or shop.

ovaire, n.m. ovary.

ovale, adj. and n.m. oval.

ovation, n.f. ovation.

oxygène, n.m. oxygen.

P

pacage, n.m. land used for pasture.

pacificateur, 1. adj. pacifying. 2. n.m. peacemaker.

pacification, n.f. peace-making.

pacifier, vb. pacify, appease, soothe.

pacifique, adj. pacific, peaceful, peaceable.

pacifisme, n.m. pacifism.

pacotille, n.f. small wares.

pacte, n.m. covenant, pact.

pactiser, vb. make a pact, compromise.

pagaie, n.f. paddle.

pagaïe, n.f. disorder, rush.

paganisme, n.m. paganism.

pagayer, vb. paddle.

pagayeur, n.m. paddler.

page, 1. n.m. page (boy). 2. n.f. page (in book).

pages centrales, n.f.pl. centerfold.

pagination, n.f. pagination.

paginer, vb. number pages.

pagode, n.f. pagoda.

paiement, payement, n.m. payment.

païen, adj. and n.m. pagan, heathen.

paillard, adj. lewd, indecent.

paillasse, n.f. mattress of straw, ticking.

paillasson, n.m. (door-)mat.

paille, n.f. straw; defect (in gems).

paillette, n.f. spangle; defect.

pain, n.m. bread, loaf. petit p., roll.

pair, 1. n.m. peer. 2. adj. even, equal.

paire, n.f. pair.

pairesse, n.f. peeress.

pairie, n.f. peerage.

paisible, adj. peaceful.

paître, vb. graze.

paix, n.f. peace.

palabre, n.m. palaver.

palais, n.m. palace; palate.

palan, n.m. gear for hoisting.

palatal, adj. and n.m. palatal.

pale, n.f. blade, stake.

pâle, adj. pale.

palefrenier, n.m. groom.

palet, n.m. quoit.

paletot, n.m. overcoat.

pâleur, n.f. paleness.

palier, n.m. stair landing.

pâlir, vb. grow pale or dim.

palissade, n.f. paling, fence.

pâlissant, adj. becoming pale.

palme, n.f. palm.

palmier, n.m. palm (tree).

palpable, adj. palpable.

palper, vb. touch, feel.

palpitant, adj. fluttering, palpitating.

palpiter, vb. flutter, beat, palpitate.

paludéen, adj. marshy.

pâmer, vb. se p., faint.

pamphlet, n.m. pamphlet, satire.

pamphlétaire, n.m. pamphleteer.

pamplemousse, n.m. grapefruit.

pan, n.m. side, piece, flap.

panacée, n.f. panacea.

panache, n.m. plume.

panais, n.m. parsnip.

pandit, n.m. pundit.

pané, adj. dotted with bread crumbs.

panier, n.m. basket.

panique, n.f. and adj. panic.

panne, n.f. fat, lard; accident.

panneau, n.m. panel.

panse, n.f. paunch, cud.

pansement, n.m. dressing.

panser, vb. groom; dress.

pantalon, n.m. trousers.

panteler, vb. pant, gasp.

panthère, n.f. panther.

pantomime, n.f. pantomime.

pantoufle, n.f. slipper.

pantoufler, vb. act silly.

paon (pân), n.m. peacock.

papal, adj. papal.

papauté, n.f. papacy.

pape, n.m. pope.

paperasse, n.f. waste paper; official documents.

paperassier, adj. scribbling, petty.

papeterie, n.f. stationery.

papetier, n.m. stationer.

papier, n.m. paper.

papier à notes, n.m. notepaper.

papier à tapisser, n.m. wallpaper.

papier peint, n.m. wallpaper.

papillon, n.m. butterfly.

papillonner, vb. flutter, trifle.

papoter, vb. prate, prattle.

pâque, n.f. Passover.

paquebot, n.m. small liner, packet.

pâquerette, n.f. daisy.

Pâques, n.m. Easter.

paquet, n.m. package, parcel, bundle; deck (cards).

par, prep. by; through.

parabole, n.f. parabola; parable.

parachute, n.m. parachute.

parade, n.f. parade, procession.

parader, vb. parade, show off.

paradis, n.m. paradise.

paradoxal, adj. paradoxical.

paradoxe, n.m. paradox.

paraffine, n.f. paraffin.

parage, n.m. ancestry, descent; locality.

paragraphe, n.m. paragraph.

paraître, vb. appear, seem.

parallèle, adj. and n.m.f. parallel.

paralyser, vb. paralyze.

paralysie, n.f. paralysis.

paralytique, adj. and n.m.f. paralytic.

paramètre, n.m. parameter.

parangon, n.m. model, paragon.

paraphraser, vb. paraphrase.

parapluie, n.m. umbrella.

parasite, n.m. parasite.

paratonnerre, n.m. lightning rod.

paravent, n.m. screen.

parc (-k), n.m. park.

parcelle, n.f. part, instalment.

parce que, conj. because.

parchemin, n.m. parchment.

parcimonie, n.f. parsimony.

parcourir, vb. run through.

parcours, n.m. course, journey.

pardessus, n.m. overcoat.

par-dessus, adv. and prep. above, over.

pardon, 1. n.m. pardon, forgiveness. 2. interj. sorry!

pardonner (à), vb. forgive, pardon.

pardonneur, n.m. pardoner.

pare-boue, n.m. mudguard.

pare-chocs, n.m. bumper.

pareil, adj. like.

parent, n.m. relative; (pl.) parents.

parenté, n.f. relationship.

parenthèse, n.f. parenthesis.

parer, vb. attire, deck out; parry.

paresse, n.f. sloth.

paresser, vb. laze, waste time.

paresseux, adj. lazy.

parfaire, vb. complete, finish up.

parfait, adj. perfect.

parfois, adv. sometimes.

parfum, n.m. perfume.

parfumé, adj. fragrant.

parfumer, vb. perfume.

parfumerie, n.f. perfumery.

pari, n.m. bet.

parier, vb. bet.

parieur, n.m. one who bets.

Parisien, n.m. Parisian.

parisien, adj. Parisian.

parité, n.f. equality, parity.

parjure, n.m. perjury.

parjurer, vb. se p., commit perjury.

parlant, adj. speaking, chatty.

parlement, n.m. parliament.

parlementaire, adj. parliamentary.

parlementer, vb. parley.

parler, vb. talk, speak.

parleur, n.m. one who speaks or talks.

parloir, n.m. parlor.

parmi, prep. among.

parodie, n.f. parody.

parodier, vb. parody, imitate.

parol, n.f. wall lining.

paroisse, n.f. parish.

paroissial, adj. parochial.

parole, n.f. speech, word.

prendre la p., take the floor.

paroxysme, n.m. fit of violence.

parquer, vb. park, enclose.

parquet, n.m. floor.

parqueterie, n.f. parquetry.

parrain, n.m. godfather.

parsemer, vb. spread, strew.

part, n.f. share, part. de la p. de, on behalf of. quelque p., somewhere. nulle p., nowhere. faire p. à, share; inform.

partage, n.m. partition, sharing, share.

partager, vb. share, divide.

partance, n.f. going, sailing.

partant, n.m. one who leaves.

partenaire, n.m.f. partner.

parti, n.m. party.

partial, adj. partial.

partialité, n.f. bias, partiality.

participant, adj. and n.m. participant.

participation, n.f. participation, share.

participe, n.m. participle.

participer à, vb. partake of, take part in.

particularité, n.f. peculiarity.

particule, n.f. particle.

particulier, adj. particular, private, peculiar, special.

partie, n.f. part, party.

partiel, adj. partial.

partir, vb. depart, leave, go (come) away, sail.

partisan, n.m. partisan, follower.

partitif, adj. partitive.

partition, n.f. score.

partout, adv. everywhere, throughout. p. où, wherever.

parure, n.f. ornament.

parvenir, vb. reach.

parvenu, n.m. upstart.

pas, 1. n.m. step, pace. faux p., slip. 2. adv. not. p. du tout, not at all.

passable, adj. fair.

passage, n.m. aisle, passage, alley.

passager, 1. n.m. passenger. 2. adj. passing, fugitive.

passant, n.m. passer-by.

passavant, n.m. permit.

passe, n.f. passing, permit.

passé, adj. and n.m. past.

passe-partout, n.m. skeleton key, passport.

passeport, n.m. passport.

passer, vb. pass; go by; spend; strain. se p. de, go without.

passereau, n.m. sparrow.

passerelle, n.f. bridge.

passe-temps, n.m. pastime.

passible, adj. capable of feeling.

passif, adj. and n.m. passive.

passion, n.f. passion.

passionné, adj. passionate.

passionnel, adj. concerning or due to passion.

passionner, vb. interest, excite.

se p., be eager or excited over.

passoire, n.f. device for straining.

pastel, n.m. crayon.

pastèque, n.f. watermelon.

pasteur, n.m. pastor.

pasteuriser, vb. pasteurize.

pastille, n.f. lozenge, cough drop.

pastoral, adj. pastoral.

pataud, adj. awkward.

patauger, vb. flounder.

pâte, n.f. paste, dough, batter.

pâté, n.m. block; pie.

patenôtre, n.f. (Lord's) prayer.

patent, adj. patent, evident.

patente, n.f. license.

patenter, vb. license.

paterne, adj. paternal.

paternel, adj. paternal.

paternité, n.f. fatherhood.

pâteux, adj. pasty, thick, muddy.

pathétique, adj. pathetic.

pathologie, n.f. pathology.

patience, n.f. patience.

patient, adj. and n.m. patient.

patin, n.m. skate.

patiner, vb. skate.

patineur, n.m. skater.

pâtir, vb. suffer.

pâtisserie, n.f. pastry.

patois, n.m. dialect, gibberish.

pâtre, n.m. shepherd.

patriarche, n.m. patriarch.

patricien, adj. and n.m. patrician.

patrie, n.f. native country, homeland.

patrimoine, n.m. patrimony.

patriote, n.m.f. patriot.

patriotique, adj. patriotic.

patriotisme, n.m. patriotism.

patron, n.m. employer; boss; model, pattern; patron.

patronat, n.m. management, employers.

patronner, vb. patronize, provide for.

patrouille, n.f. patrol.

patrouiller, vb. patrol

patte, n.f. paw, leg, flap.

pâturage, n.m. pasture.

pâture, n.f. fodder, pasture.

paume, n.f. palm.

paupière, n.f. eyelid.

pause, n.f. pause.

pauvre, adj. poor.

pauvreté, n.f. poverty.

pavaner, vb. se p., swagger, strut.

pavé, n.m. pavement.

paver, vb. pave.

pavillon, n.m. pavilion.

pavot, n.m. poppy.

paye, n.f. payment, salary.

payement, n.m. payment.

payer, vb. pay, settle.

payeur, n.m. payer.

pays, n.m. country.

paysage, n.m. landscape, scenery.

paysager, adj. of the country, rural.

paysan, n.m. peasant.

Pays-Bas, les, n.m.pl. Holland; the Netherlands.

péage, n.m. toll.

peau, n.f. skin, hide.

pêche, n.f. peach; fishing.

péché, n.m. sin.

pécher, vb. sin.

pêcher, 1. vb. fish. 2. n.m. peach tree.

pêcherie, n.f. fishing place.

pécheur m., pécheresse f. 1. n. sinner. 2. adj. sinful.

pêcheur, n.m. fisherman.

pécule, n.f. savings.

pécuniaire, adj. pecuniary.

pédagogie, n.f. pedagogy.

pédale, n.f. pedal.

pédant, adj. and n.m.f. pedant, pedantic.

pédanterie, n.f. pedantry.

pédé(raste), n.m. homosexual.

pédestre, adj. pedestrian.

pédiatre, n.m. pediatrician.

pédicure, n.m. chiropodist.

peigne, n.m. comb.

peigner, vb. comb.

peignoir, n.m. dressing-gown.

peindre, vb. paint, portray, depict.

peine, n.f. pain, penalty. à p., hardly, barely; faire de la p. à, pain, vb.; valoir la p. de, be worth while to; se donner la p., take the trouble.

peiner, vb. labor; grieve.

peintre, n.m. painter.

peinture, n.f. paint, painting.

pelage, n.m. coat.

pelé, adj. bald, uncovered.

pêle-mêle, adv. pell-mell.

peler, vb. peel, pare.

pèlerin, n.m. pilgrim.

pèlerinage, n.m. pilgrimage.

pèlerine, n.f. cape.

pélican, n.m. pelican.

pelle, n.f. shovel.

pelletier, n.m. furrier.

pellicule, n.f. film.

pelote, n.f. ball, pellet.

peloton, n.m. ball; group of soldiers.

pelure, n.f. peel.

pénal, adj. penal.

pénalité, n.f. penalty.

penaud, adj. awkwardly bashful or embarrassed.

penchant, n.m. bent, liking, tendency.

pencher, vb. tilt, lean, droop. se p., bend.

pendaison, n.f. hanging (execution).

pendant, prep. during, pending. p. que, as, while.

pendiller, vb. dangle.

pendre, vb. hang.

pendule, n.m. clock; pendulum.

pénétrable, adj. penetrable.

pénétrant, adj. keen.

pénétration, n.f. penetration.

pénétrer, vb. penetrate, pervade.

pénible, adj. painful.

péninsule, n.f. peninsula.

pénitence, n.f. penance.

pénitencier, n.m. penitentiary.

pénitent, adj. and n.m. penitent.

penne, n.f. feather.

pénombre, n.f. gloom, shadow.

pensée, n.f. thought; pansy.

penser (à), vb. think (of).

penseur, n.m. thinker.

pensif, adj. thoughtful, pensive.

pension, n.f. board, pension.

pensionnaire, n.m.f. boarder.

pensionnat, n.m. boarding school.

pente, n.f. slope, slant.

pénurie, n.f. penury, scarcity.

pépier, vb. chirp.

pépin, n.m. pip, kernel.

pépinière, n.f. nursery.

pépite, n.f. nugget.

perçant, adj. sharp.

perce, n.f. boring tool.

perce-neige, n.f. snowdrop.

percepteur, n.m. tax collector.

perception, n.f. perception, collecting.

percer, vb. pierce, bore.

percevoir, vb. collect, amass, perceive.

perche, n.f. pole, perch.

percher, vb. se p., perch.

perchoir, n.m. perch.

perclus, adj. lame, crippled.

percussion, n.f. percussion.

percuter, vb. hit, strike.

perdition, n.f. perdition.

perdre, vb. lose; waste.

perdrix, n.f. partridge.

père, n.m. father.

péremptoire, adj. peremptory.

perfection, n.f. perfection.

perfectionnement, n.m. improvement, finishing.

perfectionner, vb. perfect, finish.

perfide, adj. treacherous.

perfidie, n.f. treachery.

perforation, n.f. perforation.

perforer, vb. perforate, drill.

péricliter, vb. be in danger, shake.

péril (-l), n.m. peril, danger.

périlleux, adj. perilous, dangerous.

périmètre, n.m. perimeter.

période, n.f. period, term, stage.

périodique, adj. periodic.

péripétie, n.f. shift of luck.

périr, vb. perish.

périscope, n.m. periscope.

périssable, adj. perishable.

perle, n.f. pearl, bead.

perlé, adj. pearly, perfect.

permanence, n.f. permanence.

permanent, adj. permanent.

perméable, adj. permeable.

permettre, vb. permit, allow.

permis, n.m. permit, license.

permission, n.f. permission, leave (of absence), furlough.

permissionnaire, n.m. one having a permit; one on leave.

permuter, vb. change, exchange.

pernicieux, adj. pernicious.

pérorer, vb. harangue, argue.

perpétrer, vb. commit.

perpétuel, adj. perpetual.

perpétuer, vb. perpetuate.

perplexe, adj. perplexed, undecided.

perplexité, n.f. perplexity.

perquisition, n.f. exploration, search.

perron, n.m. flight of steps.

perroquet, n.m. parrot.

perruque, n.f. wig.

perse, adj. Persian.

persécuter, vb. persecute.

persécution, n.f. persecution.

persévérance, n.f. perseverance.

persévérant, adj. persevering, resolute.

persévérer, vb. persevere.

persienne, n.f. blind, shutter.

persifler, vb. banter, ridicule.

persil, n.m. parsley.

persistance, n.f. persistence.

persistant, adj. persistent.

persister, vb. persist.

personnage, n.m. personage; character.

personnalité, n.f. personality.

personne, 1. n.f. person. 2. pron. nobody.

personnel, 1. n.m. personnel, staff. 2. adj. personal.

personnifier, vb. personify.

perspective, n.f. perspective, prospect.

perspicace, adj. discerning.

perspicacité, n.f. insight.

persuader, vb. persuade, convince, induce.

persuasif, adj. persuasive.

perte, n.f. loss, waste; (pl.) casualties.

pertinence, n.f. pertinence.

pertinent, adj. relevant, pertinent.

perturbateur, n.m. agitator, disturber.

pervers, adj. perverse, contrary.

pervertir, vb. pervert.

pesant, adj. heavy, ponderous.

pesanteur, n.f. weight, dullness.

peser, vb. weigh.

pessimisme, n.m. pessimism.

pessimiste, n.m. pessimist.

peste, n.f. pestilence; nuisance.

pestilence, n.f. pestilence, plague, nuisance.

pétale, n.m. petal.

pétiller, vb. twinkle, crackle.

petit, 1. adj. little, small, petty. 2. n.m. cub.

petite-fille, n.f. granddaughter.

petitesse, n.f. smallness, pettiness.

petit-fils (-fès), n.m. grandson.

petit-gris, n.m. fur of the squirrel.

pétition, n.f. petition.

pétitionner, vb. request, ask.

petits-enfants, n.m.pl. grandchildren.

pétrifiant, adj. petrifying.

pétrifier, vb. petrify or (se p.) become petrified.

pétrir, vb. knead, mold.

pétrole, n.m. petroleum, kerosene.

pétulance, n.f. petulance.

peu, 1. n.m. little; few. 2. adv. not. p. à p., gradually.

peuplade, n.f. tribe, clan.

peuple, n.m. people.

peupler, vb. people.

peuplier, n.m. poplar.

peur, n.f. fear. avoir p., be afraid. de p. que . . . ne, lest.

peureux, adj. shy, timid.

peut-être, adv. perhaps, maybe.

phallocratie, n.f. machismo.

phallocrate, adj. macho.

phare, n.m. beacon, lighthouse; headlight.

pharmacie, n.f. drug store, pharmacy.

pharmacien, n.m. druggist.

phase, n.f. phase.

phénix, n.m. phoenix; superior person.

phénoménal, adj. phenomenal.

phénomène, n.m. phenomenon; freak.

philanthrope, n.m. philanthropist.

philanthropie, n.f. philanthropy.

philatélie, n.f. stamp-collecting.

philosophe, n.m. philosopher.

philosophie, n.f. philosophy.

philosophique, adj. philosophical.

phobie, n.f. phobia.

phonéticien, n.m. phonetician.

phonétique, adj. and n.f. phonetic, phonetics.

phonographe, n.m. phonograph.

phoque, n.m. seal.

photocopie, n.f. photocopy.

photocopieur, n.m. photocopier.

photographe, n.m. photographer.

photographie, n.f. photograph, photography.

phrase, n.f. sentence.

phtisie, n.f. consumption.

phtisique, adj. and n.m. consumptive.

physicien, n.m. physical scientist.

physionomie, n.f. looks, expression.

physique, 1. n.f. physics. 2. adj. physical.

piailler, vb. peep, squeal.

pianiste, n.m.f. pianist.

piano, n.m. piano.

pic, n.m. peak.

picoter, vb. prick, peck.

pièce, n.f. piece, coin, patch, room. p. de théâtre, play.

pied, n.m. foot. aller à p., walk. coup de p., kick.

pied-à-terre, n.m. temporary quarters.

piédestal, n.m. pedestal.

piège, n.m. snare, trap.

pierre, n.f. stone.

pierreries, n.f.pl. jewelry, gems.

pierreux, adj. full of stone or grit.

pierrot, n.m. clown in pantomime.

piété, n.f. piety.

piétiner, vb. trample.

piéton, n.m. pedestrian.

piètre, adj. pitiful, mean, wretched.

pieu, n.m. stake, pile.

pieuvre, n.f. octopus.

pieux, adj. pious.

pigeon, n.m. pigeon, dove.

pile, n.f. stack; battery.

piler, vb. crush, blast.

pilier, n.m. pillar, column.

pillage, n.m. plundering.

piller, vb. plunder.

pilotage, n.m. piloting; driving piles.

pilote, n.m. pilot.

piloter, vb. pilot, lead.

pilule, n.f. pill.

piment, n.m. chili.

pimenter, vb. flavor, season.

pimpant, adj. stylish, smart.

pin, n.m. pine.

pinacle, n.m. pinnacle.

pince, n.f. clip; (pl.) pliers.

pinceau, n.m. paint-brush.

pince-nez, n.m. eyeglasses.

pincer, vb. pinch, nip.

pinte, n.f. pint.

pioche, n.f. pickax.

piocher, vb. dig.

piocheur, n.m. digger.

pion, n.m. pawn, peon.

pioncer, vb. nap, sleep.

pionnier, n.m. pioneer.

pipe, n.f. pipe.

piper, vb. catch, decoy, trick.

piquant, adj. sharp. mot p., quip.

pique, n.m. spade.

pique-nique, n.m. picnic.

piquer, vb. prick, sting.

piquet, n.m. picket, peg, stake.

piqûre, n.f. prick, sting, puncture.

pirate, n.m. pirate.

pirate de l'air, n.m. hijacker.

piraterie, n.f. piracy.

pire, adj. worse, worst.

pirouette, n.f. pirouette, shift.

pis, adv. worse, worst.

piscine, n.f. pool.

pissenlit, n.m. dandelion.

pistache, n.f. pistachio.

piste, n.f. track.

pistolet, n.m. pistol.

piston, n.m. piston.

pistonner, vb. help, push.

pitance, n.f. meager amount, as of food.

piteux, adj. pitiful.

pitié, n.f. pity, mercy.

pitoyable, *adj.* pitiful, miserable.

pitre, *n.m.* clown.

pittoresque, *adj.* picturesque, colorful.

pivoine, *n.f.* peony.

pivot, *n.m.* pivot.

pivoter, *vb.* turn, pivot, revolve.

pizza, *n.f.* pizza.

placard, *n.m.* closet; poster.

placarder, *vb.* post, display.

place, *n.f.* place, room.

placement, *n.m.* investment, placing.

placer, *vb.* invest, place.

placet, *n.m.* petition, demand.

placide, *adj.* placid.

placidité, *n.f.* placidness.

plafond, *n.m.* ceiling.

plage, *n.f.* beach.

plagiaire, *n.m.* one who plagiarizes.

plagiat, *n.m.* plagiarism.

plagier, *vb.* plagiarize.

plaid, *n.m.* plaid.

plaider, *vb.* plead.

plaideur, *n.m.* pleader.

plaidoirie, *n.f.* lawyer's speech.

plaie, *n.f.* wound, sore.

plaignant, *n.m.* plaintiff.

plaindre, *vb.* pity. **se p.**, complain.

plaine, *n.f.* plain.

plainte, *n.f.* complaint.

plaintif, *adj.* mournful.

plaire à, *vb.* please. **s'il vous plaît**, if you please.

plaisance, *n.f.* pleasure, ease.

plaisant, *adj.* joking.

plaisanter, *vb.* joke.

plaisanterie, *n.f.* joke.

plaisir, *n.m.* pleasure.

plan, *n.m.* plan; plane; schedule, scheme. **premier p.**, foreground.

planche, *n.f.* board, shelf, plank.

planche à roulettes, *n.f.* skateboard.

plancher, *n.m.* floor.

planer, *vb.* glide; hover.

planétaire, 1. *adj.* planetary. 2. *n.m.* planetarium.

planète, *n.f.* planet.

planeur, *n.m.* glider (plane).

plantation, *n.f.* plantation.

plante, *n.f.* plant; sole.

planter, *vb.* plant.

planteur, *n.m.* planter.

planton, *n.m.* military orderly.

plantureux, *adj.* fertile, rich.

plaque, *n.f.* plate, slab. **p. de projection**, lantern-slide.

plaquer, *vb.* plate; abandon.

plaquette, *n.f.* booklet, medal.

plastique, *adj.* plastic.

plastronner, *vb.* pose, strut jauntily.

plat, 1. *n.m.* dish, platter. 2. *adj.* flat. **œuf sur le p.**, fried egg.

platane, *n.m.* plane-tree.

plat-bord, *n.m.* gunwale.

plateau, *n.m.* plateau, tray.

plate-bande, *n.f.* flower bed.

plate-forme, *n.f.* platform.

platine, 1. *n.f.* platen, plate. 2. *n.m.* platinum.

platitude, *n.f.* flatness.

plâtras, *n.m.* rubbish, rubble.

plâtre, *n.m.* plaster.

plausible, *adj.* plausible.

plébéien, *adj.* ignoble.

plébiscite, *n.m.* plebiscite.

plein, *adj.* full, crowded.

plénier, *adj.* complete, plenary.

plénitude, *n.f.* fullness.

pleurer, *vb.* cry, weep, lament, mourn.

pleurésie, *n.f.* pleurisy.

pleurnicher, *vb.* complain, whine.

pleurs, *n.m.pl.* tears, weeping.

pleutre, *n.m.* cad, coward.

pleuvoir, *vb.* rain.

pli, *n.m.* fold, envelope, pleat, crease.

pliable, *adj.* pliable.

pliant, *n.m.* folding chair.

plier, *vb.* fold, bend.

plissement, *n.m.* fold, folding.

plisser, *vb.* pleat.

plomb, *n.m.* lead.

plomberie, *n.f.* plumbing.

plombier, *n.m.* plumber.

plongeon, *n.m.* plunge.

plonger, *vb.* plunge, dive, dip.

plongeur, *n.m.* diver; dishwasher.

plouf, *interj. and n.m.* splash, plop.

ploutocrate, *n.m.* plutocrat.

ployer, *vb.* incline, bend.

pluie, *n.f.* rain.

pluie radioactive, *n.f.* fallout.

plumage, *n.m.* feathers.

plume, *n.f.* pen, feather.

plumeau, *n.m.* feather duster.

plumer, *vb.* pluck.

plumet, *n.m.* plume.

plumeux, *adj.* feathery.

plumier, *n.m.* pen or pencil case.

plupart, *n.f.* greater part, majority. **pour la p.**, mostly.

pluralité, *n.f.* plurality.

pluriel, *adj. and n.m.* plural.

plus, *adv.* more, most. **ne ... p.**, no more. **non p.**, neither. **en p.**, extra.

plusieurs, *adj. and pron.* several.

plus-que-parfait, *n.m.* (gramm.) pluperfect.

plutôt, *adv.* rather.

pluvieux, *adj.* rainy, wet.

pneumatique, *abbr.* **pneu**, *n.m.* tire.

pneumonie, *n.f.* pneumonia.

pochade, *n.f.* hasty sketch.

poche, *n.f.* pocket.

pocher, *vb.* poach.

pochet, *vb.* pocket.

pochette, *n.f.* little pocket, handkerchief.

pochoir, *n.m.* stencil.

poêle, *n.m.* stove.

poème, *n.m.* poem.

poésie, *n.f.* poem, poetry.

poète, *n.f.* poet.

poétique, *adj.* poetic.

poids (pwä), *n.m.* weight.

poignant, *adj.* poignant, keen.

poignard, *n.m.* dagger.

poignarder, *vb.* stab.

poigne, *n.f.* grip, power.

poignée, *n.f.* handful; handle.

poignet, *n.m.* wrist; cuff.

poil (pwäl), *n.m.* hair.

poilu, 1. *adj.* hairy, strong. 2. *n.m.* French soldier.

poinçon, *n.m.* punch.

poing, *n.m.* fist.

point, *n.m.* point, dot, period, stitch. **p. de vue**, point of view. **p. du jour**, dawn. **ne ... p.**, none. **être sur le p. de**, be about to. **au p.**, in focus. **deux p.s**, colon. **p. d'interrogation**, question mark.

pointage, *n.m.* pointing; (mil.) sighting.

pointe, *n.f.* point, tip, touch (small amount).

pointer, *vb.* point, aim.

pointeur, *n.m.* pointer, checker.

pointillage, *n.m.* dotting.

pointiller, *vb.* dot; tease.

pointilleux, *adj.* fussy, precise.

pointu, *adj.* pointed.

pointure, *n.f.* size.

poire, *n.f.* pear.

poireau, *n.m.* leek.

poirier, *n.m.* pear tree.

pois, *n.m.* pea.

poison, *n.m.* poison.

poisser, *vb.* make gluey or sticky.

poisson, *n.m.* fish.

poissonnerie, *n.f.* fish store.

poissonneux, *adj.* filled with fish.

poissonnier, *n.m.* fish dealer.

poitrinaire, *adj. and n.m.* consumptive.

poitrine, *n.f.* chest.

poivre, *n.m.* pepper.

poivrer, *vb.* spice with pepper.

poivrier, *n.m.* pepper plant.

poix, *n.f.* pitch.

polaire, *adj.* polar.

pôle, *n.m.* pole.

polémique, *n.f.* argument.

poli, 1. *adj.* civil, polite. 2. *n.m.* polish.

police, *n.f.* police; (insurance) policy.

policer, *vb.* refine.

polichinelle, *n.m.* Punch (puppet).

policier, *n.m.* policeman. **roman p.**, detective story.

polir, *vb.* polish.

polisseur, *n.m.* polisher.

polisson, 1. *n.m.* gamin, scamp. 2. *adj.* running wild.

polissonnerie, *n.f.* naughty action or remark.

politesse, *n.f.* good manners.

politicien, *n.m.* politician.

politique, 1. *n.f.* policy, politics. 2. *adj.* politic, political.

polka, *n.f.* polka.

pollen, n.m. pollen.
polluer, vb. pollute.
pollution, n.f. pollution.
Pologne, n.f. Poland.
Polonais, n.m. Pole.
polonais, adj. and n.m. Polish.
poltron, 1. adj. craven, cowardly. 2. n.m.f. coward.
poltronnerie, n.f. cowardly behavior.
polygame, 1. n.m. polygamist. 2. adj. polygamous.
polygamie, n.f. polygamy.
polygone, n.m. polygon.
pommade, n.f. pomade, salve.
pomme, n.f. apple. p. de terre, potato.
pommeau, n.m. pommel.
pommette, n.f. cheekbone.
pommier, n.m. apple tree.
pompe, n.f. pump; pomp.
pomper, vb. pump.
pompeux, adj. pompous.
pompier, n.m. fireman.
pompon, n.m. pompon, tuft.
ponce, n.f. pumice.
ponctualité, n.f. punctuality.
ponctuation, n.f. punctuation.
ponctuel, adj. punctual.
ponctuer, vb. punctuate.
poney, n.m. pony.
pont, n.m. bridge; deck.
pontife, n.m. pontiff.
pont-levis, n.m. drawbridge.
ponton, n.m. pontoon.
popeline, n.f. poplin.
popote, n.f. mess (military).
populace, n.f. mob.
populaire, adj. popular.
populariser, vb. popularize.
popularité, n.f. popularity.
population, n.f. population.
populeux, adj. populous.
porc, n.m. pig, pork.
porcelaine, n.f. china.
porc-épic, n.m. porcupine.
porche, n.m. porch.
porcherie, n.f. pigpen.
pore, n.m. pore.
poreux, adj. porous.
pornographie, n.f. pornography.
port, n.m. port, harbor; carrying; postage.
portable, adj. wearable.
portail, n.m. portal.
portatif, adj. portable.
porte, n.f. door, gate.
porte-affiches, n.m. billboard.
porte-avions, n.m. aircraft carrier.
portée, n.f. range, import, scope, reach; litter. hors de p., out of reach.
portefaix, n.m. porter.
portefeuille, n.m. wallet, case, portfolio.
portemanteau, n.m. cloak rack.
portement, n.m. carrying.
porte-monnaie, n.m. purse.
porter, vb. carry, bear; wear. se p., be (in health).
porte-rame, n.m. oarlock.
porteur, n.m. porter, bearer.

portier, n.m. doorman, porter.
portière, n.f. door-curtain.
portion, n.f. portion, share.
portique, n.m. portico, porch.
porto, n.m. port wine.
portrait, n.m. portrait.
portraitiste, n.m. painter of portraits.
Portugais, n.m. Portuguese (person).
portugais, 1. n.m. Portuguese (language). 2. adj. Portuguese.
Portugal, n.m. Portugal.
pose, n.f. pose, attitude.
posé, n.f. poised, set.
peser, vb. place, stand, set, lay. se p., settle, alight.
poseur, n.m. person or thing that places or applies; affected person.
positif, adj. and n.m. positive.
position, n.f. stand, place, position.
positiviste, n.m.f. positivist.
posséder, vb. own, possess.
possesseur, n.m. possessor.
possessif, adj. and n.m. possessive.
possession, n.f. possession.
possibilité, a.f. possibility.
possible, adj. possible. tout son p., one's utmost.
postal, adj. postal.
poste, n.f. mail. mettre à la p., mail. p. restante, general delivery.
poste, n.m. post. p. d'essence, gas station. p. de secours, first-aid station.
poster, vb. post (letter); place.
postérieur, n.m. rear, posterior.
postérité, n.f. posterity.
posthume, adj. posthumous.
postiche, adj. false, unnecessary.
post-scriptum, n.m. postscript.
postulant, n.m. applicant.
postuler, vb. apply for.
posture, n.f. posture.
pot, n.m. pot, pitcher, jar.
potable, adj. drinkable.
potage, n.m. soup.
potager, adj. vegetable.
potasse, n.f. potash.
pot-de-vin, n.m. tip, bribe.
poteau, n.m. post.
potée, n.f. potful.
potence, n.f. gallows.
potentat, n.m. potentate.
potentiel, adj. and n.m. potential.
poterie, n.f. pottery.
poterne, n.f. postern.
potier, n.m. potter.
potion, n.f. potion.
potiron, n.m. pumpkin.
pou, n.m. louse.
pouce, n.m. thumb; inch.
pouding, n.m. pudding.
poudre, n.f. powder.
poudrer, vb. powder.
poudreux, adj. full of powder or dust.

poudrier, n.m. compact (cosmetic).
poudroyer, vb. be dusty.
pouilleux, adj. infected with lice.
poulailler, n.m. hen-house.
poulain, n.m. colt.
poule, n.f. hen, chicken.
poulet, n.m. chicken.
poulette, n.f. pullet.
poulie, n.f. pulley.
poulpe, n.m. octopus.
pouls, n.m. pulse.
poumon, n.m. lung.
poupe, n.f. poop (of ship).
poupée, n.f. doll.
poupin, adj. smart, chic.
pour, prep. for; in order to. p. que, so that.
pourboire, n.m. tip, gratuity.
pourceau, n.m. hog.
pour-cent, n.m. percent.
pourcentage, n.m. percentage.
pourchasser, vb. pursue.
pourfendeur, n.m. killer, bully.
pourparler, n.m. discussion, parley.
pourpoint, n.m. doublet.
pourpre, adj. purple.
pourquoi, adv. why.
pourri, adj. rotten.
pourrir, vb. rot, spoil.
pourriture, n.f. rot.
poursuite, n.f. pursuit.
poursuivant, n.m. one who sues or prosecutes.
poursuivre, vb. pursue, sue, prosecute.
pourtant, adv. however.
pourvoi, n.m. appeal (at court).
pourvoir (de), vb. provide (with), supply. p. à, cater to.
pourvoyeur, n.m. caterer, purveyor.
pourvu que, conj. provided that.
pousse, n.f. shoot, sprouting.
poussée, n.f. push.
pousser, vb. push, urge, drive; grow.
poussier, n.m. coal dust.
poussière, n.f. dust.
poussiéreux, adj. dusty.
poussin, n.m. newly-hatched chick.
poussoir, n.m. push-button.
poutre, n.f. beam.
pouvoir, 1. vb. be able, can, may. 2. n.m. power.
prairie, n.f. meadow.
praline, n.f. burnt almond.
praticable, adj. practicable.
praticien, n.m. practitioner.
pratique, 1. n.f. practice, exercise. 2. adj. practical.
pratiquer, vb. practice, exercise.
pré, n.m. meadow.
préalable, adj. preliminary.
préambule, n.m. preamble.
préau, n.m. yard, as of a prison.
préavis, n.m. advance notice.
précaire, adj. precarious.

précaution, *n.f.* precaution, discretion.

précédent, *n.m.* precedent.

précéder, *vb.* precede; come (go) before.

précepte, *n.m.* precept.

précepteur, *n.m.* tutor.

prêche, *n.m.* sermon; the Protestant religion.

prêcher, *vb.* preach.

précieux, *adj.* precious, valuable.

préciosité, *n.f.* preciosity.

précipice, *n.m.* precipice.

précipitamment, *adv.* headlong.

précipitation, *n.f.* hurry.

précipité, *adj.* hasty.

précipiter, *vb.* precipitate. se p., rush, hasten.

précis, *adj.* precise, exact, accurate.

précisément, *adv.* precisely, definitely, just so.

préciser, *vb.* state.

précision, *n.f.* accuracy, precision.

précité, *adj.* previously cited.

précoce, *adj.* precocious.

précocité, *n.f.* precociousness.

précompter, *vb.* deduct in advance.

préconçu, *adj.* preconceived.

préconiser, *vb.* extol, praise.

préconnaissance, *n.f.* foreknowledge.

précurseur, *n.m.* precursor.

prédécesseur, *n.m.* predecessor.

prédestination, *n.f.* predestination.

prédicateur, *n.m.* preacher.

prédiction, *n.f.* prediction.

prédilection, *n.f.* preference, predilection.

prédire, *vb.* foretell, predict.

prédisposer, *vb.* predispose.

prédisposition, *n.f.* predisposition.

prédominant, *adj.* predominant.

prééminence, *n.f.* preëminence.

préface, *n.f.* preface.

préfecture, *n.f.* prefecture, district.

préférable, *adj.* preferable.

préférence, *n.f.* preference.

préférer, *vb.* prefer.

préfet, *n.m.* prefect.

préfixe, *n.m.* prefix.

préfixer, *vb.* fix in advance.

prégnant, *adj.* pregnant.

préhistorique, *adj.* prehistoric.

préjudice, *n.m.* injury.

préjudiciel, *adj.* interlocutory (as in law).

préjugé, *n.m.* prejudice.

préjuger, *vb.* prejudge.

prélasser, *vb.* se p., bask, lounge.

prélat, *n.m.* prelate.

prélèvement, *n.m.* deduction in advance.

prélever, *vb.* deduct previously.

préliminaire, *adj.* preliminary.

prélude, *n.m.* prelude.

prématuré, *adj.* premature.

préméditation, *n.f.* premeditation.

préméditer, *vb.* premeditate.

prémices, *n.f.pl.* first fruits, first works.

premier, *adj.* first, foremost; early; former.

prémisse, *n.f.* premise.

prémunir, *vb.* warn, take precautions.

prendre, *vb.* take.

prénom, *n.m.* given name.

prénommé, *adj.* previously named.

préoccupation, *n.f.* care, worry.

préoccuper, *vb.* worry.

prépaiement, *n.m.* prepayment.

préparatifs, *n.m.pl.* preparation.

préparation, *n.f.* preparation.

préparatoire, *adj.* preparatory.

préparer, *vb.* prepare.

prépondérance, *n.f.* preponderance.

prépondérant, *adj.* preponderant.

préposé, *n.m.* one in charge.

préposition, *n.f.* preposition.

prérogative, *n.f.* prerogative.

près, 1. *adv.* near. **2.** *prep.* p. de, near. de p., nearby.

présage, *n.m.* omen.

présager, *vb.* (fore)bode.

presbyte, *adj.* far-sighted.

presbytère, *n.m.* parsonage, presbytery.

prescription, *n.f.* prescription.

prescrire, *vb.* prescribe.

préséance, *n.f.* precedence.

présélection, *n.f.* triage.

présence, *n.f.* presence, attendance.

présent, *adj. and n.m.* present.

présentable, *adj.* presentable.

présentation, *n.f.* presentation, introduction.

présentement, *adv.* now, at present.

présenter, *vb.* present, introduce. se p. à l'esprit, come to mind.

préservatif, *adj. and n.m.* preservative.

préservation, *n.f.* preservation.

préserver, *vb.* preserve.

présidence, *n.f.* presidency.

président, *n.m.* president, chairman.

présidente, *n.f.* chairwoman.

présidentiel, *adj.* presidential.

présider, *vb.* preside.

présomptif, *adj.* apparent, presumed.

présomptueux, *adj.* presumptuous.

presque, *adv.* almost, nearly.

presqu'île, *n.f.* peninsula.

pressage, *n.m.* pressing.

pressant, *adj.* urgent.

presse, *n.f.* press, crowd.

pressentiment, *n.m.* foreboding, misgiving.

pressentir, *vb.* foresee.

presse-papiers, *n.m.* paperweight.

presser, *vb.* press; urge; hurry.

pression, *n.f.* pressure.

pressoir, *n.m.* machine or device for squeezing.

pressurer, *vb.* squeeze, put pressure on.

prestance, *n.f.* imposing appearance.

preste, *adj.* dexterous, nimble.

prestesse, *n.f.* vivacity, nimbleness.

prestige, *n.m.* prestige, illusion.

prestigieux, *adj.* enchanting.

présumer, *vb.* presume.

présupposer, *vb.* presuppose.

prêt, 1. *n.m.* loan. **2.** *adj.* ready.

prêtable, *adj.* lendable.

prétendant, *n.m.* claimant.

prétendre, *vb.* claim.

prétendu, *adj.* supposed, so-called.

prétentieux, *adj.* pretentious.

prétention, *n.f.* claim.

prêter, *vb.* lend.

prêteur, *n.m.* lender.

prétexte, *n.m.* pretext.

prétexter, *vb.* pretend, feign.

prêtre, *n.m.* priest.

prêtresse, *n.f.* priestess.

preuve, *n.f.* proof.

preux, *adj. and n.m.* gallant, brave.

prévaloir, *vb.* prevail.

prévenance, *n.f.* attentiveness, obligingness.

prévenant, *adj.* prepossessing, obliging.

prévenir, *vb.* prevent; warn.

préventif, 1. *adj.* preventive. **2.** *n.m.* deterrent.

prévention, *n.f.* bias; prevention.

prévenu, *adj.* partial, biased.

prévision, *n.f.* forecast, expectation.

prévoir, *vb.* foresee.

prévôt, *n.m.* provost.

prévoyance, *n.f.* foresight.

prévoyant, *adj.* farseeing, prudent.

prier, *vb.* beg; pray.

prière, *n.f.* prayer.

prieur, *n.m.* prior.

prieuré, *n.m.* priory.

primaire, *adj.* primary.

primauté, *n.f.* preëminence, primacy.

prime, 1. *n.f.* premium, subsidy, **2.** *adj.* first; accented.

primer, *vb.* outdo, excel.

primeur, *n.f.* freshness, earliness.

primitif, *adj.* primitive; original.

primordial, *adj.* primordial.

prince, *n.m.* prince.

princesse, *n.f.* princess.

princier, *adj.* princely.

principal, *adj.* chief, main, principal.

principauté, *n.f.* principality.

principe, *n.m.* principle.

printanier, *adj.* of spring.

printemps, *n.m.* spring.

priorité, *n.f.* priority.

prisable, *adj.* estimable.

prise, *n.f.* grasp, hold, grip. **p. de courant,** (electric) plug.

prisée, *n.f.* appraisal.

priser, *vb.* appraise.

priseur, *n.m.* auctioneer, appraiser.

prisme, *n.m.* prism.

prison, *n.f.* jail, prison.

prisonnier, *n.m.* prisoner.

privation, *n.f.* privation, want, hardship.

privé, *adj.* private.

priver, *vb.* deprive.

privilège, *n.m.* privilege, license.

privilégier, *vb.* license.

prix, *n.m.* price, charge, fare; prize, award.

prix-courant, *n.m.* list of prices.

probabilité, *n.f.* probability, chances.

probable, *adj.* likely, probable.

probité, *n.f.* probity.

problématique, *adj.* problematical.

problème, *n.m.* problem.

procédé, *n.m.* procedure, process.

procéder, *vb.* proceed.

procédure, *n.f.* proceeding.

procès, *n.m.* trial; (law)suit.

procession, *n.f.* procession.

processionnel, *adj.* processional.

procès-verbal, *n.m.* minutes (of meeting).

prochain, 1. *n.m.* neighbor. 2. *adj.* next.

prochainement, *adv.* soon.

proche, *adj.* near, close.

proclamation, *n.f.* proclamation.

proclamer, *vb.* proclaim.

procréation, *n.f.* procreation.

procurer, *vb.* procure, get.

procureur, *n.m.* attorney.

prodigalement, *adv.* prodigally.

prodigalité, *n.f.* extravagance.

prodige, *n.m.* prodigy.

prodigieux, *adj.* wondrous.

prodigue, *adj.* extravagant, lavish, profuse.

prodiguer, *vb.* lavish.

producteur, *n.m.* producer.

productif, *adj.* productive.

production, *n.f.* production.

productivité, *n.f.* productivity.

produire, *vb.* produce, yield, breed.

produit, *n.m.* product, commodity.

proéminence, *n.f.* prominence.

proéminent, *adj.* prominent, standing out.

profane, *adj.* profane.

profaner, *vb.* misuse, debase, profane.

proférer, *vb.* say, utter.

professer, *vb.* profess.

professeur, *n.m.* professor, teacher.

profession, *n.f.* profession.

professionnel, *adj.* professional.

professoral, *adj.* professorial.

professorat, *n.m.* professorship.

profil (-1), *n.m.* profile.

profiler, *vb.* show a profile of.

profit, *n.m.* profit.

profitable, *adj.* profitable.

profiter, *vb.* profit.

profiteur, *n.m.* profiteer.

profond, *adj.* deep, profound; in-depth.

profondeur, *n.f.* depth.

profus, *adj.* profuse.

profusion, *n.f.* profusion, excess.

progéniture, *n.f.* offspring.

programme, *n.m.* program.

progrès, *n.m.* progress, advance.

progresser, *vb.* progress.

progressif, *adj.* progressive.

progressiste, *n.m.* progressive.

prohiber, *vb.* prohibit.

prohibitif, *adj.* prohibitive.

prohibition, *n.f.* prohibition.

proie, *n.f.* prey.

projecteur, *n.m.* projector.

projectile, *n.m.* missile.

projection, *n.f.* projection.

projet, *n.m.* project. **p. de loi,** bill.

projeter, *vb.* project, plan.

prolétaire, *adj.* and *n.m.* proletarian.

prolétariat, *n.m.* proletariat.

prolifération, *n.f.* proliferation.

prolifique, *adj.* prolific.

prolixe, *adj.* prolix, wordy.

prologue, *n.m.* prologue.

prolongation, *n.f.* extension, prolongation.

prolonger, *vb.* extend, prolong.

promenade, *n.f.* excursion; walk; ride.

promener, *vb.* take out. **se p.** take a walk (ride).

promeneur, *n.m.* walker.

promesse, *n.f.* promise.

promettre, *vb.* promise.

promontoire, *n.m.* promontory.

promoteur, *n.m.* promoter.

promotion, *n.f.* promotion.

promouvoir, *vb.* promote.

prompt, *adj.* prompt.

promptitude, *n.f.* quickness.

promulguer, *vb.* promulgate.

prôner, *vb.* lecture to, praise.

pronom, *n.m.* pronoun.

prononcer, *vb.* pronounce, utter; deliver.

prononciation, *n.f.* pronunciation.

pronostic, *n.m.* prognosis, prediction.

propagande, *n.f.* propaganda.

propagandiste, *n.m.* propagandist.

propagateur, *n.m.* propagator.

propagation, *n.f.* propagation.

propager, *vb.* propagate.

propension, *n.f.* inclination, propensity.

prophète, *n.m.* prophet.

prophétie, *n.f.* prophecy.

prophétique, *adj.* prophetic.

prophétiser, *vb.* prophesy.

propice, *adj.* favorable. **peu p.,** unfavorable.

propitiation, *n.f.* propitiation, conciliation.

proportion, *n.f.* proportion.

proportionné, *adj.* proportionate.

proportionnel, *adj.* proportional.

proportionner, *vb.* keep in proportion.

propos, *n.m.* subject; discourse. **à p.,** relevant. **à p. de,** with regard to.

proposable, *adj.* sutable, appropriate.

proposer, *vb.* propose; move. **se p. de,** intend, mean.

proposition, *n.f.* proposal, proposition.

propre, *adj.* proper; clean, neat: own. **peu p.,** unfit.

propreté, *n.f.* cleanliness, neatness.

propriétaire, *n.m.f.* proprietor.

propriété, *n.f.* property (landed), estate.

propulser, *vb.* push, propel.

propulseur, *n.m.* propeller.

propulsion, *n.f.* propulsion.

proroger, *vb.* postpone, extend time limit.

prosaïque (-zä ëk), *adj.* prosaic.

prosaïsme, *n.m.* prosaicness, dullness.

prosateur, *n.m.* writer of prose.

proscription, *n.f.* proscription.

proscrire, *vb.* outlaw, proscribe.

proscrit, *adj.* and *n.m.* exile(d); forbidden.

prose, *n.f.* prose.

prosodie, *n.f.* prosody.

prospecter, *vb.* search, as for gold.

prospecteur, *n.m.* prospector.

prospère, *adj.* prosperous.

prospérer, *vb.* flourish, thrive, prosper.

prospérité, *n.f.* prosperity.

prosterner, *vb.* prostrate.

prostituée, *n.f.* prostitute.

prostitution, *n.f.* prostitution.

protecteur, 1. *n.m.* protector; patron. 2. *adj.* protective.

protecteur du citoyen, *n.m.* ombudsman (in Quebec).

protection, *n.f.* protection.

protectorat, *n.m.* protectorate.

protéger, *vb.* protect, patronize, foster.

protéine, *n.f.* protein.

protestant, *adj.* and *n.m.* Protestant.

protestantisme, *n.m.* Protestantism.
protestation, *n.f.* protest.
protester. *vb.* protest.
protêt, *n.m.* protest.
prothèse, *n.f.* artificial aid, as a denture.
protocole, *n.m.* protocol.
protubérance, *n.f.* protuberance.
proue, *n.f.* prow, front.
prouesse, *n.f.* prowess.
prouver, *vb.* prove.
provenance, *n.f.* place of origin; product.
provençal, 1. *adj.* of Provence. **2.** *n.m.* language of Provence.
provende, *n.f.* provender, foodstuffs.
provenir, *vb.* come from.
proverbe, *n.m.* proverb, saying.
proverbial, *adj.* proverbial.
providence, *n.f.* providence.
providentiel, *adj.* providential.
province, *n.f.* province.
provincial, *adj. and n.m.* provincial.
provincialisme, *n.m.* provincialism.
provision, *n.f.* supply, store, provision.
provisoire, *adj.* temporary.
provocateur, *n.m.* one who provokes action.
provocation, *n.f.* provocation.
provoquer, *vb.* provoke.
proximité, *n.f.* closeness, proximity.
prude, 1. *n.f.* prude. **2.** *adj.* like a prude.
prudence, *n.f.* caution, prudence.
prudent, *adj.* cautious, prudent.
pruderie, *n.f.* prudishness.
prune, *n.f.* plum.
pruneau, *n.m.* prune.
prunelle, *n.f.* pupil (of eye).
prunier, *n.m.* plum tree.
Prusse, *n.f.* Prussia.
Prussien, *n.m.* Prussian.
prussien, *adj.* Prussian.
psalmiste, *n.m.* psalmist.
psaume, *n.m.* psalm.
psautier, *n.m.* psalm book.
pseudonyme, *n.m.* pseudonym.
psychanalyse (-k-), *n.f.* psychoanalysis.
psychédélique (-k), *adj.* psychedelic.
psychiatre (-k-), *n.m.* psychiatrist.
psychiatrie (-k-), *n.f.* psychiatry.
psychique (-k), *adj.* psychic.
psychologie (-k-), *n.f.* psychology.
psychologique (-k-), *adj.* psychological.
psychologue (-k-), *n.m.* psychologist.
psychose (-k-), *n.f.* psychosis.
puant, *adj.* foul, shameful.
puberté, *n.f.* puberty.

public, 1. *adj. m.,* **publique** *f.* public. **2.** *n.m.* public.
publication, *n.f.* publication.
publiciste, *n.m.* publicist.
publicité, *n.f.* publicity, advertisement(s).
publier, *vb.* publish, issue.
puce, *n.f.* flea.
pucelle, *n.f.* young girl, virgin.
pudeur, *n.f.* modesty.
pudique, *adj.* modest.
puer, *vb.* smell, have an offensive odor.
puéril (-l), *adj.* childish.
pugiliste, *m.* boxer.
puîné, *adj.* younger (of a brother or sister).
puis, *adv.* then.
puisard, *n.m.* cesspool.
puisatier, *n.m.* well-digger.
puiser, *vb.* draw up, derive.
puisque, *conj.* since, as.
puissamment, *adv.* very, powerfully.
puissance, *n.f.* power.
puissant, *adj.* potent, powerful, mighty.
puits (pwē), *n.m.* well; shaft.
pulluler, *vb.* breed abundantly, multiply.
pulmonaire, *adj.* pulmonary.
pulpe, *n.f.* pulp.
pulpeux, *adj.* pulpy.
pulsar, *n.m.* pulsar.
pulsation, *n.f.* pulsation, beating.
pulvérisateur, *n.m.* vaporizer, spray.
pulvériser, *vb.* spray, pulverize.
punaise, *n.f.* bedbug.
punir, *vb.* punish.
punitif, *adj.* punitive.
punition, *n.f.* punishment.
pupille (-l), *n.m.f.* ward: pupil (of the eye).
pupitre, *n.m.* desk.
pur, *adj.* pure.
purée, *n.f.* mash.
purement, *adv.* purely, solely.
pureté, *n.f.* purity.
purgatoire, *n.m.* purgatory.
purge, *n.f.* purge.
purger, *vb.* purge.
purification, *n.f.* purification.
purifier, *vb.* purify, cleanse.
puritain, *adj. and n.m.* Puritan.
purulent, *adj.* purulent.
pustule, *n.f.* pimple.
putois, *n.m.* skunk, polecat.
putréfier, *vb.* corrupt, rot, spoil.
putride, *adj.* putrid.
pygmée, *n.m.* Pygmy.
pyjama, *n.m.* pajamas.
pyramidal, *adj.* pyramidal, overwhelming.
pyramide, *n.f.* pyramid.

Q

quadrangle (kw-), *n.m.* quadrangle.

quadrillé, *adj.* checked, ruled off.
quadriphonique (kw-), *adj.* quadraphonic.
quadrupède (kw-), *n.m. and adj.* quadruped.
quadruple (kw-), *adj.* quadruple.
quai, *n.m.* pier, dock; (station) platform.
qualification, *n.f.* qualification.
qualifier, *vb.* qualify.
qualité, *n.f.* quality, nature, grade.
quand, *adv.* when.
quant à, *prep.* as to, as for.
quantité, *n.f.* amount, quantity.
quarantaine, *n.f.* quarantine.
quarante, *adj. and n.m.* forty.
quart, *n.m.* fourth, quarter.
quartier, *n.m.* district, quarter. **q. général,** headquarters.
quartz (kw-), *n.m.* quartz.
quasar, (kw-), *n.m.* quasar.
quasi, *adv.* nearly, quasi.
quatorze, *adj. and n.m.* fourteen.
quatrain, *n.m.* quatrain.
quatre, *adj. and n.m.* four.
quatre-vingt-dix, *adj. and n.m.* ninety.
quatre-vingts, *adj. and n.m.* eighty.
quatrième, *adj. and n.* fourth.
quatuor (kw-), *n.m.* quartet.
que, 1. *pron.* whom, which, that. **2.** *conj.* that, than.
quel, *adj.* which, what; of what kind.
quelconque, *adj.* of any kind.
quelque, *adj.* some, any. **q. chose,** something. **q. part,** somewhere.
quelquefois, *adv.* sometimes.
quelques, *adj.* a few.
quelques-uns, *pron.* a few.
quelqu'un, *pron.* somebody.
querelle, *n.f.* quarrel.
quereller, *vb.* quarrel (with); scold.
querelleur, 1. *n.m.* quarreler. **2.** *adj.* inclined to quarrel.
question, *n.f.* question, issue, matter.
questionner, *vb.* question.
quête, *n.f.* quest, seeking.
quêter, *vb.* seek, look for.
queue (kœ), *n.f.* tail; line. **faire la q.,** stand in line.
qui, 1. *interr. pron.* who, whom. **2.** *rel. pron.* who, which. **q. que,** whoever.
quiconque, *pron.* whoever.
quignon, *n.m.* large piece of bread.
quincaillerie, *n.f.* hardware.
quinine, *n.f.* quinine.
quintal, *n.m.* unit of weight (100 kilograms).
quinze, *adj. and n.m.* fifteen.
quinzième, *adj. and n.m.* fifteenth.
quittance, *n.f.* receipt.

quitte, *adj.* free, quit, released.
quitter, *vb.* quit, leave.
quoi, *pron. and interj.* what.
quoique, *conj.* though.
quote-part, *n.f.* quota.
quotidien, *adj.* daily.

R

rabais, *n.m.* reduction.
rabaisser, *vb.* diminish, lower.
rabattre, *vb.* put down, suppress, quell.
rabbin, *n.m.* rabbi.
rabbinique, *adj.* rabbinical.
rabot, *n.m.* plane.
raboter, *vb.* plane, perfect.
roboteux, *adj.* rugged.
rabougri, *adj.* puny, stunted.
raccommodage, *n.m.* fixing, mending.
raccommoder, *vb.* mend.
raccorder, *vb.* join, bring together.
raccourcir, *vb.* shorten, curtail.
raccourcissement, *n.m.* shortening, curtailing.
raccrocher, *vb.* hook up; recover.
race, *n.f.* race.
rachat, *n.m.* redemption.
racheter, *vb.* redeem.
rachitique, *adj.* rickety, affected with rickets.
rachitisme, *n.m.* rickets.
racine, *n.f.* root.
raclage, *n.m.* action of scraping.
racler, *vb.* scrape.
racoler, *vb.* recruit, esp. by fraud.
raconter, *vb.* tell, narrate, recount.
raconteur, *n.m.* story-teller.
radar, *n.m.* radar.
radeau, *n.m.* raft.
radiant, *adj.* radiant.
radiateur, *n.m.* radiator.
radical, *adj. and n.m.* radical.
radier, *vb.* radiate; erase.
radieux, *adj.* radiant, beaming, glorious.
radio, *n.f.* radio; wireless.
radio-actif, *adj.* radioactive.
radiodiffuser, *vb.* broadcast.
radio-émission, *n.f.* broadcast.
radiogramme, *n.m.* radiogram.
radiographie, *n.f.* radiography.
radis, *n.m.* radish.
radium, *n.m.* radium.
radoter, *vb.* babble, drivel.
radoub, *n.m.* refitting (of ship).
radoucir, *vb.* quiet, soften, appease.
rafale, *n.f.* blast, gust, squall.
raffermir, *vb.* make stronger or more secure.
raffinement, *n.m.* refinement.
raffiner, *vb.* refine.
raffinerie, *n.f.* refinery.
raffoler, *vb.* dote on, be mad about.
rafistoler, *vb.* mend, patch.

rafler, *vb.* carry off.
rafraîchir, *vb.* refresh.
rafraîchissement, *n.m.* refreshment.
rage, *n.f.* rage, fury.
rager, *vb.* be angry, rage.
rageur, *n.m.* irritable person.
ragoût, *n.m.* stew.
ragoûtant, *adj.* tasty, pleasing.
ragréer, *vb.* refinish, renovate.
raid, *n.m.* raid.
raide, *adj.* stiff; taut; steep.
raideur, *n.f.* stiffness.
raidir, *vb.* stiffen.
raie, *n.f.* streak; part (in hair).
raifort, *n.m.* horseradish.
rail, *n.m.* rail.
railler, *vb.* make fun of.
raillerie, *n.f.* jesting.
railleur, *n.m.* scoffer, jester.
rainure, *n.f.* groove.
rais, *n.m.* ray, spoke.
raisin, *n.m.* grape(s). r. sec, raisin.
raison, *n.f.* reason, judgment. avoir r., be right.
raisonnable, *adj.* reasonable, rational.
raisonnement, *n.m.* reason, argument.
raisonner, *vb.* reason.
rajeunir, *vb.* rejuvenate.
rajuster, *vb.* readjust.
râle, *n.m.* rail (bird); rattle in throat.
ralentir, *vb.* slacken, slow down.
râler, *vb.* rattle (in dying).
rallier, *vb.* rally.
rallonger, *vb.* make an addition to, lengthen.
ramage, *n.m.* flower pattern; chirping; babble.
ramasse, *adj.* thick-set, dumpy.
ramasser, *vb.* pick up.
ramasseur, *n.m.* collector.
rame, *n.f.* oar.
rameau, *n.m.* branch.
ramener, *vb.* bring (take) back.
rameneur, *n.m.* restorer.
ramer, *vb.* row.
rameur, *n.m.* rower.
ramifier, *vb.* divide into branches, ramify.
ramille, *n.f.* twig.
ramollir, *vb.* soften, weaken.
rampe, *n.f.* banister; ramp.
ramper, *vb.* crawl, creep.
rance, *adj. and n.m.* rancid, rancidness.
rancoeur, *n.f.* rancor.
rançon, *n.f.* ransom.
rancune, *n.f.* grudge, spite, rancor. garder de la r., bear a grudge.
rancunier, *adj.* rancorous, bitter.
rang, *n.m.* row; rank.
rangée, *n.f.* file, row.
ranger, *vb.* rank, array, (ar)range.
rapace, *adj.* predatory, greedy.
râpe, *n.f.* file, rasp.
râper, *vb.* grate.

rapide, 1. *n.m.* rapid. **2.** *adj.* rapid, fast, quick.
rapidité, *n.f.* rapidity.
rapiécer, *vb.* patch.
rapière, *n.f.* rapier.
rapin, *n.m.* art student, pupil.
rapiner, *vb.* plunder, rob.
rappel, *n.m.* recall, repeal, reminder.
rappeler, *vb.* recall, remind. se r., remember.
rapport, *n.m.* report; relation.
rapporter, *vb.* bring back; report. se r. à, relate to, refer to.
rapporteur, *n.m.* reporter, tattle-tale.
rapprochement, *n.m.* bringing close, junction.
rapprocher, *vb.* bring together. se r. de, approximate.
rapt, *n.m.* rape, kidnapping.
raquette, *n.f.* racket.
rare, *adj.* scarce, rare.
raréfier, *vb.* rarefy.
rarement, *adv.* seldom.
rareté, *n.f.* rarity, uniqueness, scarcity.
ras, *adj.* smooth-shaven, open.
raser, *vb.* shave.
rasoir, *n.m.* razor.
rassasier, *vb.* cloy, sate.
rassemblement, *n.m.* rally.
rassembler, *vb.* gather, congregate, muster.
rasseoir, *vb.* reseat. se r., be seated again.
rasséréner, *vb.* clear up (weather).
rassis, *adj.* stale.
rassurer, *vb.* reassure, comfort.
rat, *n.m.* rat.
ratatiner, *vb.* shrivel, shrink.
rate, *n.f.* spleen.
râteau, *n.m.* rake.
râteler, *vb.* rake.
râtelier, *n.m.* rack.
rater, *vb.* miss.
ratière, *n.f.* rat trap.
ratifier, *vb.* ratify.
ration, *n.f.* ration.
rationnel, *adj.* rational.
rationnement, *n.m.* rationing.
rationner, *vb.* ration.
ratissoire, *n.f.* scraper, rake.
rattacher, *vb.* fasten.
rattraper, *vb.* overtake.
rature, *n.f.* erasure.
raturer, *vb.* erase, blot out.
rauque, *adj.* hoarse, raucous.
ravage, *n.m.* havoc.
ravager, *vb.* lay waste.
ravauder, *vb.* mend, patch.
ravigoter, *vb.* enliven, refresh.
ravin, *n.m.* ravine.
ravir, *vb.* ravish; delight.
ravissant, *adj.* ravishing, charming; ravenous.
ravissement, *n.m.* rapture.
ravisseur, *n.m.* ravisher, robber.
raviver, *vb.* revive.
rayer, *vb.* streak; cross out.
rayon, *n.m.* ray, beam; shelf. r. X, X-ray.

rayonnant, adj. beaming.
rayonne, n.f. rayon.
rayonnement, n.m. radiation; radiance.
rayonner, vb. radiate, beam.
rayure, n.f. streak, blemish.
re-, ré-, prefix. re-, again.
réabonnement, n.m. renewal of subscription.
réabonner, vb. renew, resubscribe.
réaction, n.f. reaction. avion à r., jet-plane.
reactionnaire, adj. and n. reactionary.
réagir, vb. react.
réalisable, adj. realizable.
réalisation, n.f. attainment, carrying out.
réaliser, vb. realize. se r., materialize.
réaliste, 1. n.m.f. realist. 2. adj. realist, realistic.
réalité, n.f. reality.
réassurer, vb. reinsure.
rébarbatif, adj. forbidding.
rebattre, vb. repeat, beat again.
rebattu, adj. trite.
rebelle, 1. n.m.f. rebel. 2. adj. rebel, rebellious.
rebeller, vb. se r., rebel.
rébellion, n.f. rebellion.
rebondi, adj. plump.
rebondir, vb. bounce.
rebord, n.m. border, edge.
rebuffade, n.f. rebuff, rebuke.
rebut, n.m. trash, refuse, junk, rubbish.
rebuter, vb. rebuke, discard.
recéler, vb. accept stolen goods, hide.
récemment, adv. recently.
recensement, n.m. census.
recenser, vb. make a census.
récent, adj. recent.
réceptacle, n.m. receptacle.
récepteur, n.m. receiver.
réceptif, adj. receptive.
réception, n.f. reception, receipt.
recette, n.f. recipe, receipt; (pl.) returns.
receveur, n.m. conductor; receiver.
recevoir, vb. receive, get; entertain.
réchapper, vb. escape, get out.
réchaud, n.m. food warmer, chafing dish.
réchauffer, vb. warm again, excite.
recherche, n.f. inquiry, (re)search; quest.
rechercher, vb. seek again, investigate.
rechute, n.f. relapse.
récif, n.m. reef.
récipient, n.m. container.
réciproque, adj. mutual.
récit, n.m. account.
réciter, vb. recite, tell.
réclamation, n.f. complaint.
réclame, n.f. advertisement.
réclamer, vb. claim, demand.

reclus, 1. adj. withdrawn, secluded. 2. n.m. recluse.
réclusion, n.f. (solitary) confinement.
recoin, n.m. recess, corner.
récolte, n.f. crop, harvest.
récolter, vb. harvest, gather.
recommandable, adj. advisable.
recommandation, n.f. recommendation.
recommander, vb. recommend; register (letter).
recommencer, vb. start again.
récompense, n.f. reward.
récompenser, vb. reward.
réconcilier, vb. reconcile.
reconduire, vb. accompany, show out, dismiss.
reconnaissance, n.f. recognition; gratitude.
reconnaissant, adj. grateful.
reconnaître, vb. recognize; admit, acknowledge.
reconstituer, vb. rebuild, restore.
recourir, vb. resort (to).
recours, n.m. resort, recourse. avoir r. à, resort to; appeal to.
recouvrement, n.m. recovery.
recouvrer, vb. recover, retrieve.
recouvrir, vb. re-cover, cover completely.
récréation, n.f. amusement.
récréer, vb. entertain. se r., amuse oneself.
recrue, n.f. recruit.
recruter, vb. recruit.
rectangle, n.m. rectangle.
recteur, n.m. rector.
rectifier, vb. rectify, correct.
reçu, n.m. receipt.
recueil, n.m. collection, compilation.
recueillir, vb. gather, collect, glean.
recul, n.m. kick, recoil.
reculade, n.f. backing, retreat.
reculer, vb. recoil, draw back, go back.
récuser, vb. challenge, reject.
recycler, vb. recycle.
rédacteur, n.m. editor.
rédaction, n.f. editorial staff.
reddition, n.f. surrendering.
rédemption, n.f. redemption.
rédiger, vb. draw up.
redingote, n.f. frock-coat.
redire, vb. repeat, echo, reveal.
redoutable, adj. redoubtable, alarming.
redouter, vb. dread.
redresser, vb. straighten.
réduction, n.f. reduction, decrease, cut.
réduire, vb. reduce. se r. à, amount to.
réduit, n.m. retreat, hovel.
réel, adj. real, actual.
réfection, n.f. reconstruction; refreshments.
réfectoire, n.m. dining-room.
référence, n.f. reference.
référer, vb. refer.
refermer, vb. close up or again.

réfléchir, vb. reflect, consider, ponder.
reflet, n.m. reflection.
refléter, vb. reflect.
réflexe, adj. and n.m. reflex.
réflexion, n.f. reflection, consideration, thought.
refluer, vb. return to source, ebb.
reflux, n.m. ebb.
refondre, vb. cast again; remodel, improve.
réformateur, 1. adj. reforming. 2. n.m. reformer, crusader.
réforme, n.f. reform, reformation.
réformer, vb. reform.
refoulement, n.m. forcing back, retreat.
refouler, vb. drive back, repel.
réfractaire, adj. refractory.
rafraîchir, vb. freshen.
réfrigérant, n.m. refrigerator.
réfrigérer, vb. put under refrigeration.
refroidir, vb. chill, cool.
refroidissement, n.m. cooling, refrigeration, chill.
refuge, n.m. refuge.
réfugié, n.m. refugee.
réfugier, vb. se r., take refuge.
refus, n.m. refusal, denial.
refuser, vb. refuse, withhold, deny.
réfutation, n.f. rebuttal.
réfuter, vb. disprove, refute.
regagner, vb. regain, recover.
regain, n.m. regrowth, renewal.
régal, n.m. feast, repast.
régaler, vb. entertain, treat.
regard, n.m. look.
regarder, vb. look (at); concern.
régence, n.f. regency.
régénérer, vb. regenerate.
régent, adj. and n.m. regent.
régenter, vb. direct, dominate.
régime, n.m. diet; government; direction.
régiment, n.m. regiment.
région, n.f. area, region.
régional, adj. regional.
régir, vb. rule.
régisseur, n.m. manager.
registre, n.m. register, record.
règle, n.f. rule; ruler.
règlement, n.m. regulation; settlement.
réglementaire, adj. according to regulations.
régler, vb. regulate; rule; settle.
règne, n.m. reign.
régner, vb. reign.
régression, n.f. regression.
regret, n.m. regret.
regrettable, adj. regrettable.
regretter, vb. regret, be sorry for.
régulariser, vb. regularize.
régularité, n.f. regularity.
régulateur, n.m. regulator.
régulier, adj. regular.
réhabiliter, vb. rehabilitate.
rehausser, vb. enhance.

rein, n.m. kidney; (pl.) loins, back.

reine, n.f. queen.

réitérer, vb. reiterate.

rejet, n.m. rejection.

rejeter, vb. reject.

rejeton, n.m. plant shoot; scion.

rejoindre, vb. rejoin; catch up with, overtake.

réjouir, vb. rejoice, delight, cheer up.

réjouissance, n.f. festivity.

relâché, adj. loose.

relâcher, vb. relax, slacken.

relais, n.m. relay.

relater, vb. relate.

relatif, adj. relative.

relation, n.f. relation, connection.

relaxation, n.f. relaxation, release.

relayer, vb. relay.

reléguer, vb. relegate, banish.

relève, n.f. (mil.) relief, replacement.

relèvement, n.m. bearing.

relever, vb. lift; relieve; point out.

relief, n.m. relief. mettre en r., emphasize.

relier, vb. bind; link.

relieur, n.m. binder, esp. of books.

religieuse, n.f. nun.

religieux, adj. religious.

religion, n.f. religion.

reliquaire, n.m. receptacle for relic.

relique, n.f. relic.

reliure, n.f. binding.

reluire, vb. shine, glisten.

remanier, vb. redo, modify.

remarquable, adj. remarkable, noticeable.

remarque, n.f. remark.

remarquer, vb. remark; notice.

rembarrer, vb. drive back; put in one's place.

remblai, n.m. embankment.

remboursement, n.m. refund.

rembourser, vb. repay, refund.

remède, n.m. remedy, cure.

remédiable, adj. remediable.

remédier à, vb. remedy.

remerciement, n.m. thanks.

remercier, vb. thank.

remettre, vb. put back; restore; remit; pardon; deliver. se r., recover.

remise, n.f. discount; delivery.

rémission, n.f. remission.

remontrance, n.f. remonstrance.

remontrer, vb. show anew, point out error.

remords (-môr), n.m. remorse.

remorquer, vb. tow.

remorqueur, n.m. tug(boat).

rémouleur, n.m. sharpener, grinder.

remous, n.m. eddy.

rempart, n.m. bulwark, rampart.

remplaçant, n.m. substitute.

remplacer, vb. replace, substitute.

rempli, vb. tuck, hitch.

remplier, vb. take a tuck in.

remplir, vb. fill; carry out; crowd.

remporter, vb. take away, bring back.

remuer, vb. stir. se r., bustle.

renaissance, n.f. rebirth, revival.

renaître, vb. be reborn, get new life.

renard, n.m. fox; sly person.

rencontre, n.f. meeting. aller à la r. de, go to meet.

rencontrer, vb. meet; come across.

rendement, n.m. output.

rendez-vous, n.m. date, appointment.

rendre, vb. give back; repay; surrender. se r. compte de, realize.

rendu, adj. tired out, all in.

rêne, n.f. rein.

rené, adj. born-again.

renégat, adj. and n.m. renegade.

renfermer, vb. enclose.

renfler, vb. swell, inflate.

renforcer, vb. reinforce.

renfort, n.m. reinforcement, aid.

renfrogner, vb. se r. scowl, frown.

rengaine, n.f. often-told story.

renne, n.m. reindeer.

renom, n.m. renown, repute.

renommée, n.f. fame, renown.

renoncer à, vb. renounce, give up, forego.

renonciation, n.f. renunciation.

renouement, n.m. renewing, retying.

renouveau, n.m. springtime.

renouveler, vb. renew, renovate.

renouvellement, n.m. renewal.

renseignements, n.m.pl. information.

renseigner, vb. inform. se r., inquire.

rente, n.f. income; interest; annuity.

rentier, n.m. one who lives off interest on investments.

rentrée, n.f. return.

rentrer, vb. go back, go home.

renversant, adj. amazing, overwhelming.

renverser, vb. overthrow, overturn; reverse.

renvoi, n.m. dismissal; return.

renvoyer, vb. send back, return; dismiss.

repaire, n.m. den, animal's lair.

repaître, vb. feed, feast.

répandre, vb. diffuse, scatter, spill.

répandu, adj. prevalent, widespread.

reparaître, vb. reappear.

réparateur, n.m. restorer, repairer.

réparation, n.f. repair; amends.

réparer, vb. repair, make up for, make amends for.

repartie, n.f. reply, quick retort.

repartir, vb. leave again; retort.

répartir, vb. apportion, allot, distribute.

repas, n.m. meal.

repasser, vb. press; pass; look over.

repentir, 1. n.m. repentance. 2. vb. se r., repent.

répercussion, n.f. repercussion.

répercuter, vb. reverberate, echo.

repère, n.m. guiding mark.

répertoire, n.m. list, repertory.

répéter, vb. repeat; rehearse.

répétition, n.f. repetition.

répit, n.m. respite.

replacer, vb. replace.

replier, vb. fold again or up.

réplique, n.f. rejoinder; cue.

répliquer, vb. rejoin.

répondant, n.m. respondent, bail.

répondre, vb. answer, reply. r. de, vouch for.

réponse, n.f. answer, reply.

report, n.m. (in bookkeeping) amount brought forward.

reportage, n.m. reporting.

reporter, 1. n.m. reporter. 2. vb. carry or take back.

repos, n.m. rest.

reposer, vb. rest, repose.

repousser, vb. push back, repel; spurn.

repoussoir, n.m. foil.

répréhensible, adj. objectionable.

répréhension, n.f. reprehension, censure.

reprendre, vb. take back, resume.

représailles, n.f.pl. retaliation.

représentant, n.m. representative.

représentatif, adj. representative.

représentation, n.f. representation, performance.

représenter, adj. represent.

répressif, adj. repressive.

répression, n.f. repression.

réprimande, n.f. reproof, rebuke, reprimand.

réprimander, vb. chide, reprove, reprimand.

réprimer, vb. quell.

reprise, n.f. recovery; turn; darn. à plusieurs r.s, repeatedly.

repriser, vb. darn.

réprobation, n.f. reprobation.

reproche, n.m. reproach.

reprocher, vb. reproach.

reproduction, n.f. reproduction.

reproduction exacte, n.f. clone.

reproduire, vb. reproduce.

réprouver, vb. censure.

reptile, n.m. reptile.

républicain, *adj. and n.m.* republican.

république, *n.f.* republic.

répudier, *vb.* repudiate.

répugnance, *n.f.* repugnance.

répulsion, *n.f.* repulsion.

réputation, *n.f.* reputation.

réputer, *vb.* consider, esteem.

requête, *n.f.* request, plea.

requin, *n.m.* shark.

requis, *adj.* required, necessary.

réquisition, *n.f.* requisition.

rescousse, *n.f.* rescue.

réseau, *n.m.* network.

réserve, *n.f.* reserve, reservation; qualification. **de r.,** spare, extra.

réservé, *adj.* aloof, reticent.

réserver, *vb.* reserve.

réserviste, *n.f.* reservist *(mil.).*

réservoir, *n.m.* tank, reservoir.

résidant, *adj.* resident.

résidence, *n.f.* residence, dwelling.

résider, *vb.* reside.

résidu, *n.m.* residue.

résignation, *n.f.* resignation.

résigner, *vb.* resign.

résiliation, *n.f.* cancelling.

résine, *n.f.* resin.

résistance, *n.f.* endurance, resistance.

résister (à), *vb.* resist.

résolu, *adj.* resolute.

résolument, *adv.* resolutely.

résolution, *n.f.* resolution.

résonnance, *n.f.* resonnance.

résonnant, *adj.* resonant.

résonner, *vb.* resound.

résoudre, *vb.* resolve, solve.

respect (-spè), *n.m.* respect.

respectable, *adj.* decent, respectable.

respecter, *vb.* respect.

respectif, *adj.* respective.

respectueux, *adj.* respectful.

respiration, *n.f.* respiration, breathing.

respirer, *vb.* breathe.

resplendir, *vb.* gleam resplendently.

responsabilité, *n.f.* responsibility.

responsable, *adj.* responsible; accountable, liable.

ressaisir, *vb.* regain possession.

ressemblance, *n.f.* likeness.

ressembler (à), *vb.* resemble. se r., look alike.

ressentiment, *n.m.* resentment.

ressentir, *vb.* feel, resent, show.

resserrer, *vb.* tighten, compress.

ressort, *n.m.* spring, elasticity.

ressortir, *vb.* stand out.

ressource, *n.f.* resort, resource.

ressusciter, *vb.* revive, resuscitate.

restaurant, *n.m.* restaurant.

restaurateur, *n.m.* restorer; restaurant man.

restauration, *n.f.* restoration.

restaurer, *vb.* restore.

reste, *n.m.* remainder, rest, remnant.

rester, *vb.* remain, stay.

restituer, *vb.* give back, restore.

restreindre, *vb.* restrict.

restrictif, *adj.* restrictive.

restriction, *n.f.* restriction.

résultat, *n.m.* outcome, upshot, result.

résulter, *vb.* result.

résumé, *n.m.* summing up.

résumer, *vb.* sum up.

rétablir, *vb.* restore, reëstablish. se r., recover.

rétablissement, *n.m.* recovery.

retard, *n.m.* delay. en r., late; slow.

retarder, *vb.* delay, retard; be slow.

retenir, *vb.* retain; keep; hold (back); detain. se r. de, refrain from.

rétentif, *adj.* retentive.

retentir, *vb.* resound.

retentissant, *adj.* reëchoing.

réticence, *n.f.* silence, reticence.

retirer, *vb.* withdraw. se r., retire, retreat.

retoucher, *vb.* retouch, alter.

retour, *n.m.* return. de r., back.

retourner, *vb.* go back, invert, return. se r., turn around.

retrait, *n.m.* contraction, retraction.

retraite, *n.f.* retreat; privacy.

retrancher, *vb.* cut off, curtail.

rétrécir, *vb.* shrink, contract.

rétribution, *n.f.* salary, recompense.

retrousser, *vb.* turn up.

retrouver, *vb.* find; recover.

réunion, *n.f.* meeting, convention, reunion.

réunir, *vb.* unite. se r., assemble.

réussir, *vb.* succeed.

réussite, *n.f.* successful outcome.

revanche, *n.f.* revenge. en r., in return.

rêve, *n.m.* dream.

réveil, *n.m.* awaking; revival.

réveiller, *vb.* wake (up), rouse, arouse.

révélateur, **1.** *adj.* revealing. **2.** *n.m.* revealer.

révélation, *n.f.* revelation.

révéler, *vb.* disclose, reveal.

revenant, *n.m.* ghost, specter.

revendeur, *n.m.* retailer, old-clothes dealer.

revendiquer, *vb.* claim.

revenir, *vb.* come back, return, recur; amount to.

revenu, *n.m.* income, revenue.

rêver, *vb.* dream.

réverbérer, *vb.* reverberate.

révéremment, *adv.* reverently.

révérence, *n.f.* reverence; bow, curtsy.

révérend, *adj.* reverend.

révérer, *vb.* revere.

rêverie, *n.f.* dreaming, reverie.

revers, *n.m.* reverse, wrong side; lapel.

revêtir, *vb.* clothe; assume.

rêveur, **1.** *n.m.* dreamer. **2.** *adj.* pensive.

réviser, *vb.* revise.

réviseur, *n.m.* reviser, inspector.

révision, *n.f.* revision, review.

revivre, *vb.* revive.

révocation, *n.f.* revocation, annulment.

revoir, *vb.* see again. au r., good-bye.

révolte, *n.f.* revolt.

révolter, *vb.* se r., revolt.

révolution, *n.f.* revolution, turn.

révolutionnaire, *adj. and n.m.* revolutionary.

revolver, *n.m.* revolver.

révoquer, *vb.* revoke.

revue, *n.f.* review, magazine.

rez-de-chaussée, *n.m.* ground floor.

rhétorique, *n.f.* rhetoric.

rhinocéros, *n.m.* rhinoceros.

rhubarbe, *n.f.* rhubarb.

rhum, *n.m.* rum.

rhumatisme, *n.m.* rheumatism.

rhume, *n.m.* cold.

ricaner, *vb.* laugh objectionably.

riche, *adj.* rich, wealthy.

richesse, *n.f.* wealth.

ricocher, *vb.* ricochet, spring back.

rictus, *n.m.* grin.

ride, *n.f.* wrinkle, ripple.

rideau, *n.m.* curtain.

rider, *vb.* ripple, wrinkle.

ridicule, **1.** *n.m.* ridicule. **2.** *adj.* ridiculous.

ridiculiser, *vb.* ridicule.

rien, *pron.* nothing.

rieur, *n.m.* laugher.

rigide, *adj.* rigid.

rigidité, *n.f.* rigidity.

rigole, *n.f.* ditch, gutter.

rigoureux, *adj.* rigorous.

rigueur, *n.f.* rigor.

rime, *n.f.* rhyme.

rimer, *vb.* rhyme.

rince-doigts, *n.m.* finger bowl.

rincer, *vb.* rinse.

ripaille, *n.f.* feasting, revelry.

riposte, *n.f.* retort.

rire, **1.** *n.m.* laugh, laughter. **2.** *vb.* laugh.

ris, *n.m.* laugh; reef in a sail; sweetbread.

risée, *n.f.* laugh, mocking.

risible, *adj.* laughable.

risque, *n.m.* risk.

risquer, *vb.* risk.

risque-tout, *n.m.* daredevil.

rissoler, *vb.* brown, as in cooking.

rite, *n.m.* rite.

rituel, *adj.* ritual.

rivage, *n.m.* shore, bank.

rival, *adj. and n.m.* rival.

rivaliser, *vb.* compete, rival.

rivalité, *n.f.* rivalry.

rive, *n.f.* bank.

river, vb. clinch.
rivet, n.m. rivet.
rivière, n.f. river.
rixe, n.f. brawl.
riz, n.m. rice.
rizière, n.f. rice field.
robe, n.f. dress, gown, frock, robe.
robinet, n.m. faucet, tap.
robuste, adj. hardy, strong, robust.
roc, n.m. rock.
rocailleux, adj. rocky, rough.
rocher, n.m. rock.
rocheux, adj. rocky.
rock, adj. rock (music).
rôder, vb. prowl.
rôdeur, n.m. prowler.
rogner, vb. pare, trim down.
rognon, n.m. kidney.
rogue, adj. proud, arrogant.
roi, n.m. king.
rôle, n.m. role, part.
Romain, n.m. Roman.
romain, adj. Roman.
roman, n.m. novel.
romance, n.f. ballad.
romancier, n.m. novelist.
romanesque, adj. romantic.
roman-feuilleton, n.m. serial.
romanichel, n.m. gypsy.
romantique, adj. romantic.
romarin, n.m. rosemary.
rompre, vb. break.
ronce, n.f. bramble.
rond, 1. n.m. round; circle. 2. adj. round.
ronde, n.f. round, patrol.
rondeur, n.f. roundness.
ronflement, n.m. snoring, roar.
ronfler, vb. snore.
ronger, vb. gnaw; fret.
rongeur, adj. and n.m. rodent.
ronronner, vb. purr, murmur.
rosaire, n.m. rosary.
rosbif, n.m. roast beef.
rose, 1. n.f. rose. 2. adj. pink.
roseau, n.m. reed.
rosée, n.f. dew.
rosier, n.m. rosebush.
rossignol, n.m. nightingale.
rôt, n.m. roast (meat).
rotation, n.f. rotation.
rotatoire, adj. rotary.
roter, vb. belch.
rôti, n.m. roast.
rôtir, vb. roast.
rotondité, n.f. rotundity.
rotule, n.f. kneecap.
roturier, adj. commonplace, vulgar.
roublardise, n.f. cunningness.
roue, n.f. wheel.
roué, 1. n.m. rake, debauchee. 2. adj. crafty.
rouge, 1. n.m. rouge. 2. adj. red. r. foncé, maroon.
rouge-gorge, n.m. robin.
rougeole, n.f. measles.
rougeur, n.f. flush, blush.
rougir, vb. blush.
rouille, n.f. rust.
rouiller, vb. rust.
rouir, vb. soak.

rouleau, n.m. roll, roller, scroll, coil.
roulement, n.m. rolling, winding; rotation.
rouler, vb. roll, wind.
roulette, n.f. little wheel, caster.
roulis, n.m. roll.
Roumain, n.m. Rumanian (person).
roumain, 1. n.m. Rumanian (language). 2. adj. Rumanian.
Roumanie, n.f. Rumania.
rousseur, n.f. redness. tache de r., freckle.
roussir, vb. scorch.
route, n.f. road, way, course, route. en r., under way. en r. de, on the way to.
routine, n.f. routine.
routinier, adj. routine.
roux, adj. and n.m. red, reddish-brown.
royal, adj. royal, regal.
royaliste, adj. and n.m.f. royalist.
royaume, n.m. kingdom.
royauté, n.f. royalty.
ruban, n.m. ribbon, tape.
rubis, n.m. ruby.
rubrique, n.f. red ocher; heading.
ruche, n.f. hive.
rude, adj. rough, gruff, harsh; rugged.
rudesse, n.f. harshness.
rudiment, n.m. rudiment, element.
rudimentaire, adj. rudimentary.
rudoyer, vb. bully.
rue, n.f. street, road.
ruée, n.f. rush.
ruelle, n.f. lane, alley.
ruer, vb. se r., rush.
rugir, vb. roar.
rugissement, n.m. roar.
rugueux, adj. rugged, harsh.
ruine, n.f. ruin.
ruiner, vb. ruin.
ruineux, adj. ruinous.
ruisseau, n.m. brook, creek, gutter.
ruisseler, vb. stream, flow.
rumeur, n.f. rumor, noise.
ruminant, adj. and n.m. ruminant.
ruminer, vb. chew the cud.
rupture, n.f. break, rupture.
rural, adj. rural.
ruse, n.f. trick; cunning.
rusé, adj. sly, cunning.
Russe, n.m.f. Russian (person).
russe, 1. n.m. Russian (language). 2. adj. Russian.
Russie, n.f. Russia.
rusticité, n.f. rusticity, uncouthness.
rustique, adj. rustic.
rustre, adj. and n.m. boor, boorish.
rythme, n.m. rhythm.
rythmique, adj. rhythmical.

S

sabbat, n.m. Sabbath.
sable, n.m. sand.
sabler, vb. sand; quaff.
sablier, n.m. sandbox, sandman; hourglass.
sablonneux, adj. sandy.
sablonnière, n.f. sand pit.
sabord, n.m. porthole.
sabot, n.m. hoof; wooden shoe.
sabotage, n.m. sabotage.
saboter, vb. sabotage.
saboteur, n.m. saboteur; awkward bungler.
sabre, n.m. saber.
sac, n.m. sack, bag. s. à main, pocketbook. s. à air, airbag.
saccade, n.f. jerk.
saccager, vb. ransack, sack, plunder.
sacerdoce, n.m. priesthood.
sachet, n.m. sachet.
sacre, n.m. consecration, coronation.
sacré, adj. sacred.
sacrement, n.m. sacrament.
sacrer, vb. crown, consecrate; curse.
sacrifice, n.m. sacrifice.
sacrifier, vb. sacrifice.
sacrilège, n.m. sacrilege.
sacristain, n.m. sexton.
sac tyrolien, n.m. backpack.
sadisme, n.m. sadism.
sagace, adj. shrewd.
sagacité, n.f. sagacity.
sage, 1. n.m. sage. 2. adj. wise, good.
sage-femme, n.f. midwife.
sagesse, n.f. wisdom.
saignée, n.f. bleeding.
saigner, vb. bleed.
saillant, adj. prominent, projecting.
saillie, n.f. projection.
saillir, vb. protrude.
sain, adj. healthy, sound, wholesome. s. d'esprit, sane.
saindoux, n.m. lard.
saint, 1. n.m. saint. 2. adj. holy.
Saint-Esprit, n.m. Holy Ghost.
sainteté, n.f. holiness.
saisie, n.f. seizure.
saisir, vb. seize, grasp, snatch, grab.
saisissement, n.m. chill, seizure.
saison, n.f. season.
salade, n.f. salad.
saladier, n.m. salad bowl or dish.
salaire, n.m. wages, earnings, pay.
salarié, 1. adj. salaried. 2. n.m.f. person earning a salary.
sale, adj. dirty.
saler, vb. salt.
saleté, n.f. dirt.
salière, n.f. saltcellar.
salin, adj. salt, salty.
salir, vb. get dirty.

salive, *n.f.* saliva.

salle, *n.f.* (large) room, hall, auditorium, (hospital) ward. **s. de classe,** classroom. **s. de bain,** bathroom.

salon, *n.m.* parlor.

saltimbanque, *n.m.* charlatan, buffoon.

salubre, *adj.* healthful.

salubrité, *n.f.* healthfulness.

saluer, *vb.* bow, greet, salute.

salut, *n.m.* bow, salute; salvation.

salutaire, *adj.* wholesome, beneficial.

salutation, *n.f.* greeting.

salve, *n.f.* salvo, salute.

samedi, *n.m.* Saturday.

sanctifier, *vb.* hallow.

sanction, *n.f.* sanction.

sanctionner, *vb.* sanction, countenance.

sanctuaire, *n.m.* sanctuary.

sandale, *n.f.* sandal.

sang, *n.m.* blood.

sang-froid, *n.m.* calmness, composure.

sanglant, *adj.* bloody.

sangler, *vb.* strap, fasten.

sanglier, *n.m.* (wild) boar.

sanglot, *n.m.* sob.

sangloter, *vb.* sob.

sangsue, *n.f.* leech.

sanguin, *adj.* pertaining to blood.

sanguinaire, *adj.* bloodthirsty.

sanitaire, *adj.* sanitary.

sans, *prep.* without, out of. **s. doute,** without doubt. **s. plomb,** unleaded. **s. repos,** restless. **s. valeur,** worthless. **s. nom,** nameless.

sans-souci, *adj.* carefree, careless.

santé, *n.f.* health.

saper, *vb.* sap, weaken.

saphir, *n.m.* sapphire.

sapin, *n.m.* fir.

sarcasme, *n.m.* sarcasm.

sarcastique, *adj.* sarcastic.

sarcler, *vb.* weed, root out.

sardine, *n.f.* sardine.

sardonique, *adj.* sardonic.

satanique, *adj.* satanic.

satellite, *n.m.* satellite.

satin, *n.m.* satin.

satire, *n.f.* satire.

satiriser, *vb.* satirize.

satisfaction, *n.f.* satisfaction.

satisfaire, *vb.* satisfy.

satisfaisant, *adj.* satisfactory.

saturer, *vb.* saturate.

satyre, *n.m.* satyr.

sauce, *n.f.* sauce. **s. piquante,** catsup.

saucisse, *n.f.* sausage.

sauf, **1.** *prep.* but. **2.** *adj.* safe. **sain et sauf,** safe and sound.

sauf-conduit, *n.m.* safe-conduct pass.

sauge, *n.f.* sage.

saugrenu, *adj.* absurd, preposterous.

saule, *n.f.* willow.

saumon, *n.m.* salmon.

saumure, *n.f.* brine.

saut, *n.m.* spring, jump.

saute, *n.f.* wind shift.

sauter, *vb.* spring, jump, leap, skip. **faire s.,** blow up.

sauterelle, *n.f.* grasshopper.

sautiller, *vb.* hop.

sauvage, 1. *n.m.f.* savage. **2.** *adj.* wild, savage.

sauvegarde, *n.f.* safeguard.

sauvegarder, *vb.* safeguard.

sauve-qui-peut, *n.m.* stampede, panic.

sauver, *vb.* save. **se s.,** run away.

sauvetage, *n.m.* salvage.

sauveteur, *n.m.* rescuer, saver.

sauveur, *n.m.* savior, Saviour.

savane, *n.f.* prairie.

savant, 1. *n.m.* scholar. **2.** *adj.* learned.

saveur, *n.f.* flavor, savor, zest.

savoir, 1. *vb.* know, be aware, have knowledge. **vouloir s.,** wonder. **2.** *n.m.* knowledge.

savoir-faire, *n.m.* poise, ability.

savoir-vivre, *n.m.* breeding, manners.

savon, *n.m.* soap.

savonner, *vb.* soap, lather.

savourer, *vb.* relish.

savoureux, *adj.* tasty.

scabreux, *adj.* rough, harsh, indelicate.

scalper, *vb.* scalp.

scandale, *n.m.* scandal.

scandaleux, *adj.* scandalous.

scandaliser, *vb.* shock.

scander, *vb.* scan.

Scandinave, *n.m.f.* Scandinavian.

scandinave, *adj.* Scandinavian.

Scandinavie, *n.f.* Scandinavia.

scarabée, *n.m.* beetle.

scarlatine, *n.f.* scarlet fever.

sceau, *n.m.* seal.

scélérat, *n.m.* villain, criminal, knave, ruffian.

sceller, *vb.* seal.

scénario, *n.m.* scenario.

scène, *n.f.* scene, stage.

scénique, *adj.* scenic.

scepticisme, *n.m.* skepticism.

sceptique, 1. *n.m.f.* skeptic. **2.** *adj.* skeptical.

sceptre, *n.m.* scepter.

schampooing, *n.m.* shampoo.

schisme, *n.m.* schism.

sciatique, *n.f.* sciatica.

scie, *n.f.* saw.

science, *n.f.* science.

science-fiction, *n.f.* science fiction.

scientifique, *adj.* scientific.

scier, *vb.* saw.

scinder, *vb.* divide.

scintiller, *vb.* twinkle.

scission, *n.f.* cutting, division.

sclérose, *n.f.* sclerosis.

scolaire, *adj.* scholastic. **système s.,** school system.

scolastique, *adj.* scholastic.

scrofule, *n.f.* scrofula.

scrupule, *n.m.* scruple.

scrupuleux, *adj.* scrupulous.

scruter, *vb.* scan, scrutinize.

scrutin, *n.m.* ballot, poll.

sculpter (-lt-), *vb.* carve.

sculpteur (-lt-), *n.f.* sculptor.

sculpture (-lt-), *n.f.* sculpture.

se (sə), *pron.* himself, herself, itself, oneself, themselves, each other.

séance, *n.f.* sitting; session; meeting.

séant, *adj.* sitting, proper.

seau, *n.m.* pail, bucket.

sec *m.,* **sèche** *f. adj.* dry.

sécession, *n.f.* secession.

sécher, *vb.* dry.

sécheresse, *n.f.* dryness, drought.

second (-g-), *adj.* second.

secondaire (-g-), *adj.* secondary.

seconde (-g-), *n.f.* second.

seconder (-g-), *vb.* second, help.

secouer, *vb.* shake, rouse.

secourir, *vb.* relieve, succor, help.

secours, *n.m.* help, relief. **premiers s.,** first aid. **poste de s.,** first aid station. **au s.!,** help!

secousse, *n.f.* jar, shock.

secret, *adj.* and *n.m.* secret.

secrétaire, *n.m.f.* secretary.

sécréter, *vb.* secrete.

sécrétion, *n.f.* secretion.

sectaire, *adj.* sectarian.

secte, *n.f.* sect.

secteur, *n.m.* district, sector.

section, *n.f.* section.

sectionner, *vb.* cut into sections.

séculaire, *adj.* secular.

séculier, *adj.* secular, lay.

sécurité, *n.f.* safety.

sédatif, *adj.* and *n.m.* sedative.

sédentaire, *adj.* sedentary, stationary.

séditieux, *adj.* seditious.

sédition, *n.f.* sedition.

séduction, *n.f.* seduction.

séduire, *vb.* seduce, attract, allure.

séduisant, *adj.* attractive.

segment, *n.m.* segment.

ségrégation, *n.f.* segregation.

seigle, *n.m.* rye.

seigneur, *n.m.* lord, peer.

seigneurie, *n.f.* lordship.

sein, *n.m.* bosom, breast.

seize, *adj.* and *n.m.* sixteen.

seizième, *adj.* and *n.m.* sixteenth.

séjour, *n.m.* stay. **lieu de s.,** resort.

séjourner, *vb.* sojourn.

sel, *n.m.* salt.

sélection, *n.f.* selection.

selle, *n.f.* saddle.

seller, *vb.* saddle.

sellette, *n.f.* little stool or saddle.

selon, *prep.* according to.

seltz, *n.m.* **eau de s.,** soda water.

semailles, *n.f.pl.* sowing.

semaine, n.f. week; weekly pay.
semblable, adj. similar, alike.
semblant, n.m. show; appearance. **faire s.,** make believe.
sembler, vb. seem, appear.
semelle, n.f. sole.
semence, n.f. seed.
semer, vb. sow.
semestre, n.m. semester.
semeur, n.m. sower.
sémillance, n.f. briskness, liveliness.
sémitique, adj. Semitic.
semoncer, vb. lecture, scold.
sénat, n.m. senate.
sénateur, n.m. senator.
sénile, adj. senile.
sénilité, n.f. senility.
sens (-s), n.m. meaning, sense; direction.
sensation, n.f. sensation, feeling.
sensationnel, adj. sensational.
sensé, adj. sensible.
sensibilité, n.f. sensitivity.
sensible, adj. sensible, sensitive; conscious (of).
sensitif, adj. sensitive.
sensualisme, n.m. sensualism.
sensualité, n.f. sensuality.
sensuel, adj. sensual.
sentence, n.f. sentence.
sentencieux, adj. sententious.
senteur, n.f. smell.
sentier, n.m. path.
sentiment, n.m. feeling.
sentimental, adj. sentimental.
sentimentalité, n.f. sentimentality.
sentinelle, n.f. sentry.
sentir, vb. feel; smell.
séparable, adj. separable.
séparation, n.f. separation, parting.
séparé, adj. separate.
séparer, vb. separate, segregate. **se s.,** part.
sept (sèt), adj. and n.m. seven.
septembre, n.m. September.
septième (sèt-), adj. and n.m. seventh.
septique, adj. septic.
sépulcre, n.m. sepulcher.
séquestrer, vb. withdraw, remove.
serein, adj. serene, placid.
sérénade, n.f. serenade.
sérénité, n.f. serenity.
serf, 1. n.m. serf. **2.** adj. in serfdom or the like.
sergent, n.m. sergeant.
série, n.f. series.
sérieux, 1. adj. serious, sober, grave. **2.** n.m. gravity.
serin, n.m. canary.
seringue, n.f. syringe.
serment, n.m. oath.
sermon, n.m. sermon.
sermonner, vb. lecture, preach.
serpent, n.m. snake, serpent.
serpenter, vb. wind, wander.
serre, n.f. green-house; claw.
serré, adj. tight.
serre-joint, n.m. clamp.

serrer, vb. tighten, squeeze, press, crowd, shake (hands). **s. dans ses bras,** hug.
serrure, n.f. lock.
sérum, n.m. serum.
servage, n.m. servitude.
servant, 1. adj. serving. **2.** n.m. server, gunner.
servante, n.f. maid.
serviable, adj. helpful.
service, n.m. service, favor. **être de s.,** be on duty.
serviette, n.f. napkin; towel; brief case.
servile, adj. menial.
servilité, n.f. servility.
servir, vb. serve. **se s. de,** use. **ne s. à rien,** be of no use.
serviteur, n.m. attendant, servant.
servitude, n.f. slavery.
session, n.f. session.
seuil, n.m. threshold.
seul, adj. alone, only, single.
seulement, adv. only, solely.
sève, n.f. sap.
sévère, adj. severe, stern.
sévérité, n.f. severity, rigor.
sévir, vb. punish, rage.
sevrer, vb. wean, withhold.
sexe, n.m. sex.
sexisme, n.m. sexism.
sexiste, adj. sexist.
sexuel, adj. sexual.
seyant, adj. becoming.
shrapnel, n.m. shrapnel.
si, 1. adv. so, so much, yes. **si . . . que,** however (+adj.). **2.** conj. if, whether.
siècle, n.m. century.
siège, n.m. seat; siege.
siéger, vb. sit, convene, reside.
sien, pron. **le sien, la sienne,** his, hers, its.
sieste, n.f. siesta.
siffler, vb. whistle, hiss.
sifflerie, n.f. hissing, whistling.
sifflet, n.m. whistle.
signal, n.m. signal.
signalement, n.m. description, details.
signaler, vb. point out.
signature, n.f. signature.
signe, n.m. sign. **s. de la tête,** nod. **faire s. à,** beckon.
signer, vb. sign. **se s.,** cross oneself.
significatif, adj. significant, meaningful.
signification, n.f. significance, meaning.
signifier, vb. signify, mean.
silence, n.m. silence.
silencieux, adj. noiseless, silent.
silex, n.m. flint.
sillage, n.m. wake, course.
sillon, n.m. furrow.
sillonner, vb. plow.
similaire, adj. similar.
simple, adj. plain, simple, mere; no-frills.
simplicité, n.f. simplicity.
simplifier, vb. simplify.
simulation, n.f. simulation.

simuler, vb. pretend.
simultané, adj. simultaneous.
sincère, adj. candid, sincere.
sincérité, n.f. candor, sincerity.
singe, n.m. monkey; imitator.
singularité, n.f. singularity; peculiar trait.
singulier, adj. and n.m. singular; peculiar, strange.
sinistre, 1. n.m. disaster. **2.** adj. sinister.
sinon, conj. otherwise.
sinueux, adj. winding, sinuous.
sirène, n.f. siren.
sirop, n.m. syrup.
siroter, vb. sip.
site, n.m. site.
sitôt, adv. as soon (as).
situation, n.f. situation, position, location, office.
situer, vb. situate, locate.
six (sès), adj. and n.m. six.
sixième (-z-), adj. and n.m. sixth.
ski, n.m. ski. **faire du s.,** ski, vb.
skieur, n.m. skier.
smoking, n.m. dinner-jacket, tuxedo.
sobre, adj. temperate, sober.
sobriété, n.f. moderation, temperance.
sobriquet, n.m. nickname.
soc, n.m. plowshare.
sociable, adj. sociable.
social, adj. social.
socialisme, n.m. socialism.
socialiste, adj. and n.m.f. socialist.
société, n.f. society; company.
sociologie, n.f. sociology.
sociologiste, n.m. sociologist.
sœur, n.f. sister.
soi-disant, adj. so-called.
soie, n.f. silk; bristle.
soierie, n.f. silk goods.
soif, n.f. thirst. **avoir s.,** be thirsty.
soigné, adj. trim. **mal s.,** sloppy.
soigner, vb. tend, look after, take care of.
soigneux, adj. careful.
soi-même, pron. oneself.
soin, n.m. care. **prendre s. de,** take care of.
soir, n.m. evening. **hier s.,** last night. **ce s.,** tonight. **le s.,** at night.
soirée, n.f. evening.
soit, vb. so be it. **s. . . . s.,** whether . . . or. **s. que,** whether.
soixante (-s-), adj. and n.m. sixty.
soixante-dix, adj. and n.m. seventy.
sol, n.m. earth, soil, ground.
solaire, adj. solar.
soldat, n.m. soldier.
solde, n.m. balance.
sole, n.f. sole.
solécisme, n.m. solecism.
soleil, n.m. sun, sunshine. **coucher du s.,** sunset. **lever du s.,** sunrise.

solennel, *adj.* solemn.
solenniser, *vb.* solemnize.
solennité, *n.f.* solemnity.
solidaire, *adj.* jointly binding.
solidariser, *vb.* se s., unite, join together.
solidarité, *n.f.* joint responsibility.
solide, *adj. and n.m.* solid.
solidifier, *vb.* solidify.
solidité, *n.f.* solidity.
soliloque, *n.m.* soliloquy.
soliste, *n.m.* soloist.
solitaire, *adj.* lonely, lonesome.
solitude, *n.f.* solitude.
solliciter, *vb.* solicit, ask, apply.
sollicitude, *n.f.* solicitude.
soluble, *adj.* soluble.
solution, *n.f.* solution.
solvable, *adj.* solvent.
sombre, *adj.* dark, dim, gloomy, somber.
sombrer, *vb.* sink.
sommaire, *n.m.* summary.
sommation, *n.f.* appeal, summons.
somme, 1. *n.f.* amount, sum. 2. *n.m.* nap.
sommeil, *n.m.* sleep. avoir s., be sleepy.
sommeiller, *vb.* doze, slumber.
sommer, *vb.* summon.
sommet, *n.m.* top, peak, summit.
somnolence, *n.f.* drowsiness.
somnolent, *adj.* drowsy, sleepy.
somptueux, *adj.* lavish, sumptuous.
son *m.*, sa *f.*, ses *pl. adj.* his, her, its.
son, *n.m.* sound, ring; bran.
sonate, *n.f.* sonata.
sonder, *vb.* fathom; probe.
songe, *n.m.* dream.
songer à, *vb.* think of, dream.
songeur, 1. *adj.* dreamy, thoughtful. 2. *n.m.* dreamer.
sonner, *vb.* sound, ring, strike.
sonnerie, *n.f.* ringing.
sonnette, *n.f.* bell.
sonore, *adj.* sonorous.
sophiste, *n.m.* sophist.
soprano, *n.m.* soprano.
sorcellerie, *n.f.* sorcery.
sorcier, *n.m.* wizard.
sorcière, *n.f.* witch.
sordide, *adj.* sordid.
sort, *n.m.* lot.
sorte, *n.f.* sort, kind. de s. que, so that.
sortie, *n.f.* exit, way out.
sortilège, *n.m.* sorcery.
sortir, *vb.* go (come, get) out.
sot *m.*, sotte *f. adj.* silly, stupid, foolish, dumb.
sottise, *n.f.* foolishness.
sou, *n.m.* cent. sans le s., penniless.
soubassement, *n.m.* basement.
soubresaut, *n.m.* bound, jerk.
souche, *n.f.* stub, stump.
souci, *n.m.* care, worry, concern.

soucier, *vb.* se s. (de), care, worry (about).
soucieux, *adj.* anxious.
soucoupe, *n.f.* saucer.
soudain, *adj.* sudden.
soudaineté, *n.f.* suddenness.
soude, *n.f.* soda.
souder, *vb.* solder, fuse.
souffle, *n.m.* breath.
souffler, *vb.* blow.
soufflet, *n.m.* bellows; blow, slap.
souffleter, *vb.* slap one's face.
souffrance(s), *n.f. (pl.)* misery, pain, suffering.
souffrir, *vb.* suffer, bear.
soufre, *n.m.* sulphur.
souhait, *n.m.* wish.
souhaiter, *vb.* wish for.
souiller, *vb.* soil, defile.
souillure, *n.f.* stain, dirt.
soulager, *vb.* relieve, alleviate.
soûler, *vb.* fill with food and drink, inebriate.
soulever, *vb.* lift, raise, arouse.
soulier, *n.m.* shoe.
souligner, *vb.* underline.
soumettre, *vb.* submit, subdue.
soumis, *adj.* obedient, submissive.
soumission, *n.f.* submission.
soupape, *n.f.* valve.
soupçon, *n.m.* suspicion.
soupçonner, *vb.* suspect.
soupçonneux, *adj.* suspicious.
soupe, *n.f.* soup.
souper, *n.m.* supper.
soupir, *n.m.* sigh.
soupirer, *vb.* sigh. s. après, yearn for.
souple, *adj.* flexible.
souplesse, *n.f.* suppleness, pliability.
source, *n.f.* source; spring.
sourcil, *n.m.* eyebrow.
sourciller, *vb.* frown.
sourcilleux, *adj.* haughty, disdainful.
sourd, *adj.* deaf.
sourd-muet, *n.m.* deaf mute.
souricière, *n.f.* (mouse)trap.
sourire, *n.m. and vb.* smile.
souris, *n.f.* mouse.
sournois, *adj.* sly.
sous, *prep.* under.
souscription, *n.f.* subscription.
souscrire, *vb.* subscribe.
sous-estimer, *vb.* underestimate.
sous-louer, *vb.* sublet.
sous-marin, *n.m.* submarine.
sous-produit, *n.m.* by-product.
soussigné, *adj.* undersigned.
sous-sol, *n.m.* basement.
sous-titre, *n.m.* subtitle.
soustraction, *n.f.* subtraction.
soustraire, *vb.* subtract.
soutane, *n.f.* cassock.
soute, *n.f.* storeroom.
soutenir, *vb.* support, uphold, maintain; claim; back up.
soutenu, *adj.* steady.
souterrain, *adj.* underground.
soutien, *n.m.* support.
soutien-gorge, *n.m.* brassière.

souvenance, *n.f.* recall, recollection.
souvenir, 1. *n.m.* remembrance, memory. 2. *vb.* se s. de, remember.
souvent, *adv.* often.
souverain, *n.m.* ruler, sovereign.
souveraineté, *n.f.* sovereignty.
soyeux, *adj.* silky.
spacieux, *adj.* spacious.
spasme, *n.m.* spasm.
spatule, *n.f.* spatula.
spécial, *adj.* special.
spécialiser, *vb.* specialize.
spécialiste, *n.m.f.* specialist.
spécialité, *n.f.* specialty.
spécifier, *vb.* specify.
spécifique, *adj.* specific.
spécimen, *n.m.* specimen.
spectacle, *n.m.* sight, show.
spectaculaire, *adj.* spectacular.
spectateur, *n.m.* spectator.
spectre, *n.m.* ghost; spectrum.
spéculation, *n.f.* speculation.
spéculer, *vb.* speculate.
sphère, *n.f.* sphere.
spinal, *adj.* spinal.
spiral, *adj.* spiral.
spirale, *n.f.* spiral.
spirite, *n.m.f.* spiritualism.
spiritisme, *n.m.* spiritualism.
spirituel, *adj.* spiritual; witty.
spiritueux, *adj.* pertaining to alcohol.
splendeur, *n.f.* splendor.
splendide, *adj.* splendid.
spolier, *vb.* plunder, pillage.
spontané, *adj.* spontaneous.
spontanéité, *n.f.* spontaneity.
sporadique, *adj.* sporadic.
sport, *n.m.* sport.
sportif, *adj.* of sport.
squelette, *n.m.* skeleton.
stabiliser, *vb.* stabilize.
stabilité, *n.f.* stability.
stable, *adj.* stable, steady.
stage, *n.m.* period of probation.
stagflation, *n.f.* stagflation.
stagnant, *adj.* stagnant.
stalle, *n.f.* stall.
stance, *n.f.* stanza.
station, *n.f.* stand, stop, station (subway).
stationnaire, *adj.* stationary.
stationner, *vb.* park.
statique, *adj.* static.
statistique, *n.f.* statistics.
statue, *n.f.* statue.
statuer, *vb.* decree, decide.
stature, *n.f.* stature.
statut, *n.m.* statute.
sténographe, *n.m.f.* stenographer.
sténographie, *n.f.* stenography.
stéréophonique, *adj.* stereophonic.
stérile, *adj.* barren.
stériliser, *vb.* sterilize.
stéthoscope, *n.m.* stethoscope.
stigmatiser, *vb.* mark, stigmatize.
stimulant, *n.m.* stimulus.
stimuler, *vb.* stimulate.

stipuler, vb. stipulate.
stoïque, adj. and n.m.f. stoic.
store, n.m. (window) shade, blind.
stratagème, n.m. stratagem.
stratégie, n.f. strategy.
stratégique, adj. strategic.
strict (-kt), adj. severe, strict.
strier, vb. mark, streak, make grooves.
structure, n.f. structure.
stuc, n.m. stucco.
studieux, adj. studious.
stupéfait, adj. astounded.
stupéfiant, n.m. narcotic, dope.
stupéfier, vb. astound.
stupeur, n.f. amazement.
stupide, adj. stupid.
stupidité, n.f. stupidity.
style, n.m. style.
styler, vb. train, teach.
stylet, n.m. stiletto.
stylographe, stylo, n.m. fountain pen.
suavité, n.f. suavity.
subalterne, adj. and n.m.f. junior (rank).
subdiviser, vb. subdivide.
subir, vb. undergo, bear.
subit, adj. sudden.
subjectif, adj. subjective.
subjonctif, adj. and n.m. subjunctive.
subjuguer, vb. subdue, overcome.
sublime, adj. sublime, exalted.
submerger, vb. submerge, flood.
subordonné, adj. and n.m. subordinate.
subordonner, vb. subordinate.
subreptice, adj. surreptitious.
subséquent, adj. subsequent.
subside, n.m. subsidy.
subsister, vb. subsist, live.
substance, n.f. substance.
substantiel, adj. substantial.
substantif, n.m. noun.
substituer, vb. substitute.
substitution, n.f. substitution.
subtil (-l), adj. subtle.
subtilité, n.f. subtlety.
subvention, n.f. grant, subsidy.
subventionner, vb. subsidize.
subversif, adj. subversive.
suc, n.m. juice.
succéder à, vb. succeed, follow.
succès, n.m. success; hit.
successeur, n.m. successor.
successif, adj. successive.
succession, n.f. succession.
succion, n.f. suction.
succomber, vb. succumb.
succursale, n.f. branch office.
sucer, vb. suck.
sucre, n.m. sugar.
sucrer, vb. add sugar.
sud (-d), n.m. south.
sudation, n.f. sweating.
sud-est, n.m. southeast.
sud-ouest, n.m. southwest.
Suède, n.f. Sweden.
Suédois, n.m. Swede.
suédois, adj. and n.m. Swedish.
suer, vb. sweat.

sueur, n.m. sweat.
suffire, vb. suffice.
suffisance, n.f. adequacy, conceit.
suffisant, adj. sufficient, adequate; conceited.
suffixe, n.m. suffix.
suffoquer, vb. suffocate.
suffrage, n.m. suffrage.
suggérer, vb. suggest.
suggestion, n.f. suggestion.
suicide, n.m. suicide.
suicider, vb. se s., kill oneself.
suie, n.f. soot.
suif, n.m. tallow.
suinter, vb. seep.
Suisse, 1. n.m. Swiss. **2.** n.f. Switzerland.
suisse, adj. Swiss.
suite, n.f. sequence; retinue; *(pl.)* results, aftermath. **et ainsi de s.,** and so on. **tout de s.,** at once.
suivant, 1. n.m. follower. **2.** adj. next, following, subsequent. **3.** prep. by, according to.
suivi, adj. followed, coherent.
suivre, vb. follow; attend. **faire s.,** forward.
sujet, 1. n.m. subject; topic. **2.** adj. subject. **s. à,** liable to.
sujétion, n.f. subjection, slavery.
superbe, adj. superb, magnificent.
superficie, n.f. surface.
superficiel, adj. superficial, shallow.
superflu, adj. superfluous.
supérieur, adj. and n.m. superior, higher, upper; senior.
supériorité, n.f. superiority.
superlatif, adj. and n.m. superlative.
superstar, n.m. superstar.
superstitieux, adj. superstitious.
superstition, n.f. superstition.
suppléant, adj. and n.m. assistant, substitute.
suppléer, vb. substitute.
supplément, n.m. supplement.
supplémentaire, adj. extra. **heures s.s,** overtime.
supplice, n.m. punishment, torture.
supplier, vb. beseech, entreat, beg, supplicate.
support, n.m. support, stand.
supporter, vb. support, bear, stand, endure.
supposer, vb. suppose, assume.
supposition, n.f. assumption, conjecture, supposition.
suppôt, n.m. implement, tool, agent.
suppression, n.f. suppression.
supprimer, vb. suppress, put down, take out.
supputation, n.f. computation.
supputer, vb. compute.
suprématie, n.f. supremacy.
suprême, adj. supreme.
sur, prep. on, upon, over.
sûr, adj. safe, sure, secure.

surabonder, vb. be very abundant.
suranné, adj. out-of-date.
surcroît, n.m. addition.
surdité, n.f. deafness.
suret, adj. sour.
sûreté, n.f. safety, security, reliability.
surface, n.f. surface, area.
surgélateur, n.m. deep freeze.
surgir, vb. spring up, arise.
surhumain, adj. superhuman.
surintendant, n.m. superintendent.
sur-le-champ, adv. at once, immediately.
surmener, vb. overwork.
surmonter, vb. overcome, surmount.
surnaturel, adj. and n.m. supernatural.
surnom, n.m. nickname.
surpasser, vb. surpass.
surplis, n.m. surplice.
surplomber, vb. overhang.
surplus, n.m. surplus, excess.
surprendre, vb. surprise.
surprise, n.f. surprise.
sursaut, n.m. start.
sursauter, vb. give a start.
sursis, n.m. delay, putting off.
surtaxe, n.f. surtax.
surtout, 1. n.m. overcoat. **2.** adv. above all.
surveillance, n.f. supervision, watch.
surveillant, n.m. superintendent.
surveiller, vb. supervise, watch over.
survenir, vb. happen.
survie, n.f. survival.
survivance, n.f. survival.
survivre, vb. survive.
susceptible, adj. susceptible; liable.
suspect (-kt), adj. suspicious.
suspecter, vb. suspect.
suspendre, vb. suspend, hang, sling.
suspension, n.f. suspension.
suspicion, n.f. suspicion.
sustenter, vb. sustain, bulwark.
svelte, adj. slender, slim.
syllabe, n.f. syllable.
sylphe, n.m. sylph.
sylphide, n.f. sylph.
sylvestre, adj. sylvan, woody.
sylviculture, n.f. forestry.
symbole, n.m. symbol.
symboliser, vb. symbolize.
symétrie, n.f. symmetry.
sympathie, n.f. sympathy. **avoir de la s. pour,** like.
sympathique, adj. congenial, likeable.
sympathiser, vb. sympathize.
symphonie, n.f. symphony.
symptôme, n.m. symptom.
synchroniser, vb. synchronize.
syndical, adj. of a trade-union.
syndicat, n.m. syndicate **s. ouvrier,** trade-union.
syndrome, n.m. syndrome.
synonyme, n.m. synonym.
syntaxe, n.f. syntax.

synthèse, *n.f.* synthesis.
synthétique, *adj.* synthetic.
systématique, *adj.* systematic.
système, *n.m.* system.

T

tabac (-bǎ), *n.m.* tobacco.
tabernacle, *n.m.* tabernacle.
table, *n.f.* table. **t. des matières**, index.
tableau, *n.m.* picture. **t. noir**, blackboard.
tabler, *vb.* count on, depend.
tablette, *n.f.* tablet.
tablier, *n.m.* apron.
tabou, *n.m.* taboo.
tabouret, *n.m.* stool.
tache, *n.f.* spot, stain, blot, smear.
tâche, *n.f.* task; assignment.
tacher, *vb.* spot, stain, blot.
tâcher, *vb.* try.
tacite, *adj.* tacit, silent.
taciturne, *adj.* unspeaking.
tact (-kt), *n.m.* tact.
tacticien, *n.m.* tactician.
tactique, 1. *adj.* of tactics, tactical. 2. *n.f.* tactics.
taffetas, *n.m.* taffeta.
tale, *n.f.* pillowcase.
taillade, *n.f.* slash.
taille, *n.f.* waist, figure, size.
tailler, *vb.* trim, cut.
tailleur, *n.m.* tailor.
taire, *vb.* keep quiet. **se t.**, be silent.
talent, *n.m.* ability, talent.
talon, *n.m.* heel.
talus, *n.m.* slope.
tambour, *n.m.* drum.
tambourin, *n.m.* tambourine.
tamis, *n.m.* sieve.
tampon, *n.m.* plug, pad.
tamponner, *vb.* plug; run together.
tan, *n.m.* tan (leather).
tandis que, *conj.* while, whereas.
tangible, *adj.* tangible.
tanguer, *vb.* cover with pitch.
tant, *adv.* so much, so many. **t. que**, as long as.
tante, *n.f.* aunt.
tantième, *n.m.* part, percentage.
tantôt, *adv.* presently, soon.
tapage, *n.m.* din.
tapageur, *adj.* rowdy.
taper, *vb.* pat, knock, tap; type.
tapir, *vb.* se t., squat, cower, lurk.
tapis, *n.m.* carpet, rug.
tapisserie, *n.f.* tapestry.
tapissier, *n.m.* upholsterer.
taquiner, *vb.* tease.
taquinerie, *n.f.* teasing.
tard, *adv.* late.
tarder, *vb.* delay.
tardif, *adj.* slow, tardy, late.
tarière, *n.f.* auger.
tarif, *n.m.* scale of charges;

rate; fare. **t. douanier**, tariff.
tartan, *n.m.* plaid.
tarte, *n.f.* pie.
tartre, *n.m.* tartar.
tas, *n.m.* heap, pile.
tasse, *n.f.* cup.
tasser, *vb.* pack, fill up.
tâter, *vb.* feel.
tâtonner, *vb.* grope.
taudis, *n.m.* hovel.
taupe, *n.f.* mole.
taureau, *n.m.* bull.
taux, *n.m.* rate.
taverne, *n.f.* tavern.
taxe, *n.f.* tax. **t. (à la) valeur ajoutée**, value-added tax.
taxer, *vb.* tax, assess.
taxi, *n.m.* cab, taxi.
te (tə), *pron.* you, yourself.
technicien, *n.m.* technician.
technique, 1. *n.f.* technique. 2. *adj.* technical.
technologie, *n.f.* technology.
teindre, *vb.* dye.
teint, *n.m.* complexion.
teinte, *n.f.* tint, shade.
teinter, *vb.* tint, stain.
teinture, *n.f.* dye.
teinturier, *n.m.* dry-cleaner, dyer.
tel, *adj.* such.
télégramme, *n.m.* telegram.
télégraphe, *n.m.* telegraph.
télégraphie, *n.f.* telegraphy. **t. sans fil**, *abbrev.* T.S.F., radio, wireless.
télégraphier, *vb.* telegraph.
téléphone, *n.m.* telephone. **coup de t.**, ring.
téléphoner, *vb.* telephone.
télescope, *n.m.* telescope.
télescoper, *vb.* crash, run together.
télévision, *n.f.* television.
tellement, *adv.* so much.
téméraire, *adj.* rash.
témoignage, *n.m.* testimony, token.
témoigner, *vb.* testify.
témoin, *n.m.* witness.
tempe, *n.f.* temple.
tempérament, *n.m.* temper, temperament.
tempérance, *n.f.* temperance.
tempérant, *adj.* temperate.
température, *n.f.* temperature.
tempéré, *adj.* temperate.
tempérer, *vb.* moderate, calm, lessen.
tempête, *n.f.* storm, tempest.
tempétueux, *adj.* tempestuous.
temple, *n.m.* temple.
temporaire, *adj.* temporary.
temporiser, *vb.* temporize, evade.
temps (täN), *n.m.* time; weather.
tenace, *adj.* tenacious.
ténacité, *n.f.* tenacity.
tenailles, *n.f.pl.* tongs.
tendance, *n.f.* tendency, trend, leaning.
tendre, 1. *adj.* tender, fond, loving. 2. *vb.* tend, extend.

tendresse, *n.f.* tenderness, fondness.
tendu, *adj.* tense; uptight.
ténèbres, *n.f.pl.* gloom, darkness.
ténébreux, *adj.* dismal.
teneur, *n.m.* t. de livres, bookkeeper.
tenir, *vb.* hold.
tennis (-s), *n.m.* tennis.
ténor, *n.m.* tenor.
tension, *n.f.* strain; stress.
tentacule, *n.m.* tentacle.
tentatif, *adj.* tentative.
tentation, *n.f.* temptation.
tentative, *n.f.* attempt.
tente, *n.f.* tent; awning.
tenter, *vb.* tempt, try, attract.
tenture, *n.f.* wallcovering.
tenue, *n.f.* rig; conduct, manners.
ténuité, *n.f.* tenuity, unimportance.
térébenthine, *n.f.* turpentine.
terme, *n.m.* term, period; end.
terminaison, *n.f.* ending.
terminer, *vb.* end.
terminologie, *n.f.* terminology.
terminus, *n.m.* terminus.
terne, *adj.* drab, dull, dim, dingy.
ternir, *vb.* tarnish, dull.
terrain, *n.m.* ground(s).
terrasse, *n.f.* terrace.
terrasser, *vb.* heap up, embank; knock down, conquer.
terre, *n.f.* earth, ground, land. **pomme de t.**, potato. **à t.**, ashore.
terrestre, *adj.* earthly.
terreur, *n.f.* terror, fright, fear.
terrible, *adj.* terrible, awful, tremendous.
terrifier, *vb.* terrify.
territoire, *n.m.* territory.
terroir, *n.m.* soil.
terroriser, *vb.* terrorize.
tertre, *n.m.* mound.
tesson, *n.m.* broken piece, fragment.
testament, *n.m.* testament, will.
testateur, *n.m.* testator.
tête, *n.f.* head. **tenir t. à**, cope with.
téter, *vb.* suck.
téton, *n.m.* breast.
texte, *n.m.* text.
textile, *adj.* textile.
textuel, *adj.* textual.
texture, *n.f.* texture.
thé, *n.m.* tea.
théâtral, *adj.* theatrical.
théâtre, *n.m.* theater.
théière, *n.f.* teapot.
thème, *n.m.* theme.
théologie, *n.f.* theology.
théorie, *n.f.* theory.
théorique, *adj.* theoretical.
thermomètre, *n.m.* thermometer.
thésauriser, *vb.* hoard.
thèse, *n.f.* thesis.
thym, *n.m.* thyme.

ticket, n.m. check, ticket, coupon.

tiède, adj. lukewarm.

tiédir, vb. make or become cool.

tien, pron. le tien, la tienne, yours.

tiers, n.m. third.

Tiers Monde, n.m. Third World.

tige, n.f. stem, stalk.

tigre, n.m. tiger.

tilleul, n.m. linden, limetree.

timbre, n.m. stamp. t.-poste, postage stamp.

timbrer, vb. stamp.

timide, adj. timid, shy, coy, bashful.

timidité, n.f. timidity.

timoré, adj. timorous.

tintamarre, n.m. racket.

tinter, vb. ring, knell, tinkle.

tirailleur, n.m. sharpshooter.

tire, n.f. pull, yank.

tire-bouchon, n.m. corkscrew.

tirer, vb. draw, pull; shoot.

tiret, n.m. blank.

tiroir, n.m. drawer.

tisane, n.f. drink, broth.

tisser, vb. weave.

tisserand, n.m. weaver.

tissu, n.m. web; cloth; fabric.

titre, n.m. title, right.

titrer, vb. invest with a title.

toast (-t), n.m. toast.

toaster, vb. toast.

toile, n.f. web; canvas; linen.

toilette, n.f. toilet; dressing, dress.

toison, n.f. fleece.

toit, n.m. roof.

toiture, n.f. roofing.

tolérance, n.f. tolerance.

tolérer, vb. tolerate, bear.

tomate, n.f. tomato.

tombe, n.f. grave.

tombeau, n.m. tomb.

tombée, n.f. fall, decline.

tomber, vb. fall. laisser t., drop.

ton, n.m. tone, pitch.

ton m., ta f., tes pl. adj. your.

tondeuse, n.f. (lawn) mower.

tondre, vb. shear; mow.

tonique, adj. and n.m. tonic.

tonne, n.f. ton; barrel.

tonneau, n.m. cask, barrel.

tonner, vb. thunder.

tonnerre, n.m. thunder.

topaze, n.f. topaz.

topographie, n.f. topography.

torche, n.f. torch.

tordre, vb. twist, wrench, wring. se t., writhe.

torpeur, n.f. torpor.

torpille, n.f. torpedo.

torrent, n.m. torrent.

torride, adj. torrid.

torse, n.m. torso.

tort, n.m. wrong. avoir t., be wrong.

tortiller, vb. twist, wiggle.

tortu, adj. crooked.

tortue, n.f. turtle, tortoise.

torture, n.f. torture.

torturer, vb. torture.

tôt, adv. soon, early.

total, adj. and n.m. total.

totalisateur, n.m. adding machine.

totaliser, vb. total, add up.

totalitaire, adj. totalitarian.

totalité, n.f. entirety.

touchant, prep. concerning.

touche, n.f. key.

toucher, 1. n.m. touch. 2. vb. touch; collect; affect; border on.

touffe, n.f. tuft, bunch.

touffu, adj. bushy.

toujours, adv. always, still, ever, yet.

toupie, n.f. top (child's toy).

tour, 1. n.m. turn; trick; stroll. faire le t. de, go around. 2. n.f. tower.

tourbe, n.f. rabble.

tourbillon, n.m. whirl. t. d'eau, whirlpool. t. de vent, whirlwind.

tourbillonner, vb. whirl.

tourelle, n.f. turret.

touriste, n.m.f. tourist.

tourment, n.m. torment.

tourmenter, vb. torment.

tourne-disques, n.m. record player.

tournedos, n.f. beefsteak.

tournée, n.f. round.

tourner, vb. turn, revolve, spin.

tournesol, n.m. sunflower.

tournevis, n.m. screwdriver.

tournoi, n.m. tournament.

tournure, n.f. figure.

tousser, vb. cough.

tout, 1. adj.m. toute f., tous m.pl., toutes f.pl. all, each every. 2. pron. everything. t. les deux, both. t. d'un coup, all at once. t. de même, all the same. pas du t., not at all.

toutefois, adv. however.

tout-puissant, adj. almighty.

toux, n.f. cough.

toxique, adj. toxic.

tracasser, vb. worry.

trace, n.f. trace, step, track, footprint.

tracer, vb. outline, trace.

tracteur, n.m. tractor.

traction, n.f. traction.

tradition, n.f. tradition.

traditionnel, adj. traditional.

traducteur, n.m. translator.

traduction, n.f. translation.

traduire, vb. translate.

trafic, n.m. traffic.

trafiquer, vb. traffic, carry on dealings.

tragédie, n.f. tragedy.

tragique, adj. tragic.

trahir, vb. betray.

trahison, n.f. treason.

train, n.m. train.

traînard, n.m. loiterer, dawdler.

traîne, n.f. train of dress.

traîneau, n.m. sled, sleigh.

traîner, vb. drag, haul.

traire, vb. milk.

trait, n.m. feature; draft; shot. t. d'union, hyphen.

traité, n.m. treaty.

traitement, n.m. treatment.

traiter, vb. treat, deal.

traître, n.m. traitor.

traîtrise, n.f. treachery.

trajet, n.m. crossing.

trame, n.f. web (woof); plan, plot.

tramer, vb. devise.

tramway, n.m. streetcar.

tranchant, adj. sharp, crisp.

tranche, n.f. slice.

tranchée, n.f. trench.

trancher, vb. cut.

tranquille (-l), adj. quiet. laisser t., leave alone.

tranquilliser (-l-), vb. soothe, make tranquil.

tranquillité (-l-), n.f. quiet, stillness.

transaction, n.f. transaction.

transe, n.f. fright, fear.

transférer, vb. transfer.

transformer, vb. transform.

transfuser, vb. transfuse.

transfusion, n.f. transfusion.

transition (-z-), n.f. transition.

transitoire (-z-), adj. transitory.

transmettre, vb. transmit, convey, send.

transparent, adj. transparent.

transpiration, n.f. perspiration.

transpirer, vb. perspire.

transplanter, vb. transplant.

transport, n.m. transfer, transport, transportation; bliss, ecstasy.

transporter, vb. transport, transfer, convey.

transposer, vb. transpose.

transsexuel, adj. transsexual.

travail, n.m. work, job, labor.

travailler, vb. work.

travailleur, 1. n.m. worker, laborer. 2. adj. industrious.

travée, n.f. span.

travers, n.m. breadth. à t., across, through. de t., askance, awry.

traversée, n.f. crossing.

traverser, vb. cross.

traversin, n.m. bolster.

travesti, n.f. transvestite.

travestir, vb. disguise.

trébucher, vb. stumble, trip.

trèfle, n.m. clover; club (cards).

treillis, n.m. denim.

treize, adj. and n.m. thirteen.

tréma, n.m. dieresis.

tremblement, n.m. trembling. t. de terre, earthquake.

trembler, vb. tremble, shake, quake.

trembloter, vb. quiver.

trémousser, vb. flutter.

trempe, n.f. temper, cast.

tremper, vb. soak, drench, temper.

trente, adj. and n.m. thirty.

trépasser, vb. die.

trépied, n.m. tripod, trivet.

très, *adv.* very.

trésor, *n.m.* treasure, treasury; darling.

trésorier, *n.m.* treasurer.

tressaillement, *n.m.* thrill; start.

tressaillir, *vb.* thrill; start.

tresse, *n.f.* braid.

tresser, *vb.* braid.

tréteau, *n.m.* trestle.

trève, *n.f.* truce.

triangle, *n.m.* triangle.

tribade, *n.f.* Lesbian.

tribu, *n.f.* tribe.

tribulation, *n.f.* tribulation.

tribut, *n.m.* tribute.

tributaire, *adj.* tributary.

tricher, *vb.* cheat.

tricherie, *n.f.* cheating.

tricoter, *vb.* knit.

trier, *vb.* sort.

trimestre, *n.m.* term.

trimestriel, *adj.* quarterly.

trinquer, *vb.* touch glasses in making a toast.

triomphant, *adj.* triumphant.

triomphe, *n.m.* triumph.

triompher, *vb.* triumph.

triple, *adj.* and *n.m.* triple.

tripoter, *vb.* fiddle with, dabble in; bother.

triste, *adj.* sad.

tristesse, *n.f.* sadness.

trivial, *adj.* trivial.

trivialité, *n.f.* triviality.

troc, *n.m.* barter.

trois, *adj.* and *n.m.* three.

troisième, *adj.* third.

trompe, *n.f.* horn, trumpet, elephant's trunk.

trompe l'œil, *n.m.* make-believe, sham.

tromper, *vb.* deceive, cheat. **se t.,** be wrong, make a mistake.

tromperie, *n.f.* deceit.

trompette, *n.f.* trumpet.

trompeur, *adj.* deceitful.

tronc, *n.m.* trunk.

trône, *n.m.* throne.

trop, *adv.* too; too much, too many.

trophée, *n.m.* trophy.

tropical, *adj.* tropical.

tropique, *n.m.* tropic.

troquer, *vb.* barter, dicker, trade.

trot, *n.m.* trot.

trotter, *vb.* trot.

trottiner, *vb.* trot, jog.

trottoir, *n.m.* sidewalk.

trou, *n.m.* hole.

trouble, *n.m.* disturbance, riot.

troublé, *adj.* anxious, worried.

troubler, *vb.* perturb.

trouer, *vb.* pierce, bore.

troupe, *n.f.* troop.

troupeau, *n.m.* herd, flock, drove.

troupier, *n.m.* soldier, trooper.

trousseau, *n.m.* bunch; outfit.

trousser, *vb.* truss up, turn up.

trouvaille, *n.f.* discovery.

trouver, *vb.* find. **se t.,** be located.

truc, *n.m.* trick; thing.

truelle, *n.f.* trowel.

truite, *n.f.* trout.

truquer, *vb.* fake.

trust, *n.m.* trust.

T.S.F., *n.f.* radio.

tu, *pron.* you.

tube, *n.m.* tube, pipe.

tuberculeux, *adj.* tuberculous.

tuberculose, *n.f.* tuberculosis.

tuer, *vb.* kill.

tuerie, *n.f.* slaughter, massacre.

tuile, *n.f.* tile.

tulipe, *n.f.* tulip.

tuméfier, *vb.* make swollen.

tumulte, *n.m.* tumult, turmoil, uproar.

tunique, *n.f.* tunic.

tunnel, *n.f.* tunnel.

Turc *m.,* **Turque** *f.n.* Turk.

turc, *n.m.* Turkish (language).

turc *m.,* **turque** *f. adj.* Turkish.

Turquie, *n.f.* Turkey.

tutelle, *n.f.* tutelage, protection.

tuteur, *n.m.* guardian.

tutoyer, *vb.* use "tu" (familiar form) to.

tuyau, *n.f.* pipe; hose.

tympan, *n.m.* eardrum.

type, *n.m.* type; fellow, guy.

typique, *adj.* typical.

tyran, *n.m.* tyrant.

tyrannie, *n.f.* tyranny.

tyranniser, *vb.* tyrannize.

tzigane, *n.* gypsy.

U

ubiquité, *n.f.* ubiquity.

ulcère, *n.m.* ulcer.

ultérieur, *adj.* ulterior, further.

ultime, *adj.* ultimate, last.

un *m.,* **une** *f.* **1.** *art.* a. **2.** *adj.* and *n.m.* one.

unanime, *adj.* unanimous.

unanimité, *n.f.* unanimity.

unifier, *vb.* unify.

uniforme, *adj.* and *n.m.* uniform.

union, *n.f.* union.

unique, *adj.* unique; only.

unir, *vb.* unite.

unisexuel, *adj.* unisex.

unisson, *n.m.* unison.

unité, *n.f.* unit, unity.

univers, *n.m.* universe.

universel, *adj.* universal.

université, *n.f.* university, college.

urbain, *adj.* urban.

urgence, *n.f.* urgency.

urgent, *adj.* urgent, pressing.

urne, *n.f.* urn; ballot box.

urticaire, *n.f.* hives.

usage, *n.m.* use; custom.

usager, *adj.* for daily use.

usé, *adj.* shabby, worn-out.

user, *vb.* wear out.

usine, *n.f.* factory.

ustensile, *n.f.* utensil.

usuel, *adj.* usual.

usure, *n.f.* wear and tear; usury; interest.

usurper, *vb.* usurp.

utile, *adj.* helpful, useful.

utilisation, *n.f.* use.

utiliser, *vb.* use.

utilité, *n.f.* utility.

utopie, *n.f.* utopia.

V

vacance, *n.* vacancy; *(pl.)* vacation.

vacarme, *n.m.* uproar.

vaccin, *n.m.* vaccine.

vacciner, *vb.* vaccinate.

vache, *n.f.* cow.

vaciller (-l-), *vb.* waver.

vacuité, *n.f.* emptiness, vacuity.

vagabond, *adj.* vagrant.

vagabonder, *vb.* roam, tramp.

vague, **1.** *n.f.* wave. **2.** *adj.* vague.

vaguer, *vb.* wander.

vaillant, *adj.* valiant, brave, gallant.

vain, *adj.* idle, vain, futile.

vaincre, *vb.* defeat.

vainqueur, *n.m.* victor.

vaisseau, *n.m.* ship.

vaisselle, *n.f.* dishes.

valeur, *n.f.* valor; value, worth; *(pl.)* securities.

valeureux, *adj.* brave, valorous.

valide, *adj.* valid.

valise, *n.f.* suitcase.

vallée, *n.f.* valley.

vallon, *n.m.* valley, vale.

valoir, *vb.* be worth. **v. mieux,** be better.

valse, *n.f.* waltz.

vandale, *n.m.f.* vandal.

vanille, *n.f.* vanilla.

vanité, *n.f.* conceit, vanity.

vaniteux, *adj.* vain.

vantard, *adj.* boastful.

vanter, *vb.* extol. **se v.,** boast, brag.

vapeur, **1.** *n.m.* steamship. **2.** *n.f.* vapor, steam.

vaporisateur, *n.f.* vaporizer, spray.

variation, *n.f.* variation, change.

varicelle, *n.f.* chicken-pox.

varier, *vb.* vary.

variété, *n.f.* variety.

variole, *n.f.* smallpox.

vase, *n.m.* vase, jar, pot.

vasectomie, *n.f.* vasectomy.

vaseux, *adj.* slimy.

vassal, *n.f.* vassal.

vaste, *adj.* vast, spacious.

vaurien, *n.m.* worthless person, idler.

veau, *n.m.* calf.

végéter, *vb.* vegetate.

véhicule, *n.m.* vehicle.

veille, *n.f.* eve, day before.

veiller, *vb.* watch over, sit up.

veine, *n.f.* vein; luck.

velours, *n.m.* velvet. **v. côtelé,** corduroy.

velouté, adj. like velvet.

velu, adj. hairy.

vendange, n.f. vintage.

vendeur, n.m. seller; clerk, salesman.

vendre, vb. sell.

vendredi, n.m. Friday.

vénéneux, adj. poisonous.

vénérer, vb. venerate.

vengeance, n.f. revenge.

venger, vb. avenge. se v., get revenge.

venimeux, adj. poisonous.

venin, n.m. poison.

venir, vb. come. v. de, have just. . . . à v., forthcoming.

vent, n.m. wind.

vente, n.f. sale.

venteux, adj. windy.

ventilateur, n.m. fan.

ventiler, vb. ventilate.

ventre, n.m. belly.

venue, n.f. advent, arrival.

vêpres, n.f.pl. vespers.

ver (-r), n.m. worm.

véracité, n.f. veracity.

véranda, n.f. porch.

verbe, n.m. verb.

verbeux, adj. wordy, verbose.

verdeur, n.f. greenness, sharpness, vigor.

verdict (-kt), n.m. verdict.

verdir, vb. make or become green.

verge, n.f. rod.

verger, n.m. orchard.

vérification, n.f. check.

vérifier, vb. check, confirm.

véritable, adj. genuine, real.

vérité, n.f. truth.

vermine, n.f. vermin.

vernir, vb. varnish.

vernis, n.m. varnish.

vérole, n.f. petite v., smallpox.

verre, n.m. glass.

verrou, n.m. bolt.

verrouiller, vb. bolt.

vers, 1. n.m. verse. 2. prep. toward.

verse, adj. tomber à v., pour.

verser, vb. pour, shed.

versifier, vb. versify.

version, n.f. version, translation.

vert, adj. green.

vertical, adj. upright, vertical.

vertige, n.m. dizziness.

vertigineux, adj. dizzy.

vertu, n.f. virtue.

vertueux, adj. virtuous.

verveux, adj. lively, animated.

vessie, n.f. bladder.

veste, n.f. jacket.

vestiaire, n.m. cloak-room.

vestibule, n.m. hall, lobby.

vestige, n.m. vestige, remains.

veston, n.m. jacket, coat.

vêtement, n.m. garment; (pl.) clothes.

vétéran, n.m. veteran.

vétérinaire, n.m. veterinary.

vêtir, vb. clothe.

véto, n.m. veto.

veuf, n.m. widower.

veuve, n.f. widow.

vexation, n.f. vexation.

vexer, vb. vex.

viaduc, n.m. viaduct.

viande, n.f. meat.

vibrant, adj. vibrant, vibrating.

vibration, n.f. vibration.

vibrer, vb. vibrate.

vicaire, n.m. vicar.

vice, n.m. vice.

vice-roi, n.m. viceroy.

vicieux, adj. vicious.

vicomte, n.m. viscount.

victime, n.f. victim.

victoire, n.f. victory.

victorieux, adj. victorious.

vidange, n.f. emptying, cleaning.

vide, 1. n.m. emptiness, vacuum, blank, gap. 2. adj. empty, void, vacant, blank.

vidéodisque, n.m. videodisc.

vider, vb. empty, drain.

vie, n.f. life.

vieil, adj. old.

vieillard, n.m. old man.

vieille, 1. n.f. old woman. 2. adj. (f.) old.

vieillesse, n.f. old age.

vieillir, vb. age.

vierge, n.f. virgin.

vieux, adj.m. old.

vif m., vive f. adj. lively, quick, brisk, bright, vivacious.

vif-argent, n.m. quicksilver.

vigie, n.f. lookout man or station.

vigilance, n.f. vigilance.

vigilant, adj. watchful.

vigne, n.f. vine; vineyard.

vigoureux, adj. lusty, hardy, vigorous.

vigueur, n.f. vigor, force.

vil (-l), adj. vile.

vilain, adj. ugly, mean, wicked.

village (-l-), n.m. village.

ville (-l-), n.f. city, town.

villégiature (-l-), n.f. country holiday.

vin, n.m. wine.

vinaigre, n.m. vinegar.

vindicatif, adj. vindictive.

vingt (văn), adj. and n.m. twenty.

vingtaine (văn-), n.f. score.

vingtième (văn-), adj. and n.m. twentieth.

violateur, n.m. violator.

violation, n.f. violation.

violemment, adj. violently.

violence, n.f. violence.

violent, adj. violent.

violer, vb. violate.

violet, adj. purple, violet.

violette, n.f. violet.

violon, n.m. violin.

vipère, n.f. viper.

virgule, n.f. comma.

viril (-l), adj. manly.

virilité, n.f. manhood.

virtuel, adj. virtual.

virtuose, n.m.f. virtuoso.

virus (-s), n.m. virus.

vis (-s), n.f. screw.

visa, n.m. visa.

visage, n.m. face.

vis-à-vis, adv. opposite, across from.

viser, vb. aim.

visibilité, n.f. visibility.

visible, adj. visible.

visière, n.f. visor; keenness.

vision, n.f. vision.

visionnaire, adj. and n.m.f. visionary.

visite, n.f. call, visit.

visiter, vb. visit.

visiteur, n.m. visitor.

visqueux, adj. viscous, sticky.

visser, vb. screw.

visuel, adj. visual.

vital, adj. vital.

vitalité, n.f. vitality.

vitamine, n.f. vitamin.

vite, adv. quick, fast.

vitesse, n.f. speed, rate; gear. changer de v., shift gears.

vitrail, n.m. (church) window.

vitre, n.f. pane.

vitrine, n.f. display case, shop-window.

vitupération, n.f. vituperation.

vivace, adj. long-lived; perennial (of plant).

vivacité, n.f. vivacity.

vivant, adj. alive.

vivement, adv. quickly, smartly, vividly.

vivre, vb. live.

vocabulaire, n.m. vocabulary.

vocal, adj. vocal.

vocation, n.f. vocation.

vœu (vœ), n.m. vow.

vogue, n.f. vogue.

voici, vb. here is, behold.

voie, n.f. track, road. v. d'eau, leak.

voilà, vb. there is; behold.

voile, n.m. veil; sail.

voiler, vb. veil, hide.

voilure, n.f. sails.

voir, vb. see. faire v., show.

voirie, n.m. dump.

voisin, 1. n.m. neighbor. 2. adj. nearby, adjoining.

voisinage, n.m. neighborhood.

voisiner, vb. act like a neighbor.

voiture, n.f. car, carriage. en v.!, all aboard!

voix, n.f. voice.

vol, n.m. flight; theft, robbery; ripoff.

volage, adj. fickle.

volaille, n.f. fowl, poultry.

volatil, adj. volatile.

volcan, n.m. volcano.

volcanique, adj. volcanic.

volée, n.f. flight, covey; herd.

voler, vb. fly; steal, rob; rip off.

volet, n.m. shutter, blind.

voleur, n.m. thief, robber.

vol frété, n.m. charter flight.

volontaire, 1. n.m. volunteer. 2. adj. voluntary, volunteer.

volonté, n.f. will.

volontiers, adv. gladly, willingly.

voltigement, n.m. flutter.

voltiger, vb. flutter; hover.

volubilité, *n.f.* volubility, glibness.

volume, *n.m.* volume.

volumineux, *adj.* bulky.

volupté, *n.f.* pleasure, voluptuousness.

vomir, *vb.* vomit.

vorace, *adj.* voracious.

votant, *n.m.* voter.

vote, *n.m.* vote.

voter, *vb.* vote.

votre *sg.,* **vos** *pl. adj.* your.

vôtre, *pron.* le v., yours.

vouer, *vb.* vow.

vouloir, *vb.* want, wish, will. v. dire, mean. v. savoir, wonder. v. bien, be willing. en v. à, bear a grudge against.

vous, *pron.* you, yourself.

voûte, *n.f.* vault.

voûter, *vb.* arch.

voyage, *n.m.* journey, trip.

voyager, *vb.* travel.

voyageur, *n.m.* traveler, passenger.

voyageur de banlieue, *n.m.* commuter.

voyant, 1. *n.m.* clairvoyant. **2.** *adj.* gaudy, flashy.

voyelle, *n.f.* vowel.

vrai, *adj.* true, real.

vraisemblable, *adj.* probable, likely.

vraisemblance, *n.f.* probability.

vue, *n.f.* view, sight.

vue d'ensemble, *n.f.* overview.

vulcaniser, *vb.* vulcanize.

vulgaire, *adj.* vulgar, coarse, rude.

vulgarité, *n.f.* vulgarity.

vulnérable, *adj.* vulnerable.

W, X, Y, Z

wagon, *n.m.* coach, car.

wagon-lits, *n.m.* sleeping car.

wagon-restaurant, *n.m.* diner, dining-car.

watt, *n.m.* watt.

xérès (k-), *n.m.* sherry.

xylophone (ks-), *n.m.* xylophone.

y, *adv.* there, in it, to it.

yacht, *n.m.* yacht.

zèbre, *n.m.* zebra.

zèle, *n.m.* zeal.

zélé, *adj.* zealous.

zénith, *n.m.* zenith.

zéro, *n.m.* zero.

zézayer, *vb.* lisp.

zibeline, *n.f.* sable.

zigzaguer, *vb.* zigzag.

zodiaque, *n.m.* zodiac.

zone, *n.f.* zone, district.

zoologie, *n.f.* zoology.

zoologique, *adj.* zoological. jardin z., zoo.

English-French

A

a, *art.* un *m.*, une *f.*

aardvark, *n.* aardvark *m.*

abacus, *n.* abaque *m.*

abandon, *vb.* abandonner.

abandon, *n.* abandon *m.*

abandoned, *adj.* abandonné.

abandonment, *n.* abandon *m.*

abase, *vb.* abaisser; avilir.

abasement, *n.* abaissement *m.;* avilissement *m.*

abash, *vb.* déconcerter.

abate, *vb.* diminuer.

abatement, *n.* diminution *f.*

abbess, *n.* abbesse *f.*

abbey, *n.* abbaye *f.*

abbot, *n.* abbé *m.*

abbreviate, *vb.* abréger.

abbreviation, *n.* abréviation *f.*

abdicate, *vb.* abdiquer.

abdication, *n.* abdication *f.*

abdomen, *n.* abdomen *m.*

abdominal, *adj.* abdominal.

abduct, *vb.* enlever.

abduction, *n.* enlèvement *m.*

abductor, *n.* ravisseur *m.*

aberrant, *adj.* aberrant, égaré.

aberration, *n.* égarement *m.*

abet, *vb.* aider, encourager, appuyer.

abetment, *n.* encouragement *m.,* appui *m.*

abettor, *n.* aide *m.,* complice *m.*

abeyance, *n.* suspension *f.*

abhor, *vb.* détester.

abhorrence, *n.* aversion extrême *f.,* horreur *f.*

abhorrent, *adj.* odieux, répugnant (à).

abide, *vb.* (tolerate) supporter; (remain) demeurer; (a. by the law) respecter la loi.

abiding, *adj.* constant, durable.

ability, *n.* talent *m.*

abject, *adj.* abject.

abjuration, *n.* abjuration *f.*

abjure, *vb.* abjurer, renoncer à.

abjurer, *n.* personne *f.* qui abjure.

ablative, *adj. and n.* ablatif *m.*

ablaze, *adj.* en feu, en flammes.

able, *adj.* capable; (to be a.) pouvoir.

able-bodied, *adj.* fort, robuste.

able-bodied seaman, *n.* marin de première classe *m.*

ablution, *n.* ablution *f.*

ably, *adv.* capablement.

abnegate, *vb.* nier.

abnegation, *n.* abnégation *f.*

abnormal, *adj.* anormal.

abnormality, *n.* irrégularité *f.*

abnormally, *adv.* anormalement.

aboard, 1. *adv.* (naut.) à bord; (all a.) en voiture. 2. *prep.* à bord de.

abode, *n.* demeure *f.*

abolish, *vb.* abolir.

abolishment, *n.* abolissement *m.*

abolition, *n.* abolition *f.*

abominable, *adj.* abominable.

abominate, *vb.* abominer.

abomination, *n.* abomination *f.*

aboriginal, *adj.* aborigène, primitif.

abortion, *n.* avortement *m.*

abortive, *adj.* abortif, manqué.

abound, *vb.* abonder (en).

about, 1. *adv.* (approximately) à peu près; (around) autour; (to be a. to) être sur le point de. 2. *prep.* (concerning) au sujet de; (near) auprès de; (around) autour de.

about-face, *n.* volte-face *f.*

above, 1. *adv.* au-dessus. 2. *prep.* (higher than) au-dessus de; (more than) plus de.

aboveboard, *adj. and adv.* ouvertement, franchement.

abrasion, *n.* abrasion *f.*

abrasive, *adj.* abrasif.

abreast, *adv.* de front.

abridge, *vb.* abréger.

abridgment, *n.* abrégé *m.,* réduction *f.*

abroad, *adv.* à l'étranger.

abrogate, *vb.* abroger.

abrogation, *n.* abrogation *f.*

abrupt, *adj.* brusque; (steep) escarpé.

abruptly, *adv.* brusquement, subitement.

abruptness, *n.* brusquerie *f.,* précipitation *f.*

abscess, *n.* abcès *m.*

abscond, *vb.* disparaître, se dérober.

absence, *n.* absence *f.*

absent, *adj.* absent.

absentee, *n.* absent *m.,* manquant *m.*

absinthe, *n.* absinthe *f.*

absolute, *adj.* absolu.

absolutely, *adv.* absolument.

absoluteness, *n.* pouvoir absolu *m.;* arbitraire *m.*

absolution, *n.* absolution *f.*

absolutism, *n.* absolutisme *m.*

absolve, *vb.* absoudre.

absorb, *vb.* absorber.

absorbed, *adj.* absorbé, préoccupé.

absorbent, *n. and adj.* absorbant *m.*

absorbing, *adj.* absorbant, préoccupant.

absorption, *n.* absorption *f.*

abstain from, *vb.* s'abstenir de.

abstemious, *adj.* abstème.

abstinence, *n.* abstinence *f.*

abstract, 1. *n.* (book) extrait *m.* 2. *adj.* abstrait.

abstracted, *adj.* détaché, pensif.

abstraction, *n.* abstraction *f.*

abstruse, *adj.* caché, abstrus.

abundance, *n.* abondance *f.*

abundant, *adj.* abondant.

abundantly, *adv.* abondamment.

absurd, *adj.* absurde.

absurdity, *n.* absurdité *f.*

absurdly, *adv.* absurdement.

abuse, 1. *n.* (misuse) abus *m.;* (insult) injures *f.pl.* 2. *vb.* abuser de, injurier.

abusive, *adj.* (insulting) injurieux.

abusively, *adv.* abusivement, injurieusement.

abut, *vb.* s'embrancher (sur), aboutir (à).

abutment, *n.* contrefort *m.;* (of a bridge) culée *f.*

abyss, *n.* abîme *m.*

academic, *adj.* académique.

academic freedom, *n.* liberté de l'enseignement *f.*

academy, *n.* académie *f.*

acanthus, *n.* acanthe *f.*

accede, *vb.* consentir.

accelerate, *vb.* accélérer.

acceleration, *n.* accélération *f.*

accelerator, *n.* accélérateur *m.*

accent, *n.* accent *m.*

accentuate, *vb.* accentuer.

accept, *vb.* accepter.

acceptability, *n.* acceptabilité *f.*

acceptable, *adj.* acceptable.

acceptably, *adv.* agréablement.

acceptance, *n.* acceptation *f.*

access, *n.* accès *m.*

accessible, *adj.* accessible.

accessory, *n. and adj.* accessoire *m.*

accident, *n.* accident *m.*

accidental, *adj.* accidentel.

accidentally, *adv.* accidentellement, par hasard.

acclaim, *vb.* acclamer.

acclamation, *n.* acclamation *f.*

acclimate, *vb.* acclimater.

acclivity, *n.* montée *f.,* rampe *f.*

accolade, *n.* accolade *f.*

accommodate, *vb.* (lodge) loger; (oblige) obliger.

accommodating, *adj.* accommodant, obligeant.

accommodation, *n.* (lodging) logement *m.*

accompaniment, *n.* accompagnement *m.*

accompanist, *n.* accompagnateur *m.,* accompagnatrice *f.*

accompany, *vb.* accompagner.

accomplice, *n.* complice *m.f.*

accomplish, *vb.* accomplir.

accomplished, *adj.* accompli, achevé.

accord, *n.* accord *m.*

accordance, *n.* conformité *f.*

accordingly, *adv.* (correspondingly) à l'avenant; (therefore) donc.

according to, *prep.* selon.

accordion, *n.* accordéon *m.*

accost, *vb.* aborder.

account, *n.* (comm.) compte *m.;* (narrative) récit *m.*

accountable for, *adj.* responsable de.

accountant, n. comptable m.

account for, vb. rendre compte de.

accounting, n. comptabilité f.

accouter, vb. habiller, équiper.

accouterments, n. équipements m.pl., accoutrements m.pl.

accredit, vb. accréditer.

accretion, n. accroissement m.

accrual, n. accroissement m.

accrue, vb. provenir.

accumulate, vb. entasser.

accumulation, n. entassement m.

accumulative, adj. (thing) qui s'accumule, (person) qui accumule.

accumulator, n. accumulateur m., accumulatrice f.

accuracy, n. précision f.

accurate, adj. précis.

accursed, adj. maudit, exécrable.

accusation, n. accusation f.

accusative, n. and adj. accusatif m.

accuse, vb. accuser.

accused, n. and adj. accusé m., accusée f.

accuser, n. accusateur m., accusatrice f.

accustom, vb. accoutumer.

accustomed, adj. accoutumé, habituel.

ace, n. as m.

acerbity, n. acerbité f., âpreté f.

acetate, n. acétate m.

acetic acid, n. acide acétique m.

acetylene, n. acétylène m.

ache, 1. n. douleur f. 2. vb. faire mal à.

achieve, vb. accomplir.

achievement, n. accomplissement m.

acid, adj. and n. acide m.

acidify, vb. acidifier.

acidity, n. acidité f.

acidosis, n. acidose f.

acid test, n. épreuve concluante f.

acidulous, adj. acidulé.

acknowledge, vb. reconnaître; (a. receipt of) accuser réception de.

acme, n. comble m., apogée m.

acne, n. acné f.

acolyte, n. acolyte m.

acorn, n. gland m.

acoustics, n. acoustique f.

acquaint, vb. informer (de); (be a.d with) connaître.

acquaintance, n. connaissance f.

acquainted, adj. connu, familier (avec).

acquiesce in, vb. acquiescer à.

acquiescence, n. acquiescement m.

acquire, vb. acquérir.

acquirement, n. acquis m., acquisition f.

acquisition, n. acquisition f.

acquisitive, adj. porté à acquérir.

acquit, vb. acquitter.

acquittal, n. acquittement m.

acre, n. arpent m., acre f.

acreage, n. superficie f.

acrid, adj. âcre.

acrimonious, adj. acrimonieux.

acrimony, n. acrimonie f., aigreur f.

acrobat, n. acrobate m.f.

across, 1. prep. à travers; (on the other side of) de l'autre côté de. 2. adv. en travers.

acrostic, n. acrostiche m.

act, 1. n. acte m. 2. vb. (do) agir; (play) jouer; (behave) se conduire.

acting, 1. n. (theater) jeu m.; feinte f. 2. adj. (taking the place of) suppléant; (comm.) gérant.

actinism, n. actinisme m.

actinium, n. actinium m.

action, n. action f.

activate, vb. activer.

activation, n. activation f.

activator, n. activateur m.

active, adj. actif.

activity, n. activité f.

actor, n. acteur m.

actress, n. actrice f.

actual, adj. réel.

actuality, n. réalité f., actualité f.

actually, adv. réellement, véritablement, en effet.

actuary, n. actuaire m.

actuate, vb. mettre en action, animer.

acumen, n. finesse f., pénétration f.

acupuncture, n. acuponcture f.

acute, adj. (geom.) aigu m., aiguë f.; (mind) fin.

acutely, adv. vivement, d'une manière poignante.

acuteness, n. finesse f., vivacité f.

adage, n. adage m., proverbe m.

adamant, adj. indomptable.

Adam's apple, n. pomme d'Adam f.

adapt, vb. adapter.

adaptable, adj. adaptable.

adaptability, n. faculté d'adaptation f.

adaptation, n. adaptation f.

adapter, n. qui adapte.

adaptive, adj. adaptable.

add, vb. (join) ajouter; (arith.) additionner.

adder, n. vipère f.

addict, n. personne adonnée à f.

addict oneself to, vb. s'adonner à.

addition, n. addition f.

additional, adj. additionel.

addle, 1. vb. corrompre, rendre couvi (of eggs). 2. adj. couvi, pourri.

address, 1. n. (on letters, etc.) adresse f.; (speech) discours

m. 2. vb. (a letter) adresser; (a person) adresser la parole à.

addressee, n. destinataire m.f.

adduce, vb. alléguer, avancer.

adenoid, adj. and n. adénoïde f.

adeptly, adv. habilement, adeptement.

adeptness, n. habileté f.

adequacy, n. suffisance f.

adequate, adj. suffisant.

adequately, adv. suffisamment, convenablement.

adhere, vb. adhérer.

adherence, n. adhérence f., attachement m.

adherent, n. adhérent m.

adhesion, n. adhésion f.

adhesive, adj. adhésif.

adhesiveness, n. propriété d'adhérer f.

adieu, n. and adv. adieu m.

adjacent, adj. adjacent.

adjective, n. adjectif m.

adjoin, vb. adjoindre, être contigu (à).

adjourn, vb. ajourner, tr. s'ajourner, intr.

adjournment, n. ajournement m.

adjunct, n. and adj. adjoint m., accessoire m.

adjust, vb. ajuster, arranger, régler.

adjuster, n. ajusteur m.

adjustment, n. ajustement m., accommodement m.

adjutant, n. capitaine adjudant major m.

administer, vb. administrer.

administration, n. administration f.

administrative, adj. administratif.

administrator, n. administrateur m.

admirable, adj. admirable.

admirably, adv. admirablement.

admiral, n. amiral m.

admiralty, n. amirauté f.

admiration, n. admiration f.

admire, vb. admirer.

admirer, n. admirateur m.

admiringly, adv. avec admiration.

admissible, adj. admissible.

admission, n. (entrance) entrée f.; (confession) aveu m.

admit, vb. (let in) laisser entrer; (confess) avouer.

admittance, n. entrée f.

admittedly, adv. de l'aveu de tout le monde.

admixture, n. mélange m.

admonish, vb. réprimander.

admonition, n. admonition f., avertissement m.

ado, n. fracas m.

adolescence, n. adolescence f.

adolescent, adj. and n. adolescent m.f.

adopt, vb. adopter.

adoption, n. adoption f.

adorable, adj. adorable.

adoration, n. adoration f.

adore, vb. adorer.

adorn, vb. orner.

adornment, n. ornement m.

adrenal glands, n.pl. capsules surrénales f.pl.

adrenalin, n. adrénaline f.

adrift, adv. (naut.) à la dérive.

adroit, adj. adroit.

adulate, vb. aduler.

adulation, n. adulation f.

adult, adj. and n. adulte m.f.

adulterant, n. adultérant n.

adulterate, vb. adultérer; (of wines, milk, etc.) fralater.

adulterer, n. adultère m.

adulteress, n. femme adultère f.

adultery, n. adultère m.

advance, 1. n. (motion forward) avancement m.; (progress) progrès m.; (pay) avances f.pl.; (in a.) d'avance. 2. vb. avancer.

advanced, adj. avancé.

advancement, n. avancement m., progrès m.

advantage, n. avantage m.

advantageous, adj. avantageux.

advantageously, adv. avantageusement.

advent, n. venue f.; (eccles.) Avent m.

adventitious, adj. adventice, fortuit.

adventure, n. aventure f.

adventurer, n. aventurier m.

adventurous, adj. aventureux.

adventurously, adv. aventureusement.

adverb, n. adverbe m.

adverbial, adj. adverbial.

adversary, n. adversaire m.

adverse, adj. adverse.

adversely, adv. défavorablement, d'une manière hostile.

adversity, n. adversité f.

advert, vb. faire allusion (à).

advertise, vb. annoncer; (a. a product) faire de la réclame pour un produit.

advertisement, n. publicité f.; (in a paper) annonce f.; (on a wall) affiche f.

advertiser, n. personne qui fait de réclame f.

advertising, n. publicité f., annonce (newspaper) f.

advice, n. conseil m.; (comm.) avis m.

advisability, n. convenance f., utilité f.

advisable, adj. recommandable.

advisably, adv. convenablement.

advise, vb. conseiller.

advisedly, adv. de propos délibéré.

advisement, n. délibération.

advocacy, n. défense f., plaidoyer m.

advocate, 1. n. (law) avocat m.; (supporter) défenseur m. 2. vb. appuyer.

aegis, n. égide f.

aerate, vb. aérer.

aeration, n. aération f.

aerial, adj. aérien.

aerially, adv. d'une manière aérienne.

aerie, n. aire f.

aeronautics, n. aéronautique f.

aesthetic, adj. esthétique.

afar, adv. loin, de loin.

affability, n. affabilité f.

affable, adj. affable.

affably, adv. affablement.

affair, n. affair f.

affect, vb. (move) toucher; (concern) intéresser; (pretend) affecter.

affectation, n. affectation f.

affected, adj. maniéré.

affecting, adj. touchant, émouvant.

affection, n. affection f.

affectionate, adj. affectueux.

affectionately, adv. affectueusement.

afferent, adj. afférent.

affiance, vb. fiancer.

affidavit, n. attestation (sous serment) f.

affiliate, vb. affilier.

affiliation, n. affiliation f.

affinity, n. affinité f.

affirm, vb. affirmer.

affirmation, n. affirmation f.

affirmative, adj. affirmatif.

affirmatively, adv. affirmativement.

affix, vb. apposer.

afflict, vb. affliger (de).

affliction, n. affliction f.

affluence, n. affluence f., opulence f.

affluent, adj. affluent, opulent.

afford, vb. (have the means to) avoir les moyens de.

affray, n. bagarre m., tumulte m.

affront, 1. n. affront m. 2. vb. insulter.

afield, adv. aux champs, en campagne.

afire, adv. en feu.

afloat, adv. à flot, en train.

aforementioned, adj. mentionné plus haut, susdit.

aforesaid, adj. susdit, ledit.

afraid, pred. adj. (be afraid) avoir peur.

Africa, n. Afrique f.

African, 1. n. Africain m. 2. adj. africain.

aft, adv. à l'arrière.

after, 1. adv. and prep. après. 2. conj. après que.

aftereffect, n. effet m.

aftermath, n. suites f. pl.

afternoon, n. après-midi m. or f.

afterthought, n. réflexion tardive f.

afterward, adv. ensuite.

again, adv. de nouveau, encore; (again and again) maintes et maintes fois.

against, prep. contre.

agape, adv. bouche bée.

agate, n. agate f.

age, 1. n. âge m. 2. vb. vieillir.

aged, adj. vieux, âgé.

ageism, n. attitude discriminative basée sur l'âge f.

ageless, adj. qui ne vieillit jamais.

agency, n. (comm.) agence f.

agenda, n. ordre du jour m., agenda m.

agent, n. agent m.

agglutinate, vb. agglutiner.

agglutination, n. agglutination f.

aggrandize, vb. agrandir.

aggrandizement, n. agrandissement m.

aggravate, vb. (intensify) aggraver; (exasperate) exaspérer.

aggravation, n. aggravation f., agacement m.

aggregate, n. masse f.

aggregation, n. agrégation f., assemblage m.

aggression, n. agression f.

aggressive, adj. agressif.

aggressively, adv. agressivement.

aggressiveness, n. caractère agressif m.

aggressor, n. agresseur m.

aghast, adj. consterné.

agile, adj. agile.

agility, n. agilité f.

agitate, vb. agiter.

agitation, n. agitation f.

agitator, n. agitateur m.

agnostic, n. and adj. agnostique m.

ago, adv. il y a (always precedes).

agonized, adj. torturé, déchirant.

agony, n. (anguish) angoisse f.; (death agony) agonie f.

agrarian, adj. agraire, agrarien.

agree, vb. être d'accord.

agreeable, adj. agréable.

agreeably, adv. agréablement.

agreement, n. accord m.

agriculture, n. agriculture f.

ahead, 1. adv. and interj. en avant. 2. prep. (ahead of) en avant de.

aid, 1. n. aide f.; (first aid) premiers secours; (first-aid station) poste de secours. 2. vb. aider.

aide, n. aide m., assistant m.

ail, vb. intr. être souffrant.

ailment, n. indisposition f.

aim, 1. n. (fig.) but m. 2. vb. viser.

aimless, adj. sans but.

aimlessly, adv. sans but, à la dérive.

air, 1. n. air m.; (a. force) aviation f.; (by a. mail) par avion; (in the open a.) en plein air. 2. vb. aérer.

airbag, n. (in automobiles) sac à air m.

air base, n. champs d'aviation m.

airborne, *adj.* par voie de l'air.
air-condition, *vb.* climatiser.
air-conditioning, *n.* climatisation *f.*
aircraft, *n.* avions *m.pl.*; (**aircraft carrier**) porte-avions *m.*
air fleet, *n.* aéroflotte.
air gun, *n.* fusil à vent.
airing, *n.* aérage *m.,* tour *m.*
air line, *n.* ligne aérienne *f.*
air liner, *n.* avion *m.*
air mail, *n.* poste aérienne *f.*
airplane, *n.* avion *m.*
air pollution, *n.* pollution de l'air *f.*
airport, *n.* aéroport *m.*
air pressure, *n.* pression d'air *f.*
air raid, *n.* raid aérien *m.*
airsick, *adj.* (**to be a.**) avoir le mal d'air.
airtight, *adj.* imperméable à l'air, étanche.
airy, *adj.* (**well aired**) aéré; (**light**) léger.
aisle, *n.* (**passageway**) passage *m.;* (*arch.*) bas côté *m.*
ajar, *adv.* entr'ouvert.
akin, *adj.* allié (à), parent (de).
alacrity, *n.* empressement *m.*
alarm, *n.* alarme *f.*
alarmist, *n.* alarmiste *m.*
albino, *n.* albinos *m.*
album, *n.* album *m.*
alcohol, *n.* alcool *m.*
alcoholic, *adj.* alcoolique.
alcove, *n.* (**recess**) niche *f.;* (**sleeping alcove**) alcôve *f.*
ale, *n.* bière *f.*
alert, *adj.* alerte.
alfalfa, *n.* luzerne *f.*
algebra, *n.* algèbre *f.*
alias, **1.** *n.* nom d'emprunt *m.* **2.** *adv.* autrement nommé, dit.
alibi, *n.* alibi *m.*
alien, *adj.* étranger.
alienate, *vb.* aliéner.
alight, *vb.* (**descend**) descendre; (**stop after descent**) s'abattre.
align, *vb.* aligner.
alike, **1.** *adj.* semblable; (**be alike**) se ressembler. **2.** *adv.* également.
alimentary canal, *n.* canal alimentaire *m.*
alive, *adj.* vivant.
alkali, *n.* alcali *m.*
alkaline, *adj.* alcalin.
all, **1.** *adj.* tout *m.sg.,* toute *f.sg.,* tous *m.pl.,* toutes *f.pl.* **2.** *adv. and pron.* (**everything**) tout; (**above all**) surtout; (**all at once**) tout d'un coup; (**all the same**) tout de même; (**that's all**) c'est tout; (**not at all**) pas du tout; (**everybody**) tous; (**all of you**) vous tous.
allay, *vb.* apaiser.
allegation, *n.* allégation *f.*
allege, *vb.* alléguer.
allegiance, *n.* fidélité *f.*
allegory, *n.* allégorie *f.*
allergy, *n.* allergie *f.*
alleviate, *vb.* soulager.

alley, *n.* (**in town**) ruelle *f.;* (**blind alley**) cul-de-sac *m.*
alliance, *n.* alliance *f.*
allied, *adj.* allié.
alligator, *n.* alligator *m.*
allocate, *vb.* assigner.
allot, *vb.* (**grant**) accorder; (**distribute**) répartir.
allotment, *n.* partage *m.,* lot *m.*
allow, *vb.* (**permit**) permettre; (**admit**) admettre; (**grant**) accorder; (**allow for**) tenir compte de.
allowance, *n.* (**money granted**) allocation *f.;* (**food**) ration *f.;* (**tolerance**) tolérance *f.;* (**pension**) rente *f.;* (**weekly allowance**) semaine *f.*
alloy, *n.* alliage *m.*
all right, *adv.* très bien.
allude to, *vb.* faire allusion à.
allure, *vb.* séduire.
allusion, *n.* allusion *f.*
ally, **1.** *n.* allié *m.* **2.** *vb.* allier.
almanac, *n.* almanach *m.*
almighty, *adj.* tout-puissant.
almond, *n.* amande *f.*
almost, *adv.* presque.
alms, *n.* aumône *f.*
aloft, *adv.* en haut.
alone, *adj.* seul; (**let alone**) laisser tranquille.
along, **1.** *prep.* le long de. **2.** *adv.* (**come along!**) venez donc!
alongside, *prep.* le long de.
aloof, **1.** *adv.* à l'écart. **2.** *adj.* réservé.
aloud, *adv.* à haute voix.
alpaca, *n.* alpaga (**fabric**) *m.;* alpaca (**animal**) *m.*
alphabet, *n.* alphabet *m.*
alphabetical, *adj.* alphabétique.
alphabetize, *vb.* alphabétiser.
Alps, *n.pl.* Alpes *f.pl.*
already, *adv.* déjà.
also, *adv.* aussi.
altar, *n.* autel *m.*
alter, *vb.* changer.
alteration, *n.* modification *f.*
alternate, **1.** *n.* remplaçant *m.* **2.** *adj.* alternatif. **3.** *vb.* alterner.
alternative, *n.* alternative *f.*
although, *conj.* bien que.
altitude, *n.* altitude *f.*
altogether, *adv.* tout à fait.
altruism, *n.* altruisme *m.*
alum, *n.* alun *m.*
aluminum, *n.* aluminium *m.*
always, *adv.* toujours.
amalgam, *n.* amalgame *n.*
amalgamate, *vb.* amalgamer.
amass, *vb.* amasser.
amateur, *n.* amateur *m.*
amaze, *vb.* étonner.
amazement, *n.* stupeur *f.*
amazing, *adj.* étonnant.
ambassador, *n.* ambassadeur *m.,* ambassadrice *f.*
amber, *n.* ambre *m.*
ambidextrous, *adj.* ambidextre.
ambiguity, *n.* ambiguïté *f.*
ambiguous, *adj.* ambigu *m.,* ambiguë *f.*

ambition, *n.* ambition *f.*
ambitious, *adj.* ambitieux.
ambulance, *n.* ambulance *f.*
ambulatory, *adj.* ambulatoire.
ambush, *n.* embuscade *f.*
ameliorate, *vb.* améliorer.
amenable, *adj.* responsable, soumis (à), sujet (à).
amend, *vb.* amender.
amendment, *n.* amendement *m.*
amenity, *n.* aménité *f.,* agrément *m.*
America, *n.* Amérique *f.;* (**North A.**) A. du Nord; (**South A.**) A. du Sud.
American, **1.** *n.* Américain *m.* **2.** *adj.* américain.
amethyst, *n.* améthyste *f.*
amiable, *adj.* aimable.
amicable, *adj.* amical.
amid, *prep.* au milieu de.
amidships, *adv.* par le travers.
amiss, *adv.* de travers.
amity, *n.* amitié *f.*
ammonia, *n.* ammoniaque *f.*
ammunition, *n.* munitions (*f.pl.*) de guerre.
amnesia, *n.* amnésie *f.*
amnesty, *n.* amnistie *f.*
amniocentesis, *n.* amniocentèse *f.*
amoeba, *n.* amibe *f.*
among, *prep.* parmi, entre.
amoral, *adj.* amoral.
amorous, *adj.* amoureux.
amorphous, *adj.* amorphe.
amortize, *vb.* amortir.
amount, **1.** *n.* (**sum**) somme *f.;* (**quantity**) quantité *f.* **2.** *vb.* (**amount to**) se réduire à.
ampere, *n.* ampère *m.*
amphibian, *n.* amphibie *m.*
amphibious, *adj.* amphibie.
amphitheater, *n.* amphithéâtre *m.*
ample, *adj.* ample.
amplify, *vb.* amplifier.
amputate, *n.* amputer.
amputee, *n.* amputé *m.*
amuse, *vb.* amuser.
amusement, *n.* amusement *m.*
an, *art.* un *m.,* une *f.*
anachronism, *n.* anachronisme *m.*
analogous, *adj.* analogue.
analogy, *n.* analogie *f.*
analysis, *n.* analyse *f.*
analyst, *n.* analyste *m.*
analytic, *adj.* analytique.
analyze, *vb.* analyser.
anarchy, *n.* anarchie *f.*
anatomy, *n.* anatomie *f.*
ancestor, *n.* ancêtre *m.*
ancestral, *adj.* d'ancêtres, héréditaire.
ancestry, *n.* aïeux, *m.pl.*
anchor, **1.** *vb.* ancrer. **2.** *n.* ancre *f.*
anchorage, *n.* mouillage *m.,* ancrage *m.*
anchovy, *n.* anchois *m.*
ancient, *adj.* ancien *m.,* ancienne *f.*
and, *conj.* et.

anecdote, n. anecdote f.

anemia, n. anémie f.

anesthetic, adj. and n. anesthésique m.

anesthetist, n. anesthésiste m.

anew, adv. de nouveau.

angel, n. ange m.

anger, n. colère f.

angle, 1. n. angle m.; (at an angle) en biais. 2. vb. (fish) pêcher à la ligne.

angry, adj. fâché; (to get angry) se fâcher.

anguish, n. angoisse f.

angular, adj. anguleux.

aniline, n. aniline f.

animal, n. and adj. animal m.

animate, vb. animer.

animated, adj. animé.

animated cartoon, n. dessin animé m.

animation, n. animation f.

animosity, n. animosité f.

anise, n. anis m.

ankle, n. cheville f.

annals, n.pl. annales f.pl.

annex, n. (to a building) dépendance f.

annexation, n. annexion f.

annihilate, vb. anéantir.

anniversary, n. anniversaire m.

annotate, vb. annoter.

annotation, n. annotation f.

announce, vb. annoncer.

announcement, n. annonce f.

announcer, n. speaker m.

annoy, vb. (vex) contrarier; (bore) ennuyer.

annoyance, n. contrariété f.

annual, adj. annuel.

annuity, n. annuité f., rente annuelle f.

annul, vb. annuler.

anode, n. anode f.

anoint, vb. oindre.

anomalous, adj. anomal, irrégulier.

anonymous, adj. anonyme.

another, adj. and pron. un autre m., une autre f.; (one another) l'un l'autre.

answer, vb. répondre.

answer, n. réponse f.

answerable, adj. responsable (de), susceptible de réponse.

ant, n. fourmi f.

antacid, adj. antiacide.

antagonism, n. antagonisme m.

antagonist, n. antagoniste m.

antagonistic, adj. en opposition (à), hostile (à), opposé (à).

antagonize, vb. s'opposer à.

antarctic, adj. antarctique.

antecedent, adj. and n. antécédent m.

antedate, vb. antidater.

antelope, n. antilope f.

antenna, n. antenne f.

anterior, adj. antérieur.

anteroom, n. antichambre m. or f.

anthem, n. (national) hymne national m.

anthology, n. anthologie f.

anthracite, n. anthracite m.

anthrax, n. anthrax m.

anthropology, n. anthropologie f.

antiaircraft, adj. contre-avion.

antibody, n. anticorps m.

antic, n. bouffonerie f.

anticipate, vb. (advance) anticiper; (expect) s'attendre à; (foresee) prévoir.

anticipation, n. anticipation f.

anticlerical, adj. anticlérical.

anticlimax, n. anticlimax m.

antidote, n. antidote m.

antimony, n. antimoine m.

antinuclear, adj. antinucléaire.

antipathy, n. antipathie f.

antiquated, adj. antique.

antique, n. antique m.; (antique dealer) antiquaire m.

antiquity, n. antiquité f.

antiseptic, adj. and n. antiseptique m.

antisocial, adj. antisocial.

antitoxin, n. antitoxine f.

antler, n. andouiller m.

anvil, n. enclume f.

anxiety, n. anxiété f.

anxious, adj. inquiet m., inquiète f.

any, 1. adj. (in questions, for "some") du m.sg., de la f.sg., des pl.; (not . . . any) ne . . . pas de; (no matter which) n'importe quel; (every) tout. 2. pron. (any of it or them, with verb) en.

anybody, pron. (somebody) quelqu'un; (somebody, implying negation) personne; (not . . . anybody) ne . . . personne; (no matter who) n'importe qui.

anyhow, adv. en tout cas; d'une manière quelconque.

anyone, pron. see anybody.

anything, pron. (something) quelque chose; (something, implying negation) rien; (not . . . anything) ne . . . rien; (no matter what) n'importe quoi.

anyway, adv. see anyhow.

anywhere, adv. n'importe où.

apart, 1. adv. à part. 2. prep. (apart from) en dehors de.

apartheid, n. ségrégation des populations noire et blanche, f.

apartment, n. appartement m.

apathetic, adj. apathique.

apathy, n. apathie f.

ape, n. 1. n. singe m. 2. vb. singer.

aperture, n. ouverture f.

apex, n. sommet m.

aphorism, n. aphorisme m.

apiary, n. rucher m.

apiece, adv. chacun.

apologetic, adj. use verb s'excuser.

apologist, n. apologiste m.

apologize for, vb. s'excuser de.

apology, n. excuses f. pl.

apoplectic, adj. apoplectique.

apoplexy, n. apoplexie f.

apostate, n. apostat m.

apostle, n. apôtre m.

apostolic, adj. apostolique.

appall, vb. épouvanter.

apparatus, n. appareil m.

apparel, n. habillement m.

apparent, adj. apparent.

apparition, n. apparition f.

appeal, 1. n. appel m. 2. vb. (a. to) en appeler à.

appear, vb. (become visible) apparaître; (seem) sembler.

appearance, n. (apparition) apparition f.; (semblance) apparence f.; (aspect) aspect m.

appease, vb. apaiser.

appeaser, n. personne qui apaise.

appellant, n. appelant m.

appellate, adj. d'appel.

appendage, n. accessoire m., apanage m.

appendectomy, n. appendéctomie f.

appendicitis, n. appendicite f.

appendix, n. appendice m.

appetite, n. appétit m.

appetizer, n. (drink) apéritif m.

appetizing, adj. appétissant.

applaud, vb. applaudir.

applause, n. applaudissements m.pl.

apple, n. pomme f.

applesauce, n. compote (f.) de pommes.

appliance, n. appareil m.

applicable, adj. applicable.

applicant, n. postulant m.

application, n. (request) demande f.

applied, adj. appliqué.

apply, vb. (a. to somebody) s'adresser à; (a. for a job) solliciter; (put on) appliquer; (a. oneself) s'appliquer.

appoint, vb. (a person) nommer; (time, place) désigner.

appointment, n. (meeting) rendez-vous m.; (make an a. with) donner un rendezvous à; (nomination) nomination f.

apportion, vb. répartir.

apposition, n. apposition f.

appraisal, n. évaluation f.

appraise, vb. priser.

appreciable, adj. appréciable.

appreciate, vb. apprécier.

appreciation, n. appréciation f.

apprehend, vb. saisir.

apprehension, n. (seizure) arrestation f.; (understanding) compréhension f.; (fear) appréhension f.

apprehensive, adj. craintif.

apprentice, n. apprenti m.

apprise, vb. prévenir, informer.

approach, 1. n. approche f.; (make approaches to) faire des avances à. 2. vb. s'approcher de.

approachable, adj. abordable, accessible.

approbation, n. approbation f.

appropriate, 1. adj. convenable. 2. vb. s'approprier.

appropriation, n. appropriation f.

approval, n. approbation f.

approve, vb. approuver.

approximate, 1. adj. approximatif. 2. vb. se rapprocher (de).

approximately, adv. approximativement, à peu près.

approximation, n. approximation f.

appurtenance, n. appartenance f., dépendance f.

apricot, n. abricot m.

April, n. avril m.

apron, n. tablier m.

apropos, adj. à propos.

apse, n. abside f.

apt, adj. (likely to) sujet à; (suitable for) apte à; (appropriate) à propos; (clever) habile.

aptitude, n. aptitude f.

aquarium, n. aquarium m.

aquatic, adj. aquatique.

aqueduct, n. aqueduc m.

aqueous, adj. aqueux.

aquiline, adj. aquilin.

Arab, 1. n. Arabe m.f. 2. adj. arabe.

Arabic, adj. and n. arabe m.

arable, adj. arable, labourable.

arbiter, n. arbitre m.

arbitrary, adj. arbitraire.

arbitrate, vb. arbitrer.

arbitration, n. arbitrage m.

arbitrator, n. arbitre m.

arbor, n. (bower) berceau m.

arboreal, adj. arboricole.

arc, n. arc m.

arcade, n. arcade f.

arch, 1. n. arc m.; (of bridge) arche f. 2. adj. espiègle.

archaeology, n. archéologie f.

archaic, adj. archaïque.

archbishop, n. archevêque m.

archdiocese, n. archidiocèse m.

archduke, n. archiduc m.

archer, n. archer m.

archery, n. tir à l'arc m.

archipelago, n. archipel m.

architect, n. architecte m.

architectural, adj. architectural.

architecture, n. architecture f.

archives, n. archives f.pl.

archway, n. voûte f., passage (sous une voûte) m.

arctic, adj. arctique.

ardent, adj. ardent.

ardor, n. ardeur f.

arduous, adj. difficile.

area, n. (geom.) aire f.; (locality) région f.; (surface) surface f.

area code, n. indicatif interurbain m.

arena, n. arène f.

argentine, adj. argentin.

argue, vb. (reason) argumenter; (indicate) prouver; (discuss) discuter.

argument, n. (reasoning) argument m.; (dispute) discussion f.

argumentative, adj. disposé à argumenter, raisonneur.

aria, n. air m., chanson f.

arid, adj. aride.

arise, vb. (move upward) s'élever; (originate from) provenir de.

aristocracy, n. aristocratie f.

aristocrat, n. aristocrate m.f.

aristocratic, adj. aristocratique.

arithmetic, n. arithmétique f.

ark, n. arche f.

arm, 1. n. (limb) bras m.; (weapon) arme f. 2. vb. armer.

armament, n. armement m.

armchair, n. fauteuil m.

armed forces, n. forces armées f.pl.

armful, n. brassée f.

armhole, n. emmanchure f., entournure f.

armistice, n. armistice m.

armor, n. armure f.

armory, n. (drill hall) salle (f.) d'exercice.

armpit, n. aisselle f.

arms, n. armes f.pl.

army, n. armée f.

arnica, n. arnica f.

aroma, n. arome m.

aromatic, adj. aromatique.

around, 1. adv. autour. 2. prep. autour de.

arouse, vb. (stir) soulever; (awake) réveiller.

arraign, vb. accuser, poursuivre en justice.

arrange, vb. arranger.

arrangement, n. arrangement m.

array, n. (military) rangs m.pl.; (display) étalage m.

array, vb. ranger.

arrear, n. arriéré m.

arrest, 1. n. (capture) arrestation f.; (military) arrêts m.pl.; (halt) arrêt m. 2. vb. arrêter.

arrival, n. arrivée f.

arrive, vb. arriver.

arrogance, n. arrogance f.

arrogant, adj. arrogant.

arrogate, vb. usurper, (to oneself) s'arroger.

arrow, n. flèche f.

arrowhead, n. pointe de flèche f.; (plant) sagittaire f.

arsenal, n. arsenal m.

arsenic, n. arsenic m.

arson, n. crime d'incendie m.

art, n. art m.; (fine arts) beaux-arts.

arterial, adj. artériel.

arteriosclerosis, n. artériosclérose f.

artery, n. artère f.

artesian well, n. puits artésien m.

artful, adj. (crafty) artificieux; (skillful) adroit.

arthritis, n. arthrite f.

artichoke, n. artichaut m.

article, n. article m.

articulate, vb. articuler.

articulation, n. articulation f.

artifice, n. artifice m.

artificial, adj. artificiel.

artificiality, n. nature artificielle f.

artillery, n. artillerie f.

artisan, n. artisan m.

artist, n. artiste m.

artistic, adj. artistique.

artistry, n. habileté f.

artless, adj. ingénu, naïf.

as, 1. adv. comme; (as . . . as) aussi . . . que; (as much as) autant que; (such as) tel que. 2. conj. (so . . . as) de façon à; (while) pendant que; (since) puisque; (progress) à mesure que. 3. prep. (as to) quant à.

asbestos, n. asbeste m.

ascend, vb. monter.

ascendancy, n. ascendant m.

ascendant, adj. ascendant, supérieur.

ascent, n. montée f.; (of a mountain) ascension f.

ascertain, vb. s'assurer (de).

ascetic, n. ascétique m.

ascribe, vb. attribuer.

ash, n. cendre f.; (tree) frêne m.

ashamed, adj. honteux; (be a. of) avoir honte de.

ashen, adj. cendré, gris pâle.

ashes, n. cendres f.pl.

ashore, adv. à terre; (go a.) débarquer.

ash-tray, n. cendrier m.

Asia, n. Asie f.

Asian, 1. n. Asiatique m.f. 2. adj. asiatique.

aside, adv. de côté.

ask, vb. demander à; (invite) inviter.

askance, adv. de travers, obliquement.

asleep, adj. endormi.

asparagus, n. asperges f.pl.

aspect, n. aspect m.

asperity, n. aspérité f., rudesse f.

aspersion, n. aspersion f.

asphalt, n. asphalte m.

asphyxia, n. asphyxie f.

asphyxiate, vb. asphyxier.

aspirant, n. aspirant m., candidat m.

aspirate, vb. aspirer.

aspiration, n. aspiration f.

aspirator, n. aspirateur m.

aspire, vb. aspirer.

ass, n. âne m., ânesse f.

assail, vb. assaillir.

assailable, adj. attaquable.

assailant, n. assaillant m.

assassin, n. assassin m.

assassinate, vb. assassiner.

assassination, n. assassinat m.

assault, n. assaut m.

assay, 1. n. essai m., vérification f., épreuve f. 2. vb. essayer.

assemblage, n. assemblage m.

assemble, vb. assembler, tr.; s'assembler, intr.

assembly, n. assemblée f.

assent, 1. n. assentiment m. **2.** vb. consentir.

assert, vb. affirmer.

assertion, n. assertion f.

assertive, adj. assertif.

assertiveness, n. qualité d'être assertif.

assess, vb. (tax) taxer; (evaluate) évaluer.

assessor, n. assesseur m.

assets, n.pl. (comm.) actif m.; (property) biens m.pl.

asseverate, vb. affirmer solennellement.

asseveration, n. affirmation f.

assiduous, adj. assidu.

assiduously, adv. assidûment.

assign, vb. assigner.

assignable, adj. assignable, transférable.

assignation, n. assignation f.; rendez-vous m.

assignment, n. (law) cession f.; (school) tâche f.

assimilate, vb. assimiler, tr.; s'assimiler, intr.

assimilation, n. assimilation f.

assimilative, adj. assimilatif, assimilateur.

assistance, n. aide f.

assistant, n. aide m.f.

assist in, vb. aider à.

associate, vb. associer, tr.; s'associer, intr.

association, n. association f.

assonance, n. assonance f.

assort, vb. assortir.

assorted, adj. assorti.

assortment, n. assortiment m.

assuage, vb. adoucir, apaiser.

assume, vb. (take) prendre; (appropriate) s'arroger; (feign) simuler; (suppose) supposer.

assuming, adj. prétentieux, arrogant.

assumption, n. supposition f.; (eccles.) Assomption f.

assurance, n. assurance f.

assure, vb. assurer.

assured, adj. assuré.

assuredly, adv. assurément.

aster, n. aster m.

asterisk, n. astérisque m.

astern, adv. à l'arrière, de l'arrière.

asteroid, n. astéroïde m.

asthma, n. asthme m.

astigmatism, n. astigmatisme m.

astir, adj. agité, debout.

astonish, vb. étonner.

astonishment, n. étonnement m.

astound, vb. stupéfier.

astral, adj. astral.

astray, adv. égaré; (go a.) s'égarer.

astride, adv. à califourchon.

astringent, n. and adj. astringent m.

astrology, n. astrologie f.

astronaut, n. astronaute m.

astronomy, n. astronomie f.

astute, adj. fin.

asunder, adv. (apart) écartés; (to pieces) en morceaux.

asylum, n. asile m.

asymmetry, n. asymétrie f.

at, prep. (time, place, price) à; (someone's house, shop, etc.) chez.

ataxis, n. ataxie f.

atheist, n. athée m.f.

athlete, n. athlète m.f.

athletic, adj. athlétique.

athletics, n. sports m.pl.

athwart, adv. de travers.

Atlantic, adj. atlantique.

Atlantic Ocean, n. océan Atlantique m.

atlas, n. atlas m.

atmosphere, n. atmosphère f.

atmospheric, adj. atmosphérique.

atoll, n. atoll m.

atom, n. atome m.

atomic, adj. atomique.

atomic bomb, n. bombe atomique f.

atomic energy, n. énergie atomique f.

atomic theory, n. théorie atomique f.

atomic warfare, n. guerre atomique f.

atomic weight, n. poids atomique m.

atonal, adj. atonal.

atone for, vb. expier.

atonement, n. expiation f.

atrocious, adj. atroce.

atrocity, n. atrocité f.

atrophy, n. atrophie f.

atropine, n. atropine f.

attach, vb. attcher.

attaché, n. attaché m.

attachment, n. attachement m.; (device) accessoire m.

attack, 1. n. attaque f. **2.** vb. attaquer.

attacker, n. agresseur m.

attain, vb. atteindre.

attainable, adj. qu'on peut atteindre.

attainment, n. (realization) réalisation f.; (knowledge) connaissance f.

attempt, n. tentative f.

attend, vb. (give heed to) faire attention à; (medical) soigner; (serve) servir; (meeting) assister à; (lectures) suivre; (see to) s'occuper de.

attendance, n. service m.; présence f.

attendant, n. serviteur m.; (retinue) suite f.

attention, n. attention f.; (pay attention to) faire attention à.

attentive, adj. attentif.

attentively, adv. attentivement.

attenuate, vb. atténuer.

attest, vb. attester.

attic, n. grenier m.

attire, 1. n. costume m. **2.** vb. parer, tr.; se parer, intr.

attitude, n. attitude f.

attorney, n. avoué m.

attract, vb. attirer.

attraction, n. attraction f.

attractive, adj. attrayant.

attributable, adj. attributable, imputable.

attribute, n. attribut m.

attrition, n. attrition f.

attune, vb. accorder, mettre à l'unisson.

auction, n. vente (f.) aux enchères.

auctioneer, n. commissaire-priseur m.

audacious, adj. audacieux.

audacity, n. audace f.

audible, adj. intelligible.

audience, n. (listeners) auditoire m.; (interview) audience f.

audiovisual, adj. audiovisuel.

audit, 1. vb. vérifier (des comptes). **2.** n. vérification (des comptes) f.

audition, n. audition f.

auditor, n. vérificateur m., censeur m.

auditorium, n. salle f.

auditory, adj. auditif.

auger, n. tarière f.

augment, vb. augmenter.

augur, vb. augurer.

August, n. août m.

aunt, n. tante f.

auspice, n. auspice m.

auspicious, adj. de bon augure.

austere, adj. austère.

austerity, n. austérité f.

Australia, n. Australie f.

Australian, 1. n. Australien m. **2.** adj. australien.

Austria, n. Autriche f.

Austrian, 1. n. Autrichien m. **2.** adj. autrichien.

authentic, adj. authentique.

authenticate, vb. authentiquer, valider.

authenticity, n. authenticité f.

author, n. auteur m.

authoritarian, adj. autoritaire.

authoritative, adj. autoritaire.

authoritatively, adv. avec autorité, en maître.

authority, n. autorité f.

authorization, n. autorisation f.

authorize, vb. autoriser.

auto, n. auto f.

autobiography, n. autobiographie f.

autocracy, n. autocratie f.

autocrat, n. autocrate m.

autograph, 1. n. autographe m. **2.** vb. autographier.

automatic, adj. automatique.

automatically, adv. automatiquement.

automobile, n. automobile f.

automotive, adj. automoteur.

autonomously, adv. d'une manière autonome.

autonomy, n. autonomie f.

autopsy, n. autopsie f.

autumn, n. automne m.

auxiliary, adj. auxiliaire.

avail, vb. servir; (be of no a.) ne servir à rien.

available, *adj.* disponible.

avalanche, *n.* avalanche *f.*

avarice, *n.* avarice *f.*

avariciously, *adv.* avec avarice.

avenge, *vb.* venger.

avenger, *n.* vengeur *m.,* vengeresse *f.*

avenue, *n.* avenue *f.*

average, 1. *n.* moyenne *f.* **2.** *adj.* moyen.

averse, *adj.* opposé.

aversion, *n.* aversion *f.*

avert, *vb.* détourner.

aviary, *n.* volière *f.*

aviation, *n.* aviation *f.*

aviator, *n.* aviateur *m.*

aviatrix, *n.* aviatrice *f.*

avid, *adj.* avide.

avocation, *n.* distraction *f.,* profession *f.,* métier *m.*

avoid, *vb.* éviter.

avoidable, *adj.* évitable.

avoidance, *n.* action d'éviter *f.*

avow, *vb.* avouer.

avowal, *n.* aveu *m.*

avowed, *adj.* avoué, confessé.

avowedly, *adj.* de son propre aveu, ouvertement.

await, *vb.* attendre.

awake, *vb.* éveiller, *tr.;* s'éveiller, *intr.*

awaken, *vb. see* awake.

award, 1. *n.* (prize) prix *m.;* (law) sentence *f.* **2.** *vb.* décerner.

aware, *adj.* (be a.) savoir; (not to be a.) ignorer.

awash, *adv.* dans l'eau.

away, *adv.* loin; (go a.) s'en aller; (a. from) absent de.

awe, *n.* crainte *f.*

awesome, *adj.* inspirant du respect.

awful, *adj.* terrible.

awhile, *adv.* pendant quelque temps.

awkward, *adj.* (clumsy) gauche; (embarrassing) embarrassant.

awning, *n.* tente *f.*

awry, *adv.* de travers.

ax, *n.* hache *f.*

axiom, *n.* axiome *m.*

axis, *n.* axe *m.*

axle, *n.* essieu *m.*

ayatollah, *n.* ayatollah *m.*

azure, *n.* azur *m.*

azure, *adj.* azuré.

B

babble, *vb.* babiller.

babbler, *n.* babillard *m.*

babe, *n.* enfant *m.* or *f.*

baboon, *n.* babouin *m.*

baby, *n.* bébé *m.*

babyish, *adj.* enfantin.

bachelor, *n.* célibataire *m.*

bacillus, *n.* bacille *m.*

back, 1. *n.* dos *m.* **2.** *vb.* (b. up, go b.) reculer; (uphold) soutenir. **3.** *adv.* en arrière.

backbone, *n.* épine dorsale *f.*

backer, *n.* partisan *m.*

backfire, *vb.* donner des retours de flamme, retomber (sur).

background, *n.* fond *m.*

backhand, *adj.* donné avec le revers de la main.

backing, *n.* soutien *m.*

backlash, *n.* réaction conservatrice *f.*

backlog, *n.* réserve *f.*

back out, *vb.* se retirer.

backpack, *n.* sac tyrolien *m.*

backstage, *adv.* dans les coulisses.

backward, *adj.* en arrière.

backwardness, *n.* rétard *m.*

backwards, *adv.* en arrière.

backwater, 1. *n.* eau stagnante *f.* **2.** *vb.* aller en arrière (dans l'eau).

backwoods, *n.* forêts vierges *f.pl.*

bacon, *n.* porc *(m.)* salé et fumé.

bacteriologist, *n.* bactériologue *m.*

bacteriology, *n.* bactériologie *f.*

bacterium, *n.* bactérie *f.*

bad, *adj.* mauvais; (wicked) méchant.

badge, *n.* insigne *m.*

badger, *vb.* ennuyer.

badness, *n.* mauvaise qualité *f.;* (wickedness) méchanceté *f.*

baffle, *vb.* déconcerter.

bafflement, *n.* confusion *f.,* frustration *f.*

bag, *n.* sac *m.;* (suitcase) valise *f.*

baggage, *n.* bagage *m.*

baggage cart, *n.* (airport) chariot *m.*

baggy, *adj.* bouffant.

bagpipe, *n.* cornemuse *f.*

bail, 1. *n.* (law) caution *f.* **2.** *vb.* (b. out water) vider (l'eau).

bailiff, *n.* huissier *m.*

bait, *n.* appât *m.*

bake, *vb.* faire cuire au four, *tr.*

baker, *n.* boulanger *m.*

bakery, *n.* boulangerie *f.*

baking, *n.* boulangerie *f.*

balance, 1. *n.* (equilibrium) équilibre *m.;* (bank) solde *m.;* account, scales) balance *f.* **2.** *vb.* balancer, *tr.*

balcony, *n.* balcon *m.;* (theater) galerie *f.*

bald, *adj.* chauve.

baldness, *n.* calvitie *f.;* (fig.) sécheresse *f.*

bale, *n.* balle *f.*

balk, *vb.* frustrer.

balky, *adj.* regimbé.

ball, *n.* (games, bullet) balle *f.;* (round object) boule *f.;* (dance) bal *m.*

ballad, *n.* (song) romance *f.;* (poem) ballade *f.*

ballast, *n.* lest *m.*

ball bearing, *n.* roulement à billes *m.*

ballerina, *n.* ballérina *f.*

ballet, *n.* ballet *m.*

balloon, *n.* ballon *m.*

ballot, *n.* scrutin *m.*

ballroom, *n.* salon de bal *m.*

balm, *n.* baume *m.*

balmy, *adj.* embaumé; doux *m.,* douce *f.*

balsa, *n.* balsa *f.*

balsam, *n.* baume *m.*

balustrade, *n.* balustrade *f.*

bamboo, *n.* bambou *m.*

ban, 1. *n.* ban *m.* **2.** *vb.* mettre au ban, *tr.*

banal, *adj.* banal.

banana, *n.* banane *f.*

band, *n.* bande *f.;* (music) orchestre *m.*

bandage, *n.* bandage *m.*

bandanna, *n.* foulard (de soie de couleur) *m.*

bandbox, *n.* carton (de modiste) *m.*

bandit, *n.* bandit *m.*

bandmaster, *n.* chef de musique *m.*

bandsman, *n.* musicien *m.*

bandstand, *n.* kiosque *m.*

baneful, *adj.* pernicieux.

bang, *vb.* frapper.

bang, *n.* coup *m.*

banish, *vb.* bannir.

banishment, *n.* bannissement *m.*

banister, *n.* rampe *f.*

bank, *n.* banque *f.;* (river) rive *f.*

bankbook, *n.* livret de banque *m.*

banker, *n.* banquier *m.*

banking, *n.* banque *f.,* affaires de banque *f.pl.*

bank note, *n.* billet de banque *m.*

bankrupt, *adj. and n.* failli *m.*

bankruptcy, *n.* faillite *f.*

banner, *n.* bannière *f.*

banquet, *n.* banquet *m.*

banter, 1. *n.* badinage *m.* **2.** *vb.* badiner, railler.

baptism, *n.* baptême *m.*

baptismal, *adj.* baptismal.

Baptist, *n.* Baptiste *m.*

baptistery, *n.* baptistère *f.*

baptize, *vb.* baptiser.

bar, *n.* (drinks) bar *m.;* (metal) barre *f.;* (law) barreau *m.*

barb, *n.* barbillon *m.*

barbarian, barbarous, *adj. and n.* barbare *m.f.*

barbarism, *n.* barbarie *f.;* (gramm.) barbarisme *m.*

barber, *n.* coiffeur *m.*

barbiturate, *n.* barbiturat *m.*

bare, 1. *adj.* nu. **2.** *vb.* découvrir.

bareback, *adv.* à dos nu.

barefoot, *adv.* nu-pieds.

barely, *adv.* à peine.

bareness, *n.* nudité *f.*

bargain, *n.* marché *m.*

bargain, *vb.* marchander.

barge, *n.* chaland *m.*

barium, *n.* barium *m.*

bark, 1. *n.* (tree) écorce *f.;*

(dog) aboiement *m.* **2.** *vb.* (dog) aboyer.

barley, *n.* orge *f.*

barn, *n.* (grain) grange *f.;* (livestock) étable *f.*

barnacle, *n.* anatife (shellfish) *m.;* barnache (goose) *f.*

barnyard, *n.* basse-cour *f.*

barometer, *n.* baromètre *m.*

barometric, *adj.* barométrique.

baron, *n.* baron *m.*

baroness, *n.* baronne *f.*

baronial, *adj.* baronnial, seigneurial.

baroque, *adj.* baroque.

barracks, *n.* caserne *f.*

barrage, *n.* barrage *m.*

barred, *adj.* barré, empêché, exclus, défendu.

barrel, *n.* tonneau *m.*

barren, *adj.* stérile.

barrenness, *n.* stérilité *f.*

barricade, *n.* barricade *f.*

barrier, *n.* barrière *f.*

barroom, *n.* buvette *f.,* comptoir *m.,* bar *m.*

bartender, *n.* barman *m.*

barter, *n.* troc *m.*

base, 1. *n.* base *f.* **2.** *adj.* bas *m.,* basse *f.*

baseball, *n.* baseball *m.*

baseboard, *n.* moulure de base *f.*

basement, *n.* sous-sol *m.*

baseness, *n.* bassesse *f.*

bashful, *adj.* timide.

bashfully, *adv.* timidement, modestement.

bashfulness, *n.* timidité *f.,* modestie *f.*

basic, *adj.* fondamental.

basin, *n.* (wash) cuvette *f.;* (river) bassin *m.*

basis, *n.* base *f.*

bask, se chauffer *intr.*

basket, *n.* (with handle) panier *m.;* (without handle) corbeille *f.*

bass, *n.* (music) basse *f.;* (fish) bar *m.*

bassinet, *n.* bercelonnette *f.*

bassoon, *n.* basson *m.*

bastard, *n.* bâtard *m., (law)* enfant naturel *m.*

baste, *vb.* (cooking) arroser; (sewing) faufiler.

bat, *n.* (animal) chauve-souris *f.;* (baseball) batte *f.*

batch, *n.* fournée *f.*

bate, *vb.* rabattre, diminuer.

bath, *n.* bain *m.*

bathe, *vb.* se baigner.

bather, *n.* baigneur *m.*

bathrobe, *n.* peignoir *(m.)* de bain.

bathroom, *n.* salle *(f.)* de bain.

bathtub, *n.* baignoire *f.*

baton, *n.* bâton *m.*

battalion, *n.* bataillon *m.*

batter, *n.* (cooking) pâte *f.*

battery, *n.* (military) batterie *f.;* (electric) pile *f.*

battle, *n.* bataille *f.*

battle, *vb.* lutter.

battlefield, *n.* champ *(m.)* de bataille.

battleship, *n.* cuirassé *m.*

bauxite, *n.* bauxite *f.*

bawl, *vb.* brailler.

bay, *n.* (geography) baie *f.;* (plant) laurier *m.*

bayonet, *n.* baïonnette *f.*

bazaar, *n.* bazar *m.*

be, *vb.* être.

beach, *n.* plage *f.*

beachhead, *n.* (haut de) plage *f.*

beacon, *n.* phare *m.*

bead, *n.* perle *f.*

beading, *n.* ornement de grains *m.*

beady, *adj.* comme un grain, couvert de grains.

beak, *n.* bec *m.*

beaker, *n.* gobelet *m.,* coupe *f.*

beam, 1. *n.* (construction) poutre *f.;* (light) rayon *m.* **2.** *vb.* rayonner.

beaming, *adj.* rayonnant.

bean, *n.* haricot *m.*

bear, 1. *n.* ours *m.* **2.** *vb.* (carry) porter; (endure) supporter; (birth) enfanter.

bearable, *adj.* supportable.

beard, *n.* barbe *f.*

bearded, *adj.* barbu.

beardless, *adj.* imberbe.

bearer, *n.* porteur *m.*

bearing, *n.* (person) maintien *m.;* (machinery) coussinet *m.;* (naut.) relèvement *m.*

bearskin, *n.* peau d'ours *f.*

beast, *n.* bête *f.*

beat, 1. *vb.* battre. **2.** *n.* battement *m.*

beaten, *adj.* battu.

beatify, *vb.* béatifier.

beating, *n.* battement *m.,* rossée *f.*

beau, *n.* galant *m.*

beautiful, *adj.* beau (bel) *m.,* belle *f.*

beautifully, *adv.* admirablement.

beautify, *vb.* embellir.

beauty, *n.* beauté *f.*

beaver, *n.* castor *m.*

becalm, *vb.* calmer, apaiser; (naut.) abriter.

because, *conj.* parce que.

beckon, *vb.* faire signe (à).

become, *vb.* devenir.

becoming, *adj.* convenable; (dress) seyant.

bed, *n.* lit *m.*

bedbug, *n.* punaise *f.*

bedclothes, *n.* couvertures *f.pl.*

bedding, *n.* literie *f.*

bedfellow, *n.* camarade de lit *m.*

bedizen, *vb.* parer, attifer.

bedridden, *adj.* alité.

bedrock, *n.* roche solide *f.*

bedroom, *n.* chambre *(f.)* à coucher.

bedside, *n.* bord du lit *m.*

bedspread, *n.* dessus *(m.)* de lit.

bedstead, *n.* bois de lit *m.,* couchette *f.*

bedtime, *n.* heure *(f.)* de se coucher.

bee, *n.* abeille *f.*

beef, *n.* bœuf *m.*

beefsteak, *n.* bifteck *m.,* tournedos *m.*

beehive, *n.* ruche *f.*

beer, *n.* bière *f.*

beeswax, *n.* cire jaune *f.*

beet, *n.* betterave *f.*

beetle, *n.* scarabée *m.*

befall, *vb.* arriver (à).

befit, *vb.* convenir (à).

befitting, *adj.* convenable.

before, 1. *adv.* (place) en avant; (time) avant. **2.** *prep.* (place) devant; (time) avant. **3.** *conj.* avant que.

beforehand, *adv.* d'avance.

befriend, *vb.* aider; traiter en ami.

befuddle, *vb.* embrouiller, déconcerter.

beg, *vb.* (of beggar) mendier; (ask) prier.

beget, *vb.* engendrer, produire.

beggar, *n.* mendiant *m.*

beggarly, *adj.* chétif, misérable.

begin, *vb.* commencer.

beginner, *n.* commençant *m.*

beginning, *n.* commencement *m.*

beguile, *vb.* tromper, séduire.

behalf, *n.* (on b. of) de la part de; (in b. of) en faveur de.

behave, *vb.* se conduire.

behavior, *n.* conduite *f.*

behead, *vb.* décapiter.

behind, *adv. and prep.* derrière.

behind, *n.* derrière *m.*

behold, 1. *vb.* voir. **2.** *interj.* voici.

beige, *adj.* beige.

being, *n.* être *m.*

bejewel, *vb.* orner de bijoux.

belated, *adj.* attardé.

belch, *vb.* éructer.

belfry, *n.* clocher *m.,* beffroi *m.*

Belgian, 1. *n.* Belge *m.f.* **2.** *adj.* belge.

Belgium, *n.* Belgique *f.*

belie, *vb.* démentir.

belief, *n.* croyance *f.;* (confidence) confiance *f.*

believable, *adj.* croyable.

believe, *vb.* croire.

believer, *n.* croyant *m.*

belittle, *vb.* rabaisser.

bell, *n.* (house) sonnette *f.;* (church) cloche *f.*

bellboy, *n.* chasseur *m.*

bell buoy, *n.* bouée sonore *f.*

belligerence, *n.* belligérance *f.*

belligerent, *adj. and n.* belligérant *m.*

belligerently, *adv.* d'une manière belligérante.

bellow, *vb.* mugir.

bellows, *n.* soufflet *m.*

bell-tower, *n.* clocher *m.*

belly, *n.* ventre *m.*

belongings, *n.* effets, *m.pl.*

belong to, *vb.* appartenir (à).

beloved, *adj. and n.* chéri *m.*

below, 1. *adv.* en bas. **2.** *prep.* au-dessous de.

belt, *n.* ceinture *f.*

bench, *n.* banc *m.*

bend, *vb.* plier; (curve) courber *tr.*

beneath, *see* below.

benediction, *n.* bénédiction *f.*

benefactor, *n.* bienfaiteur *m.*

benefactress, *n.* bienfaitrice *f.*

beneficent, *adj.* bienfaisant.

beneficial, *adj.* salutaire.

beneficiary, *n.* bénéficiaire *m.*

benefit, 1. (favor) bienfait *m.;* (advantage) bénéfice *m.*

benevolence, *n.* bienveillance *f.*

benevolent, *adj.* bienveillant.

benevolently, *adv.* bénévolement.

benign, *adj.* bénin *m.* bénigne *f.*

benignity, *n.* bénignité *f.*

bent, *n.* penchant *m.*

benzene, *n.* benzène *m.*

benzine, *n.* benzine *f.*

bequeath, *vb.* léguer.

bequest, *n.* legs *m.*

berate, *vb.* gronder.

bereave, *vb.* priver (de).

bereavement, *n.* privation *f.,* perte *f.,* deuil *m.*

beriberi, *n.* béribéri *m.*

berry, *n.* baie *f.*

berth, *n.* couchette *f.*

beseech, *vb.* supplier.

beseechingly, *adv.* en suppliant.

beset, *vb.* attaquer, presser, assiéger.

beside, *prep.* à côté de.

besides, *adv.* en outre.

besiege, *vb.* assiéger.

besieged, *adj.* assiégé.

besieger, *n.* assiégeant *m.*

besmirch, *vb.* tacher, salir.

best, 1. *adj.* (le) meilleur. **2.** *adv.* (le) mieux.

bestial, *adj.* bestial.

bestir, *vb.* remuer.

best man, *n.* garçon d'honneur (at weddings) *m.*

bestow, *vb.* accorder.

bestowal, *n.* dispensation *f.*

bet, 1. *n.* pari *m.* **2.** *vb.* parier.

betake (oneself), *vb.* se rendre.

betray, *vb.* trahir.

betroth, *vb.* fiancer.

betrothal, *n.* fiançailles *f.pl.*

better, 1. *adj.* meilleur. **2.** *adv.* mieux.

between, *prep.* entre.

bevel, 1. *n.* en biseau. **2.** *vb.* biaiser.

beverage, *n.* boisson *f.*

bewail, *vb.* lamenter, pleurer.

beware of, *vb.* prendre garde à.

bewilder, *vb.* égarer.

bewildered, *adj.* égaré.

bewildering, *adj.* déconcertant.

bewilderment, *n.* égarement *m.*

bewitch, *vb.* ensorceler.

beyond, 1. *adv.* au delà. **2.** *prep.* au delà de.

biannual, *adj.* semestriel.

bias, *n.* (slant) biais *m.;* (prejudice) prévention *f.*

bib, *n.* bavette *f.*

Bible, *n.* Bible *f.*

biblical, *adj.* biblique.

bibliography, *n.* bibliographie *f.*

bicarbonate, *n.* bicarbonat *m.*

bicentennial, *n.* and *adj.* bicentenaire *m.*

biceps, *n.* biceps *m.*

bicker, *vb.* se quereller, se chamailler.

bicycle, *n.* bicyclette *f.*

bicyclist, *n.* cycliste *m.*

bid, 1. *n.* (auction) enchère *f.;* (bridge) appel *m.* **2.** *vb.* (order) ordonner; (invite) inviter.

bidder, *n.* enchérisseur *m.*

bide, *vb.* (live) demeurer; (wait) attendre.

bier, *n.* corbillard *m.,* civière *f.*

bifocal, *adj.* bifocal.

big, *adj.* grand.

bigamy, *n.* bigamie *f.*

bigot, *n.* bigot *m.*

bigotry, *n.* bigoterie *f.*

bilateral, *adj.* bilatéral.

bile, *n.* bile *f.*

bilingual, *adj.* bilingue.

bilious, *adj.* bilieux.

bill, *n.* (restaurant) addition *f.;* (hotel, profession) note *f.;* (money) billet *(m.)* de banque; (poster) affiche *f.;* (politics) projet *(m.)* de loi; (b. of fare) carte *(f.)* du jour; (bird) bec *m.*

billet, *n.* (mil.) billet de logement *m.*

billfold, *n.* portefeuille *m.*

billiard balls, *n.pl.* billes *n.pl.*

billiards, *n.* billard *m.*

billion, *n.* billion *m.*

bill of health, *n.* patente de santé *f.*

bill of lading, *n.* connaissement *m.*

bill of sale, *n.* lettre de vente *f.,* acte de propriété *m.*

billow, *n.* grande vague *f.,* lame *f.*

bimetallic, *adj.* bimétallique.

bimonthly, *adj.* and *adv.* bimensuel.

bin, *n.* coffre *m.*

bind, *vb.* lier; (books) relier.

bindery, *n.* atelier de reliure *m.*

binding, 1. *n.* (book) reliure *f.* **2.** *adj.* obligatoire.

binocular, *adj.* binoculaire.

binoculars, *n.pl.* binocle *m.*

biochemistry, *n.* biochimie *f.*

biodegradable, *adj.* sujet à la putréfaction.

biofeedback, *n.* biofeedback *m.,* information reçue par un organisme pendant un processus biologique *f.*

biographer, *n.* biographe *m.*

biographical, *adj.* biographique.

biography, *n.* biographie *f.*

biological, *adj.* biologique.

biologically, *adv.* biologiquement.

biology, *n.* biologie *f.*

bipartisan, *adj.* représentant les deux partis.

biped, *n.* bipède *m.*

bird, *n.* oiseau *m.*

birdlike, *adj.* comme un oiseau.

bird of prey, *n.* oiseau de proie *m.*

birth, *n.* naissance *f.*

birth control, *n.* contrôle des naissances *m.*

birthday, *n.* anniversaire *(m.)* de naissance.

birthmark, *n.* tache de naissance *f.*

birthplace, *n.* lieu *(m.)* de naissance.

birth rate, *n.* natalité *f.*

birthright, *n.* droit d'aînesse *m.*

biscuit, *n.* (hard) biscuit *m.;* (soft) petit pain *(m.)* au lait.

bisect, *vb.* couper en deux.

bishop, *n.* évêque *m.*

bishopric, *n.* évêché *m.*

bismuth, *n.* bismuth *m.*

bison, *n.* bison *m.*

bit, *n.* (piece) morceau *m.;* (a b. (of)) un peu (de); (harness) mors *m.;* unité unique d'information *f.*

bitch, *n.* chienne *f.*

bite, 1. *n.* morsure *f.* **2.** *vb.* mordre.

biting, *adj.* mordant.

bitter, *adj.* amer.

bitterly, *adv.* amèrement, avec amertume.

bitterness, *n.* amertume *f.*

bivouac, *n.* bivouac *m.*

biweekly, *adj.* and *adv.* tous les quinze jours.

black, *adj.* noir.

Black, *n.* and *adj.* (for person) nègre *m.;* négresse *f.*

blackberry, *n.* mûre *(f.)* de ronce.

blackbird, *n.* merle *m.*

blackboard, *n.* tableau *(m.)* noir.

blacken, *vb.* noircir.

black eye, *n.* oeil poché *m.*

blackguard, *n.* gredin *m.,* polisson *m.,* salaud *m.*

blackmail, *n.* chantage *m.*

black market, *n.* marché noir *m.*

blackout, *n.* blackout *m.*

blacksmith, *n.* forgeron *m.*

bladder, *n.* vessie *f.*

blade, *n.* (sword, knife) lame *f.;* (grass) brin *m.*

blame, 1. *n.* blâme *m.* **2.** *vb.* blâmer.

blameless, *adj.* innocent, sans tache.

blanch, *vb.* blanchir, pâlir.

bland, *adj.* doux *m.,* douce *f.*

blank, 1. *n.* (space) blanc *m.;* (void) vide *m.;* (printing) tiret *m.* **2.** *adj.* (page) blanc *m.,* blanche *f.;* (empty) vide.

blanket, *n.* couverture *f.*

blare, n. son (de la trompette) m., rugissement m.

blare, vb. retentir, intr.

blaspheme, vb. blasphémer.

blasphemer, n. blasphémateur m.

blasphemous, adj. blasphématoire.

blasphemy, n. blasphème m.

blast, n. (wind) rafale f.; (mine) explosion f.

blatant, adj. criard, bruyant.

blaze, 1. n. flambée f. 2. vb. flamber.

blazing, adj. enflammé, flamboyant.

bleach, vb. décolorer, tr.

bleak, adj. morne.

bleakness, n. froideur f.

bleed, vb. saigner.

blemish, n. défaut m.

blend, 1. n. mélange m. 2. vb. mêler tr.

blended, adj. mélangé.

bless, vb. bénir.

blessed, adj. béni.

blessing, n. bénédiction f.

blight, 1. vb. flétrir, détruire, nieller, brouir. 2. n. brouissure f., flétrissure f.

blind, 1. n. store m. 2. adj. aveugle; (b. alley) cul-de-sac m.

blindfold, adj. and adv. les yeux bandés.

blinding, adj. aveuglant.

blindly, adv. aveuglément.

blindness, n. cécité f.

blink, vb. clignoter.

bliss, n. béatitude f.

blissful, adj. bienheureux.

blissfully, adv. heureusement.

blister, n. ampoule f.

blithe, adj. gai, joyeux.

blizzard, n. tempête (f.) de neige.

bloat, vb. boursoufler.

bloc, n. bloc m.

block, 1. n. bloc m.; (houses) pâté m. 2. vb. bloquer.

blockade, n. blocus m.

blond, adj. and adj. blond m.

blood, n. sang m.

bloodhound, n. limier m.

bloodless, adj. exsangue, sans effusion de sang.

blood plasma, n. plasma du sang m.

blood poisoning, n. empoisonnement du sang m.

blood pressure, n. tension artérielle f.

bloodshed, n. effusion (f.) de sang.

bloodshot, adj. injecté de sang.

bloodthirsty, adj. sanguinaire.

bloody, adj. sanglant.

bloom, 1. n. fleur f. 2. vb. fleurir.

blooming, 1. n. floraison f. 2. adj. fleurissant.

blossom, see bloom.

blot, 1. n. tache f. 2. vb. (spot) tacher; (dry ink) sécher l'encre.

blotch, n. tache f.

blotchy, adj. couvert de taches.

blotter, n. buvard m.

blouse, n. blouse f.

blow, 1. n. coup m. 2. vb. souffler; (b. out) éteindre; (b. over) passer; (b. up) faire sauter, tr.

blowout, n. éclatement (m.) de pneu.

blubber, 1. vb. pleurer comme un veau. 2. n. graisse de baleine f.

bludgeon, 1. n. matraque f. 2. vb. donner des coups de matraque.

blue, adj. bleu.

blue jeans, n. blue jeans m.pl.

blueprint, n. dessin négatif m.

bluff, n. bluff m.

bluffer, n. bluffeur m.

blunder, n. bévue f.

blunderer, n. maladroit m.

blunt, adj. (blade) émoussé; (person) brusque.

bluntly, adv. brusquement.

bluntness, n. brusquerie f.

blur, vb. (smear) barbouiller.

blush, 1. n. rougeur f. 2. vb. rougir.

bluster, n. rodomontade f., fanfaronnade f.

boar, n. (wild) sanglier m.

board, 1. n. (plank) planche f.; (daily meals) pension f.; (boat) bord m.; (politics) ministère m.; (administration) conseil m.

boarder, n. pensionnaire m.f.

boast (of), vb. se vanter (de).

boaster, n. vantard m.

boastful, adj. vantard.

boastfulness, n. vantardise f.

boat, n. bateau m.

boathouse, n. garage (à bateaux) m.

boatswain, n. maître d'équipage m.

bob, vb. (hair) couper court.

bobbin, n. bobine f.

bode, vb. présager.

bodice, n. corsage m.

bodily, adj. corporel.

body, n. corps m.

bodyguard, n. garde (f.) du corps.

bog, 1. n. marécage m. 2. vb. embourber.

Bohemia, n. (geographical) Bohème f.; (fig.) bohème f.

Bohemian, 1. n. (geographical) Bohémien m.; (fig.) bohème m.f. 2. adj. (geographical) bohémien; (fig.) bohème.

boil, 1. vb. bouillir, intr.; faire bouillir, tr. 2. n. (med.) furoncle m., (popular) clou m.

boiler, n. chaudière f.

boisterous, adj. (person) bruyant.

boisterously, adv. bruyamment.

bold, adj. hardi.

boldface, adj. (type) caractères gras m.pl.

boldly, adv. hardiment, avec audace.

boldness, n. hardiesse f.

bologna, n. saucisson (m.) de Bologne.

bolster, n. traversin m.

bolster up, vb. soutenir.

bolt, 1. n. verrou m. 2. vb. verrouiller.

bomb, n. bombe f.

bombard, vb. bombarder.

bombardier, n. bombardier m.

bombardment, n. bombardement m.

bomber, n. avion (m.) de bombardement.

bombproof, adj. à l'épreuve des bombes.

bombshell, n. bombe f.

bombsight, n. viseur de lancement m.

bonbon, n. bonbon m.

bond, n. lien m.; (law, finance) obligation f.

bondage, n. servitude f.

bonded, adj. entreposé.

bone, n. os m.

boneless, adj. sans os.

bonfire, n. feu (m.) de joie.

bonnet, n. chapeau m.

bonus, n. gratification f.

bony, adj. osseux.

book, n. livre m.

bookbindery, n. atelier de reliure m.

bookcase, n. bibliothèque f.

bookkeeper, n. teneur (m.) de livres.

bookkeeping, n. comptabilité f.

booklet, n. opuscule m.

bookseller, n. libraire m.; (second-hand) bouquiniste m.

bookstore, bookshop, n. librairie f.

boon, n. bienfait m., don m.

boor, n. rustre m.

boorish, adj. rustre.

boost, vb. (push) pousser; (praise) louer.

boot, n. bottine f.

bootblack, n. cireur m.

booth, n. (fair) baraque f.; (telephone) cabine f.

booty, n. butin m.

border, n. bord m.; (of country) frontière f.

borderline, adj. touchant (à), avoisinant.

bore, vb. (make a hole) forer; (annoy) ennuyer.

boredom, n. ennui m.

boric acid, n. acide borique m.

boring, adj. ennuyeux.

born, 1. adj. né. 2. vb. (be b.) naître.

born-again, adj. rené.

borough, n. (administration) circonscription électorale f.; (large village) bourg m.

borrower, n. emprunteur m.

borrow from, vb. emprunter à.

bosom, n. sein m.

boss, 1. n. patron m. 2. vb. diriger.

bossy, *adj.* comme un patron, impérieux.

botanical, *adj.* botanique.

botany, *n.* botanique *f.*

botch, 1. *n.* ravaudage *m.* 2. *vb.* ravauder, faire une mauvaise besogne.

both, *adj. and pron.* tous (les) deux *m.*, toutes (les) deux *f.*

bother, 1. *n.* ennui *m.* 2. *vb.* gêner.

bothersome, *adj.* gênant.

bottle, *n.* bouteille *f.*

bottom, *n.* fond *m.*

bottomless, *adj.* sans fond.

bough, *n.* branche *f.*

bouillon, *n.* bouillon *m.*

boulder, *n.* galet *m.*

boulevard, *n.* boulevard *m.*

bounce, *vb.* (ball) rebondir.

bound, 1. *n.* (limit) borne *f.*; (jump) bond *m.* 2. *vb.* (limit) borner; (jump) bondir.

boundary, *n.* frontière *f.*

bound for, *adj.* en route pour.

boundless, *adj.* sans bornes, illimité.

boundlessly, *adv.* sans bornes.

bounteous, *adj.* généreux, bienfaisant.

bounty, *n.* largesse *f.*; (premium) prime *f.*

bouquet, *n.* bouquet *m.*

bourgeois, *adj.* bourgeois.

bout, *n.* (fever) accès *m.*

bovine, *n.* bovine *f.*; *adj.* bovin.

bow, *n.* (weapon) arc *m.*; (violin) archet *m.*; (curtsy) révérence *f.*; (ship) avant *m.*

bow, *vb.* incliner, *tr.*

bowels, *n.* entrailles *f.pl.*

bowl, 1. *n.* bol *m.* 2. *vb.* jouer aux boules.

bowlegged, *adj.* à jambes arquées.

bowler, *n.* joueur de boule *m.*

box, *n.* boîte *f.*; (theater) loge *f.*

boxcar, *n.* wagon de marchandises *m.*

boxer, *n.* boxeur *m.*

boxing, *n.* boxe *f.*

box office, *n.* bureau *(m.)* de location.

boy, *n.* garçon *m.*

boycott, *vb.* boycotter.

boyhood, *n.* première jeunesse *f.*

boyish, *adj.* enfantin, puéril.

boyishly, *adv.* comme un gamin.

brace, 1. *vb.* fortifier. 2. *n.* vilebrequin (tool) *m.*, paire *f.*, couple *m.*

bracelet, *n.* bracelet *m.*

bracket, *n.* (wall) console *f.*; (printing) crochet *f.*

brag, *vb.* se vanter.

braggart, *n.* fanfaron *m.*

braid, *n.* (hair) tresse *f.*; (sewing) galon *m.*

brain, *n.* cerveau *m.*; (brains) cervelle *f.*

brainy, *adj.* intelligent.

brake, *n.* frein *m.*

bran, *n.* son *m.*

branch, *n.* branche *f.*

brand, *n.* marque *f.*

brandish, *vb.* brandir.

brand-new, *adj.* tout neuf.

brandy, *n.* eau-de-vie *f.*

brash, *adj.* impertinent.

brass, *n.* cuivre *(m.)* jaune.

brassiere, *n.* soutien-gorge *m.*

brat, *n.* gosse *m.f.*

bravado, *n.* bravade *f.*

brave, *adj.* courageux.

bravery, *n.* courage *m.*

brawl, *n.* rixe *f.*

brawn, *n.* partie charnue *f.*, muscles *m.pl.*

bray, *vb.* braire.

brazen, *adj.* (person) effronté.

Brazil, *n.* Brésil *m.*

breach, *n.* infraction *f.*; *(mil.)* brèche *f.*

bread, *n.* pain *m.*

breadth, *n.* largeur *f.*

break, 1. *n.* rupture *f.*; (pause) interruption *f.* 2. *vb.* rompre, briser, casser.

breakable, *adj.* cassable.

breakage, *n.* cassure *f.*, rupture *f.*

breakfast, *n.* (petit) déjeuner *m.*

breakwater, *n.* brise-lames *m.*, jetée *f.*

breast, *n.* poitrine *f.*, sein *m.*

breath, *n.* haleine *f.*; *(fig.,* wind) souffle *m.*

breathe, *vb.* respirer.

breathless, *adj.* (out of breath) essoufflé.

breathlessly, *adv.* hors d'haleine.

bred, *adj.* élevé.

breeches, *n.* pantalon *m.sg.*

breed, *vb.* produire; (livestock) élever.

breeder, *n.* (raiser) éleveur *m.*

breeding, *n.* (manners) éducation *f.*; (animals) élevage *m.*

breeze, *n.* brise *f.*

breezy, *adj.* (windy) venteux; (manner) dégagé.

brevity, *n.* brièveté *f.*

brew, *vb.* (beer) brasser; (tea) faire infuser, *tr.*

brewery, *n.* brasserie *f.*

briar, *n.* ronce *f.*

bribe, *vb.* corrompre.

briber, *n.* corrupteur *m.*

bribery, *n.* corruption *f.*

brick, *n.* brique *f.*

bricklaying, *n.* maçonnerie *f.*

bricklike, *adj.* comme une brique.

bridal, *adj.* nuptial.

bride, *n.* mariée *f.*

bridegroom, *n.* marié *m.*

bridesmaid, *n.* demoiselle *(f.)* d'honneur.

bridge, *n.* pont *m.*; (boat) passerelle *f.*; (cards) bridge *m.*

bridged, *adj.* lié.

bridgehead, *n.* tête de pont *f.*

bridle, *n.* bride *f.*

brief, *adj.* bref *m.*, brève *f.*

brief case, *n.* serviette *f.*

briefly, *adv.* brièvement.

briefness, *n.* brièveté *f.*

brier, *n.* bruyère *f.*, ronces *f.pl.*

brig, *n.* brick *m.*

brigade, *n.* brigade *f.*

bright, *adj.* vif *m.*, vive *f.*; intelligent.

brighten, *vb.* faire briller, *tr.*

brightness, *n.* éclat *m.*

brilliance, *n.* éclat *m.*

brilliant, *adj.* brillant.

brim, *n.* bord *m.*

brine, *n.* saumure *f.*

bring, *vb.* (thing) apporter; (person) amener; (b. about) amener, causer.

brink, *n.* bord *m.*

briny, *adj.* salé.

brisk, *adj.* vif *m.*, vive *f.*

brisket, *n.* poitrine (meat) *f.*

briskly, *adv.* vivement.

briskness, *n.* vivacité *f.*

bristle, *n.* soie *f.*

bristly, *adj.* hérissé (de), poilu.

British, *adj.* britannique.

British Empire, *n.* Empire Britannique *m.*

British Isles, *n.* Îles Britanniques *f.pl.*

brittle, *adj.* fragile.

broad, *adj.* large.

broadcast, *vb.* radiodiffuser.

broadcast, *n.* radio-émission *f.*

broadcaster, *n.* speaker *m.*

broadcloth, *n.* drap *(m.)* fin.

broaden, *vb.* élargir.

broadly, *adv.* largement.

broadminded, *adj.* large d'esprit.

broadside, *n.* côte *f.*, bordée *f.*

brocade, *n.* brocart *m.*

brocaded, *adj.* de brocart.

broil, *vb.* griller.

broiler, *n.* gril *m.*

broken-hearted, *adj.* qui a le coeur brisé.

broker, *n.* courtier *m.*; (stock-b.) agent *(m.)* de change.

brokerage, *n.* courtage *m.*

bronchial, *adj.* bronchique.

bronchitis, *n.* bronchite *f.*

bronze, *n.* bronze *m.*

brooch, *n.* broche *f.*

brood, 1. *n.* couvée *f.* 2. *vb.* couver.

brook, *n.* ruisseau *m.*

broom, *n.* balai *m.*

broomstick, *n.* manche à balai *m.*

broth, *n.* bouillon *m.*

brothel, *n.* bordel *m.*, maison mal famée *f.*

brother, *n.* frère *m.*

brotherhood, *n.* fraternité *f.*

brother-in-law, *n.* beau-frère *m.*

brotherly, *adj.* fraternel.

brow, *n.* front *m.*

brown, *adj.* brun.

browse, *vb.* (animals) brouter; (books) feuilleter (des livres).

bruise, 1. *n.* meurtrissure *f.* 2. *vb.* meurtrir.

brunette, *adj. and n.* brune *f.*

brunt, *n.* choc *m.*

brush, n. brosse f.; (paint-b.) pinceau m.
brushwood, n. broussailles f.pl.
brusque, adj. brusque.
brusquely, adv. brusquement.
brutal, adj. brutal.
brutality, n. brutalité f.
brutalize, vb. abrutir.
brute, n. brute f.
bubble, 1. n. bulle f. 2. vb. bouillonner.
buck, n. daim m.; (male) mâle m.
bucket, n. seau m.
buckle, n. boucle f.
buckram, n. bougran m.
buckshot, n. chevrotine f.
buckwheat, n. sarrasin m., blé noir m.
bud, 1. n. bourgeon m. 2. vb. bourgeonner.
budding, adj. en herbe.
budge, vb. bouger.
budget, n. budget m.
buffalo, n. buffle m.
buffer, n. tampon m.
buffet, n. (sideboard) buffet m.
buffoon, n. bouffon m.
bug, n. insecte m.
bugle, n. clairon m.
build, vb. bâtir.
builder, n. (buildings) entrepreneur m.; (ships) constructeur m.
building, n. bâtiment m.
bulb, n. (electricity) ampoule f.; (botany) bulbe m.
bulge, n. bosse f.
bulk, n. masse f.
bulkhead, n. cloison étanche f.
bulky, adj. volumineux.
bull, n. taureau m.
bulldog, n. bouledogue m.
bulldozer, n. machine à refouler f.
bullet, n. balle f.
bulletin, n. bulletin m.
bulletproof, adj. à l'épreuve des balles.
bullfinch, n. bouvreuil m.
bullion, n. lingot m.
bully, vb. rudoyer.
bulwark, n. rempart m.
bum, n. fainéant m.
bumblebee, n. bourdon m.
bump, 1. n. (blow) coup m.; (protuberance) bosse f. 2. vb. cogner.
bumper, n. (auto) pare-chocs m.
bun, n. brioche f.
bunch, n. (flowers) bouquet m.; (grapes) grappe f.; (keys) trousseau m.
bundle, n. paquet m.
bungle, vb. bousiller.
bunion, n. cor m.
bunk, n. couchette f.
bunny, n. lapin m.
bunting, n. drapeaux m.pl.
buoy, n. bouée f.
buoyant, adj. qui a du ressort.
burden, n. fardeau m.
burdensome, adj. onéreux.
bureau, n. (office) bureau m.;

(chest of drawers) commode f.
burglar, n. cambrioleur m.
burglarize, vb. cambrioler.
burglary, n. vol (m.) avec effraction.
burial, n. enterrement m.
burlap, n. gros canevas m.
burly, adj. corpulent.
burn, vb. brûler.
burner, n. bec m.
burning, adj. brûlant.
burnish, vb. brunir, polir.
burrow, n. terrier m.
burst, vb. éclater.
bury, vb. enterrer.
bus, n. autobus m.
bush, n. buisson m.
bushel, n. boisseau m.
bushy, adj. buissonneux; (hair) touffu.
busily, adv. activement.
business, n. affaire f.; (comm.) affaires f.pl.
businesslike, adj. pratique.
businessman, n. homme (m.) d'affaires.
business-woman, n. femme (f.) d'affaires.
bust, n. buste m.
bustle, vb. se remuer.
busy, adj. occupé.
busybody, n. officieux m.
but, conj. mais; (only) ne . . . que; (except) sauf.
butcher, n. boucher m.
butchery, n. tuerie f., massacre m.
butler, n. maître (m.) d'hôtel.
butt, n. bout m., (of jokes) plastron m.
butter, n. beurre m.
buttercup, n. bouton d'or m.
butterfly, n. papillon m.
buttermilk, n. babeurre m.
butterscotch, n. caramel au beurre m.
buttock, n. fesse f.
button, n. bouton m.
buttonhole, n. boutonnière f.
buttress, n. contrefort m.; (flying b.) arc-boutant m.
buxom, adj. (of women) aux formes rebondies.
buy, vb. acheter.
buyer, n. acheteur m.
buzz, 1. n. bourdonnement m. 2. vb. bourdonner.
buzzard, n. buse f.
buzzer, n. trompe f., sirène f.
by, prep. (through) par; (near) près de.
by-and-by, adv. bientôt.
bygone, adj. passé, d'autrefois.
bylaw, n. règlement local m.
by-pass, 1. n. route d'évitement f. 2. vb. faire un détour.
by-product, n. sous-produit m.
bystander, n. spectateur m.
byte, n. unité fondamentale de données f.
byway, n. sentier détourné m.

C

cab, n. (taxi) taxi m.; (horse) fiacre m.
cabaret, n. cabaret m.
cabbage, n. chou m.
cabin, n. (hut) cabane f.; (boat) cabine f.
cabinet, n. cabinet m.
cabinetmaker, n. ébéniste m.
cable, 1. n. câble m. 2. vb. câbler.
cablegram, n. câblogramme m.
cachet, n. cachet m.
cackle, 1. n. caquet m. 2. vb. caqueter.
cacophony, n. cacophonie f.
cactus, n. cactus m.
cad, n. mufle m.
cadaver, n. cadavre m.
cadaverous, adj. cadavérique.
cadence, n. cadence f.
cadet, n. cadet m.
cadmium, n. cadmium m.
cadre, n. cadre m.
café, n. café, (-restaurant) m.
cafeteria, n. restaurant m.
caffeine, n. caféine f.
cage, n. cage f.
caged, adj. mis en cage.
caisson, n. caisson m.
cajole, vb. cajoler.
cake, n. gâteau m.
calamitous, adj. calamiteux, désastreux.
calamity, n. calamité f.
calcify, vb. calcifier.
calcium, n. calcium m.
calculable, adj. calculable.
calculate, vb. calculer.
calculating, adj. qui fait des calculs.
calculation, n. calcul m.
calculus, n. calcul m.
caldron, n. chaudron m.
calendar, n. calendrier m.
calender, n. calandre f.
calf, n. veau m.
calfskin, n. en peau de veau.
caliber, n. calibre m.
calico, n. calicot m.
calisthenic, adj. callisthénique.
calisthenics, n. callisthénie f.
calk, vb. ferrer à glace.
call, 1. n. appel m.; (visit) visite f. 2. vb. appeler; (call on) faire visite à.
calligraphy, n. calligraphie f.
calling, n. vocation f., profession f.
calling card, n. carte de visite f.
callously, adv. d'une manière insensible.
callousness, n. insensibilité f.
callow, adj. blanc-bec.
callus, n. callosité f.
calm, 1. adj. calme. 2. vb. calmer.
calmly, adv. calmement.
calmness, n. calme m., tranquillité f.
caloric, adj. calorique.
calorie, n. calorie f.

calorimeter, n. calorimètre m.

calumniate, vb. calomnier.

calumny, n. calomnie f.

Calvary, n. Calvaire m.

calve, vb. vêler.

calyx, n. calice m.

camaraderie, n. camaraderie f.

cambric, n. batiste f.

camel, n. chameau m.

camellia, n. camélia m.

camel's hair, n. poil de chameau m.

cameo, n. camée m.

camera, n. appareil photographique m.

camouflage, vb. camoufler.

camouflaged, adj. camouflé.

camouflaging, adj. camouflant.

camp, 1. n. camp m.; (holiday camp) camping m. 2. vb. camper.

campaign, n. campagne f.

camper, n. qui fait du camping.

camphor, n. camphre m.

camphor ball, n. balle de camphre f.

campus, n. terrains (m.pl.) de l'université.

can, 1. n. (food) boîte f.; (general) bidon m. 2. vb. (be able) pouvoir; (put in a can) conserver.

Canada, n. Canada m.

Canadian, 1. n. Canadien m. 2. adj. canadien.

canal, n. canal m.

canalize, vb. canaliser.

canapé, n. canapé m.

canard, n. canard m.

canary, n. serin m.

Canary Islands, n. Îles Canaries f.pl.

cancel, vb. annuler; (erase) biffer.

cancellation, n. annulation f.

cancer, n. cancer m.

candelabrum, n. candélabre m.

candid, adj. sincère.

candidacy, n. candidature f.

candidate, n. candidat m.

candidly, adv. franchement.

candidness, n. candeur f.

candied, adj. candi.

candle, n. bougie f.; (church) cierge m.

candler, n. fabricant de chandelles m.

candlestick, n. chandelier m.

candor, n. sincérité f.

candy, n. bonbon m.

cane, n. canne f.

canine, adj. canin.

canister, n. boîte à thé f.

canker, n. chancre m.

cankerworm, n. ver rongeur m.

canned, adj. conservé en boîtes (de fer blanc).

canner, n. travailleur dans une conserverie m.

cannery, n. conserverie f.

cannibal, adj. and n. cannibale m.f.

canning, n. mise en conserve, en boîtes (de fer blanc) f.

cannon, n. canon m.

cannonade, n. cannonade f.

cannoneer, n. canonier m.

cannot, vb. ne peut pas.

canny, adj. avisé, rusé.

canoe, n. canot m.

canon, n. chanoine m.; canon (rule) m.

canonical, adj. canonique.

canonize, vb. canoniser.

canopy, n. dais m.

cant, n. hypocrisie f.

can't, vb. ne peut pas.

cantaloupe, n. melon m., cantaloup m.

canteen, n. cantine f.; bidon m.

canter, 1. n. petit galop m. 2. vb. aller au petit galop.

cantonment, n. cantonnement m.

canvas, n. toile f.

canvass, 1. n. sollicitation f. 2. vb. solliciter; (discuss) débattre.

canyon, n. gorge f., défilé m.

cap, n. bonnet m.; (peaked) casquette f.

capability, n. capacité f.

capable, adj. capable.

capably, adv. capablement.

capacious, adj. ample, spacieux.

capacity, n. capacité f.

caparison, 1. n. caparaçon m. 2. vb. caparaçonner.

cape, n. (geography) cap m.; (cloak) cape f.

caper, 1. n. bond m.; (plant) câpre f. 2. vb. bondir.

capillary, adj. capillaire.

capital, adj. capital.

capital, n. (finance) capital m.; (city) capitale f.; (letter) majuscule f.; (architecture) chapiteau m.

capitalism, n. capitalisme m.

capitalist, n. capitaliste m.f.

capitalistic, adj. capitaliste.

capitalization, n. capitalisation f.

capitalize, vb. capitaliser.

capitulate, vb. capituler.

capon, n. chapon m.

caprice, n. caprice m.

capricious, adj. capricieux.

capriciously, adv. capricieusement.

capriciousness, n. caractère capricieux m., humeur fantasque f.

capsize, vb. chavirer, intr.; faire chavirer, tr.

capsule, n. capsule f.

captain, n. capitaine m.

caption, n. en-tête m.

captious, adj. chicaneur.

captivate, vb. captiver.

captivating, adj. séduisant.

captive, adj. and n. captif m.

captivity, n. captivité f.

captor, n. capteur m.

capture, 1. n. capture f. 2. vb. capturer.

car, n. (auto) voiture f.; (train) wagon m.

caracul, n. caracul m.

carafe, n. carafe f.

caramel, n. caramel m.

carat, n. carat m.

caraway, n. carvi m., cumin (des prés) m.

carbide, n. carbure m.

carbine, n. carabine f.

carbohydrate, n. carbohydrate m.

carbon, n. carbone m.

carbon dioxide, n. acide carbonique m.

carbon monoxide, n. oxyde de carbone m.

carbon paper, n. papier carbone m.

carbuncle, n. escarboucle f., charbon (med.) m.

carburetor, n. carburateur m.

carcass, n. carcasse f.

carcinogenic, adj. cancérogène.

card, n. carte f.

cardboard, n. carton m.

cardiac, adj. cardiaque.

cardigan, n. gilet de tricot m.

cardinal, n. cardinal m.

care, 1. n. (worry) souci m.; (attention) attention f.; (take c.!) faites attention!; (charge) soin m.; (take c. of) prendre soin de 2. vb. (c. about) se soucier de; (c. for) aimer; (look after) soigner.

careen, vb. caréner.

career, n. carrière f.

carefree, adj. insouciant.

careful, adj. soigneux.

carefully, adv. soigneusement, attentivement.

carefulness, n. soin m., attention f.

careless, adj. insouciant.

carelessly, adv. nonchalamment, négligemment.

carelessness, n. insouciance f., négligence f.

caress, 1. n. caresse f. 2. vb. caresser.

caretaker, n. concierge m.f.

cargo, n. cargaison f.

caricature, n. caricature f.

caries, n. carie f.

carillon, n. carillon m.

carload, n. voiturée f.

carnal, adj. charnel.

carnation, n. œillet m.

carnival, n. carnaval m.

carnivorous, adj. carnivore.

carol, n. (Xmas c.) noël m.

carouse, vb. faire la fête.

carpenter, n. charpentier m.

carpet, n. tapis m.

carpeting, n. pose de tapis f.

car pool, n. groupe de personnes qui voyagent régulièrement ensemble en auto m.

carriage, n. (vehicle) voiture f.; (bearing) maintien m.; (transport) transport m.

carrier, n. porteur m., messager m.

carrier pigeon, n. pigeon voyageur m.

carrot, *n.* carotte *m.*

carrousel, *n.* carrousel *m.*

carry, *vb.* porter; (c. on) continuer; (c. out) exécuter; (c. through) mener à bonne fin.

cart, *n.* charrette *f.*

cartage, *n.* charriage *m.*, transport *m.*

cartel, *n.* cartel *m.*

carter, *n.* charretier *m.*

cartilage, *n.* cartilage *m.*

carton, *n.* carton *m.*

cartoon, *n.* dessin satirique *m.*

cartoonist, *n.* caricaturiste *m.*

cartridge, *n.* cartouche *f.*

carve, *vb.* (art) sculpter; (meat) découper.

carver, *n.* découpeur *m.*, sculpteur *m.*

carving, *n.* découpage *m.*, sculpture *f.*

cascade, *n.* cascade *f.*

case, *n.* (instance, state of things) cas *m.*; (law) cause *f.*; (packing) caisse *f.*; (holder) étui *m.*; (in any c.) en tout cas.

cash, 1. *n.* espèces *f.pl.*; (C.O.D.) livraison contre remboursement *f.* 2. *vb.* (c. a check) toucher.

cashier, *n.* caissier *m.*

cashmere, *n.* cachemire *m.*

casing, *n.* revêtement *m.*, enveloppe *f.*

casino, *n.* casino *m.*

cask, *n.* tonneau *m.*

casket, *n.* cassette *f.*

casserole, *n.* casserole *f.*

cassette, *n.* cassette *f.*

cast, 1. *n.* (throw) coup *m.*; (characteristic) trempe *f.*; (theater) distribution *f.*; (c. from mold) moulage *m.*; (hue) nuance *f.* 2. *vb.* (throw) jeter; (metal) couler.

castaway, *n.* naufragé *m.*, rejeté *m.*

caste, *n.* caste *f.*

caster, *n.* fondeur *m.*

castigate, *vb.* châtier, punir.

cast iron, *n.* fonte *f.*

castle, *n.* château *m.*

castoff, *adj.* abandonné.

casual, *adj.* (accidental) casuel; (person) insouciant.

casually, *adv.* fortuitement, en passant.

casualness, *n.* nonchalance *f.*

casualties, *n.* (mil.) pertes *f.pl.*

cat, *n.* chat *m.*, chatte *f.*

cataclysm, *n.* cataclysme *m.*

catacomb, *n.* catacombe *f.*

catalogue, *n.* catalogue *m.*

catapult, *n.* catapulte *f.*

cataract, *n.* cataracte *f.*

catarrh, *n.* catarrhe *m.*

catastrophe, *n.* catastrophe *f.*

catch, *vb.* attraper; (seize, understand) saisir.

catcher, *n.* qui attrape.

catchword, *n.* mot d'ordre *m.*

catchy, *adj.* (musical air) facile à retenir; (question) insidieuse.

catechism, *n.* catéchisme *m.*

catechize, *vb.* catéchiser.

categorical, *adj.* catégorique.

category, *n.* catégorie *f.*

cater, *vb.* pourvoir à.

caterpillar, *n.* chenille *f.*

catgut, *n.* corde à boyau *f.*

catharsis, *n.* catharsis *f.*, (med.) purgation *f.*

cathartic, *adj.* cathartique, purgatif.

cathedral, *n.* cathédrale *f.*

cathode, *n.* cathode *f.*

Catholic, *adj.* catholique.

Catholic Church, *n.* Église catholique *f.*

Catholicism, *n.* catholicisme *m.*

cat nap, *n.* somme *m.*

catsup, *n.* sauce piquante *f.*

cattle, *n.* bétail *m.*, bestiaux *m.pl.*

cattleman, *n.* éleveur de bétail *m.*

catwalk, *n.* coursive *f.*

causation, *n.* causation *f.*

cause, *n.* cause *f.*

causeway, *n.* chaussée *f.*

caustic, *adj.* caustique.

cauterize, *vb.* cautériser.

cautery, *n.* cautère *m.*

caution, *n.* prudence *f.*

caution, *vb.* avertir.

cautious, *adj.* prudent.

cavalcade, *n.* cavalcade *f.*

cavalier, *adj.* and *n.* cavalier *m.*

cavalry, *n.* cavalerie *f.*

cave, *n.* caverne *f.*

cave-in, *n.* effondrement *m.*

cavern, *n.* caverne *f.*

caviar, *n.* caviar *m.*

cavity, *n.* cavité *f.*

cease, *vb.* cesser (de).

ceaseless, *adj.* incessant, continuel.

cedar, *n.* cèdre *m.*

cede, *vb.* céder.

ceiling, *n.* plafond *m.*

celebrant, *n.* célébrant *m.*

celebrate, *vb.* célébrer.

celebration, *n.* célébration *f.*

celebrity, *n.* célébrité *f.*

celerity, *n.* célérité *f.*, vitesse *f.*

celery, *n.* céleri *m.*

celestial, *adj.* céleste.

celibacy, *n.* célibat *m.*

celibate, *adj.* célibataire.

cell, *n.* cellule *f.*

cellar, *n.* cave *f.*

cellist, *n.* violoncelliste *m.*

cello, *n.* violoncelle *m.*

cellophane, *n.* cellophane *f.*

cellular, *adj.* cellulaire.

celluloid, *n.* celluloïd *m.*

cellulose, *n.* cellulose *f.*

Celtic, *adj.* celtique.

cement, 1. *n.* ciment *m.* 2. *vb.* cimenter.

cemetery, *n.* cimetière *m.*

censor, 1. *n.* censeur *m.* 2. *vb.* censurer.

censorious, *adj.* critique, hargneux.

censorship, *n.* censure *f.*

censure, *n.* censure *f.*

census, *n.* recensement *m.*

cent, *n.* cent *m.*; (per c.) pour cent.

centenary, centennial, *adj.* and *n.* centenaire *n.*

center, *n.* centre *m.*

centerfold, *n.* pages centrales *f.pl.*

centerpiece, *n.* pièce de milieu *f.*

centigrade, *adj.* centigrade.

centigrade thermometer, *n.* thermomètre centigrade *m.*

central, *adj.* central.

centralize, *vb.* centraliser.

century, *n.* siècle *m.*

century plant, *n.* agave d'Amérique *m.*

ceramic, *adj.* céramique.

ceramics, *n.* céramique *f.*

cereal, *adj.* and *n.* céréale *f.*

cerebral, *adj.* cérébral.

ceremonial, *adj.* and *n.* cérémonial *m.*

ceremonious, *adj.* cérémonieux.

ceremony, *n.* cérémonie *f.*

certain, *adj.* certain.

certainly, *adv.* certainement.

certainty, *n.* certitude *f.*

certificate, *n.* certificat *m.*; (birth c.) acte de naissance.

certification, *n.* certification *f.*

certified, *adj.* certifié, diplômé, breveté.

certifier, *n.* (personne) qui certifie.

certify, *vb.* certifier.

certitude, *n.* certitude *f.*

cervical, *adj.* cervical.

cervix, *n.* cervix *m.*

cessation, *n.* cessation *f.*, suspension *f.*

cession, *n.* cession *f.*

cesspool, *n.* fosse d'aisances *f.*

chafe, *vb.* frictionner.

chaff, 1. *n.* menue paille *f.*; (colloq.) blague *f.* 2. *vb.* blaguer.

chafing dish, *n.* réchaud *m.*

chagrin, *n.* chagrin *m.*

chain, *n.* chaîne *f.*

chain reaction, *n.* réaction caténaire *f.*

chain store, *n.* succursale de grand magasin *f.*

chair, *n.* chaise *f.*; (arm-c.) fauteuil *m.*

chairman, *n.* président *m.*

chairmanship, *n.* présidence *f.*

chairperson, *n.* président *m.*; présidente *f.*

chairwoman, *n.* présidente *f.*

chalice, *n.* calice *m.*

chalk, *n.* craie *f.*

chalky, *adj.* de craie, calcaire.

challenge, *n.* défi *m.*

challenge, *vb.* défier; (dispute) contester.

challenger, *n.* qui fait un défi, prétendant *m.*

chamber, *n.* chambre *f.*

chamberlain, *n.* chambellan *m.*

chambermaid, n. femme de chambre f.

chamber music, n. musique de chambre f.

chameleon, n. caméléon m.

chamois, n. chamois m.

champ, vb. ronger, mâcher.

champion, n. champion m.

championship, n. championnat m.

chance, n. chance f.; (by c.) par hasard.

chancel, n. sanctuaire m., choeur m.

chancellery, n. chancellerie f.

chancellor, n. chancelier m.

chandelier, n. lustre m.

change, 1. n. changement m.; (money) monnaie f.; (exchange) change m. 2. vb. changer.

changeable, adj. changeant.

changeability, n. variabilité f.

changer, n. changeur m.

channel, n. canal m.; (the English C.) la Manche f.

chant, 1. n. chant m. 2. vb. chanter.

chaos, n. chaos m.

chaotic, adj. chaotique.

chap, n. (on skin) gerçure f.; (young man) gars m.

chapel, n. chapelle f.

chaperon, n. (person) duègne f.; chaperon m.

chaplain, n. aumônier m.

chapman, n. colporteur m.

chapped, adj. gercé.

chapter, n. chapitre m.

char, vb. carboniser.

character, n. caractère m.; (in fiction) personnage m.; (role) rôle m.

characteristic, 1. n. trait caractéristique m. 2. adj. caractéristique.

characteristically, adv. d'une manière caractéristique.

characterization, n. action de caractériser f.

characterize, vb. caractériser.

charcoal, n. charbon (m.) de bois.

charge, 1. n. (guns, legal, office) charge f.; (price) prix m.; (care) soin m. 2. vb. charger; (c. with) charger de; (price) demander.

charger, n. grand plat m.; cheval de bataille m.

chariot, n. char m., chariot m.

charioteer, n. conducteur de chariot m.

charisma, n. charisme m.

charitable, adj. charitable.

charitableness, n. bienveillance f.

charitably, adv. charitablement.

charity, n. charité f.

charlatan, n. charlatan m.

charlatanism, n. charlatanisme m.

charm, 1. n. charme m. 2. vb. charmer.

charmer, n. charmeur m., enchanteur m.

charming, adj. charmant.

charred, adj. carbonisé.

chart, n. (map) carte f.; (graph) graphique m.

charter, 1. n. charte f. 2. vb. (boat) affréter.

charter flight, n. vol frété m.; charter m.

charwoman, n. femme de journée f., femme de ménage f.

chase, 1. n. chasse f. 2. vb. chasser.

chaser, n. chasseur m.; ciseleur m.

chasm, n. abîme m.

chassis, n. chassis m.

chaste, adj. chaste.

chasten, vb. châtier, corriger.

chasteness, n. pureté f.

chastise, vb. châtier.

chastisement, n. châtiment m.

chastity, n. chasteté f.

chat, 1. n. causette f. 2. vb. causer.

chateau, n. château m.

chattel, n. bien m., meuble m.

chatter, 1. n. bavardage m. 2. vb. bavarder.

chatterbox, n. bavard m.

chauffeur, n. chauffeur m.

cheap, adj. (inexpensive) bon marché, (mean) de peu de valeur.

cheapen, vb. déprécier.

cheaply, adv. à bon marché.

cheapness, n. bon marché m., bas prix m.; basse qualité f.

cheat, vb. tromper; (at games) tricher.

cheater, n. tricheur m., trompeur m.

check, 1. n. (restraint) frein m.; (verification) vérification f.; (stub) ticket m.; (bill) addition f.; (bank draft) chèque m. 2. vb. (stop) arrêter; (restrain) modérer; (verify) vérifier; (luggage) enregistrer.

checker, n. enregistreur m., contrôleur m.

checkers, n. jeu de dames m.

checkmate, 1. n. échec et mat m. 2. vb. mater.

cheek, n. joue f.

cheer, 1. n. (applause) hourra m. 2. vb. (acclaim) acclamer; (c. up, tr.) réjouir.

cheerful, cheery, adj. gai.

cheerfully, adv. gaiement, de bon cœur.

cheerfulness, n. gaieté f., bonne humeur f.

cheerless, adj. triste, morne, sombre.

cheery, adj. gai, joyeux.

cheese, n. fromage m.

cheesecloth, n. gaze f.

cheesy, adj. fromageux.

chemical, adj. chimique.

chemically, adv. chimiquement.

chemist, n. chimiste m.f.

chemistry, n. chimie f.

chemotherapy, n. chimiothérapie f.

chenille, n. chenille f.

cherish, vb. chérir.

cherry, n. cerise f.

cherub, n. chérubin m.

chess, n. échecs m.pl.

chessman, n. pièce f.

chest, n. (box) coffre m.; (body) poitrine f.; (c. of drawers) commode f.

chestnut, n. châtaigne f.

chevron, n. chevron m.

chew, vb. mâcher.

chewer, n. mâcheur m.

chic, adj. chic.

chicanery, n. chicane f., chicanerie f.

chick, n. poussin m.

chicken, n. poulet m.

chicken-hearted, adj. peureux.

chicken-pox, n. varicelle f.

chicle, n. chiclé m.

chicory, n. chicorée f.

chide, vb. gronder, réprimander.

chief, 1. n. chef m. 2. adj. principal.

chiefly, adv. surtout, principalement.

chieftain, n. chef de clan m.

chiffon, n. chiffon m.

chilblain, n. engelure f.

child, n. enfant m.f.

childbirth, n. enfantement m.

childhood, n. enfance f.

childish, adj. enfantin.

childishness, n. puérilité f., enfantillage m.

childless, adj. sans enfant.

childlessness, n. l'état d'être sans enfants.

childlike, adj. comme un enfant, en enfant.

Chile, n. Chili m.

Chilean, 1. n. Chilien m.; 2. adj. chilien.

chili, n. piment m.

chill, 1. n. froid m.; (shiver) frisson m. 2. vb. refroidir.

chilliness, n. froid m., frisson m.

chilly, adj. un peu froid.

chime, 1. n. carillon m. 2. vb. carillonner.

chimney, n. cheminée f.

chimney sweep, n. ramoneur m.

chimpanzee, n. chimpanzé m.

chin, n. menton m.

China, n. Chine f.

china, n. (ware) porcelaine f.

chinchilla, n. chinchilla m.

Chinese, 1. n. (person) Chinois m.; (language) chinois m. 2. adj. chinois.

chink, n. fente f., crevasse f.

chintz, n. perse f.

chip, n. éclat m.; (potato c.s) frites f.pl.

chipmunk, n. tamias m.

chiropodist, n. pédicure m.

chiropractor, n. chiropracteur m.

chirp, vb. pépier, gazouiller.

chisel, 1. vb. ciseler. 2. n. ciseau m.
chivalrous, adj. chevaleresque.
chivalry, n. chevalerie f.
chive, n. ciboulette f.
chloride, n. chlorure m.
chlorine, n. chlore m.
chloroform, n. chloroforme m.
chlorophyll, n. chlorophylle m.
chockfull, adj. plein comme un œuf.
chocolate, n. chocolat m.
choice, n. choix m.
choir, n. chœur m.
choke, vb. étouffer.
choker, n. foulard m.
cholera, n. choléra m.
choleric, adj. cholérique.
choose, vb. choisir.
chop, 1. n. (meat) côtelette f. 2. vb. couper.
chopper, n. couperet m.
choppy, adj. (sea) clapoteux.
chopstick, n. baguette f., bâtonnet m.
choral, adj. choral.
chord, n. (music) accord m.
chore, n. travail (m.) de ménage.
choreography, n. choréographie f.
chorister, n. choriste m. enfant de chœur m.
chortle, vb. glousser de joie.
chorus, n. chœur m.
chowder, n. (sorte de) bouillabaisse f.
christen, vb. baptiser.
Christendom, n. chrétienté f.
christening, n. baptême m.
Christian, adj. and n. chrétien m.
Christianity, n. christianisme m.
Christmas, n. Noël m.
chromatic, adj. chromatique.
chromium, n. chrome m.
chromosome, n. chromosome m.
chronic, adj. chronique.
chronically, adv. chronologiquement.
chronicle, n. chronique f.
chronological, adj. chronologique.
chronology, n. chronologie f.
chrysalis, n. chrysalide f.
chrysanthemum, n. chrysanthème m.
chubby, adj. joufflu.
chuck, n. petite tape f., gloussement (de volaille) m.
chuckle, vb. rire tout bas.
chug, 1. n. souffle m. (d'une machine à vapeur). 2. vb. souffler.
chum, n. camarade m., copain m.
chummy, adj. familier, intime.
chunk, n. gros morceau m.
chunky, adj. en gros morceaux.
church, n. église f.
churchman, n. homme d'église m., ecclésiastique m.
churchyard, n. cimetière m.

churn, vb. baratter.
chute, n. glissière f.
chutney, n. chutney m.
cicada, n. cigale f.
cider, n. cidre m.
cigar, n. cigare m.
cigarette, n. cigarette f.
cilia, n. cils m.pl.
ciliary, adj. ciliaire.
cinch, n. (it's a c.) c'est facile.
cinchona, n. quinquina m.
cinder, n. cendre f.
cinema, n. cinéma m.
cinematic, adj. cinématographique.
cinnamon, n. cannelle f.
cipher, n. chiffre m.; (nought) zéro m.
circle, 1. n. cercle n. 2. vb. entourer (de).
circuit, n. circuit m.
circuitous, adj. détourné, sinueux.
circuitously, adv. d'une manière détournée, par des détours.
circular, adj. circulaire.
circularize, vb. envoyer des circulaires.
circulate, vb. circuler, tr.; faire circuler, intr.
circulation, n. circulation f.
circulator, n. circulateur m.
circulatory, adj. circulaire, circulatoire.
circumcise, vb. circoncire.
circumcision, n. circoncision f.
circumference, n. circonférence f.
circumlocution, n. circonlocution f.
circumscribe, vb. circonscrire.
circumspect, adj. circonspect.
circumstance, n. (condition) circonstance f.; (financial) moyens m.pl.
circumstantial, adj. circonstancié.
circumstantially, adv. en détail.
circumvent, vb. circonvenir.
circumvention, n. circonvention f.
circus, n. cirque m.
cirrhosis, n. cirrhose f.
cistern, n. citerne f.
citadel, n. citadelle f.
citation, n. citation f.
cite, vb. citer.
citizen, n. citoyen m.
citizenry, n. tous les citoyens m.pl.
citizenship, n. droit (m.) de cité.
citric acid, n. acide citrique m.
city, n. ville f.; cité f.
civic, adj. civique.
civics, n. instruction (f.) civique.
civil, adj. civil; (polite) poli; (c. servant) fonctionnaire m.

civil service, n. administration (civile) f.
civil war, n. guerre civile f.
clad, adj. habillé, vêtu.
claim, 1. n. (demand) demande f.; (right) droit m. 2. vb. (demand) réclamer, prétendre; (insist) soutenir.
claimant, n. réclamateur m., prétendant m.
clairvoyance, n. clairvoyance f.
clairvoyant, n. voyant m.
clam, n. palourde f., mollusque m.
clamber, vb. grimper.
clammy, adj. visqueux, moite.
clamor, n. clameur f.
clamorous, adj. bruyant.
clamp, 1. n. (metal) crampon m.; (carpentry) serre-joint m. 2. vb. cramponner, serrer.
clan, n. clan m., clique f., coterie f.
clandestine, adj. clandestin.
clandestinely, adv. clandestinement.
clang, 1. n. cliquetis m., son métallique m. 2. vb. résonner.
clangor, n. cliquetis m.
clannish, adj. de clan.
clap, vb. (applaud) applaudir.
clapboard, n. bardeau m.
clapper, n. claqueur m., battant (of a bell) m.
claque, n. claque f.
claret, n. vin rouge de Bordeaux m.
clarification, n. clarification f.
clarify, vb. (lit.) clarifier; (fig.) éclaircir.
clarinet, n. clarinette f.
clarinetist, n. clarinettiste m.
clarion, n. clairon m.
clarity, n. clarté f.
clash, 1. vb. choquer, tr.; s'entre-choquer, intr. 2. n. choc m.
clasp, 1. n. agrafe f.; (embrace) étreinte f. 2. vb. agrafer, étreindre.
class, n. classe f.
classic, classical, adj. classique.
classicism, n. classicisme m.
classifiable, adj. classifiable.
classification, n. classification f.
classify, vb. classifier, classer.
classmate, n. camarade (m.) de classe.
classroom, n. salle (f.) de classe.
clatter, n. bruit m.
clause, n. clause f.
claustrophobia, n. claustrophobie f.
claw, n. griffe f.
claw-hammer, n. marteau à dent m.
clay, n. argile f., glaise f.
clean, 1. adj. propre. 2. vb. nettoyer.
clean-cut, adj. net, fin.
cleaner, n. (dry-c.) teinturier m.

cleanliness, cleanness, *n.* propreté *f.*

cleanse, *vb.* nettoyer, curer.

cleanser, *n.* chose qui nettoie *f.*, détersif *m.*, cureur *m.*

clear, 1. *adj.* clair. 2. *vb.* (c. up) déblayer; (profit) gagner; (get over) franchir; (weather, *intr.*) s'éclaircir.

clear-cut, *adj.* nettement dessiné.

clearing, *n.* (open place) clairière *f.*, éclaircissement *m. (comm.)* acquittement *m.*, (woods) éclaircie *f.*

clearing house, *n.* banque de virement *f.*, chambre de compensation *f.*

clearly, *adv.* clairement, nettement, évidemment.

clearness, *n.* clarté *f.*, netteté *f.*

cleat, *n.* fer *m.*, (*naut.*) taquet *m.*

cleavage, *n.* fendage *m.*, scission *f.*

cleave, *vb.* (split) fendre; (adhere) adhérer.

cleaver, *n.* fendeur (person) *m.*; fendoir *m.*, couperet (instrument) *m.*

cleft, *n.* fente *f.*

clemency, *n.* clémence *f.*

clench, *vb.* serrer.

clergy, *n.* clergé *m.*

clergyman, *n.* ecclésiastique *m.*

clerical, *adj.* (clergy) clérical; (business) de bureau.

clericalism, *n.* cléricalisme *m.*

clerk, *n.* (business) employé *m.*; (store) commis *m.*; (law, *eccles.*) clerc *m.*

clerkship, *n.* place de clerc *f.*, place de commis *f.*

clever, *adj.* habile.

cleverly, *adv.* habilement.

cleverness, *n.* adresse *f.*

clew, *n.* fil *m.*

cliché, *n.* cliché *m.*

click, 1. *n.* cliquetis *m.*, déclic *m.* 2. *vb.* cliqueter.

client, *n.* client *m.*

clientele, *n.* clientèle *f.*

cliff, *n.* falaise *f.*

climactic, *adj.* arrivé à son apogée.

climate, *n.* climat *m.*

climatic, *adj.* climatique.

climax, *n.* comble *m.*

climb, 1. *n.* montée *f.* 2. *vb.* monter, grimper.

climber, *n.* grimpeur *m.*, ascensioniste *m.*

clinch, *vb.* river; (settle) conclure.

cling, *vb.* s'accrocher.

clinging, *adj.* qui se cramponne, qui s'accroche (à).

clinic, *n.* clinique *f.*

clinical, *adj.* clinique.

clinically, *adv.* d'une manière clinique.

clip, 1. *vb.* couper. 2. *n.* pince *f.*

clipper, *n.* rogneur *m.*, tondeuse (instrument) *f.*, (*naut.*) fin voilier *m.*

clipping, *n.* coupure *f.*

clique, *n.* clique *f.*

cloak, *n.* manteau *m.*; (cloakroom) vestiaire *m.*

clock, *n.* horloge *f.*; (two o'clock) deux heures.

clockwise, *adv.* dans le sens des aiguilles d'une montre.

clockwork, *n.* mouvement (*m.*) d'horlogerie.

clod, *n.* motte (*f.*) de terre; (person) lourdaud *m.*

clog, *vb.* entraver.

cloister, *n.* cloître *m.*

clone, *n.* reproduction exacte *f.*

close, 1. *adj.* (closed) fermé; (narrow) étroit; (near) proche; (secret) réservé. 2. *vb.* fermer. 3. *adv.* tout près. 4. *prep.* (c. to) près de.

closely, *adv.* de près, étroitement.

closeness, *n.* proximité *f.*, lourdeur (of the weather) *f.*, réserve *f.*

closet, *n.* (room) cabinet *m.*; (clothes) placard *m.*

clot, *n.* (blood) caillot *m.*

cloth, *n.* étoffe *f.*

clothe, *vb.* vêtir (de); habiller *m.*

clothes, *n.* habits *m.pl.*

clothespin, *n.* pince *f.*

clothier, *n.* drapier *m.*, tailleur *m.*

clothing, *n.* vêtements *m.pl.*

cloud, *n.* nuage *m.*

cloudburst, *n.* trombe *f.*, rafale de pluie *f.*

cloudiness, *n.* état nuageux *m.*, obscurité *f.*

cloudless, *adj.* sans nuage.

cloudy, *adj.* nuageux, couvert.

clout, 1. *n.* gifle *f.*, tape *f.* 2. *vb.* gifler, taper.

clove, *n.* clou (*m.*) de girofle.

clover, *n.* trèfle *m.*

clown, *n.* bouffon *m.*

clownish, *adj.* rustre, grossier, de payan.

cloy, *vb.* rassasier.

club, *n.* (society) club *m.*, société *f.*, cercle *m.*; (stick) massue *f.*; (golf) crosse *f.*; (cards) trèfle *m.*

clubfoot, *n.* pied bot *m.*

clue, *n.* fil *m.*

clump, *n.* (trees) bosquet *m.*; massif *m.*

clumsiness, *n.* gaucherie *f.*, maladresse *f.*

clumsy, *adj.* gauche.

cluster, 1. *n.* (people) groupe *m.*; (fruit) grappe *f.*; (flowers, trees) bouquet *m.* 2. *vb.* se grouper.

clutch, 1. *n.* (claw) griffe *f.*; (auto) embrayage *m.* 2. *vb.* saisir.

clutter, *vb.* encombrer.

coach, 1. *n.* (carriage) carrosse *m.*; (train) wagon *m.*; (sports) entraîneur *m.* 2. *vb.* (sports) entraîner; (school) donner des leçons particulières à.

coachman, *n.* cocher *m.*

coagulate, *vb.* se coaguler.

coagulation, *n.* coagulation *f.*

coal, *n.* charbon (*m.*) de terre, houille *f.*

coalesce, *vb.* se fondre, se fusionner, s'unir.

coalition, *n.* coalition *f.*

coal tar, *n.* goudron de houille *m.*

coarse, *adj.* grossier.

coarsen, *vb.* rendre plus grossier.

coarseness, *n.* grossièreté *f.*

coast, *n.* côte *f.*

coastal, *adj.* de la côte, littoral.

coaster, *n.* caboteur *m.*, dessous de carafe *m.*

coast guard, *n.* garde-côtes *m.*

coat, 1. *n.* (man) pardessus *m.*; (woman) manteau *m.*; (paint) couche *f.* 2. *vb.* (c. with) revêtir de.

coating, *n.* couche *f.*, enduit *m.*, étoffe pour habits *f.*

coat of arms, *n.* écusson *m.*, cotte d'armes *f.*

coax, *vb.* cajoler.

cobalt, *n.* cobalt *m.*

cobbler, *n.* savetier *m.*, cordonnier *m.*

cobblestone, *n.* pierre du pavé *f.*

cobra, *n.* cobra *m.*

cobweb, *n.* toile (*f.*) d'araignée.

cocaine, *n.* cocaïne *f.*

cock, 1. *n.* (fowl) coq *m.*; (male) mâle *m.* 2. *vb.* faire de l'œil.

cocker spaniel, *n.* épagneul cocker *m.*

cockeyed, *adj.* louche.

cockhorse, *n.* dada *m.*

cockroach, *n.* blatte *f.*

cocksure, *adj.* sûr et certain.

cocktail, *n.* cocktail *m.*

cocky, *adj.* suffisant.

cocoa, *n.* cacao *m.*

coconut, *n.* noix (*f.*) de coco; coco *m.*

cocoon, *n.* cocon *m.*

cod, *n.* morue *f.*

coddle, *vb.* dorloter.

code, *n.* code *m.*

codeine, *n.* codéine *f.*

codfish, *n.* morue *f.*

codify, *vb.* codifier.

cod-liver oil, *n.* huile de foie de morue *f.*

coeducation, *n.* enseignement mixte *m.*

coequal, *adj.* égal.

coerce, *vb.* contraindre.

coercion, *n.* coercition *f.*, contrainte *f.*

coercive, *adj.* coercitif.

coexist, *vb.* coexister.

coffee, *n.* café *m.*

coffer, *n.* coffre *m.*

coffin, *n.* cercueil *m.*

cog, *n.* dent *f.*

cogent, *adj.* puissant, fort.

cogitate, *vb.* méditer, penser.

cognizance, *n.* connaissance *f.*

cognizant, *adj.* instruit, (*law*) compétent.

cogwheel, n. roue d'engrenage f.

coherent, adj. cohérent.

cohesion, n. cohésion f.

cohesive, adj. cohésif.

cohort, n. cohorte f.

coiffure, n. coiffure f.

coil, n. rouleau m.

coin, n. pièce (f.) de monnaie.

coinage, n. monnayage m., monnaie f.

coincide, vb. coïncider.

coincidence, n. coïncidence f.

coincident, adj. coïncident.

coincidental, adj. coïncident, d'accord (avec).

coincidentally, adv. par coïncidence.

colander, n. passoire f.

cold, 1. n. (temperature) froid m.; (medical) rhume m. 2. adj. froid; (it is cold) il fait froid; (feel cold) avoir froid.

cold-blooded, adj. de sang froid.

coldly, adv. froidement.

coldness, n. froideur f.

collaborate, vb. collaborer.

collaboration, n. collaboration f.

collaborator, n. collaborateur m.

collapse, 1. n. effrondrement m.; (med.) affaissement m. 2. vb. s'effrondrer; (med.) s'affaisser.

collar, n. col m.; (dog) collier m.

collarbone, n. clavicule f.

collate, vb. collationner, comparer.

collateral, adj. and n. collatéral m.

collation, n. collation f., comparaison f., repas froid m.

colleague, n. collègue m.f.

collect, vb. rassembler.

collection, n. collection f.; (money) collecte f.

collective, adj. collectif.

collectively, adv. collectivement.

collector, n. (art) collectionneur m.; (tickets) contrôleur m.

college, n. collège m.; (higher education) université f.

collegiate, adj. de collège, collégial.

collide, vb. se heurter (contre).

colliery, n. houillère f., mine de charbon f.

collision, n. collision f.

colloquial, adj. familier.

colloquialism, n. expression de style familier f.

colloquially, adv. en style familier.

colloquy, n. colloque m., entretien m.

collusion, n. collusion f., connivence f.

colon, n. (gramm.) deux points m.pl.

colonel, n. colonel m.

colonial, adj. colonial.

colonist, n. colon m.

colonization, n. colonisation f.

colonize, vb. coloniser.

colony, n. colonie f.

color, 1. n. couleur f. 2. vb. colorer, tr.

coloration, n. coloris m.

colored, adj. coloré, de couleur, colorié.

colorful, adj. coloré, pittoresque.

coloring, n. coloris m., couleur f.

colorless, adj. sans couleur, incolore, terne.

colossal, adj. colossal.

colt, n. poulain m.

colter, n. coutre m.

column, n. colonne f.

columnist, n. journaliste (qui a sa rubrique à lui) m.

coma, n. coma m.

comb, 1. n. peigne m. 2. vb. peigner.

combat, n. combat m.

combatant, adj. and n. combattant m.

combative, adj. combatif.

combination, n. combinaison f.

combination lock, n. serrure à combinaisons f.

combine, vb. combiner, tr.

combustible, adj. and n. combustible m.

combustion, n. combustion f.

come, vb. venir; (c. about) arriver; (c. across) rencontrer; (c. away) partir; (c. back) revenir; (c. down) descendre; (c. in) entrer; (c. out) sortir; (c. up) monter.

comedian, n. comédien m.

comedienne, n. comédienne f.

comedy, n. comédie f.

comely, adj. avenant.

comet, n. comète f.

comfort, 1. n. (mental) consolation f.; (material) confort m. 2. vb. consoler.

comfortable, adj. commode.

comfortably, adv. confortablement, commodément.

comforter, n. consolateur m.

comfortingly, adv. d'une manière réconfortante.

comfortless, adj. sans consolation, inconsolable, désolé.

comic, comical, adj. comique.

comic strip, n. dessein comique m.

coming, n. venue f., arrivée f., approche f.

comma, n. virgule f.

command, 1. n. commandement m. 2. vb. commander (à).

commandeer, vb. réquisitionner.

commander, n. commandant m.

commander in chief, n. généralissime m.

commandment, n. commandement m.

commemorate, vb. commémorer.

commemoration, n. célébration f., commémoration f.

commemorative, adj. commémoratif.

commence, vb. commencer.

commencement, n. (school) distribution (f.) des diplômes.

commend, vb. (entrust) recommander; (praise) louer.

commendable, adj. louable, recommandable.

commendably, adv. d'une manière louable.

commendation, n. louange f.

commensurate, adj. proportionné.

comment, 1. n. commentaire m. 2. vb. commenter.

commentator, n. commentateur m.

commerce, n. commerce m.

commercial, adj. commercial.

commercialism, n. commercialisme m.

commercialize, vb. commercialiser.

commercially, adv. commercialement.

commiserate, vb. plaindre, avoir pitié de.

commissary, n. (person) commissaire m.; (supply store) dépôt (m.) de vivres.

commission, n. (assignment) commande f.; (officer) brevet m.; (committee, percentage) commission f.

commissioner, n. commissaire m.

commit, vb. commettre.

commitment, n. engagement m.

committee, n. comité m.

commodious, adj. spacieux.

commodity, n. produit m., commodité f., denrée f.

common, adj. commun; (vulgar) vulgaire.

common law, n. droit coutumier m.

commonly, adv. communément, ordinairement.

commonness, n. vulgarité f.

commonplace, n. lieu-commun m.

commonwealth, n. état m.

commotion, n. agitation f.

communal, adj. communal.

commune, n. commune f.

communicable, adj. communicable.

communicant, n. communiant m.

communicate, vb. communiquer.

communication, n. communication f.

communicative, adj. communicatif.

communion, n. communion f.

communiqué, n. communiqué m.

communism, n. communisme m.

communist, adj. and n. communiste m.f.

communistic, adj. communiste.

community, n. communauté f.

commutation, n. commutation f.

commute, vb. changer, (law) commuer.

commuter, n. voyageur de banlieue m.

compact, 1. n. (agreement) accord m.; (cosmetic) poudrier m. **2.** adj. compact.

compactness, n. compacité f.

companion, n. compagnon m., compagne f.

companionable, adj. sociable.

companionship, n. camaraderie f.

company, n. compagnie f.

comparable with, adj. comparable à.

comparative, adj. and n. comparatif m.

comparatively, adv. comparativement, relativement.

compare, vb. comparer.

comparison, n. comparaison f.

compartment, n. compartiment m.

compass, n. (naut.) boussole f.; (geom.) compas m.

compassion, n. compassion f.

compassionate, adj. compatissant.

compassionately, adv. avec compassion.

compatible, adj. compatible.

compatriot, n. compatriote m.f.

compel, vb. forcer.

compensate, vb. compenser.

compensation, n. compensation f.

compensatory, adj. compensateur.

compete, vb. rivaliser.

competence, n. compétence f.

competent, adj. capable.

competently, adv. convenablement, avec compétence.

competition, n. concurrence f.

competitor, n. concurrent m.

compile, vb. compiler.

complacency, n. contentement (m.) de soi-même.

complacent, adj. content de soi-même.

complacently, adv. avec un air (un ton) suffisant.

complain, vb. se plaindre.

complainer, n. plaignant m., réclameur m.

complainingly, adv. d'une manière plaignante.

complaint, n. plainte f.

complement, n. complément m.

complete, adj. complet.

completely, adv. complètement, tout à fait.

completeness, n. état complet m., perfection f.

completion, n. achèvement m.

complex, adj. and n. complexe m.

complexion, n. teint m.

complexity, n. complexité f.

compliance, n. acquiescement m.

compliant, adj. complaisant, accommodant.

complicate, vb. compliquer.

complicated, adj. compliqué.

complication, n. complication f.

complicity, n. complicité f.

compliment, n. compliment m.

complimentary, adj. flatteur, de félicitations.

comply with, vb. se conformer à.

component, adj. and n. composant m.

comport, vb. s'accorder (avec), convenir (à).

compose, vb. composer.

composed, adj. composé, calme, tranquille.

composer, n. compositeur m.

composite, adj. composé.

composition, n. composition f.

compost, n. compost m., terreau m.

composure, n. calme m., tranquillité f., sang-froid m.

compote, n. compote f.

compound, 1. adj. and n. composé m. **2.** vb. composer.

comprehend, vb. comprendre.

comprehensible, adj. compréhensible, intelligible.

comprehension, n. compréhension f.

comprehensive, adj. compréhensif.

compress, 1. n. compresse f. **2.** vb. comprimer, tr.

compressed, adj. comprimé.

compression, n. compression f.

compressor, n. compresseur m.

comprise, vb. comprendre.

compromise, 1. n. compromis m. **2.** vb. compromettre.

compromiser, n. comprometteur m.

compulsion, n. contrainte f.

compulsive, adj. coercitif, obligatoire.

compulsory, adj. obligatoire.

compunction, n. componction f.

computation, n. supputation f.

compute, vb. supputer.

computer, n. ordinateur m.

computerize, vb. informatiser.

computer science, n. informatique f.

comrade, n. camarade m.f.

comradeship, n. camaraderie f.

concave, adj. concave.

conceal, vb. cacher.

concealment, n. action (f.) de cacher.

concede, vb. concéder.

conceit, n. vanité f.

conceited, adj. vaniteux, suffisant.

conceivable, adj. concevable.

conceivably, adv. d'une manière concevable.

conceive, vb. concevoir.

concentrate, vb. concentrer tr.

concentration camp, n. camp de concentration m.

concept, n. concept m.

conception, n. conception f.

concern, 1. n. (what pertains to one) affaire f.; (comm.) entreprise f.; (solicitude) souci m. **2.** vb. concerner; (c. oneself with) s'intéresser à; (be c.ed about) s'inquiéter de.

concerning, prep. concernant.

concert, n. concert m.

concerted, adj. concerté.

concession, n. concession f.

conciliate, vb. concilier.

conciliation, n. conciliation f.

conciliator, n. conciliateur m.

conciliatory, adj. conciliant, conciliatoire.

concise, adj. concis.

concisely, adv. avec concision, succinctement.

conciseness, n. concision f.

conclave, n. conclave m.

conclude, vb. conclure.

conclusion, n. conclusion f.

conclusive, adj. concluant.

conclusively, adv. d'une manière concluante.

concoct, vb. préparer.

concomitant, 1. adj. concomitant. **2.** n. accessoire m.

concord, n. concorde f.

concordat, n. concordat m.

concourse, n. concours m., affluence f.

concrete, 1. n. béton m. **2.** adj. concret.

concretely, adv. d'une manière concrète.

concreteness, n. état concret m.

concubine, n. concubine f.

concur, vb. (events) concourir; (persons) être d'accord.

concurrence, n. assentiment m., concours m.

concurrent, adj. concourant.

concussion, n. secousse f., ébranlement m.

condemn, vb. condamner.

condemnable, adj. condamnable.

condemnation, n. condamnation f.

condensation, n. condensation f.

condense, vb. condenser, tr.

condenser, n. condenseur m.

condescend, vb. condescendre.

condescendingly, adv. avec condescendance.

condescension, n. condescendance f.

condiment, n. condiment m., assaisonnement m.

condition, 1. n. condition f. **2.** vb. conditionner.

conditional, adj. and n. conditionnel m.

conditionally, *adv.* conditionnellement.
condolence, *n.* condoléance *f.*
condole with, *vb.* faire ses condoléances à.
condominium, *n.* condominium *m.*
conducive, *adj.* favorable.
conduct, 1. *n.* conduite *f.* 2. *vb.* conduire.
conductivity, *n.* conductivité *f.*
conductor, *n.* conducteur *m.;* (bus) receveur *m.;* (rail) chef *(m.)* de train; (music) chef *(m.)* d'orchestre.
conduit, *n.* conduit *m.,* tuyau *m.*
cone, *n.* cône *m.*
confection, *n.* confection *f.;* (sweet) bonbon *m.*
confectioner, *n.* confiseur *m.*
confectionery, *n.* confiserie *f.*
confederacy, confederation, *n.* confédération *f.*
confederate, *adj.* and *n.* confédéré *m.*
confer, *vb.* conférer.
conference, *n.* (meeting) entretien *m.;* (congress) congrès *m.*
confess, *vb.* avouer; *(eccles.)* confesser, *tr.*
confession, *n.* confession *f.*
confessional, *n.* confessional *m.*
confessor, *n.* confesseur *m.*
confetti, *n.* confetti *m.*
confidant, *n.* confident *m.*
confidante, *n.* confidente *f.*
confide, *vb.* confier (à), *tr.*
confidence, *n.* (trust) confiance *f.;* (secret) confidence *f.*
confident, *adj.* confiant.
confidential, *adj.* confidentiel.
confidentially, *adv.* confidentiellement.
confidently, *adv.* avec confiance.
confine, *vb.* (banish) confiner; (limit) limiter.
confirm, *vb.* confirmer.
confirmation, *n.* confirmation *f.*
confirmed, *adj.* invétéré, incorrigible.
confiscate, *vb.* confisquer.
confiscation, *n.* confiscation *f.*
conflagration, *n.* conflagration *f.,* incendie *m.*
conflict, *n.* conflit *m.*
conform, *vb.* conformer, *tr.*
conformation, *n.* conformation *f.,* conformité *f.*
conformer, *n.* conformiste *m.*
conformist, *n.* conformiste *m.*
conformity, *n.* conformité *f.*
confound, *vb.* confondre; (c. him!) que le diable l'emporte!
confront, *vb.* confronter.
confuse, *vb.* confondre.
confusion, *n.* confusion *f.*
congeal, *vb.* congeler, *tr.*
congealment, *n.* congélation *f.*
congenial, *adj.* (person) sympathique; (thing) convenable.
congenital, *adj.* congénital.

congenitally, *adv.* d'une manière congénitale.
congestion, *n.* *(med.)* congestion *f.;* (traffic) encombrement *m.*
conglomerate, *adj.* congloméré.
conglomeration, *n.* conglomération *f.*
congratulate, *vb.* féliciter (de).
congratulation, *n.* félicitation *f.*
congratulatory, *adj.* de félicitation.
congregate, *vb.* rassembler, *tr.*
congregation, *n.* assemblée *f.*
congress, *n.* congrès *m.*
congressional, *adj.* congressionnel.
conic, *adj.* conique.
conjecture, *n.* conjecture *f.*
conjugal, *adj.* conjugal.
conjugate, *vb.* conjuguer.
conjugation, *n.* conjugaison *f.*
conjunction, *n.* conjonction *f.*
conjunctive, *adj.* conjonctif.
conjunctivitis, *n.* conjonctivite *f.*
conjure, *vb.* conjurer.
connect, *vb.* joindre.
connection, *n.* connexion *f.;* (social) relations *f.pl.;* (train) correspondance *f.*
connivance, *n.* connivence *f.*
connive, *vb.* conniver (à).
connoisseur, *n.* connaisseur *m.*
connotation, *n.* connotation *f.*
connote, *vb.* signifier, vouloir dire.
connubial, *adj.* conjugal, du mariage.
conquer, *vb.* conquérir.
conquerable, *adj.* qui peut être vaincu, domptable.
conqueror, *n.* conquérant *m.*
conquest, *n.* conquête *f.*
conscience, *n.* conscience *f.*
conscientious, *adj.* consciencieux.
conscientiously, *adv.* consciencieusement.
conscious, *adj.* conscient.
consciously, *adv.* sciemment, en parfaite connaissance.
consciousness, *n.* conscience *f.*
conscript, *adj.* and *n.* conscrit *m.*
conscription, *n.* conscription *f.*
consecrate, *vb.* consacrer.
consecration, *n.* consécration *f.*
consecutive, *adj.* consécutif.
consecutively, *adv.* consécutivement, de suite.
consensus, *n.* consensus *m.,* assentiment général *m.*
consent, 1. *n.* consentement *m.* 2. *vb.* consentir.
consequence, *n.* conséquence *f.*
consequent, *adj.* conséquent.
consequential, *adj.* conséquent, logique.
consequently, *adv.* par conséquent.
conservation, *n.* conservation *f.*

conservatism, *n.* conservatisme *m.*
conservative, *adj.* (politics) conservateur; *(comm.)* prudent.
conservatively, *adv.* d'une manière conservatrice.
conservatory, *n.* conservatoire *m.*
conserve, *vb.* conserver.
consider, *vb.* considérer.
considerable, *adj.* considérable.
considerably, *adv.* considérablement.
considerate, *adj.* plein d'égards.
considerately, *adv.* avec égards, avec indulgence.
consideration, *n.* considération *f.*
considering, *prep.* vu que, attendu que.
consign, *vb.* consigner.
consignment, *n.* expédition *f.,* consignation *f.*
consistency, *n.* consistance *f.*
consistent, *adj.* consistant.
consist of, *vb.* consister en.
consolation, *n.* consolation *f.*
console, *vb.* consoler.
consolidate, *vb.* consolider.
consommé, *n.* consommé *m.*
consonant, *n.* consonne *f.*
consort, 1. *n.* compagnon *m.,* époux *m.* 2. *vb.* s'associer (à).
conspicuous, *adj.* en évidence.
conspicuously, *adv.* visiblement, éminemment.
conspicuousness, *n.* éclat *m.,* position éminente *f.*
conspiracy, *n.* conspiration *f.*
conspirator, *n.* conspirateur *m.*
conspire, *vb.* conspirer.
conspirer, *n.* conspirateur *m.*
constancy, *n.* constance *f.,* fermeté *f.*
constant, *adj.* constant.
constantly, *adv.* constamment.
constellation, *n.* constellation *f.*
consternation, *n.* consternation *f.*
constipation, *n.* constipation *f.*
constituency, *n.* circonscription électorale *f.*
constituent, *adj.* constituant.
constitute, *vb.* constituer.
constitution, *n.* constitution *f.*
constitutional, *adj.* constitutionnel.
constrain, *vb.* contraindre.
constrained, *adj.* contraint.
constraint, *n.* contrainte *f.,* gêne *f.*
constrict, *vb.* resserrer.
construct, *vb.* construire.
construction, *n.* construction *f.*
constructive, *adj.* constructif.
constructively, *adv.* constructivement, par induction.
constructor, *n.* constructeur *m.*
construe, *vb.* interpréter.
consul, *n.* consul *m.*
consular, *adj.* consulaire.

consulate, n. consulat m.

consult, vb. consulter.

consultant, n. conseiller m.

consultation, n. consultation f.

consume, vb. consumer.

consumer, n. consommateur m.

consummate, 1. adj. consommé. 2. vb. consommer.

consummation, n. consommation f.

consumption, n. consommation f.; (med.) phtisie f.

consumptive, adj. poitrinaire, tuberculeux.

contact, n. contact m.

contagion, n. contagion f.

contagious, adj. contagieux.

contain, vb. contenir.

container, n. récipient m.

contaminate, vb. contaminer.

contaminated, adj. contaminé.

contemplate, vb. contempler.

contemplation, n. contemplation f.

contemplative, adj. contemplatif.

contemporary, adj. contemporain.

contempt, n. mépris m.

contemptible, adj. méprisable.

contemptuous, adj. méprisant.

contemptuously, adv. avec mépris, dédaigneusement.

contend, vb. (struggle) lutter; (maintain) soutenir.

contender, n. compétiteur m., concurrent m.

content, n. (satisfaction) contentement m.; (c.s) contenu m.

contented with, adj. content de.

contention, n. contention f., lutte f.

contentment, n. contentement m.

contest, 1. n. (struggle) lutte f.; (competition) concours m. 2. vb. contester.

contestable, adj. contestable.

contestant, n. concurrent m., disputant m.

context, n. contexte m.

contiguous, adj. contigu.

continence, n. continence f., retenue f.

continent, adj. and n. continent m.

continental, adj. continental.

contingency, n. contingence f.

contingent, adj. contingent.

continual, adj. continuel.

continuation, n. continuation f.

continue, vb. continuer.

continuity, n. continuité f.

continuous, adj. continu.

continuously, adv. continûment, sans interruption.

contort, vb. tordre, défigurer.

contortionist, n. contortionniste m.

contour, n. contour m.

contraband, n. contrebande f.

contraception, n. limitation des naissances f.

contract, 1. n. contrat m. 2. vb. contracter, tr.

contracted, adj. contracté, resserré.

contraction, n. contraction f.

contractor, n. entrepreneur m.

contradict, vb. contredire.

contradictable, adj. qui peut être contredit.

contradiction, n. contradiction f., démenti m.

contradictory, adj. contradictoire.

contraption, n. machin m.

contrary, adj. and n. contraire m.; (on the c.) au contraire.

contrast, 1. n. contraste m. 2. vb. mettre en contraste, tr.; contraster, intr.

contribute, vb. contribuer.

contribution, n. contribution f.

contributive, adj. contributif.

contributor, n. contribuant m.

contributory, adj. contribuant.

contrite, adj. contrit, pénitent.

contrition, n. contrition f.

contrivance, n. combinaison f., invention f., artifice m.

contrive, vb. inventer, imaginer, arranger.

control, 1. n. autorité f.; (machinery) commande f. 2. vb. gouverner; (check) contrôler.

controllable, adj. vérifiable, gouvernable.

controller, n. contrôleur m.

controversial, adj. de controverse, polémique.

controversy, n. controverse f.

contusion, n. contusion f.

conundrum, n. devinette f., énigme f.

convalescence, n. convalescence f.

convalescent, adj. convalescent.

convene, vb. assembler, tr.

convenience, n. convenance f.; (comfort) commodité f.

convenient, adj. commode.

conveniently, adv. commodément.

convent, n. couvent m.

convention, n. convention f.

conventional, adj. conventionnel.

conventionally, adv. par convention.

converge, vb. converger.

convergence, n. convergence f.

convergent, adj. convergent.

conversant, adj. versé (dans), familier (avec).

conversation, n. conversation f.

conversational, adj. de conversation.

conversationalist, n. causeur m.

converse, vb. converser.

conversely, adv. réciproquement.

convert, vb. convertir, tr.

converter, n. convertisseur m.

convertible, adj. convertible (of things), convertissable (of persons).

convex, adj. convexe.

convey, vb. (transport) transporter; (transmit) transmettre.

conveyance, n. transport m.

conveyor, n. transporteur m., conducteur (électrique) m.

convict, 1. n. forçat m. 2. vb. condamner.

conviction, n. (condemnation) condamnation f.; (persuasion) conviction f.

convince, vb. convaincre.

convincing, adj. convaincant.

convincingly, adv. d'une manière convaincante.

convivial, adj. jovial, joyeux.

convocation, n. convocation f.

convoke, vb. convoquer.

convoy, n. convoi m.

convulse, vb. convulser, bouleverser.

convulsion, n. convulsion f.

convulsive, adj. convulsif.

cook, 1. n. cuisinier m. 2. vb. cuire, intr.; faire cuire, tr.

cookbook, n. livre de cuisine m.

cookie, n. gâteau sec m.

cool, adj. frais m., fraîche f.

cooler, n. rafraîchissoir m., réfrigérant m.

coolness, n. fraîcheur f.

coop, n. cage (f.) à poules.

coöperate, vb. coopérer.

coöperation, n. coopération f.

coöperative, 1. n. coopérative f. 2. adj. coopératif.

coöperatively, adj. d'une manière coopérative.

coördinate, vb. coordonner.

coördination, n. coordination f.

coördinator, n. coordinateur m.

cop, 1. n. (slang) flic m. 2. vb. (colloquial) attraper, pincer.

cope with, vb. tenir tête à.

copier, n. machine à copier f.

copious, adj. copieux.

copiously, adv. copieusement.

copiousness, n. abondance f.

copper, n. cuivre m.

copperplate, n. cuivre plané m.; taille-douce f.

copy, 1. n. copie f. 2. vb. copier.

copyist, n. copiste m., imitateur m.

copyright, n. droit (m.) d'auteur.

coquetry, n. coquetterie f.

coquette, n. coquette f.

coral, n. corail m.; pl. coraux.

cord, n. corde f.

cordial, adj. and n. cordial m.

cordiality, n. cordialité f.

cordially, adv. cordialement.

cordon, n. cordon m.

cordovan, adj. cordovan.

corduroy, m. velours côtelé m.

core, n. cœur m.

cork, n. (botany) liège m.; (stopper) bouchon m.

corkscrew, n. tire-bouchon m.

corn, n. maïs m.

cornea, n. cornée f.

corner, n. coin m.

cornerstone, n. pierre angulaire f.

cornet, n. cornet m.

cornetist, n. cornettiste m.

cornice, n. corniche f.

cornucopia, n. corne d'abondance f.

corollary, n. corollaire m.

coronary, adj. coronaire.

coronation, n. couronnement m.

coroner, n. coroner m.

coronet, n. (petite) couronne f.

corporal, n. (mil.) caporal m.

corporate, adj. de corporation.

corporation, n. corporation f.

corps, n. corps m.

corpse, n. cadavre m.

corpulent, adj. corpulent, gros.

corpuscle, n. corpuscule m.

corral, n. corral m.

correct, 1. adj. correct. 2. vb. corriger.

correction, n. correction f.

corrective, 1. adj. correctif. 2. n. correctif m.

correctly, adv. correctement, justement.

correctness, n. correction f.

correlate, vb. être en corrélation, intr.; mettre en corrélation, tr.

correlation, n. corrélation f.

correspond, vb. correspondre.

correspondence, n. correspondance f.

correspondent, n. correspondant m.

corridor, n. couloir m.

corroborate, vb. corroborer.

corroboration, n. corroboration f., confirmation f.

corroborative, adj. coroboratif.

corrode, vb. corroder.

corrosion, n. corrosion f.

corrugate, vb. rider, plisser.

corrupt, 1. adj. corrompu. 2. vb. corrompre.

corruptible, adj. corruptible.

corruption, n. corruption f.

corruptive, adj. corruptif.

corsage, n. corsage m.

corset, n. corset m.

cortege, n. cortège m.

corvette, n. corvette f.

cosmetic, adj. and n. cosmétique m.

cosmic, adj. cosmique.

cosmic rays, n. rayons cosmiques m.pl.

cosmopolitan, adj. and n. cosmopolite m.f.

cosmos, n. cosmos m.

cost, 1. n. coût m. 2. vb. coûter.

costliness, n. haut prix m., somptuosité f.

costly, adj. coûteux.

costume, n. costume m.

costumer, n. costumier m.

cot, n. (berth) couchette f.; (folding) lit-cage m.

coterie, n. coterie f., clique f.

cotillion, n. cotillon m

cottage, n. chaumière f.

cotton, n. coton m.

cottonseed, n. graine de coton f.

couch, n. divan m.

cougar, n. couguar f.

cough, 1. n. toux f. 2. vb. tousser.

could, vb. pouvait, pourrait.

council, n. conseil m.

councilman, n. conseiller m.

counsel, 1. n. conseil m. 2. vb. conseiller.

counselor, n. conseiller m.

count, 1. n. (calculation) compte m.; (title) comte m. 2. vb. compter.

countenance, n. expression f.

counter, 1. n. (shop) comptoir m. 2. adv. (c. to) à l'encontre de.

counteract, vb. neutraliser.

counteraction, n. action contraire f.

counterattack, n. contre-attaque f.

counterbalance, 1. n. contrepoids m. 2. vb. contre-balancer.

counterfeit, 1. adj. (money) faux m., fausse f. 2. n. contrefaire.

countermand, vb. contremander.

counteroffensive, n. contre-offensive f.

counterpart, n. contre-partie f.

countess, n. comtesse f.

countless, adj. innombrable.

country, n. (nation) pays m.; (opposed to town) campagne f.; (native c.) patrie f.

countryman, n. (of same c.) compatriote m.f.; (rustic) campagnard m.

county, n. comté m.

coupé, n. coupé m.

couple, 1. n. couple f. 2. vb. coupler.

coupon, n. coupon m.

courage, n. courage m.

courageous, adj. courageux.

courier, n. courrier m.

course, n. cours m.; (of c.) bien entendu; (route) route f.; (meal) service m.

court, 1. n. cour f. 2. vb. faire la cour à.

courteous, adj. courtois.

courtesy, n. courtoisie f.

courthouse, n. palais de justice m.

courtier, n. courtisan m.

courtly, adj. de cour, élégant, courtois.

courtmartial, n. conseil de guerre m.

courtroom, n. salle d'audience f.

courtship, n. cour f.

courtyard, n. cour f.

cousin, n. cousin m., cousine f.

covenant, n. pacte m.

cover, 1. n. (book, comm., blanket) couverture f.; (pot) couvercle m.; (shelter) abri m.; (envelope) pli m.; (mil.) couvert m. 2. vb. couvrir.

coverage, n. couverture f.

covering, n. couverture f., enveloppe f.

covet, vb. convoiter.

covetous, adj. avide, avaricieux.

cow, n. vache f.

coward, adj. lâche.

cowardice, n. lâcheté f.

cowboy, n. (U.S.A.) cowboy m.

cower, vb. se blottir.

cow hand, n. vacher m.

cowhide, n. peau (f.) de vache.

coxswain, n. patron de chaloupe m., barreur m.

coy, adj. timide.

cozy, adj. confortable.

crab, n. crabe m.

crab apple, n. pomme sauvage f.

crack, 1. n. (fissure) fente f.; (noise) craquement m. 2. vb. tr. (glass, china) fêler; (nuts) casser; (noise) faire craquer. 3. vb. intr. (split) se fendiller; (noise) craquer.

cracked, adj. fendu, fêlé.

cracker, n. biscuit m.

cracking, n. craquement m., claquement m.

crackup, n. crach m.

cradle, n. berceau m.

craft, n. (skill) habileté f.; (trade) métier m.; (boat) embarcation f.

craftsman, n. artisan m.

craftsmanship, n. habileté, technique f.

crafty, adj. rusé, astucieux.

crag, n. rocher à pic m., rocher escarpé m.

cram, vb. remplir, farcir.

cramp, n. (med.) crampe f.; (mechanical) crampon m.

cranberry, n. canneberge f., airelle f.

crane, n. grue f.

cranium, n. crâne m.

crank, n. manivelle f.

cranky, adj. d'humeur difficile.

cranny, n. crevasse f., fente f.

craps, n. (slang) jeu de dés m.

crapshooter, n. (slang) joueur aux dés m.

crash, 1. n. (noise) fracas m.; (accident) accident m. 2. vb. tomber avec fracas, intr.

crate, n. caisse f.

crater, n. cratère m.

crave for, vb. désirer ardemment.

craven, adj. lâche, poltron.

craving, n. désir ardent m., besoin impérieux m.

crawl, vb. (reptiles) ramper; (persons) se traîner.

crayon, *n.* pastel *m.*

crazed, *adj.* fou, dément.

crazy, *adj.* fou *m.,* folle *f.*

creak, *vb.* grincer.

creaky, *adj.* qui crie, qui grince.

cream, *n.* crème *f.*

creamery, *n.* crèmerie *f.*

creamy, *adj.* crémeux, de crème.

crease, 1. *n.* pli *m.* **2.** *vb.* froisser, *tr.*

create, *vb.* créer.

creation, *n.* création *f.*

creative, *adj.* créateur *m.,* créatrice *f.*

creator, *n.* créateur *m.,* créatrice *f.*

creature, *n.* créature *f.*

credence, *n.* créance *f.,* croyance *f.*

credentials, *n.* lettres (*f.pl.*) de créance; (student, servant) certificat *m.*

credibility, *n.* crédibilité *f.*

credible, *adj.* croyable.

credit, *n.* crédit *m.;* (merit) honneur *m.*

creditable, *adj.* estimable.

creditably, *adv.* honorablement.

credit card, *n.* carte de crédit *f.*

creditor, *n.* créancier *m.*

credo, *n.* credo *m.*

credulity, *n.* crédulité *f.*

credulous, *adj.* crédule.

creed, *n.* (belief) croyance *f.,* (theology) credo *m.*

creek, *n.* ruisseau *m.*

creep, *vb.* (reptiles, insects, plants) ramper; (persons) se glisser.

cremate, *vb.* incinérer.

crematory, *n.* crématorium *m.*

creosote, *n.* créosote *f.*

crepe, *n.* crêpe *m.*

crescent, *n.* croissant *m.*

crest, *n.* crête *f.*

crestfallen, *adj.* abattu, découragé.

cretonne, *n.* cretonne *f.*

crevice, *n.* crevasse *f.*

crew, *n.* (boat) équipage *m.;* (gang) équipe *f.*

crib, *n.* (child's bed) lit (*m.*) d'enfant; (manger) mangeoire *f.*

cricket, *n.* (insect) grillon *m.;* (game) cricket *m.*

crier, *n.* crieur *m.,* huissier *m.*

crime, *n.* crime *m.*

criminal, *adj.* criminel.

criminologist, *n.* criminologue *m.*

criminology, *n.* criminologie *f.*

crimson, *adj.* and *n.* cramoisi *m.*

cringe, *vb.* faire des courbettes, se tapir, s'humilier.

crinkle, 1. *n.* pli *m.,* sinuosité *f.* **2.** *vb.* serpenter, former en zigzag.

cripple, 1. *n.* estropié *m.* **2.** *vb.* estropier.

crisis, *n.* crise *f.*

crisp, *adj.* (food) croquant; (manner) tranchant.

crispness, *n.* frisure *f.*

crisscross, *adj.* and *adv.* entrecroisé.

criterion, *n.* critérium *m.*

critic, *n.* critique *m.*

criticism, *n.* critique *f.*

criticize, *vb.* critiquer.

critique, *n.* critique *f.*

croak, *vb.* (frogs) coasser; (crows, persons) croasser.

crochet, 1. *vb.* broder au crochet. **2.** *n.* crochet *m.*

crock, *n.* pot (*m.*) de terre.

crockery, *n.* faïence *f.*

crocodile, *n.* crocodile *m.*

crocodile tears, *n.* larmes de crocodiles *f.pl.*

crone, *n.* vieille femme *f.*

crony, *n.* vieux camarade *m.,* compère *m.*

crook, *n.* (thief) escroc *m.,* voleur *m.*

crooked, *adj.* tortu.

croon, *vb.* chantonner, fredonner.

crop, *n.* récolte *f.*

croquet, *n.* (jeu de) croquet *m.*

croquette, *n.* croquette *f.*

cross, 1. *n.* croix *f.* **2.** *adj.* maussade. **3.** *vb.* croiser, *tr.;* (c. oneself) se signer; (c. out) rayer; (go across) traverser.

crossbreed, *n.* race croisée *f.*

cross-examine, *vb.* contre-examiner.

cross-eye, *adj.* louche.

cross-fertilization, *n.* croisement *m.*

cross-purpose, *n.* opposition *f.,* contradiction *f.,* malentendu *m.*

cross section, *n.* coupe en travers *f.*

crossword puzzle, *n.* mots croisés *m.pl.*

crotch, *n.* fourche *f.,* fourchet *m.*

crouch, *vb.* s'accroupir.

croup, *n.* croupe *f.;* (med.) croup *m.*

croupier, *n.* croupier *m.*

crouton, *n.* crouton *m.*

crow, *n.* (bird) corneille *f.;* (cock-c.) chant (*m.*) du coq. **2.** *vb.* chanter.

crowd, *n.* foule *f.*

crowd, *vb.* serrer, *tr.;* (c. with) remplir de.

crowded, *adj.* (streets, etc.) encombré.

crown, 1. *n.* couronne *f.;* (of head) sommet *m.;* (of hat) calotte *f.* **2.** *vb.* couronner.

crown prince, *n.* prince héritier *m.*

crow's-foot, *n.* patte d'oie (near the eye) *f.;* (naut.) araignée *f.*

crucial, *adj.* crucial.

crucible, *n.* creuset *m.*

crucifix, *n.* crucifix *m.*

crucifixion, *n.* crucifixion *f.,* crucifiement *m.*

crucify, *vb.* crucifier.

crude, *adj.* (unpolished) grossier; (metals, etc.) brut.

crudeness, *n.* crudité *f.*

cruel, *adj.* cruel.

cruelty, *n.* cruauté *f.*

cruet, *n.* burette *f.*

cruise, *n.* croisière *f.*

cruiser, *n.* croiseur *m.*

crumb, *n.* (small piece) miette *f.;* (not crust) mie *f.*

crumble, *vb.* émietter, *tr.*

crumple, *vb.* chiffonner, *tr.*

crunch, 1. *vb.* croquer, broyer, **2.** *n.* grincement *m.*

crusade, *n.* croisade *f.*

crusader, *n.* croisé *m.*

crush, *vb.* écraser.

crust, *n.* croûte *f.*

crustacean, *adj.* crustacé.

crusty, *adj.* couvert d'une croûte; (fig.) bourru, maussade.

crutch, *n.* béquille *f.*

cry, 1. *n.* cri *m.* **2.** *vb.* (shout) crier; (weep) pleurer.

crying, *adj.* criant.

cryosurgery, *n.* cryochirurgie *f.*

crypt, *n.* crypte *f.*

cryptic, *adj.* occulte, secret.

cryptography, *n.* cryptographie *f.*

crystal, *n.* cristal *m.*

crystalline, *adj.* cristallin.

crystallize, *vb.* cristalliser, *tr.*

cub, *n.* petit *m.* (d'un animal).

Cuba, *n.* Cuba *m.*

Cuban, 1. *n.* Cubain *m.* **2.** *adj.* cubain.

cubbyhole, *n.* retraite *f.,* cachette *f.,* placard *m.*

cube, *n.* cube *m.*

cubic, *adj.* cubique.

cubicle, *n.* compartiment *m.,* cabine *f.*

cubic measure, *n.* mesures de volume *f.pl.*

cubism, *n.* cubisme *m.*

cuckoo, *n.* coucou *m.;* (fig.) niais *m.*

cucumber, *n.* concombre *m.*

cud, *n.* bol alimentaire *m.,* panse *f.,* chique (of tobacco) *f.*

cuddle, *vb.* serrer (dans ses bras), *tr.*

cudgel, 1. *n.* bâton *m.,* gourdin *m.,* trique *f.* **2.** *vb.* bâtonner.

cue, *n.* (theater) réplique *f.;* (hint) mot *m.*

cuff, *n.* poignet *m.*

cuisine, *n.* cuisine *f.*

culinary, *adj.* culinaire, de cuisine.

cull, *vb.* cueillir, recueillir.

culminate, *vb.* culminer.

culmination, *n.* point culminant *m.*

culpable, *adj.* coupable.

culprit, *n.* coupable *m.f.*

cult, *n.* culte *m.*

cultivate, *vb.* cultiver.

cultivated, *adj.* cultivé.

cultivation, n. culture f.
cultivator, n. cultivateur m.
cultural, adj. cultural.
culture, n. culture f.
cumbersome, adj. encombrant.
cumulative, adj. cumulatif.
cunning, 1. n. (guile) ruse f.; (skill) adresse f. 2. adj. rusé; (attractive) charmant.
cup, n. tasse f.
cupboard, n. armoire f.
cupidity, n. cupidité f.
curable, adj. guérissable.
curator, n. conservateur m.
curb, 1. n. (horse) gourmette f.; (pavement) bord m. 2. vb. (horse) gourmer; (fig.) brider.
curbstone, n. garde-pavé m.
curd, n. lait caillé m.
curdle, vb. cailler.
cure, 1. n. (healing) guérison f.; (remedy) remède m. 2. vb. guérir.
curfew, n. couvre-feu m.
curio, n. curiosité f.
curiosity, n. curiosité f.
curious, adj. curieux.
curl, 1. n. boucle f. 2. vb. friser.
curly, adj. frisé.
currant, n. groseille f.
currency, n. monnaie f.
current, adj. and n. courant m.
currently, adv. couramment.
curriculum, n. programme d'études m., plan d'études m.
curry, n. cari m.
curse, 1. n. (malediction) malédiction f.; (oath) juron m.; (scourge) fléau m. 2. vb. maudire; (swear) jurer.
cursed, adj. maudit.
cursory, adj. rapide, superficiel.
curt, adj. brusque.
curtail, vb. raccourcir.
curtain, n. rideau m.
curtsy, n. révérence f.
curvature, n. courbure f.
curve, 1. n. courbe f. 2. vb. courber, tr.
cushion, n. coussin m.
cuspidor, n. crachoir m.
custard, n. crème f.
custodian, n. gardien m.
custody, n. (care) garde f.; (arrest) détention f.
custom, n. coutume f.
customary, adj. habituel.
customer, n. client m.
custom-house, customs, n. douane f.
customs-officer, n. douanier m.
cut, 1. n. (wound) coupure f.; (clothes, hair) coupe f.; (reduction) réduction f. 2. vb. couper.
cutaneous, adj. cutané.
cute, adj. gentil m., gentille f.
cut glass, n. cristal m.
cuticle, n. cuticule f.
cutlery, n. coutellerie f.
cutlet, n. côtelette f.
cutout, n. découpage m., coupe

cutter, n. coupeur m., coupeuse f.
cutthroat, n. coupe-jarret m.
cutting, 1. n. incision f. 2. adj. incisif, tranchant.
cyclamate, n. cyclamate m.
cycle, 1. n. cycle m. 2. vb. faire de la bicyclette.
cyclist, n. cycliste m.
cyclone, n. cyclone m.
cyclotron, n. cyclotron m.
cylinder, n. cylindre m.
cylindrical, adj. cylindrique.
cymbal, n. cymbale f.
cynic, n. cynique m.
cynical, adj. cynique.
cynicism, n. cynisme m.
cypress, n. cyprès m.
cyst, n. kyste m.

D

dab, 1. n. coup léger m., tape f. 2. vb. toucher légèrement.
dabble, vb. humecter, faire l'amateur.
dad, n. papa m.
daffodil, n. narcisse m.
daffy, adj. niais, sot.
dagger, n. poignard m.
dahlia, n. dahlia m.
daily, adj. quotidien.
daintiness, n. délicatesse f.
dainty, adj. délicat.
dairy, n. laiterie f.
dairyman, n. crémier m.
dais, n. estrade f.
daisy, n. marguerite f.
dale, n. vallon m., vallée f.
dam, n. digue f.
damage, 1. n. dommage m. 2. vb. endommager.
damask, n. damas m.
damnation, n. damnation f.
damp, adj. humide.
dampen, vb. humecter.
dampness, n. humidité f., moiteur f.
damsel, n. demoiselle f., jeune fille f.
dance, 1. n. danse f. 2. vb. danser.
dancer, n. danseur m.
dandelion, n. pissenlit m.
dandruff, n. pellicules f.pl.
dandy, 1. n. dandy m. 2. adj. élégant.
danger, n. danger m.
dangerous, adj. dangereux.
dangle, vb. pendiller, intr.
Dane, n. Danois m.
Danish, adj. and n. danois m.
dapper, adj. pimpant, petit et vif.
dappled, adj. pommelé.
dare, vb. oser.
daredevil, n. casse-cou m.
daring, adj. audacieux.
dark, adj. sombre.
darken, vb. obscurcir, tr.
dark horse, n. tocard m.
darkness, n. obscurité f.

darkroom, n. chambre noire f.
darling, adj. and n. chéri m.
darn, 1. n. reprise f. 2. vb. repriser.
darning needle, n. aiguille à repriser f.
dart, 1. n. dard m.; (sewing) pince f. 2. vb. se précipiter.
dash, 1. n. (energy) fougue f.; (pen) trait m. 2. vb. (throw) lancer; (destroy) détruire; (rush) se précipiter.
dashboard, n. tablier m.
dashing, adj. fougueux, brillant, superbe.
data, n. données f.pl.
data processing, n. élaboration f.
date, 1. n. date f.; (appointment) rendez-vous m.; (fruit) datte f. 2. vb. dater.
date line, n. ligne de changement de date f.
daub, 1. n. barbouillage m. 2. vb. barbouiller.
daughter, n. fille f.
daughter-in-law, n. belle-fille f.
daunt, vb intimider.
dauntless, adj. intrépide, indomptable.
dauntlessly, adv. d'une manière intrépide.
davenport, n. divan m.
dawdle, vb. flâner, muser.
dawn, n. aube f.
day, n. jour m.; (span of day) journée f.
daydream, n. rêverie f.
daylight, n. lumière (f.) du jour.
daylight-saving time, n. l'heure d'été f.
daze, vb. étourdir.
dazzle, vb. éblouir.
deacon, n. diacre m.
dead, adj. mort.
deaden, vb. amortir.
dead end, n. cul de sac m., impasse f.
dead letter, n. lettre morte f.
deadline, n. ligne de délimitation f.
deadlock, n. impasse f.
deadly, adj. mortel.
deadwood, n. bois mort m.
deaf, adj. sourd.
deafen, vb. assourdir.
deaf-mute, adj. sourd-muet.
deafness, n. surdité f.
deal, 1. n. (great d.) beaucoup; (business) affair f.; (cards) donne f. 2. vb. (d. with) traiter; (d. out) distribuer.
dealer, n. marchand m.
dean, n. doyen m.
dear, adj. and n. cher m.
dearly, adv. chèrement.
dearth, n. disette f.
death, n. mort f.
deathless, adj. impérissable.
deathly, adj. mortel.
debacle, n. débâcle f.
debase, vb. avilir.
debatable, adj. discutable.

debate, 1. n. débat m. 2. vb. discuter.

debater, n. orateur parlementaire m., argumentateur m.

debauch, 1. n. débauche f. 2. vb. débaucher, corrompre.

debenture, n. obligation f.

debilitate, vb. débiliter, affaiblir.

debit, n. débit m.

debonair, adj. courtois et jovial.

debris, n. débris m.pl.

debt, n. dette f.

debtor, n. débiteur m.

debunk, vb. dégonfler.

debut, n. début m.

debutante, n. débutante f.

decade, n. période (f.) de dix ans.

decadence, n. décadence f.

decadent, adj. décadent.

decaffeinated, adj. décaféiné.

decalcomania, m. décalcomanie f.

decanter, n. carafe f.

decapitate, vb. décapiter.

decay, 1. n. décadence f.; (state of ruin) délabrement m.; (teeth) carie f. 2. vb. tomber en décadence.

deceased, adj. défunt.

deceit, n. tromperie f.

deceitful, adj. trompeur.

deceive, vb. tromper.

deceiver, n. imposteur.

December, n. décembre m.

decency, n. décence f.

decent, adj. décent.

decentralization, n. décentralisation f.

decentralize, vb. décentraliser.

deception, n. tromperie f., duperie f.

deceptive, adj. décevant, trompeur.

decibel, n. décibel m.

decide, vb. décider.

decided, adj. décidé, prononcé.

deciduous, adj. à feuillage caduc.

decimal, adj. décimal.

decimate, vb. décimer.

decipher, vb. déchiffrer.

decision, n. décision f.

decisive, adj. décisif.

deck, n. (boat) pont m.; (cards) paquet m.

deck hand, n. matelot de pont m.

declaim, vb. déclamer.

declamation, n. déclamation f.

declaration, n. déclaration f.

declarative, adj. explicatif, (law) déclaratif.

declare, vb. déclarer.

declension, n. déclinaison f.

decline, vb. décliner.

decode, vb. déchiffrer.

décolleté, adj. décolleté.

decompose, vb. décomposer, tr.

decongestant, adj. décongestionnant.

decor, n. décor m.

decorate, vb. décorer.

decoration, n. décoration f.

decorative, adj. décoratif.

decorator, n. décorateur m.

decorous, adj. bienséant, convenable.

decorum, n. décorum m.

decoy, 1. n. leurre m. 2. vb. leurrer.

decrease, 1. n. diminution f. 2. vb. diminuer.

decree, n. décret m.

decrepit, adj. décrépit.

decry, vb. décrier, dénigrer.

dedicate, vb. dédier.

dedication, n. dédicace f.

deduce, vb. déduire.

deduct, vb. déduire.

deduction, n. déduction f.

deductive, adj. déductif.

deed, n. action f.; (law) acte (m.) notarié.

deem, vb. juger.

deep, adj. profond.

deepen, vb. approfondir, tr.

deep freeze, n. surgélateur m.

deeply, adv. profondément.

deep-rooted, adj. enraciné.

deer, n. cerf m.

deerskin, n. peau de daim f.

deface, vb. défigurer.

defamation, n. diffamation f.

defame, vb. diffamer.

default, n. défaut m.

defeat, 1. n. défaite f. 2. vb. vaincre.

defeatism, n. défaitisme m.

defect, n. défaut m.

defection, n. défection f.

defective, adj. défectueux.

defend, vb. défendre.

defendant, n. défendeur m.

defender, n. défenseur m.

defense, n. défense f.

defenseless, adj. sans défense.

defensible, adj. défendable, soutenable.

defensive, adj. défensif.

defer, vb. (put off) différer; (show deference) déférer.

deference, n. déférence f.

deferential, adj. plein de déférence, respectueux.

defiance, n. défi m.

defiant, adj. de défi.

deficiency, n. insuffisance f.

deficient, adj. insuffisant.

deficit, n. déficit m.

defile, vb. souiller.

define, vb. définir.

definite, adj. défini.

definitely, adv. d'une manière déterminée.

definition, n. définition f.

definitive, adj. définitif.

deflate, vb. dégonfler.

deflation, n. dégonflement m.

deflect, vb. faire dévier, détourner.

deform, vb. déformer.

deformity, n. difformité f.

defraud, vb. frauder.

defray, vb. payer.

defrost, vb. déglacer.

defroster, n. déglaceur m.

deft, adj. adroit.

defy, vb. défier.

degenerate, vb. dégénérer.

degeneration, n. dégénérescence f.

degradation, n. dégradation f.

degrade, vb. dégrader.

degree, n. degré m.

dehydrate, vb. déshydrater.

deify, vb. déifier.

deign, vb. daigner.

deity, n. divinité f.

dejected, adj. abattu.

dejection, n. abattement m.

delay, 1. n. retard m. 2. vb. retarder, tr.; tarder, intr.

delectable, adj. délectable.

delegate, 1. n. délégué m. 2. vb. déléguer.

delegation, n. délégation f.

delete, vb. rayer, biffer.

deliberate, 1. adj. délibéré. 2. vb. délibérer.

deliberately, adv. de propos délibéré.

deliberation, n. délibération f.

deliberative, adj. délibératif.

delicacy, n. délicatesse f.

delicate, adj. délicat.

delicious, adj. délicieux.

delight, 1. n. délices f.pl. 2. vb. enchanter.

delightful, adj. charmant.

delineate, vb. esquisser, dessiner.

delinquency, n. délit m.

delinquent, adj. and n. délinquant m.

delirious, adj. délirant.

deliver, vb. délivrer; (speech) prononcer.

deliverance, n. délivrance f.

delivery, n. (child) accouchement m.; (speech) débit m.; (goods) livraison f.; (letters) distribution f.; (general d.) poste restante f.

delouse, vb. épouiller.

delude, vb. tromper.

deluge, n. déluge m.

delusion, n. illusion f.

de luxe, adv. de luxe.

delve, vb. creuser, pénétrer.

demagogue, n. démagogue m.

demand, 1. n. demande f. 2. vb. demander; (as right or by force) exiger.

demarcation, n. démarcation f.

demean, vb. comporter.

demeanor, n. maintien m.

demented, adj. fou m., folle f.

demerit, n. démérite m.

demigod, n. demi-dieu m.

demilitarize, vb. démilitariser.

demise, n. décès m., mort f.

demobilization, n. démobilisation f.

demobilize, vb. démobiliser.

democracy, n. démocratie f.

democrat, n. démocrate m.f.

democratic, adj. démocratique.

demolish, vb. démolir.

demolition, n. démolition f.

demon, n. démon m.

demonstrable, *adj.* démonstrable.

demonstrate, *vb.* démontrer.

demonstration, *n.* démonstration *f.*

demonstrative, *adj.* démonstratif.

demonstrator, *n.* démonstrateur *m.*

demoralize, *vb.* démoraliser.

demote, *vb.* réduire à un grade inférieur.

demur, *vb.* hésiter, s'opposer à.

demure, *adj.* posé, d'une modestie affectée.

den, *n.* antre *m.*, repaire *m.*

denaturalize, *vb.* dénaturaliser.

denature, *vb.* dénaturer.

denial, *n.* dénégation *f.*; (refusal) refus *m.*

denim, *n.* treillis *m.*

Denmark, *n.* Danemark *m.*

denomination, *n.* dénomination *f.*; (religion) confession *f.*

denominator, *n.* dénominateur *m.*

denote, *vb.* dénoter.

denouement, *n.* dénouement *m.*

denounce, *vb.* dénoncer.

dense, *adj.* dense; (stupid) bête.

density, *n.* densité *f.*

dent, *n.* bosselure *f.*

dental, *adj.* dentaire; (gramm.) dental.

dentifrice, *n.* dentifrice *m.*

dentist, *n.* dentiste *m.*

dentistry, *n.* art du dentiste *m.*, dentisterie *f.*

denture, *n.* dentier *m.*, râtelier *m.*

denude, *vb.* dénuder.

denunciation, *n.* dénonciation *f.*

deny, *vb.* nier.

deodorant, *n.* désodorisant *m.*

deodorize, *vb.* désodoriser, désinfecter.

depart, *vb.* partir, s'en aller, quitter.

department, *n.* département *m.*; (government) ministère *m.*; (d. store) grand magasin *m.*

departmental, *adj.* départemental.

departure, *n.* départ *m.*

depend on, *vb.* dépendre de; (rely) compter sur.

dependability, *n.* confiance que l'on inspire *f.*

dependable, *adj.* digne de confiance.

dependence, *n.* dépendance *f.*, confiance *f.*

dependent, *adj.* dépendant.

depict, *vb.* peindre.

depiction, *n.* description *f.*

deplete, *vb.* épuiser.

deplorable, *adj.* déplorable.

deplore, *vb.* déplorer.

depopulate, *vb.* dépeupler.

deport, *vb.* déporter.

deportation, *n.* déportation *f.*

deportment, *n.* maintien *m.*

depose, *vb.* déposer.

deposit, 1. *n.* dépôt *m.* 2. *vb.* déposer.

depositor, *n.* déposant *m.*

depository, *n.* dépôt *m.*, dépositaire *m.*

depot, *n.* dépôt *m.*, gare *f.*

deprave, *vb.* dépraver, corrompre.

depravity, *n.* dépravation *f.*, corruption *f.*

deprecate, *vb.* désapprouver, s'opposer à.

depreciate, *vb.* déprécier.

depreciation, *n.* dépréciation *f.*

depredation, *n.* déprédation *f.*, pillage *m.*

depress, *vb.* (lower) abaisser; (fig.) abattre.

depressed, *adj.* abattu, bas.

depression, *n.* dépression *f.*; (personal) abattement *m.*; (comm.) crise *f.*

deprive, *vb.* priver.

depth, *n.* profondeur *f.*

depth charge, *n.* grenade sousmarine *f.*

deputy, *n.* délégué *m.*; (politics) député *m.*

derail, *vb.* dérailler.

derange, *vb.* déranger.

deranged, *adj.* dérangé, troublé.

derelict, 1. *n.* vaisseau abandonné *m.*, épave *f.* 2. *adj.* abandonné, délaissé.

dereliction, *n.* abandon *m.*

deride, *vb.* tourner en dérision.

derision, *n.* dérision *f.*

derisive, *adj.* dérisoire.

derivation, *n.* dérivation *f.*, origine *f.*

derivative, *n.* dérivatif *f.*

derive, *vb.* dériver.

dermatology, *n.* dermatologie *f.*

derogatory, *adj.* dérogatoire.

derrick, *n.* grue *f.*

descend, *vb.* descendre.

descendant, *n.* descendant *m.*

descent, *n.* descente *f.*

describe, *vb.* décrire.

description, *n.* description *f.*

descriptive, *adj.* descriptif.

desecrate, *vb.* profaner.

desensitize, *vb.* désensibiliser.

desert, 1. *n.* (place) désert *m.*; (merit) mérite *m.* 2. *vb.* déserter.

deserter, *n.* déserteur *m.*

desertion, *n.* abandon *m.*; (military) désertion *f.*

deserve, *vb.* mériter.

deserving, *adj.* méritoire, de mérite.

design, 1. *n.* (project) dessein *m.*; (architecture) projet *m.* 2. *vb.* dessiner; (d. for) destiner à.

designate, *vb.* désigner.

designation, *n.* désignation *f.*

designedly, *adv.* à dessein.

designer, *n.* dessinateur *m.*

designing, *adj.* intrigant, artificieux.

desirable, *adj.* désirable.

desire, 1. *n.* désir *m.* 2. *vb.* désirer.

desirous, *adj.* désireux.

desist, *vb.* cesser.

desk, *n.* (office) bureau *m.*; (school) pupitre *m.*

desolate, *adj.* désolé.

desolation, *n.* désolation *f.*

despair, 1. *n.* désespoir *m.* 2. *vb.* désespérer.

desperado, *n.* désespéré *m.*, cerveau brûlé *m.*

desperate, *adj.* désespéré.

desperation, *n.* désespoir *m.*

despicable, *adj.* méprisable.

despise, *vb.* mépriser.

despite, *prep.* en dépit de.

despondent, *adj.* découragé.

despot, *n.* despote *m.*

despotic, *adj.* despotique.

despotism, *n.* despotisme *m.*

dessert, *n.* dessert *m.*

destination, *n.* destination *f.*

destine, *vb.* destiner.

destiny, *n.* destin *m.*

destitute, *adj.* (deprived) dénué; (poor) indigent.

destitution, *n.* destitution *f.*

destroy, *vb.* détruire.

destroyer, *n.* destructeur *m.*; (naval) contre-torpilleur *m.*

destructible, *adj.* destructible.

destruction, *n.* destruction *f.*

destructive, *adj.* destructif.

desultory, *adj.* à bâtons rompus, décousu.

detach, *vb.* détacher.

detachment, *n.* détachement *m.*

detail, *n.* détail *m.*

detain, *vb.* retenir; (in prison) détenir.

detect, *vb.* découvrir.

detection, *n.* découverte *f.*

detective, *n.* agent *(m.)* de la police secrète; (d. novel) roman policier.

detente, *n.* détente *f.*

detention, *n.* détention *f.*

deter, *vb.* détourner, empêcher (de), dissuader (de).

detergent, *n.* détersif *m.*

deteriorate, *vb.* détériorer, *tr.*

deterioration, *n.* détérioration *f.*

determination, *n.* détermination *f.*

determine, *vb.* déterminer.

determined, *adj.* déterminé.

determinism, *n.* déterminisme *m.*

deterrence, *n.* préventif *m.*

deterrent, *n. and adj.* préventif *m.*

detest, *vb.* détester.

dethrone, *vb.* détrôner.

detonate, *vb.* détoner.

detour, *n.* détour *m.*

detract, *vb.* enlever, ôter (à), dénigrer, déroger (à).

detriment, *n.* détriment *m.*, préjudice *m.*

detrimental, adj. préjudiciable, nuisible (à).

devaluate, vb. dévaluer, déprécier.

devastate, vb. dévaster.

develop, vb. développer, tr.

developer, n. (photography) révélateur m.

developing nation, n. nation en cours de développement f.

development, n. développement m.

deviate, vb. dévier, s'écarter (de).

deviation, n. déviation f., écart m.

device, n. expédient m.

devil, n. diable m.

devilish, adj. diabolique.

devious, adj. détourné.

devise, vb. (plan) combiner; (plot) tramer.

devitalize, vb. dévitaliser.

devoid, adj. dépourvu.

devote, vb. consacrer.

devoted, adj. dévoué.

devotee, n. dévot m., dévote f.

devotion, n. (religious) dévotion f.; (to person or thing) dévouement m.

devour, vb. dévorer.

devout, adj. dévot.

dew, n. rosée f.

dewy, adj. de rosée.

dexterity, n. dextérité f.

dexterous, adj. adroit.

diabetes, n. diabète m.

diabolic, adj. diabolique.

diadem, n. diadème m.

diagnose, vb. diagnostiquer.

diagnosis, n. diagnose f.

diagnostic, adj. diagnostique.

diagonal, adj. diagonal.

diagonally, adv. diagonalement.

diagram, n. diagramme m.

dial, 1. n. cadran m. 2. vb. (d. a number) composer.

dialect, n. dialecte m.

dialogue, n. dialogue m.

diameter, n. diamètre m.

diametrical, adj. diamétral.

diamond, n. diamant m.; (shape) losange m.; (cards) carreau m.

diaper, n. (babies) couche f.

diaphragm, n. diaphragme m.

diarrhea, n. diarrhée f.

diary, n. journal m.

diathermy, n. diathermie f.

diatribe, n. diatribe f.

dice, n. dés m.pl.

dicker, vb. marchander.

dictaphone, n. machine à dicter f.

dictate, vb. dicter.

dictation, n. dictée f.

dictator, n. dictateur m.

dictatorial, adj. dictatorial.

dictatorship, n. dictature f.

diction, n. diction f.

dictionary, n. dictionnaire m.

didactic, adj. didactique.

die, 1. n. dé m. 2. vb. mourir.

die-hard, n. intransigent m., ultra m.

diet, n. régime m.

dietary, adj. diététique.

dietetics, n. diététique f.

dietitian, n. diététicien m.

differ, vb. différer.

difference, n. différence f.

different, adj. différent.

differential, adj. différentiel.

difficult, adj. difficile.

difficulty, n. difficulté f.

diffident, adj. hésitant, timide.

diffuse, adj. diffus.

diffusion, n. diffusion f.

dig, vb. bêcher; (hole) creuser.

digest, vb. digérer.

digestible, adj. digestible.

digestion, n. digestion f.

digestive, adj. and n. digestif m.

digital, adj. (in watches, etc.) digital.

digitalis, n. digitaline f.

dignified, adj. plein de dignité.

dignify, vb. honorer, élever.

dignitary, n. dignitaire m.

dignity, n. dignité f.

digress, vb. faire une digression.

digression, n. digression f.

dike, n. (ditch) fossé m.; (dam) digue f.

dilapidated, adj. délabré.

dilapidation, n. délabrement m.

dilate, vb. dilater, tr.

dilatory, adj. dilatoire, lent, négligent.

dilemma, n. dilemme m.

dilettante, n. dilettante m., amateur m.

diligence, n. diligence f.

diligent, adj. diligent.

dill, n. aneth m.

dilute, vb. diluer.

dim, adj. (light, sight) faible; (color) terne.

dime, n. un dixième de dollar m.

dimension, n. dimension f.

diminish, vb. diminuer.

diminution, n. diminution f.

diminutive, 1. adj. tout petit. 2. n. (gramm.) diminutif m.

dimness, n. (weakness) faiblesse f.; (darkness) obscurité f.

dimple, n. (face) fossette f.

din, n. tapage m.

dine, vb. dîner.

diner, dining-car, n. wagon-restaurant m.

dingy, adj. défraîchi; (color) terne.

dinner, n. dîner m.; (d. jacket) smoking m.

dinosaur, n. dinosaurien m.

diocese, n. diocèse m.

dip, vb. plonger.

diphtheria, n. diphtérie f.

diploma, n. diplôme m.

diplomacy, n. diplomatie f.

diplomat, n. diplomate m.

diplomatic, adj. diplomatique.

dipper, n. cuiller (f.) à pot.

dire, adj. affreux.

direct, vb. (guide) diriger; (address) adresser.

direct, adj. direct.

direct current, n. courant continu m.

direction, n. direction f.; (orders) instructions f.pl.

directional, adj. de direction.

directive, 1. n. directif m. 2. adj. dirigeant.

directly, adv. directement.

directness, n. rectitude f.; (frankness) franchise f.

director, n. directeur m.

directorate, n. conseil d'administration m.

directory, n. annuaire m.

dirge, n. chant funèbre m.

dirigible, adj. and n. dirigeable m.

dirt, n. saleté f.

dirty, adj. sale.

disability, n. incapacité f., impuissance f.

disable, vb. mettre hors de combat, tr.

disabled, adj. invalide.

disabuse, vb. désabuser.

disadvantage, n. désavantage m.

disagree, vb. être en désaccord.

disagreeable, adj. désagréable.

disagreement, n. désaccord m.

disappear, vb. disparaître.

disappearance, n. disparition f.

disappoint, vb. désappointer.

disappointment, n. désappointement m.

disapproval, n. désapprobation f.

disapprove, vb. désapprouver.

disarm, vb. désarmer.

disarmament, n. désarmement m.

disarray, n. désarroi m., désordre m.

disassemble, vb. démonter, désassembler.

disaster, n. désastre m.

disastrous, adj. désastreux.

disavow, vb. désavouer.

disavowal, n. désaveu m.

disband, vb. congédier, tr.; se débander, intr.

disbar, vb. rayer du tableau des avocats.

disbelieve, vb. ne pas croire, refuser de croire.

disburse, vb. débourser.

discard, vb. mettre de côté.

discern, vb. discerner.

discerning, adj. judicieux, éclairé.

discernment, n. discernement m.

discharge, 1. n. décharge f.; (mil.) congé m. 2. vb. décharger; (mil.) congédier.

disciple, n. disciple m.

disciplinarian, n. disciplinaire m.

disciplinary, adj. disciplinaire.

discipline, n. discipline f.

disclaim, vb. désvouer, nier.

disclaimer, n. désaveu m.

disclose, vb. révéler.
disclosure, n. révélation f.
disco, adj. disco.
discolor, vb. décolorer.
discomfiture, n. défaite f., déroute f.
discomfort, n. malaise m.
disconcert, vb. déconcerter.
disconnect, vb. déchunir.
disconnected, adj. (electricity) hors circuit.
disconsolate, adj. désolé.
discontent, n. mécontentement m.
discontented, adj. mécontent.
discontinue, vb. discontinuer.
discord, n. discorde f.
discordant, adj. discordant, en désaccord.
discotheque, n. discothèque f.
discount, n. escompte m.; (reduction) remise f.
discourage, vb. décourager.
discouragement, n. découragement m.
discourse, n. discours m.
discourteous, adj. impoli.
discourtesy, n. impolitesse f.
discover, vb. découvrir.
discoverer, n. découvreur m.
discovery, n. découverte f.
discredit, 1. n. discrédit m. 2. vb. discréditer.
discreditable, adj. déshonorant, peu honorable.
discreet, adj. discret.
discrepancy, n. contradiction f.
discretion, n. discrétion f.
discriminate, vb. distinguer.
discrimination, n. discernement m., jugement m.
discursive, adj. discursif, sans suite.
discuss, vb. discuter.
discussion, n. discussion f.
disdain, n. dédain m.
disdainful, adj. dédaigneux.
disease, n. maladie f.
disembark, vb. débarquer.
disembody, vb. dépouiller du corps.
disenchantment, n. désenchantement m.
disengage, vb. dégager.
disentangle, vb. démêler.
disfavor, n. défaveur f.
disfigure, vb. défigurer, enlaidir.
disfranchise, vb. priver du droit de vote.
disgorge, vb. dégorger.
disgrace, n. disgrâce f.
disgraceful, adj. honteux.
disgruntled, adj. mécontent, de mauvaise humeur.
disguise, 1. n. déguisement m. 2. vb. dégoûter.
dish, n. plat m.; (wash the dishes) laver la vaisselle.
dishcloth, n. torchon m.
dishearten, vb. décourager.
dishonest, adj. malhonnête.
dishonesty, n. malhonnêteté f.
dishonor, n. déshonneur m.

dishonorable, adj. (action) déshonorant.
disillusion, n. désillusion f.
disinfect, vb. désinfecter.
disinfectant, n. désinfectant m.
disinherit, vb. déshériter.
disintegrate, vb. désagréger.
disinterested, adj. désintéressé.
disjointed, adj. désarticulé, disloqué.
disk, n. disque m.
dislike, 1, n. aversion f. 2. vb. ne pas aimer.
dislocate, vb. disloquer.
dislodge, vb. déloger.
disloyal, adj. infidèle.
disloyalty, n. infidélité f., perfidie f.
dismal, adj. sombre.
dismantle, vb. dépouiller (de).
dismay, n. consternation f.
dismember, vb. démembrer.
dismiss, vb. congédier.
dismissal, n. renvoi m.
dismount, vb. descendre.
disobedience, n. désobéissance f.
disobedient, adj. désobéissant.
disobey, vb. désobéir à.
disorder, n. désordre m.
disorderly, adj. désordonné.
disorganize, vb. désorganiser.
disown, vb. désavouer.
disparage, vb. déprécier, dénigrer.
disparate, adj. disparate.
disparity, n. inégalité f.
dispassionate, adj. calme.
dispatch, 1. n. (business) expédition f.; (speed) promptitude f.; (message) dépêche f. 2. vb. expédier.
dispatcher, n. expéditeur m.
dispel, vb. dissiper.
dispensable, adj. dont on peut se passer.
dispensary, n. dispensaire m.
dispensation, n. dispensation f.
dispense, vb. distribuer, dispenser.
dispersal, n. dispersion f.
disperse, vb. disperser.
displace, vb. déplacer.
displaced person, n. réfugié m.
displacement, n. déplacement m.
display, 1. n. (show) exposition f.; (shop, ostentation) étalage m. 2. vb. étaler.
displease, vb. déplaire à.
disposable, adj. disponible.
disposal, n. disposition f.
dispose, vb. disposer.
disposition, n. disposition f.; (character) caractère m.
dispossess, vb. déposséder, exproprier.
disproportion, n. disproportion f.
disproportionate, adj. disproportionné.
disprove, vb. réfuter.
disputable, adj. contestable, disputable.
dispute, 1. n. (discussion) dis-

cussion f.; (quarrel) dispute f. 2. vb. (se) disputer.
disqualify, vb. (sports) disqualifier.
disregard, vb. ne tenir aucun compte de.
disrepair, n. délabrement m.
disreputable, adj. déshonorant, honteux.
disrespect, n. irrévérence f.
disrespectful, adj. irrespectueux.
disrobe, vb. déshabiller, dévêtir.
disrupt, vb. faire éclater, rompre.
dissatisfaction, n. mécontentement m.
dissatisfy, vb. mécontenter.
dissect, vb. disséquer.
dissemble, vb. dissimuler.
disseminate, vb. disséminer.
dissension, n. dissension f.
dissent, vb. différer.
dissertation, n. dissertation f., discours m.
disservice, n. mauvais service rendu m.
dissimilar, adj. dissemblable.
dissipate, vb. dissiper.
dissipated, adj. dissipé.
dissipation, n. dissipation f.
dissociate, vb. désassocier, dissocier.
dissolute, adj. dissolu.
dissolution, n. dissolution f.
dissolve, vb. dissoudre, tr.
dissonance, n. dissonance f., désaccord m.
dissonant, adj. dissonant.
dissuade, vb. dissuader.
distance, n. distance f.
distant, adj. distant.
distaste, n. dégoût m.
distasteful, adj. désagréable.
distemper, 1. n. maladie des chiens f. 2. vb. peindre en détrempe.
distend, vb. dilater, gonfler.
distill, vb. distiller.
distillation, n. distillation f.
distiller, n. distillateur m.
distillery, n. distillerie f.
distinct, adj. distinct.
distinction, n. distinction f.
distinctive, adj. distinctif.
distinctly, adv. distinctement, clairement.
distinguish, vb. distinguer.
distinguished, adj. distingué.
distort, vb. déformer.
distract, vb. (divert) distraire; (upset) affoler.
distracted, adj. affolé, bouleversé.
distraction, n. (diversion) distraction f.; (madness) folie f.
distraught, adj. affolé, éperdu, hors de soi.
distress, 1. n. détresse f. 2. vb. affliger.
distressing, adj. affligeant, pénible, désolant.
distribute, vb. distribuer.
distribution, n. distribution f.

distributor, n. distributeur m.
district, n. (region) contrée f.; (administration) district m.; (town) quartier m.
distrust, 1. n. méfiance f. 2. vb. se méfier de.
distrustful, adj. méfiant.
disturb, vb. déranger.
disturbance, n. dérangement m.
disunite, vb. désunir.
disuse, n. désuétude f.
ditch, n. fossé m.
ditto, adv. idem, de même.
diva, n. diva f.
divan, n. divan m.
dive, vb. plonger.
dive bomber, n. avion de bombardement qui fait des vols piqués m.
diver, n. plongeur m.
diverge, vb. diverger.
divergence, n. divergence f.
divergent, adj. divergent.
diverse, adj. divers.
diversion, n. (amusement) divertissement m.
diversity, n. diversité f.
divert, vb. (turn aside) détourner; (amuse) divertir.
divest, vb. ôter, dépouiller, priver.
divide, vb. diviser.
divided, adj. divisé, séparé.
dividend, n. dividende m.
divine, adj. divin.
divinity, n. divinité f.
divisible, adj. divisible.
division, n. division f.
divisive, adj. qui divise, qui sépare.
divorce, 1. n. divorce m. 2. vb. divorcer.
divorcee, n. divorcé m., divorcée f.
divulge, vb. divulguer.
dizziness, n. vertige m.
dizzy, adj. pris de vertige.
do, vb. faire; (how d. you d.?) comment allez-vous?
docile, adj. docile.
dock, n. bassin m.
docket, n. registre m., bordereau m.
dockyard, n. chantier de construction de navires m.
doctor, n. docteur m.
doctorate, n. doctorat m.
doctrinaire, adj. doctrinaire.
doctrine, n. doctrine f.
document, n. document m.
documentary, adj. documentaire.
documentation, n. documentation f.
dodge, vb. esquiver, éluder.
doe, n. daine f.
doeskin, n. peau de daim f.
dog, n. chien m.
dogfight, n. combat de chiens m., mêlée générale f.
dogged, adj. obstiné, tenace.
doggerel, n. poésie burlesque f.
doghouse, n. chenil m.
dogma, n. dogme m.

dogmatic, adj. dogmatique.
dogmatism, n. dogmatisme m.
dolly, n. petit napperon m.
doldrum, n. (naut.) zone des calmes f., cafard m.
dole, 1. n. pitance f.; aumône f. 2. vb. distribuer parcimonieusement.
doleful, adj. lugubre.
doll, n. poupée f.
dollar, n. dollar m.
dolorous, adj. douloureux.
dolphin, n. dauphin m.
domain, n. domaine m.
dome, n. dôme m.
domestic, adj. domestique.
domesticate, vb. domestiquer, apprivoiser.
domicile, n. domicile m.
dominance, n. dominance f., prédominance f.
dominant, adj. dominant.
dominate, vb. dominer.
domination, n. domination f.
domineer, vb. se montrer tyrannique.
domineering, adj. impérieux.
dominion, n. domination f.; (territory) possessions f.pl.
domino, n. domino m.
don, vb. endosser, revêtir.
donate, vb. donner.
donation, n. donation f.
done, vb. fait.
donkey, n. âne m.
don't, vb. ne faites pas!, ne fais pas!
doom, vb. condamner.
doomsday, n. (jour du) jugement dernier m.
door, f. porte f.; (d.-keeper) concierge m.f.
doorman, n. portier m.
doorstep, n. seuil m., pas de la porte m.
doorway, n. (baie de) porte f., encadrement de la porte m.
dope, n. stupéfiant m.
dormant, adj. endormi, assoupi.
dormer, n. lucarne f.
dormitory, n. maison (f.) d'étudiants.
dosage, n. dosage m.
dose, n. dose f.
dossier, n. dossier m.
dot, n. point m.
dotage, n. radotage m.
dote, vb. radoter; (d. on) aimer excessivement.
double, 1. adj. and n. double m. 2. vb. doubler.
double-breasted, adj. croisé.
double-cross, vb. duper, tromper.
double-dealing, n. duplicité f.
double time, n. pas gymnastique m.
doubly, adv. doublement.
doubt, 1. n. doute m. 2. vb. douter (de).
doubtful, adj. douteux.
doubtless, adv. sans doute.
dough, n. pâte f.

doughnut, n. pet (m.) de nonne.
dour, adj. austère.
douse, vb. plonger, tremper.
dove, n. colombe f.
dowager, n. douairière f.
dowdy, adj. dans élégance, qui manque de chic.
dowel, 1. n. goujon m. 2. vb. goujonner.
down, 1. n. duvet m. 2. adv. en bas. 3. prep. (along) le long de.
downcast, adj. (look) baissé.
downfall, n. chute f.
downhearted, adj. découragé, déprimé.
downhill, 1. n. descente f. 2. adj. en pente, incliné.
downpour, n. averse f.
downright, adv. tout à fait.
downstairs, adv. en bas.
downtown, adv. en ville.
downtrodden, adj. opprimé, piétiné.
downward, adj. descendant.
downy, adj. duveteux.
dowry, n. dot f.
doze, vb. sommeiller.
dozen, n. douzaine f.
drab, adj. (color) gris; (dull) terne.
draft, 1. n. (drawing) dessin m.; (mil.) conscription f.; (air) courant (m.) d'air. 2. vb. (mil.) appeler sous le drapeau.
draftee, n. conscrit m.
draftsman, n. dessinateur m.
drafty, adj. plein de courante d'air.
drag, vb. traîner.
dragnet, n. drague f., seine f., chalut m.
dragon, n. dragon m.
drain, vb. drainer, tr.; s'écouler, intr.
drainage, n. drainage m.
dram, n. drachme f., goutte f.
drama, n. drame m.
dramatic, adj. dramatique.
dramatics, n. théâtre m.
dramatist, n. dramaturge m.
dramatize, vb. dramatiser.
dramaturgy, n. dramaturgie f.
drape, vb. draper.
drapery, n. draperie f.
drastic, adj. drastique.
draught, n. traction f.; trait m.
draw, vb. (pull) tirer; (sketch) dessiner.
drawback, n. inconvénient m.
drawbridge, n. pont-levis m.
drawer, n. tiroir m.
drawing, n. dessin m.
drawl, 1. n. voix (f.) traînante. 2. vb. traîner la voix.
dray, n. camion m.
drayman, n. camionneur m.
dread, 1. n. crainte f. 2. vb. redouter.
dreadful, adj. affreux.
dreadfully, adv. terriblement, affreusement.
dream, n. rêve m.

dreamer, n. rêveur m.

dreamy, adj. rêveur m., rêveuse f.

dreary, adj. morne.

dredge, vb. draguer.

dreg, n. lie f.

drench, vb. tremper.

dress, 1. n. robe f. 2. vb. habiller, tr.; s'habiller, intr.

dresser, n. commode f.

dressing, n. toilette f.; (surgical) pansement m.

dressing gown, n. robe de chambre f., peignoir m.

dressmaker, n. couturière f.

dress rehearsal, n. répétition générale f.

drier, n. sécheur m., dessécheur m.

drift, vb. (boat) dériver; (person) se laisser aller.

driftwood, n. bois flottant m.

drill, 1. n. (tool) foret m.; (exercise) exercice m. 2. vb. (hole) forer; (exercise) exercer, tr.; faire l'exercice, intr.

drink, 1. n. boisson f. 2. vb. boire.

drinkable, adj. potable.

drip, vb. dégoutter.

dripping, 1. n. dégouttement m. 2. adj. ruisselant.

drive, 1. n. promenade (f.) en voiture; (energy) énergie f. 2. vb. (auto, animals) conduire; (force) pousser.

drivel, n. bave f.

driver, n. (auto) chauffeur m.

drizzle, 1. n. bruine f. 2. vb. bruiner.

dromedary, n. dromadaire m.

drone, 1. n. abeille mâle f.; bourdonnement m. 2. vb. bourdonner.

droop, vb. pencher.

drop, 1. n. goutte f.; (fall) chute f. 2. vb. tomber, intr.; laisser tomber, tr.

dropout, n. étudiant qui quitte l'école avant de recevoir son diplôme m.

dropper, n. compte-gouttes m.

dropsy, n. hydropisie f.

drought, n. sécheresse f.

drove, n. troupeau m.

drown, vb. noyer, tr.

drowse, vb. s'assoupir.

drowsiness, n. somnolence f.

drowsy, adj. somnolent.

drudge, vb. s'éreinter.

drug, n. drogue f.

druggist, n. pharmacien m.

drug store, n. pharmacie f.

drum, n. tambour m.; (ear) tympan m.

drum major, n. tambour-major m.

drummer, n. tambour m.

drumstick, n. baguette de tambour f.

drunk, adj. ivre.

drunkard, n. ivrogne m.

drunkenness, n. ivresse f.; (habitual) ivrognerie f.

dry, 1. adj. sec m., sèche f. 2. vb. sécher.

dry-clean, vb. nettoyer à sec.

dry dock, 1. n. cale sèche f. 2. vb. mettre en cale sèche.

dry goods, n. articles de nouveautés m.pl.

dryness, n. sécheresse f.

dual, adj. double.

dualism, n. dualité f., dualisme m.

dubious, adj. douteux.

duchess, n. duchesse f.

duchy, n. duché m.

duck, n. canard m.

duct, n. conduit m.

ductile, adj. ductile.

dud, 1. adj. incapable. 2. n. obus qui a raté m.

due, adj. dû m., due f.

duel, n. duel m.

duelist, n. duelliste m.

duet, n. duo m.

duffel bag, n. sac pour les vêtements de rechange m.

dugout, n. abri-caverne m.

duke, n. duc m.

dukedom, n. duché m.

dulcet, adj. doux, suave.

dull, adj. (boring) ennuyeux.

dullard, n. lourdaud m.

dullness, n. (monotony) monotonie f.

duly, adv. dûment.

dumb, adj. muet m., muette f.; (stupid) sot m., sotte f.

dumbwaiter, n. monte-plats m.

dumfound, vb. abasourdir, interdire.

dummy, n. (dressmaking) mannequin m.; (cards) mort m.

dump, n. voirie f.

dumpling, n. boulette (de pâte) f.

dun, vb. importuner, talonner.

dunce, n. crétin m.

dunce cap, n. bonnet d'âne m.

dune, n. dune f.

dung, n. fiente f.; (agriculture) fumier m.

dungaree, n. salopette f., bleus m.pl.

dungeon, n. cachot m.

dupe, 1. n. dupe f. 2. vb. duper.

duplex, adj. double.

duplicate, 1. n. double m. 2. vb. faire le double de.

duplication, n. duplication f.

duplicity, n. duplicité f.

durable, adj. durable.

durability, n. durabilité f.

duration, n. durée f.

duress, n. contrainte f., coercition f.

during, prep. pendant.

dusk, n. crépuscule m.

dusky, adj. sombre.

dust, 1. n. poussière f. 2. vb. épousseter.

dustpan, n. ramasse-poussière m.

dust storm, n. tourbillon de poussière m.

dusty, adj. poussiéreux.

Dutch, adj. and n. hollandais m.

Dutchman, n. Hollandais m.

dutiful, adj. respectueux, fidèle.

dutifully, adv. avec soumission.

duty, n. (moral, legal) devoir m.; (tax) droit m.; (be on d.) être de service.

duty-free, adj. exempt de droits.

dwarf, adj. and n. nain m.

dwell, vb. demeurer.

dwindle, vb. diminuer.

dye, 1. n. teinture f. 2. vb. teindre.

dyer, n. teinturier m.

dyestuff, n. matière colorante f.

dynamic, adj. dynamique.

dynamics, n. dynamique f.

dynamite, n. dynamite f.

dynamo, n. dynamo f.

dynasty, n. dynastie f.

dysentery, n. dysenterie f.

dyslexia, n. dyslexie f.

dyspepsia, n. dyspepsie f.

dyspeptic, adj. dyspeptique.

E

each, 1. adj. chaque. 2. pron. chacun m., chacune f.; (e. other) l'un l'autre.

eager, adj. ardent.

eagerly, adv. ardemment, avidement.

eagerness, n. empressement m.

eagle, n. (bird) aigle m.; (mil.) aigle f.

eaglet, n. aiglon m.

ear, n. oreille f.

earache, n. mal d'oreille m.

eardrum, n. tympan m.

earl, n. comte m.

early, 1. adj. (of morning) matinal; (first) premier. 2. adv. de bonne heure; tôt.

earmark, 1. n. marque distinctive f. 2. vb. marquer, assigner.

earn, vb. gagner.

earnest, adj. sérieux.

earnestly, adv. sérieusement, sincèrement.

earnestness, n. gravité f., sérieux m.

earnings, n. salaire m.

earphone, n. casque (téléphonique) m.

earring, n. boucle (f.) d'oreille.

earshot, n. portée de voix f.

earth, n. terre f.

earthenware, n. poterie f., argile cuite f.

earthly, adj. terrestre.

earthquake, n. tremblement (m.) de terre.

earthworm, n. ver de terre m.

earthy, adj. terreux.

ease, n. aise f.; (with e.) avec facilité.

easel, n. chevalet m.

easily, adv. facilement.

easiness, n. facilité f.

east, n. est m.

Easter, n. Pâques m.

easterly, adj. d'est, vers l'est.

eastern, adj. de l'est, oriental.

eastward, adv. vers l'est.

easy, adj. facile; (of manners) aisé.

easygoing, adj. insouciant, peu exigeant, accommodant.

eat, vb. manger.

eaves, n. avant-toit m.

eavesdrop, vb. écouter aux portes.

ebb, n. (water) reflux m.; (decline) déclin m.

ebony, n. ébène m.

ebullient, adj. bouillonnant.

eccentric, adj. excentrique.

eccentricity, n. excentricité f.

ecclesiastic, adj. and n. ecclésiastique m.

ecclesiastical, adj. ecclésiastique.

echelon, n. échelon m.

echo, n. écho m.

eclipse, n. éclipse f.

ecological, adj. écologique.

ecology, n. écologie f.

economic, adj. économique.

economical, adj. (person) économe.

economics, n. économie (f.) politique.

economist, n. économiste m.

economize, vb. économiser.

economy, n. économie f.

ecru, n. écru m.

ecstasy, n. (religious) extase f.; (fig.) transport m.

ecumenical, adj. œcuménique.

eczema, n. eczéma m.

eddy, n. remous m.

edge, n. bord m.; (blade) fil m.

edging, n. pose f., bordure f.

edgy, adj. d'un air agacé.

edible, adj. comestible.

edict, n. édit m.

edifice, n. édifice m.

edify, vb. édifier.

edition, n. édition f.

editor, n. (text) éditeur m.; (paper) rédacteur m.

editorial, n. article (m.) de fond.

educate, vb. (upbringing) élever; (knowledge) instruire.

education, n. éducation f.; (schooling) instruction f.

educator, n. éducateur m.

eel, n. anguille f.

efface, vb. effacer.

effect, 1. n. effet m. 2. vb. effectuer.

effective, adj. (having effect) efficace; (in effect) effectif.

effectively, adv. efficacement, effectivement.

effectiveness, n. efficacité f.

effectual, adj. efficace.

effeminate, adj. efféminé.

effervesce, vb. être en effervescence, pétiller d'animation.

effete, adj. épuisé, caduc.

efficacious, adj. efficace.

efficacy, n. efficacité f.

efficiency, n. (person) compétence f.; (machine) rendement m.

efficient, adj. (person) capable.

efficiently, adv. efficacement, avec compétence.

effigy, n. effigie f.

effort, n. effort m.

effortless, adj. sans effort.

effrontery, n. effronterie f.

effulgent, adj. resplendissant.

effusive, adj. démonstratif.

egg, n. œuf m.; (boiled e.) œuf à la coque; (fried e.) œuf sur le plat; (poached e.) œuf poché; (scrambled e.) œuf brouillé.

eggplant, n. aubergine f.

egoism, n. égoïsme m.

egotism, n. égotisme m.

egotist, n. égotiste m.

Egypt, n. Égypte m.

Egyptian, 1. n. Égyptien m. 2. adj. égyptien.

eight, adj. and n. huit m.

eighteen, adj. and n. dix-huit m.

eighteenth, adj. and n. dix-huitième m.f.

eighth, adj. and n. huitième m.f.

eightieth, adj. quatre-vingtième.

eighty, adj. and n. quatre-vingts m.

either, 1. adj. (each of two) chaque; (one or other) l'un ou l'autre. 2. pron. chacun; l'un ou l'autre. 3. conj. (e. . . . or) ou . . . ou . . .

ejaculate, vb. éjaculer, prononcer.

eject, vb. (throw) jeter.

ejection, n. jet m., éjection f., expulsion f.

eke, vb. suppléer à, subsister pauvrement.

elaborate, 1. adj. minutieux. 2. vb. élaborer.

elapse, vb. (time) s'écouler.

elastic, adj. and n. élastique m.

elasticity, n. élasticité f.

elate, vb. exalter, transporter.

elated, adj. exalté.

elation, n. exaltation f.

elbow, n. coude m.

elbowroom, n. aisance des coudes f.

elder, adj. and n. aîné m.

elderberry, n. baie de sureau f.

elderly, adj. d'un certain âge.

eldest, adj. aîné.

elect, vb. élire.

election, n. élection f.

electioneer, vb. faire une campagne électorale.

elective, adj. électif.

electorate, n. électorat m., les votants m.pl.

electric, electrical, adj. électrique.

electric chair, n. fauteuil électrique m.

electric eel, n. anguille électrique f.

electrician, n. électricien m.

electricity, n. électricité f.

electrocardiogram, n. électrocardiogramme m.

electrocute, vb. électrocuter.

electrode, n. électrode f.

electrolysis, n. électrolyse f.

electron, n. électron m.

electronics, n. électronique f.

electroplate, 1. vb. plaquer. 2. adj. plaqué.

elegance, n. élégance f.

elegant, adj. élégant.

elegiac, adj. élégiaque.

elegy, n. élégie f.

element, n. élément m.

elemental, elementary, adj. élémentaire.

elephant, n. éléphant m.

elephantine, adj. éléphantin.

elevate, vb. élever.

elevation, n. élévation f.

elevator, n. ascenseur m.

eleven, adj. and n. onze m.

eleventh, adj. and n. onzième m.f.

elf, n. elfe m.

elfin, adj. d'elfe.

elicit, vb. tirer, faire jaillir.

eligibility, n. éligibilité f.

eligible, adj. éligible.

eliminate, vb. éliminer.

elimination, n. élimination f.

elixir, n. élixir m.

elk, n. élan m.

elm, n. orme m.

elocution, n. élocution f.

elongate, vb. allonger, étendre.

elope, vb. s'enfuir.

eloquence, n. éloquence f.

eloquent, adj. éloquent.

eloquently, adv. d'une manière éloquente.

else, 1. adj. autre; (someone e.) quelqu'un d'autre. 2. adv. autrement.

elsewhere, adv. ailleurs.

elucidate, vb. élucider, éclaircir.

elude, vb. éluder.

elusive, adj. évasif, insaisissable.

emaciated, adj. émacié.

emanate, vb. émaner.

emancipate, vb. émanciper.

emancipation, n. émancipation f.

emancipator, n. émancipateur m.

emasculate, vb. émasculer.

embalm, vb. embaumer.

embankment, n. levée f.

embargo, n. embargo m.

embark, vb. embarquer, tr.

embarrass, vb. embarrasser.

embarrassing, adj. embarrassant.

embarrassment, n. embarras m.

embassy, n. ambassade f.

embellish, vb. embellir.

embellishment, n. embellissement m.

ember, n. braise f., charbon ardent m.

embezzle, vb. détourner.

embitter, vb. aigrir, envenimer.

emblazon, vb. blasonner.

emblem, n. emblème m.

emblematic, adj. emblématique.

embody, vb. incarner, incorporer.

emboss, vb. graver en relief, travailler en bosse.

embrace, 1. n. étreinte f. **2.** vb. embrasser.

embroider, vb. broder.

embroidery, n. broderie f.

embroil, vb. embrouiller.

embryo, n. embryon m.

embryology, n. embryologie f.

embryonic, adj. embryonnaire.

emerald, n. émeraude f.

emerge, vb. émerger.

emergency, n. circonstance (f.) critique.

emergent, adj. émergent.

emery, n. émeri m.

emetic, n. émétique m.

emigrant, n. émigrant m.

emigrate, vb. émigrer.

emigration, n. émigration f.

eminence, n. éminence f.

eminent, adj. éminent.

emissary, n. émissaire m.

emission control, n. appareil pour limiter l'émission de vapeurs nuisibles m.

emit, vb. émettre.

emollient, adj. émollient.

emolument, n. traitement m.

emotion, n. émotion f.

emotional, adj. émotif; (excitable) émotionnable.

emperor, n. empereur m.

emphasis, n. (impressiveness) force f.; (stress) accent m.

emphasize, vb. mettre en relief.

emphatic, adj. (manner) énergique.

empire, n. empire m.

empirical, adj. empirique.

employ, vb. employer.

employee, n. employé m.

employer, n. patron m.

employment, n. emploi m.

empower, vb. autoriser.

empress, n. impératrice f.

emptiness, n. vide m.

empty, 1. adj. vide. **2.** vb. vider.

emulate, vb. émuler.

emulsion, n. émulsion f.

enable, vb. mettre à même (de).

enact, vb. (law) décréter; (play) jouer.

enactment, n. promulgation f., acte législatif m.

enamel, n. émail m., pl. émaux.

enamor, vb. amouracher.

encamp, vb. camper, faire camper.

encampment, n. campement m., camp m.

encephalitis, n. encéphalite f.

encephalon, n. encéphale m.

enchant, vb. enchanter.

enchanting, adj. ravissant.

enchantment, n. enchantement m.

encircle, vb. entourer.

enclose, vb. enclore; (in letter) joindre.

enclosure, n. enclos m.; (in letter) pièce (f.) jointe.

encompass, vb. entourer.

encounter, vb. rencontrer.

encourage, vb. encourager.

encouragement, n. encouragement m.

encroach, vb. empiéter.

encumber, vb. encombrer.

encumbrance, n. encombre m.

encyclical, n. encyclique f.

encyclopedia, n. encyclopédie f.

end, 1. n. fin f.; (extremity) bout m.; (aim) but m. **2.** vb. finir.

endanger, vb. mettre en danger.

endear, vb. rendre cher.

endearment, n. charme m., attrait m.

endeavor, 1. n. effort m. **2.** vb. s'efforcer.

endemic, adj. endémique.

ending, n. terminaison f.

endless, adj. sans fin.

endocrine gland, n. glande endocrine f.

endorse, vb. (sign) endosser; (support) appuyer.

endorsement, n. (signing) endossement m.; (approval) approbation f.

endow, vb. doter.

endowment, n. dotation f., fondation f.

endurance, n. résistance f.

endure, vb. supporter.

enduring, adj. durable.

enema, n. lavement m.

enemy, adj. and n. ennemi m.

energetic, adj. énergique.

energy, n. énergie f.

enervate, vb. énerver, affaiblir.

enervation, n. affaiblissement m.

enfold, vb. envelopper.

enforce, vb. imposer; (law) exécuter.

enforcement, n. exécution f.

enfranchise, vb. affranchir, accorder le droit de vote.

engage, vb. engager, tr.; (become e.d, to be married) se fiancer.

engaged, adj. occupé, pris; fiancé.

engagement, n. engagement m.; (marriage) fiançailles f.pl.

engaging, adj. attrayant, séduisant.

engender, vb. engendrer.

engine, n. machine f.; (train) locomotive f.; (motor) moteur m.

engineer, n. (profession) ingénieur m.; (engine operator)

mécanicien m.; (mil.) soldat (m.) du génie.

engineering, n. génie m.

England, n. Angleterre f.

English, adj. and n. anglais m.

Englishman, n. Anglais m.

Englishwoman, n. Anglaise f.

engrave, vb. graver.

engraver, n. graveur m.

engraving, n. gravure f.

engross, vb. (absorb) absorber.

engrossing, adj. absorbant.

enhance, vb. rehausser.

enigma, n. énigme f.

enigmatic, adj. énigmatique.

enjoin, vb. enjoindre.

enjoy, vb. jouir de; (e. oneself) s'amuser.

enjoyable, adj. agréable.

enjoyment, n. jouissance f.

enlace, vb. enlacer.

enlarge, vb. agrandir, tr.

enlargement, n. agrandissement m.

enlarger, n. agrandisseur m., amplificateur m.

enlighten, vb. éclairer.

enlightenment, n. éclaircissement m.

enlist, vb. enrôler, tr.

enlisted man, n. gradé m.

enlistment, n. enrôlement m.

enliven, vb. animer.

enmesh, vb. engrener, embarrasser.

enmity, n. inimitié f.

ennoble, vb. anoblir.

ennui, n. ennui m.

enormity, n. énormité f.

enormous, adj. énorme.

enough, adj. and adv. assez (de).

enrage, vb. faire enrager.

enrapture, vb. ravir, enchanter.

enrich, vb. enrichir.

enroll, vb. enrôler.

enrollment, n. enrôlement m.

ensemble, n. ensemble m.

enshrine, vb. enchâsser.

ensign, n. (navy) enseigne m.

enslave, vb. asservir.

ensnare, vb. prendre au piège.

ensue, vb. s'ensuivre.

entail, vb. (involve) entraîner; (law) substituer.

entangle, vb. empêtrer.

enter, vb. entrer (dans).

enterprise, n. entreprise f.

enterprising, adj. entreprenant.

entertain, vb. (amuse) amuser; (receive) recevoir.

entertainment, n. amusement m.

enthrall, vb. captiver, ensorceler.

enthusiasm, n. enthousiasme m.

enthusiast, n. enthousiaste m.f.

enthusiastic, adj. enthousiaste.

entice, vb. attirer.

entire, adj. entier.

entirely, adv. entièrement.

entirety, n. totalité f.

entitle, vb. donner droit à; (book) intituler.

entity, n. entité f.

entomb, vb. enterrer, ensevelir.

entrails, n. entrailles f.pl.

entrain, vb. embarquer en chemin de fer.

entrance, n. entrée f.

entrant, n. débutant m., inscrit m.

entrap, vb. attraper, prendre au piège.

entreat, vb. supplier.

entreaty, n. instance f.

entrench, vb. retrancher.

entrust to, vb. confier à.

entry, n. (entrance) entrée f.; (recording) inscription f.

enumerate, vb. énumérer.

enumeration, n. énumération f.

enunciate, vb. énoncer.

enunciation, n. énonciation f.

envelop, vb. envelopper.

envelope, n. enveloppe f.

enviable, adj. enviable.

envious, adj. envieux.

environment, n. milieu m.

environmentalist, n. écologiste m.; environnementaliste m.

environmental protection, n. protection de l'environnement f.

environs, n. environs m.pl., alentours m.pl.

envisage, vb. envisager.

envoy, n. envoyé m.

envy, 1. n. envie f. 2. vb. envier.

eon, n. éon m.

ephemeral, adj. éphémère.

epic, 1. n. épopée f. 2. adj. épique.

epicure, n. gourmet m.

epidemic, n. épidémie f.

epidermis, n. épiderme m.

epigram, n. épigramme f.

epilepsy, n. épilepsie f.

epilogue, n. épilogue m.

episode, n. épisode m.

epistle, n. épître f.

epitaph, n. épitaphe f.

epithet, n. épithète f.

epitome, n. épitomé m., résumé m.

epitomize, vb. résumer, abréger.

epoch, n. époque f.

equable, adj. uniforme, régulier.

equal, adj. égal; (be e. to) être à la hauteur de.

equality, n. égalité f.

equalize, vb. égaliser, tr.

equanimity, n. tranquillité d'esprit f., équanimité f., sérénité f.

equate, vb. égaler, mettre en équation.

equation, n. équation f.

equator, n. équateur m.

equatorial, adj. équatorial.

equestrian, adj. équestre.

equidistant, adj. équidistant.

equilateral, adj. équilatéral.

equilibrium, n. équilibre m.

equinox, n. équinoxe m.

equip, vb. équiper.

equipment, n. équipement m.

equitable, adj. équitable, juste.

equity, n. équité f.

equivalent, adj. and n. équivalent m.

equivocal, adj. équivoque.

equivocate, vb. équivoquer.

era, n. ère f.

eradicate, vb. déraciner.

eradicator, n. effaceur m., grattoir m.

erase, vb. effacer.

eraser, n. gomme f.

erasure, n. rature f.

erect, adj. droit.

erection, n. érection f., construction f.

erectness, n. attitude droite f.

ermine, n. hermine f.

erode, vb. éroder, ronger.

erosion, n. érosion f.

erosive, adj. érosif.

erotic, adj. érotique.

err, vb. errer.

errand, n. course f.

errant, adj. errant.

erratic, adj. irrégulier, excentrique.

erring, adj. égaré, dévoyé.

erroneous, adj. erroné.

error, n. erreur f.

erudite, adj. érudit.

erudition, n. érudition f.

erupt, vb. entrer en éruption.

eruption, n. éruption f.

escalate, vb. escalader.

escalator, n. escalier roulant m.

escapade, n. escapade f.

escape, 1. n. fuite f. 2. vb. échapper.

escapism, n. évasion f., échappement m.

eschew, vb. éviter, s'abstenir.

escort, n. (mil.) escorte f.; (to a lady) cavalier m.

esculent, adj. comestible.

escutcheon, n. écusson m.

esoteric, adj. ésotérique.

especial, adj. spécial.

espionage, n. espionnage m.

espousal, n. adoption f., adhésion (à) f.

espouse, vb. épouser, embrasser (une cause).

Eskimo, 1. n. Esquimau m., Esquimaude f. 2. adj. esquimau m., esquimaude f.

esquire, n. écuyer m.; titre honorifique d'un "gentleman" m.

essay, 1. n. essai m.; (school) composition f. 2. vb. essayer.

essayist, n. essayiste m.

essence, n. essence f.

essential, adj. essentiel.

essentially, adv. essentiellement.

establish, vb. établir.

establishment, n. établissement m.

estate, n. (condition, class) état m.; (wealth) biens m.pl.; (land) propriété f.

esteem, 1. n. estime f. 2. vb. estimer.

estimable, adj. estimable.

estimate, 1. n. estimation f.; (comm.) devis m. 2. vb. estimer.

estimation, n. (opinion) jugement m.

estrange, vb. aliéner.

estuary, n. estuaire m.

etching, n. gravure (f.) à l'eau-forte.

eternal, adj. éternel.

eternity, n. éternité f.

ether, n. éther m.

ethereal, adj. éthéré.

ethical, adj. moral.

ethics, n. éthique f.

Ethiopia, n. Éthiopie f.

ethnic, adj. ethnique.

etiquette, n. étiquette f.

Etruscan, 1. n. Étrusque m.f. 2. adj. étrusque.

etymology, n. étymologie f.

eucalyptus, n. eucalyptus m.

eugenic, adj. eugénésique.

eugenics, n. eugénisme m., eugénique f.

eulogize, vb. faire l'éloge de.

eulogy, n. panégyrique m.

eunuch, n. eunuque m.

euphonious, adj. mélodieux, euphonique.

Europe, n. Europe f.

European, 1. n. Européen m. 2. adj. européen.

euthanasia, n. euthanasie f.

evacuate, vb. évacuer.

evacuee, n. évacué m.

evade, vb. éluder.

evaluate, vb. évaluer.

evaluation, n. évaluation f.

evanescent, adj. évanescent, éphémère.

evangelist, n. évangéliste m.

evaporate, vb. évaporer, tr.

evaporation, n. évaporation f.

evasion, n. subterfuge m.

evasive, adj. évasif.

eve, n. veille f.

even, 1. adj. égal; (number) pair. 2. adv. même.

evening, n. soir m.; (span of e.) soirée f.

evenness, n. égalité f.

event, n. événement m.; (eventuality) cas m.

eventful, adj. plein d'événements.

eventual, adj. (ultimate) définitif; (contingent) éventuel.

ever, adv. (at all times) toujours; (at any time) jamais.

everglade, n. région marécageuse (de la Floride) f.

evergreen, adj. à feuilles persistantes, toujours vert.

everlasting, adj. éternel.

every, adj. (each) chaque; (all) tous les m.; toutes les f.

everybody, everyone, pron. tout le monde; chacun.

everyday, adj. de tous les jours.

everything, pron. tout.

everywhere, adv. partout.

evict, vb. expulser.

eviction, n. éviction f., expulsion f.

evidence, n. évidence f.; (proof) preuve f.

evident, adj. évident.

evidently, adv. évidemment.

evil, n. mal m.

evil, adj. mauvais.

evince, vb. démontrer.

eviscerate, vb. éviscérer.

evoke, vb. évoquer.

evolution, n. évolution f.

evolutionist, n. évolutionniste m.

evolve, vb. évoluer, développer.

ewe, n. agnelle f.

exact, adj. exact.

exacting, adj. (person) exigeant.

exactly, adv. exactement.

exaggerate, vb. exagérer.

exaggerated, adj. exagéré.

exaggeration, n. exagération f.

exalt, vb. exalter; (raise) élever.

exaltation, n. exaltation f.

examination, n. examen m.

examine, vb. examiner.

example, n. exemple m.

exasperate, vb. exaspérer.

exasperation, n. exaspération f.

excavate, vb. creuser.

exceed, vb. excéder.

exceedingly, adv. extrêmement.

excel, vb. exceller, intr.

excellence, excellency, n. excellence f.

excellent, adj. excellent.

excelsior, n. copeaux d'emballage m.pl.

except, 1. vb. excepter. 2. prep. excepté, sauf.

exception, n. exception f.

exceptional, adj. exceptionnel.

excerpt, n. extrait m.

excess, n. excès m.; (surplus) excédent m.

excessive, adj. excessif.

exchange, 1. n. échange m.; (money) change m. 2. vb. échanger.

exchangeable, adj. échangeable.

excise, vb. contribution indirecte f., régie f.

excitable, adj. émotionnable, excitable.

excite, vb. exciter.

excitement, n. agitation f.

exclaim, vb. s'écrier.

exclamation, n. exclamation f.

exclamation point or mark, n. point d'exclamation m.

exclude, vb. exclure.

exclusion, n. exclusion f.

exclusive, adj. exclusif; (stylish) sélect.

excommunicate, vb. excommunier.

excommunication, n. excommunication f.

excoriate, vb. excorier, écorcher.

excrement, n. excrément m.

excruciating, adj. atroce, affreux.

exculpate, vb. disculper, exonérer.

excursion, n. excursion f.

excusable, adj. excusable.

excuse, 1. n. excuse f. 2. vb. excuser.

execrable, adj. exécrable, abominable.

execute, vb. exécuter.

execution, n. exécution f.

executioner, n. bourreau m.

executive, adj. and n. exécutif m.

executive mansion, n. maison présidentielle f.

executor, n. exécuteur m.

exemplary, adj. exemplaire.

exemplify, vb. expliquer par des exemples.

exempt, 1. adj. exempt. 2. vb. exempter.

exercise, 1. n. exercice m. 2. vb. exercer.

exert, vb. employer; (e. oneself) s'efforcer de.

exertion, n. effort m.

exhale, vb. exhaler.

exhaust, 1. n. (machines) échappement m. 2. vb. épuiser.

exhaustion, n. épuisement m.

exhaustive, adj. complet, approfondi.

exhibit, vb. (pictures, etc.) exposer; (show) montrer.

exhibition, n. exposition f.

exhibitionism, n. exhibitionnisme m.

exhilarate, vb. égayer.

exhort, vb. exhorter.

exhortation, n. exhortation f.

exhume, vb. exhumer.

exigency, n. exigence f.

exile, 1. n. exil m.; (person) exilé m. 2. vb. exiler.

exist, vb. exister.

existence, n. existence f.

existent, adj. existant.

exit, n. sortie f.

exodus, n. exode m.

exonerate, vb. exonérer.

exorbitant, adj. exorbitant.

exorcise, vb. exorciser.

exotic, adj. exotique.

expand, vb. étendre, tr.; (dilate) dilater, tr.

expanse, n. étendue f.

expansion, n. expansion f.

expansive, adj. expansif.

expatiate, vb. discourir.

expatriate, vb. expatrier.

expect, vb. s'attendre à; (await) attendre.

expectancy, n. attente f.

expectation, n. attente f.; (hope) espérance f.

expectorate, vb. expectorer.

expediency, n. convenance f.

expedient, n. expédient m.

expedite, vb. activer, accélérer.

expedition, n. expédition f.

expel, vb. expulser.

expend, vb. (money) dépenser; (use up) épuiser.

expenditure, n. dépense f.

expense, n. dépense f.; (expenses) frais m.pl.

expensive, adj. coûteux, cher.

expensively, adv. coûteusement.

experience, 1. n. expérience f. 2. vb. éprouver.

experienced, adj. expérimenté.

experiment, n. expérience f.

experimental, adj. expérimental.

expert, adj. and n. expert m.

expiate, vb. expier.

expiration, n. expiration f.

expire, vb. expirer.

explain, vb. expliquer.

explanation, n. explication f.

explanatory, adj. explicatif.

expletive, n. explétif m.

explicit, adj. explicite.

explode, vb. (burst) éclater, intr.

exploit, 1. n. exploit m. 2. vb. exploiter.

exploitation, n. exploitation f.

exploration, n. exploration f.

exploratory, adj. exploratif.

explore, vb. explorer.

explorer, n. explorateur m.

explosion, n. explosion f.

explosive, adj. and n. explosif m.

exponent, n. interprète m.

export, 1. n. (exportation) exportation f.; (exported object) article (m.) d'exportation. 2. vb. exporter.

exportation, n. exportation f.

expose, vb. exposer.

exposé, n. exposé m.

exposition, n. exposition f.

expository, adj. expositoire.

expostulate, vb. faire des remontrances à.

exposure, n. exposition f.

expound, vb. exposer.

express, 1. adj. exprès. 2. vb. exprimer.

expressage, n. frais d'expédition m.pl.

expression, n. expression f.

expressive, adj. expressif.

expressly, adv. expressément.

expressman, n. agent de messageries m.

expropriate, vb. exproprier.

expulsion, n. expulsion f.

expunge, vb. effacer, rayer.

expurgate, vb. expurger, épurer.

exquisite, adj. exquis.

extant, adj. existant.

extemporaneous, adj. improvisé, impromptu.

extend, vb. étendre; (prolong) prolonger.

extension, n. extension f.

extensive, adj. étendu.

extensively, adv. largement, considérablement.

extent, n. étendue f.; (to some e.) jusqu'à un certain point.

extenuate, vb. (tire out) exténuer; (diminish) atténuer.

exterior, adj. and n. extérieur m.

exterminate, vb. exterminer.

extermination, n. extermination f.

external, adj. externe.

extinct, adj. éteint.

extinction, n. extinction f.

extinguish, vb. éteindre.

extirpate, vb. extirper.

extol, vb. vanter.

extort, vb. extorquer.

extortion, n. extorsion f.

extortioner, n. extorqueur m.

extra, adj. (additional) supplémentaire; (spare) de réserve.

extra-, prefix. (outside of) en dehors de; (intensive) extra-.

extract, 1. n. extrait m. 2. vb. extraire.

extraction, n. extraction f., origine f.

extradite, vb. extrader.

extraneous, adj. étranger à.

extraordinary, adj. extraordinaire.

extravagance, n. extravagance f.; (money) prodigalité f.

extravagant, adj. extravagant; (money) prodigue.

extravaganza, m. œuvre fantaisiste f.

extreme, adj. and n. extrême m.

extremity, n. extrémité f.

extricate, vb. dégager, tirer.

extrovert, n. extroverti m.

exuberant, adj. exubérant.

exude, vb. exsuder.

exult, vb. exulter.

exultant, adj. exultant, joyeux.

eye, n. œil m.pl. yeux.

eyeball, n. globe (m.) de l'œil.

eyebrow, n. sourcil m.

eyeglass, n. lorgnon m.

eyeglasses, n. lunettes f.pl.

eyelash, n. cil m.

eyelet, n. œillet m.

eyelid, n. paupière f.

eyesight, n. vue f.

eyewitness, n. témoin oculaire m.

F

fable, n. fable f.

fabric, n. (structure) édifice m.; (cloth) tissu m.

fabricate, vb. fabriquer.

fabrication, n. fabrication f.

fabulous, adj. fabuleux.

façade, n. façade f.

face, 1. n. figure f. 2. vb. faire face à.

facet, n. facette f.

facetious, adj. facétieux.

face value, n. valeur nominale f.

facial, adj. facial.

facile, adj. facile.

facilitate, vb. faciliter.

facility, n. facilité f.

facing, n. revêtement m., revers m.

facsimile, n. fac-similé m.

fact, n. fait m.; (as a matter of f.) en effet.

faction, n. faction f.

factor, n. facteur m.

factory, n. fabrique f.

factual, adj. effectif, positif.

faculty, n. faculté f.

fad, n. marotte f.

fade, vb. intr. se faner; (color) se décolorer; (f. away) s'évanouir.

fagged, adj. épuisé, fatigué.

fail, vb. manquer; (not succeed) échouer.

failing, 1. n. manquement m. 2. adj. faiblissant. 3. prep. au défaut de.

faille, n. faille f.

failure, n. (lack) défaut m.; (want of success) insuccès m.

faint, 1. adj. faible. 2. vb. s'évanouir.

faintly, adv. faiblement, timidement, légèrement.

fair, 1. n. foire m. 2. adj. (beautiful) beau m., belle f.; (blond) blond; (honest) juste; (pretty good) passable.

fairly, adv. honnêtement, impartialement.

fairness, n. (honesty) honnêteté f.

fairy, n. fée f.

fairyland, n. pays des fées m.

faith, n. foi f.

faithful, adj. fidèle.

faithless, adj. infidèle.

fake, vb. truquer.

faker, n. truqueur m.

falcon, n. faucon m.

falconry, n. fauconnerie f.

fall, 1. n. chute f.; (autumn) automne m. 2. vb. tomber.

fallacious, adj. fallacieux.

fallacy, n. fausseté f.

fallen, adj. tombé, déchu.

fallible, adj. faillible.

fallout, n. pluie radioactive f.

fallow, adj. en jachère.

false, adj. faux m., fausse f.

falsehood, n. mensonge m.

falseness, n. fausseté f.

falsetto, n. and adj. fausset m.

falsification, n. falsification f.

falsify, vb. falsifier.

falter, vb. hésiter.

fame, n. renommée f.

famed, adj. célèbre, renommé, fameux.

familiar, adj. familier.

familiarity, n. familiarité f.

familiarize, vb. familiariser.

family, n. famille f.

famine, n. (food) disette f.; (general) famine f.

famished, adj. affamé.

famous, adj. célèbre.

fan, n. éventail m.; (mechanical) ventilateur m.

fanatic, adj. and n. fanatique m.

fanatical, adj. fanatique.

fanaticism, n. fanatisme m.

fanciful, adj. fantastique, fantaisiste.

fancy, 1. n. fantaisie f. 2. vb. se figurer.

fanfare, n. fanfare f.

fang, n. croc (of a dog) m., crochet (of a snake) m.

fantastic, adj. fantastique.

fantasy, n. fantaisie f.

far, adv. loin; (so f.) jusqu'ici; (as f. as) autant que; (much) beaucoup; (by f.) de beaucoup.

faraway, adj. lointain.

farce, n. farce f.

farcical, adj. bouffon.

fare, 1. n. (price) prix m.; (food) chère f. 2. vb. aller.

farewell, interj. and n. adieu m.

far-fetched, adj. forcé.

far-flung, adj. très étendu, vaste.

farina, n. farine f.

farm, n. ferme f.

farmer, n. fermier m.

farmhouse, n. maison (f.) de ferme.

farming, n. culture f.

farmyard, n. cour de ferme f.

far-reaching, adj. de grande envergure.

far-sighted, adj. clairvoyant.

farther, 1. adj. plus éloigné. 2. adv. plus loin.

farthest, adj. and adv. le plus lointain.

fascinate, vb. fasciner.

fascination, n. fascination f.

fascism, n. fascisme m.

fashion, n. mode f.; (manner) manière f.

fashionable, adj. à la mode.

fast, 1. adj. jeûne m. 2. adj. (speedy) rapide; (firm) en avance; (of clock) en avance. 3. vb. jeûner. 4. adv. (quickly) vite; (firmly) ferme.

fasten, vb. attacher, tr.

fastener, n. fermeture f.

fastening, n. attache f.

fastidious, adj. difficile.

fat, adj. gras m., grasse f.

fatal, adj. fatal; (deadly) mortel.

fatality, n. fatalité f.

fatally, adv. fatalement, mortellement.

fate, n. destin m.

fateful, adj. fatal.

father, n. père m.

fatherhood, n. paternité f.

father-in-law, n. beau-père m.

fatherland, n. patrie f.

fatherless, adj. sans père.

fatherly, adj. paternel.

fathom, 1. n. (naut.) brasse f. 2. vb. sonder.

fatigue, n. fatigue f.

fatten, vb. engraisser.

fatty, adj. graisseux.

fatuous, adj. sot.

faucet, n. robinet m.

fault, n. (mistake) faute f.; (defect) défaut m.

faultfinding, n. disposition à critiquer f.

faultless, adj. sans défaut.

faultlessly, adv. d'une manière impeccable.

faulty, adj. défectueux.

favor, 1. n. faveur f. **2.** vb. favoriser.

favorable, adj. favorable.

favored, adj. favorisé.

favorite, adj. and n. favori, m., favorite f.

favoritism, n. favoritisme m.

fawn, n. faon m.

faze, vb. bouleverser.

fear, 1. n. crainte f. **2.** vb. craindre.

fearful, adj. (person) craintif; (thing) effrayant.

fearless, adj. intrépide.

fearlessness, n. intrépidité f.

feasible, adj. faisable.

feast, n. fête f.; (banquet) festin m.

feat, n. exploit m.

feather, n. plume f.

feathered, adj. emplumé.

feathery, adj. plumeux.

feature, n. trait m.

February, n. février m.

fecund, adj. fécond.

federal, adj. fédéral.

federation, n. fédération f.

fedora, n. chapeau mou m.

fee, n. (for professional services) honoraires m.pl.; (school) frais m.pl.

feeble, adj. faible.

feeble-minded, adj. d'esprit faible.

feebleness, n. faiblesse f.

feed, 1. n. nourriture f. **2.** vb. nourrir, tr.

feedback, n. action de contrôle en retour f.

feel, vb. sentir, tr.; (touch) tâter.

feeling, n. sentiment m.

feign, vb. feindre.

felicitate, vb. féliciter.

felicitous, adj. heureux.

felicity, n. félicité f.

feline, adj. félin.

fell, adj. funeste.

fellow, n. (general) homme m., garçon m.; (companion) compagnon m.

fellowship, n. camaraderie f.; (university) bourse (f.) universitaire.

felon, n. criminel m.

felony, n. crime m.

felt, n. feutre m.

female, 1. n. (person) femme f.; (animals, plants) femelle f. **2.** adj. féminin, femelle.

feminine, adj. féminin.

femininity, n. féminéité f.

fence, 1. n. clôture f. **2.** vb. (en-

close) enclore; (sword, foil) fair de l'escrime.

fencer, n. escrimeur m.

fencing, n. escrime f.

fender, n. garde-boue m.; (fireplace) garde-feu m.

ferment, vb. fermenter.

fermentation, n. fermentation f.

fern, n. fougère f.

ferocious, adj. féroce.

ferociously, adv. d'une manière féroce.

ferocity, n. férocité f.

ferry, n. passage (m.) en bac; (f. boat) bac m.

fertile, adj. fertile.

fertility, n. fertilité f.

fertilization, n. fertilisation f.

fertilize, vb. fertiliser.

fervency, n. ardeur f.

fervent, adj. fervent.

fervently, adv. ardemment.

fervid, adj. fervent.

fervor, n. ferveur f.

fester, vb. suppurer.

festival, n. fête f.

festive, adj. de fête.

festivity, n. réjouissance f.

festoon, 1. n. feston m. **2.** vb. festonner.

fetal, adj. foetal.

fetch, vb. (go and get) aller chercher; (bring) apporter.

fetching, adj. attrayant.

fete, vb. fêter.

fetid, adj. fétide.

fetish, n. fétiche m.

fetlock, n. fanon m.

fetter, 1. n. lien m., chaîne f. **2.** vb. enchaîner.

fetus, n. fœtus m.

feud, n. inimitié f.; (historical) fief m.

feudal, adj. féodal.

feudalism, n. régime féodal m.

fever, n. fièvre f.

feverish, adj. fiévreux.

feverishly, adv. fébrilement, fiévreusement.

few, 1. adj. peu de; (a f.) quelques. **2.** pron. peu; (a f.) quelques-uns.

fiancé, n. fiancé m.

fiasco, n. fiasco m.

fiat, n. décret m.

fib, n. petit mensonge m.

fiber, n. fibre f.

fiberboard, n. fibre de bois m.

fibrous, adj. fibreux.

fickle, adj. volage.

fickleness, n. inconstance f.

fiction, n. fiction f.; (literature) romans m.pl.

fictional, adj. de romans.

fictitious, adj. fictif, imaginaire.

fictitiously, adv. d'une manière factice.

fiddle, 1. n. violon m. **2.** vb. jouer du violon.

fiddlesticks, interj. quelle blague!

fidelity, n. fidélité f.

fidget, vb. se remuer.

field, n. champ m.

fiend, n. démon m.

fiendish, adj. diabolique, infernal.

fierce, adj. féroce.

fiery, adj. ardent.

fiesta, n. fête f.

fife, n. fifre m.

fifteen, adj. and n. quinze m.

fifteenth, adj. and n. quinzième m.

fifth, adj. and n. cinquième m.

fifty, adj. and n. cinquante m.

fig, n. figue f.

fight, 1. n. combat m.; (struggle) lutte f.; (quarrel) dispute f. **2.** vb. combattre; se disputer.

fighter, n. combattant m.

figment, n. invention f.

figurative, adj. figuré.

figuratively, adv. au figuré.

figure, 1. n. figure f.; (of body) tournure f.; (math.) chiffre m. **2.** vb. figurer; calculer.

figured, adj. à dessin.

figurehead, n. homme de paille m.

figure of speech, n. façon de parler f.

figurine, n. figurine f.

filament, n. filament m.

filch, vb. escamoter.

file, 1. n. (tool) lime f.; (row) file f.; (papers) liasse f.; (for papers, etc.) classeur m.; (f.s) archives f.pl. **2.** vb. (tool) limer; (papers) classer; (f. off) défiler.

filial, adj. filial.

filigree, n. filigrane m.

filings, n. limaille f.

fill, vb. remplir, tr.

fillet, n. (band) bandeau m.; (meat, fish) filet m.

filling, n. remplissage m.

filling station, n. poste d'essence m.

film, n. (cinema) film m.; (photo) pellicule f.

filmy, adj. couvert d'une pellicule.

filter, 1. n. filtre m. **2.** vb. filtrer.

filth, n. ordure f.

filthy, adj. immonde; obscène.

fin, n. nageoire f.

final, adj. final.

finale, n. finale m.

finalist, n. finaliste m.

finality, n. finalité f.

finally, adv. finalement, enfin.

finance, 1. n. finance f. **2.** vb. financer.

financial, adj. financier.

financier, n. financier m.

find, vb. trouver.

fine, 1. n. amende f. **2.** adj. (beautiful) beau m., belle f.; (pure, thin) fin. **3.** vb. mettre à l'amende.

fine arts, n. beaux arts m.pl.

finery, n. parure f.

finesse, 1. n. finesse f. **2.** vb. finasser.

finger, *n.* doigt *m.*

finger bowl, *n.* rince-bouche *m.*

fingernail, *n.* ongle *m.*

fingerprint, *n.* empreinte digitale *f.*

finicky, *adj.* affété.

finish, *vb.* finir.

finished, *adj.* fini, achevé.

finite, *adj.* fini.

Finland, *n.* Finlande *f.*

Finn, *n.* Finlandais, Finnais *m.*

Finnish, 1. *n.* Finnois *m.* 2. *adj.* finlandais, finnois.

fir, *n.* sapin *m.*

fire, 1. *n.* feu *m.;* (burning of house, etc.) incendie *m.* 2. *vb.* (weapon) tirer.

fire alarm, *n.* avertisseur d'incendie *m.*

firearm, *n.* arme (*f.*) à feu.

firedamp, *n.* grisou *m.*

fire engine, *n.* pompe à incendie *f.*

fire escape, *n.* échelle de sauvetage *f.*

fire extinguisher, *n.* extincteur *m.*

firefly, *n.* luciole *f.*

fireman, *n.* pompier *m.*

fireplace, *n.* cheminée *f.*

fireproof, *adj.* à l'épreuve du feu.

fireside, *n.* coin du feu *m.*

firewood, *n.* bois de chauffage *m.*

fireworks, *n.* feu (*m.*) d'artifice.

firm, 1. *n.* maison (*f.*) de commerce. 2. *adj.* ferme.

firmness, *n.* fermeté *f.*

first, 1. *adj.* premier. 2. *adv.* d'abord.

first-aid, *n.* premiers secours *m.pl.*

first-class, *adj.* de premier ordre.

first-hand, *adj.* de première main.

first-rate, *adj.* de premier ordre.

fiscal, *adj.* fiscal.

fish, 1. *n.* poisson *m.* 2. *vb.* pêcher.

fisherman, *n.* pêcheur *m.*

fishery, *n.* pêcherie *f.*

fishhook, *n.* hameçon *m.*

fishing, *n.* pêche *f.*

fishmonger, *n.* marchand de poisson *m.*

fishwife, *n.* marchande de poisson *f.*

fishy, *adj.* de poisson; (slang) louche.

fission, *n.* fission *f.*

fissure, *n.* fente *f.*

fist, *n.* poing *m.*

fistic, *adj.* au poing.

fit, 1. *n.* accès *m.* 2. *adj.* (suitable) convenable; (capable) capable; (**f. for**) propre à. 3. *vb.* (befit) convenir à; (clothes) aller à; (adjust) ajuster, *tr.*

fitful, *adj.* agité, irrégulier.

fitness, *n.* à-propos *m.;* (person) aptitude *f.*

fitting, 1. *n.* ajustage *m.* 2. *adj.* convenable.

five, *adj. and n.* cinq *m.*

fix, 1. *n.* embarras *m.* 2. *vb.* fixer; (repair) réparer.

fixation, *n.* fixation *f.*

fixed, *adj.* fixe.

fixture, *n.* object (*m.*) d'attache.

flabby, *adj.* flasque.

flaccid, *adj.* flasque.

flag, *n.* drapeau *m.;* (stone) dalle *f.*

flagellate, *vb.* flageller.

flagging, 1. *n.* relâchement *m.* 2. *adj.* qui s'affaiblit.

flagon, *n.* flacon *m.*

flagpole, *n.* mât de drapeau *m.*

flagrant, *adj.* flagrant.

flagrantly, *adv.* d'une manière flagrante.

flagship, *n.* vaisseau amiral *m.*

flagstone, *n.* dalle *f.*

flail, 1. *n.* fléau *m.* 2. *vb.* battre au fléau.

flair, *n.* flair *m.*

flake, *n.* (snow) flocon *m.*

flamboyant, *adj.* flamboyant.

flame, 1. *n.* flamme *f.* 2. *vb.* flamboyer.

flame thrower, *n.* lanceur de flammes *m.*

flaming, *adj.* flamboyant.

flamingo, *n.* flamant *m.*

flank, *n.* flanc *m.*

flannel, *n.* flanelle *f.*

flap, 1. *n.* (wing) coup *m.;* (pocket) patte *f.;* (table) battant *m.* 2. *vb.* battre.

flare, *vb.* flamboyer.

flare-up, 1. *n.* emportement *m.* 2. *vb.* s'emporter.

flash, *n.* éclair *m.*

flashcube, *n.* flash-cube *m.*

flashiness, *n.* faux brillant *m.,* éclat superficiel *m.*

flashlight, *n.* (lighthouse) feu (*m.*) à éclats; (pocket) lampe (*f.*) de poche.

flashy, *adj.* voyant.

flask, *n.* gourde *f.*

flat, 1. *n.* appartement *m.* 2. *adj.* plat *m.,* platte *f.*

flatcar, *n.* wagon en plateforme *m.*

flatness, *n.* (evenness) égalité *f.;* (dullness) platitude *f.*

flatten, *vb.* aplatir.

flatter, *vb.* flatter.

flatterer, *n.* flatteur *m.*

flattery, *n.* flatterie *f.*

flattop, *n.* porte-avion *m.*

flaunt, *vb.* parader, étaler.

flavor, *n.* (taste) saveur *f.;* (fragrance) arome *m.*

flavoring, *n.* assaisonnement *m.*

flavorless, *adj.* fade.

flaw, *n.* défaut *m.*

flawless, *adj.* sans défaut, parfait.

flawlessly, *adv.* d'une manière impeccable.

flax, *n.* lin *m.*

flay, *vb.* écorcher.

flea, *n.* puce *f.*

fleck, 1. *n.* tache *f.* 2. *vb.* tacheter (de).

fledgling, *n.* oisillon *m.*

flee, *vb.* s'enfuir.

fleece, *n.* toison *f.*

fleecy, *adj.* laineux, moutonneux.

fleet, *n.* flotte *f.*

fleeting, *adj.* fugitif.

flesh, *n.* chair *f.*

fleshy, *adj.* charnu.

flex, *vb.* fléchir.

flexibility, *n.* flexibilité *f.*

flexible, *adj.* flexible.

flicker, 1. *n.* lueur (*f.*) vacillante. 2. *vb.* trembloter.

flier, *n.* aviateur *m.*

flight, *n.* (flying) vol *m.;* (fleeing) fuite *f.*

flight attendant, *n.* hôtesse de l'air *f.*

flighty, *adj.* étourdi.

flimsy, *adj.* sans solidité.

flinch, *vb.* reculer, broncher.

fling, *vb.* jeter.

flint, *n.* (lighter) pierre (*f.*) à briquet; (mineral) silex *m.*

flippant, *adj.* léger.

flippantly, *adv.* légèrement.

flirt, *vb.* flirter.

flirtation, *n.* flirt *m.*

float, *vb.* flotter.

flock, 1. *n.* troupeau *m.* 2. *vb.* accourir.

flog, *vb.* fouetter.

flood, *n.* inondation *f.*

floodgate, *n.* écluse *f.*

floodlight, *n.* lumière à grand flots *f.*

floor, *n.* plancher *m.;* (**take the f.**) prendre la parole; (story) étage *m.*

flooring, *n.* plancher *m.,* parquet *m.*

floorwalker, *n.* inspecteur du magasin *m.*

flop, 1. *vb.* faire plouf, s'effondrer. 2. *n.* fiasco *m.*

floral, *adj.* floral.

florid, *adj.* fleuri, vermeil.

florist, *n.* fleuriste *m.f.*

flounce, 1. *n.* volant *m.* 2. *vb.* se démener.

flounder, *n.* flet *m.*

flour, *n.* farine *f.*

flourish, *vb.* prospérer.

flow, *vb.* couler.

flower, 1. *n.* fleur *f.* 2. *vb.* fleurir.

flowerpot, *n.* pot à fleurs *m.*

flowery, *adj.* fleuri.

fluctuate, *vb.* osciller.

fluctuation, *n.* fluctuation *f.*

flue, *n.* tuyau de cheminée *m.*

fluency, *n.* facilité *f.*

fluent, *adj.* (**be a f. speaker of . . .**) parler . . . couramment.

fluid, *adj and n.* fluide *m.*

fluidity, *n.* fluidité *f.*

flunk, *vb.* coller, recaler.

flunkey, *n.* laquais *m.*

fluorescent lamp, *n.* lampe fluorescente *f.*

fluoroscope, *n.* fluoroscope *f.*

flurry, 1. *n.* agitation *f.* **2.** *vb.* agiter.

flush, *n.* (redness) rougeur *f.;* (plumbing) chasse *f.*

flute, *n.* flûte *f.*

flutter, 1. *n.* (bird) voltigement *m.;* (agitation) agitation *f.* **2.** *vb.* s'agiter; (heart) palpiter.

flux, *n.* flux *m.*

fly, 1. *n.* mouche *f.* **2.** *vb.* voler.

foam, *n.* écume *f.*

focal, *adj.* focal.

focus, 1. *n.* foyer *m.;* (in f.) au point. **2.** *vb.* (photo) mettre au point.

fodder, *n.* fourrage *m.*

foe, *n.* ennemi *m.*

fog, *n.* brouillard *m.*

foggy, *adj.* brumeux.

foil, *n.* (sheet) feuille *f.;* (set-off) repoussoir *m.;* (fencing) fleuret *m.*

foist, *vb.* fourrer.

fold, 1. *n.* pli *m.* **2.** *vb.* plier.

folder, *n.* (booklet) prospectus *m.*

foliage, *n.* feuillage *m.*

folio, *n.* in-folio *m.*

folk, *n.* gens *m.f.pl.*

folklore, *n.* folk-lore *m.*

follicle, *n.* follicule *m.*

follow, *vb.* suivre.

follower, *n.* disciple *m.*

folly, *n.* folie *f.*

foment, *vb.* fomenter.

fond, *adj.* tendre; (be f. of) aimer.

fondant, *n.* fondant *m.*

fondle, *vb.* caresser.

fondly, *adv.* tendrement.

fondness, *n.* tendresse *f.*

food, *n.* nourriture *f.*

foodstuff, *n.* comestible *m.*

fool, *n.* sot *m.,* sotte *f.;* (jester) bouffon *m.*

foolhardiness, *n.* témérité *f.*

foolhardy, *adj.* téméraire.

foolish, *adj.* sot *m.,* sotte *f.*

foolproof, *adj.* à toute épreuve.

foolscap, *n.* papier écolier *m.*

foot, *n.* pied *m.*

footage, *n.* métrage *m.*

football, *n.* football *m.,* ballon *m.*

foothill, *n.* colline basse *f.*

foothold, *n.* point d'appui *m.*

footing, *n.* pied *m.,* point d'appui *m.*

footlights, *n.* rampe *f.*

footnote, *n.* note *f.*

footprint, *n.* empreinte de pas *f.*

footsore, *adj.* aux pieds endoloris.

footstep, *n.* pas *m.*

footstool, *n.* tabouret *m.*

footwork, *n.* jeu de pieds *m.*

fop, *n.* fat *m.*

for, 1. *prep.* pour. **2.** *conj.* car.

forage, 1. *n.* fourrage *m.* **2.** *vb.* fourrager.

foray, *n.* razzia *f.*

forbear, *vb.* (avoid) s'abstenir de; (be patient) montrer de la patience.

forbearance, *n.* patience *f.*

forbid, *vb.* défendre (à).

forbidding, *adj.* rébarbatif.

force, 1. *n.* force *f.* **2.** *vb.* forcer.

forced, *adj.* forcé.

forceful, *adj.* énergique.

forcefulness, *n.* énergie *f.,* vigueur *f.*

forceps, *n.* forceps *m.*

forcible, *adj.* forcé.

ford, 1. *n.* gué *m.* **2.** *vb.* traverser à gué.

fore, *adj.* antérieur, de devant.

fore, *n.* avant *m.*

fore and aft, *adv.* de l'avant à l'arrière.

forearm, *n.* avant-bras *m.*

forebears, *n.* ancêtres *m.pl.*

forebode, *vb.* présager.

foreboding, 1. *n.* mauvais augure *m.,* pressentiment *m.* **2.** *adj.* qui présage le mal.

forecast, 1. *n.* prévision *f.* **2.** *vb.* prévoir.

forecaster, *n.* pronostiqueur *m.*

forecastle, *n.* gaillard *m.*

foreclose, *vb.* exclure, forclore.

forefather, *n.* ancêtre *m.*

forefinger, *n.* index *m.*

forefront, *n.* premier rang *m.*

foregone, *adj.* décidé d'avance.

foreground, *n.* premier plan *m.*

forehead, *n.* front *m.*

foreign, *adj.* étranger.

foreign aid, *n.* aide aux pays étrangers *f.*

foreigner, *n.* étranger *m.*

foreleg, *n.* jambe antérieure *f.*

foreman, *n.* contremaître *m.*

foremost, *adj.* premier.

forenoon, *n.* matinée *f.*

forensic, *adj.* judiciaire.

forerunner, *n.* avant-coureur *m.*

foresee, *vb.* prévoir.

foreseeable, *adj.* que l'on peut prévoir.

foreshadow, *vb.* présager.

foresight, *n.* prévoyance *f.*

forest, *n.* forêt *f.*

forestall, *vb.* anticiper, devancer.

forester, *n.* forestier *m.*

forestry, *n.* sylviculture *f.*

foretaste, *n.* avant-goût *m.*

foretell, *vb.* prédire.

forever, *adv.* pour toujours.

forevermore, *adv.* à jamais.

foreword, *n.* avant-propos *m.*

forfeit, *vb.* forfaire.

forfeiture, *n.* perte par confiscation *f.,* forfaiture *f.*

forgather, *vb.* se réunir.

forge, 1. *n.* forge *f.* **2.** *vb.* forger; (signature, money) contrefaire.

forger, *n.* faussaire *m.,* falsificateur *m.*

forgery, *n.* faux *m.*

forget, *vb.* oublier.

forgetful, *adj.* oublieux.

forget-me-not, *n.* myosotis *m.*

forgive, *vb.* pardonner (à).

forgiveness, *n.* pardon *m.*

forgo, *vb.* renoncer à.

fork, *n.* fourchette *f.;* (tool, road) fourche *f.*

forlorn, *adj.* (hopeless) désespéré; (forsaken) abandonné.

form, 1. *n.* forme *f.;* (blank) formule *f.* **2.** *vb.* former.

formal, *adj.* formel.

formaldehyde, *n.* formaldéhyde *f.*

formality, *n.* formalité *f.*

formally, *adv.* formellement.

format, *n.* format *m.*

formation, *n.* formation *f.*

formative, *adj.* formatif.

former, 1. *adj.* précédent; (with latter) premier. **2.** *pron.* le premier.

formerly, *adv.* autrefois, jadis, auparavant.

formidable, *adj.* formidable.

formless, *adj.* informe.

formula, *n.* formule *f.*

formulate, *vb.* formuler.

formulation, *n.* formulation *f.*

forsake, *vb.* abandonner.

forsythia, *n.* forsythie *f.*

fort, *n.* fort *m.*

forte, *n.* fort *m.*

forth, *adv.* en avant; (and so f.) et ainsi de suite.

forthcoming, *adv.* à venir.

forthright, 1. *adj.* tout droit. **2.** *adv.* carrément, nettement.

forthwith, *adv.* sur-le-champ, tout de suite.

fortieth, *adj. and n.* quarantième *m.*

fortification, *n.* fortification *f.*

fortify, *vb.* fortifier, renforcer.

fortissimo, *adv.* fortissimo.

fortitude, *n.* courage *m.*

fortnight, *n.* quinzaine *f.*

fortress, *n.* forteresse *f.*

fortuitous, *adj.* fortuit.

fortunate, *adj.* heureux.

fortune, *n.* fortune *f.*

fortuneteller, *n.* diseur de bonne aventure *m.*

forty, *adj. and n.* quarante *m.*

forum, *n.* (Roman) forum *m.*

forward, 1. *adj.* en avant; (advanced) avancé; (bold) hardi. **2.** *adv.* en avant. **3.** *vb.* (letter) faire suivre.

forwardness, *n.* empressement *m.,* effronterie *f.*

fossil, *n.* fossile *m.*

fossilize, *vb.* fossiliser.

foster, *vb.* nourrir.

foul, *adj.* (dirty) sale; (disgusting) dégoûtant; (obscene) ordurier; (abominable) infâme.

found, *vb.* fonder.

foundation, *n.* fondation *f.;* (theory) fondement *m.*

founder, *n.* fondateur *m.*

foundling, *n.* enfant trouvé.

foundry, *n.* fonderie *f.*

fountain, *n.* fontaine *f.*

fountainhead, *n.* source *f.*

fountain pen, *n.* stylo-(graphe) *m.*

four, *adj. and n.* quatre *m.*

four-in-hand, n. attelage à quatre m.

fourscore, adj. quatre-vingts.

foursome, n. à quatre.

fourteen, adj. and n. quatorze m.

fourth, adj. quatrième m.; (fraction) quart m.

fourth estate, n. quatrième état m.

fowl, n. volaille f.

fox, n. renard m.

foxglove, n. digitale f.

foxhole, n. renardière f.

fox terrier, n. fox-terrier m.

fox trot, n. fox-trot m.

foxy, adj. rusé.

foyer, n. foyer m.

fracas, n. fracas m.

fraction, n. fraction f.

fracture, n. fracture f.

fragile, adj. fragile.

fragment, n. fragment m.

fragmentary, adj. fragmentaire.

fragrance, n. parfum m.

fragrant, adj. parfumé.

frail, adj. frêle.

frailty, n. faiblesse f.

frame, n. (picture) cadre m.; (structure) structure f.

frame-up, 1. n. coup monté m. 2. vb. monter un coup.

framework, n. charpente f.

France, n. France f.

franchise, n. droit (m.) électoral.

frank, adj. franc m., franche f.

frankfurter, n. saucisse (f.) de Francfort.

frankincense, n. encens m.

frankly, adv. franchement.

frankness, n. franchise f.

frantic, adj. frénétique.

fraternal, adj. fraternel.

fraternally, adv. fraternellement.

fraternity, n. fraternité f.

fraternization, n. fraternisation f.

fraternize, vb. fraterniser.

fratricide, n. fratricide m.

fraud, n. fraude f.; (person) imposteur m.

fraudulent, adj. frauduleux.

fraudulently, adv. frauduleusement.

fraught, adj. chargé (de), plein, gros.

fray, 1. n. bagarre f. 2. vb. érailler.

freak, n. (whim) caprice m.; (abnormality) phénomène m.

freckle, n. tache de rousseur f.

freckled, adj. taché de rousseur.

free, 1. adj. libre; (without cost) gratuit. 2. vb. libérer, affranchir.

freedom, n. liberté f.

free lance, 1. journaliste ou politicien indépendant m. 2. vb. faire du journalisme indépendant.

freestone, n. pêche dont la

chair n'adhère pas au noyau f.

free verse, n. vers libre m.

free will, n. libre arbitre m.

freeze, vb. geler.

freezer, n. glacière f.; congélateur m.

freezing point, n. point de congélation m.

freight, n. fret m.

freightage, n. frètement m.

freighter, n. affréteur m.

French, adj. and n. français m.

French leave, n. filer à l'anglaise.

Frenchman, n. Français m.

French toast, n. tranche de pain frite f.

Frenchwoman, n. Française f.

frenzied, adj. affolé, frénétique.

frenzy, n. frénésie f.

frequency, n. fréquence f.

frequent, 1. adj. fréquent. 2. vb. fréquenter.

frequently, adv. fréquemment.

fresco, n. fresque f.

fresh, adj. frais m., fraîche f.; (new, recent) nouveau; nouvel m., nouvelle f.

freshen, vb. refraîchir.

freshman, n. étudiant de première année m.

freshness, n. fraîcheur f.

fresh-water, adj. d'eau douce.

fret, vb. ronger, tr.

fretful, adj. chagrin.

fretfully, adv. avec irritation.

fretfulness, n. irritabilité f.

friar, n. moine m., frère religieux m.

fricassee, n. fricassée f.

friction, n. friction f.

Friday, n. vendredi m.

friend, n. ami m., amie f.

friendless, adj. sans amis.

friendliness, n. disposition (f.) amicale.

friendly, adj. amical.

friendship, n. amitié f.

fright, n. effroi m.

frighten, vb. effrayer.

frightful, adj. affreux.

frigid, adj. glacial.

Frigid Zone, n. zone glaciale f.

frill, 1. n. volant m.; affectation f. 2. vb. plisser.

frilly, adj. froncé, ruché.

fringe, n. frange f.

frisky, adj. folâtre.

frivolity, n. frivolité f.

frivolous, adj. frivole.

frivolousness, n. frivolité f.

frock, n. robe f.; (monk's) froc m.

frog, n. grenouille f.

frolic, vb. folâtrer.

from, prep. de; (time) depuis.

front, n. front m.; (front part) devant m.; (in f. of) devant.

frontage, n. étendue de devant f.

frontal, adj. frontal, de face.

frontier, n. frontière f.

frost, n. gelée f.

frostbite, n. gelure f.

frosting, n. glaçage m.

frosty, adj. gelé, glacé.

froth, 1. n. écume f. 2. vb. écumer.

frown, vb. froncer les sourcils.

frowzy, adj. mal tenu, peu soigné.

frozen, adj. gelé.

fructify, vb. fructifier.

frugal, adj. frugal.

frugality, n. frugalité f.

fruit, n. fruit m.

fruitful, adj. fructueux.

fruition, n. réalisation f., jouissance f., fructification f.

fruitless, adj. infructueux.

frustrate, vb. faire échouer.

frustration, n. frustration f.

fry, vb. frire, intr.; faire frire, tr.

fryer, n. casserole f.

fuchsia, n. fuchsia m.

fudge, 1. n. espèce de fondant américain. 2. interj. bah!

fuel, n. combustible m.

fugitive, adj. fugitif.

fugue, n. fugue f.

fulcrum, n. pivot m., point d'appui m.

fulfill, vb. accomplir.

fulfillment, n. accomplissement m.

full, adj. plein.

fullback, n. arrière m.

full dress, adj. en tenue de cérémonie.

fullness, n. plénitude f.

fully, adv. pleinement.

fulminate, vb. fulminer.

fulmination, n. fulmination f.

fumble, vb. tâtonner.

fume, n. fumée f.

fumigate, vb. désinfecter.

fumigator, n. fumigateur m.

fun, n. (amusement) amusement m.; (have f.) s'amuser; (joke) plaisanterie f.; (make f. of) se moquer de.

function, n. fonction f.

functional, adj. fonctionnel.

functionary, n. fonctionnaire m.

fund, n. fonds m.

fundamental, adj. fondamental.

funeral, n. funérailles f.pl.

funereal, adj. funèbre, funéraire.

fungicide, n. fongicide m.

fungus, n. fongus m.

funnel, n. entonnoir m.; (smoke-stack) cheminée f.

funny, adj. drôle.

fur, n. fourrure f.

furious, adj. furieux.

furlong, n. furlong m.

furlough, n. permission f.

furnace, n. fourneau m.

furnish, vb. fournir; (house) meubler.

furnishings, n. ameublement m.

furniture, n. meubles m.pl.

furor, n. fureur f.

furred, adj. fourré.

furrier, n. fourreur m.

furrow, n. sillon m.

furry, adj. qui ressemble à la fourrure.

further, 1. adj. ultérieur. **2.** adv. (distance) plus loin; (extent) davantage.

furtherance, n. avancement m.

furthermore, adv. en outre.

fury, n. furie f.

fuse, vb. fondre.

fuselage, n. fuselage m.

fusillade, n. fusillade f.

fusion, n. fusion f., fusionnement m.

fuss, n. **(make a f.)** faire des histoires.

fussy, adj. difficile.

futile, adj. futile.

futility, n. futilité f.

future, 1. n. avenir m.; (gramm.) futur m. **2.** adj. futur.

futurity, n. avenir m.

futurology, n. futurologie f.

fuzz, n. duvet m., flou m.

fuzzy, adj. flou, frisotté.

G

gab, vb. jaser.

gabardine, n. gabardine f.

gable, n. pignon m.

gadabout, n. coureur m.

gadfly, n. taon m.

gadget, n. truc m.

gag, 1. vb. bâillonner. **2.** n. blague f., bobard m.; bâillon m.

gaiety, n. gaieté f.

gaily, adv. gaiement.

gain, 1. n. gain m. **2.** vb. gagner.

gainful, adj. profitable, rémunérateur.

gainfully, adv. profitablement.

gainsay, vb. contredire.

gait, n. allure f.

gala, n. fête de gala f.

galaxy, n. galaxie f., assemblée brillante f.

gale, n. grand vent m.

gall, n. (bile) fiel m.; (sore) écorchure f.

gallant, adj. (brave) vaillant; (with ladies) galant.

gallantly, adv. galamment.

gallantry, n. vaillance f., galanterie f.

gall bladder, n. vésicule biliaire f.

galleon, n. galion m.

gallery, n. galerie f.

galley, n. galère f., (naut.) cuisine f., (typographic) galée f.

galley proof, n. épreuve en première f.

Gallic, adj. gaulois.

gallivant, vb. courailler.

gallon, n. gallon m.

gallop, 1. n. galop m. **2.** vb. galoper.

gallows, n. potence f.

gallstone, n. calcul biliaire m.

galore, adv. à foison, à profusion.

galosh, n. galoche f.

galvanize, vb. galvaniser.

gamble, 1. n. jeu (m.) de hasard. **2.** vb. jouer.

gambler, n. joueur m.

gambling, n. jeu m.

gambol, 1. n. gambade f. **2.** vb. gamboler.

game, n. jeu m.; (hunting) gibier m.

gamely, adv. courageusement, crânement.

gameness, n. courage m., crânerie f.

gamin, n. gamin m.

gamut, n. gamme f.

gamy, adj. giboyeux.

gander, n. jars m.

gang, n. bande f.; (workers) équipe f.

gangling, adj. dégingandé.

gangplank, n. passerelle f.

gangrene, n. gangrène f.

gangrenous, adj. gangreneux.

gangster, n. gangster m.

gangway, n. passage m., passavant m.

gap, n. (opening) ouverture f.; (empty space) vide m.

gape, vb. rester bouche bée.

garage, n. garage m.

garb, 1. n. vêtement m., costume m. **2.** vb. vêtir, habiller.

garbage, n. ordures f.pl.

garble, vb. tronquer, altérer.

garden, n. jardin m.

gardener, n. jardinier m.

gardenia, n. gardénia m.

gargle, 1. n. gargarisme f. **2.** vb. se gargariser.

gargoyle, n. gargouille f.

garish, adj. voyant.

garland, n. guirlande f.

garlic, n. ail m.

garment, n. vêtement m.

garner, vb. mettre en grenier.

garnet, n. grenat m.

garnish, vb. garnir.

garnishee, n. tiers-saisi m.

garnishment, n. saisie-arrêt f.

garret, n. mansarde f.

garrison, n. garnison f.

garrote, 1. n. garrotte f. **2.** vb. garrotter.

garrulous, adj. bavard, loquace.

garter, n. jarretière f.

gas, n. gaz m.

gaseous, adj. gazeux.

gash, 1. n. coupure f., entaille f. **2.** vb. couper, entailler.

gasket, n. garcette f.

gasless, adj. sans gaz.

gas mask, n. masque à gaz m.

gasohol, n. essence (f.) fabriquée avec de l'alcool.

gasoline, n. essence f.

gasp, vb. (astonishment) sursauter; (lack of breath) haleter.

gassy, adj. gazeux, bavard.

gastric, adj. gastrique.

gastric juice, n. suc gastrique m.

gastritis, n. gastrite f.

gastronomically, adv. d'une manière gastronomique.

gastronomy, n. gastronomie f.

gate, n. (city) porte f.; (with bars) barrière f.; (wrought-iron) grille f.

gateway, n. porte f., entrée f.

gather, vb. rassembler, tr.; recueillir, tr.

gathering, n. rassemblement m.

gaudily, adv. de manière voyante.

gaudiness, n. éclat criard m., ostentation f.

gaudy, adj. voyant.

gaunt, adj. décharné.

gauntlet, n. gantelet m.

gauze, n. gaze f.

gavel, n. marteau m.

gavotte, n. gavotte f.

gawky, adj. dégingandé.

gay, 1. adj. gai. **2.** homosexuel n. **3.** pédé(raste) m.

gaze, vb. regarder fixement.

gazelle, n. gazelle f.

gazette, n. gazette f.

gazetteer, n. gazetier m., répertoire géographique m.

gear, n. (implements, device) appareil m.; (machines) engrenage m.; (in g.) engrené; (g. change) changement (m.) de vitesse.

gearing, n. engrenage m.

gearshift, n. changement de vitesse m.

gelatin, n. gélatine f.

gelatinous, adj. gélatineux.

geld, vb. châtrer.

gelding, n. animal châtré m.

gem, n. pierre (f.) précieuse.

gender, n. genre m.

gene, n. déterminant d'hérédité m.

genealogical, adj. généalogique.

genealogy, n. généalogie f.

general, adj. and n. général m.

generality, n. généralité f.

generalization, n. généralisation f.

generalize, vb. généraliser.

generally, adv. généralement.

generalship, n. stratégie f.

generate, vb. engendrer, générer.

generation, n. génération f.

generic, adj. générique.

generosity, n. générosité f.

generous, adj. généreux.

generously, adv. généreusement.

genetic, adj. génétique.

genetics, n. génétique f.

genial, adj. sympathique.

geniality, n. jovialité f., bienveillance f.

genially, adv. affablement.

genital, adj. génital.

genitals, n. organes génitaux m.pl.

genitive, n. and adj. génitif m.

genius, n. génie m.

genocide, n. génocide m.

genre, n. genre m.

genteel, adj. de bon ton.

gentian, n. gentiane f.

gentile, n. gentil m.

gentility, n. prétention à la distinction f.

gentle, adj. doux m., douce f.

gentleman, n. monsieur m. pl. messieurs; (character) galant homme m.

gentlemanly, adj. comme il faut, bien élevé.

gentlemen's agreement, n. convention verbale f.

gentleness, n. douceur f.

gently, adv. doucement.

gentry, n. petite noblesse f.

genuflect, vb. faire des génuflexions.

genuine, adj. véritable.

genuinely, adv. véritablement.

genuineness, n. authenticité f.

genus, n. genre m.

geographer, n. géographe m.

geographical, adj. géographique.

geography, n. géographie f.

geometric, adj. géométrique.

geometry, n. géométrie f.

geopolitics, n. géopolitique f.

geranium, n. géranium m.

germ, n. germe m.

German, 1. n. (person) Allemand m.; (language) allemand m. **2.** adj. allemand.

germane, adj. approprié.

Germanic, adj. allemand, germanique.

German measles, n. rougeole bénigne f.

Germany, n. Allemagne f.

germicide, n. microbicide m.

germinal, adj. germinal.

germinate, vb. germer.

gestate, vb. enfanter.

gestation, n. gestation f.

gesticulate, vb. gesticuler.

gesticulation, n. gesticulation f.

gesture, n. geste m.

get, vb. (obtain) obtenir; (receive) recevoir; (take) prendre; (become) devenir; (arrive) arriver; (g. in) entrer; (g. off) descendre; (g. on, agree) s'entendre; (g. on, go up) monter; (g. out) sortir; (g. up) se lever.

getaway, n. fuite f.

geyser, n. geyser m.

ghastly, adj. horrible.

ghost, n. (specter) revenant m.; (Holy G.) Saint-Esprit m.

ghost writer, n. collaborateur anonyme m., nègre m.

ghoul, n. goule f., vampire m.

giant, n. géant m.

gibberish, n. baragouin m.

gibbon, n. gibbon m.

gibe, 1. n. raillerie f. **2.** vb. railler.

giblet, n. abatis (de volaille) m.

giddy, adj. étourdi.

gift, n. don m.; (present) cadeau m.

gifted, adj. doué.

gigantic, adj. géant, gigantesque.

giggle, vb. rire nerveusement, glousser.

gigolo, n. gigolo m.

gild, vb. dorer.

gill, n. ouïes (of fish) f.pl.

gilt, 1. n. dorure f. **2.** adj. doré.

gilt-edged, adj. doré sur tranche.

gimcrack, 1. n. camelote f. **2.** adj. de camelote.

gimlet, n. vrille f.

gin, n. genièvre m.

ginger, n. gingembre m.

ginger ale, n. boisson gazeuse au gingembre f.

gingerly, adv. avec précaution.

gingersnap, n. biscuit au gingembre m.

gingham, n. guingan m.

giraffe, n. girafe f.

gird, vb. ceindre.

girder, n. support m.

girdle, n. gaine f.

girl, n. jeune fille f.

girlish, adj. de jeune fille.

girth, n. sangle f., circonférence f., corpulence f.

gist, n. fond m., essence f.

give, vb. donner; (g. back) rendre; (g. in) céder; (g. out) distribuer; (g. up) renoncer à.

give-and-take, adv. donnant donnant.

given, adj. donné.

given name, n. nom de baptême m.

giver, n. donneur m.

gizzard, n. gésier m.

glacé, adj. glacé.

glacial, adj. glaciaire.

glacier, n. glacier m.

glad, adj. heureux.

gladden, vb. réjouir.

glade, n. clairière f., éclaircie f.

gladiolus, n. glaïeul m.

gladly, adv. volontiers.

gladness, n. joie f.

Gladstone bag, n. sac américain m.

glamour, n. éclat m.

glance, n. coup (m.) d'œil.

gland, n. glande f.

glandular, adj. glandulaire.

glare, 1. n. (light) clarté f.; (stare) regard (m.) enflammé. **2.** vb. (shine) briller; (look) jeter des regards enflammés.

glaring, adj. éclatant, flagrant, voyant, manifeste.

glass, n. verre m.

glass-blowing, n. soufflage m.

glasses, n. lunettes f.pl.

glassful, n. verre m., verrée f.

glassware, n. verrerie f.

glassy, adj. vitreux.

glaucoma, n. glaucome m.

glaze, 1. n. lustre m. **2.** vb. vitrer.

glazier, n. vitrier m.

gleam, 1. n. lueur f. **2.** vb. luire.

glee, n. allégresse f.

glee club, n. chœur d'hommes m.

gleeful, adj. joyeux, allègre.

glen, n. vallon m., ravin m.

glib, adj. spécieux.

glide, vb. glisser; (plane) planer.

glider, n. planeur m.

glimmer, 1. n. faible lueur f. **2.** vb. jeter une faible lueur.

glimmering, adj. faible, vacillant.

glimpse, vb. entrevoir.

glint, 1. n. éclair m., reflet m. **2.** vb. entreluire, étinceler.

glitter, vb. étinceler.

gloat, vb. se régaler de.

global, adj. global.

globe, n. globe m.

globetrotter, n. globe trotter m.

globular, adj. globulaire, globuleux.

globule, n. globule f.

glockenspiel, n. glockenspiel m.

gloom, n. (darkness) ténèbres f.pl.; (sadness) tristesse f.

gloomy, adj. sombre.

glorification, n. glorification f.

glorify, vb. glorifier.

glorious, adj. glorieux; (weather) radieux.

glory, n. gloire f.

gloss, 1. n. lustre m., vernis m. **2.** vb. lustrer, glacer.

glossary, n. glossaire m.

glossy, adj. lustré, glacé.

glove, n. gant m.

glow, n. (light) lumière f.; (heat) chaleur f.

glowing, adj. embrasé, rayonnant.

glowingly, adv. en termes chaleureux.

glowworm, n. ver luisant m.

glucose, n. glucose f.

glue, 1. n. colle (f.) forte. **2.** vb. coller.

glum, adj. maussade.

glumness, n. air maussade m., tristesse f.

glut, 1. n. assouvissement m., excès m., pléthore f. **2.** vb. assouvir, rassasier, gorger.

glutinous, adj. glutineux.

glutton, n. gourmand m.

gluttonous, adj. gourmand, goulu.

glycerin, n. glycérine f.

gnarl, n. loupe f., nœud m.

gnash, vb. grincer.

gnat, n. moucheron m.

gnaw, vb. ronger.

gnu, n. gnou m.

go, vb. aller; (g. away) s'en aller; (g. back) retourner; (g. by) passer; (g. down) descendre; (g. in) entrer; (g. on) continuer; (g. out) sortir; (g. up) monter; (g. without) se passer de.

goad, 1. n. aiguillon m. **2.** vb. aiguillonner, piquer.

goal, n. but m.

goat, n. chèvre f.

goatee, n. barbiche f.

goatherd, n. chevrier m.

goatskin, n. peau de chèvre f.

gobble, vb. avaler goulûment, dévorer.

gobbler, n. avaleur m.; dindon m.

go-between, n. intermédiaire m.

goblet, n. gobelet m.

goblin, n. gobelin m., lutin m.

God, n. Dieu m.

godchild, n. filleul m.

goddess, n. déesse f.

godfather, n. parrain m.

godless, adj. athée, impie, sans Dieu.

godlike, adj. comme un dieu, divin.

godly, adj. dévot, pieux, saint.

godmother, n. marraine f.

godsend, n. aubaine f., bienfait du ciel m.

Godspeed, interj. bon voyage!

go-getter, n. homme d'affaires énergique m., arriviste m.

goiter, n. goitre m.

gold, n. or m.

gold brick, n. attrape-niais m.

golden, adj. d'or.

goldenrod, n. solidage m.

golden rule, n. règle par excellence f.

gold-filled, adj. aurifié, en (or) doublé.

goldfinch, n. chardonneret m.

goldfish, n. poisson rouge m.

gold leaf, n. feuille d'or f., or battu m.

goldsmith, n. orfèvre m.

gold standard, n. étalon or m.

golf, n. golf m.

gondola, n. gondole f.

gondolier, n. gondolier m.

gone, adj. disparu, parti.

gong, n. gong m.

gonorrhea, n. gonorrhée f., blennorrhagie f.

good, adj. bon m., bonne f.

good, n. bien m.; (goods) marchandises f.pl.

good-bye, n. and interj. adieu m.

Good Friday, n. Vendredi Saint m.

good-hearted, adj. qui a un bon cœur, compatissant.

good-humored, adj. de bonne humeur, plein de bonhomie.

good-looking, adj. beau, joli.

good-natured, adj. au bon naturel, accommodant.

goodness, n. bonté f.

good will, n. bonne volonté f.

goose, n. oie f.

gooseberry, n. groseille verte f.

gooseneck, n. col de cygne m.

goose step, n. pas d'oie m.

gore, 1. n. (dress) chanteau m., soufflet m.; (blood) sang coagulé m. 2. vb. corner.

gorge, n. gorge f.

gorgeous, adj. splendide.

gorilla, n. gorille m.

gory, adj. sanglant, ensanglanté.

gosling, n. oison m.

gospel, n. évangile m.

gossamer, n. filandre f., gaze légère f.

gossip, 1. n. bavardage m. 2. vb. bavarder.

Gothic, adj. gothique.

gouge, 1. n. gouge f. 2. vb. gouger.

gourd, n. gourde f., courge f.

gourmand, n. gourmand m.

gourmet, n. gourmet m.

govern, vb. gouverner.

governess, n. gouvernante f.

government, n. gouvernement m.

governmental, adj. gouvernemental.

governor, n. gouvernant m.

governorship, n. fonctions de gouverneur f.pl., temps de gouvernement m.

gown, n. robe f.

grab, vb. saisir.

grace, n. grâce f.

graceful, adj. gracieux.

gracefully, adv. avec grâce.

graceless, adj. sans grâce, gauche.

gracious, adj. gracieux; (merciful) miséricordieux.

grackle, n. mainate m.

grade, 1. n. grade m.; (quality) qualité f.; 2. vb. classer.

grade crossing, n. passage à niveau m.

gradual, adj. graduel.

gradually, adv. graduellement.

graduate, vb. graduer; (school) prendre ses grades.

graft, n. corruption f.

grail, n. graal m.

grain, n. grain m.

gram, n. gramme m.

grammar, n. grammaire f.

grammarian, n. grammairien m.

grammar school, n. école primaire f.

grammatical, adj. grammatical.

gramophone, n. phonographe.

granary, n. grenier m.

grand, adj. grandiose; (in titles) grand; (fine, colloq.) épatant.

grandchild, n. petit-fils m.; petite-fille f.; petits-enfants m.pl.

granddaughter, n. petite-fille f.

grandee, n. grand m.

grandeur, n. grandeur f.

grandfather, n. grand-père m.

grandiloquent, adj. grandiloquent.

grandiose, adj. grandiose.

grand jury, n. jury d'accusation m.

grandly, adv. grandement, magnifiquement.

grandmother, n. grand'mère f.

grand opera, n. grand opéra m.

grandson, n. petit-fils m.

grandstand, n. grande tribune f.

granger, n. régisseur m.

granite, n. granit m.

granny, n. bonne-maman f.

grant, 1. n. concession f.; (money) subvention f. 2. vb. accorder; (admit) admettre.

granular, adj. en grains, granulé.

granulate, vb. granuler, grener.

granulation, n. granulation f.

granule, n. granule m.

grape, n. raisin m.

grapefruit, n. pamplemousse f.

grapeshot, n. mitraille f.

grapevine, n. treille f.

graph, n. courbe f.

graphic, adj. graphique, pittoresque.

graphite, n. graphite m.

graphology, n. graphologie f.

grapple, 1. n. grappin m.; lutte f. 2. vb. accrocher; en venir aux prises.

grasp, 1. n. (hold) prise f. 2. vb. saisir.

grasping, adj. avide, cupide.

grass, n. herbe f.

grasshopper, n. sauterelle f.

grassy, adj. herbeux, verdoyant.

grate, 1. n. grille f. 2. vb. (cheese, etc.) râper; (make noise) grincer.

grateful, adj. reconnaissant.

gratify, vb. contenter, satisfaire.

grating, 1. n. grille f. 2. vb. grinçant, discordant.

gratis, adv. gratis, gratuitement.

gratitude, n. gratitude f.

gratuitous, adj. gratuit.

gratuity, n. (tip) pourboire m.

grave, 1. n. tombe f. 2. adj. grave.

gravel, n. gravier m.

gravely, adv. gravement, sérieusement.

gravestone, n. pierre sépulcrale f., tombe f.

graveyard, n. cimetière m.

gravitate, vb. graviter.

gravitation, n. gravitation f.

gravity, n. gravité f.

gravure, n. gravure f.

gravy, n. jus m.

gray, adj. gris.

grayish, adj. grisâtre.

gray matter, n. substance grise f., cendrée f.

graze, vb. paître.

grazing, n. pâturage m.

grease, 1. n. graisse f. 2. vb. graisser.

great, adj. grand.

Great Dane, n. grand Danois m.

greatness, n. grandeur f.

Greece, n. Grèce f.

greediness, n. gourmandise f.

greedy, adj. gourmand.

Greek, n. (person) Grec m., Grecque f.; (language) grec

m. 2. adj. grec m., grecque f.
green, adj. vert.
greenery, n. verdure f.
greenhouse, n. serre f.
greet, vb. saluer.
greeting, n. salutation f.; (reception) accueil m.
gregarious, adj. grégaire.
grenade, n. grenade f.
grenadine, n. grenadine f.
greyhound, n. lévrier m.
grid, n. gril m.
griddle, n. gril m.
gridiron, n. gril m.
grief, n. chagrin m.
grievance, n. grief m.
grieve, vb. affliger, tr.; chagriner, tr.
grievous, adj. douloureux.
grill, 1. n. gril m. 2. vb. griller.
grillroom, n. grill-room f.
grim, adj. sinistre.
grimace, n. grimace f.
grime, n. saleté f., noirceur f.
grimy, adj. sale, noirci, encrassé.
grin, n. large sourire m.
grind, vb. (crush) moudre; (sharpen) aiguiser.
grindstone, n. meule f.
gringo, n. Anglo-américain m.
grip, n. prise f.
gripe, vb. saisir, empoigner; grogner.
grisly, adj. hideux, horrible.
grist, n. blé à moudre m., mouture f.
gristle, n. cartilage m.
grit, n. grès m., sable m.; (fig.) cran f., courage m.
grizzled, adj. grison, grisonnant.
groan, 1. n. gémissement m. 2. vb. gémir.
grocer, n. épicier m.
grocery, n. épicerie f.
grog, n. grog m.
groggy, adj. gris, titubant.
groin, n. aine f.
groom, 1. n. (horses) palefrenier m.; (bridegroom) nouveau marié m. 2. vb. (horses) panser.
groove, n. rainure f.
grope, vb. tâtonner.
grosgrain, adj. de grosgrain.
gross, adj. (bulky) gros m., grosse f.; (coarse) grossier; (comm.) brut.
grossly, adv. grossièrement.
grossness, n. grossièreté f., énormité f.
grotesque, adj. and n. grotesque m.
grotto, n. grotte f.
grouch, 1. n. maussaderie f.; grogneur m. 2. vb. grogner.
ground, n. (earth) terre f.; (territory) terrain m.; (reason) raison f.; (background) fond m.
ground hog, n. marmotte d'Amérique f.
groundless, adj. sans fondement.

ground swell, n. houle f., lame de fond f.
groundwork, n. fondement m., fond m., base f.
group, 1. n. groupe m. 2. vb. grouper, tr.
groupie, n. groupie f.; membre d'un groupe de jeunes filles m.
grouse, 1. n. tétras m. 2. vb. grogner.
grove, n. bocage m., bosquet m.
grovel, vb. ramper, se vautrer.
grow, vb. croître; (persons) grandir; (become) devenir; (cultivate) cultiver.
growl, vb. grogner.
grown, adj. fait, grand.
grownup, adj. and n. grand m., adulte m.f.
growth, n. croissance f.; (increase) accroissement m.
grub, 1. n. larve f., ver blanc m.; (slang) nourriture f. 2. vb. défricher, fouiller.
grubby, adj. véreux, (fig.) sale.
grudge, n. rancune f.
gruel, n. gruau m.
gruesome, adj. lugubre, terrifiant.
gruff, adj. bourru.
grumble, vb. grommeler.
grumpy, adj. bourru, morose.
grunt, 1. n. grognement m. 2. vb. grogner.
guarantee, 1. n. garantie f. 2. vb. garantir.
guarantor, n. garant m.
guaranty, n. garantie f.
guard, 1. n. garde f. 2. vb. garder.
guarded, adj. prudent, circonspect, réservé.
guardhouse, n. corps de garde m., poste m.
guardian, n. gardien m.; (law) tuteur m.
guardianship, n. tutelle f.
guardsman, n. garde m.
guava, n. goyave f.
gubernatorial, adj. du gouverneur, du gouvernement.
guerrilla, n. guérilla f.
guess, 1. n. conjecture f. 2. vb. deviner.
guesswork, n. conjecture f.
guest, n. invité m.
guffaw, 1. n. gros rire m. 2. vb. s'esclaffer.
guidance, n. direction f.
guide, 1. n. guide m. 2. vb. guider.
guidebook, n. guide m.
guidepost, n. poteau indicateur m.
guild, n. corporation f., corps de métier m.
guile, n. astuce f., artifice m.
guillotine, n. guillotine f.
guilt, n. culpabilité f.
guiltily, adv. criminellement.
guiltless, adj. innocent.
guilty, adj. coupable.
guimpe, n. guimpe f.

guinea fowl, n. pintade f.
guinea pig, n. cobaye m.
guise, n. guise f., façon f.
guitar, n. guitare f.
gulch, n. ravin m.
gulf, n. (geog.) golfe m.; (fig.) gouffre m.
gull, n. mouette f.
gullet, n. gosier m.
gullible, adj. crédule, facile à duper.
gully, n. ravin m.
gulp, 1. n. goulée f., gorgée f., trait m. 2. vb. avaler, gober.
gum, n. gomme f.; (teeth) gencive f.
gumbo, n. gombo m.
gummy, adj. gommeux.
gun, n. (cannon) canon m.; (rifle) fusil m.
gunboat, n. canonnière f.
gunman, n. partisan armé m., voleur armé m., bandit m.
gunner, n. artilleur m.
gunpowder, n. poudre (f.) à canon.
gunshot, n. portée de fusil f.
gunwale, n. plat-bord m.
gurgle, vb. faire glouglou, gargouiller.
guru, n. gourou f.
gush, 1. n. jaillissement m. 2. vb. jaillir.
gusher, n. source jaillissante f., personne exubérante f.
gusset, n. gousset m., soufflet m.
gust, n. (wind) rafale f.
gustatory, adj. gustatif.
gusto, n. goût m., délectation f., verve f.
gusty, adv. venteux, orageux.
gut, 1. n. boyau m., intestin m. 2. vb. éventrer, vider.
gutter, n. (roof) gouttière f.; (street) ruisseau m.
guttural, adj. guttural.
guy, 1. n. type m., individu m. 2. vb. se moquer de.
guzzle, vb. ingurgiter, boire avidement.
gym, n. gymnase m.
gymnasium, n. gymnase m.
gymnast, n. gymnaste m.
gymnastic, adj. gymnastique.
gymnastics, n. gymnastique f.
gynecology, n. gynécologie f.
gypsum, n. gypse m.
gypsy, n. gitane m.f.
gyrate, vb. tournoyer.
gyroscope, n. gyroscope m.

H

habeas corpus, n. habeas corpus m.
haberdasher, n. chemisier m., mercier m.
haberdashery, n. chemiserie f., mercerie f.
habiliment, n. habillement m., apprêt m.
habit, n. habitude f.

habitable, *adj.* habitable.

habitat, *n.* habitat *m.*

habitation, *n.* habitation *f.*

habitual, *adj.* habituel.

habituate, *vb.* habituer, accoutumer.

habitué, *n.* habitué *m.*

hack, 1. *n.* (tool) pioche *f.*; (horse) cheval (*m.*) de louage; (vehicle) voiture (*f.*) de louage. 2. *vb.* (**h. up**) hacher; (notch) entailler.

hackneyed, *adj.* banal, rebattu.

hacksaw, *n.* scie à métaux *f.*

haddock, *n.* aigle fin *m.*

haft, *n.* manche *m.*, poignée *f.*

hag, *n.* vieille sorcière *f.*

haggard, *adj.* hagard.

haggle, *vb.* marchander.

hagridden, *adj.* tourmenté par le cauchemar.

hail, 1. *n.* grêle *f.* 2. *vb.* (weather) grêler; (salute) saluer; (come from) venir de. 3. *interj.* salut.

Hail Mary, *n.* Ave Maria *m.*

hailstone, *n.* grêlon *m.*

hailstorm, *n.* tempête de grêle *f.*

hair, *n.* cheveux *m.pl.*; (single, on head) cheveu *m.*; (on body, animals) poil *m.*

haircut, *n.* coupe (*f.*) de cheveux.

hairdo, *n.* coiffure *f.*

hairdresser, *n.* coiffeur *m.*

hairline, *n.* délié *m.*

hairpin, *n.* épingle (*f.*) à cheveux.

hair-raising, *adj.* horripilant, horrifique.

hair's-breadth, *n.* l'épaisseur d'un cheveu *f.*

hairspray, *n.* laque *f.*

hairy, *adj.* velu, poilu.

halcyon, 1. *n.* alcyon *m.* 2. *adj.* calme.

hale, *adj.* sain.

half, 1. *n.* moitié *f.* 2. *adj.* demi. 3. *adv.* à moitié.

half-and-half, *n.* moitié de l'un, moitié de l'autre *f.*

halfback, *n.* demi-arrière *m.*

half-baked, *adj.* à moitié cuit, inexpérimenté, incomplet.

half-breed, *n.* métis *m.*

half brother, *n.* frère de père *m.*, frère de mère *m.*

half dollar, *n.* demi-dollar *m.*

half-hearted, *adj.* sans enthousiasme.

half-mast, *adv.* à mi-mât.

halfpenny, *n.* petit sou *m.*

halfway, *adv.* à mi-chemin.

half-wit, *n.* niais *m.*, sot *m.*

halibut, *n.* flétan *m.*

hall, *n.* (large room) salle *f.*; (entrance) vestibule *m.*

hallmark, *n.* contrôle *m.*

hallow, *vb.* sanctifier.

Halloween, *n.* la veille de la Toussaint *f.*

hallucination, *n.* hallucination *f.*

hallway, *n.* corridor *m.*, vestibule *m.*

halo, *n.* auréole *f.*

halt, 1. *n.* halte *f.* 2. *vb.* arrêter, tr.

halter, *n.* licou *m.*, longe *f.*, corde *f.*

halve, *vb.* diviser en deux, partager en deux.

halyard, *n.* drisse *f.*

ham, *n.* jambon *m.*

hamlet, *n.* hameau *m.*

hammer, 1. *n.* marteau *m.* 2. *vb.* marteler.

hammock, *n.* hamac *m.*

hamper, 1. *n.* pannier *m.* 2. *vb.* embarrasser, gêner.

hamstring, *vb.* couper le jarret à, couper les moyens à.

hand, *n.* main *f.*

handball, *n.* balle *f.*

handbook, *n.* manuel *m.*

handcuff, 1. *n.* menotte *f.* 2. *vb.* mettre les menottes à.

handful, *n.* poignée *f.*

handicap, *n.* handicap *m.*, désavantage *m.*

handicraft, *n.* métier *m.*

handiwork, *n.* main-d'œuvre *f.*

handkerchief, *n.* mouchoir *m.*

handle, 1. *n.* manche *m.* 2. *vb.* manier.

handle bar, *n.* guidon *m.*

handmade, *adj.* fait à la main, fabriqué à la main.

handmaid, *n.* servante *f.*

hand organ, *n.* orgue portatif *m.*, orgue de Barbarie *m.*

handout, *n.* aumône *f.*; compte rendu communiqué à la presse *m.*

hand-pick, *vb.* trier à la main, éplucher à la main.

handsome, *adj.* beau *m.*, belle *f.*

hand-to-hand, *adj.* corps à corps.

handwriting, *n.* écriture *f.*

handy, *adj.* (person) adroit; (thing) commode; (at hand) sous la main.

handy man, *n.* homme à tout faire *m.*, bricoleur *m.*, factotum *m.*

hang, *vb.* pendre.

hangar, *n.* hangar *m.*

hangdog, *adj.* avec une mine patibulaire, avec un air en dessous.

hanger-on, *n.* dépendant *m.*, parasite *m.*

hang glider, *n.* glisseur duquel l'usager pend *m.*

hanging, 1. *n.* suspension *f.*, pendaison *f.* 2. *adj.* suspendu, pendant.

hangman, *n.* bourreau *m.*

hangnail, *n.* envie *f.*

hangout, *n.* repaire *m.*, nid *m.*

hang-over, *n.* reste *m.*, reliquat *m.*

hangup, *n.* difficulté psychologique *f.*

hank, *n.* écheveau *m.*, torchette *f.*

hanker, *vb.* désirer vivement, convoiter.

haphazard, *adv.* au hasard.

happen, *vb.* (take place) arriver; (chance to be) se trouver.

happening, *n.* évènement *m.*

happily, *adv.* heureusement.

happiness, *n.* bonheur *m.*

happy, *adj.* heureux.

happy-go-lucky, *adj.* sans souci, insouciant.

harakiri, *n.* hara-kiri *m.*

harangue, 1. *n.* harangue *f.* 2. *vb.* haranguer.

harass, *vb.* harceler, tracasser.

harbinger, *n.* avant-coureur *m.*, précurseur *m.*

harbor, *n.* (refuge) asile *m.*; (port) port *m.*

hard, 1. *adj.* dur; (difficult) difficile. 2. *adv.* fort.

hard-bitten, *adj.* tenace dur à cuire.

hard-boiled, *adj.* dur, tenace, boucané.

hard coal, *n.* anthracite *m.*

harden, *vb.* durcir.

hard-headed, *adj.* pratique, positif.

hard-hearted, *adj.* insensible, impitoyable, au cœur dur.

hardiness, *n.* robustesse *f.*, vigueur *f.*

hardly, *adv.* (in a hard manner) durement; (scarcely) à peine; (h. ever) presque jamais.

hardness, *n.* dureté *f.*; (difficulty) difficulté *f.*

hardship, *n.* privation *f.*

hardtack, *n.* galette *f.*, biscuit de mer *m.*

hardware, *n.* quincaillerie *f.*

hardwood, *n.* bois dur *m.*

hardy, *adj.* robuste.

hare, *n.* lièvre *m.*

harebrained, *adj.* écervelé, étourdi.

harelip, *n.* bec-de-lièvre *m.*

harem, *n.* harem *m.*

hark, 1. *vb.* prêter l'oreille à. 2. *interj.* écoutez!

Harlequin, *n.* Arlequin *m.*

harlot, *n.* prostituée *f.*, fille de joie *f.*

harm, 1. *n.* mal *m.* 2. *vb.* nuire à.

harmful, *adj.* nuisible.

harmless, *adj.* inoffensif.

harmonic, *adj.* harmonique.

harmonica, *n.* harmonica *m.*

harmonious, *adj.* harmonieux.

harmonize, *vb.* harmoniser.

harmony, *n.* harmonie *f.*

harness, 1. *n.* harnais *m.* 2. *vb.* harnacher.

harp, *n.* harpe *f.*

harpoon, 1. *n.* harpon *m.* 2. *vb.* harponner.

harridan, *n.* vieille sorcière *f.*, vieille mégère *f.*

harrow, *vb.* herser; (fig.) tourmenter.

harry, *vb.* harceler.

harsh, *adj.* rude.

harshness, n. rudesse f.

harvest, 1. n. moisson f. 2. vb. moissoner.

hash, 1. n. hachis m., émincé m. 2. vb. hacher (de la viande).

hashish, n. hachisch m.

hasn't, vb. n'a pas.

hassle, 1. vb. harceler. 2. n. harcèlement m.

hassock, n. agenouilloir m.

haste, n. hâte f.

hasten, vb. hâter, tr.

hastily, adv. à la hâte.

hasty, adj. précipité.

hat, n. chapeau m.

hatch, vb. (hen) couver; (egg) éclore.

hatchery, n. établissement de pisiculture m.

hatchet, n. hachette f.

hate, vb. haïr.

hateful, adj. odieux.

hatred, n. haine f.

haughtiness, n. arrogance f., hauteur f.

haughty, adj. hautain.

haul, vb. traîner.

haunch, n. hanche f., cuissot m.

haunt, vb. hanter.

have, vb. avoir; (h. to, necessity) devoir.

haven, n. havre m.; (refuge) asile m.

haven't, n. n'ont pas.

havoc, n. ravage m.

hawk, n. faucon m.

hawker, n. colporteur m., marchand ambulant m.

hawser, n. haussière f., amarre f.

hawthorn, n. aubépine f.

hay, n. foin m.

hay fever, n. fièvre des foins f.

hayfield, n. champs de foin m.

hayloft, n. fenil m., grenier m.

haystack, n. meule de foin f.

hazard, 1. n. hasard m. 2. vb. hasarder, risquer.

hazardous, adj. hasardeux.

haze, n. brume (f.) légère.

hazel, n. noisetier m.; couleur de noisette f.

hazy, adj. brumeux, nébuleux.

he, pron. il; (alone, stressed, with another subject) lui.

head, n. tête f.

headache, n. mal (m.) de tête.

headband, n. bandeau m.

headfirst, adv. la tête la première.

headgear, n. garniture de tête f., coiffure f.

head-hunting, n. chasse aux têtes f.

heading, n. rubrique f.

headlight, n. phare m., projecteur m.

headlong, adv. la tête la première.

headman, n. chef m.

headmaster, n. directeur m., principal m.

head-on, adj. and adv. de front.

headquarters, n. (mil.) quartier (m.) général; (comm.) bureau (m.) principal.

headstone, n. pierre angulaire f.

headstrong, adj. volontaire, têtu, entêté.

headwaters, n. cours supérieur (d'une rivière) m., eau d'amont f.

headway, n. progrès m.

headwork, n. travail de tête m., travail intellectuel m.

heady, adj. impétueux, capiteux.

heal, vb. guérir.

health, n. santé f.

healthful, adj. salubre.

healthy, adj. sain.

heap, 1. n. tas m. 2. vb. entasser.

hear, vb. entendre.

hearing, n. audition f.; ouïe f.

hearsay, n. ouï-dire m.

hearse, n. catafalque m., corbillard m.

heart, n. cœur m.

heartache, n. chagrin m., peine de cœur f.

heartbreak, n. déchirement de cœur m.

heartbroken, adj. avec le cœur brisé, navré.

heartburn, n. brûlures d'estomac f.pl., aigreur f.

heartfelt, adj. sincère, qui va au cœur.

hearth, n. foyer m., âtre m.

heartless, adj. sans cœur, insensible, sans pitié.

heart-rending, adj. à fendre le cœur, navrant, déchirant.

heartsick, adj. écœuré.

heart-stricken, adj. frappé au cœur, navré.

heart-to-heart, adj. à cœur ouvert, intime.

hearty, adj. cordial.

heat, 1. n. chaleur f. 2. vb. chauffer.

heated, adj. chaud, chauffé, animé.

heath, n. bruyère f., lande f.

heathen, adj. and n. païen m., païenne f.

heather, n. bruyère f., brande f.

heatstroke, n. coup de chaleur m.

heat wave, n. vague de chaleur f., onde calorifique f.

heave, vb. (lift) lever; (utter) pousser; (rise) se soulever, intr.

heaven, n. ciel m., pl. cieux.

heavenly, adj. céleste.

heavy, adj. lourd.

heavyweight, n. poids lourd m.

Hebrew, 1. n. (language) hébreu m. 2. adj. hébreu.

heckle, vb. poser des questions embarrassantes.

hectare, n. hectare m.

hectic, adj. (restless) agité.

hectograph, 1. n. hectographe m., autocopiste m. 2. vb. hectographier, autocopier.

hedge, n. haie f.

hedgehog, n. hérisson m.

hedgehop, vb. voler à ras de terre.

hedgerow, n. bordure de haies f.

hedonism, n. hédonisme m.

heed, 1. n. attention f. 2. vb. faire attention à.

heedless, adj. étourdi, imprudent, insouciant.

heel, n. talon m.

hefty, adj. fort, solide, costaud.

hegemony, n. hégémonie f.

heifer, n. génisse f.

height, n. hauteur f.

heighten, vb. rehausser, augmenter.

heinous, adj. odieux, atroce, abominable.

heir, n. héritier m.

heir apparent, n. héritier présomptif m.

heirloom, n. meuble m. (or bijou m.) de famille.

heir presumptive, n. héritier présomptif m.

helicopter, n. hélicoptère m.

heliocentric, adj. héliocentrique.

heliograph, n. héliographe m.

heliotrope, n. héliotrope m.

helium, n. hélium m.

hell, n. enfer m.

Hellenism, n. hellénisme m.

hellish, adj. infernal, diabolique.

hello, interj. (telephone) allô.

helm, n. barre (f.) du gouvernail.

helmet, n. casque m.

helmsman, n. homme de barre m., timonier m.

help, 1. n. aide f. 2. vb. aider; (at table) servir. 3. interj. au secours!

helper, n. aide m.f.

helpful, adj. (person) serviable; (thing) utile.

helpfulness, n. serviabilité f., utilité f.

helping, 1. n. portion f. 2. adj. secourable.

helpless, adj. (forlorn) délaissé; (powerless) impuissant.

helter-skelter, adv. pêle-mêle, en désordre.

hem, 1. n. ourlet m. 2. vb. ourler.

hematite, n. hématite f.

hemisphere, n. hémisphère m.

hemlock, n. ciguë f.

hemoglobin, n. hémoglobine f.

hemophilia, n. hémophilie f.

hemorrhage, n. hémorragie f.

hemorrhoid, n. hémorroïde f.

hemp, n. chanvre m.

hemstitch, 1. n. ourlet m. 2. vb. ourler.

hen, n. poule f.

hence, adv. (time, place) d'ici; (therefore) de là.

benceforth, adv. désormais.

henchman, n. homme de confiance m., acolyte m., satellite m.

henequen, n. henequen m.

henna, 1. n. henné m. 2. vb. teindre au henné.

henpeck, vb. mener par le bout du nez.

hepatic, adj. hépatique.

hepatica, n. hépatique f.

her, 1. adj. son m., sa f., ses pl. 2. pron. (direct) la; (indirect) lui; (alone, stressed, with prep.) elle.

herald, n. héraut m.

heraldic, adj. héraldique.

heraldry, n. l'héraldique f.

herb, n. herbe f.

herbaceous, adj. herbacé.

herbarium, n. herbier m.

herculean, adj. herculéen.

herd, n. troupeau m.

here, adv. ici; (h. is) voici.

hereabout, adv. par ici, près d'ici.

hereafter, adv. dorénavant.

hereby, adv. par ceci, par ce moyen, par là.

hereditary, adj. héréditaire.

heredity, n. hérédité f.

herein, adv. ici; (h. enclosed) ci-enclus.

heresy, n. hérésie f.

heretic, n. hérétique m.f.

heretical, adj. hérétique.

hereto, adv. ci-joint.

heretofore, adv. jusqu'ici.

herewith, adv. avec ceci, ci-joint.

heritage, n. héritage m., patrimoine m.

hermetic, adj. hermétique.

hermit, n. ermite m.

hermitage, n. ermitage m.

hernia, n. hernie f.

hero, n. héros m.

heroic, adj. héroïque.

heroically, adv. héroïquement.

heroin, n. héroïne f.

heroine, n. héroïne f.

heroism, n. héroïsme m.

heron, n. héron m.

herpes, n. herpès m.

herring, n. hareng m.

herringbone, n. arête de hareng f.

hers, pron. le sien m., la sienne f.

herself, pron. elle-même; (reflexive) se.

hertz, n. hertz m.

hesitancy, n. hésitation f., incertitude f.

hesitant, adj. hésitant, irrésolu.

hesitate, vb. hésiter.

hesitation, n. hésitation f.

heterodox, adj. hétérodoxe.

heterodoxy, n. hétérodoxie f.

heterogeneous, adj. hétérogène.

heterosexual, adj. hétérosexuel.

hew, vb. couper, tailler.

hexagon, n. hexagone m.

heyday, n. apogée m., beaux jours m.pl.

hiatus, n. lacune f.

hibernate, vb. hiberner, hiverner.

hibernation, n. hibernation f.

hibiscus, n. hibiscus m.

hiccup, 1. n. hoquet m. 2. vb. hoqueter.

hickory, n. noyer (blanc) d'Amérique m.

hide, vb. cacher, tr.

hide, n. peau f.

hideous, adj. hideux.

hide-out, n. cachette f., lieu de retraite m.

hierarchical, adj. hiérarchique.

hierarchy, n. hiérarchie f.

hieroglyphic, adj. hiéroglyphique.

high, adj. haut.

highbrow, n. intellectuel m.

high fidelity, n. haute fidélité f.

high-handed, adj. arbitraire, tyrannique.

high-hat, vb. traiter de haut en bas.

highland, n. haute terre f.

highlight, 1. n. clou m. 2. vb. mettre en relief.

highly, adv. extrêmement.

high-minded, adj. à l'esprit élevé, généreux.

Highness, n. (title) Altesse f.

high school, n. lycée m.

high seas, n. haute mer f.

high-strung, adj. nerveux, impressionable.

high tide, n. marée haute f.

highway, n. grande route f.

hijacker, n. pirate de l'air m.

hike, n. excursion (f.) à pied.

hilarious, adj. hilare.

hilariousness, n. hilarité f.

hilarity, n. hilarité f.

hill, n. colline f.

hilt, n. poignée f., garde f.

him, pron. (direct) le; (indirect) lui; (alone, stressed, with prep.) lui.

himself, pron. lui-même; (reflexive) se.

hinder, vb. (impede) gêner; (prevent) empêcher.

hindmost, adj. dernier.

hindquarter, n. arrière-main m., arrière-train m.

hindrance, n. empêchement m., obstacle m., entrave f.

Hindu, 1. n. Hindou m. 2. adj. hindou.

hinge, n. gond m.

hint, 1. n. allusion f. 2. vb. insinuer.

hinterland, n. hinterland m., arrière-pays m.

hip, n. hanche f.

hippodrome, n. hippodrome m.

hippopotamus, n. hippopotame m.

hire, vb. louer; (servant) engager.

hireling, n. mercenaire m., stipendié m.

his, 1. adj. son m., sa f., ses pl. 2. pron. le sien m., la sienne f.

Hispanic, adj. hispanique.

hiss, vb. siffler.

historian, n. historien m.

historic, adj. historique.

historical, adj. historique.

history, n. histoire f.

histrionic, adj. histrionique, théâtral.

histrionics, n. parade d'émotions f., démonstration peu sincère f.

hit, 1. n. coup m.; (success) succès m. 2. vb. frapper.

hitch, 1. n. (obstacle) anicroche f. 2. vb. (fasten) accrocher, tr.

hither, 1. adv. ici. 2. adj. le plus rapproché.

hitherto, adv. jusqu'ici.

hive, n. ruche f.

hives, n. éruption f., varicelle pustuleuse f., urticaire f.

hoard, 1. n. amas m. 2. vb. amasser; (money) thésauriser.

hoarse, adj. enroué.

hoax, n. mystification f.

hobble, vb. boitiller, clopiner, entraver.

hobbyhorse, n. dada m., cheval de bois m.

hobgoblin, n. lutin m., esprit follet m.

hobnail, 1. n. caboche f., clou à ferrer m. 2. vb. ferrer.

hobnob, vb. boire avec, fréquenter.

hobo, n. vagabond m., clochard m., ouvrier ambulant m.

hock, n. jarret m.

hockey, n. hockey m.

hocuspocus, n. passe-passe m.

hod, n. auge f.

hodgepodge, n. mélange confus m.

hoe, 1. n. houe f. 2. vb. houer.

hog, n. porc m.

hogshead, n. tonneau m., barrique f.

hog-tie, vb. lier les quatre pattes.

hoist, 1. n. treuil m., grue f. 2. vb. hisser.

hold, 1. n. prise f.; (ship) cale f. 2. vb. tenir; (contain) contenir; (h. back) retenir; (h. up) arrêter, détenir, entraver.

holdup, n. arrêt m., suspension f.; coup à main armée m.

hole, n. trou m.

holiday, n. jour (m.) de fête; fête f.; (h.s) vacances f.pl.

holiness, n. sainteté f.

Holland, n. les Pays-Bas m.pl., Hollande f.

hollow, adj. and n. creux m.

holly, n. houx m.

hollyhock, n. passe-rose f., rose-trémière f.

holocaust, n. holocauste m.

hologram, n. hologramme m.

holography, n. holographie f.

holster, n. étui m.

holy, adj. saint.

Holy See, n. Saint-Siège m.

Holy Spirit, n. Saint-Esprit m.

Holy Week, n. semaine sainte f.

homage, n. hommage m.

home, n. maison f.; (hearth) foyer (m.) domestique; (at h.) à la maison, chez soi.

homeland, n. patrie f.

homeless, adj. sans foyer, sans asile, sans abri.

homelike, adj. qui resemble au foyer domestique.

homely, adj. laid.

homemade, adj. fait à la maison.

home rule, n. autonomie f.

homesick, adj. nostalgique.

homespun, adj. (étoffe) de fabrication domestique, fait à la maison, simple.

homestead, n. ferme f., bien de famille m.

homeward, adj. de retour.

homework, n. travail fait à la maison m., devoirs m.pl.

homicide, n. homicide m.

homily, n. homélie f.

homing pigeon, n. pigeon messager m.

hominy, n. bouillie de farine de maïs f., semoule de maïs f.

homogeneous, adj. homogène.

homonym, n. homonyme m.

homosexual, n. and adj. homosexuel m.

Honduras, n. Honduras m.

hone, vb. aiguiser, affiler.

honest, adj. honnête.

honestly, adv. honnêtement, de bonne foi.

honesty, n. honnêteté f.

honey, n. miel m.

honeybee, n. abeille domestique f.

honeycomb, 1. n. rayon de miel m. 2. vb. cribler, affouiller.

honeydew melon, n. melon m.

honeymoon, n. lune (f.) de miel.

honeysuckle, n. chèvre-feuille m.

honor, 1. n. honneur m. 2. vb. honorer.

honorable, adj. honorable.

honorary, adj. honoraire.

hood, n. capuchon m.; (vehicle) capote f.

hoodlum, n. voyou m.

hoodwink, vb. tromper, bander les yeux à.

hoof, n. sabot m.

hook, 1. n. croc m.; (fishing) hameçon m. 2. vb. accrocher.

hooked, adj. crochu, recourbé.

hooked rug, n. tapis à points noués simples m.

hookworm, n. ankylostome m.

hoop, n. cercle m.

hoop skirt, n. jupe à paniers f., vertugadin m.

hoot, 1. n. ululation f., hulule-

---

ment m., huée f. 2. vb. hululer, huer.

hop, 1. n. (plant) houblon m. 2. vb. sautiller.

hope, 1. n. espérance f., espoir m. 2. vb. espérer.

hopeful, adj. plein d'espoir.

hopeless, adj. désespéré.

hopelessness, n. désespoir m., état désespéré m.

hopscotch, n. marelle f.

horde, n. horde f.

horizon, n. horizon m.

horizontal, adj. horizontal.

hormone, n. hormone f.

horn, n. corne f.; (music) cor m.

hornet, n. frelon m., guêpe-frelon f.

horny, adj. corné, calleux.

horoscope, n. horoscope m.

horrendous, adj. horrible, horripilant.

horrible, adj. horrible.

horrid, adj. affreux.

horrify, vb. horrifier.

horror, n. horreur f.

horse, n. cheval m.

horseback, n. (on h.) à cheval.

horsefly, n. taon m.

horsehair, n. crin m.

horseman, n. cavalier m.

horsemanship, n. équitation f., manège m.

horseplay, n. jeu de mains m., badinage grossière f.

horsepower, n. puissance en chevaux f.

horseradish, n. raifort m.

horseshoe, n. fer à cheval m.

horsewhip, 1. n. cravache f. 2. vb. cravacher, sangler.

hortatory, adj. exhortatif.

horticulture, n. horticulture f.

hose, n. (pipe) tuyau m.; (stockings) bas m.pl.

hosiery, n. bonneterie f.

hospitable, adj. hospitalier.

hospital, n. hôpital m.

hospitality, n. hospitalité f.

hospitalization, n. hospitalisation f.

hospitalize, vb. hospitaliser.

host, n. hôte m.

hostage, n. otage m.

hostel, n. hôtellerie f., auberge f.

hostelry, n. hôtellerie f., auberge f.

hostess, n. hôtesse f.

hostile, adj. hostile.

hostility, n. hostilité f.

hot, adj. chaud.

hotbed, n. couche f., foyer ardent m.

hot dog, n. saucisse chaude.

hotel, n. hôtel m.

hot-headed, adj. impétueux, exalté, emporté.

hothouse, n. serre f.

hound, 1. n. chien (m.) de chasse. 2. vb. poursuivre, pourchasser.

hour, n. heure f.

hourglass, n. sablier m.

---

hourly, adv. à chaque heure, à l'heure.

house, n. maison f.; (legislature) chambre f.

housefly, n. mouche domestique f.

household, n. (family) famille f.; (servants) domestiques m.pl.

housekeeper, n. gouvernante f.

housekeeping, n. ménage m., économie domestique f.

housemaid, n. fille de service f., bonne f., femme de chambre f.

housewife, n. ménagère f.

housework, n. ménage m.

hovel, n. taudis m., bicoque f.

hover, vb. planer.

hovercraft, n. aéroglisseur m.

how, adv. comment; (h. much) combien (de); (in exclamation) comme.

however, adv. (in whatever way) de quelque manière que; (with adj.) si . . . que; (nevertheless) cependant.

howitzer, n. obusier m.

howl, vb. hurler.

hub, n. moyeu m., centre m.

hubbub, n. vacarme m., tintamarre m.

huckleberry, n. airelle f.

huddle, 1. n. tas confus m., fouillis m. 2. vb. entasser.

hue, n. couleur f.

huff, 1. n. emportement m., accès de colère m. 2. vb. gonfler, enfler.

hug, 1. n. étreinte f. 2. vb. serrer dans ses bras.

huge, adj. énorme.

hulk, n. carcasse f., ponton m.

hull, n. coque f., corps m.

hullabaloo, n. vacarme m.

hum, vb. (insect) bourdonner; (sing) fredonner.

human, humane, adj. humain.

humanism, n. humanisme m.

humanitarian, adj. humanitaire.

humanities, n. humanités f.pl.

humanity, n. humanité f.

humanly, adv. humainement.

humble, adj. humble.

humbug, n. blague f., tromperie f., fumisterie f.

humdrum, adj. monotone, assommant.

humid, adj. humide.

humidify, vb. humidifier.

humidor, n. boîte à cigares f.

humiliate, adj. humilier.

humiliation, n. humiliation f.

humility, n. humilité f.

humor, n. (wit) humour m.; (medical, mood) humeur f.

humorous, adj. (witty) humoristique; (funny) drôle.

hump, n. bosse f.

humpback, n. bossu m.

humus, n. humus m., terreau m.

hunch, 1. n. bosse f.; pressentiment m. 2. vb. arrondir, voûter.

hunchback, n. bossu m.

hundred, adj. and n. cent m.

hundredth n. and adj. centième m.

Hungarian, 1. n. (person) Hongrois m.; (language) hongrois m. 2. adj. hongrois.

Hungary, n. Hongrie f.

hunger, n. faim f.

hungry, adj. affamé; (be h.) avoir faim.

hunk, n. gros morceau m.

hunt, vb. chasser.

hunter, n. chasseur m.

hunting, n. chasse f.

huntress, n. chasseuse f., chasseresse f.

hurdle, n. claie f.

hurl, vb. lancer.

hurricane, n. ouragan m.

hurry, 1. n. hâte f.; (in a h.) à la hâte. 2. vb. presser, tr.; se presser, intr.

hurt, vb. faire mal (à).

hurtful, adj. nuisible, pernicieux, préjudiciable.

hurtle, vb. se choquer, se heurter.

husband, n. mari m.

husbandry, n. agriculture f., économie f.

hush, 1. interj. chut! paix! 2. vb. taire, imposer silence à.

husk, 1. n. cosse f., gousse f. 2. vb. écosser, éplucher.

husky, adj. cossu; rauque, enroué.

hustle, vb. bousculer, se presser.

hut, n. cabane f.

hutch, n. huche f., clapier m.

hyacinth, n. jacinthe f.

hybrid, n. hybride m.

hydrangea, n. hortensia m.

hydrant, n. prise d'eau f., bouche d'incendie f.

hydraulic, adj. hydraulique.

hydrochloric acid, n. acide chlorhydrique m.

hydroelectric, adj. hydroélectrique.

hydrogen, n. hydrogène m.

hydrophobia, n. hydrophobie f.

hydroplane, n. hydroplane m.

hydrotherapy, n. hydrothérapie f.

hyena, n. hyène f.

hygiene, n. hygiène f.

hygienic, adj. hygiénique.

hymn, n. (song, anthem) hymne m.; (church) hymne f.

hymnal, n. hymnaire m., receuil d'hymnes m.

hyperacidity, n. hyperacidité f.

hyperbole, n. hyperbole f.

hypercritical, adj. hypercritique.

hypersensitive, adj. hypersensible.

hypertension, n. hypertension f.

hyphen, n. trait d'union m.

hyphenate, vb. mettre un trait d'union à.

hypnosis, n. hypnose f.

hypnotic, adj. hypnotique.

hypnotism, n. hypnotisme m.

hypnotize, vb. hypnotiser.

hypochondria, n. hypocondrie f.

hypochondriac, n. and adj. hypocondriaque m.

hypocrisy, n. hypocrisie f.

hypocrite, n. hypocrite m.f.

hypocritical, adj. hypocrite.

hypodermic, adj. hypodermique.

hypotenuse, n. hypoténuse f.

hypothesis, n. hypothèse f.

hypothetical, adj. hypothétique.

hysterectomy, n. hystérectomie f.

hysteria, n. hystérie f.

hysterical, adj. hystérique.

I

I, pron. je; (alone, stressed, with another subject) moi.

iambic, adj. iambique.

Iberia, n. Ibérie f.

ice, n. glace f.

iceberg, n. iceberg m., gros bloc de glace m.

ice-box, n. glacière f.

ice cream, n. glace f.

ice skate, 1. n. patin à glace m. 2. vb. patiner.

ichthyology, n. ichtyologie f.

icing, n. glacé m.

icon, n. icone f.

icy, adj. glacial.

idea, n. idée f.

ideal, adj. and n. idéal m.

idealism, n. idéalisme m.

idealist, n. idéaliste m.f.

idealistic, adj. idéaliste.

idealize, vb. idéaliser.

ideally, adv. idéalement, en idée.

identical (with), adj. identique (à).

identifiable, adj. identifiable.

identification, n. identification f.

identify, vb. identifier.

identity, n. identité f.

ideology, n. idéologie f.

idiocy, n. idiotie f., idiotisme m.

idiom, n. (language) idiome m.; (peculiar expression) idiotisme m.

idiot, adj. and n. idiot m.

idiotic, adj. idiot.

idle, adj. (unoccupied) désœuvré; (lazy) paresseux; (futile) vain.

idleness, n. oisiveté f.

idol, n. idole f.

idolatry, n. idolâtrie f.

idolize, vb. idolâtrer.

idyl, n. idylle f.

idyllic, adj. idyllique.

if, conj. si.

ignite, vb. allumer, mettre en feu.

ignition, n. ignition f., allumage m.

ignoble, adj. ignoble; (low birth) plébéien.

ignominious, adj. ignominieux.

ignoramus, n. ignorant m., ignare m.

ignorance, n. ignorance f.

ignorant, adj. ignorant; (be i. of) ignorer.

ignore, vb. feindre d'ignorer.

ill, 1. n. mal. 2. adj. (sick) malade; (bad) mauvais. 3. adv. mal.

illegal, adj. illégal.

illegible, adj. illisible.

illegibly, adv. illisiblement.

illegitimacy, n. illégitimité f.

illegitimate, adj. illégitime.

illicit, adj. illicite.

illiteracy, n. analphabétisme m.

illiterate, adj. illettré.

illness, n. maladie f.

illogical, adj. illogique.

illuminate, vb. illuminer.

illumination, n. illumination f., enluminure f.

illusion, n. illusion f.

illusive, adj. illusoire.

illustrate, vb. illustrer.

illustration, n. illustration f.; (example) exemple m.

illustrative, adj. explicatif, qui éclaircit.

illustrious, adj. illustre.

ill will, adj. mauvais vouloir m., malveillance f.

image, n. image f.

imagery, n. images f.pl, langage figuré m.

imaginable, adj. imaginable.

imaginary, adj. imaginaire.

imagination, n. imagination f.

imaginative, adj. imaginatif.

imagine, vb. imaginer, tr.

imam, n. imam m.

imbecile, n. imbécile m.

imitate, vb. imiter.

imitation, n. imitation f.

imitative, adj. imitatif.

immaculate, adj. immaculé, sans tache.

immanent, adj. immanent.

immaterial, adj. immatériel, incorporel, sans conséquence.

immature, adj. pas mûr, prématuré.

immediate, adj. immédiat.

immediately, adv. immédiatement, tout de suite.

immense, adj. immense.

immerse, vb. immerger, plonger.

immigrant, n. immigrant m., immigré m.

immigrate, vb. immigrer.

imminent, adj. imminent.

immobile, adj. fixe, immobile.

immobilize, vb. immobiliser.

immoderate, adj. immodéré, intempéré, outré.

immodest, adj. immodeste, impudique, présomptueux.
immoral, adj. immoral.
immorality, n. immoralité f.
immorally, adv. immoralement.
immortal, adj. and n. immortel m.
immortality, n. immortalité f.
immortalize, vb. immortaliser.
immovable, adj. fixe, immuable, inébranlable.
immunity, n. exemption f., immunité f.
immunize, vb. immuniser.
immutable, adj. immuable, inaltérable.
impact, n. choc m., impact m.
impair, vb. affaiblir, altérer, compromettre.
impale, vb. empaler.
impart, vb. donner, communiquer, transmettre.
impartial, adj. impartial.
impatience, n. impatience f.
impatient, adj. impatient.
impeach, vb. attaquer, accuser, récuser.
impede, vb. entraver, empêcher.
impediment, n. entrave f., obstacle m., empêchement f.
impel, vb. pousser, forcer.
impenetrable, adj. impénétrable.
impenitent, adj. impénitent.
imperative, 1. n. (gramm.) impératif m. 2. adj. impératif (gramm.); urgent, impérieux.
imperceptible, adj. imperceptible.
imperfect, adj. and n. imparfait m.
imperfection, n. imperfection f.
imperial, adj. impérial.
imperialism, n. impérialisme m.
imperil, vb. mettre en péril, exposer au danger.
imperious, adj. impérieux, arrogant.
impersonate, vb. personnifier, représenter.
impersonation, n. personnification f., incarnation f.
impersonator, n. personnificateur m.
impertinence, n. impertinence f.
impervious, adj. impénétrable, imperméable.
impetuous, adj. impétueux.
impetus, n. élan m., vitesse acquise f.
impinge, vb. se heurter à, empiéter sur.
implacable, adj. implacable.
implant, vb. inculquer, implanter.
implement, n. outil m.
implicate, vb. impliquer, entremêler.
implication, n. implication f.
implicit, adj. implicite.
implied, adj. implicite, tacite.

implore, vb. implorer.
imply, vb. impliquer.
impolite, adj. impoli.
imponderable, adj. impondérable.
import, 1. n. article (m.) d'importation; importation f. 2. vb. importer.
importance, n. importance f.
important, adj. important.
importation, n. importation f.
importune, vb. importuner.
impose (on), vb. imposer (à).
imposition, n. imposition f.
impossibility, n. impossibilité f.
impossible, adj. impossible.
impotence, n. impuissance f.
impotent, adj. impuissant.
impoverish, vb. appauvrir.
impregnable, adj. imprenable, inexpugnable.
impregnate, vb. imprégner, féconder.
impresario, n. imprésario m.
impress, vb. (imprint) imprimer; (affect) faire une impression à.
impression, n. impression f.
impressive, adj. impressionnant.
imprison, vb. emprisonner.
imprisonment, n. emprisonnement m.
improbable, adj. improbable.
impromptu, adv., adj. and n. impromptu m.
improper, adj. (inaccurate) impropre; (unbecoming) malséant.
improve, vb. améliorer, tr.
improvement, n. amélioration f.
improvise, vb. improviser.
impudent, adj. insolent, effronté, impertinent.
impugn, vb. attaquer, contester, impugner.
impulse, n. impulsion f.
impulsion, n. impulsion f.
impulsive, adj. impulsif.
impunity, n. impunité f.
impure, adj. impur.
impurity, n. impureté f.
impute, vb. imputer.
in, prep. en; (with art. or adj.) dans; (town) à.
inadvertent, adj. inattentif, négligent, involontaire.
inalienable, adj. inaliénable.
inane, adj. inepte, niais, bête.
inaugural, adj. inaugural.
inaugurate, vb. inaugurer.
inauguration, n. inauguration f.
Inca, n. Inca m.
incandescence, n. incandescence f.
incandescent, adj. incandescent.
incantation, n. incantation f., conjuration f.
incapacitate, vb. rendre incapable, priver de capacité légale.

incarcerate, vb. incarcérer, emprisonner.
incarnate, 1. vb. incarner. 2. adj. incarné, fait chair.
incarnation, n. incarnation f.
incendiary, 1. n. incendiaire m. 2. adj. incendiaire, séditieux.
incense, n. encens m.
incentive, n. stimulant m., aiguillon m.
inception, n. commencement m., début m.
incessant, adj. incessant, continuel.
incest, n. inceste m.
inch, n. pouce m.
incidence, n. incidence f.
incident, n. incident m.
incidental, adj. fortuit.
incidentally, adv. incidemment, en passant.
incinerator, n. incinérateur m.
incipient, adj. naissant, qui commence.
incision, n. incision f., entaille f.
incisive, adj. incisif, tranchant.
incisor, n. incisive f.
incite, vb. inciter, instiguer.
inclination, n. inclinaison f., penchant m.
incline, vb. incliner.
inclose, see enclose.
include, vb. comprendre.
inclusive, adj. inclusif.
incognito, adj. and adv. incognito.
income, n. revenu m.
incomparable, adj. incomparable.
inconvenience, 1. n. inconvénient m. 2. vb. incommoder.
inconvenient, adj. incommode.
incorporate, vb. incorporer.
incorrigible, adj. incorrigible.
increase, 1. n. augmentation f. 2. vb. augmenter.
incredible, adj. incroyable.
incredulity, n. incrédulité f.
incredulous, adj. incrédule.
increment, n. augmentation m., accroissement m.
incriminate, vb. incriminer.
incrimination, n. incrimination f.
incrust, vb. incruster.
incubator, n. incubateur m.
inculcate, vb. inculquer.
incumbency, n. période d'exercice f., charge f.
incumbent, 1. n. titulaire m., bénéficiaire m. 2. adj. couché, posé, appuyé.
incur, vb. encourir.
incurable, adj. incurable.
indebted, adj. endetté.
indeed, adv. en effet.
indefatigable, adj. infatigable, inlassable.
indefinite, adj. indéfini.
indefinitely, adv. indéfiniment.
indelible, adj. indélébile, ineffaçable.
indemnify, vb. garantir, indemniser, dédommager.

indemnity, n. garantie f., indemnité f., dédommagment m.

indent, vb. denteler, découper, entailler.

indentation, n. découpage m., renfoncement m., endentement m.

independence, n. indépendance f.

independent, adj. indépendant.

in-depth, adj. profond.

index, n. index m.

India, n. Inde f.

Indian, 1. n. Indien m. 2. adj. indien.

indicate, vb. indiquer.

indication, n. indication f.

indicative, adj. and n. indicatif m.

indicator, n. indicateur m.

indict, vb. accuser, inculper.

indictment, n. accusation f., inculpation f., réquisitoire m.

indifference, n. indifférence f.

indifferent, adj. indifférent.

indigenous, adj. indigène.

indigent, adj. indigent, pauvre.

indigestion, n. dyspepsie f., indigestion f.

indignant, adj. indigné.

indignation, n. indignation f.

indignity, n. indignité f., affront m.

indirect, adj. indirect.

indiscreet, adj. indiscret.

indiscretion, n. imprudence f.

indiscriminate, adj. aveugle, qui ne fait pas de distinction.

indispensable, adj. indispensable.

indisposed, adj. peu enclin, peu disposé, indisposé, souffrant.

individual, 1. n. individu m. 2. adj. individuel.

individuality, n. individualité f.

individually, adv. individuellement.

indivisible, adj. indivisible.

indoctrinate, vb. endoctriner, instruire.

indolent, adj. indolent, paresseux.

Indonesia, n. Indonésie f.

indoor, adj. d'intérieur.

indoors, adv. à la maison.

indorse, vb. endosser, appuyer, sanctionner.

induce, vb. (persuade) persuader; (produce) produire.

induct, vb. installer, conduire.

induction, n. induction f.; installation f.

inductive, adj. inductif.

indulge, vb. contenter, favoriser.

indulgence, n. indulgence f.

indulgent, adj. indulgent.

industrial, adj. industriel.

industrialist, n. industriel m.

industrious, adj. travailleur.

industry, n. industrie f.; (diligence) assiduité f.

ineligible, adj. inéligible.

inept, adj. inepte, mal à propos.

inert, adj. inerte, apathique.

inertia, n. inertie f.

inevitable, adj. inévitable.

inexplicable, adj. inexplicable.

infallible, adj. infaillible.

infamous, adj. infâme.

infamy, n. infamie f.

infancy, n. (première) enfance f.

infant, n. enfant m.f.

infantile, adj. enfantin, infantile.

infantryman, n. soldat d'infanterie m., fantassin m.

infatuated, adj. infatué, entiché.

infect, vb. infecter.

infection, n. infection f.

infectious, adj. infectieux, infect, contagieux.

infer, vb. déduire.

inference, n. inférence f.

inferior, adj. and n. inférieur m.

inferiority complex, n. complexe d'infériorité m.

infernal, adj. infernal.

inferno, n. enfer m.

infest, vb. infester.

infidel, n. infidèle m., incroyant m.

infidelity, n. infidélité f.

infiltrate, vb. infiltrer.

infinite, adj. and n. infini m.

infinitesimal, adj. infinitésimal.

infinitive, n. infinitif m.

infinity, n. infinité f.

infirm, adj. infirme, faible, maladif.

infirmary, n. infirmerie f.

infirmity, n. infirmité f.

inflame, vb. enflammer, tr.

inflammable, adj. inflammable.

inflammation, n. inflammation f.

inflammatory, adj. incendiaire, inflammatoire.

inflate, vb. gonfler.

inflation, n. (currency) inflation f.

inflection, n. inflection f.

inflict, vb. (penalty) infliger.

infliction, n. infliction f., châtiment m.

influence, n. influence f.

influential, adj. influent.

influenza, n. grippe f., influenza f.

inform, vb. (tell) informer.

informal, adj. (without formality) sans cérémonie.

information, n. renseignements m.pl.

infringe, vb. enfreindre, violer.

infuriate, vb. rendre furieux.

ingenious, adj. ingénieux.

ingenuity, n. ingéniosité f.

ingredient, n. ingrédient m.

inhabit, vb. habiter.

inhabitant, n. habitant m.

inhale, vb. inhaler, aspirer, humer.

inherent, adj. inhérent.

inherit, vb. hériter.

inheritance, n. héritage m.

inhibit, vb. empêcher; (psychology) inhiber.

inhibition, n. inhibition f., défense expresse f., prohibition f.

inhuman, adj. inhumain.

inimical, adj. ennemi, hostile, défavorable.

inimitable, adj. inimitable.

iniquity, n. iniquité f.

initial, 1. n. initiale f. 2. adj. initial.

initiate, vb. (begin) commencer; (admit) initier.

initiation, n. commencement m., début m., initiation f.

initiative, n. initiative f.

inject, vb. injecter.

injection, n. injection f.

injunction, n. injonction f., ordre m.

injure, vb. (harm) nuire à; (wound) blesser; (damage) abîmer.

injurious, adj. (harmful) nuisible; (offensive) injurieux.

injury, n. (person) préjudice m.; (body) blessure f.; (thing) dommage m.

injustice, n. injustice f.

ink, n. encre f.

inland, adj. and n. intérieur m.

inlet, n. entrée f., admission f., débouché m.

inmate, n. habitant m., hôte m., pensionnaire m.

inn, n. auberge f.

inner, adj. intérieur.

innocence, n. innocence f.

innocent, adj. innocent.

innocuous, adj. inoffensif.

innovation, n. innovation f.

innuendo, n. insinuation f., allusion malveillante f.

innumerable, adj. innombrable.

inoculate, vb. inoculer.

inoculation, n. inoculation f., vaccination préventive f.

input, n. informations fournies à un informateur f.pl.

inquest, n. enquête f.

inquire (about), vb. se renseigner (sur).

inquiry, n. (investigation) recherche f.; (question) demande f.; (official) enquête f.

inquisition, n. Inquisition f.; enquête f., recherche f.

inquisitive, adj. curieux, questionneur, indiscret.

inroad, n. incursion f., invasion f. empiètement m.

insane, adj. fou m., folle f.

insanity, n. folie f., insanité f., démence f.

inscribe, vb. inscrire, graver.

inscription, n. inscription f.

insect, n. insecte m.

insecticide, n. insecticide m.

inseparable, adj. inséparable.

insert, vb. insérer.

insertion, n. insertion f.

inside, 1. n. dedans m., 2. adj. intérieur. 3. prep. à l'intérieur de. 4. adv. (en) dedans.

insidious, adj. insidieux.

insight, n. perspicacité f., pénétration f.

insignia, n. insignes m.pl.

insignificance, n. insignifiance f.

insignificant, adj. insignifiant.

insinuate, vb. insinuer.

insinuation, n. insinuation f.

insipid, adj. insipide, fade.

insist, vb. insister.

insistence, n. insistance f.

insistent, adj. qui insiste, importun.

insolence, n. insolence f.

insolent, adj. insolent.

insomnia, n. insomnie f.

inspect, vb. examiner, inspecter.

inspection, n. inspection f.

inspector, n. inspecteur m.

inspiration, n. inspiration f.

inspire, vb. inspirer.

install, vb. installer.

installation, n. installation f., montage m.

installment, n. acompte m., versement partiel m., payement à compte m.

instance, n. exemple m.

instant, n. instant m.

instantaneous, adj. instantané.

instantly, adv. à l'instant.

instead, adv. au lieu de cela.

instead of, prep. au lieu de.

instigate, vb. instiguer.

instill, vb. instiller, faire pénétrer, inculquer.

instinct, n. instinct m.

instinctive, adj. instinctif.

institute, vb. instituer.

institution, n. institution f.

instruct, vb. instruire.

instruction, n. instruction f.

instructive, adj. instructif.

instructor, n. (mil.) instructeur m.; (university) chargé (m.) de cours.

instrument, n. instrument m.

instrumental, adj. instrumental, contributif (à).

insufferable, adj. insupportable, intolérable.

insufficient, adj. insuffisant.

insular, adj. insulaire.

insulate, vb. isoler.

insulation, n. isolement m.

insulator, n. isolant m., isolateur m.

insulin, n. insuline f.

insult, 1. vb. insulter. 2. n. insulte f.

insuperable, adj. insurmontable.

insurance, n. assurance f.

insure, vb. assurer.

insurgent, adj. and n. insurgé m.

insurrection, n. insurrection f., soulèvement m.

intact, adj. intact.

intangible, adj. intangible, impalpable.

integral, adj. intégrant.

integrate, vb. intégrer, compléter, rendre entier.

integrity, n. intégrité f.

intellect, n. (mind) esprit m.; (faculty) intellect m.

intellectual, adj. and n. intellectuel m.

intelligence, n. intelligence f.; (information) renseignements m.pl.

intelligent, adj. intelligent.

intelligentsia, n. l'intelligence f.

intelligible, adj. intelligible.

intend, vb. avoir l'intention de; (destine for) destiner à.

intense, adj. intense.

intensity, n. intensité f.

intensive, adj. intensif.

intent on, adj. (absorbed in) absorbé dans; (determined to) déterminé à.

intention, n. intention f.

intentional, adj. intentionnel, voulu, fait exprès.

intercede, vb. intervenir, intercéder.

intercept, vb. intercepter, capter.

intercourse, n. commerce m., relations f.pl., rapports m.pl

interdict, vb. interdire, prohiber.

interest, 1. n. intérêt m. 2. vb. intéresser.

interesting, adj. intéressant.

interface, n. entreface f.

interfere, vb. (person) intervenir (dans); (i. with, hinder) gêner.

interference, n. (person) intervention f.

interim, adv. entre temps, en attendant.

interior, adj. and n. intérieur m.

interject, vb. lancer, émettre.

interjection, n. interjection f.

interlude, n. intermède m., interlude m.

intermarry, vb. se marier.

intermediary, n. intermédiaire m.f.

intermediate, adj. and n. intermédiaire m.f.

interment, n. enterrement m.

intermission, n. interruption f., relâche f.; (theater) entr'acte m.

intermittent, adj. intermittent.

intern, 1. n. interne m. 2. vb. interner.

internal, adj. interne.

international, adj. international.

internationalism, n. internationalisme m.

interne, n. interne m.

interpose, vb. interposer, tr.

interpret, vb. interpréter.

interpretation, n. interprétation f.

interpreter, n. interprète m.f.

interrogate, vb. interroger, questionner.

interrogation, n. interrogation f.

interrogative, 1. adj. interrogateur. 2. n. interrogatif m.

interrupt, vb. interrompre.

interruption, n. interruption f.

intersect, vb. entrecouper, intersecter, entrecroiser.

intersection, n. intersection f.

intersperse, vb. entremêler, parsemer, intercaler.

interval, n. intervalle m.

intervene, vb. intervenir.

intervention, n. intervention f.

interview, n. entrevue f.; (press) interview m. or f.

intestine, n. intestin m.

intimacy, n. intimité f.

intimate, adj. intime.

intimidate, vb. intimider.

intimidation, n. intimidation f.

into, prep. en; (with art. or adj.) dans.

intonation, n. intonation f.

intone, vb. entonner, psalmodier.

intoxicate, vb. enivrer.

intoxication, n. intoxication f., ivresse f.

intravenous, adj. intraveineux.

intrepid, adj. intrépide, brave, courageux.

intricacy, n. complexité f., nature compliquée f.

intricate, adj. compliqué.

intrigue, n. intrigue f.

intrinsic, adj. intrinsèque.

introduce, vb. (bring in) introduire; (present) présenter.

introduction, n. introduction f.; (presenting) présentation f.

introductory, adj. introductoire, d'introduction.

introspection, n. introspection f., recueillement m.

introvert, n. introverti m.

intrude on, vb. importuner.

intruder, n. intrus m.

intuition, n. intuition f.

intuitive, adj. intuitif.

inundate, vb. inonder.

invade, vb. envahir.

invader, n. envahisseur m., transgresseur m.

invalid, adj. and n. infirme m.f.

invariable, adj. invariable.

invasion, n. invasion f.

invective, n. invective f.

inveigle, vb. attirer, séduire, leurrer.

invent, vb. inventer.

invention, n. invention f.

inventive, adj. inventif, trouveur.

inventor, n. inventeur m.

inventory, n. inventaire m.

invertebrate, 1. n. invertébré m. 2. adj. invertébré.

invest, vb. investir; (money) placer.

investigate, vb. faire des recherches (sur).

investigation, n. investigation f.

investment, n. placement m.

inveterate, adj. invétéré, enraciné.

invidious, adj. odieux, haïssable, ingrat.

invigorate, vb. fortifier, vivifier.

invincible, adj. invincible.

invisible, adj. invisible.

invitation, n. invitation f.

invite, vb. inviter.

invocation, n. invocation f.

invoice, n. facture f.

invoke, vb. invoquer.

involuntary, adj. involontaire.

involve, vb. (implicate) impliquer; (entail) entraîner.

invulnerable, adj. invulnérable.

inward, adj. intérieur.

iodine, n. iode m.

Iran, n. Iran m.

Iraq, n. Irak m.

irate, adj. en colère, courroucé, furieux.

Ireland, n. Irlande f.

iridium, n. iridium m.

iris, n. iris m.

Irish, adj. irlandais.

Irishman, n. Irlandais m.

irk, vb. ennuyer.

iron, n. fer m.

ironworks, n. fonderie de fonte f., usine métallurgique f.

irony, n. ironie f.

irrational, adj. irrationnel, déraisonnable, absurde.

irrefutable, adj. irréfutable, irrécusable.

irregular, adj. irrégulier.

irregularity, n. irrégularité f.

irrelevant, adj. non pertinent, hors de propos.

irresistible, adj. irrésistible.

irresponsible, adj. irresponsable.

irreverent, adj. irrévérent, irrévérencieux.

irrevocable, adj. irrévocable.

irrigate, vb. irriguer, arroser.

irrigation, n. irrigation f.

irritability, n. irritabilité f.

irritable, adj. irritable, irascible.

irritant, n. irritant m.

irritate, vb. irriter.

irritation, n. irritation f.

Islam, n. Islam m.

Islamic, adj. islamique.

island, n. île f.

isolate, vb. isoler.

isolation, n. isolement m.

isolationist, n. isolationniste m.

isosceles, adj. isocèle.

Israel, n. Israël m.

Israeli, n. Israéli m.

issuance, n. délivrance f.

issue, 1. n. (way out, end) issue f.; (result) résultat m.; (question) question f.; (money, bonds) émission f. 2. vb. (come out) sortir; (publish) publier; (money) émettre.

isthmus, n. isthme m.

it, pron. (subject) il m.; elle f.; (object) le m., la f.; (of it) en; (in it, to it) y.

Italian, 1. n. (person) Italien m.; (language) italien m. 2. adj. italien.

Italy, n. Italie f.

itch, 1. n. démangeaison f. 2. vb. démanger.

item, n. (article) article m.; (detail) détail m.

itemize, vb. détailler.

itinerant, adj. ambulant.

itinerary, n. itinéraire m.

its, 1. adj. son m., sa f., ses pl. 2. pron. le sien m., la sienne f.

itself, pron. lui-même m., elle-même f.; (reflexive) se.

ivory, n. ivoire m.

ivy, n. lierre m.

J

jab, n. coup m., coup sec m. 2. vb. piquer, donner un coup sec.

jackal, n. chacal m.

jackass, n. âne m.; idiot m.

jacket, n. (man) veston m.; (woman) jaquette f.

jackknife, n. couteau de poche m.

jack-of-all-trades, n. maître Jacques m., factotum m., homme à tous les métiers m.

jade, n. rosse f., haridelle f.; drôlesse f., coureuse f.; jade m.

jaded, adj. surmené, éreinté, blasé, fatigué.

jagged, adj. déchiqueté, entaillé, dentelé.

jaguar, n. jaguar m.

jail, n. prison f.

jailer, n. gardien m., geôlier m.

jam, 1. n. foule f., presse f., embouteillage m.; confiture f. 2. vb. serrer, presser.

jamb, n. jambage m., montant m., chambranle m.

jangle, 1. n. querelle f., chamaille f.; cliquetis m. 2. vb. se quereller, se chamailler; cliqueter.

janitor, n. concierge m.

January, n. janvier m.

Japan, n. Japon m.

Japanese, 1. n. (person) Japonais m.; (language) japonais m. 2. adj. japonais.

jar, 1. n. (container) pot m.; (sound) son m.) discordant; (shock) secousse f. 2. vb. secouer, heurter.

jargon, n. jargon m.

jasmine, n. jasmin m.

jaundice, n. jaunisse f.

jaunt, n. petite excursion f., balade f.

javelin, n. javelot m., javeline f.

jaw, n. mâchoire f.

jay, n. geai m.

jaywalk, vb. se promener d'une façon distraite ou imprudente.

jazz, n. jazz m.

jealous, adj. jaloux.

jealousy, n. jalousie f.

jeans, n. jeans m.pl.

jeer, 1. n. raillerie f.; moquerie f., huée f. 2. vb. se moquer de, huer.

jelly, n. gelée f.

jellyfish, n. méduse f.

jeopardize, vb. exposer au danger, mettre en danger, hasarder.

jeopardy, n. danger m., péril m.

jerk, n. saccade f.

jerkin, n. justaucorps m., pourpoint m.

jerky, adj. saccadé, coupé.

jersey, n. jersey m., tricot de laine m.

Jerusalem, n. Jérusalem m.

jest, 1. plaisanterie f., raillerie f., badinage m. 2. vb. plaisanter, railler, badiner.

jester, n. railleur m., farceur m., bouffon m.

Jesuit, n. jésuite m.

Jesus, n. Jésus m.

jet, n. (mineral) jais m.; (water, gas) jet m.; (j. plane) avion (m.) à réaction.

jet lag, n. désorientation physiologique produite par le décalage d'heures.

jetsam, n. épaves f.pl.

jettison, vb. se délester.

jetty, n. jetée f., môle m.

Jew, n. Juif m., Juive f.

jewel, n. bijou m.

jeweler, n. bijoutier m., jouaillier m.

jewelry, n. bijouterie f.

Jewish, adj. juif m., juive f.

jib, n. foc m.

jibe, vb. être en accord, s'accorder.

jiffy, n. instant m., clin d'oeil m.

jig, 1. n. gigue f.; calibre m., gabarit m. 2. danser la gigue, sautiller.

jilt, vb. délaisser, plaquer, planter.

jingle, 1. n. tintement m., cliquetis m. 2. vb. tinter, cliqueter.

jinx, n. porte-malheur m.

jittery, adj. très nerveux.

job, n. (work) travail m.; (employment) emploi m.

jobber, n. intermédiaire m., marchandeur m., sous-traitant m.

jockey, n. jockey m.

jocular, adj. facétieux, jovial, rieur.

jocund, adj. enjoué.

jodhpurs, n. pantalon d'équitation m.

jog, 1. n. coup m., secousse f., cahot m. 2. vb. pousser, secouer, cahoter.

joggle, 1. *n.* petite secousse *f.* **2.** *vb.* secouer légèrement.

join, *vb.* (things) joindre; (group, etc.) se joindre à.

joiner, *n.* menuisier *m.*

joint, 1. *n.* joint *m.* **2.** *adj.* (in common) commun; (in partnership) co-.

jointly, *adv.* ensemble, conjointement.

joist, *n.* solive *f.*, poutre *f.*

joke, 1. *n.* plaisanterie *f.* **2.** *vb.* plaisanter.

joker, *n.* farceur *m.*, blagueur *m.;* joker *m.*

jolly, *adj.* joyeux.

jolt, 1. *n.* cahot *m.*, choc *m.*, secousse *f.* **2.** *vb.* cahoter, secouer, ballotter.

jonquil, *n.* jonquille *f.*

jostle, *vb.* coudoyer *tr.*

jounce, 1. *n.* cahot *m.*, secousse *f.* **2.** *vb.* cahoter.

journal, *n.* journal *m.*

journalism, *n.* journalisme *m.*

journalist, *n.* journaliste *m.*

journey, 1. *n.* voyage *m.* **2.** *vb.* voyager.

journeyman, *n.* compagnon *m.*

jovial, *adj.* jovial, gai.

jowl, *n.* mâchoire *f.*

joy, *n.* joie *f.*

joyful, *adj.* joyeux.

joyous, *adj.* joyeux.

jubilant, *adj.* réjoui, jubilant, exultant.

jubilee, *n.* jubilé *m.*

Judaism, *n.* judaïsme *m.*

judge, 1. *n.* juge *m.* **2.** *vb.* juger.

judgment, *n.* jugement *m.*

judicial, *adj.* judiciaire.

judiciary, *adj.* judiciaire.

judicious, *adj.* judicieux, sensé.

jug, *n.* cruche *f.*

juggle, *vb.* jongler.

jugular, *adj.* jugulaire.

juice, *n.* jus *m.*

juicy, *adj.* juteux.

July, *n.* juillet *m.*

jumble, 1. *n.* brouillamini *m.*, fouillis *m.*, fatras *m.* **2.** *vb.* brouiller, mêler confusément.

jump, 1. *n.* saut *m.* **2.** *vb.* sauter.

junction, *n.* jonction *f.;* (rail) embranchement *m.*

juncture, *n.* jointure *f.*, jonction *f.*, conjoncture *f.*

June, *n.* juin *m.*

jungle, *n.* jungle *f.*, brousse *f.*

junior, *adj. and n.* (age) cadet *m.;* (rank) subalterne *m.*

juniper, *n.* genévrier *m.*, genièvre *m.*

junk, *n.* (waste) rebut *m.*

junket, *n.* jonchée *f.;* festin *m.;* partie de plaisir *f.*

jurisdiction, *n.* juridiction *f.*

jurisprudence, *n.* jurisprudence *f.*

jurist, *n.* juriste *m.*, légiste *m.*

juror, *n.* juré *m.*, membre du jury *m.*

jury, *n.* jury *m.*

just, 1. *adj.* juste. **2.** *adv.* (ex-actly) juste; (barely) à peine; (have j.) venir de.

justice, *n.* justice *f.*

justifiable, *adj.* justifiable, justifié.

justification, *n.* justification *f.*

justify, *vb.* justifier.

jut, *vb.* être en saillie.

jute, *n.* jute *m.*

juvenile, *adj.* juvénile.

K

kale, *n.* chou *m.*

kaleidoscope, *n.* kaléidoscope *m.*

kangaroo, *n.* kangourou *m.*

karakul, *n.* karakul *m.*, caracul *m.*

karat, *n.* carat *m.*

karate, *n.* karaté *m.*

keel, *n.* quille *f.*

keen, *adj.* (edge) aiguisé; (pain, point) aigu; (look, mind) pénétrant; (k. on) enthousiaste de.

keep, *vb.* tenir; (reserve, protect, retain) garder; (remain) rester; (continue) continuer à.

keeper, *n.* gardien *m.*

keepsake, *n.* souvenir *m.*

keg, *n.* caque *f.*, barillet *m.*, tonnelet *m.*

kennel, *n.* chenil *m.*

kerchief, *n.* fichu *m.*, mouchoir *m.*

kernel, *n.* (grain) grain *m.;* (nut) amande *f.;* (fig.) noyau *m.*

kerosene, *n.* pétrole *m.*

ketchup, *n.* sauce piquante à base de tomates *f.*

kettle, *n.* bouilloire *f.*

kettledrum, *n.* timbale *f.*

key, *n.* clef, clé *f.;* (piano, typewriter) touche *f.*

keyhole, *n.* entrée de clef *f.*

khaki, *n.* kaki *m.*

kick, 1. *n.* coup (*m.*) de pied; (gun) recul *m.* **2.** *vb.* donner un coup de pied à.

kid, *n.* (animal, skin) chevreau *m.;* (child) gosse *m.f.*

kidnap, *vb.* enlever de vive force.

kidnaper, *n.* auteur de l'enlèvement *m.*, ravisseur *m.*

kidney, *n.* rein *m.;* (food) rognon *m.*

kidney bean, *n.* haricot nain *m.*

kill, *vb.* tuer.

killer, *n.* tueur *m.*, meurtrier *m.*

kiln, *n.* four (céramique) *m.*, séchoir *m.*

kilocycle, *n.* kilocycle *m.*

kilohertz, *n.* kilohertz *m.*

kilowatt, *n.* kilowatt *m.*

kilt, *n.* kilt *m.*

kimono, *n.* kimono *m.*

kin, *n.* (relation) parent *m.*

kind, 1. *n.* genre *m.* **2.** *adj.* aimable.

kindergarten, *n.* jardin d'enfants *m.*, école maternelle *f.*

kindle, *vb.* allumer, *tr.*

kindling, *n.* allumage *m.*, bois d'allumage *m.*

kindly, *adv.* avec bonté.

kindness, *n.* bonté *f.*

kindred, 1. *n.* parenté *f.*, affinité *f.* **2.** *adj.* analogue.

kinetic, *adj.* cinétique.

king, *n.* roi *m.*

kingdom, *n.* royaume *m.*

kink, 1. *n.* nœud *m.*, tortillement *m.* **2.** *vb.* se nouer.

kiosk, *n.* kiosque *m.*

kipper, *n.* kipper *m.*, hareng légèrement salé et fumé *m.*

kiss, 1. *n.* baiser *m.* **2.** *vb.* baiser.

kitchen, *n.* cuisine *f.*

kite, *n.* cerf-volant *m.*

kitten, *n.* petit chat *m.*

kleptomania, *n.* kleptomanie *f.*

kleptomaniac, *n.* kleptomane *m.*

knack, *n.* tour de main *m.*, talent *m.*, truc *m.*

knapsack, *n.* havresac *m.*

knead, *vb.* pétrir, malaxer.

knee, *n.* genou *m.*

kneecap, *n.* genouillère *f.*

kneel, *vb.* s'agenouiller.

knell, *n.* glas *m.*

knickers, *n.* pantalon *m.*, culotte *f.*

knife, *n.* couteau *m.*

knight, *n.* chevalier *m.*

knit, *vb.* (with needles) tricoter.

knock, 1. *n.* coup *m.* **2.** *vb.* frapper.

knot, *n.* nœud *m.*

knotty, *adj.* plein de nœuds.

know, *vb.* savoir; (be acquainted with) connaître.

knowledge, *n.* connaissance *f.;* (learning) savoir *m.*

knuckle, *n.* articulation du doigt *f.*, jointure du doigt *f.*

kodak, *n.* kodak *m.*

Korea, *n.* Corée *f.*

L

label, *n.* étiquette *f.*

labor, 1. *n.* travail *m.;* (workers) ouvriers *m.pl.* **2.** *vb.* peiner.

laboratory, *n.* laboratoire *m.*

laborer, *n.* travailleur *m.*

laborious, *adj.* laborieux.

labor union, *n.* syndicat *m.*

laburnum, *n.* cytise *m.*

labyrinth, *n.* labyrinthe *m.*

lace, *n.* dentelle *f.;* (string) lacet *m.*

lacerate, *vb.* lacérer, déchirer.

laceration, *n.* lacération *f.*

lack, 1. *n.* manque *m.* **2.** *vb.* manquer de.

lackadaisical, *adj.* affecté.

laconic, *adj.* laconique.

lacquer, *n.* vernis-laque *m.*

lactic, *adj.* lactique.

lactose, *n.* lactose *f.*

lacy, *adj.* de dentelle.

ladder, *n.* échelle *f.*

ladle, *n.* cuiller à pot *f.*

lady, *n.* dame *f.*

ladybug, *n.* coccinelle *f.*

lag behind, *vb.* rester en arrière.

lagoon, *n.* lagune *f.*

laid-back, *adj.* décontracté.

lair, *n.* tanière *f.*, repaire *m.*

laissez faire, *n.* laissez faire *m.*

laity, *n.* les laïques *m.pl.*

lake, *n.* lac *m.*

lamb, *n.* agneau *m.*

lame, *adj.* boiteux.

lament, *vb.* se lamenter (sur); (mourn) pleurer.

lamentable, *adj.* lamentable, déplorable.

lamentation, *n.* lamentation *f.*

laminate, *vb.* laminer, écacher.

lamp, *n.* lampe *f.*

lampoon, 1. *n.* pasquinade *f.* satire *f.* 2. *vb.* lancer des satires.

lance, *n.* lance *f.*

land, 1. *n.* terre *f.* 2. *vb.* (boat) débarquer; (plane) atterrir.

landholder, *n.* propriétaire foncier *m.*

landing, *n.* débarquement *m.*, mise à terre *f.*

landlord, *n.* propriétaire *m.f.*

landmark, *n.* borne *f.*

landscape, *n.* paysage *m.*

landslide, *n.* éboulement *m.*

landward, *adv.* vers la terre.

lane, *n.* (country) sentier *m.*; (town) ruelle *f.*

language, *n.* langue *f.*; (form of expression) langage *m.*

languid, *adj.* languissant.

languish, *vb.* languir.

languor, *n.* langueur *f.*

lanky, *adj.* grand et maigre.

lanolin, *n.* lanoline *f.*

lantern, *n.* lanterne *f.*

lap, *n.* genoux *m.pl.*

lapel, *n.* revers *m.*

lapin, *n.* lapin *m.*

lapse, 1. *n.* (of time) laps *m.*; (error) faute *f.* 2. *vb.* passer.

larceny, *n.* larcin *m.*, vol *m.*

lard, *n.* saindoux *m.*

large, *adj.* grand.

largely, *adv.* en grande partie.

largo, *n.* largo *m.*

lariat, *n.* lasso *m.*

lark, *n.* alouette *f.*

larkspur, *n.* pied d'alouette *m.*, delphinium *m.*

larva, *n.* larve *f.*

laryngitis, *n.* laryngite *f.*

larynx, *n.* larynx *m.*

lascivious, *adj.* lascif.

laser, *n.* laser *m.*

lash, 1. *n.* (whip) lanière *f.*; (blow) coup (*m.*) de fouet. 2. *vb.* fouetter.

lass, *n.* jeune fille *f.*

lassitude, *n.* lassitude *f.*

lasso, *n.* lasso *m.*

last, 1. *adj.* dernier; (at l.) enfin. 2. *vb.* durer.

lasting, *adj.* durable.

latch, *n.* loquet *m.*

late, *adj. and adv.* (on in day, etc.) tard; (after due time) en retard; (dead) feu; (recent) dernier.

lately, *adv.* dernièrement.

latent, *adj.* latent, caché.

lateral, *adj.* latéral.

lath, *n.* latte *f.*

lathe, *n.* tour *m.*

lather, 1. *n.* (soap) mousse *f.*; (horse) écume *f.*

Latin, 1. *n.* (person) Latin *m.*; (language) latin *m.* 2. *adj.* latin.

latitude, *n.* latitude *f.*

latrine, *n.* latrine *f.*

latter, *adj. and pron.* dernier.

lattice, *n.* treillis *m.*

laud, *vb.* louer.

laudable, *adj.* louable.

laudanum, *n.* laudanum *m.*

laudatory, *adj.* élogieux.

laugh, laughter, *n.* rire *m.*

laughable, *adj.* risible.

launch, 1. *n.* (boat) chaloupe *f.* 2. *vb.* lancer, *tr.*

launder, *vb.* blanchir.

laundry, *n.* (works) blanchisserie *f.*; (washing) lessive *f.*

laundryman, *n.* blanchisseur *m.*

laureate, *adj. and n.* lauréat *m.f.*

laurel, *n.* laurier *m.*

lava, *n.* lave *f.*

lavaliere, *n.* lavallière *f.*

lavatory, *n.* lavabo *m.*; cabinet (*m.*) de toilette.

lavender, *n.* lavande *f.*

lavish, 1. *adj.* (person) prodigue; (thing) somptueux. 2. *vb.* prodiguer.

law, *n.* loi *f.*; (jurisprudence) droit *m.*

lawful, *adj.* légal.

lawless, *adj.* sans loi.

lawn, *n.* pelouse *f.*

lawsuit, *n.* procès *m.*

lawyer, *n.* (counselor) avocat *m.*; (attorney) avoué *m.*; (jurist) jurisconsulte *m.*

lax, *adj.* lâche, mou, relâché.

laxative, *n.* laxatif *m.*

laxity, *n.* relâchement *m.*

lay, *vb.* poser.

layer, *n.* couche *f.*

layman, *n.* laïque *m.*

lazy, *adj.* paresseux.

lead, 1. *n.* plomb *m.*; (pencil) mine *f.* 2. *vb.* mener, conduire.

leaden, *adj.* de plomb.

leader, *n.* chef *m.*

lead pencil, *n.* crayon à la mine de plomb *m.*

leaf, *n.* feuille *f.*

leaflet, *n.* feuillet *m.*

leafy, *adj.* feuillu.

league, *n.* (compact) ligue *f.*; (measure) lieue *f.*

League of Nations, *n.* La Société des Nations *f.*

leak, 1. *n.* (liquid) fuite *f.*; (boat) voie *f.*) d'eau. 2. *vb.* fuir; faire eau.

leakage, *n.* fuite d'eau *f.*

leaky, *adj.* qui coule, qui fait eau.

lean, 1. *adj.* maigre. 2. *vb. intr.* (l. against) s'appuyer sur; (stoop) se pencher. 3. *vb.tr.* appuyer.

leap, *vb.* sauter.

leap year, *n.* année bissextile *f.*

learn, *vb.* apprendre.

learned, *adj.* savant, docte.

learning, *n.* science *f.*, instruction *f.*, érudition *f.*

lease, *n.* bail *m.*

leash, *n.* laisse *f.*, attache *f.*

least, 1. *n.* moins *m.* 2. *adj.* (le) moindre. 3. *adv.* (le) moins.

leather, *n.* cuir *m.*

leathery, *adj.* coriace.

leave, 1. *n.* permission *f.* 2. *vb.* laisser; (go away from) quitter.

leaven, 1. *n.* levain *m.* 2. *vb.* faire lever, modifier.

lecherous, *adj.* lascif, libertin.

lecture, *n.* conférence *f.*

lecturer, *n.* conférencier *m.*

ledge, *n.* bord *m.*; (of rocks) chaîne *f.*

ledger, *n.* grand livre *m.*

lee, *n.* côté (*m.*) sous le vent.

leech, *n.* sangsue *f.*

leek, *n.* poireau *m.*

leer, 1. *n.* oeillade *f.*, regard de côté *m.* 2. *vb.* lorgner.

leeward, *adj. and adv.* sous le vent.

left, *adj. and n.* gauche *f.*; (on, to the l.) à gauche.

leftist, *n.* gaucher *m.*

left wing, *n.* l'aile gauche *f.*

leg, *n.* (man, horse) jambe *f.*; (most animals) patte *f.*

legacy, *n.* legs *m.*

legal, *adj.* légal.

legalize, *vb.* rendre légal.

legation, *n.* légation *f.*

legend, *n.* légende *f.*

legendary, *adj.* légendaire.

legible, *adj.* lisible.

legion, *n.* légion *f.*

legislate, *vb.* faire les lois.

legislation, *n.* législation *f.*

legislator, *n.* législateur *m.*

legislature, *n.* législature *f.*

legitimate, *adj.* légitime.

legume, *n.* légume *m.*

leisure, *n.* loisir *m.*

leisurely, *adv.* à loisir.

lemon, *n.* citron *m.*

lemonade, *n.* citron (*m.*) pressé.

lend, *vb.* prêter.

length, *n.* (dimension) longueur *f.*; (time) durée *f.*

lengthen, *vb.* allonger, *tr.*

lengthwise, *adv.* en long.

lengthy, *adj.* assez long.

lenient, *adj.* indulgent.

lens, n. lentille f.; (camera) objectif m.

Lent, n. carême m.

Lenten, adj. de carême.

lentil, n. lentille f.

lento, adv. lento.

leopard, n. léopard m.

leper, n. lépreux m.

leprosy, n. lèpre f.

lesbian, 1. adj. lesbien. 2. n. lesbienne f.; tribade f.

lesion, n. lésion f.

less, 1. adj. (smaller) moindre; (not so much) moins de. 2. adv. (l. than) moins (de).

lessen, vb. diminuer.

lesser, adj. moindre.

lesson, n. leçon f.

lest, conj. de peur que ... (ne).

let, vb. laisser; (lease) louer.

letdown, n. déception f.

lethal, adj. mortel.

lethargic, adj. léthargique.

lethargy, n. léthargie f.

letter, n. lettre f.

letterhead, n. en-tête de lettre m.

lettuce, n. laitue f.

levee, n. lever m.

level, 1. adj. (flat) égal; (l. with) au niveau de. 2. n. niveau m.

lever, n. levier m.

levity, n. légèreté f.

levy, 1. n. levée f. 2. vb. lever.

lewd, adj. impudique.

lexicon, n. lexique m.

liability, n. responsabilité f.

liable, adj. (responsible for) responsable de; (subject to) sujet à.

liar, n. menteur m.

libation, n. libation f.

libel, n. diffamation f.

libelous, adj. diffamatoire.

liberal, adj. libéral; (generous) généreux.

liberalism, n. libéralisme m.

liberality, n. libéralité f.

liberate, vb. libérer.

libertine, 1. n. libre-penseur m. 2. adj. libertin.

liberty, n. liberté f.

libidinous, adj. libidineux.

libido, n. libido m.

librarian, n. bibliothécaire m.

library, n. bibliothèque f.

libretto, n. livret m.

license, n. permis m.; (tradesmen) patente f.; (abuse of freedom) licence f.

licentious, adj. licencieux.

lick, vb. lécher.

licorice, n. réglisse f.

lid, n. couvercle m.

lie, 1. n. mensonge f. 2. vb. (fib) mentir; (recline) être couché; (l. down) se coucher; (be situated) se trouver.

lien, n. privilège m.

lieutenant, n. lieutenant m.

life, n. vie f.

lifeboat, n. bateau de sauvetage m.

life buoy, n. bouée de sauvetage m.

lifeguard, n. garde du corps m.

life insurance, n. assurance sur la vie f.

lifeless, adj. sans vie.

life preserver, n. appareil de sauvetage.

life style, n. manière de vivre f.

lifetime, n. vie f., vivant m.

lift, vb. lever.

ligament, n. ligament m.

ligature, n. ligature f.

light, 1. n. lumière f. 2. adj. (not heavy) léger; (not dark) clair. 3. vb. allumer, tr.

lighten, vb. (relieve) alléger, tr.; (brighten) éclairer, tr.

lighthouse, n. phare m.

lightly, adv. légèrement.

lightness, n. légèreté f.

lightning, n. (flash of) éclair m.

lightship, n. bateau-feu m.

lignite, n. lignite m.

likable, adj. agréable.

like, 1. adj. pareil. 2. vb. aimer; plaire à. 3. prep. comme.

likelihood, n. probabilité f.

likely, adj. probable.

liken, vb. comparer.

likeness, n. ressemblance f.

likewise, adv. de même.

lilac, n. lilas m.

lilt, 1. n. forte cadence f. 2. vb. chanter gaiement.

lily, n. lis m.; (l. of the valley) muguet m.

limb, n. membre m.; (tree) grosse branche f.

limber, 1. adj. souple, flexible. 2. vb. assouplir.

limbo, n. limbes m.pl.

lime, n. (mineral) chaux f.; (tree) tilleul m.; (fruit) lime f.

limelight, n. lumière oxhydrique f.

limestone, n. pierre à chaux f., calcaire m.

limewater, n. eau de chaux f.

limit, 1. n. limite f. 2. vb. limiter.

limitation, n. limitation f.

limitless, adj. sans limite, sans bornes.

limousine, n. limousine f.

limp, 1. adj. flasque. 2. vb. boiter.

limpid, adj. limpide.

linden, n. tilleul m.

line, n. ligne f.

lineage, n. lignée f., race f.

lineal, adj. linéaire.

linen, n. (cloth) toile f.; (sheets, etc.) linge m.

linger, vb. s'attarder.

lingerie, n. lingerie f.

linguist, n. linguiste m.

linguistic, adj. linguistique.

linguistics, n. linguistique f.

liniment, n. liniment m.

lining, n. (clothes) doublure f.

link, 1. n. (chain) chaînon m.; (fig.) lien m. 2. vb. (re)lier.

linoleum, n. linoléum m.

linseed, n. graine de lin f.

lint, n. charpie f.

lion, n. lion m.

lip, n. lèvre f.

liquefy, vb. liquéfier.

liqueur, n. liqueur f.

liquid, adj. and n. liquide m.

liquidate, vb. liquider.

liquidation, n. liquidation f., acquittement m.

liquor, n. boisson (f.) alcoolique.

lisle, n. fil d'Écosse m.

lisp, vb. zézayer.

list, 1. n. liste f. 2. vb. enregistrer.

listen (to), vb. écouter.

listless, adj. inattentif.

litany, n. litanie f.

literacy, n. degré d'aptitude à lire et à écrire m.

literal, adj. littéral.

literary, adj. littéraire.

literate, adj. lettré.

literature, n. littérature f.

lithe, adj. flexible, pliant.

lithograph, vb. lithographier.

lithography, n. lithographie f.

litigant, n. plaideur m.

litigation, n. litige m.

litmus, n. tournesol m.

litter, n. (vehicle, animals' bedding) litière f.; (disorder) fouillis m.; (animals' young) portée f.

little, 1. n. and adv. peu m. 2. adj. (small) petit; (not much) peu (de).

liturgical, adj. liturgique.

liturgy, n. liturgie f.

live, vb. vivre.

livelihood, n. vie f., subsistance f., gagne-pain m.

lively, adj. vif m., vive f.

liven, vb. animer, activer.

liver, n. foie m.

livery, n. livrée f.

livestock, n. bétail m.

livid, adj. livide, blême.

lizard, n. lézard m.

llama, n. lama m.

lo, interj. voilà.

load, 1. n. (cargo) charge f.; (burden) fardeau m. 2. vb. charger.

loaf, 1. n. pain m. 2. vb. flâner.

loafer, n. fainéant m.

loam, n. terre grasse f.

loan, 1. n. (thing) prêt m.; (borrowing) emprunt m. 2. vb. prêter.

loath, adj. fâché, peiné.

loathe, vb. détester.

loathing, n. dégoût m.

loathsome, adj. dégoûtant.

lobby, n. (hall) vestibule m.

lobe, n. lobe m.

lobster, n. homard m.

local, adj. local.

locale, n. localité f., scène f.

locality, n. localité f.

localize, vb. localiser.

locate, vb. localiser.

location, n. placement m.

lock, 1. n. (door) serrure f.;

(hair) mèche f. 2. vb. fermer à clef.

locker, n. armoire f.; (baggage) consigne automatique f.

locket, n. médaillon m.

lockjaw, n. tétanos m.

locksmith, n. serrurier m.

locomotion, n. locomotion f.

locomotive, n. locomotive f.

locust, n. sauterelle f.

locution, n. locution f.

lode, n. filon m.

lodge, vb. loger.

lodger, n. locataire m.

lodging, n. logement m.

loft, n. grenier m.

lofty, adj. élevé; (proud) hautain.

log, n. (wood) bûche f.; (boat) loch m.

loge, n. loge f.

logic, n. logique f.

logical, adj. logique.

loins, n. reins m.pl.

loiter, vb. flâner.

lollipop, n. sucre d'orge m.

London, n. Londres m.

lone, lonely, lonesome, adj. solitaire.

loneliness, n. solitude f.

long, 1. adj. long m., longue f. 2. adv. longtemps.

longevity, n. longévité f.

long for, vb. désirer ardemment.

longing, n. désir ardent m.

longitude, n. longitude f.

longitudinal, adj. longitudinal.

look, 1. n. regard m.; aspect m. 2. vb. (l. at) regarder; (l. for) chercher; (l. after) soigner; (seem) paraître.

looking glass, n. miroir m.

loom, 1. n. métier m. 2. vb. se dessiner.

loop, n. boucle f.

loophole, n. meurtrière f., échappatoire f.

loose, adj. (not tight) lâche; (detached) détaché; (morals) relâché.

loosen, vb. desserrer.

loot, 1. n. butin m. 2. vb. piller.

lop, vb. élaguer, ébrancher.

loquacious, adj. loquace.

lord, n. seigneur m.; (title) lord m.

lordship, n. seigneurie f.

lorgnette, n. lorgnette f.

lose, vb. perdre.

loss, n. perte f.

lot, n. (fortune) sort m.; (land) terrain m.; (much) beaucoup.

lotion, n. lotion f.

lottery, n. loterie f.

lotus, n. lotus m., lotos m.

loud, 1. adj. fort; (noisy) bruyant. 2. adv. haut.

lounge, 1. n. sofa m.; hall m. 2. vb. flâner.

louse, n. pou m.

lout, n. rustre m.

louver, n. auvent m.

lovable, adj. aimable.

love, 1. n. amour m. 2. vb. aimer.

lovely, adj. beau m., belle f.

lover, n. amoureux m.

low, adj. bas m., basse f.

lowboy, n. commode basse f.

lowbrow, adj. terre à terre.

lower, vb. baisser.

lowly, adj. humble.

loyal, adj. loyal.

loyalist, n. loyaliste m.

loyalty, n. loyauté f.

lozenge, n. pastille f.

lubricant, n. lubrifiant m.

lubricate, vb. lubrifier.

lucid, adj. lucide.

luck, n. chance f.

lucky, adj. (person) heureux.

lucrative, adj. lucratif.

ludicrous, adj. risible.

lug, vb. traîner, tirer.

luggage, n. bagages m.pl.

lukewarm, adj. tiède.

lull, n. moment (m.) de calme.

lullaby, n. berceuse f.

lumbago, n. lumbago m.

lumber, n. bois (m.) de charpente.

luminous, adj. lumineux.

lump, n. (gros) morceau m.

lumpy, adj. grumeleux.

lunacy, n. folie f.

lunar, adj. lunaire.

lunatic, adj. aliéné m.

lunch, 1. n. déjeuner m. 2. vb. déjeuner.

luncheon, n. déjeuner m.

lung, n. poumon m.

lunge, 1. n. botte f. 2. vb. se fendre.

lurch, 1. n. embardée f. 2. vb. faire une embardée.

lure, vb. (animal) leurrer; (attract) attirer.

lurid, adj. blafard, sombre.

lurk, vb. se cacher.

luscious, adj. délicieux.

lush, adj. luxuriant.

lust, n. luxure f.

luster, n. lustre m.

lustful, adj. lascif, sensuel.

lustrous, adj. brillant, lustré.

lusty, adj. vigoreux.

lute, n. luth m.

Lutheran, n. Luthérien m.

luxuriant, adj. exubérant.

luxurious, adj. (thing) luxueux.

luxury, n. luxe m.

lying, n. mensonge m.

lymph, n. lymphe f.

lynch, vb. lyncher.

lyre, n. lyre f.

lyric, adj. lyrique.

lyricism, n. lyrisme m.

M

macaroni, n. macaroni m.

machine, n. machine f.

machine gun, n. mitrailleuse f.

machinery, n. machines f.pl; (fig.) mécanisme m.

machinist, n. machiniste m.

machismo, n. phallocratie f.

macho, 1. adj. phallocrate. 2. n. homme phallocrate m.

mackerel, n. maquereau m.

mackinaw, n. mackinaw m.

mad, adj. fou m., folle f.

madam, n. madame f.

madcap, n. and adj. écervelé.

madden, vb. exaspérer.

made, adj. fait, fabriqué.

mafia, n. mafia f.

magazine, n. revue f.

magic, 1. n. magie f. 2. adj. magique.

magician, n. magicien m.

magistrate, n. magistrat m.

magnanimous, adj. magnanime.

magnate, n. magnat m.

magnesium, n. magnésium m.

magnet, n. aimant m.

magnetic, adj. magnétique.

magnificence, n. magnificence f.

magnificent, adj. magnifique.

magnify, vb. grossir.

magnitude, n. grandeur f.

mahogany, n. acajou m.

maid, n. (servant) bonne f.; (old m.) vieille fille f.

maiden, adj. de jeune fille.

mail, 1. n. courrier m. 2. vb. envoyer par la poste.

mailbox, n. boîte (f.) aux lettres.

mailman, n. facteur m.

maim, vb. estropier, mutiler.

main, adj. principal.

mainframe, n. partie centrale d'un informateur m.

mainland, n. terre (f.) ferme.

mainspring, n. grand ressort m.; mobile essentiel m.

maintain, vb. maintenir; (support) soutenir.

maintenance, n. entretien m.

maize, n. maïs m.

majestic, adj. majestueux.

majesty, n. majesté f.

major, 1. n. (mil.) commandant m.; (school) sujet (m.) principal. 2. adj. majeur.

majority, n. majorité f.

major scale, mode, or key, n. ton majeur m., mode majeur m.

make, 1. n. fabrication f. 2. vb. faire.

make-believe, 1. n. trompe l'œil m. 2. vb. feindre.

maker, n. fabricant m.

makeshift, n. expédient m.

make-up, n. (face) maquillage m.

maladjusted, adj. mal adapté, mal ajusté.

maladjustment, n. mauvaise adaptation f.

malady, n. maladie f.

malaria, n. malaria f.

male, n. and adj. mâle m.

malevolent, adj. malveillant.

malice, n. méchanceté f.

malicious, adj. méchant.

malign, vb. calomnier.

malignant, adj. malin m., maligne f.

malleable, adj. malléable.

malnutrition, n. mauvaise hygiène (f.) alimentaire.

malpractice, n. méfait m.

malt, n. malt m.

mammal, n. mammifère m.

man, n. homme m.

manage, 1. vb. tr. (administer) gérer; (conduct) diriger; (person, animal) dompter. 2. vb. intr. se tirer d'affaire; (m. to) réussir à.

management, n. direction f.

manager, n. directeur m.; (household) ménager m.

mandate, n. (politics) mandat m.

mandatory, adj. obligatoire.

mandolin, n. mandoline f.

mane, n. crinière f.

maneuver, n. manœuvre f.

manganese, n. manganèse m.

manger, n. mangeoire f.

mangle, vb. mutiler.

manhood, n. virilité f.

mania, n. (craze) manie f.; (madness) folie f.

maniac, adj. and n. fou m., folle f.

manicure, n. (person) manucure m.f.; (care of hands) soin (m.) des mains.

manifest, 1. adj. manifeste. 2. vb. manifester.

manifesto, n. manifeste m.

manifold, adj. (varied) divers; (numerous) nombreux.

manipulate, vb. manipuler.

mankind, n. genre (m.) humain.

manly, adj. viril.

manner, n. manière f.; (customs) mœurs f.pl.

mannerism, n. maniérisme m.; affectation f.

mansion, n. (country) château m.; (town) hôtel m.

manslaughter, n. homicide involontaire m.

mantel, n. (framework) manteau m.; (shelf) tablette f.

mantle, n. manteau m.

manual, adj. and n. manuel m.

manufacture, 1. n. manufacture f.; (product) produit (m.) manufacturé. 2. vb. fabriquer.

manufacturer, n. fabricant m.

manure, n. fumier m.

manuscript, adj. and n. manuscrit m.

many, 1. adj. beaucoup de, un grand nombre de; (too m.) trop de; (so m.) tant de; (how m.) combien de. 2. pron. beaucoup.

map, n. carte (f.) géographique.

maple, n. érable m.

mar, vb. gâter.

marble, n. marbre m.

march, 1. n. marche f. 2. vb. marcher.

March, n. mars m.

mare, n. jument f.

margarine, n. margarine f.

margin, n. marge f.

marijuana, n. marijuana f.; marie-jeanne f.

marinate, vb. faire mariner.

marine, 1. n. (ships) marine f.; (soldier) fusilier (m.) marin. 2. adj. marin; (insurance) maritime.

mariner, n. marin m.

marionette, n. marionnette f.

marital, adj. matrimonial.

maritime, adj. maritime.

mark, 1. n. marque f.; (target) but m.; (school) point m. 2. vb. marquer.

market, n. marché m.

market place, n. place (f.) du marché.

marmalade, n. confiture f.

maroon, 1. adj. and n. rouge (m.) foncé. 2. vb. abandonner (dans une île déserte).

marquee, n. (tente) marquise f.

marquis, n. marquis m.

marriage, n. mariage m.

married, adj. marié.

marrow, n. moelle f.

marry, vb. épouser; se marier (avec).

marsh, n. marais m.

marshal, n. maréchal m.

marshmallow, n. guimauve (plant) f.

martial, adj. martial.

martinet, n. officier strict sur la discipline m.

martyr, n. martyr m.

martyrdom, n. martyre m.

marvel, 1. n. merveille f. 2. vb. (m. at) s'étonner de.

marvelous, adj. merveilleux.

mascara, n. mascara m.

mascot, n. mascotte f.

masculine, adj. masculin.

mash, n. (food) purée f.

mask, 1. n. masque m. 2. vb. masquer.

mason, n. maçon m.

masquerade, n. mascarade f.; bal masqué m.

mass, n. masse f.

Mass, n. messe f.

massacre, 1. n. massacre m. 2. vb. massacrer.

massage, n. massage m.

masseur, n. masseur m.

massive, adj. massif.

mass meeting, n. réunion f.

mast, n. mât m.

master, 1. n. maître m. 2. vb. maîtriser.

masterpiece, n. chef-d'œuvre m.

mastery, n. maîtrise f.

masticate, vb. mâcher.

mat, n. (door) paillasson m.

match, 1. n. (for fire) allumette f.; (equal) égal m.; (marriage) mariage m.; (person to marry) parti m.; (sport) partie f. 2. vb. assortir, tr.

mate, n. (fellow-worker) camarade m.f.; (of pair) compa-

gnon m.; compagne f.; (boat) officier m.

material, 1. n. matière f.; (cloth) étoffe f. 2. adj. matériel.

materialism, n. matérialisme m.

materialize, vb. matérialiser, tr.; se réaliser, intr.

maternal, adj. maternel.

maternity, n. maternité f.

mathematical, adj. mathématique.

mathematics, n. mathématiques f.pl.

matinee, n. matinée f.

matriarch, n. femme qui porte les chausses f.

matrimony, n. mariage m.

matron, n. (institution) intendante f.

matter, 1. n. (substance) matière f.; (subject) sujet m.; (question, business) affaire f.; (what is the m.?) qu'est-ce qu'il y a? 2. vb. importer.

mattress, n. matelas m.

mature, 1. adj. mûr. 2. vb. mûrir.

maturity, n. maturité f.; (comm.) échéance f.

maudlin, adj. larmoyant.

mausoleum, n. mausolée m.

maxim, n. maxime f.

maximum, n. maximum m.

may, vb. pouvoir.

May, n. mai m.

maybe, adv. peut-être.

mayhem, n. mutilation f.

mayonnaise, n. mayonnaise f.

mayor, n. maire m.

maze, n. labyrinthe m.

me, pron. (unstressed direct and indirect) me; (alone, stressed, with prep.) moi.

meadow, n. (small) pré m.; (large) prairie f.

meager, adj. maigre.

meal, n. (repast) repas m.; (grain) farine f.

mean, 1. n. (math.) moyenne f.; (m.s financial) moyens m.pl.; (m.s way to do) moyen m. 2. adj. humble; (stingy) avare; (contemptible) méprisable. 3. vb. (signify) vouloir dire; (purpose) se proposer (de); (destine) destiner (à).

meaning, n. sens m.

meantime, meanwhile, adv. sur ces entrefaites.

measles, n. rougeole f.

measure, 1. n. mesure f. 2. vb. mesurer.

measurement, n. mesurage m.

meat, n. viande f.

mechanic, n. mécanicien m.

mechanical, 1. adj. mécanique. 2. (fig.) machinal.

mechanism, n. mécanisme m.

mechanize, vb. mécaniser.

medal, n. médaille f.

meddle, vb. se mêler (de).

media, n. organes de communication m.pl.

median, n. médian.
mediate, vb. agir en médiateur.
medical, adj. médical.
medicate, vb. médicamenter.
medicine, n. médecine m.
medieval, adj. médiéval.
mediocre, adj. médiocre.
mediocrity, n. médiocrité f.
meditate, vb. méditer.
meditation, n. méditation f.
Mediterranean, 1. adj. méditerrané. 2. n. (M. Sea) Méditerranée f.
medium, 1. n. milieu m.; (agent) intermédiaire m.; (psychic person) médium m. 2. adj. moyen.
medley, n. mélange m.
meek, adj. doux m., douce f.
meekness, n. douceur f.
meet, vb. rencontrer, tr.; (become acquainted with) faire la connaissance de; (expenses) faire face à.
meeting, n. réunion f.
megahertz, n. mégahertz m.
megaphone, n. mégaphone m.
melancholy, n. mélancolie f.
mellow, adj. moelleux.
melodious, adj. mélodieux.
melodrama, n. mélodrame m.
melody, n. mélodie f.
melon, n. melon m.
melt, vb. fondre.
meltdown, n. fusion f.
member, n. membre m.
membrane, n. membrane f.
memento, n. mémento m.
memoir, n. mémoire m.
memorable, adj. mémorable.
memorandum, n. mémorandum m.
memorial, 1. n. souvenir m., monument m. 2. adj. commémoratif.
memorize, vb. apprendre par cœur.
memory, n. mémoire f.
menace, 1. n. menace f. 2. vb. menacer.
menagerie, n. ménagerie f.
mend, vb. (clothes) raccommoder; (correct) corriger.
mendacious, adj. menteur.
mendicant, n. and adj. mendiant m.
menial, adj. servile.
menstruation, n. menstruation f.
menswear, n. habillements masculins m.pl.
mental, adj. mental.
mentality, n. mentalité f.
menthol, n. menthol m.
mention, 1. n. mention f. 2. vb. mentionner; (don't m. it) il n'y a pas de quoi.
menu, n. menu m.
mercantile, adj. mercantile.
mercenary, adj. and n. mercenaire m.
merchandise(s), n. marchandise(s) f.(pl.).
merchant, 1. n. négociant m. 2. adj. marchand.

merchant marine, n. marine marchande f.
merchandise f.
merciful, adj. miséricordieux.
merciless, adj. impitoyable.
mercury, n. mercure m.
mercy, n. miséricorde f.; (at the m. of) à la merci de.
mere, adj. simple.
merely, adv. simplement.
merge, vb. fusionner.
merger, n. fusion f.
merit, 1. n. mérite m. 2. vb. mériter.
meritorious, adj. (person) méritant; (deed) méritoire.
mermaid, n. sirène f.
merriment, n. gaieté f.
merry, adj. gai.
merry-go-round, n. carrousel m.
mesh, n. maille f.
mesmerize, n. magnétiser.
mess, 1. n. (muddle) fouillis m.; gâchis m.; (mil.) popote f. 2. vb. gâcher.
message, n. message m.
messenger, n. messager m.
messy, adj. (dirty) malpropre.
metabolism, n. métabolisme m.
metal, n. métal m.
metallic, adj. métallique.
metamorphosis, n. métamorphose f.
metaphysics, n. métaphysique f.
meteor, n. météore m.
meter, 1. n. (measure) mètre m.; (device) compteur m.
method, n. méthode f.
meticulous, adj. méticuleux.
metric, n. métrique.
metropolis, n. métropole f.
metropolitan, adj. métropolitain.
mettle, n. ardeur f.
Mexican, 1. n. Mexicain m. 2. adj. Mexicain.
Mexico, n. Mexique m.
mezzanine, n. mezzanine f.
microbe, n. microbe m.
microfiche, n. microfiche f.
microfilm, n. microfilm m.
microform, n. microforme f.
microphone, n. microphone m.
microscope, n. microscope m.
microscopic, adj. microscopique.
mid, adj. mi-.
middle, 1. n. milieu m. 2. adj. du milieu.
middle-aged, adj. d'un certain âge.
Middle Ages, n. moyen âge m.
middle class, n. classe moyenne f., bourgeoisie f.
Middle East, n. Moyen Orient m.
midget, n. nain m.
midnight, n. minuit m.
midriff, n. diaphragme m.
midwife, n. sage-femme f.
mien, n. mine f.; air m.
might, n. puissance f.
mighty, adj. puissant.
migrate, vb. émigrer.

migration, n. migration f.
mild, adj. doux m., douce f.
mildew, n. rouille f.
mile, n. mille m.
mileage, n. kilométrage m.
milestone, n. borne routière f.
militarism, n. militarisme m.
military, adj. militaire.
militia, n. milice f.
milk, n. lait m.
milkman, n. laitier m.
milky, adj. laiteux.
mill, 1. n. (grinding) moulin m.; (spinning) filature f.; (factory) usine f. 2. vb. (grind) moudre; (crowd) fourmiller.
miller, n. meunier m.
millimeter, n. millimètre m.
milliner, n. modiste f.
millinery, n. modes f.pl.
million, n. million m.
millionaire, adj. and n. millionnaire m.f.
mimic, 1. n. mime m. 2. adj. mimique. 3. vb. imiter.
mince, vb. (chop) hacher.
mind, 1. n. esprit m.; (opinion) avis m.; (desire) envie f. 2. vb. (heed) faire attention à; (listen to) écouter; (apply oneself to) s'occuper de; (take care) prendre garde; (look after) garder; (never m.) n'importe.
mindful, adj. attentif.
mine, 1. n. mine f. 2. pron. le mien m., la mienne f.
mine field, n. champ de mines m.
miner, n. mineur m.
mineral, adj. and n. minéral m.
mine sweeper, n. dragueur de mines m.
mingle, vb. mêler, tr.
miniature, n. miniature f.
miniaturize, vb. miniaturiser.
minimize, vb. réduire au minimum.
minimum, n. minimum m.
minimum wage, n. salaire minimum m.
mining, n. exploitation minière f., pose de mines f.
minister, n. ministre m.
ministry, n. ministère m.
mink, n. vison m.
minnow, n. vairon m.
minor, adj. and n. mineur m.
minority, n. minorité f.
minstrel, n. ménestrel m.
mint, n. (plant) menthe f.; (place) Hôtel (m.) de la Monnaie.
minute, 1. n. minute f.; (of meeting) procès-verbal m. 2. adj. (very small) minuscule; (detailed) minutieux.
miracle, n. miracle m.
miraculous, adj. miraculeux.
mirage, n. mirage m.
mire, n. boue f., bourbier m.
mirror, n. miroir m.
mirth, n. gaieté f.

misadventure, n. mésaventure f., contretemps m.

misappropriate, vb. détourner, dépréder.

misbehave, vb. se mal conduire.

miscellaneous, adj. divers.

mischief, n. (harm) mal m.; (mischievousness) malice f.

mischievous, adj. espiègle; (wicked) méchant.

misconstrue, vb. mal interpréter, tourner en mal.

misdemeanor, n. délit m.

miser, n. avare m.f.

miserable, adj. (unhappy) malheureux; (wretched) misérable.

miserly, adj. avare.

misery, n. (affliction) souffrance(s) f.(pl.); (poverty) misère f.

misfit, n. vêtement manqué m.; inadapté m., inapte m.

misfortune, n. malheur m.

misgiving, n. doute m.

mishap, n. mésaventure f.

mislead, vb. tromper, égarer.

misplace, vb. mal placer.

mispronounce, vb. mal prononcer, estropier.

miss, vb. manquer; (I m. you) vous me manquez.

Miss, n. mademoiselle f.

missile, n. projectile m.

mission, n. mission f.

missionary, adj. and n. missionnaire m.f.

misspell, vb. mal orthographier.

mist, n. brume f.

mistake, 1. n. erreur f. 2. vb. (misunderstand) comprendre mal; (make a mistake) se tromper (de).

mister, n. monsieur m.

mistletoe, n. gui m.

mistreat, vb. maltraiter.

mistress, n. maîtresse f.

mistrust, 1. n. méfiance f. 2. vb. se méfier de.

misty, adj. brumeux.

misunderstand, vb. mal comprendre.

misuse, vb. (misapply) faire mauvais usage (de); (maltreat) maltraiter.

mite, n. denier m., obole f.

mitigate, vb. adoucir.

mitten, n. moufle f.

mix, vb. mêler, tr.

mixture, n. mélange m.

mix-up, n. embrouillement m.

moan, 1. n. gémissement m. 2. vb. gémir.

moat, n. fossé m.

mob, n. foule f.; (pejorative) populace f.

mobile, adj. mobile.

mobilization, n. mobilisation f.

mobilize, vb. mobiliser.

mock, vb. (m. at) se moquer de; (imitate) singer.

mockery, n. moquerie f.

mod, n. à la mode.

mode, n. mode m.

model, n. modèle m.

moderate, 1. adj. modéré. 2. vb. modérer.

moderation, n. modération f.

modern, adj. moderne.

modernize, vb. moderniser.

modest, adj. modeste.

modesty, n. modestie f.

modify, vb. modifier.

modish, adj. à la mode.

modulate, vb. moduler.

moist, adj. moite.

moisten, vb. humecter.

moisture, n. humidité f.

molar, n. and adj. molaire f.

molasses, n. mélasse f.

mold, 1. n. (casting) moule m.; (mildew) moisissure f. 2. vb. (shape) mouler; (get moldy) moisir.

moldy, adj. moisi.

mole, n. (animal) taupe f.; (spot) grain (m.) de beauté.

molecule, n. molécule f.

molest, vb. molester.

mollify, vb. adoucir, apaiser.

molten, adj. fondu, coulé.

moment, n. moment m.

momentary, adj. momentané.

momentous, adj. important.

monarch, n. monarque m.

monarchy, n. monarchie f.

monastery, n. monastère m.

Monday, n. lundi m.

monetary, adj. monétaire.

money, n. argent m.; (comm.) monnaie f.

mongrel, n. métis m.

monitor, n. moniteur m.

monk, n. moine m.

monkey, n. singe m.

monologue, n. monologue m.

monoplane, n. monoplan m.

monopolize, vb. monopoliser.

monopoly, n. monopole m.

monosyllable, n. monosyllabe m.

monotone, n. monotone m.

monotonous, adj. monotone.

monotony, n. monotonie f.

monsoon, n. mousson f.

monster, n. monstre m.

monstrosity, n. monstruosité f.

monstrous, adj. monstrueux.

month, n. mois m.

monthly, adj. mensuel.

monument, n. monument m.

monumental, adj. monumental.

mood, n. humeur f.; (gramm.) mode m.

moody, adj. de mauvaise humeur.

moon, n. lune f.

moonlight, n. clair (m.) de lune.

moor, n. lande f.

mooring, n. amarrage m.

moot, adj. discutable.

mop, n. balai (m.) à laver.

moped, n. cyclomoteur m.

moral, 1. n. morale f.; (morals) moralité f. 2. adj. moral.

morale, n. moral m.

moralist, n. moraliste m.f.

morality, n. moralité f.; (ethics) morale f.

morally, adv. moralement.

morbid, adj. morbide.

more, 1. pron. en . . . davantage. 2. adj., adv. plus; (m. than) plus de; (no m.) ne . . . plus.

moreover, adv. de plus.

mores, n. mœurs f.pl.

morgue, n. morgue f.

morning, n. matin m.; (length of m.) matinée f.; (good m.) bonjour.

moron, n. idiot.

morose, adj. morose.

Morse code, n. l'alphabet Morse m.

morsel, n. morceau m.

mortal, adj. and n. mortel m.

mortality, n. mortalité f.

mortar, n. mortier m.

mortgage, 1. n. hypothèque f. 2. vb. hypothéquer.

mortician, n. entrepreneur de pompes funèbres m.

mortify, vb. mortifier.

mortuary, adj. mortuaire.

mosaic, 1. n. mosaïque f. 2. adj. en mosaïque.

Moscow, n. Moscou m.

Moslem, adj. and n. musulman m.

mosquito, n. moustique m.

moss, n. mousse f.

most, 1. n. le plus. 2. adj. le plus (de); la plupart (de). 3. adv. (with adj. and vb.) le plus; (intensive) très.

mostly, adv. pour la plupart; (time) la plupart du temps.

moth, n. (clothes) mite f.

mother, n. mère f.

mother-in-law, n. belle-mère f.

motif, n. motif m.

motion, n. mouvement m.; (gesture) signe m.; (proposal) motion f.

motionless, adj. immobile.

motion-picture, n. film m.

motivate, vb. motiver.

motive, n. motif m.

motley, 1. adj. bigarré. 2. n. livrée de bouffon m.

motor, n. moteur m.

motorboat, n. canot (m.) automobile.

motorist, n. automobiliste m.

motto, n. devise f.

mound, n. tertre m.

mount, 1. n. (hill) mont m.; (horse, structure) monture f. 2. vb. monter.

mountain, n. montagne f.

mountaineer, n. montagnard m., Alpiniste m.

mountainous, adj. montagneux.

mountebank, n. saltimbanque m., charlatan m.

mourn, vb. pleurer.

mournful, adj. triste.

mourning, n. deuil m.

mouse, n. souris f.

mouth, n. bouche f.

mouthpiece, n. embouchure f., embout m.

movable, adj. mobile.

move, vb. mouvoir, tr.; remuer; (stir) bouger; (affect with emotion) émouvoir; (change residence) déménager; (propose) proposer.

movement, n. mouvement m.

moving, 1. n. déménagement m. 2. adj. touchant.

mow, vb. faucher; (lawn) tondre.

Mr., n. M. m. (abbr. for Monsieur).

Mrs., n. Mme. f. (abbr. for Madame).

much, adj., pron. and adv. beaucoup (de); (too m.) trop (de); (so m.) tant (de); (how m.) combien (de).

mucilage, n. mucilage m.

muck, n. fumier m.

mucous, adj. muqueux.

mud, n. boue f.

muddy, adj. boueux.

muff, n. manchon m.

muffin, n. petit pain m.

muffle, vb. emmitoufler.

mug, n. gobelet m., pot m.

mulatto, n. mulâtre m.

mule, n. mulet m.

mullah, n. mollah m.

multicolored, adj. multicolore.

multinational, adj. multinational.

multiple, adj. multiple.

multiplication, n. multiplication f.

multiplicity, n. multiplicité f.

multiply, vb. multiplier, tr.

multitude, n. multitude f.

mummy, n. momie f.; maman f.

mumps, n. oreillons m.pl.

munch, vb. mâcher.

municipal, adj. municipal.

munificent, adj. munificent.

munition, n. munition(s) f.

mural, n. (painting) peinture (f.) murale.

murder, n. meurtre m.

murderer, n. meurtrier m.

murmur, 1. n. murmure m. 2. vb. murmurer.

muscle, n. muscle m.

muscular, adj. musculaire; (strong) musculeux.

muse, 1. n. muse f. 2. vb. méditer.

museum, n. musée m.

mushroom, n. champignon m.

music, n. musique f.

musical, adj. musical; (person) musicien.

musical comedy, n. comédie musicale f.

musician, n. musicien m.

Muslim, adj. and n. musulman m.

muslin, n. mousseline f.

must, vb. devoir; falloir (used impersonally, il faut que).

mustache, n. moustache f.

mustard, n. moutarde f.

muster, vb. rassembler, tr.

musty, adj. moisi, suranné.

mutation, n. mutation f.

mute, adj. muet.

mutilate, vb. mutiler.

mutiny, n. mutinerie f.

mutter, vb. grommeler.

mutton, n. mouton m.

mutual, adj. mutuel.

muzzle, n. muselière f.

my, adj. mon m., ma f., mes pl.

myopia, n. myopie f.

myriad, n. myriade f.

myrtle, n. myrte m.

myself, pron. moi-même; (reflexive) me.

mysterious, adj. mystérieux.

mystery, n. mystère m.

mystic, adj. mystique.

mystify, vb. mystifier.

myth, n. mythe m.

mythical, adj. mythique.

mythology, n. mythologie f.

N

nag, vb. gronder.

nail, 1. n. (person, animal) ongle m.; (metal) clou m. 2. vb. clouer.

naïve, adj. naïf m., naïve f.

naked, adj. nu.

name, 1. n. nom m. 2. vb. nommer.

namesake, n. homonyme m.

nap, n. petit somme m.

napkin, n. serviette f.

narcissus, n. narcisse m.

narcotic, adj. and n. narcotique m.

narrate, vb. raconter.

narrative, n. récit m.

narrow, adj. étroit.

nasal, adj. nasal.

nasty, adj. désagréable.

natal, adj. natal.

nation, n. nation f.

national, adj. national.

nationalism, n. nationalisme m.

nationality, n. nationalité f.

nationalization, n. nationalisation f.

nationalize, vb. nationaliser.

native, 1. n. natif m.; (primitive inhabitant, etc.) indigène m.f. 2. adj. natif; (place) natal; (language) maternel.

nativity, n. naissance f.

natural, adj. naturel.

naturalist, n. naturaliste m.

naturalize, vb. naturaliser.

naturalness, n. naturel m.

nature, n. nature f.

naughty, adj. méchant.

nausea, n. nausée f.

nauseous, adj. nauséeux.

nautical, adj. marin.

naval, adj. naval.

nave, n. nef f.

navigable, adj. navigable.

navigate, vb. naviguer.

navigation, n. navigation f.

navigator, n. navigateur m.

navy, n. marine f.

navy yard, n. arsenal maritime m.

near, 1. adj. proche. 2. adv. près. 3. prep. près de.

nearly, adv. de près; (almost) presque.

near-sighted, adj. myope.

neat, adj. propre.

neatness, n. propreté f.

nebula, n. nébuleuse f.

nebulous, adj. nébuleux.

necessary, adj. nécessaire.

necessity, n. nécessité f.

neck, n. cou m.

necklace, n. collier m.

necktie, n. cravate f.

nectar, n. nectar m.

need, 1. n. besoin m. 2. vb. avoir besoin de.

needful, adj. nécessaire.

needle, n. aiguille f.

needle point, n. pointe d'aiguille f.

needless, adj. inutile.

needy, adj. nécessiteux.

nefarious, adj. infâme.

negative, adj. négatif.

neglect, 1. n. négligence f. 2. vb. négliger (de).

negligee, n. négligé f.

negligent, adj. négligent.

negligible, adj. négligeable.

negotiate, vb. négocier.

negotiation, n. négociation f.

Negro, adj. and n. nègre m.

neighbor, n. voisin m.; (fellow man) prochain m.

neighborhood, n. voisinage m.

neither, 1. adj. and pron. ni l'un ni l'autre. 2. adv. non plus. 3. conj. (n. . . . nor) ni . . . ni.

neon, n. néon m.

neophyte, n. néophyte m.

nephew, n. neveu m.

nepotism, n. népotisme m.

nerve, n. nerf m.

nervous, adj. nerveux.

nervous system, n. système nerveux m.

nest, n. nid m.

nestle, vb. se nicher.

net, 1. n. filet m. 2. adj. net m., nette f.

Netherlands, the, n. les Pays-Bas m.pl., Hollande f.

network, n. réseau m.

neuralgia, n. névralgie f.

neurology, n. neurologie f.

neurotic, adj. and n. névrosé m.

neutral, adj. and n. neutre m.

neutron, n. neutron m.

neutron bomb, n. bombe à neutrons f.

never, adv. jamais.

nevertheless, adv. néanmoins.

new, adj. nouveau m., nouvelle f.; (not used) neuf m., neuve f.

news, n. (piece of news) nouvelle f.

newsboy, n. vendeur (m.) de journaux.

newscast, n. journal parlé m., informations f.pl.

newspaper, n. journal m.

newsreel, n. film d'actualité m.

New Testament, n. le Nouveau Testament m.

new year, n. nouvel an m.

next, 1. adj. prochain. 2. adv. ensuite. 3. prep. auprès de.

nibble, vb. grignoter.

nice, adj. (person) gentil; (thing) joli.

nick, n. entaille f.

nickel, n. nickel m.

nickname, n. surnom m.

nicotine, n. nicotine f.

niece, n. nièce f.

niggardly, adj. chiche.

night, n. nuit f.; (evening) soir m.

night club, n. boîte de nuit f., établissement de nuit m.

nightgown, n. chemise (f.) de nuit.

nightingale, n. rossignol m.

nightly, adv. tous les soirs; toutes les nuits.

nightmare, n. cauchemar m.

nimble, adj. agile.

nine, adj. and n. neuf m.

nineteen, adj. and n. dix-neuf m.

ninety, adj. and n. quatre-vingt-dix m.

ninth, adj. and n. neuvième m.

nip, 1. n. pincement m., pincade f. 2. vb. pincer.

nitrogen, n. nitrogène m.

no, 1. adj. pas de. 2. interj., adv. non.

nobility, n. noblesse f.

noble, adj. noble.

nobleman, n. gentilhomme m.

nobly, adv. noblement.

nobody, pron. personne.

nocturnal, adj. nocturne.

nod, 1. n. signe (m.) de la tête. 2. vb. incliner la tête.

node, n. nœud m.

no-frills, adj. simple.

noise, n. bruit m.

noiseless, adj. silencieux.

noisome, adj. puant, fétide.

noisy, adj. bruyant.

nomad, n. nomade m. and f.

nominal, adj. nominal.

nominate, vb. (appoint) nommer; (propose) désigner.

nomination, n. (appointment) nomination f.; (proposal) désignation f.

nominee, n. personne nommée f., candidat choisi m.

nonaligned, adj. (in politics) non-aligné.

nonchalant, adj. nonchalant.

noncombatant, adj. and n. non-combattant m.

noncommissioned, adj. sans brevet.

noncommittal, adj. qui n'engage à rien.

nondescript, adj. indéfinissable.

none, pron. aucun.

nonentity, n. nullité f.

non-proliferation, n. non-prolifération n.

nonresident, n. and adj. non-résident m.

nonsense, n. absurdité f.

nonstop, adj. sans arrêt.

noodles, n. nouilles f.pl.

nook, n. coin m., recoin m.

noon, n. midi m.

noose, n. nœud coulant m.

nor, conj. ni; (and not) et ne . . . pas.

normal, adj. normal.

normally, adv. normalement.

north, n. nord m.

North America, n. Amérique (f.) du Nord.

northeast, n. nord-est m.

northern, adj. du nord.

North Pole, n. pôle nord m.

northwest, n. nord-ouest m.

Norway, n. Norvège f.

Norwegian, 1. n. (person) Norvégien m.; (language) norvégien m. 2. adj. norvégien.

nose, n. nez m.

nosebleed, n. saignement du nez m.

nose dive, n. vol piqué m.

nostalgia, n. nostalgie f.

nostril, n. narine f.; (animals) naseau m.

nostrum, n. panacée f., remède de charlatan m.

not, adv. (ne) pas.

notable, adj. and n. notable m.

notation, n. notation f.

note, 1. n. note f.; (letter, finance) billet m.; (distinction) marque f. 2. vb. noter.

notebook, n. (small) carnet m.; (large) cahier m.

noted, adj. célèbre.

notepaper, n. papier à notes m.

noteworthy, adj. remarquable, mémorable.

notice, 1. n. (announcement) avis m.; (attention) attention f.; (forewarning) préavis m. 2. vb. remarquer.

noticeable, adj. remarquable; apparent.

notification, n. notification f.

notify, vb. avertir.

notion, n. idée f.

notoriety, n. notoriété f.

notorious, adj. notoire.

notwithstanding, 1. adv. tout de même. 2. prep. malgré.

noun, n. substantif m.

nourish, vb. nourrir.

nourishment, n. nourriture f.

novel, n. roman m.

novelist, n. romancier m.

novelty, n. nouveauté f.

November, n. novembre m.

novice, n. novice m.f.

now, adv. maintenant; (n. and then) de temps en temps.

nowhere, adv. nulle part.

nozzle, n. ajutage m., jet m.

nuance, n. nuance f.

nuclear, adj. nucléaire.

nuclear physics, n. physique nucléaire f.

nuclear warhead, n. cône de charge nucléaire m.

nuclear waste, n. déchets nucléaires m.pl.

nucleus, n. noyau m.

nude, adj. and n. nu m.

nugget, n. pépite f.

nuisance, n. (thing) ennui m.; (person) peste f.

nuke, 1. n. arme nucléaire f. 2. vb. détruire avec des armes nucléaires.

nullify, vb. annuler, nullifier.

number, 1. n. nombre m.; (in a series, street, etc.) numéro m. 2. vb. compter, numéroter.

numerical, adj. numérique.

numerous, adj. nombreux.

nun, n. religieuse f.

nuncio, n. nonce m.

nuptial, adj. nuptial.

nurse, 1. n. (hospital) infirmière f.; (wet-n.) nourrice f. 2. vb. soigner; (suckle) allaiter.

nursery, n. (children) chambre (f.) des enfants; (plants) pépinière f.

nurture, 1. n. nourriture f. 2. vb. nourrir, entretenir.

nut, n. noix f.; (metal) écrou m.

nutcracker, n. casse-noix m.

nutrition, n. nutrition f.

nutritious, adj. nutritif.

nutshell, n. coquille de noix f.; (in a n.) en deux mots.

nylon, n. nylon m.

nymph, n. nymphe f.

O

oak, n. chêne m.

oar, n. rame f.

oasis, n. oasis f.

oath, n. serment m.; (curse) juron m.

oatmeal, n. farine d'avoine f.

oats, n. avoine f.

obdurate, adj. obstiné, têtu.

obedience, n. obéissance f.

obedient, adj. obéissant.

obeisance, n. salut m.

obelisk, n. obélisque m.

obey, vb. obéir à.

obituary, n. nécrologe m.

object, 1. n. objet m. 2. vb. objecter.

objection, n. objection f.

objectionable, adj. répréhensible.

objective, adj. and n. objectif m.

obligation, n. obligation f.

obligatory, adj. obligatoire.

oblige, vb. obliger.

oblivion, n. oubli m.

obnoxious, adj. odieux.

obscene, *adj.* obscène.
obscure, *adj.* obscur.
obsequious, *adj.* obséquieux.
observance, *n.* observance *f.*
observation, *n.* observation *f.*
observe, *vb.* observer.
observer, *n.* observateur *m.*
obsession, *n.* obsession *f.*
obsolete, *adj.* désuet.
obstacle, *n.* obstacle *m.*
obstetrician, *n.* médecin-accoucheur *m.*
obstinate, *adj.* obstiné.
obstreperous, *adj.* tapageur.
obstruct, *vb.* obstruer.
obstruction, *n.* obstruction *f.*
obtain, *vb.* obtenir.
obtrude, *vb.* mettre en avant.
obviate, *vb.* prévenir, éviter.
obvious, *adj.* évident.
occasion, *n.* occasion *f.*
occasional, *adj.* (not regular) de temps en temps.
occult, *adj.* occulte.
occupant, *n.* occupant *m.*
occupation, *n.* occupation *f.*; (vocation) métier *m.*
occupy, *vb.* occuper.
occur, *vb.* (happen) avoir lieu; (come to the mind) se présenter à l'esprit.
occurrence, *n.* occurrence *f.*
ocean, *n.* océan *m.*
o'clock, *see* clock.
octagon, *n.* octogone *m.*
octave, *n.* octave *f.*
October, *n.* octobre *m.*
octopus, *n.* poulpe *m.*
ocular, *adj.* oculaire.
oculist, *n.* oculiste *f.*
odd, *adj.* (not even) impair; (unmatched) dépareillé; (strange) bizarre.
oddity, *n.* singularité *f.*
odds, *n.* inégalité *f.*, (betting) cote *f.*
odious, *adj.* odieux.
odor, *n.* odeur *f.*
of, *prep.* de.
off, 1. *adv.* (away) à . . . de distance; (cancelled) rompu. 2. *prep.* de.
offend, *vb.* offenser; (o. against the law) enfreindre la loi.
offender, *n.* offenseur *m.*; (law) délinquant *m.*
offense, *n.* offense *f.*; (transgression) délit *m.*
offensive, 1. *n.* offensive *f.* 2. *adj.* (mil., etc.) offensif; (word, etc.) offensant.
offer, 1. *n.* offre *f.* 2. *vb.* offrir.
offering, *n.* offre *f.*, offrande *f.*
offhand, 1. *adj.* spontané. 2. *adv.* sans préparation.
office, *n.* (service) office *m.*; (function) fonctions *f.pl.*; (room) bureau *m.*
officer, *n.* (mil.) officier *m.*; (public) fonctionnaire *m.*
official, *adj.* officiel.
officiate, *vb.* officier.
officious, *adj.* officieux.
offshore, 1. *adv.* vers le large. 2. *adj.* du côté de la terre.

offspring, *n.* descendant *m.*
often, *adv.* souvent.
oil, *n.* huile *f.*
oilcloth, *n.* toile cirée *f.*
oily, *adj.* huileux.
ointment, *n.* onguent *m.*
okay, *interj.* très bien.
old, *adj.* vieux (vieil) *m.*, vieille *f.*; (how o. are you?) quel âge avez-vous?
old-fashioned, *adj.* démodé.
Old Testament, *n.* l'Ancien Testament *m.*
olfactory, *adj.* olfactif.
oligarchy, *n.* oligarchie *f.*
olive, *n.* (tree) olivier *m.*; (fruit) olive *f.*
ombudsman, *n.* (in France) médiateur *m.*; (in Quebec) protecteur du citoyen *m.*
omelet, *n.* omelette *f.*
omen, *n.* présage *m.*
ominous, *adj.* de mauvais augure.
omission, *n.* omission *f.*
omit, *vb.* omettre.
omnibus, *n.* omnibus *m.*
omnipotent, *adj.* omnipotent, tout-puissant.
on, *prep.* sur.
once, *adv.* une fois; (formerly) autrefois; (at o., without delay) tout de suite; (at o., at the same time) à la fois.
one, 1. *adj.* un; (only) seul. 2. *n.* un *m.* 3. *pron.* un; (indefinite subject) on, (indefinite object) vous; (the o.) celui; (this o.) celui-ci; (that o.) celui-là; (which o.) lequel.
oneself, *pron.* soi-même; (reflexive) se.
one-sided, *adj.* unilatéral.
onion, *n.* oignon *m.*
onionskin, *n.* pelure d'oignon *f.*, (paper) papier pelure *m.*
only, 1. *adj.* seul. 2. *adv.* seulement.
onslaught, *n.* assaut *m.*
onward, *adj. and adv.* en avant.
opal, *n.* opale *f.*
opaque, *adj.* opaque.
open, 1. *adj.* ouvert. 2. *vb.* ouvrir.
opening, *n.* ouverture *f.*
opera, *n.* opéra *m.*
opera glasses, *n.* jumelles *f.pl.*
operate, *vb.* opérer; (put into operation) actionner.
operatic, *adj.* d'opéra.
operation, *n.* opération *f.*; (functioning) fonctionnement *m.*
operator, *n.* opérateur *m.*; (telephone) employée *f.*
operetta, *n.* opérette *f.*
opinion, *n.* opinion *f.*
opponent, *n.* adversaire *m.f.*
opportunism, *n.* opportunisme *m.*
opportunity, *n.* occasion *f.*
oppose, *vb.* (put in opposition) opposer; (resist) s'opposer à.
opposite, 1. *adj.* opposé;

vis-à-vis. 3. *prep.* en face de.
opposition, *n.* opposition *f.*
oppress, *vb.* opprimer.
oppression, *n.* oppression *f.*
oppressive, *adj.* oppressif; (heat, etc.) accablant.
optic, *adj.* optique.
optician, *n.* opticien *m.*
optimism, *n.* optimisme *m.*
optimistic, *adj.* optimiste.
option, *n.* option *f.*
optional, *adj.* facultatif.
optometry, *n.* optométrie *f.*
opulent, *adj.* opulent, riche.
or, *conj.* ou; (with negative) ni.
oracle, *n.* oracle *m.*
oral, *adj.* oral.
orange, *n.* orange *f.*
orangeade, *n.* orangeade *f.*
oration, *n.* discours *m.*
orator, *n.* orateur *m.*
oratory, *n.* art *(m.)* oratoire.
orbit, *n.* orbite *f.*
orchard, *n.* verger *m.*
orchestra, *n.* orchestre *m.*
orchid, *n.* orchidée *f.*
ordain, *vb.* ordonner.
ordeal, *n.* épreuve *f.*
order, 1. *n.* ordre *m.*; (comm.) commande *f.* 2. *vb.* ordonner; (comm.) commander.
orderly, *adj.* ordonné.
ordinance, *n.* ordonnance *f.*
ordinary, *adj. and n.* ordinaire *m.*
ordination, *n.* ordination *f.*
ore, *n.* minerai *m.*
organ, *n.* (music) orgue *m.*; (body) organe *m.*
organdy, *n.* organdi *m.*
organic, *adj.* organique.
organism, *n.* organisme *m.*
organist, *n.* organiste *m.f.*
organization, *n.* organisation *f.*
organize, *vb.* organiser.
orgy, *n.* orgie *f.*
orient, *vb.* orienter.
Orient, *n.* Orient *m.*
Oriental, 1. *n.* Oriental *m.* 2. *adj.* oriental.
orientation, *n.* orientation *f.*
origin, *n.* origine *f.*
original, *adj.* (new, unique) original; (from the origin) originel.
originality, *n.* originalité *f.*
ornament, *n.* ornement *m.*
ornamental, *adj.* ornemental.
ornate, *adj.* orné.
ornithology, *n.* ornithologie *f.*
orphan, *n.* orphelin *m.*
orphanage, *n.* orphelinat *m.*
orthodox, *adj.* orthodoxe.
orthopedics, *n.* orthopédie *f.*
osmosis, *n.* osmose *f.*
ostensible, *adj.* prétendu.
ostentation, *n.* ostentation *f.*
ostentatious, *adj.* plein d'ostentation.
ostracize, *vb.* ostraciser.
ostrich, *n.* autruche *f.*
other, *adj. and pron.* autre.
otherwise, *adv.* autrement.
ought, *vb.* devoir.
ounce, *n.* once *f.*

our, adj. notre sg., nos pl.

ours, pron. le nôtre.

ourself, pron. nous-même; (reflexive) nous.

oust, vb. évincer.

ouster, n. éviction f.

out, adv. dehors.

outbreak, n. (beginning) commencement m.; (insurrection) révolte f.

outburst, n. éruption f.

outcast, n. paria m.

outcome, n. résultat m.

outdoors, adv. dehors.

outer, adj. extérieur.

outfit, n. équipement m.

outgrowth, n. conséquence f.

outing, n. promenade f.

outlandish, adj. bizarre.

outlaw, vb. proscrire.

outlet, n. issue f.

outline, 1. n. contour m.; (general idea) aperçu m. **2.** vb. (drawing) tracer; (plan) exposer à grands traits.

out of, prep. hors de; (because of) par; (without) sans.

out-of-date, adj. suranné.

output, n. rendement m.

outrage, n. outrage m.

outrageous, adj. outrageant.

outrank, vb. occuper un rang supérieur.

outright, adv. complètement.

outrun, vb. dépasser.

outside, 1. adv. dehors. **2.** prep. en dehors de.

outskirts, n. limites f.pl.

outward, adj. extérieur.

oval, adj. and n. ovale m.

ovation, n. ovation f.

oven, n. four m.

over, 1. prep. (on) sur; (above) au-dessus de; (beyond) au delà de; (more than) plus de. **2.** adv. (all over) partout; (more) davantage; (finished) fini; (with adj.) trop.

overbearing, adj. arrogant.

overcoat, n. pardessus m.

overcome, vb. vaincre; (be overcome by) succomber à.

overdue, adj. arriéré, échu.

overflow, vb. déborder.

overhaul, vb. examiner en détail, remettre au point.

overhead, 1. adj. (comm.) général. **2.** adv. en haut.

overkill, n. exagération rhétorique f.

overlook, vb. (look on to) avoir vue sur; (neglect) négliger.

overnight, adv. pendant la nuit.

overpower, vb. (subdue) subjuguer; (crush) accabler.

overrule, vb. décider contre.

overrun, vb. envahir.

oversee, vb. surveiller.

oversight, n. inadvertance f.

overstuffed, adj. rembourré.

overt, adj. manifeste.

overtake, vb. rattraper; (accident, etc.) arriver à.

overthrow, vb. renverser.

overtime, n. heures (f.pl.) supplémentaires.

overture, n. ouverture f.

overturn, vb. renverser, tr.

overview, n. vue d'ensemble f.

overweight, n. excédent m.

overwhelm, vb. accabler (de).

overwork, vb. surmener, tr.

owe, vb. devoir.

owing, 1. prep. à cause de, en raison de. **2.** adj. dû.

owl, n. hibou m.

own, 1. adj. propre. **2.** vb. posséder; (admit) avouer; (acknowledge) reconnaître.

owner, n. propriétaire m.f.

ox, n. bœuf m.

oxygen, n. oxygène m.

oxygen mask, n. masque d'oxygène m.

oyster, n. huître f.

P

pace, 1. n. (step) pas m.; (gait) allure f. **2.** vb. arpenter.

pacific, adj. pacifique.

Pacific Ocean, n. océan Pacifique m.

pacifism, n. pacifisme m.

pacify, vb. pacifier.

pack, 1. n. paquet m.; (animals, persons) bande f. **2.** vb. emballer; (crowd) entasser.

package, n. paquet m.

pact, n. pacte m., contrat m.

pad, 1. n. (stuffing) bourrelet m.; (cotton, ink) tampon m.; (paper) bloc m. **2.** vb. (clothes) ouater; (stuff) bourrer.

padding, n. remplissage m., rembourrage m.

paddle, n. pagaie f.

paddock, n. enclos m.

pagan, adj. and n. païen m.

page, n. (book) page f.; (attendant) page m.

pageant, n. spectacle m.

pagoda, n. pagode f.

pail, n. seau m.

pain, 1. n. douleur f.; (trouble) peine f. **2.** vb. (hurt) faire mal (à); (distress) faire de la peine (à).

painful, adj. douloureux.

painstaking, adj. soigneux.

paint, 1. n. peinture f. **2.** vb. peindre.

painter, n. peintre m.

painting, n. peinture f.

pair, n. paire f.

pajamas, n. pyjama m.

palace, n. palais m.

palatable, adj. d'un goût agréable, agréable au palais.

palate, n. palais m.

palatial, adj. qui ressemble à un palais, magnifique.

pale, adj. pâle.

paleness, n. pâleur f.

palette, n. palette f.

pall, 1. n. drap funéraire m. **2.** vb. s'affadir.

pallbearer, n. porteur (d'un cordon du poêle) m.

pallid, adj. pâle, blême.

palm, n. (tree) palmier m.; (branch) palme f.; (hand) paume f.

palpitate, vb. palpiter.

paltry, adj. mesquin.

pamper, vb. choyer.

pamphlet, n. brochure f.

pan, n. (cooking) casserole f.

panacea, n. panacée f.

Pan-American, adj. panaméricain.

pancake, n. crêpe f.

pane, n. (window) vitre f.

panel, n. panneau m.

pang, n. angoisse f.

panic, n. panique f.

panorama, n. panorama m.

pant, vb. haleter.

pantomime, n. pantomime m.

pantry, n. office f.

pants, n. pantalon m.

panty hose, n. collant m.

papal, adj. papal.

paper, n. papier m.

paperback, n. livre broché m.

par, n. pair m., égalité f.

parable, n. parabole f.

parachute, n. parachute f.

parade, n. parade f.

paradise, n. paradis m.

paradox, n. paradoxe f.

paraffin, n. paraffine f.

paragraph, n. alinéa m.

parakeet, n. perruche f.

parallel, 1. n. (line) parallèle f.; (geography, comparison) parallèle m. **2.** adj. parallèle.

paralyze, vb. paralyser.

paramedic, n. assistant médical m.

parameter, n. paramètre m.

paramount, adj. souverain.

paraphrase, vb. paraphraser.

parasite, n. parasite m.

parcel, n. paquet m.; (p. post) colis postal m.

parch, vb. dessécher, tr.

parchment, n. parchemin m.

pardon, 1. n. pardon m. **2.** vb. pardonner.

pare, vb. (fruit) peler.

parent, n. père m.; mère f.; (parents) parents m.pl.

parentage, n. naissance f.

parenthesis, n. parenthèse f.

parish, n. paroisse f.

Parisian, 1. n. Parisien m. **2.** adj. parisien.

parity, n. parité f., égalité f.

park, 1. n. parc m. **2.** vb. stationner.

parley, n. conférence f., pourparler m.

parliament, n. parlement m.

parliamentary, adj. parlementaire.

parlor, n. petit salon m.

parochial, adj. paroissial; (limited in outlook) de clocher.

parody, n. parodie f.

parole, 1. *n.* parole *f.* **2.** *vb.* libérer conditionnellement.

paroxysm, *n.* paroxysme *m.*

parrot, *n.* perroquet *m.*

parsley, *n.* persil *m.*

parson, *n.* pasteur *m.*

part, 1. *n.* (of a whole) partie *f.*; (share) part *f.* **2.** *vb.* (divide) diviser; (share) partager; (of people) se séparer.

partake of, *vb.* participer à.

partial, *adj.* partiel; (favoring) partial.

participant, *adj. and n.* participant *m.*

participate, *vb.* participer.

participation, *n.* participation *f.*

participle, *n.* participe *m.*

particle, *n.* particule *f.*

particular, 1. *n.* détail *m.* **2.** *adj.* particulier; (person) exigeant.

parting, *n.* séparation *f.*; (hair) raie *f.*

partisan, *n.* partisan *m.*

partition, *n.* partage *m.*; (wall) cloison *f.*

partly, *adv.* en partie.

partner, *n.* associé *m.*

part of speech, *n.* partie (*f.*) du discours.

partridge, *n.* perdrix *f.*

party, *n.* (faction) parti *m.*; (social) réception *f.*; (group of people) groupe *m.*; (law) partie *f.*

pass, 1. *n.* (mountain) col *m.*; (permission) laissez-passer *m.* **2.** *vb.* passer.

passable, *adj.* traversable, passable, assez bon.

passage, *n.* passage *m.*

passenger, *n.* (land) voyageur *m.*; (sea, air) passager *m.*

passer-by, *n.* passant *m.*

passion, *n.* passion *f.*

passionate, *adj.* passionné.

passive, *adj. and n.* passif *m.*

passport, *n.* passeport *m.*

past, 1. *adj. and n.* passé *m.* **2.** *prep.* (beyond) au delà de; (more than) plus de; (half p. four) quatre heures et demie.

paste, 1. *n.* pâte *f.*; (glue) colle *f.* **2.** *vb.* coller.

pasteurize, *vb.* pasteuriser.

pastime, *n.* passe-temps *m.*

pastor, *n.* pasteur *m.*

pastry, *n.* pâtisserie *f.*

pasture, *n.* pâturage *m.*

pasty, *adj.* empâté, pâteux.

pat, *vb.* taper.

patch, 1. *n.* pièce *f.* **2.** *vb.* rapiécer.

patchwork, *n.* ouvrage fait de pièces disparates *m.*

patent, *n.* brevet (*m.*) d'invention.

patent leather, *n.* cuir (*m.*) verni.

paternal, *adj.* paternel.

paternity, *n.* paternité *f.*

path, *n.* sentier *m.*

pathetic, *adj.* pathétique.

pathology, *n.* pathologie *f.*

pathos, *n.* pathétique *m.*

patience, *n.* patience *f.*

patient, 1. *n.* malade *m.f.* **2.** *adj.* patient.

patio, *n.* patio *m.*

patriarch, *n.* patriarche *m.*

patriot, *n.* patriote *m.f.*

patriotic, *adj.* patriotique.

patriotism, *n.* patriotisme *m.*

patrol, *n.* patrouille *f.*

patrolman, *n.* agent (de police) *m.*, patrouilleur *m.*

patron, *n.* protecteur *m.*; (comm.) client *m.*

patronize, *vb.* protéger.

pattern, *n.* modèle *m.*; (design) dessin *m.*

pauper, *n.* indigent *m.*, pauvre *m.*, mendiant *m.*

pause, *n.* pause *f.*

pave, *vb.* paver.

pavement, *n.* pavé *m.*; (sidewalk) trottoir *m.*

pavilion, *n.* pavillon *m.*

paw, *n.* patte *f.*

pawn, 1. *n.* pion *m.* **2.** *vb.* mettre en gage, engager.

pay, 1. *n.* salaire *m.* **2.** *vb.* payer.

payment, *n.* payement *m.*

pea, *n.* pois *m.*

peace, *n.* paix *f.*

peaceable, peaceful, *adj.* paisible.

peach, *n.* pêche *f.*

peacock, *n.* paon *m.*

peak, *n.* sommet *m.*

peal, 1. *n.* retentissement *m.* **2.** *vb.* sonner, retentir.

peanut, *n.* arachide *f.*

pear, *n.* poire *f.*

pearl, *n.* perle *f.*

peasant, *n.* paysan *m.*

pebble, *n.* caillou *m.*

peck, *vb.* becqueter.

peculiar, *adj.* particulier; (unusual) singulier.

pecuniary, *adj.* pécuniaire.

pedagogue, *n.* pédagogue *m.*

pedagogy, *n.* pédagogie *f.*

pedal, *n.* pédale *f.*

pedant, *n.* pédant *m.*

peddle, *vb.* colporter.

peddler, *n.* colporteur *m.*

pedestal, *n.* piédestal *m.*

pedestrian, *n.* piéton *m.*

pediatrician, *n.* pédiatre *m.*

pedigree, *n.* généalogie *f.*

peek, 1. *n.* coup d'œil furtif *m.* **2.** *vb.* regarder à la dérobée.

peel, 1. *n.* pelure *f.* **2.** *vb.* peler.

peep, *vb.* regarder furtivement.

peer, 1. *n.* pair *m.*, pareil *m.* **2.** *vb.* scruter, regarder.

peevish, *adj.* irritable.

peg, *n.* cheville *f.*

pelt, 1. *n.* peau *f.*, fourrure *f.* **2.** *vb.* lancer, jeter.

pelvis, *n.* bassin *m.*

pen, *n.* plume *f.*

penalty, *n.* peine *f.*

penance, *n.* pénitence *f.*

penchant, *n.* penchant *m.*

pencil, *n.* crayon *m.*

pending, *prep.* pendant.

penetrate, *vb.* pénétrer.

penetration, *n.* pénétration *f.*

peninsula, *n.* péninsule *f.*

penitent, 1. *adj.* pénitent, contrit. **2.** *n.* pénitent *m.*

penknife, *n.* canif *m.*

penniless, *adj.* sans le sou.

penny, *n.* sou *m.*

pension, *n.* pension *f.*

pensive, *adj.* pensif.

pent-up, *adj.* refoulé.

penury, *n.* pénurie *f.*

people, 1. *n.* gens *m.f.pl.*; (of a country) peuple *m.* **2.** *vb.* peupler.

pepper, *n.* poivre *m.*

perambulator, *n.* voiture d'enfant *f.*

perceive, *vb.* apercevoir, *tr.*

percent, pour cent.

percentage, *n.* pourcentage *m.*

perceptible, *adj.* perceptible.

perception, *n.* perception *f.*

perch, 1. *n.* (for birds) perchoir *m.*; (fish) perche *f.* **2.** *vb.* se percher.

perdition, *n.* perte *f.*

peremptory, *adj.* péremptoire.

perennial, *adj.* perpétuel; (plant) vivace.

perfect, *adj.* parfait.

perfection, *n.* perfection *f.*

perforation, *n.* perforation *f.*

perform, *vb.* accomplir; (theater) jouer.

performance, *n.* (task) accomplissement *m.*; (theater) représentation *f.*

perfume, *n.* parfum *m.*

perfunctory, *adj.* fait pour la forme, superficiel.

perhaps, *adv.* peut-être.

peril, *n.* péril *m.*

perilous, *adj.* périlleux.

perimeter, *n.* périmètre *m.*

period, *n.* période *f.*; (full stop) point *m.*

periodic, *adj.* périodique.

periodical, *n.* périodique *m.*

periphery, *n.* périphérie *f.*

perish, *vb.* périr.

perishable, *adj.* périssable.

perjury, *n.* parjure *m.*

permanent, *adj.* permanent.

permeate, *vb.* filtrer.

permissible, *adj.* admissible.

permission, *n.* permission *f.*

permit, 1. *n.* permis *m.* **2.** *vb.* permettre.

pernicious, *adj.* pernicieux.

perpendicular, *adj.* perpendiculaire, vertical.

perpetrate, *vb.* perpétrer.

perpetual, *adj.* perpétuel.

perplex, *vb.* mettre dans la perplexité.

perplexity, *n.* perplexité *f.*, embarras *m.*

persecute, *vb.* persécuter.

persecution, *n.* persécution *f.*

perseverance, *n.* persévérance *f.*

persevere, *vb.* persévérer.

persist, *vb.* persister.

persistent, *adj.* persistant.

person, *n.* personne *f.*

personage, *n.* personnage *m.*

personal, *adj.* personnel.

personality, *n.* personnalité *f.*

personally, *adv.* personnellement.

personnel, *n.* personnel *m.*

perspective, *n.* perspective *f.*

perspiration, *n.* transpiration *f.*

perspire, *vb.* transpirer.

persuade, *vb.* persuader.

persuasive, *adj.* persuasif.

pertain, *vb.* appartenir.

pertinent, *adj.* pertinent.

perturb, *vb.* troubler.

peruse, *vb.* lire attentivement.

pervade, *vb.* pénétrer.

perverse, *adj.* entêté (dans l'erreur).

perversion, *n.* perversion *f.*

pessimism, *n.* pessimisme *m.*

pestilence, *n.* pestilence *f.*

pet, *n.* (animal) animal (*m.*) familier.

petal, *n.* pétale *m.*

petition, *n.* pétition *f.*

petroleum, *n.* pétrole *m.*

petticoat, *n.* jupon *m.*

petty, *adj.* insignifiant.

phantom, *n.* fantôme *m.*

pharmacist, *n.* pharmacien *m.*

pharmacy, *n.* pharmacie *f.*

phase, *n.* phase *f.*

phenomenal, *adj.* phénoménal.

phenomenon, *n.* phénomène *m.*

philanthropy, *n.* philanthropie *f.*

philosopher, *n.* philosophe *m.*

philosophical, *adj.* philosophique.

philosophy, *n.* philosophie *f.*

phobia, *n.* phobie *f.*

phonograph, *n.* phonographe *m.*

photocopier, *n.* photocopieur *m.*

photocopy, *n.* photocopie *f.*

photograph, photography, *n.* photographie *f.*

phrase, *n.* phrase *f.*

physical, *adj.* physique.

physician, *n.* médecin *m.*

physics, *n.* physique *f.*

pianist, *n.* pianiste *m.f.*

piano, *n.* piano *m.*

pick, *vb.* (choose) choisir; (gather) cueillir.

pickles, *n.* conserves (*f.pl.*) au vinaigre.

picnic, *n.* pique-nique *m.*

picture, *n.* tableau *m.*; (motion picture) film *m.*

picturesque, *adj.* pittoresque.

pie, *n.* tarte *f.*

piece, *n.* morceau *m.*

pier, *n.* jetée *f.*; quai *m.*

pierce, *vb.* percer.

piety, *n.* piété *f.*

pig, *n.* cochon *m.*

pigeon, *n.* pigeon *m.*

pigeonhole, *n.* (for papers, etc.) case *f.*

pile, 1. *n.* (construction) pieu *m.*; (heap) tas *m.* 2. *vb.* entasser.

pilgrim, *n.* pèlerin *m.*

pilgrimage, *n.* pèlerinage *m.*

pill, *n.* pilule *f.*

pillar, *n.* pilier *m.*

pillow, *n.* oreiller *m.*

pilot, *n.* pilote *m.*

pimple, *n.* bouton *m.*

pin, 1. *n.* épingle *f.* 2. *vb.* épingler.

pinch, *vb.* pincer.

pine, 1. *n.* pin *m.* 2. *vb.* languir.

pineapple, *n.* ananas *m.*

pink, *adj. and n.* rose *m.*

pinnacle, *n.* pinacle *m.*

pint, *n.* pinte *f.*

pioneer, *n.* pionnier *m.*

pious, *adj.* pieux.

pipe, *n.* tuyau *m.*; (smoking pipe) *f.*

piper, *n.* (bagpipe) joueur (*m.*) de cornemuse.

piquant, *adj.* piquant.

pirate, *n.* pirate *m.*

pistol, *n.* pistolet *m.*

piston, *n.* piston *m.*

pit, *n.* fosse *f.*

pitch, 1. *n.* (substance) poix *f.*; (throw) jet *m.*; (height) hauteur *f.*; (music) ton *m.* 2. *vb.* (throw) lancer.

pitcher, *n.* (vessel) cruche *f.*; (baseball) lanceur *m.*

pitfall, *n.* trappe *f.*

pitiful, *adj.* pitoyable.

pitiless, *adj.* impitoyable.

pity, 1. *n.* pité *f.*; (what a p.!) quel dommage! 2. *vb.* plaindre.

pivot, *n.* pivot *m.*, axe *m.*

pizza, *n.* pizza *f.*

place, 1. *n.* endroit *m.*; (locality) lieu *m.*; (position occupied) place *f.* 2. *vb.* mettre.

placid, *adj.* placide.

plague, *n.* (disease) peste *f.*; (*fig.*) fléau *m.*

plaid, *n.* (blanket) plaid *m.*; (textile) tartan *m.*

plain, 1. *n.* plaine *f.* 2. *adj.* (clear) clair; (simple) simple; (of person) quelconque.

plaintiff, *n.* demandeur *m.*

plan, 1. *n.* plan *m.* 2. *vb.* faire le plan de.

plane, *n.* (surface) plan *m.*; (tool) rabot *m.*; (tree) platane *m.*; (airplane) avion *m.*

planet, *n.* planète *f.*

plank, *n.* planche *f.*

plant, 1. *n.* plante *f.* 2. *vb.* planter.

plantation, *n.* plantation *f.*

planter, *n.* planteur *m.*

plasma, *n.* plasma *m.*

plaster, *n.* plâtre *m.*

plastic, *adj.* plastique.

plate, *n.* plaque *f.*; (for eating) assiette *f.*

plateau, *n.* plateau *m.*

platform, *n.* plate-forme *f.*; (railroad) quai *m.*

platter, *n.* plat *m.*

plausible, *adj.* plausible.

play, 1. *n.* jeu *m.*; (drama) pièce (*f.*) de théâtre. 2. *vb.* jouer; (game) jouer à; (instrument) jouer de.

player, *n.* joueur *m.*; (theater) acteur *m.*

playful, *adj.* enjoué.

playground, *n.* (children) terrain (*m.*) de jeu.

playmate, *n.* camarade (*m.f.*) de jeu.

playwright, *n.* dramaturge *m.*

plea, *n.* défense *f.*; (excuse) excuse *f.*

plead, *vb.* plaider; (allege) alléguer.

pleasant, *adj.* agréable.

please, *vb.* plaire à; (satisfy) contenter; (if you p.) s'il vous plaît.

pleasure, *n.* plaisir *m.*

pleat, *n.* pli *m.*

pledge, *n.* gage *m.*; (promise) engagement *m.*

plentiful, *adj.* abondant.

plenty, *n.* abondance *f.*

pliable, *adj.* pliable.

pliers, *n.* pinces *f.pl.*

plight, *n.* état *m.*

plot, *n.* (literature) intrigue *f.*; (conspiracy) complot *m.*

plow, 1. *n.* charrue *f.* 2. *vb.* labourer.

pluck, *n.* courage *m.*

plug, *n.* tampon *m.*; (electric) prise (*f.*) de courant.

plum, *n.* prune *f.*

plumber, *n.* plombier *m.*

plume, *n.* panache *m.*

plump, *adj.* grassouillet.

plunder, *vb.* piller.

plunge, 1. *n.* plongeon *m.* 2. *vb.* plonger.

plural, *adj. and n.* pluriel *m.*

plus, *n.* plus *m.*

pneumonia, *n.* pneumonie *f.*

poach, *vb.* (of eggs) pocher.

poacher, *n.* braconnier *m.*

pocket, *n.* poche *f.*

pocketbook, *n.* sac (*m.*) à main.

poem, *n.* poésie *f.*; (long) poème *f.*

poet, *n.* poète *m.*

poetic, *adj.* poétique.

poetry, *n.* poésie *f.*

poignant, *adj.* poignant.

point, 1. *n.* point *m.*; (sharp end) pointe *f.* 2. *vb.* (gun, etc.) pointer; (indicate) désigner.

pointed, *adj.* pointu; (ironical) mordant.

poise, *n.* équilibre *m.*

poison, 1. *n.* poison *m.* 2. *vb.* empoisonner.

poisonous, *adj.* empoisonné; (plant) vénéneux; (animal) venimeux.

Poland, *n.* Pologne *f.*

polar, *adj.* polaire.

polar bear, *n.* ours (*m.*) blanc.

Pole, *n.* Polonais *m.*

pole, *n.* (geography) pôle *m.*; (wood) perche *f.*

police, *n.* police *f.*

policeman, n. agent (m.) de police.

policy, n. politique f.; (insurance) police f.

Polish, adj. and n. polonais m.

polish, vb. polir; (shoes) cirer.

polite, adj. poli.

politic, political, adj. politique.

politician, n. politicien m.

politics, n. politique f.

poll, n. (voting) scrutin m.

pollen, n. pollen m.

pollute, vb. polluer.

polygamy, n. polygamie f.

pomp, n. pompe f.

pompous, adj. pompeux.

pond, n. étang m.

ponder, vb. réfléchir.

ponderous, adj. pesant.

pony, n. poney m.

pool, n. mare f.; (swimming) piscine f.

poor, adj. pauvre.

pop, n. petit bruit (m.) sec.

pope, n. pape m.

popular, adj. populaire.

popularity, n. popularité f.

population, n. population f.

porch, n. véranda f.

pore, 1. n. pore m. 2. vb. (p. over) s'absorber dans.

pork, n. porc m.

pornography, n. pornographie f.

porous, adj. poreux.

port, n. (harbor) port m.; (naut.) bâbord m.; (wine) porto m.

portable, adj. portatif.

portal, n. portail m.

portfolio, n. portefeuille m.

portion, n. portion f.

portrait, n. portrait m.

portray, vb. (paint) peindre; (describe) dépeindre.

Portugal, n. Portugal m.

Portuguese, 1. n. (person) Portugais m.; (language) portugais m. 2. adj. portugais.

pose, 1. n. pose f. 2. vb. poser.

position, n. position f.

positive, 1. n. positif m. 2. adj. positif.

possess, vb. posséder.

possession, n. possession f.

possibility, n. possibilité f.

possible, adj. possible.

possibly, adv. il est possible que . . .; (perhaps) peut-être.

post, 1. n. (mail) poste f.; (wood) poteau m.; (place) poste m. 2. vb. (mail) mettre à la poste; (placard) afficher.

postage, n. affranchissement m.

postal, adj. postal.

post card, n. carte (f.) postale.

poster, n. affiche f.

posterior, adj. postérieur.

posterity, n. postérité f.

post office, n. bureau (m.) de poste.

postpone, vb. remettre.

postscript, n. post-scriptum m.

posture, n. posture f.

pot, n. pot m.; (saucepan) marmite f.; (marijuana) herbe f., kif m.

potato, n. pomme (f.) de terre.

potent, adj. puissant.

potential, adj. and n. potentiel m.

pottery, n. poterie f.

pouch, n. sac m.

poultry, n. volaille f.

pound, n. livre f.

pour, vb. verser; (rain) tomber à verse.

poverty, n. pauvreté f.

powder, n. poudre f.

power, n. pouvoir m.; (nation, mathematics) puissance f.

powerful, adj. puissant.

powerless, adj. impuissant.

practical, adj. pratique.

practically, adv. pratiquement.

practice, 1. n. (exercise) exercice m.; (habit) habitude f.; (not theory) pratique f. 2. vb. pratiquer; (piano, etc.) s'exercer (à).

practiced, adj. expérimenté.

prairie, n. savane f.

praise, 1. n. éloge m. 2. vb. louer.

prank, n. fredaine f.

pray, vb. prier.

prayer, n. prière f.

preach, vb. prêcher.

preacher, n. prédicateur m.

precarious, adj. précaire.

precaution, n. précaution f.

precede, vb. précéder.

precedent, n. précédent m.

precept, n. précepte m.

precious, adj. précieux.

precipice, n. précipice m.

precipitate, vb. précipiter.

precise, adj. précis.

precision, n. précision f.

preclude, vb. empêcher.

precocious, adj. précoce.

predecessor, n. prédécesseur m.

predestination, n. prédestination f.

predicament, n. situation (f.) difficile.

predict, vb. prédire.

predispose, vb. prédisposer.

predominant, adj. prédominant.

prefabricate, vb. préfabriquer.

preface, n. préface f.

prefer, vb. préférer.

preferable, adj. préférable.

preference, n. préférence f.

prefix, n. préfixe m.

pregnant, adj. enceinte.

prejudice, n. préjugé m.

preliminary, adj. préliminaire.

prelude, n. prélude m.

premature, adj. prématuré.

premeditate, vb. préméditer.

premier, n. premier ministre m.

première, n. première f.

premise, n. (place) lieux m.pl.; (logic) prémisse f.

premium, n. prix m.

preparation, n. préparation f.; préparatifs m.pl.

preparatory, adj. préparatoire.

prepare, vb. préparer, tr.

preponderant, adj. prépondérant.

preposition, n. préposition f.

preposterous, adj. absurde.

prerequisite, n. nécessité (f.) préalable.

prescribe, vb. prescrire.

prescription, n. prescription f.; (medical) ordonnance f.

presence, n. présence f.

present, 1. adj. and n. présent m. 2. vb. présenter.

presentable, adj. présentable.

presentation, n. présentation f.

presently, adv. tout à l'heure.

preservative, adj. and n. préservatif m.

preserve, 1. n. (jam) confiture f. 2. vb. (protect) préserver; (keep) conserver.

preside, vb. présider.

president, n. président m.

press, 1. n. presse f. 2. vb. presser; (iron) repasser.

pressure, n. pression f.

prestige, n. prestige m.

presume, vb. présumer.

presumptuous, adj. présomptueux.

pretend, vb. (claim, aspire) prétendre; (feign) simuler.

pretense, n. faux semblant m.

pretentious, adj. prétentieux.

pretext, n. prétexte m.

pretty, adj. joli.

prevail, vb. prévaloir; (p. upon) décider.

prevalent, adj. répandu.

prevent, vb. (impede) empêcher; (forestall) prévenir.

prevention, n. empêchement m.

preventive, adj. préventif.

previous, adj. antérieur.

prey, n. proie f.

price, n. prix m.

priceless, adj. inestimable.

prick, 1. n. piqûre f. 2. vb. piquer.

pride, n. orgueil m.

priest, n. prêtre m.

prim, adj. affecté.

primary, adj. premier; (school, geology) primaire.

prime, 1. n. comble m. 2. adj. premier, de première qualité. 3. vb. amorcer.

primitive, adj. primitif.

prince, n. prince m.

princess, n. princesse f.

principal, adj. principal.

principle, n. principe m.

print, 1. n. (mark) empreinte f.; (book) impression f.; (photo) épreuve f. 2. vb. imprimer.

printout, n. feuille imprimée produite par un ordinateur f.

priority, n. priorité f.

prism, n. prisme m.

prison, n. prison f.

prisoner, *n.* prisonnier *m.*

privacy, *n.* retraite *f.*

private, *adj.* particulier; (not public) privé.

privation, *n.* privation *f.*

privilege, *n.* privilège *m.*

prize, *n.* prix *m.*

probability, *n.* probabilité *f.*

probable, *adj.* probable.

probe, *vb.* sonder.

problem, *n.* problème *m.*

procedure, *n.* procédé *m.*

proceed, *vb.* procéder; (advance) avancer.

process, *n.* (method) procédé *m.;* (progress) développement *m.*

procession, *n.* cortège *m.;* (religious) procession *f.*

proclaim, *vb.* proclamer.

proclamation, *n.* proclamation *f.*

procure, *vb.* procurer.

prodigal, *adj. and n.* prodigue *m.*

prodigy, *n.* prodige *m.*

produce, *vb.* produire.

product, *n.* produit *m.*

production, *n.* production *f.*

productive, *adj.* productif.

profane, *adj.* profane.

profess, *vb.* professer.

profession, *n.* profession *f.*

professional, *adj.* professionnel.

professor, *n.* professeur *m.*

proficient, *adj.* capable.

profile, *n.* profil *m.*

profit, 1. *n.* profit *m.* 2. *vb.* profiter.

profitable, *adj.* profitable.

profound, *adj.* profond.

profuse, *adj.* (of thing) profus; (of person) prodigue.

program, *n.* programme *m.*

progress, *n.* progrès *m.;* (motion forward) marche *f.*

progressive, *adj.* progressif.

prohibit, *vb.* défendre.

prohibition, *n.* défense *f.*

prohibitive, *adj.* prohibitif.

project, 1. *n.* projet *m.* 2. *vb.* projeter; (jut out) faire saillie.

projection, *n.* projection *f.;* (jutting out) saillie *f.*

projector, *n.* projecteur *m.*

proliferation, *n.* prolifération *f.*

prolong, *vb.* prolonger.

prominent, *adj.* saillant.

promiscuous, *adj.* (indiscriminate) sans distinction.

promise, 1. *n.* promesse *f.* 2. *vb.* promettre.

promote, *vb.* (raise) promouvoir; (encourage) encourager.

promotion, *n.* promotion *f.*

prompt, *adj.* prompt.

pronoun, *n.* pronom *m.*

pronounce, *vb.* prononcer.

pronunciation, *n.* prononciation *f.*

proof, *n.* (evidence) preuve *f.;* (test) épreuve *f.*

prop, *n.* appui *m.*

propaganda, *n.* propagande *f.*

propagate, *vb.* propager, *tr.*

propeller, *n.* hélice *f.*

proper, *adj.* propre; (respectable, fitting) convenable.

property, *n.* propriété *f.*

prophecy, *n.* prophétie *f.*

prophesy, *vb.* prophétiser.

prophet, *n.* prophète *m.*

prophetic, *adj.* prophétique.

proportion, *n.* proportion *f.*

proportionate, *adj.* proportionné.

proposal, *n.* proposition *f.;* demande (*f.*) en mariage.

propose, *vb.* proposer, *tr.*

proposition, *n.* (proposal, grammar) proposition *f.;* (undertaking) affaire *f.*

proprietor, *n.* propriétaire *m.f.*

prosaic, *adj.* prosaïque.

proscribe, *vb.* proscrire.

prose, *n.* prose *f.*

prosecute, *vb.* poursuivre.

prospect, *n.* perspective *f.*

prospective, *adj.* en perspective.

prosper, *vb.* prospérer.

prosperity, *n.* prospérité *f.*

prosperous, *adj.* prospère.

prostitute, 1. *n.* prostituée *f.* 2. *vb.* prostituer.

prostrate, *adj.* prosterné.

protect, *vb.* protéger.

protection, *n.* protection *f.*

protective, *adj.* protecteur.

protector, *n.* protecteur *m.*

protégé, *n.* protégé *m.*

protein, *n.* protéine *f.*

protest, 1. *n.* protestation *f.;* (comm.) protêt *m.* 2. *vb.* protester.

Protestant, *adj. and n.* protestant *m.*

protocol, *n.* protocole *m.*

protrude, *vb.* saillir.

prove, *vb.* prouver; (test) éprouver.

proverb, *n.* proverbe *m.*

provide (with) *vb.* pourvoir (de), *tr.*

providence, *n.* (foresight) prévoyance *f.;* (divine) providence *f.*

province, *n.* province *f.*

provincial, *adj. and n.* provincial *m.*

provision, *n.* (stock) provision *f.*

provocation, *n.* provocation *f.*

provoke, *vb.* provoquer; (irritate) irriter.

prowess, *n.* prouesse *f.*

prowl, *vb.* rôder.

proximity, *n.* proximité *f.*

prudence, *n.* prudence *f.*

prudent, *adj.* prudent.

prune, *n.* pruneau *m.*

Prussia, *n.* Prusse *f.*

Prussian, 1. *n.* Prussien *m.* 2. *adj.* prussien.

pry, *vb.* fureter.

psalm, *n.* psaume *m.*

psychedelic, *adj.* psychédélique.

psychiatry, *n.* psychiatrie *f.*

psychoanalysis, *n.* psychanalyse *f.*

psychology, *n.* psychologie *f.*

psychological, *adj.* psychologique.

ptomaine, *n.* ptomaïne *f.*

public, 1. *n.* public *m.* 2. *adj.* public *m.,* publique *f.*

publication, *n.* publication *f.*

publicity, *n.* publicité *f.*

publish, *vb.* publier.

publisher, *n.* éditeur *m.*

pudding, *n.* pouding *m.*

puddle, *n.* flaque *f.*

puff, *n.* (smoke etc.) bouffée *f.*

pull, *vb.* tirer.

pulley, *n.* poulie *f.*

pulp, *n.* pulpe *f.*

pulpit, *n.* chaire *f.*

pulsar, *n.* pulsar *m.*

pulsate, *vb.* battre.

pulse, *n.* pouls *m.*

pump, 1. *n.* pompe *f.* 2. *vb.* pomper.

pumpkin, *n.* potiron *f.*

pun, *n.* calembour *m.*

punch, 1. *n.* (tool) poinçon *m.;* (blow) coup (*m.*) de poing; (beverage) punch *m.* 2. *vb.* (pierce) percer; (pummel) gourmer.

punctual, *adj.* ponctuel.

punctuate, *vb.* ponctuer.

puncture, *n.* piqûre *f.*

punish, *vb.* punir.

punishment, *n.* punition *f.*

pupil, *n.* (school) élève *m.f.;* (eye) pupille *f.*

puppet, *n.* marionnette *f.*

puppy, *n.* petit chien *m.*

purchase, 1. *n.* achat *m.* 2. *vb.* acheter.

pure, *adj.* pur.

puree, *n.* purée *f.*

purge, *vb.* purger.

purify, *vb.* purifier.

purity, *n.* pureté *f.*

purple, *adj.* violet.

purpose, *n.* but *m.;* **(to the p.)** à propos.

purposely, *adv.* exprès.

purse, *n.* bourse *f.*

pursue, *vb.* poursuivre.

pursuit, *n.* poursuite *f.;* (occupation) occupation *f.;* **(plane)** avion (*m.*) de chasse.

push, 1. *n.* poussée *f.* 2. *vb.* pousser.

put, *vb.* mettre.

puzzle, 1. *n.* problème *m.* 2. *vb.* embarrasser.

pyramid, *n.* pyramide *f.*

Q

quadraphonic, *adj.* quadriphonique.

quail, *n.* caille *f.*

quaint, *adj.* (strange) étrange.

quake, *vb.* trembler.

qualification, *n.* (reservation) réserve *f.;* (aptitude) compétence f.; (description) qualification f.

qualify, vb. qualifier; (modify) modifier.

quality, n. qualité f.

qualm, n. scrupule m.

quantity, n. quantité f.

quarantine, n. quarantaine f.

quarrel, 1. n. querelle f. 2. vb. se quereller.

quarry, n. carrière f.

quarter, 1. n. quart m.; (district, moon, beef) quartier m.

quarterly, adj. trimestriel.

quartet, n. quatuor m.

quartz, n. quartz m.

quasar, n. quasar m.

quaver, vb. chevroter.

queen, n. reine f.

queer, adj. bizarre.

quell, vb. réprimer.

quench, vb. éteindre.

query, n. question f.

quest, n. recherche f.

question, 1. n. question f. 2. vb. interroger; (raise questions) mettre en doute.

questionable, adj. douteux.

question mark, n. point (m.) d'interrogation.

questionnaire, n. questionnaire m.

quick, 1. adj. rapide; (lively) vif. 2. adv. vite.

quicken, vb. accélérer.

quiet, 1. n. tranquillité f. 2. adj. tranquille.

quilt, n. courtepointe f.

quinine, n. quinine f.

quip, n. mot (m.) piquant.

quit, vb. quitter.

quite, adv. tout à fait.

quiver, vb. trembloter.

quiz, 1. n. petit examen m. 2. vb. examiner.

quorum, n. quorum m.

quota, n. (share) quote-part f.; (immigration, etc.) contingent m.

quotation, n. citation f.; (comm.) cote f.

quote, vb. citer.

R

rabbi, n. rabbin m.

rabbit, n. lapin m.

rabble, n. tourbe f.

rabid, adj. enragé.

race, 1. n. (people) race f.; (contest) course f. 2. vb. lutter à la course (avec).

race-track, n. piste f.

rack, n. râtelier m.; (torture) chevalet (m.) de torture.

racket, n. (tennis) raquette f.; (noise) tintamarre m.

radar, n. radar m.

radiance, n. éclat m.

radiant, adj. radieux.

radiate, vb. irradier.

radiation, n. rayonnement m.

radiator, n. radiateur m.

radical, adj. and n. radical m.

radio, n. télégraphie (f.) sans fil (commonly T.S.F.).

radioactive, adj. radio-actif.

radish, n. radis m.

radium, n. radium m.

radius, n. rayon m.

raft, n. radeau m.

rafter, n. chevron m.

rag, n. chiffon m.

rage, n. rage f.

ragged, adj. en haillons.

ragweed, n. ambroisie f.

raid, n. (police) descente f.; (mil.) raid m.

rail, n. (bar) barre f.; (railroad) rail m.

railroad, n. chemin (m.) de fer.

rain, 1. n. pluie f. 2. vb. pleuvoir.

rainbow, n. arc-en-ciel m.

raincoat, n. imperméable m.

rainfall, n. chute (f.) de pluie.

rainy, adj. pluvieux.

raise, vb. (bring up, erect, promote) élever; (lift) lever; (plants) cultiver.

raisin, n. raisin (m.) sec.

rake, 1. n. râteau m. 2. vb. râteler.

rally, n. (mil.) ralliement m.; (meeting) rassemblement m.

ram, n. bélier m.

ramble, vb. rôder; (speech) divaguer.

ramp, n. rampe f.

rampart, n. rempart m.

rancid, adj. rance.

random, n. hasard m.

range, n. (scope) étendue f.; (mountains) chaîne f.; (distance) portée f.; (stove) fourneau m.

rank, 1. n. rang m. 2. vb. ranger, tr.

ransack, vb. (search) fouiller; (pillage) saccager.

ransom, n. rançon f.

rap, 1. n. coup m. 2. vb. frapper.

rapid, adj. and n. rapide m.

rapture, n. ravissement m.

rare, adj. rare.

rascal, n. coquin m.

rash, 1. n. éruption f. 2. adj. téméraire.

raspberry, n. framboise f.

rat, n. rat m.

rate, 1. n. taux m.; (speed) vitesse f.; (at any r.) en tout cas; (first-r.) de premier ordre. 2. vb. estimer.

rather, adv. plutôt.

ratify, vb. ratifier.

ration, n. ration f.

rational, adj. raisonnable; (mathematics, philosophy) rationnel.

rattle, n. (toy) hochet m.; (noise) fracas m.

rave, vb. délirer; (r. about) s'extasier sur.

raven, n. corbeau m.

raw, adj. cru.

ray, n. rayon m.

rayon, n. rayonne f.

razor, n. rasoir m.

reach, 1. n. portée f. 2. vb. atteindre; (extend) étendre, tr.; (arrive) arriver à.

react, vb. réagir.

reaction, n. réaction f.

reactionary, adj. réactionnaire.

read, vb. lire.

reader, n. (person) lecteur m.; (book) livre (m.) de lecture.

readily, adv. promptement.

ready, adj. prêt.

real, adj. réel.

realist, n. réaliste m.f.

reality, n. réalité f.

realization, n. réalisation f.

realize, vb. (notice) s'apercevoir de; (make real) réaliser, tr.

really, adv. vraiment.

realm, n. royaume m.

reap, vb. moissonner.

rear, 1. n. (hind part) queue f.; (mil.) arrière-garde f. 2. adj. situé à l'arrière. 3. vb. élever.

reason, 1. n. raison f. 2. vb. raisonner.

reasonable, adj. raisonnable.

reassure, vb. rassurer.

rebate, n. rabais m.

rebel, 1. adj. and n. rebelle m.f. 2. vb. se rebeller.

rebellion, n. rébellion f.

rebellious, adj. rebelle.

rebirth, n. renaissance f.

rebound, n. rebond m.

rebuke, 1. n. réprimande f. 2. vb. réprimander.

rebuttal, n. réfutation f.

recall, vb. (call back) rappeler; (remember) se rappeler.

recede, vb. s'éloigner.

receipt, n. (for payment) quittance f.

receive, vb. recevoir.

receiver, n. (phone) récepteur m.

recent, adj. récent.

receptacle, n. réceptacle m.

reception, n. réception f.; (welcoming) accueil m.

receptive, adj. réceptif.

recess, n. recoin m.; (Parliament) vacances f.pl.; (school) récréation f.

recipe, n. recette f.

reciprocate, vb. payer de retour.

recite, vb. réciter.

reckless, adj. téméraire.

reckon, vb. compter.

reclaim, v. (person) corriger; (land) défricher.

recline, vb. reposer, tr.

recognition, n. reconnaissance f.

recognize, vb. reconnaître.

recoil, vb. reculer.

recollect, vb. se rappeler.

recommend, vb. recommander.

recommendation, n. recommandation f.

recompense, n. récompense f.

reconcile, vb. réconcilier.

record, 1. *n.* (register) registre *m.;* (mention) mention *f.;* (known facts of person) antécédents *m.pl.;* (sports) record *m.;* (phonograph) disque *m.* 2. *vb.* enregistrer.

record player, *n.* tourne-disques *m.*

recount, *vb.* raconter.

recover, *vb.* recouvrer; (from illness) se rétablir.

recovery, *n.* recouvrement *m.;* (health) rétablissement *m.*

recruit, 1. *n.* recrue *f.* 2. *vb.* recruter.

rectangle, *n.* rectangle *m.*

rectify, *vb.* rectifier.

recuperate, *vb.* se rétablir, *intr.*

recur, *vb.* revenir.

recycle, *vb.* recycler.

red, *adj. and n.* rouge *m.*

redeem, *vb.* racheter.

redemption, *n.* rachat *m.;* (theology) rédemption *f.*

redress, 1. *n.* justice *f.* 2. *vb.* redresser, réparer; faire justice à.

reduce, *vb.* réduire.

reduction, *n.* réduction *f.;* (on price) remise *f.*

reed, *n.* roseau *m.;* (music) anche *f.*

reef, *n.* récif *m.*

reel, *n.* bobine *f.*

refer, *vb.* référer.

referee, *n.* arbitre *m.*

reference, *n.* référence *f.*

refill, *vb.* remplir (à nouveau).

refine, *vb.* raffiner.

refinement, *n.* raffinement *m.*

reflect, *vb.* réfléchir.

reflection, *n.* réflexion *f.*

reform, 1. *n.* réforme *f.* 2. *vb.* réformer, *tr.*

reformation, *n.* réforme *f.*

refractory, *adj.* réfractaire.

refrain from, *vb.* se retenir de.

refresh, *vb.* rafraîchir.

refreshment, *n.* rafraîchissement *m.*

refrigerator, *n.* frigidaire *m.*

refuge, *n.* refuge *m.*

refugee, *n.* réfugié *m.*

refund, 1. *n.* remboursement *m.* 2. *vb.* rembourser.

refusal, *n.* refus *m.*

refuse, 1. *n.* rebut *m.* 2. *vb.* refuser.

refute, *vb.* réfuter.

regain, *vb.* regagner.

regal, *adj.* royal.

regard, 1. *n.* égard *m.;* (regards, compliments) amitiés *f.pl.* 2. *vb.* regarder.

regardless, *adj.* sans se soucier de.

regent, *adj. and n.* régent *m.*

regime, *n.* régime *m.*

regiment, *n.* régiment *m.*

region, *n.* région *f.*

register, 1. *n.* registre *m.* 2. *vb.* enregistrer; (letter) recommander.

registration, *n.* enregistrement *m.*

regret, 1. *n.* regret *m.* 2. *vb.* regretter.

regular, *adj.* régulier.

regularity, *n.* régularité *f.*

regulate, *vb.* régler.

regulation, *n.* règlement *m.*

regulator, *n.* régulateur *m.*

rehabilitate, *vb.* réhabiliter.

rehearse, *vb.* répéter.

reign, 1. *n.* règne *m.* 2. *vb.* régner.

rein, *n.* rêne *f.*

reindeer, *n.* renne *m.*

reinforce, *vb.* renforcer.

reinforcement, *n.* renfort *m.*

reject, *vb.* rejeter.

rejoice, *vb.* réjouir, *tr.*

rejoin, *vb.* (join again) rejoindre; (reply) répliquer.

relapse, *n.* rechute *f.*

relate, *vb.* raconter; (have reference to) se rapporter (à); **(relate to)** entrer en rapport avec.

relation, *n.* relation *f.;* (relative) parent *m.*

relative, 1. *n.* parent *m.* 2. *adj.* relatif.

relax, *vb.* relâcher.

relay, 1. *n.* relais *m.* 2. *vb.* relayer.

release, 1. *n.* délivrance *f.* 2. *vb.* libérer.

relent, *vb.* se laisser attendrir.

relevant, *adj.* pertinent.

reliability, *n.* sûreté *f.*

reliable, *adj.* digne de confiance.

reliant, *adj.* confiant.

relic, *n.* relique *f.*

relief, *n.* (ease) soulagement *m.;* (help) secours *m.;* (projection) relief *m.*

relieve, *vb.* (ease) soulager; (help) secourir.

religion, *n.* religion *f.*

religious, *adj.* religieux.

relinquish, *vb.* abandonner.

relish, 1. *n.* goût *m.* 2. *vb.* goûter.

reluctant, *adj.* peu disposé (à).

rely upon, *vb.* compter sur.

remain, *vb.* rester.

remainder, *n.* reste *m.*

remark, 1. *n.* remarque *f.* 2. *vb.* remarquer.

remarkable, *adj.* remarquable.

remedy, 1. *n.* remède *m.* 2. *vb.* remédier à.

remember, *vb.* se souvenir de.

remembrance, *n.* souvenir *m.*

remind of, *vb.* rappeler à (person recalling).

reminisce, *vb.* raconter ses souvenirs.

remit, *vb.* remettre.

remnant, *n.* reste *m.,* vestige *m.,* (of cloth) coupon *m.*

remorse, *n.* remords *m.*

remote, *adj.* éloigné; (vague) vague.

removable, *adj.* transportable.

removal, *n.* enlèvement *m.*

remove, *vb.* enlever.

rend, *vb.* déchirer.

render, *vb.* rendre.

rendezvous, *n.* rendez-vous *m.*

renew, *vb.* renouveler.

renewal, *n.* renouvellement *m.*

renounce, *vb.* (give up) renoncer à; (repudiate) répudier.

renovate, *vb.* renouveler.

renown, *n.* renommée *f.*

rent, 1. *n.* loyer *m.* 2. *vb.* louer.

repair, 1. *n.* réparation *f.* 2. *vb.* réparer.

repay, *vb.* (give back) rendre; (refund) rembourser.

repeat, *vb.* répéter.

repel, *vb.* repousser.

repent, *vb.* se repentir (de).

repentance, *n.* repentir *m.*

repertoire, *n.* répertoire *m.*

repetition, *n.* répétition *f.*

replace, *vb.* (place again) replacer; (take place of) remplacer.

reply, 1. *n.* réponse *f.* 2. *vb.* répondre.

report, 1. *n.* rapport *m.;* (rumor) bruit *m.* 2. *vb.* rapporter; (inform against) dénoncer.

repose, *n.* repos *m.*

represent, *vb.* représenter.

representation, *n.* représentation *f.*

representative, 1. *n.* représentant *m.;* (politics) député *m.* 2. *adj.* représentatif.

repress, *vb.* réprimer.

reprimand, *n.* réprimande *f.*

reproach, 1. *n.* reproche *m.* 2. *vb.* faire des reproches à.

reproduce, *vb.* reproduire, *tr.*

reproduction, *n.* reproduction *f.*

reproof, *n.* réprimande *f.*

reprove, *vb.* réprimander.

reptile, *n.* reptile *m.*

republic, *n.* république *f.*

republican, *adj. and n.* républicain *m.*

repulsive, *adj.* répulsif.

reputation, *n.* réputation *f.*

repute, 1. *n.* renom *m.* 2. *vb.* réputer.

request, 1. *n.* requête *f.* 2. *vb.* demander.

require, *vb.* exiger.

requirement, *n.* exigence *f.*

requisite, *adj.* nécessaire.

requisition, *n.* réquisition *f.*

rescue, 1. *n.* délivrance *f.* 2. *vb.* délivrer.

research, *n.* recherche *f.*

resemble, *vb.* ressembler à.

resent, *vb.* être froissé de.

reservation, *n.* réserve *f.*

reserve, 1. *n.* réserve *f.* 2. *vb.* réserver.

reservoir, *n.* réservoir *m.*

reside, *vb.* résider.

residence, *n.* résidence *f.*

resident, 1. *n.* habitant *m.* 2. *adj.* résidant.

resign, *vb.* résigner; (from post) se démettre (de).

resignation, *n.* résignation *f.;* (from post) démission *f.*

resist, vb. résister (à).

resistance, n. résistance f.

resolute, adj. résolu.

resolution, n. résolution f.

resolve, vb. résoudre.

resonant, adj. résonnant.

resort, 1. n. (resource) ressource f.; (recourse) recours m.; (place) lieu m. de séjour. 2. vb. avoir recours.

resound, vb. résonner.

resource, n. ressource f.

respect, 1. n. respect m.; (reference) rapport m. 2. vb. respecter.

respectable, adj. respectable.

respectful, adj. respectueux.

respective, adj. respectif.

respiration, n. respiration f.

respite, n. répit m.

respond, vb. répondre.

response, n. réponse f.

responsibility, n. responsabilité f.

responsible, adj. responsable.

rest, 1. n. (repose) repos m.; (remainder) reste m.; (the r., the others) les autres m.f.pl. 2. vb. se reposer.

restaurant, n. restaurant m.

restful, adj. qui repose.

restless, adj. (anxious) inquiet.

restoration, n. restauration f.

restore, vb. remettre; (repair) restaurer.

restrain, vb. contenir.

restraint, n. contrainte f.

restrict, vb. restreindre.

result, 1. n. résultat m. 2. vb. résulter.

resume, vb. reprendre.

résumé, n. résumé m.

resurrect, vb. ressusciter.

retail, n. détail m.

retain, vb. retenir.

retaliate, vb. user de représailles.

retard, vb. retarder.

reticent, adj. réservé.

retina, n. rétine f.

retire, vb. se retirer.

retort, n. riposte f.

retreat, 1. n. retraite f. 2. vb. se retirer.

retrieve, vb. recouvrer.

retrospect, n. renvoi m., (in retrospect) coup d'œil rétrospectif m.

return, 1. n. retour m.; (returns, comm.) recettes f.pl. 2. vb. (give back) rendre; (go back) retourner; (come back) revenir.

reunion, n. réunion f.

reveal, vb. révéler.

revel, vb. s'ébattre.

revelation, n. révélation f.

revelry, n. bacchanale f.

revenge, 1. n. vengeance f. 2. vb. (r. oneself) se venger.

revenue, n. revenu m.

reverberate, vb. réverbérer, réfléchir, répercuter.

revere, vb. révérer.

reverence, n. révérence f.

reverend, adj. révérend.

reverent, adj. respectueux.

reverie, n. rêverie f.

reverse, 1. n. (opposite) contraire m.; (defeat, medal) revers m.; (gear) marche (f.) arrière. 2. vb. renverser.

revert, vb. revenir.

review, n. revue f.

revise, vb. réviser.

revision, n. révision f.

revival, n. renaissance f.; (religious) réveil m.

revive, vb. revivre, intr.; faire revivre, tr.

revoke, vb. révoquer.

revolt, 1. n. révolte f. 2. vb. se révolter.

revolution, n. révolution f.

revolutionary, adj. révolutionnaire.

revolve, vb. tourner, intr.

revolver, n. revolver m.

reward, 1. n. récompense f. 2. vb. récompenser.

rheumatism, n. rhumatisme m.

rhinoceros, n. rhinocéros m.

rhubarb, n. rhubarbe f.

rhyme, 1. n. rime f. 2. vb. rimer.

rhythm, n. rythme m.

rhythmical, adj. rythmique.

rib, n. côte f.

ribbon, n. ruban m.

rice, n. riz m.

rich, adj. riche.

rid, vb. débarrasser.

riddle, n. énigme f.

ride, 1. n. promenade f. 2. vb. (horse) aller à cheval; (vehicle) aller en voiture.

rider, n. (on horse) cavalier m.

ridge, n. crête f.

ridicule, 1. n. ridicule m. 2. vb. se moquer de.

ridiculous, adj. ridicule.

rifle, n. fusil m.

rig, 1. n. (vessel) gréement m.; (outfit) tenue f. 2. vb. gréer.

right, 1. n. droit m.; (not left) droite f. 2. adj. (straight, not left) droit; (correct, proper) juste; (be r., of person) avoir raison; (all r.) c'est bien. 3. adv. (straight) droit; (not left) à droite; (justly) bien.

righteous, adj. juste.

righteousness, n. justice f.

right of way, n. droit de passage m., (automobiles) priorité de passage f.

rigid, adj. rigide.

rigor, n. rigueur f.

rigorous, adj. rigoureux.

rim, n. bord m.; (wheel) jante f.

ring, 1. n. anneau m.; (ornament) bague f.; (circle) cercle m.; (arena) arène f.; (sound) son m.; (phone) coup (m.) de téléphone. 2. vb. sonner.

rinse, vb. rincer.

riot, n. émeute f.

rip, 1. n. fente f. 2. vb. fendre, tr.

ripe, adj. mûr.

ripen, vb. mûrir.

ripoff, 1. n. vol m. 2. vb. voler.

ripple, 1. n. (on water) ride f. 2. vb. rider, tr.

rise, 1. n. (ground) montée f.; (increase) augmentation f.; (rank) avancement m. 2. vb. se lever.

risk, 1. n. risque m. 2. vb. risquer.

rite, n. rite m.

ritual, n. rituel.

rival, 1. adj. and n. rival m. 2. vb. rivaliser avec.

rivalry, n. rivalité f.

river, n. fleuve m.

rivet, n. rivet m.

road, n. route f.

roam, vb. errer (par).

roar, vb. (person) hurler; (lion) rugir; (bull, sea) mugir; (thunder, cannon) gronder; (laughter) éclater de.

roast, 1. n. rôti m. 2. vb. rôtir.

rob, vb. voler.

robber, n. voleur m.

robbery, n. vol m.

robe, n. robe f.

robin, n. rouge-gorge m.

robot, n. automate m.

robust, adj. robuste.

rock, 1. n. rocher m. 2. vb. balancer; (child) bercer. 3. adj. (musique) rock.

rocker, n. (chair) chaise (f.) à bascule.

rocket, n. fusée f.

rocky, adj. rocheux.

rod, n. verge f.

rodent, adj. and n. rongeur m.

roe, n. (animal) chevreuil m.; (of fish) œufs (m.pl.) de poisson.

rogue, n. coquin m.

roguish, adj. coquin.

role, n. rôle m.

roll, 1. n. rouleau m.; (bread) petit pain m.; (list) liste f.; (r.-call) appel m.; (boat) roulis m. 2. vb. rouler.

roller, n. rouleau m.

Roman, 1. n. Romain m. 2. adj. romain.

romance, n. roman (m.) de chevalerie.

romantic, adj. romanesque; (poetry, music) romantique.

romp, 1. n. tapage m. 2. vb. batifoler.

roof, n. toit m.

room, n. (space) place f.; (private use) chambre f.; (public use) salle f.

roommate, n. camarade (m.f.) de chambre.

rooster, n. coq m.

root, 1. n. racine f.; (source) source f. 2. vb. enraciner, tr.

rope, n. corde f.

rosary, n. rosaire m.

rose, n. rose f.

rosin, n. colophane f.

rosy, *adj.* de rose.

rot, 1. *n.* pourriture *f.* 2. *vb.* pourrir.

rotary, *adj.* rotatoire.

rotate, *vb.* tourner.

rotation, *n.* rotation *f.*

rotten, *adj.* pourri.

rouge, *n.* rouge *m.*

rough, *adj.* rude; (sea weather) gros *m.*, grosse *f.*

round, 1. *adj.* rond; (r. trip) l'aller (*m.*) et le retour. 2. *n.* rond *m.;* (circuit) tournée *f.*

rouse, *vb.* (wake) réveiller; (stir up) secouer.

rout, *n.* (mil.) déroute *f.*

route, *n.* route *f.*

routine, *n.* routine *f.*

rove, *vb.* errer (par).

rover, *n.* rôdeur *m.*

row, 1. *n.* rang *m.;* dispute *f.* 2. *vb.* ramer.

rowboat, *n.* barque *f.*

rowdy, *adj.* tapageur.

royal, *adj.* royal.

royalty, *n.* royauté *f.;* (of author) droits (*m.pl.*) d'auteur.

rub, *vb.* frotter.

rubber, *n.* caoutchouc *m.*

rubbish, *n.* rebuts *m.pl.;* (nonsense) bêtises *f.pl.*

ruby, *n.* rubis *m.*

rudder, *n.* gouvernail *m.*

ruddy, *adj.* rouge.

rude, *adj.* (rough) rude; (impolite) impoli.

rudiment, *n.* rudiment *m.*

rue, *vb.* regretter.

ruffian, *n.* bandit *m.*

ruffle, *n.* (frill) fraise *f.*

rug, *n.* tapis *m.*

rugged, *adj.* (rough) rude; (uneven) raboteux.

ruin, 1. *n.* ruine *f.* 2. *vb.* ruiner.

ruinous, *adj.* ruineux.

rule, 1. *n.* règle *f.;* (authority) autorité *f.* 2. *vb.* gouverner; (decide) décider.

ruler, *n.* souverain *m.;* (for lines) règle *f.*

rum, *n.* rhum *m.*

Rumania, *n.* Roumanie *f.*

Rumanian, 1. *n.* (person) Roumain *m.;* (language) roumain *m.* 2. *adj.* roumain.

rumba, *n.* rumba *f.*

rumble, *vb.* gronder.

rumor, *n.* rumeur *f.*

run, *vb. intr.* courir; (of engine) marcher; (of colors) déteindre; (of liquids) couler; (r. away) s'enfuir.

run-down, *adj.* épuisé.

rung, *n.* échelon *m.*

runner, *n.* (person) coureur *m.;* (table) chemin (*m.*) de table.

rupture, *n.* rupture *f.*

rural, *adj.* rural.

rush, 1. *n.* (haste) hâte *f.;* (onrush) ruée *f.;* (air, water) coup *m.;* (plant) jonc *m.* 2. *vb.* se précipiter, *intr.*

Russia, *n.* Russie *f.*

Russian, 1. *n.* (person) Russe *m.f.;* (language) russe *m.* 2. *adj.* russe.

rust, 1. *n.* rouille *f.* 2. *vb.* rouiller, *tr.*

rustic, *adj.* rustique.

rustle, *n.* (leaves) bruissement *m.;* (skirt) frou-frou *m.*

rusty, *adj.* rouillé.

rut, *n.* ornière *f.*

ruthless, *adj.* impitoyable.

rye, *n.* seigle *m.*

S

Sabbath, *n.* sabbat *m.*

saber, *n.* sabre *m.*

sable, *n.* zibeline *f.*

sabotage, 1. *n.* sabotage *m.* 2. *vb.* saboter.

saboteur, *n.* saboteur *m.*

saccharin, *n.* saccharine *f.*

sachet, *n.* sachet *m.*

sack, 1. *n.* sac *m.* 2. *vb.* saccager.

sacrament, *n.* sacrement *m.*

sacred, *adj.* sacré.

sacrifice, 1. *n.* sacrifice *m.* 2. *vb.* sacrifier.

sacrilege, *n.* sacrilège *m.*

sad, *adj.* triste.

sadden, *vb.* attrister, *tr.*

saddle, *n.* selle *f.*

sadism, *n.* sadisme *m.*

safe, 1. *n.* coffre-fort *m.* 2. *adj.* sûr; (s. and sound) sain et sauf; (s. from) à l'abri de.

safeguard, *vb.* sauvegarder.

safety, *n.* sûreté *f.*

safety pin, *n.* épingle (*f.*) anglaise.

sage, *n.* (person) sage *m.;* (plant) sauge *f.*

sail, 1. *n.* voile *f.* 2. *vb.* naviguer; (depart) partir.

sailboat, *n.* canot (*m.*) à voiles.

sailor, *n.* marin *m.*

saint, *n. adj. and n.* saint *m.*

sake, *n.* (for the s. of) pour l'amour de.

salad, *n.* salade *f.*

salary, *n.* appointements *m.pl.*

sale, *n.* vente *f.*

salesman, *n.* vendeur *m.*

sales tax, *n.* impôt sur les ventes *m.*

saliva, *n.* salive *f.*

salmon, *n.* saumon *m.*

salt, 1. *n.* sel *m.* 2. *vb.* saler.

salute, 1. *n.* salut *m.* 2. *vb.* saluer.

salvage, *n.* sauvetage *m.*

salvation, *n.* salut *m.*

salve, *n.* onguent *m.*

same, 1. *adj. and pron.* même. 2. *adv.* de même.

sample, *n.* échantillon *m.*

sanatorium, *n.* sanatorium *m.*

sanctify, *vb.* sanctifier.

sanction, *n.* sanction *f.*

sanctity, *n.* sainteté *f.*

sanctuary, *n.* sanctuaire *m.*

sand, *n.* sable *m.*

sandal, *n.* sandale *f.*

sandwich, *n.* sandwich *m.*

sandy, *adj.* sablonneux.

sane, *adj.* sain d'esprit.

sanitary, *adj.* sanitaire.

sanitation, *n.* hygiène *f.*

sanity, *n.* santé (*f.*) d'esprit.

Santa Claus, *n.* Bonhomme Noël *m.*

sap, *n.* sève *f.*

sapphire, *n.* saphir *m.*

sarcasm, *n.* sarcasme *m.*

sarcastic, *adj.* sarcastique.

sardine, *n.* sardine *f.*

sash, *n.* ceinture *f.;* (window) châssis *m.*

satellite, *n.* satellite *m.*

satin, *n.* satin *m.*

satire, *n.* satire *f.*

satisfaction, *n.* satisfaction *f.*

satisfactory, *adj.* satisfaisant.

satisfy, *vb.* satisfaire.

saturate, *vb.* saturer.

Saturday, *n.* samedi *m.*

sauce, *n.* sauce *f.*

saucer, *n.* soucoupe *f.*

saucy, *adj.* impertinent.

sausage, *n.* saucisse *f.*

savage, *adj. and n.* sauvage *m.f.*

save, *vb.* sauver; (put aside) mettre de côté; (economize) épargner.

savior, *n.* sauveur *m.*

savor, *n.* saveur *f.*

savory, *adj.* savoureux.

saw, 1. *n.* scie *f.* 2. *vb.* scier.

say, *vb.* dire.

scab, *n.* croûte *f.*, gale *f.*

scaffold, *n.* échafaud *m.*

scald, *vb.* échauder.

scale, 1. *n.* (fish) écaille *f.;* (balance) balance *f.;* (series, graded system, map) échelle *f.;* (music) gamme *f.* 2. *vb.* escalader.

scalp, 1. *n.* cuir (*m.*) chevelu. 2. *vb.* scalper.

scan, *vb.* (examine) scruter; (verse) scander.

scandal, *n.* scandale *m.*

scandalous, *adj.* scandaleux.

Scandinavia, *n.* Scandinavie *f.*

Scandinavian, 1. *n.* Scandinave *m.f.* 2. *adj.* scandinave.

scant(y), *adj.* limité, faible.

scar, *n.* cicatrice *f.*

scarce, *adj.* rare.

scare, *vb.* effrayer.

scarf, *n.* écharpe *f.*

scarlet, *adj. and n.* écarlate *f.;* (s. fever) scarlatine *f.*

scathing, *adj.* cinglant.

scatter, *vb.* éparpiller.

scavenger, *n.* boueur *m.*

scenario, *n.* scénario *m.*

scene, *n.* scène *f.*

scenery, *n.* (theater) décors *m.pl.;* (landscape) paysage *m.*

scent, 1. *n.* parfum *m.*, odeur *f.* 2. *vb.* flairer, sentir.

schedule, *n.* plan *m.*

scheme, *n.* plan *m.*

scholar, *n.* savant *m.*

scholarship, *n.* (school) bourse *f.*

school, *n.* école *f.*

sciatica, *n.* sciatique *f.*

science, n. science f.
science fiction, n. science-fiction f.
scientist, n. homme (m.) de science.
scissors, n. ciseaux m.pl.
scoff at, vb. se moquer de.
scold, vb. gronder.
scoop out, vb. évider.
scope, n. (extent) portée f.; (outlet) carrière f.
scorch, vb. roussir.
score, n. (games) points m.pl.; (twenty) vingtaine f.; (music) partition f.
scorn, 1. n. mépris m. 2. vb. mépriser.
scornful, adj. dédaigneux.
Scotch, Scottish, adj. écossais.
Scotchman, Scotsman, Écossais m.
Scotland, n. Ecosse f.
scour, vb. nettoyer.
scourge, n. fléau m.
scout, n. éclaireur m.; (boy s.) boy-scout m.
scowl, vb. se renfrogner.
scramble, vb. avancer péniblement.
scrap, 1. n. petit morceau m. 2. vb. mettre au rebut.
scrape, scratch, 1. n. égratignure f. 2. vb. gratter.
scream, 1. n. cri m. 2. vb. crier.
screen, n. écran m.; (folding s.) paravent m.
screw, 1. n. vis f. 2. vb. visser, tr.
screwdriver, n. tournevis m.
scribble, vb. griffonner.
scroll, n. rouleau m.
scrub, vb. frotter.
scruple, n. scrupule m.
scrupulous, adj. scrupuleux.
scrutinize, vb. scruter.
sculptor, n. sculpteur m.
sculpture, n. sculpture f.
scythe, n. faux f.
sea, n. mer f.
seabed, n. lit de la mer f.
seacoast, n. littoral m.
seal, 1. n. (animal) phoque m.; (stamp) sceau m. 2. vb. sceller.
seam, n. couture f.
seaport, n. port (m.) de mer.
search, 1. n. recherche f. 2. vb. chercher.
seasickness, n. mal (m.) de mer.
season, 1. n. saison f. 2. vb. assaisonner.
seat, 1. n. siège m. 2. vb. asseoir.
second, 1. n. seconde f. 2. adj. second, deuxième.
secondary, adj. secondaire.
secret, adj. and n. secret m.
secretary, adj. secrétaire m.f.
sect, n. secte f.
section, n. section f.
sectional, adj. régional.
secular, adj. (church) séculier; (time) séculaire.
secure, 1. adj. sûr. 2. vb. (make

s.) mettre en sûreté; (make fast) fixer; (obtain) obtenir.
security, n. sûreté f.; (comm., law) caution f.; (finance, pl.) valeurs f.pl.
sedative, adj. and n. sédatif m.
seduce, vb. séduire.
see, vb. voir.
seed, n. semence f.; (vegetables, etc.) graine f.
seek, vb. chercher.
seem, vb. sembler.
seep, vb. suinter.
segment, n. segment m.
segregate, vb. séparer.
seize, vb. saisir.
seldom, adv. rarement.
select, vb. choisir.
selection, n. sélection f.
self, n. moi m., personne f.
selfish, adj. égoïste.
selfishness, n. égoïsme m.
sell, vb. vendre, tr.
semantics, n. sémantique f.
semester, n. semestre m.
semicircle, n. demi-cercle m.
semicolon, n. point (m.) et virgule (f.).
seminary, n. séminaire m.
senate, n. sénat m.
senator, n. sénateur m.
send, vb. envoyer; (s. back) renvoyer.
senile, adj. sénile.
senior, adj. and n. (age) aîné m.; (rank) supérieur m.
senior citizen, n. personne du troisième âge f.
sensation, n. sensation f.
sensational, adj. sensationnel.
sense, n. sens m.
sensible, adj. (wise) sensé; (appreciable) sensible.
sensitive, adj. sensible.
sensual, adj. sensuel.
sentence, n. (gramm.) phrase f.; (law) sentence f.
sentiment, n. sentiment m.
sentimental, adj. sentimental.
separate, 1. adj. séparé. 2. vb. séparer, tr.
separation, n. séparation f.
September, n. septembre m.
sequence, n. suite f.
serenade, n. sérénade f.
serene, adj. serein.
sergeant, n. sergent m.
serial, n. roman-feuilleton m.
series, n. série f.
serious, adj. sérieux.
sermon, n. sermon m.
serpent, n. serpent m.
serum, n. sérum m.
servant, n. (domestic) domestique m.f.; (public) employé m.
serve, vb. servir.
service, n. service m.; (church) office m.
servitude, n. servitude f.
session, n. session f.
set, 1. n. ensemble m. 2. adj. fixe; (decided) résolu. 3. vb. tr. (put) mettre; (regulate) régler; (jewels) monter; (fix)

fixer. 4. vb. intr. (sun, etc.) coucher; (s. about) se mettre à.
settle, vb. (establish) établir, tr.; (fix) fixer; (decide) décider; (arrange) arranger; (pay) payer; (s. down to, intr.) se mettre à.
settlement, n. (colony) colonie f.; (accounts) règlement m.
settler, n. colon m.
seven, adj. and n. sept m.
seventeen, adj. and n. dix-sept m.
seventh, adj. and n. septième m.
seventy, adj. and n. soixante-dix m.
sever, vb. séparer, couper.
several, adj. and pron. plusieurs.
severe, adj. sévère.
severity, n. sévérité f.
sew, vb. coudre.
sewer, n. égout m.
sex, n. sexe m.
sexism, n. sexisme m.
sexist, adj. sexiste.
sexton, n. sacristain m.
sexual, adj. sexuel.
shabby, adj. (clothes) usé; (person) mesquin.
shade, 1. n. ombre f.; (colors) nuance f.; (window) store m. 2. vb. ombrager.
shadow, n. ombre f.
shady, adj. ombragé; (not honest) louche.
shaft, n. (mine) puits m.
shaggy, adj. poilu, hirsute.
shake, vb. tr. secouer; (s. hands) serrer la main à.
shall, vb. (use future of verb).
shallow, adj. peu profond.
shame, n. honte f.
shameful, adj. honteux.
shampoo, n. schampooing m.
shape, 1. n. forme f. 2. vb. former.
share, 1. n. part f.; (finance) action f. 2. vb. partager.
shark, n. requin m.
sharp, adj. (cutting) tranchant; (clever) fin; (piercing) perçant; (music) dièse.
sharpen, vb. aiguiser.
shatter, vb. briser.
shave, vb. raser, tr.
shawl, n. châle m.
she, pron. elle.
sheaf, n. (grain) gerbe f.
shear, vb. tondre.
shears, n. cisailles f.pl.
sheath, n. étui m.
shed, 1. n. hangar m. 2. vb. verser.
sheep, n. mouton m.
sheet, n. (bed) drap m.; (paper, metal) feuille f.
shelf, n. rayon m.
shell, n. coquille f.; (of building) carcasse f.; (explosive) obus m.
shellac, n. laque f.

shelter, 1. n. abri m. 2. vb. abriter.

shepherd, n. berger m.

sherbet, n. sorbet m.

sherry, n. xérès m.

shield, n. bouclier m.

shift, 1. n. (change) changement m.; (workers) équipe f.; (expedient) expédient m.; (shirt) chemise f. 2. vb. changer; (s. gears) changer de vitesse.

shine, vb. briller, intr.; (shoes) cirer.

shiny, adj. luisant.

ship, n. navire m.; (large) vaisseau m.

shipment, n. envoi m.

shirk, vb. esquiver.

shirt, n. chemise f.

shiver, 1. n. frisson m. 2. vb. frissonner.

shock, 1. n. choc m. 2. vb. choquer.

shoe, n. soulier m.

shoelace, n. lacet m.

shoemaker, n. cordonnier m.

shoot, vb. tirer; (person) fusiller; (hit) atteindre; (rush) se précipiter.

shop, 1. n. boutique f.; (factory) atelier m. 2. vb. faire des emplettes.

shore, n. rivage m.

short, adj. court.

shortage, n. manque m.

shorten, vb. raccourcir.

shorthand, n. sténographie f.

shot, n. coup m.

should, vb. devoir (in conditional).

shoulder, n. épaule f.

shout, 1. n. cri m. 2. vb. crier.

shove, vb. pousser.

shovel, n. pelle f.

show, 1. n. (exhibition) exposition f.; (spectacle, performance) spectacle, performance) spectacle m.; (semblance) semblant m.; (display) parade f. 2. vb. montrer, tr.

shower, n. averse f.

shrapnel, n. shrapnel m.

shrewd, adj. sagace.

shriek, n. cri (m.) perçant.

shrill, adj. aigu.

shrimp, n. crevette f.

shrine, n. châsse f.

shrink, vb. rétrécir, tr.

shroud, n. linceul m.

shrub, n. arbrisseau m.

shudder, 1. n. frisson m. 2. vb. frissonner.

shun, vb. fuir.

shut, vb. fermer.

shutter, n. volet m.

shy, adj. timide.

sick, adj. malade.

sickness, n. maladie f.

side, n. côté f.

sidewalk, n. trottoir m.

siege, n. siège m.

sieve, n. tamis m.

sift, vb. cribler.

sigh, 1. n. soupir m. 2. vb. soupirer.

sight, n. vue f.; (spectacle) spectacle m.

sightseeing, n. tourisme m.

sign, 1. n. signe m.; (placard) enseigne f. 2. vb. signer.

signal, n. signal m.

signature, n. signature f.

significance, n. (meaning) signification f.; (importance) importance f.

significant, adj. significatif.

signify, vb. signifier.

silence, n. silence m.

silent, adj. silencieux.

silk, n. soie f.

silken, adj. de soie.

silly, adj. sot m., sotte f.

sliver, 1. n. argent m. 2. adj. d'argent.

silverware, n. argenterie f.

similar, adj. semblable.

simple, adj. simple.

simplicity, n. simplicité f.

simplify, vb. simplifier.

simply, adv. simplement.

simultaneous, adj. simultané.

sin, 1. n. péché m. 2. vb. pécher.

since, 1. adv., prep. depuis. 2. conj. (time) depuis que; (cause) puisque.

sincere, adj. sincère.

sincerity, n. sincérité f.

sinful, adj. (person) pécheur m., pécheresse f.; (act) coupable.

sing, vb. chanter.

singer, n. chanteur m.

single, adj. (only one) seul; (particular) particulier; (not married) célibataire.

singular, adj. and n. singulier m.

sinister, adj. sinistre.

sink, 1. n. évier m. 2. vb. enfoncer, tr.; (vessel) couler au fond; (diminish, weaken) baisser.

sinner, n. pécheur m., pécheresse f.

sinus, n. sinus m.

sip, vb. siroter.

sir, n. monsieur m.; (title) Sir m.

sirloin, n. aloyau m.

sister, n. sœur f.

sister-in-law, n. belle-sœur f.

sit, vb. (s. down) s'asseoir; (be seated) être assis.

site, n. emplacement m.

situate, vb. situer.

situation, n. situation f.

six, adj. and n. six m.

sixteen, adj. and n. seize m.

sixteenth, adj. and n. seizième m.

sixth, adj. and n. sixième m.

sixty, adj. and n. soixante m.

size, n. grandeur f.; (person) taille f.; (shoes, gloves) pointure f.

skate, 1. n. patin m. 2. vb. patiner.

skateboard, n. planche à roulettes f.

skeleton, n. squelette m.

skeptic, n. sceptique m.f.

skeptical, adj. sceptique.

sketch, 1. n. croquis m. 2. vb. esquisser.

ski, 1. n. ski m. 2. vb. faire du ski.

skill, n. adresse f.

skillful, adj. adroit.

skim, vb. (milk) écrémer; (book) feuilleter; (surface) effleurer.

skin, 1. n. peau f. 2. vb. écorcher.

skip, vb. sauter.

skirt, n. jupe f.

skull, n. crâne m.

sky, n. ciel m.

skyscraper, n. gratte-ciel m.

slab, n. dalle f.

slack, adj. lâche.

slacken, vb. (slow up) ralentir; (loosen) relâcher.

slacks, n. pantalon m.

slander, 1. n. calomnie f. 2. vb. calomnier.

slang, n. argot m.

slant, 1. n. (slope) pente f.; (bias) biais m. 2. vb. incliner.

slap, n. claque f.

slash, n. taillade f.

slate, n. ardoise f.

slaughter, 1. n. (people) massacre m.; (animals) abattage m. 2. vb. massacrer; abattre.

slave, n. esclave m.f.

slavery, n. esclavage m.

slay, vb. tuer.

sled, n. traîneau m.

sleep, 1. n. sommeil m.; (go to s.) s'endormir. 2. vb. dormir.

sleepy, adj. somnolent; (be s.) avoir sommeil.

sleet, 1. n. grésil m. 2. vb. grésiller.

sleeve, n. manche f.

sleigh, n. traîneau m.

slender, adj. mince; svelte.

slice, n. tranche f.

slide, 1. n. (sliding) glissade f.; (microscope) lamelle f.; (lantern) plaque (f.) de projection. 2. vb. glisser.

slight, adj. léger; mince.

slim, adj. svelte.

sling, 1. n. fronde f.; (medical) écharpe f. 2. vb. (throw) lancer; (hang) suspendre.

slip, 1. n. (sliding) glissade f.; (tongue, pen) lapsus m.; (mistake) faux pas m.; (paper) fiche f.; (garment) combinaison f. 2. vb. glisser; (err) faire une faute.

slipper, n. pantoufle f.

slippery, adj. glissant.

slit, 1. n. fente f. 2. vb. fendre.

slogan, n. mot (m.) d'ordre; (politics) cri (m.) de guerre.

slope, 1. n. pente f. 2. vb. incliner.

sloppy, adj. (slushy) bourbeux; (slovenly) mal soigné.

slot, n. fente f.

slow, adj. lent; (clock) en retard.

slowness, n. lenteur f.

sluggish, adj. paresseux.

slumber, vb. sommeiller.

sly, adj. (crafty) rusé; (secretive) sournois.

smack, n. (a bit) soupçon m.; (noise) claquement m.

small, adj. petit.

smallpox, n. petite vérole f.

smart, 1. adj. (clever) habile; (stylish) élégant. **2.** vb. cuire.

smash, vb. briser, tr.

smear, 1. n. tache f. **2.** vb. salir.

smell, 1. n. odeur f. **2.** vb. sentir.

smelt, n. éperlan m. **2.** vb. fondre.

smile, n., vb. sourire m.

smite, vb. frapper.

smoke, 1. n. fumée f. **2.** vb. fumer.

smolder, vb. couver.

smooth, 1. adj. lisse. **2.** vb. lisser.

smother, vb. étouffer.

smuggle, vb. faire passer en contrebande.

snack, n. casse-croute m.

snag, n. obstacle (m.) caché.

snail, n. escargot m.

snake, n. serpent m.

snap, 1. n. (bite) coup (m.) de dents; (sound) coup (m.) sec. **2.** vb.tr. (with teeth) happer; (sound) faire claquer.

snapshot, n. cliché m.

snare, n. piège m.

snarl, vb. grogner.

snatch, vb. saisir.

sneak, vb. se glisser furtivement.

sneer, vb. ricaner.

sneeze, 1. n. éternuement m. **2.** vb. éternuer.

snob, n. snob m.

snore, vb. ronfler.

snow, 1. n. neige f. **2.** vb. neiger.

snug, adj. confortable.

so, adv. si; tellement; (thus) ainsi; (s. that) de sorte que.

soak, vb. tremper.

soap, n. savon m.

soar, vb. prendre son essor.

sob, 1. n. sanglot m. **2.** vb. sangloter.

sober, adj. (moderate) sobre; (sedate) sérieux; (not drunk) qui n'est pas ivre.

sociable, adj. sociable.

social, adj. social.

socialism, n. socialisme m.

socialist, adj. and n. socialiste m.f.

society, n. société f.

sociology, n. sociologie f.

sock, n. chaussette f.

socket, n. douille f.

sod, n. motte f.

soda, n. soude f.; (s.-water) eau (f.) de Seltz.

sofa, n. canapé m.

soft, adj. doux m., douce f.; (yielding) mou m., molle f.

soften, vb. amollir, tr.

soil, 1. n. terroir m. **2.** vb. souiller.

sojourn, 1. n. séjour m. **2.** vb. séjourner.

solace, n. consolation f.

solar, adj. solaire.

soldier, n. soldat m.

sole, n. (shoe) semelle f.; (fish) sole f.

solemn, adj. solennel.

solemnity, n. solennité f.

solicit, vb. solliciter.

solicitous, adj. empressé.

solid, adj. and n. solide m.

solidity, n. solidité f.

solitary, adj. solitaire.

solitude, n. solitude f.

solo, n. solo m.

solution, n. solution f.

solve, vb. résoudre.

solvent, adj. (comm.) solvable.

somber, adj. sombre.

some, 1. adj. quelque; (partitive) de. **2.** pron. certains; (with verb) en.

somebody, someone, pron. quelqu'un.

something, pron. quelque chose m.

some time, adv. (past) autrefois; (future) quelque jour.

sometimes, adv. quelquefois.

somewhat, adv. quelque peu.

somewhere, adv. quelque part.

son, n. fils m.

song, n. chant m.; (light s.) chanson f.

son-in-law, n. gendre m.

soon, adv. bientôt, tôt.

soot, n. suie f.

soothe, vb. calmer.

sophisticated, adj. blasé.

soprano, n. soprano m.

sordid, adj. sordide.

sore, adj. (aching) douloureux; (have a s. throat, etc.) avoir mal à . . . .

sorrow, n. douleur f.

sorrowful, adj. (person) affligé.

sorry, 1. adj. fâché; (be s.) regretter. **2.** interj. pardon!

sort, 1. n. sorte f. **2.** vb. trier.

soul, n. âme f.

sound, 1. n. son m. **2.** adj. (healthy) sain, solide. **3.** vb. sonner.

soup, n. potage m.

sour, adj. aigre.

source, n. source f.

south, n. sud m.

southeast, n. sud-est m.

southern, adj. du sud.

South Pole, n. pôle sud m.

southwest, n. sud-ouest m.

souvenir, n. souvenir m.

sow, vb. semer.

space, n. espace m.

space shuttle, n. navette spatiale f.

spacious, adj. spacieux.

spade, n. bêche f.; (cards) pique m.

Spain, n. Espagne f.

span, n. (hand) empan m.; (bridge) travée f.

Spaniard, n. Espagnol m.

Spanish, adj. and n. espagnol m.

spank, vb. fesser.

spanking, n. fessée f.

spare, 1. adj. (in reserve) de réserve. **2.** vb. épargner.

spark, n. étincelle f.

sparkle, vb. étinceler.

sparrow, n. moineau m.

spasm, n. spasme m.

speak, vb. parler.

speaker, n. (public) orateur m.

special, adj. spécial.

specialist, n. spécialiste m.f.

specially, adv. spécialement.

specialty, n. spécialité f.

species, n. espèce f.

specific, adj. spécifique.

specify, vb. spécifier.

specimen, n. spécimen m.

spectacle, n. spectacle m.

spectacular, adj. spectaculaire.

spectator, n. spectateur m.

speculate, vb. spéculer.

speculation, n. spéculation f.

speech, n. (address) discours m.; (utterance) parole f.

speed, n. vitesse f.

speedy, adj. rapide.

spell, 1. n. (incantation) charme m.; (period) période f. **2.** vb. épeler.

spend, vb. (money) dépenser; (time) passer.

sphere, n. sphère f.

spice, n. épice f.

spider, n. araignée f.

spike, n. pointe f.

spill, vb. répandre tr.

spin, vb. (thread) filer; (twirl) tourner.

spinach, n. épinards m.pl.

spine, n. épine f.; (backbone) épine (f.) dorsale.

spiral, 1. n. spirale f. **2.** adj. spiral.

spirit, n. esprit m.

spiritual, adj. spirituel.

spiritualism, n. spiritisme m.

spit, 1. n. (saliva) crachat m.; (for roast) broche f. **2.** vb. cracher.

spite, n. dépit m.; (in s. of) malgré.

splash, vb. éclabousser.

splendid, adj. splendide.

splendor, n. splendeur f.

splinter, n. éclat m.

split, vb. fendre.

spoil, 1. n. butin m. **2.** vb. gâter.

sponge, n. éponge f.

sponsor, n. (law) garant m.

spontaneous, adj. spontané.

spontaneity, n. spontanéité f.

spool, n. bobine f.

spoon, n. cuiller f.

spoonful, n. cuillerée f.

sporadic, adj. sporadique.

sport, n. sport m.; (fun) jeu m.

spot, 1. n. (stain) tache f.

(place) endroit *m.* 2. *vb.* tacher; (recognize) reconnaître.

spouse, *n.* époux *m.,* épouse *f.*

spout, 1. *n.* (teapot, etc.) bec *m.* 2. *vb.* jaillir.

sprain, *n.* entorse *f.*

sprawl, *vb.* s'étaler.

spray, *n.* (sea) embrun *m.*

spread, 1. *n.* étendue *f.* 2. *vb.* étendre, *tr.*

spree, *n.* (be on a s.) faire la noce.

sprightly, *adj.* éveillé.

spring, 1. *n.* (season) printemps *m.;* (source) source *f.;* (leap) saut *m.;* (device) ressort *m.* 2. *vb.* (leap) sauter; (water) jaillir.

sprinkle, *vb.* asperger.

spry, *adj.* alerte.

spur, 1. *n.* éperon *m.* 2. *vb.* éperonner.

spurious, *adj.* faux *m.*

spurn, *vb.* repousser.

spurt, *n.* jet *m.* 2. *vb.* jaillir.

spy, *n.* espion *m.*

squad, *n.* escouade *f.*

squadron, *n.* escadron *m.*

squalid, *adj.* misérable.

squall, *n.* rafale *f.*

squander, *vb.* gaspiller.

square, 1. *n.* (geom.) carré *m.;* (in town) place *f.* 2. *adj.* carré.

squat, *vb.* s'accroupir.

squeak, *vb.* crier.

squeeze, *vb.* serrer; (lemon) presser.

squirrel, *n.* écureuil *m.*

squirt, *vb.* seringuer.

stab, *vb.* poignarder.

stability, *n.* stabilité *f.*

stable, 1. *n.* écurie *f.* 2. *adj.* stable.

stack, *n.* (hay) meule *f.;* (pile) pile *f.;* (chimney) souche *f.*

staff, *n.* (stick) bâton *m.;* (mil.) état-major *m.;* (personnel) personnel *m.*

stage, *n.* (theater) scène *f.;* (in development) période *f.;* (stopping-place) étape *f.*

stagflation, *n.* stagflation *f.*

stagger, *vb.* (totter) chanceler.

stagnant, *adj.* stagnant.

stain, 1. *n.* tache *f.* 2. *vb.* (spot) tacher; (color) teinter.

stairs, *n.* escalier *m.*

stake, 1. *n.* (post) pieu *m.;* (at s.) en jeu. 2. *vb.* (gaming) mettre au jeu.

stale, *adj.* (bread) rassis.

stalk, *n.* tige *f.*

stall, *n.* (stable, church) stalle *f.*

stamina, *n.* vigueur *f.*

stammer, *vb.* bégayer.

stamp, 1. *n.* timbre(-poste) *m.* 2. *vb.* (letter) timbrer; (with foot) frapper du pied.

stampede, *n.* sauve-qui-peut *n.*

stand, 1. *n.* (position) position *f.;* (resistance) résistance *f.;* (stall) étalage *m.;* (vehicles) station *f.* 2. *vb.* *tr.* (put)

poser; (endure) supporter. 3. *vb. intr.* (upright) se tenir debout (be situated, be) se trouver; (stop) s'arrêter.

standard, *n.* (flag) étendard *m.;* (measure, etc.) étalon *m.;* (living, etc.) niveau *m.*

star, *n.* étoile *f.;* (movie) vedette *f.*

starch, *n.* amidon *m.*

stare, *vb.* regarder fixement.

stark, *adj.* pur.

start, 1. *n.* (beginning) commencement *m.;* (surprise, etc.) tressaillement *m.* 2. *vb.* commencer, tressaillir.

startle, *vb.* effrayer.

starvation, *n.* faim *f.*

starve, *vb. intr.* mourir de faim.

state, 1. *n.* état *m.* 2. *vb.* déclarer.

statement, *n.* déclaration *f.*

statesman, *n.* homme (*m.*) d'état.

static, *adj.* statique.

station, *n.* (railroad) gare *f.;* (bus, subway) station *f.*

stationary, *adj.* stationnaire.

stationery, *n.* papeterie *f.*

statistics, *n.* statistique *f.*

statue, *n.* statue *f.*

stature, *n.* stature *f.*

statute, *n.* statut *m.*

stay, *vb.* rester.

steady, *adj.* ferme; (constant) soutenu.

steak, *n.* bifteck *m.*

steal, *vb.* voler.

steam, *n.* vapeur *f.*

steamboat, *n.* bateau (*m.*) à vapeur.

steamship, *n.* vapeur *m.*

steel, *n.* acier *m.*

steep, *adj.* raide.

steeple, *n.* clocher *m.*

steer, 1. *n.* jeune bœuf *m.* 2. *vb.* gouverner.

stem, *n.* (plant) tige *f.*

stenographer, *n.* sténographe *m.f.*

stenography, *n.* sténographie *f.*

step, *n.* pas *m.;* (of staircase) marche *f.*

stereophonic, *adj.* stéréophonique.

sterile, *adj.* stérile.

stern, *adj.* sévère.

stethoscope, *n.* stéthoscope *m.*

stew, *n.* ragoût *m.*

steward, *n.* (airline) garçon *m.*

stewardess, *n.* (airline) hôtesse de l'air *f.*

stick, 1. *n.* bâton *m.* 2. *vb.* (paste) coller, *tr.;* (remain) rester.

sticky, *adj.* gluant.

stiff, *adj.* raide.

stiffness, *n.* raideur *f.*

stifle, *vb.* étouffer.

still, 1. *adj.* tranquille. 2. *adv.* encore. 3. *conj.* cependant.

stillness, *n.* tranquillité *f.*

stimulant, *n.* stimulant *m.*

stimulate, *vb.* stimuler.

stimulus, *n.* stimulant *m.*

sting, 1. *n.* piqûre *f.* 2. *vb.* (prick) piquer; (smart) cuire.

stingy, *adj.* mesquin.

stir, 1. *vb.* remuer; (person, intr.) bouger. 2. *n.* mouvement *m.*

stitch, 1. *n.* (sewing) point *m.;* (knitting) maille *f.* 2. *vb.* coudre.

stock, *n.* (goods on hand) marchandises *f.pl.;* (finance) valeurs *f.pl.*

stockbroker, *n.* agent de change *m.*

stock exchange, *n.* Bourse *f.*

stocking, *n.* bas *m.*

stole, *n.* étole *f.*

stomach, *n.* estomac *m.*

stone, *n.* pierre *f.*

stool, *n.* escabeau *m.*

stoop, *vb.* se pencher.

stop, 1. *n.* arrêt *m.* 2. *vb.* arrêter, *tr.;* (prevent) empêcher (de); (cease) cesser.

storage, *n.* emmagasinage *m.*

store, 1. *n.* (shop) magasin *m.;* (supply) provision *f.* 2. *vb.* emmagasiner.

storm, *n.* orage *m.*

stormy, *adj.* orageux.

story, *n.* histoire *f.;* (floor) étage *m.*

stout, *adj.* gros *m.,* grosse *f.*

stove, *n.* fourneau *m.*

straight, *adj. and adv.* droit.

straighten, *vb.* redresser.

strain, 1. *n.* effort *m.* 2. *vb.* (stretch) tendre; (filter) passer.

strait, *n.* (geographical) détroit *m.*

strand, *n.* plage *f.*

strange, *adj.* étrange; (foreign) étranger.

stranger, *n.* étranger *m.*

strangle, *vb.* étrangler.

strap, *n.* courroie *f.*

strategic, *adj.* stratégique.

strategy, *n.* stratégie *f.*

straw, *n.* paille *f.*

strawberry, *n.* fraise *f.*

stray, *adj.* égaré.

streak, 1. *n.* raie *f.* 2. *vb.* rayer.

stream, *n.* courant *m.;* (small river) ruisseau *m.*

streamline, *vb.* caréner.

street, *n.* rue *f.*

strength, *n.* force *f.*

strengthen, *vb.* fortifier.

strenuous, *adj.* énergique.

streptococcus, *n.* streptocoque *m.*

stress, 1. *n.* force *f.;* tension *f.;* (gramm.) accent *m.* 2. *vb.* accentuer.

stretch, *vb.* étendre, *tr.*

stretcher, *n.* brancard *m.*

strict, *adj.* strict.

stride, *n.* enjambée *f.*

strife, *n.* lutte *f.*

strike, 1. *n.* grève *f.* 2. *vb.* frapper; (match, *tr.*) allumer; (clock) sonner; (workers) se mettre en grève.

string, *n.* ficelle *f.*; (music) corde *f.*

string bean, *n.* haricot vert *m.*

strip, 1. *n.* bande *f.* 2. *vb.* dépouiller.

stripe, *n.* bande *f.*; (mil.) galon *m.*

strive, *vb.* s'efforcer (de).

stroke, 1. *n.* coup *m.* 2. *vb.* caresser.

stroll, *n.* tour *m.*

strong, *adj.* fort.

structure, *n.* structure *f.*

struggle, 1. *n.* lutte *f.* 2. *vb.* lutter.

stub, *n.* souche *f.*

stubborn, *adj.* opiniâtre, obstiné, têtu.

student, *n.* étudiant *m.*

studio, *n.* atelier *m.*

studious, *adj.* studieux.

study, 1. *n.* étude *f.*; (room) cabinet (*m.*) de travail. 2. *vb.* étudier.

stuff, 1. *n.* (materials) matériaux *m.pl.*; (textile) étoffe *f.* 2. *vb.* bourrer; (cooking) farcir.

stuffing, *n.* bourre *f.*; (cooking) farce *f.*

stumble, *vb.* trébucher.

stump, *n.* (tree) souche *f.*

stun, *vb.* étourdir.

stunt, *n.* tour (*m.*) de force.

stupid, *adj.* stupide.

stupidity, *n.* stupidité *f.*

sturdy, *adj.* vigoureux.

stutter, *vb.* bégayer.

style, *n.* style *m.*

stylish, *adj.* élégant.

subconscious, *adj.* subconscient.

subdue, *vb.* subjuguer.

subject, 1. *n.* sujet *m.* 2. *adj.* (people, country) assujetti; (liable) sujet. 3. *vb.* assujettir.

sublimate, *vb.* sublimer.

sublime, *adj.* sublime.

submarine, *n.* sous-marin *m.*

submerge, *vb.* submerger.

submission, *n.* soumission *f.*

submit, *vb.* soumettre, *tr.*

subnormal, *adj.* sous-normal.

subordinate, *adj.* and *n.* subordonné *m.*

subscribe, *vb.* (consent, support) souscrire; (to paper, etc.) s'abonner.

subscription, *n.* souscription *f.*; (to paper, etc.) abonnement *m.*

subsequent, *adj.* subséquent.

subsidy, *n.* subvention *f.*

substance, *n.* substance *f.*

substantial, *adj.* substantiel; (well-to-do) aisé.

substitute, 1. *n.* remplaçant *m.* 2. *vb.* substituer.

substitution, *n.* substitution *f.*

subterfuge, *n.* subterfuge *m.*, faux-fuyant *m.*

subtle, *adj.* subtil.

subtract, *vb.* soustraire.

suburb, *n.* faubourg *m.*

subversive, *adj.* subversif.

subway, *n.* métro(politain) *m.*

succeed, *vb.* (come after) succéder à; (be successful) réussir (à).

success, *n.* succès *m.*

successful, *adj.* heureux.

succession, *n.* succession *f.*

successive, *adj.* successif.

successor, *n.* successeur *m.*

succumb, *vb.* succomber.

such, *adj.* tel; (intensive, s. a + *adj.*) un ... aussi + *adj.*

suck, *vb.* sucer.

suction, *n.* succion *f.*

sudden, *adj.* soudain.

sue, *vb.* poursuivre.

suffer, *vb.* souffrir.

suffice, *vb.* suffire.

sufficient, *adj.* suffisant.

suffocate, *vb.* suffoquer.

sugar, *n.* sucre *m.*

suggest, *vb.* suggérer.

suggestion, *n.* suggestion *f.*

suicide, 1. *n.* suicide *m.* 2. *vb.* (commit s.) se suicider, *intr.*

suit, 1. *n.* (law) procès *m.*; (clothes) complet *m.*; (cards) couleur *f.* 2. *vb.* convenir (à).

suitable, *adj.* convenable.

suitcase, *n.* valise *f.*

sum, *n.* somme *f.*

summary, 1. *n.* résumé *m.*, abrégé *m.* 2. *adj.* sommaire, immédiat.

summer, *n.* été *m.*

summon, *vb.* (convoke) convoquer; (bid to come) appeler.

sun, *n.* soleil *m.*

sunburn, *n.* hâle *m.*

Sunday, *n.* dimanche *m.*

sunny, *adj.* ensoleillé.

sunshine, *n.* soleil *m.*

superb, *adj.* superbe.

superficial, *adj.* superficiel.

superfluous, *adj.* superflu.

superintendent, *n.* surveillant *m.*

superior, *adj.* and *n.* supérieur *m.*

superiority, *n.* supériorité *f.*

supernatural, *adj.* and *n.* surnaturel *m.*

supersede, *vb.* remplacer.

superstar, *n.* superstar *f.*

superstition, *n.* superstition *f.*

superstitious, *adj.* superstitieux.

supervise, *vb.* surveiller.

supper, *n.* souper *m.*

supplement, *n.* supplément *m.*

supply, 1. *n.* approvisionnement *m.*; (provision) provision *f.* 2. *vb.* fournir (de).

support, 1. *n.* appui *m.* 2. *vb.* soutenir; (bear) supporter; (back up) appuyer.

suppose, *vb.* supposer.

suppress, *vb.* supprimer.

suppression, *n.* suppression *f.*

supreme, *adj.* suprême.

sure, *adj.* sûr.

surface, *n.* surface *f.*

surge, *n.* houle *f.*

surgeon, *n.* chirurgien *m.*

surgery, *n.* chirurgie *f.*

surpass, *vb.* surpasser.

surplus, *n.* surplus *m.*

surprise, 1. *n.* surprise *f.* 2. *vb.* surprendre.

surrender, *vb.* rendre, *tr.*

surround, *vb.* entourer.

survey, *vb.* contempler; (investigate) examiner.

survival, *n.* survivance *f.*

survive, *vb.* survivre.

susceptible, *adj.* susceptible (de).

suspect, *vb.* soupçonner.

suspend, *vb.* suspendre.

suspense, *n.* incertitude *f.*; (in s.) en suspens.

suspension, *n.* suspension *f.*

suspicion, *n.* soupçon *m.*

suspicious, *adj.* soupçonneux; (questionable) suspect.

sustain, *vb.* soutenir.

swallow, 1. *n.* (bird) hirondelle *f.* 2. *vb.* avaler.

swamp, *n.* marais *m.*

swan, *n.* cygne *m.*

swarm, *n.* essaim *m.*

sway, 1. *n.* (rule) domination *f.*; (motion) oscillation *f.* 2. *vb.* gouverner.

swear, *vb.* jurer.

sweat, 1. *n.* sueur *f.* 2. *vb.* suer.

Sweden, *n.* Suède *m.*

Swede, *n.* Suède *m.*

Swedish, *adj.* and *n.* suédois *m.*

sweep, 1. *n.* (bend) courbe *f.*; (movement) mouvement (*m.*) circulaire. 2. *vb.* balayer.

sweepstakes, *n.* poule *f.*

sweet, *adj.* doux *m.*, douce *f.*; sucré.

sweetheart, *n.* amant *m.*, amante *f.*

sweetness, *n.* douceur *f.*

swell, *vb.* gonfler, *tr.*; enfler, *tr.*

swift, *adj.* rapide.

swim, *vb.* nager.

swindle, *vb.* escroquer.

swine, *n.* cochon *m.*

swing, *vb.* balancer, *tr.*

Swiss, 1. *n.* Suisse *m.* 2. *adj.* suisse, helvétique.

switch, *n.* (electric) interrupteur *m.*

Switzerland, *n.* Suisse *f.*

sword, *n.* épée *f.*

syllable, *n.* syllabe *f.*

symbol, *n.* symbole *m.*

symbolic, *adj.* symbolique.

sympathetic, *adj.* compatissant.

sympathy, *n.* compassion *f.*

symphony, *n.* symphonie *f.*

symptom, *n.* symptôme *m.*

synchronize, *vb.* synchroniser, *tr.*

syndicate, *n.* syndicat *m.*

syndrome, *n.* syndrome *m.*

synonym, *n.* synonyme *m.*

synthetic, *adj.* synthétique.

syringe, *n.* seringue *f.*

syrup, *n.* sirop *m.*

system, *n.* système *m.*

systematic, *adj.* systématique.

T

tabernacle, n. tabernacle m.

table, n. table f.

tablecloth, n. nappe f.

tablespoon, n. cuiller (f.) à bouche.

tablet, n. tablette f.

tack, 1. n. (nail) broquette f. 2. vb. clouer.

tact, n. tact m.

tag, n. étiquette f.

tail, n. queue f.

tailor, n. tailleur m.

take, vb. prendre; (lead) conduire; (carry) porter.

tale, n. conte m.

talent, n. talent m.

talk, 1. n. conversation f. 2. vb. parler.

talkative, adj. bavard.

tall, adj. grand.

tame, adj. (animal) apprivoisé.

tamper, vb. toucher à.

tan, n. (leather) tan m.; (skin) hâle m.

tangible, adj. tangible.

tangle, n. embrouillement m.

tank, n. réservoir m.; (mil.) char (m.) d'assaut.

tap, 1. n. (water) robinet m.; (knock) petit coup m. 2. vb. frapper légèrement.

tape, n. ruban m.

tape recorder, n. magnétophone m.

tapestry, n. tapisserie f.

tar, n. goudron m.

target, n. cible f.

tariff, n. tarif m.

tarnish, vb. ternir, tr.

task, n. tâche f.

taste, 1. n. goût m. 2. vb. goûter.

tasty, adj. savoureux.

taut, adj. raide.

tavern, n. taverne f.

tax, 1. n. impôt m. 2. vb. imposer.

taxi, n. taxi m.

taxpayer, n. contribuable m.

tea, n. thé m.

teach, vb. enseigner; (to do) apprendre à.

teacher, n. instituteur m.; (school) professeur m.

team, n. (animals) attelage m.; (people) équipe f.

teapot, n. théière f.

tear, 1. n. larme f.; (rip) déchirure f. 2. vb. déchirer.

tease, vb. taquiner.

teaspoon, n. cuiller (f.) à thé.

technical, adj. technique.

technique, n. technique f.

tedious, adj. ennuyeux.

telegram, n. télégramme m.

telegraph, n. télégraphe m.

telephone, 1. n. téléphone m. 2. vb. téléphoner.

telescope, n. télescope m.

televise, vb. téléviser.

television, n. télévision f.

tell, vb. dire; (story, etc.) raconter.

teller, n. (bank) caissier m.

temper, n. (humor) humeur f.; (lose one's t.) s'emporter; (anger) colère f.; (metals) trempe f.

temperament, n. tempérament m.

temperamental, adj. instable.

temperance, n. tempérance f.

temperate, adj. (habit) sobre; (climate) tempéré.

temperature, n. température f.

tempest, n. tempête f.

temple, n. temple m.; (forehead) tempe f.

temporary, adj. temporaire.

tempt, vb. tenter.

temptation, n. tentation f.

ten, adj. and n. dix m.

tenant, n. locataire m.f.

tend, vb. tendre, intr.; (care for) soigner.

tendency, n. tendance f.

tender, adj. tendre.

tenderness, n. tendresse f.

tendon, n. tendon m.

tennis, n. tennis m.

tenor, n. (music) ténor m.

tense, adj. tendu.

tension, n. tension f.

tent, n. tente f.

tentative, adj. tentatif, expérimental.

tenth, adj. and n. dixième m.

term, n. terme m.; (school) trimestre m.; (conditions) conditions f.pl.

terrace, n. terrasse f.

terrible, adj. terrible.

terrify, vb. terrifier.

territory, n. territoire m.

terror, n. terreur f.

test, 1. n. épreuve f. 2. vb. mettre à l'épreuve.

testament, n. testament m.

testify, vb. témoigner (de); (declare) affirmer.

testimony, n. témoignage m.

text, n. texte m.

textile, adj. textile.

texture, n. texture f.

than, conj. que; (with numerals) de.

thank, vb. remercier; (t. you) merci.

thankful, adj. reconnaissant.

that sg., those pl. 1. adj. ce cet m., cette f., ces pl.; (opposed to this) ce . . . -là, etc. 2. demonstrative pron. celui-là m., celle-là f., ceux-là m.pl. celles-là f. celles-là; (object not named) cela, abbr. ça; (what is t.?) qu'est-ce que c'est que ça? 3. relative pron. qui (subject); que (object). 4. conj. que; (purpose) pour que.

the, art. le m., la f., les pl.

theater, n. théâtre m.

theft, n. vol m.

their, adj. leur sg., leurs pl.

theirs, pron. le leur m., la leur f., les leurs pl.

them, pron. eux m., elles f.; (unstressed, with verb) les (direct), leur (indirect).

theme, n. thème m.

themselves, pron. eux-mêmes m., elles-mêmes f.; (reflexive) se.

then, adv. alors; (after that) ensuite.

thence, adv. (place) de là; (reason) pour cette raison.

theology, n. théologie f.

theoretical, adj. théorique.

theory, n. théorie f.

therapy, n. thérapie f.

there, adv. là; (with verb) y.

therefore, adv. donc.

thermometer, n. thermomètre m.

these, see this.

they, pron. ils m., elles f.

thick, adj. épais.

thicken, vb. épaissir, tr.

thickness, n. épaisseur f.

thief, n. voleur m.

thigh, n. cuisse f.

thimble, n. dé m.

thin, adj. mince.

thing, n. chose f.

think (of), vb. penser (à).

thinker, n. penseur m.

third, 1. n. tiers m. 2. adj. troisième.

Third World, n. Tiers Monde m.

thirst, n. soif f.

thirsty, adj. (be t.) avoir soif.

thirteen, adj. and n. treize m.

thirty, adj. and n. trente m.

this, sg. these pl. 1. adj. ce, cet m., cette f., ces pl.; (opposed to that) ce . . . -ci, etc. 2. demonstrative pron. celui-ci m., celle-ci f., ceux-ci m.pl., celles-ci f.pl.; (object not named) ceci.

thorough, adj. complet.

those, see that.

though, conj. quoique.

thought, n. pensée f.

thoughtful, adj. pensif.

thousand, adj. and n. mille m.

thread, n. fil m.

threat, n. menace f.

threaten, vb. menacer.

three, adj. and n. trois m.

thrift, n. économie f.

thrill, 1. n. tressaillement m. 2. vb. tressaillir, intr.; faire frémir, tr.

thrive, vb. prospérer.

throat, n. gorge f.

throne, n. trône m.

through, prep. and adv. à travers; (be t.) avoir fini.

throughout, adv. partout.

throw, vb. jeter.

thrust, vb. pousser.

thumb, n. pouce m.

thunder, 1. n. tonnerre m. 2. vb. tonner.

Thursday, n. jeudi m.

thus, adv. ainsi.

thwart, vb. contrarier.

ticket, n. billet m.

tickle, vb. chatouiller.

ticklish, adj. chatouilleux.

tide, n. marée f.

tidy, adj. (person) ordonné; (thing) en bon ordre.

tie, 1. n. lien m.; (neck-t.) cravate f. 2. vb. attacher; (bind) lier; (knot) nouer.

tier, n. gradin m.

tiger, n. tigre m.

tight, adj. serré; (drunk) gris.

tighten, vb. serrer.

tile, n. (roof) tuile f.

till, 1. prep. jusqu'a. 2. conj. jusqu'à ce que.

tilt, vb. pencher.

timber, n. (building) bois (m.) de construction.

time, n. temps m.; (occasion) fois f.; (clock) heure f.; (what t. is it?) quelle heure est-il?; (have a good t.) s'amuser bien.

timetable, n. horaire m.

timid, adj. timide.

timidity, n. timidité f.

tin, n. étain m.

tint, n. teinte f.

tiny, adj. tout petit.

tip, 1. n. (money) pourboire m.; (end) bout m. 2. vb. (money) donner un pourboire à; (t. over) renverser.

tire, 1. n. (car, etc.) pneumatique (abbr. pneu) m. 2. vb. fatiguer.

tired, adj. fatigué.

tissue, n. tissu m.

title, n. titre m.

to, prep. à; (in order pour t.).

tobacco, n. tabac m.

today, adv. aujourd'hui.

toe, n. orteil m.

together, adv. ensemble.

toil, vb. travailler dur.

toilet, n. toilette f.

token, n. témoignage m.; (coin) jeton m.

tolerance, n. tolérance f.

tolerant, adj. tolérant.

tolerate, vb. tolérer.

tomato, n. tomate f.

tomb, n. tombeau m.

tomorrow, adv. demain.

ton, n. tonne f.

tone, n. ton m.

tongue, n. langue f.

tonic, adj. and n. tonique m.

tonight, adv. cette nuit; (evening) ce soir.

tonsil, n. amygdale f.

too, adv. trop; (also) aussi.

tool, n. outil m.

tooth, n. dent m.

toothache, n. mal (m.) de dents.

toothbrush, n. brosse (f.) à dents.

top, n. (mountain, etc.) sommet m.; (table) dessus m.

topcoat, n. pardessus m.

topic, n. sujet m.

torch, n. torche f.

torment, 1. n. tourment m. 2. vb. tourmenter.

torrent, n. torrent m.

torture, 1. n. torture f. 2. vb. torturer.

toss, vb. (throw) jeter; s'agiter, intr.

total, adj. and n. total m.

totalitarian, adj. totalitaire.

touch, 1. n. (touching) attouchement m.; (sense) toucher m.; (small amount) pointe f.; (contact) contact m. 2. vb. toucher.

tough, adj. dur.

tour, n. tour m.

tourist, n. touriste m.f.

tournament, n. tournoi m.

tow, vb. remorquer.

toward, prep. (place, time) vers; (feelings, etc.) envers.

towel, n. serviette f.

tower, n. tour f.

town, n. ville f.

toy, n. jouet m.

trace, n. trace f.

track, n. piste f.; (railroad) voie f.

tract, n. (space) étendue f.

tractor, n. tracteur m.

trade, 1. n. commerce m.; (job) métier m. 2. vb. commercer.

trader, n. commerçant m.

tradition, n. tradition f.

traditional, adj. traditionnel.

traffic, n. circulation f.

tragedy, n. tragédie f.

tragic, adj. tragique.

trail, n. trace f.

train, 1. n. train m.; (dress) traîne f.; (retinue) suite f. 2. vb. (sports) entraîner, tr.; (mil.) exercer, tr.

traitor, n. traître m.

tramp, n. (steps) bruit (m.) de pas; (person) chemineau m.

tranquil, adj. tranquille.

tranquillity, n. tranquillité f.

transaction, n. opération f.

transfer, 1. n. transport m.; (ticket) billet (m.) de correspondance. 2. vb. transférer, tr.

transform, vb. transformer.

transfusion, n. transfusion f.

transition, n. transition f.

translate, vb. traduire.

translation, n. traduction f.

transmit, vb. transmettre.

transparent, adj. transparent.

transport, transportation, 1. n. transport m. 2. vb. transporter.

transsexual, adj. transsexuel.

transvestite, n. travesti.

trap, 1. n. piège m. 2. vb. prendre au piège.

trash, n. (rubbish) rebut m.

travel, 1. n. voyage m. 2/ vb. voyager.

traveler, n. voyageur m.

traveler's check, n. chèque de voyage m.

tray, n. plateau m.

treacherous, adj. traître.

tread, vb. marcher.

treason, n. trahison f.

treasure, n. trésor m.

treasurer, n. trésorier m.

treasury, n. trésor m.

treat, vb. traiter.

treatment, n. traitement m.

treaty, n. traité m.

tree, n. arbre m.

tremble, vb. trembler.

tremendous, adj. terrible.

trench, n. tranchée f.

trend, n. tendance f.

trespass, vb. empiéter.

triage, n. présélection f.

trial, n. (law) procès m.; (test) épreuve f.

triangle, n. triangle m.

tribulation, n. tribulation f.

tributary, 1. n. (river) affluent m. 2. adj. tributaire.

tribute, n. tribut m.

trick, 1. n. ruse f. 2. vb. duper.

tricky, adj. astucieux.

trifle, n. bagatelle f.

trigger, n. détente f.

trim, 1. adj. soigné. 2. vb. (put in order) arranger; (adorn) garnir; (cut) tailler.

trinket, n. breloque f.

trip, 1. n. voyage m. 2. vb. trébucher.

triple, adj. and n. triple m.

trite, adj. rebattu.

triumph, n. triomphe m.

triumphant, adj. triomphant.

trivial, adj. trivial.

trolley-car, n. tramway m.

troop, n. troupe f.

trophy, n. trophée m.

tropic, n. tropique m.

trot, 1. n. trot m. 2. vb. intr. trotter.

trouble, 1. n. (misfortune) malheur m.; (difficulty) difficulté f.; (inconvenience, medical) dérangement m. 2. vb. (worry) inquiéter, tr.; (inconvenience) déranger; (afflict) affliger.

troublesome, adj. gênant.

trough, n. auge f.

trousers, n. pantalon m.

trousseau, n. trousseau m.

trout, n. truite f.

truce, n. trêve f.

truck, n. camion m.

true, adj. vrai.

truly, adv. vraiment.

trumpet, n. trompette f.

trunk, n. (clothes) malle f.; (body, tree) tronc m.

trust, 1. n. confiance f.; (business) trust m. 2. vb. se confier à; (entrust) confier.

trustworthy, adj. digne de confiance.

truth, n. vérité f.

truthful, adj. sincère.

try, vb. essayer; (law) mettre en jugement.

tryst, n. rendez-vous m.

T-shirt, n. maillot m.

tub, n. baignoire f.

tube, n. tube m.

tuberculosis, *n.* tuberculose *f.*

tuck, *n.* (fold) pli *m.*

Tuesday, *n.* mardi *m.*

tug, 1. *n.* (boat) remorqueur *m.* 2. *vb.* (pull) tirer; (boat) remorquer.

tuition, *n.* (prix de l')enseignement *m.*

tulip, *n.* tulipe *f.*

tumble, *vb.* (fall) tomber.

tumor, *n.* tumeur *f.*

tumult, *n.* tumulte *m.*

tuna, *n.* thon *m.*

tune, 1. *n.* air *m.*; (concord, harmony) accord *m.* 2. *vb.* accorder.

tunnel, *n.* tunnel *m.*

turban, *n.* turban *m.*

turf, *n.* gazon *m.*

Turk, *n.* Turc *m.*, Turque *f.*

turkey, *n.* dindon *m.*

Turkey, *n.* Turquie *f.*

Turkish, 1. *n.* turc *m.* 2. *adj.* turc *m.*, turque *f.*

turmoil, *n.* tumulte *m.*

turn, 1. *n.* tour *m.*; (road) détour *m.* 2. *vb.* tourner.

turnip, *n.* navet *m.*

turret, *n.* tourelle *f.*

turtle, *n.* tortue *f.*

tutor, *n.* précepteur *m.*

twelfth, *adj.* and *n.* douzième *m.*

twelve, *adj.* and *n.* douze *m.*

twentieth, *adj.* and *n.* vingtième *m.*

twenty, *adj.* and *n.* vingt *m.*

twice, *adv.* deux fois.

twig, *n.* brindille *f.*

twilight, *n.* crépuscule *m.*

twin, *adj.* and *n.* jumeau *m.*, jumelle *f.*

twine, *n.* ficelle *f.*

twinkle, *vb.* scintiller.

twist, *vb.* tordre.

two, *adj.* and *n.* deux *m.*

type, 1. *n.* type *m.*; (printing) caractère *m.* 2. *vb.* taper à la machine.

typewriter, *n.* machine (*f.*) à écrire.

typhoid fever, *n.* fièvre (*f.*) typhoïde.

typical, *adj.* typique.

typist, *n.* dactylo(graphe) *m.f.*

tyranny, *n.* tyrannie *f.*

tyrant, *n.* tyran *m.*

U

udder, *n.* mamelle *f.*

ugliness, *n.* laideur *f.*

ugly, *adj.* laid.

ulcer, *n.* ulcère *m.*

ulterior, *adj.* ultérieur.

ultimate, *adj.* dernier.

umbrella, *n.* parapluie *m.*

umpire, *n.* arbitre *m.f.*

unable, *adj.* incapable; (u. to) dans l'impossibilité de.

unanimous, *adj.* unanime.

uncertain, *adj.* incertain.

uncle, *n.* oncle *m.*

unconscious, 1. *n.* inconscient *m.* 2. *adj.* (aware) inconscient; (faint) sans connaissance; (u. of) sans conscience de.

uncover, *vb.* découvrir.

under, 1. *prep.* sous. 2. *adv.* audessous.

underestimate, *vb.* sous-estimer.

undergo, *vb.* subir.

underground, *adj.* souterrain.

underline, *vb.* souligner.

underneath, *adv.* en dessous.

undershirt, *n.* gilet (*m.*) de dessous.

understand, *vb.* comprendre.

undertake, *vb.* entreprendre.

undertaker, *n.* entrepreneur (*m.*) de pompes funèbres.

underwear, *n.* vêtements (*m.pl.*) de dessous.

undo, *vb.* défaire.

undress, *vb.* déshabiller, *tr.*

uneasy, *adj.* gêné.

uneven, *adj.* inégal.

unexpected, *adj.* inattendu.

unfair, *adj.* injuste.

unfit, *adj.* peu propre (à).

unfold, *vb.* déplier.

unforgettable, *adj.* inoubliable.

unfortunate, *adj.* malheureux.

unhappy, *adj.* malheureux.

uniform, *adj.* and *n.* uniforme *n.*

unify, *vb.* unifier.

union, *n.* union *f.*

unique, *adj.* unique.

unisex, *adj.* unisexuel.

unit, *n.* unité *f.*

unite, *vb.* unir, *tr.*

United Nations, *n.* Nations Unies *f.pl.*

United States, *n.* États-Unis *m.pl.*

unity, *n.* unité *f.*

universal, *adj.* universel.

universe, *n.* univers *m.*

university, *n.* université *f.*

unleaded, *adj.* sans plomb.

unless, *conj.* à moins que . . . ne.

unlike, *adj.* dissemblable.

unload, *vb.* décharger.

unlock, *vb.* ouvrir.

untie, *vb.* dénouer.

until, *conj.* jusqu'à ce que.

unusual, *adj.* insolite.

up, *prep.* vers le haut de.

uphold, *vb.* soutenir.

upholster, *vb.* tapisser.

upon, *prep.* sur.

upper, *adj.* supérieur.

upright, *adj.* droit.

uproar, *n.* vacarme *m.*

upset, *vb.* renverser.

upstairs, *adv.* en haut.

uptight, *adj.* tendu.

upward, 1. *adj.* dirigé en haut. 2. *adv.* en montant.

urge, *vb.* (beg) prier.

urgency, *n.* urgence *f.*

urgent, *adj.* urgent.

us, *pron.* nous.

use, 1. *n.* usage *m.* 2. *vb.* employer; se servir de.

useful, *adj.* utile.

useless, *adj.* inutile.

usher, *n.* huissier *m.*

usual, *adj.* usuel.

utensil, *n.* utensile *m.*

utilize, *vb.* utiliser, se servir de.

utmost, 1. *n.* le plus; (all one can) tout son possible. 2. *adj.* (greatest) le plus grand.

utter, 1. *adj.* absolu. 2. *vb.* prononcer; (cry) pousser.

utterance, *n.* émission *f.*

V

vacancy, *n.* vide *m.*, vacance *f.*

vacant, *adj.* vide.

vacate, *vb.* quitter, évacuer.

vacation, *n.* vacances *f.pl.*

vaccinate, *vb.* vacciner.

vaccine, *n.* vaccin *m.*

vacuum, *n.* vide *m.*; (v. cleaner) aspirateur *m.*

vagrant, *adj.* vagabond.

vague, *adj.* vague.

vain, *adj.* vain.

valiant, *adj.* vaillant.

valid, *adj.* valide.

valise, *n.* valise *f.*

valley, *n.* vallée *f.*

valor, *n.* valeur *f.*

valuable, *adj.* de valeur.

value, 1. *n.* valeur *f.* 2. *vb.* évaluer.

value-added tax, *n.* taxe à la valeur ajoutée *f.*

valve, *n.* soupape *f.*

vandal, *n.* vandale *m.f.*

vanguard, *n.* avant-garde *f.*

vanilla, *n.* vanille *f.*

vanish, *vb.* s'évanouir.

vanity, *n.* vanité *f.*

vanquish, *vb.* vaincre.

vapor, *n.* vapeur, *f.*

variation, *n.* variation *f.*

varied, *adj.* varié.

variety, *n.* variété *f.*

various, *adj.* divers.

varnish, *n.* vernis *m.*

vary, *vb.* varier.

vase, *n.* vase *m.*

vasectomy, *n.* vasectomie *f.*

vassal, *n.* vassal *m.*

vast, *adj.* vaste.

vat, *n.* cuve *f.*

vault, *n.* voûte *f.*

vegetable, *n.* légume *m.*

vehement, *adj.* véhément.

vehicle, *n.* véhicule *m.*

veil, *n.* voile *m.*

vein, *n.* veine *f.*

velocity, *n.* vitesse *f.*

velvet, *n.* velours *m.*

vengeance, *n.* vengeance *f.*

vent, *n.* ouverture *f.*

ventilate, *vb.* ventiler.

venture, 1. *n.* aventure *f.* 2. *vb.* hasarder, *tr.*

verb, *n.* verbe *m.*

verbose, *adj.* verbeux.

verdict, *n.* verdict *m.*

verge, *n.* bord *m.*

verify, *vb.* vérifier.

versatile, *adj.* versatile.

verse, *n.* vers *m.pl.;* (line of poetry) vers *m.*

version, *n.* version *f.*

vertical, *adj.* vertical.

very, *adv.* très.

vessel, *n.* vaisseau *m.*

vest, *n.* gilet *m.*

veteran, *n.* vétéran *m.*

veto, *n.* véto *m.*

vex, *vb.* vexer.

viaduct, *n.* viaduc *m.*

vibrate, *vb.* vibrer.

vibration, *n.* vibration *f.*

vice, *n.* vice *m.*

vicinity, *n.* voisinage *m.*

vicious, *adj.* méchant.

victim, *n.* victime *f.*

victor, *n.* vainqueur *m.*

victorious, *adj.* victorieux.

victory, *n.* victoire *f.*

videodisc, *n.* vidéodisque *m.*

videotape, *n.* bande vidéo *f.*

view, *n.* vue *f.*

vigil, *n.* veille *f.*

vigilant, *adj.* vigilant.

vigor, *n.* vigueur *f.*

vile, *adj.* vil, abominable.

village, *n.* village *m.*

villain, *n.* scélérat *m.*

vindicate, *vb.* défendre.

vine, *n.* vigne *f.*

vinegar, *n.* vinaigre *m.*

vineyard, *n.* vigne *f.*

vintage, *n.* (grapes gathered) vendange *f.;* (year of wine) année *f.*

violate, *vb.* violer.

violation, *n.* violation *f.*

violence, *n.* violence *f.*

violent, *adj.* violent.

violet, 1. *n.* violette *f.* 2. *adj.* violet.

violin, *n.* violon *m.*

virgin, *n.* vierge *f.*

virile, *adj.* viril.

virtual, *adj.* vrai.

virtue, *n.* vertu *f.*

virtuous, *adj.* vertueux.

virus, *n.* virus *m.*

visa, *n.* visa *m.*

visible, *adj.* visible.

vision, *n.* vision *f.*

visit, 1. *n.* visite *f.* 2. *vb.* visiter.

visitor, *n.* visiteur *m.*

visual, *adj.* visuel.

vital, *adj.* vital.

vitality, *n.* vitalité *f.*

vitamin, *n.* vitamine *f.*

vivacious, *adj.* vif *m.,* vive *f.*

vivid, *adj.* vif *m.,* vive *f.*

vocabulary, *n.* vocabulaire *m.*

vocal, *adj.* vocal.

vogue, *n.* vogue *f.*

voice, *n.* voix *f.*

void, *adj.* (law) nul.

volcano, *n.* volcan *m.*

volume, *n.* volume *m.*

voluntary, *adj.* volontaire.

volunteer, 1. *n.* volontaire *m.* 2. *vb.* s'engager.

vomit, *vb.* vomir.

vote, 1. *n.* vote *m.* 2. *vb.* voter.

voter, *n.* votant *m.*

vouch for, *vb.* répondre de.

vow, *n.* vœu *m.*

vowel, *n.* voyelle *f.*

voyage, *n.* voyage *m.*

vulgar, *adj.* vulgaire.

vulnerable, *adj.* vulnérable.

W

wade, *vb.* traverser à gué.

waffle, *n.* gaufre (américaine) *f.*

wag, *vb.* agiter.

wage, *vb.* (war) faire la guerre.

wages, *n.* salaire *m.*

wagon, *n.* chariot *m.*

wail, *vb.* gémir.

waist, *n.* taille *f.*

wait (for), *vb.* attendre.

waiter, *n.* garçon *m.*

wake (up), *vb.* réveiller, *tr.;* s'éveiller, *intr.*

walk, 1. *n.* promenade *f.* 2. *vb.* marcher; (take a w.) se promener.

wall, *n.* mur *m.*

wallcovering, *n.* tenture *f.*

wallet, *n.* portefeuille *m.*

wallpaper, *n.* papier peint *m.;* papier à tapisser *m.*

walnut, *n.* noix *f.*

walrus, *n.* morse *m.*

waltz, *n.* valse *f.*

wander, *vb.* errer.

want, 1. *n.* besoin *m.* 2. *vb.* vouloir.

war, *n.* guerre *f.*

ward, *n.* (hospital) salle *f.;* (charge) pupille *m.f.*

ware, *n.* marchandises *f.pl.*

warlike, *adj.* guerrier.

warm, 1. *adj.* chaud; (be w.) avoir chaud. 2. *vb.* chauffer.

warmth, *n.* chaleur *f.*

warn, *vb.* avertir.

warning, *n.* avertissement *m.*

warp, *vb.* détourner.

warrant, 1. *n.* mandat *m.* 2. *vb.* garantir.

warrior, *n.* guerrier *m.*

warship, *n.* navire *(m.)* de guerre.

wash, *vb.* laver, *tr.*

washing machine, *n.* laveuse mécanique *f.*

washroom, *n.* salle de bain *f.*

wasp, *n.* guêpe *f.*

waste, 1. *n.* (money) gaspillage *m.;* (time) perte *f.;* (rubbish) déchets *m.pl.* 2. *vb.* gaspiller, perdre.

watch, 1. *n.* (timepiece) montre *f.;* (guard) garde *f.* 2. *vb.* veiller, garder.

watchful, *adj.* vigilant.

watchmaker, *n.* horloger *m.*

watchman, *n.* gardien *m.*

water, *n.* eau *f.*

waterbed, *n.* aqualit *m.*

water color, *n.* aquarelle *f.*

waterfall, *n.* chute *(f.)* d'eau.

waterproof, *adj.* imperméable.

wave, 1. *n.* (sea) vague *f.;* (sound) onde *f.;* (permanent w.) ondulation *(f.)* permanente. 2. *vb.* agiter; (hair) onduler.

waver, *vb.* vaciller.

wax, *n.* cire *f.*

way, *n.* (road) chemin *m.;* (distance) distance *f.;* (direction) côté *m.;* (manner) manière *f.*

we, *pron.* nous.

weak, *adj.* faible.

weaken, *vb.* affaiblir.

weakness, *n.* faiblesse *f.*

wealth, *n.* richesse *f.*

wealthy, *adj.* riche.

weapon, *n.* arme *f.*

wear, *vb.* porter.

weary, *adj.* las.

weasel, *n.* belette *f.*

weather, *n.* temps *m.*

weave, *vb.* tisser.

weaver, *n.* tisserand *m.*

web, *n.* (fabric) tissu *m.;* (spider) toile *f.*

wedding, *n.* noces *f.pl.*

wedge, *n.* coin *m.*

Wednesday, *n.* mercredi *m.*

weed, *n.* mauvaise herbe *f.*

week, *n.* semaine *f.*

weekday, *n.* jour *(m.)* de semaine.

week end, *n.* week-end *m.,* fin de semaine *f.*

weekly, *adj.* hebdomadaire.

weep, *vb.* pleurer.

weigh, *vb.* peser.

weight, *n.* poids *m.*

weird, *adj.* mystérieux.

welcome, *adj.* bienvenu.

welfare, *n.* bien-être *m.*

well, 1. *n.* (water) puits *m.* 2. *adv.* bien.

well-known, *adj.* bien connu.

west, *n.* ouest *m.*

western, *adj.* de l'ouest.

westward, *adv.* vers l'ouest.

wet, 1. *adj.* mouillé; (weather) pluvieux. 2. *vb.* mouiller.

whale, *n.* baleine *f.*

what, 1. *adj.* quel. 2. *pron.* (relative, that which) ce qui (subject), ce que (object); (interrogative) qu'est-ce qui; quoi. 3. *interj.* quoi!

whatever, 1. *adj.* quelque . . . qui (subject), . . . que (object). 2. *pron.* quoi qui (subject), . . . que (object).

wheat, *n.* blé *m.*

wheel, *n.* roue *f.*

when, *conj.* quand.

whenever, *conj.* toutes les fois que.

where, *conj.* où.

wherever, *conj.* partout où.

whether, *conj.* soit que; (if) si.

which, 1. *adj.* quel. 2. *pron.* (relative) qui; lequel; (interrogative) lequel.

whichever, *pron.* n'importe lequel.

while, *conj.* pendant que; (whereas) tandis que.

whim, *n.* caprice *m.,* lubie *f.*

whip, *n.* fouet *m.*

whirl, *vb.* faire tourner, *tr.;* tourner sur soi, *intr.*

whirlpool, *n.* tourbillon *(m.)* d'eau.

whirlwind, *n.* tourbillon *(m.)* de vent.

whisker, *n.* (man) favori *m.;* (animals) moustache *f.*

whiskey, *n.* whiskey *m.*

whisper, *vb.* chuchoter.

whistle, 1. *n.* sifflet *m.* 2. *vb.* siffler.

white, *adj.* blanc *m.,* blanche *f.*

who, *pron.* qui.

whoever, *pron.* qui que.

whole, *adj.* entier.

wholesale, *adj. and adv.* en gros.

wholesome, *adj.* sain.

wholly, *adv.* entièrement.

whom, *pron.* (relative) que; lequel; (interrogative) qui.

whose, *pron.* (relative) dont; (interrogative) de qui.

why, *adv.* pourquoi.

wicked, *adj.* méchant.

wickedness, *n.* méchanceté *f.*

wide, *adj.* large.

widen, *vb.* élargir, *tr.*

widespread, *adj.* répandu.

widow, *n.* veuve *f.*

widower, *n.* veuf *m.*

width, *n.* largeur *f.*

wield, *vb.* manier.

wife, *n.* femme *f.*

wig, *n.* perruque *f.*

wild, *adj.* sauvage.

wilderness, *n.* désert *m.*

wildlife, *n.* faune *f.*

will, 1. *n.* volonté *f.;* (last w.) testament *m.* 2. *vb.* vouloir; (bequeath) léguer.

willful, *adj.* obstiné.

willing, *adj.* bien disposé.

wilt, *vb.* flétrir.

win, *vb.* gagner.

wind, *n.* vent *m.*

window, *n.* fenêtre *f.;* (shop) devanture *f.*

windy, *adj.* venteux.

wine, *n.* vin *m.*

wing, *n.* aile *f.*

wink, 1. *n.* clin *(m.)* d'œil. 2. *vb.* clignoter.

winner, *n.* gagnant *m.*

winter, *n.* hiver *m.*

wipe, *vb.* essuyer.

wire, *n.* fil *(m.)* de fer.

wireless, *n.* télégraphie *(f.)* sans fil *(abbr.* T.S.F.).

wisdom, *n.* sagesse *f.*

wise, *adj.* sage.

wish, 1. *n.* désir *m.* 2. *vb.* désirer.

wit, *n.* esprit *m.*

witch, *n.* sorcière *f.*

with, *prep.* avec.

withdraw, *vb.* retirer, *tr.*

wither, *vb.* flétrir.

withhold, *vb.* refuser.

within, *adv.* dedans.

without, *prep.* sans.

witness, *n.* témoin *m.*

witty, *adj.* spirituel.

wizard, *n.* sorcier *m.*

woe, *n.* malheur *m.*

wolf, *n.* loup *m.*

woman, *n.* femme *f.*

womb, *n.* matrice *f.*

wonder, *vb.* (ask oneself) se demander; (be surprised) être étonné.

wonderful, *adj.* merveilleux.

woo, *vb.* faire la cour à.

wood, *n.* bois *m.*

wooden, *adj.* de bois.

wool, *n.* laine *f.*

woolen, *adj.* de laine.

word, *n.* mot *m.*

work, 1. *n.* travail *m.* 2. *vb.* travailler.

worker, *n.* travailleur *m.*

workman, *n.* ouvrier *m.*

world, *n.* monde *m.*

worldly, *adj.* mondain.

world-wide, *adj.* mondial.

worm, *n.* ver *m.*

worn, *adj.* usé.

worry, 1. *n.* souci *m.* 2. *vb.* tracasser, préoccuper, *tr.*

worse, 1. *adj.* pire. 2. *adv.* pis.

worship, 1. *n.* culte *m.* 2. *vb.* adorer.

worst, 1. *adj.* (le) pire. 2. *adv.* (le) pis.

worth, *n.* valeur *f.;* (be w. while to) valoir la peine de.

worthless, *adj.* indigne; (without value) sans valeur.

worthy, *adj.* digne.

would, *vb.* vouloir.

wound, 1. *n.* blessure *f.* 2. *vb.* blesser.

wrap, *vb.* envelopper.

wrapping, *n.* couverture *f.*

wrath, *n.* courroux *m.*

wreath, *n.* couronne *f.*

wreck, *n.* (ship) naufrage *m.;* (remains) débris *m.pl.*

wrench, *vb.* tordre.

wrestle, *vb.* lutter.

wretched, *adj.* misérable.

wring, *vb.* tordre.

wrinkle, *n.* ride *f.*

wrist, *n.* poignet *m.*

wrist watch, *n.* montre-bracelet *f.*

write, *vb.* écrire.

writer, *n.* écrivain *m.*

writhe, *vb.* se tordre.

wrong, 1. *n.* tort *m.* 2. *adj.* faux *m.,* fausse *f.;* (be w.) avoir tort.

X, Y, Z

x-rays, *n.* rayons X *m.pl.*

xylophone, *n.* xylophone *m.*

yacht, *n.* yacht *m.*

yam, *n.* igname *f.*

yard, *n.* (house, etc.) cour *f.;* (lumber, etc.) chantier *m.;* (measure) yard *m.*

yarn, *n.* fil *m.*

yawn, 1. *n.* bâillement *m.* 2. *vb.* bâiller.

year, *n.* an *m.;* (duration) année *f.*

yearly, *adj.* annuel.

yearn for, *vb.* soupirer après.

yell, *vb.* hurler.

yellow, *adj. and n.* jaune *m.*

yes, *adv.* oui; (after negative question) si.

yesterday, *adv.* hier.

yet, 1. *adv.* encore. 2. *conj.* néanmoins.

yield, *vb.* (resign, submit) céder; (produce) produire.

yoke, *n.* joug *m.*

yolk, *n.* jaune *m.*

you, *pron.* vous; (familiar, *sg.*) tu.

young, *adj.* jeune.

your, *adj.* votre *sg.,* vos *pl.;* (familiar form) ton *m.sg.,* ta *f.sg.,* tes *pl.*

yours, *pron.* le vôtre; (familiar form) le tien *m.,* la tienne *f.*

yourself, *pron.* vous-même; (familiar form) toi-même; (reflexive) vous, te.

youth, *n.* jeunesse *f.*

youthful, *adj.* (young) jeune; (of youth) de jeunesse.

zap, *vb.* frapper d'une façon soudaine et inattendue.

zeal, *n.* zèle *m.*

zealous, *adj.* zélé.

zebra, *n.* zèbre *m.*

zero, *n.* zéro *m.*

zest, *n.* entrain *m.;* (taste) saveur *f.*

zip code, *n.* code postal *m.*

zone, *n.* zone *f.*

zoo, *n.* jardin *(m.)* zoologique.